WORLD
WAR
I
A Short History

Michael J. Lyons

North Dakota State University

PRENTICE HALL, *Englewood Cliffs, New Jersey 07632*

Library of Congress Cataloging-in-Publication-Data
Lyons, Michael J., (date)

World War I: a short history / Michael J. Lyons
    p.   cm.
  Includes bibliographical references and index.
  ISBN-0-13-953514-4 (pbk.)
  1. World War, 1914-1918.   I. Title.   II. Title: World War One.
III. Title: World War 1.
  D521.L82   1994
  940.3--dc20   93-19794
                                                         CIP

Acquisitions Editor: Steve Dalphin
Editorial/production supervision and
   electronic page make up: Elizabeth Best
Marketing Manager: Chris Freitag
Copy Editor: James Tully
Cover Designer: Karen Salzbach
Electronic maps: Mary Lyons
Production Coordinator: Kelly Behr
Editorial Assistant: Caffie Risher

 © 1994 by Prentice-Hall, Inc.
A Paramount Communications Company
Englewood Cliffs, New Jersey 07632

Printed in the United States of America

10 9 8 7 6 5 4 3 2 1

ISBN 0-13-953514-4

Prentice-Hall International (UK) Limited, *London*
Prentice-Hall of Australia Pty. Limited, *Sydney*
Prentice-Hall Canada Inc., *Toronto*
Prentice-Hall Hispanoamericana, S.A., *Mexico*
Prentice-Hall of India Private Limited, *New Delhi*
Prentice-Hall of Japan, Inc., *Tokyo*
Simon & Schuster Asia Pte. Ltd., *Singapore*
Editora Prentice-Hall do Brasil, Ltda., *Rio de Janeiro*

To Mary, Mike, and Nancy

CONTENTS

PREFACE

Eighty years have passed since Europe stumbled into World War I. Few people realized in the fateful summer of 1914 that this conflict would eclipse all previous wars both in scope and in horror. It initiated the world into the age of modern warfare and revealed the appalling capability of a highly industrialized society to inflict disaster on itself with the aid of a new and terrible technology. The battered generation that survived the four years of slaughter and devastation that followed represented both a somber aftermath and a tragic prelude to an even greater conflict. And, although World War II came to overshadow its predecessor, World War I was the real turning point in the history of the twentieth century. It changed Europe and the world so fundamentally and created such instability that it paved the way for the second conflict and all the new problems that it spawned.

The story of how Europe blundered into the abyss of 1914 and engaged in the ghastly orgy of death and destruction has been told many times before. But, as in the case of World War II, few of the multitude of books in print are suitable for the college classroom. Most general histories are far too long, while the innumerable scholarly monographs on more selective topics are usually intended for an audience of professional historians. In World War II: A Short History, which Prentice Hall first published in 1989, I presented a general history of that conflict in a relatively brief format and in a manner that I hoped would be informative, interesting, and clear to both students and the general reader, while still being useful to the professional historian. Members of all three audiences responded positively to that effort, encouraging me to undertake a similar treatment of World War I. Again I have sought to produce a narrative that is clear, informative, and readable. The reader will determine whether I have succeeded.

Any general history of World War I must offer an analysis of the factors, both long-range and immediate, that helped plunge Europe and ultimately much of the rest of the world into hostilities. This process is one of the most controversial topics in all of history. My first three chapters focus on the many developments that helped create an atmosphere conducive to the outbreak of war over a period of several decades before 1914. Although these "long-range causes" seem to imply that the conflict was inevitable, the actual descent into violence came as the result of the failure of the European powers to solve the crisis that erupted in the summer of 1914. Chapter 4 attempts to provide a balanced account of the tragic mistakes, moves, and countermoves during that crisis which led directly to the outbreak of war.

The majority of the remaining chapters deal with the conflict itself, including not only strategy and tactics on the various fighting fronts but also the belligerent powers' resort to "total war." By taking this approach, they sought to mobilize all their resources, both material and human, for the awesome task of securing victory. In pursuit of that elusive goal, millions of people lost their lives and millions more were maimed or suffered psychological wounds, which that generation referred to erroneously as "shell shock." Never before, and seldom since, has the world experienced such concentrated carnage, while the drain on the economies and national wealth of the belligerents was also unprecedented. The immense strain of this awful struggle produced many momentous changes and none more far-reaching than the Russian Revolution in 1917 and the

triumph of communism in that country. In that same year the United States entered the war, and its vast financial and economic resources as well as its abundant supply of personnel left no doubt that it had emerged as the leading power in the world.

The final two chapters relate the grim effects of the war, including the peace settlement as well as the political and economic disruption, and in some cases chaos, that developed in the wake of the conflict. Europe and the world would never be the same again.

I must express gratitude to a number of people for their support of this project. My thanks go especially to Steve Dalphin, executive editor of Prentice Hall's College Division, for providing the opportunity to undertake the task. I am also indebted to the readers who found my manuscript worthy of publication. A special acknowledgment goes to A. Harding Ganz of the Ohio State University, Newark Campus, for his wise criticism and many valuable suggestions. My daughter, Mary, a professional artist, performed a most beneficial service by drawing many of the maps that make the narrative more meaningful. Amy Ochoa, our departmental secretary, carried out the yeoman work of preparing the finished version of the manuscript. She always demonstrated exceptional efficiency, speed, and good humor despite my seemingly insatiable appetite for revision.

I also wish to acknowledge the support of my friend, colleague and department chair Larry Peterson as well as Robert Littlefield, who, as acting dean of the College of Humanities and Social Sciences, granted me release time to pursue this enterprise. My friend and colleague, David Danbom extended his encouragement as well as the constant example of his devotion to research and writing. Joan, my charming wife, great friend, and exceptional travel companion, as always was a major source of inspiration. She also remained remarkably tolerant of the stacks of notes, books, and general debris that for so long adorned my working area at home. My children, Mike and Nancy as well as Mary, all provided their most welcome support and warm encouragement. Finally, I must express a bit of stubborn pride in the fact that, in an age of computers, I typed all of my many drafts on a venerable 1949 model Smith Corona portable with a broken x key. As for errors, I have tried with all my might to banish them altogether. I am sure, nevertheless, that some still lurk in the following pages. Of course, I alone am responsible for them.

1

EUROPE BEFORE 1914: THE POLITICAL, SOCIAL, AND ECONOMIC SETTING

In early 1914, the continent of Europe was the focal point of the entire world, a distinction it had enjoyed for centuries. To be sure, the United States had recently become the leading industrial power, but in most forms of human endeavor it still looked to Europe for inspiration. Most of the world's great industrial, military, and naval powers were European states. Much of the remainder of the globe was still subject to European domination in the form of colonies and spheres of influence. Europe's trade was massive and worldwide in scope. Its intellectual and cultural achievements was still the envy of most other countries. All of this would change dramatically as the result of a conflict that broke out on the Continent in the summer of 1914. It proved to be of unprecedented ferocity and lasted more than four years. The generation that suffered through it called it the Great War. We remember it as World War I.

There had never been a war remotely like it. In terms of lives lost, destruction inflicted, and revolutionary impact on the survivors, it was unique. In the following years historians tried to explain the causes of this appalling catastrophe, and the answers proved elusive. Even though the better part of a century has elapsed since the conflict began, the question of who or what was responsible still remains highly controversial.

AN ATMOSPHERE FOR WAR

It is clear that the war began because the leaders of the European Great Powers made a number of crucial decisions during a crisis triggered by the assassination of the Archduke Francis Ferdinand, heir to the throne of Austria-Hungary, on June 28, 1914. But these fateful actions were conditioned to a large extent by other factors that had created an atmosphere in which war was a distinct possibility, although hardly inevitable. Some of these factors had their origin long before 1914 in the political, economic, and social development of Europe during the nineteenth century.

Among them were the often turbulent relations between the Great Powers and the rise of nationalism in Central Europe. The various European countries had engaged in political and economic rivalry, both on the Continent and in other parts of the world, for centuries. By the mid-eighteenth century five of these nations had emerged as Great Powers—Britain, France, Austria, Prussia, and Russia. For most of the remainder of that century an almost perfect balance of power prevailed among them. But, during the period of Napoleon Bonaparte's rule in

the early nineteenth century, France completely upset the balance and dominated the Continent for the better part of a decade. Napoleon's excessive ambition eventually led to disaster, however, and the other four Great Powers joined forces to defeat him by 1815. The subsequent peace settlement stripped France of its conquests but refrained from depriving the country of any of its original territory. France kept its position as one of the five Great Powers in the newly restored European equilibrium.

Two of the Great Powers, Austria and Prussia, shared a distinction that set them apart from the others. The Austrians and Prussians were ethnically German, even though both countries included non-Germans within their borders. For centuries Austria

FIGURE 1–1 Napoleon Bonaparte. National Archives

and Prussia had been the two most powerful of the 300 separate German states that comprised the exceedingly loose federation known as the Holy Roman Empire. But Napoleon had sharply reduced the number of German states by merging many of the smaller units with larger ones, and in 1806 he abolished the Holy Roman Empire altogether. Following Napoleon's defeat, the peacemakers at the Congress of Vienna chose not to restore the empire. Instead, they created the German Confederation, consisting of only 39 states, which were almost as loosely linked as those of the defunct empire.

In creating the German Confederation, the peacemakers had spurned the pleas of a nationalist movement that had developed among certain elements of the German states during the period of Napoleonic control. German nationalists urged an end to the centuries-old political fragmentation of Germany by the creation of a united and powerful German nation. But their desires conflicted with those of the conservative statesmen who drafted the peace settlement of 1815. These men feared nationalism as a force that would bring renewed turmoil to the Europe they were trying to stabilize after almost 25 years of war. Their alarm increased as nationalism also took root in Italy. The Italian peninsula, like Germany, had experienced political division for many centuries, and during the period of Napoleon's ascendancy, Italian nationalists had dreamed of a united Italy. The Congress of Vienna shattered their hopes by restoring a dozen separate Italian states and placing two of them—Lombardy and Venetia—under Austrian rule. Austria, Prussia, and Russia also shared a mutual desire to stifle the growth of Polish nationalism. The three Great Powers of Eastern Europe had erased Poland from the map by partitioning its territory among themselves in the late eighteenth century. Each of

them had much to lose if a revived Polish state should somehow rise from the grave.

The rulers of Austria found nationalism especially distasteful. The Austrian Empire consisted of a collection of territories in Central Europe inhabited by many different ethnic groups. Over the centuries the House of Hapsburg, the ruling dynasty of Austria, had gradually gained authority over these peoples. But the ruling group, the Austrian Germans, represented a relatively small minority of the total population in this multinational empire. In 1815, the Hapsburgs saw nationalism as a danger to the very existence of their country. While nationalism posed the prospect of unity for Germany, Italy, and Poland, it held the potential to destroy the Austrian Empire, fragmenting it into small states, none of which could remotely approach the status of a great power. Not surprisingly, Austrian leaders remained bitter enemies of nationalism in general. Success for a nationalist movement anywhere in Europe would pose an example for the various ethnic groups within the Austrian Empire. But in 1815 nationalism remained only a potential threat. It had not yet taken root in most of the national groups of the empire. As the years passed, however, the situation changed, and dissatisfaction over Austrian domination increased.

NATIONALISM AND REVOLUTION

Try as they might, the Hapsburgs could not permanently prevent victories for the cause of nationalism. Three waves of revolutions struck various parts of Europe in the 1820s, 1830, and most emphatically in 1848. Some of these uprisings were inspired by nationalism. A Greek revolt against Turkish rule in 1821 led to the creation of an independent Greece, and in 1830 the new state of Belgium gained freedom from the Netherlands. In

1848 revolution erupted in France as well as the Italian and German states, including both Prussia and Austria. Italian nationalists hoped to create a united Italy, while in Germany an assembly of representatives from the various states actually drafted a constitution for a united Germany. Nationalist revolts also broke out among the Czechs and Magyars (Hungarians) within the Austrian Empire. The former sought cultural autonomy and local self-government in the Czech-inhabited region of Bohemia. The latter initially demanded autonomy within the lands constituting the Hapsburg-ruled Kingdom of Hungary but later fought for outright independence.

All of the revolutions of 1848 caught by surprise the conservative governments of the countries involved. There was a universal tendency for the rulers to panic and either flee into exile or grant concessions. But the victories of the revolutions were short-lived. The rebels fell victim to squabbling among themselves, opening the way to conservative counterrevolutions. By 1849, most of the revolutions had failed, and conservative regimes had regained power. For the time being, there was to be no united Italy or Germany, no autonomous Bohemia or independent Hungary.

But the cause of nationalism did not die. In Italy, it found a new leader in Camillo di Cavour, premier of the northern Italian state of Piedmont-Sardinia. Under his direction, Piedmont-Sardinia gained an alliance with Napoleon III of France in 1858. This pact led to a victorious war with Austria the following year, even though Napoleon deserted his Italian ally after the initial successful battles and made a separate peace. By 1861, a united Italy had emerged, although the northeastern province of Venetia remained under Austrian rule and Rome continued to be governed by the pope, who had the protection of a French

military garrison. The new Italy won recognition as a Great Power, but in view of its limited economic and military resources, it was perhaps only an honorary member of the Great Power club.

GERMAN UNIFICATION

Within a decade a united Germany also came into existence, but the new German state did not include Austria. Hapsburg antagonism to nationalism had made certain that if Germany were ever to be unified, it would be done under Prussia's leadership. For many years Prussia deferred to Austria and remained almost as hostile to German nationalism as were the Hapsburgs. But, in 1862, Otto von Bismarck, an exceptionally able leader, became the chief minister in the Prussian government of King William I and soon became the architect of German unity. A conservative Prussian aristocrat and originally not a German nationalist at all, he seemed an unlikely candidate for this role. In fact, his first aim was not to unify Germany but to strengthen Prussian power within the German Confederation.

Although his intentions are not completely clear, it appears that Bismarck actually thought in terms of enticing the Austrians into an agreement which would partition Germany along the Main River, with Prussia dominant in the north and Austria in the south. But when the Hapsburgs, who had long thwarted all attempts at greater German unity, showed no interest in such a settlement, he resorted to armed conflict instead— the Austro-Prussian War of 1866. Bismarck prepared for the war by skillful diplomatic maneuvering, which discouraged the other Great Powers from supporting Austria and even lured Italy into joining Prussia in the conflict. With the enemy isolated, the Prussian army, led by its brilliant chief of staff, General Helmuth von Moltke, won a decisive victory over Austrian forces in the Battle of Königgrätz (or Sadowa), and Austria agreed to an armistice.

In the ensuing peace settlement, Bismarck took no territory from the Hapsburgs for Prussia but forced Austria to give up its membership in the German Confederation. He then dissolved the Confederation and established a new North German Confederation that was clearly under Prussian domination. Italy received Venetia as its reward for siding with Prussia.

While winning his victory over Austria, Bismarck recognized the growing support of many Germans for a united Germany. He decided to satisfy their desires by merging the remaining south German states with the North German Confederation. But

he was determined that this united Germany would bear the unmistakable imprint of Prussian power and would be headed by the Prussian royal family, the Hohenzollern dynasty.

Bismarck's new ambition brought Prussia into conflict with France. The French looked with growing concern on the rapid increase in Prussia's strength, seeing it as a threat to their own expansionist ambitions as well as a danger to France itself. In July 1870, Bismarck engineered a diplomatic crisis and provoked France into declaring war on Prussia. The Franco-Prussian War resulted in disaster for France as Moltke again led Prussia to victory. His troops outmaneuvered the French, encircled one army, then another, and forced each of them

FIGURE 1–2 Otto von Bismarck, architect of German Unification. National Archives

to surrender. Although France's cause was hopeless by early September, it fought on until early 1871.

When the war began, the south German states rallied to Prussia's aid, as Bismarck had expected, and agreed to join in a united German state. In January 1871, while Prussian troops besieged Paris, representatives of the German states met in the Hall of Mirrors of the nearby Palace of Versailles, proclaimed the creation of a German Empire and crowned the Prussian king, William I, emperor (kaiser). Bismarck received the position of chancellor in the new German government. The subsequent Treaty of Frankfurt forced the French to give up their northeastern province of Alsace, along with part of neighboring Lorraine on the northwest, to the new Germany. Alsace was a German-speaking area as was much of the ceded territory in Lorraine, but for strategic reasons, some French-speaking portions of the latter province also were included. These changes were far from welcome to the majority of the people of Alsace-Lorraine, who considered themselves French. The loss of these provinces also embittered France toward Germany and created a lasting impediment to the development of friendly relations between the two powers.

Bismarck's diplomatic maneuvering and the Prussian army's swift and spectacular victories over Austria and France had dramatically transformed the map of Europe. For the first time since the Middle Ages a united German Empire dominated the center of the European continent. The sudden appearance of the new state also posed the greatest threat to the balance of power since the days of Napoleon. Germany at its birth was already the strongest military and economic power on the continent of Europe. As such, it created concern, not only in Austria and France but also among the other Great Powers.

Austria's defeat at the hands of Prussia had led earlier to a reorganization of the Hapsburg Empire. The unhappy conclusion to the war once again raised the spectre of the subject nationalities attempting to break away. In the *Ausgleich* (Compromise) of 1867, the Austrians attempted to stabilize the situation by granting equality to the Magyars, the most powerful of the subject national groups within what now became the dual monarchy of Austria-Hungary. Henceforth, the Austrians continued to control the western portions, including Austria and Bohemia, as well as the northeastern province of Galicia, which contained a population of Poles and Ruthenes. The Magyars dominated most of the eastern part of the empire, which was referred to as Hungary, even though less than half its people were Magyars. The head of the Hapsburg family, Francis Joseph, was both emperor of Austria and king of Hungary. Each of the two portions of the empire had its own government for domestic affairs, while the agreement provided common ministers for foreign, military, naval, and economic affairs for the empire as a whole.

This agreement maintained the territorial integrity of the empire, and Austria-Hungary remained a significant power, but the Magyars' good fortune made other nationalities within the empire envious and, as the years passed, they agitated for similar concessions. If it had been up to the Austrians alone, their pleas might have been granted, but the Magyars bitterly opposed all such proposals, not only in Hungary but also in Austrian-controlled parts of the empire. They feared that concessions by the Austrians would lead to similar demands among their own subject nationalities, whom they intended to dominate permanently. In the face of this opposition, the Austrians were reluctant to push proposals for reform that might prompt the Magyars to break their ties with Austria and establish a completely separate state.

GROWTH OF INDUSTRIALIZATION

But the victory of nationalism in Italy and Germany was only one of the momentous changes taking place in Europe during the nineteenth century. Another was the growth of industrialization and its impact upon European society and politics. The Industrial Revolution had begun in Britain during the second half of the eighteenth century. It basically involved the mechanization of industry by the use of machinery powered by the newly developed steam engine. The process began in the cotton textile industry and gradually spread to other industries. Factories replaced small workshops and home-based manufacturing as the main centers of industry for the first time. Small towns grew into industrialized cities within a few decades.

Britain remained the only industrialized country until after 1830 when the Industrial Revolution took root on the Continent, making its first inroads in Belgium and France. By the 1850s it was spreading into western Germany and northern Italy. After completion of the unification process, German industrialization made such rapid strides that the new Germany soon challenged Britain's industrial leadership. Across the Atlantic, the United States experienced even more spectacular industrial progress during the same decades. By 1914, America ranked first in industrial production, followed by Germany, while Britain had dropped to third. Britain retained its lead in foreign trade, however, as well as its position as the world's foremost financial center and continued to invest huge amounts of capital in many parts of the globe. France, Austria,

and Russia also made progress in industrialization, although they lagged far behind the three industrial giants. Italy ranked even lower. In the Far East, during the last few decades of the nineteenth century Japan became the first non-Western country to undergo an industrial revolution, but despite its remarkable progress, it also trailed the Big Three by a lengthy margin.

The growth of industrialization altered the structure of European society dramatically. The industrialists, who invested capital in the new industries and managed them, became the most important element of the middle class, or *bourgeoisie*, as the French called it. The middle class also included the commercial and professional groups and had been gradually developing in importance since the Middle Ages. Traditionally, it had been a relatively prosperous class between the landowning and politically dominant aristocracy at the summit of the social pyramid and the economically hard-pressed and politically powerless peasantry at the bottom.

THE MIDDLE CLASS AND LIBERALISM

Although the middle class had long been an important element in the economies of the more well-developed countries of Europe, generally speaking it had been able to do little to challenge the ascendancy of the aristocracy in the political systems of Europe. But during the nineteenth century the growing economic prominence of the industrial middle class, along with increasing political ambitions on the part of professional groups, posed a threat to the aristocratic stranglehold on government. As the century progressed, the middle class became identified with the political ideology known as *liberalism*. Liberalism had developed largely out of ideas that had circulated in

Britain during the seventeenth and eighteenth centuries and had become prominent during the French Revolution in the late eighteenth century.

Liberalism varied from country to country, but in general it favored freedom of the individual from excessive government control and the guarantee of basic civil rights as well as governments based on written constitutions. It also stood for limitations on the powers of kings and other rulers and the establishment of elected parliaments to share in the political process. At first, liberals thought in terms of limiting the right to vote in parliamentary elections to the social classes of substantial economic means—the aristocracy and the middle class. But during the course of the nineteenth century, liberals came to support a democratic system in which at least all adult males could vote for representation in parliament. Almost no one thought in terms of giving women the vote until the early twentieth century. The more radical of the Continental liberals also disavowed monarchy and favored a republican form of government.

British liberals strongly advocated a *laissez faire* approach to the economy, which provided for freedom of enterprise and strengthened the economic position of middle-class industrialists. They believed the economy should function as much as possible without government regulation and in accordance with what they considered natural economic laws, such as that of supply and demand. In other words, the economy should be left to the direction of the middle-class industrialists. The fact that individual entrepreneurs had essentially carried out the industrialization of Britain, without government sponsorship, strongly influenced their approach.

On the Continent, where the Industrial Revolution came much later, industry found it difficult to compete with more well-developed British firms. In some countries the middle class was small and investment capital scarce. As a result, governments often took the lead in encouraging industrial development. Liberals supported this activity and were less attached to a strict *laissez faire* economy. Liberals in Germany and Italy were also usually nationalists and deeply involved in the movements toward political unification. Indeed, the economic basis for German unity was already evolving as a result of the creation in 1834 of a customs union for all of Germany with the exception of Austria, which characteristically had refused to join.

For many years governments dominated by the conservative landowning aristocracy blocked liberal demands for reform. Thus, liberalism, with its desire for change, and conservatism, with its opposition to change, frequently came into conflict. At times, liberals in various Continental countries embraced actual revolution. But the uprisings of the first half of the nineteenth century, more often than not, failed. Nevertheless, as the middle class grew larger and more powerful economically, its political influence mounted, and liberalism gradually made progress toward its goals by working through the established political systems. But the degree of success varied considerably. It was greatest in the countries that industrialized first and traditionally had more highly developed middle classes, most notably Britain and France. These countries also moved more rapidly in the direction of democracy.

Britain had possessed a parliament since the Middle Ages, and some members of the middle class enjoyed the right to vote long before the nineteenth century. Most of the remainder gained admission to the electorate in 1832, and by 1884 parliament had extended voting rights to virtually all adult males. But the British remained loyal to their limited monarchy. Britain's system was a model of stability. After 1859, it featured an essentially two-party system in which either the Conservatives or Liberals usually held a majority in parliament for several years at a time and controlled all positions in the cabinet, the actual policy-making body. This stability enabled Britain to maintain remarkable continuity in policy.

France experienced no fewer than five changes in its form of government during the 55 years after 1815, alternating among monarchy, republic, and even a restoration of an imperial system similar to Napoleon's with his nephew as emperor. But in 1870 France became a republic for the third time and remained so until 1940. The inability to develop a consensus on the basic form of government among the French people contributed to chronic instability in the Third Republic. The new system provided for a president as head of state, a parliamentary body elected by universal manhood suffrage, and a cabinet headed by a premier. But, unlike Britain, the Third Republic featured a multiparty system that also contributed to instability. Under this system no single party ever maintained a majority in parliament. As a result, French cabinets contained ministers from various parties and depended on coalitions of those parties to support their policies in parliament. Since these coalitions usually did not hold together for long, cabinets fell from power with alarming regularity. This instability often made it difficult for France to maintain continuity in policy.

Although liberals gained concessions in Germany and Austria-Hungary during the second half of the nineteenth century and in Russia in the early twentieth century, the monarchs of these countries retained extensive powers. Germany also had a parliament, the Reichstag, but Bismarck proved able to manipulate the political parties in such a way as to wield strong influence over it, despite the existence of a system of manhood suf-frage. Austria and Hungary each had its own parliament, although neither system functioned democratically. When Italy emerged as a united state in 1861, it adopted a limited monarchy as its form of government, complete with parliament and liberal constitution. But the electorate did not become democratic until 1912. Russia finally gained a parliament (the Duma) after a revolution in 1905, but its powers remained limited.

Hostility between the liberal middle class and the conservative aristocracy continued in most countries, but as conservatives yielded to more and more liberal demands, the gulf between them narrowed to some extent, especially in Britain. They also held at least two things in common—possession of wealth and fear of the social classes below them. Aristocratic landowners in many countries aspired to maintain their domination over the peasantry and shared middle-class concern regarding the growth of socialism among industrial workers.

PLIGHT OF THE WORKING CLASS

The industrial working class came into being as a direct result of the Industrial Revolution and the need for masses of workers in the factories as well as coal and iron mines. But, whereas the Industrial Revolution brought wealth and prestige to middle-class industrialists, its rewards were far fewer for the workers. To be sure, industrialization was not without benefit to them. Most importantly, it provided large numbers of jobs that helped to offset a rapid increase in European population, starting in the eighteenth century and continuing into the nineteenth. Without the Industrial Revolution, many people would have had no means of making a living.

Industrialization, nevertheless, caused serious problems for workers. Their working days were excessively long, as many as 16 hours being common at first. Working conditions were often poor and wages low, although higher than those of agricultural laborers in the countryside. Industrial cities grew with amazing rapidity and quite haphazardly, spawning extensive slums with poorly built and overcrowded housing, inadequate water and sanitation facilities, and a lack of recreational areas. Air pollution and soot-encrusted buildings added to the gloomy aspect of many urban centers. Generally speaking, however, the most extreme manifestations of these problems appeared in Britain in the early days of industrialization.

Despite the prevalence of these problems, middle-class industrialists, for the most part, were reluctant to deal with them. Economists explained why government efforts to provide remedies would disrupt the natural laws governing the economic marketplace and would only make matters worse. Employers and economists alike looked with disfavor on attempts to organize workers in labor unions, which could agitate for shorter working hours, higher wages, and better conditions.

In Britain, humanitarian reformers pressured the government to help the working class. Reforms were forthcoming, although on a slow, piecemeal basis. They included the legalization of trade unions in 1825, a whole series of laws that gradually shortened working hours in factories and mines, starting in 1833, and still others providing for better sanitation of cities. Eventually, many British liberals began to move away from their devotion to *laissez faire* and also supported reforms in behalf of the working class. Reform continued with the extension of the right to vote to workers in 1867 and later the enactment of legislation granting insurance for industrial accidents, old age pensions, and health insurance. Wages gradually rose as well, without government intervention,

and the purchasing power of these wages increased as prices declined during the last few decades of the nineteenth century.

Generally speaking, a reformist tradition was slower to develop on the Continent, although Bismarck actually introduced the first large-scale social welfare program in the 1880s. Labor unions remained illegal in many countries until late in the nineteenth century and in Russia until the early twentieth century. As a result, Continental workers gradually fell under the influence of still another of the great political ideologies of the nineteenth century—socialism. Although various types of socialism developed, the most successful was the version preached by Karl Marx.

THE GOSPEL OF MARXISM

Marx believed that the proletariat, as he called the working class, was locked in a continuing struggle with the middle-class industrialists. Marx saw no real improvement coming through either the capitalistic economy or through European political systems. Indeed, Marx predicted that conditions for workers would grow steadily worse, but he also saw a bleak future for capitalism in the long run. Capitalism, he insisted, contained the seeds of its own destruction: cutthroat competition between rival capitalists and the tendency of the system to fluctuate between periods of prosperity and periods of depression. He foresaw the number of capitalists steadily dwindling as a result of these tendencies. Eventually, the working class would rise in revolution to overthrow both the prevailing economic and political systems. The capitalists would be too few and too weak to resist successfully.

After securing what Marx considered an inevitable victory, the workers would establish a temporary dictatorship of the proletariat that would take over the means of production and redistribute wealth on the basis of need. When the dictatorship finished its work, classes would cease to exist, and with the coming of a classless society, the need for the dictatorship would disappear, and the state would "wither away."

To prepare the way for the inevitable revolution, Marx advocated formation of socialist political parties. But, even though he issued his first plea for the proletariat to unite in his *Communist Manifesto*, published in 1848, Marxist Socialist parties did not come into existence until the 1870s. Once established in various European states, these parties, usually called Social Democrats, gained many recruits from the working-class. Marx also helped organize an International Workingmen's Association in 1864, hoping that this "First International" would link all working-class organizations in a common cause. But he soon quarreled with virtually every other socialist leader, and the International disbanded in 1876. After Marx's death in 1883, the Marxist Socialist parties organized the "Second International," which served as a coordinating body for the cause of revolutionary socialism.

Before long, however, both the International and the parties themselves fell victim to a fundamental split between two factions: revisionists and orthodox Marxists. Revisionists pointed to the fact that, contrary to Marxist theory, the middle class showed no signs of weakening, and the condition of the working class had actually improved in recent decades. They favored working with other reform-minded parties to improve working-class conditions even more and to do so within the established political systems. Perhaps revolution would prove unnecessary. Orthodox Marxists were scandalized by what they considered a revisionist betrayal of the revolutionary principle and refused to compromise with the existing governments. But, despite their opposition, by the early twentieth century,

it appeared that the future of socialism lay with the revisionists.

European liberals accepted the revisionist olive branch with mixed emotions. To be sure, many of them supported reform legislation that also gained the backing of revisionists. But liberals usually refused to cooperate formally with socialists and remained suspicious of their ultimate objectives. Conservatives shared their skepticism of socialism but also distrusted the liberals and generally opposed reform legislation sponsored by either group. There were exceptions to this tendency, however, most notably Bismarck's far-reaching program of social welfare legislation on behalf of the German working class in the 1880s. But Bismarck took this step in an attempt to undercut the appeal of socialism to the working class. He also sponsored legislation aimed at weakening the German Social Democratic party at the same time that he was creating his system of state paternalism. Neither tactic worked. Social Democrats continued to grow stronger, but now most of them were content to work within the system.

DECLINE OF LIBERALISM

By the late nineteenth century, the middle class was no longer united in support of liberalism. The upper middle class, consisting of wealthy industrialists and financiers, gravitated more and more to conservative parties. These groups disliked the liberal flirtation with socialism and support for reform legislation. They also were often attracted by the increasingly nationalistic tone taken by the conservatives. Elements of the lower middle class, including small shopkeepers and "white collar workers" in the lower levels of both business and government, came to feel increasingly alienated from liberalism. They feared "Big Business" as well as "Big Labor" as threats to their rather precarious position on the bottom fringe of the middle class. Some of them supported parties that claimed to be defenders of the "little man" of the lower middle class. These parties and those who supported them often sought scapegoats for their problems, a tendency that usually took the form of anti-Semitism.

Although liberalism had declined by the early twentieth century and both conservatism and socialism had increased in strength, their followers did not feel secure. All three political movements continued to view each other with mutual suspicion, an attitude that contributed greatly to the existence of a tense atmosphere during the last decades before the outbreak of World War I.

2

THE GREAT POWERS
AND THE GROWTH
OF TENSION

Social and political divisions within individual countries became intertwined with other sources of tension that affected relations between the Great Powers in the late nineteenth and early twentieth centuries and helped to create an ever more explosive atmosphere. These included the continued growth of nationalism, economic and imperialistic rivalry, and the creation of two potentially hostile alliance systems.

NATIONALISM

Nationalism during this period was of a particularly unpleasant type. Early nineteenth-century nationalists, while preaching their right to create unified nation-states, generally had not contended that their ethnic groups were superior to others. Instead, they cherished a romantic vision of many nation-states existing harmoniously in

keeping with the "brotherhood of man." This idealistic nationalism became a casualty of the failure of the revolutions of 1848.

In the following years advocates of national unification placed their emphasis on a more practical, indeed brutal, strategy. The German term *Realpolitik*, meaning practical or realistic politics, characterized this new approach and implied the use of any means to achieve the desired end. It was this type of nationalism that ultimately united Italy and Germany. During the next few decades, it also reflected the attitudes of at least the more virulent nationalist groups in the various Great Powers as well as in many of the smaller ones. And, it was present in the attitudes of some of the nationalities that were still subject to the rule of the Ottoman Empire and Austria-Hungary. This hard-edged nationalism stressed the superiority of one's own nationality. It bore the imprint of Social Darwinism, an especially ugly interpretation of relations between human beings, which gained considerable popularity and influenced policies of many governments during this period. Social Darwinism represented a corruption of Charles Darwin's theory of evolution. While Darwin stressed the struggle for existence among various species of plants and animals, the British philosopher Herbert Spencer and his followers applied the concept of the struggle for existence to economic competition in which only the ruthless would survive. Later, Social Darwinists extended this approach to international relations, which they saw as a constant and vicious competition between rival powers pursuing political and economic aggrandizement at the expense of others.

Superheated nationalism was present in the Pan-German League, which expressed its desire to unite the Austrians and other Germans in Eastern Europe with those of the German Empire. It also influenced the Pan-Slav movement. Pan-Slavism looked forward to the freeing of Slavic peoples from Turkish and Austro-Hungarian rule and their association in a sort of mystical union under the leadership of the Slavs of Russia. Intense nationalism was present, too, in the French dreams of *revanche* (revenge) against Germany for the forced separation of Alsace-Lorraine from France. And, it could be detected in the British tendency to idealize the achievements of the Anglo-Saxon "race." Sometimes internal governmental policies reflected this type of nationalism, most notably the "Russification" program, which sought to force the Russian language and customs on the subject nationalities of the Russian Empire and in the attempt to "Magyarize" the other ethnic groups of Hungary.

Recent historical research indicates, however, that earlier observers may have overstated the extent of intense nationalistic feeling among the populations of the European powers. It may not have been as widespread as was once believed. But clearly it had taken root among many especially vocal groups and definitely influenced the approach of governments to foreign policy in the last few decades before the outbreak of World War I.

ECONOMIC RIVALRY

Economic rivalry also contributed to the atmosphere of tension existing among the European powers. Germany's sudden and enormous growth in economic strength created growing concern among its neighbors. France, in addition to memories of defeat at the hands of Prussia and its continuing grievance over the loss of Alsace-Lorraine, lagged far behind Germany in industrial production. The French had made progress in developing their iron and steel industry and were pioneers in manufacturing automobiles, but in 1914 their industrial output totaled only 40 percent of Germany's. French production also ranked far behind that of the United States and Britain and even trailed Russia in certain areas.

To be sure, France enjoyed some advantages. It specialized in producing high-quality goods and was rich in capital. Because of limited investment opportunities in the domestic economy, the French invested much of this capital in other countries. In 1914, their foreign investments ranked only behind those of Britain and far ahead of Germany. Nevertheless, it was unmistakably clear that France was falling further behind its powerful neighbor to the east in most major economic indices. Even more alarming was the fact that Germany could greatly outproduce France in the realm of war materiel. To make matters worse, the French birth rate lagged far behind that of Germany. In 1914, its population hovered around 40 million, while Germany's had reached 67 million.

But France was not the only country to worry about Germany's rapid economic rise. Britain mourned the sudden loss of its own industrial leadership. Although substantially ahead of its nearest competitor in 1880, in the following years Britain's annual growth rate declined, while those of the United States and Germany rose sharply. American output surpassed Britain's by 1900, and by 1913 Germany produced more than twice as much iron and steel as the British. Britain remained the leader in foreign commerce, but its share of world trade dwindled from 23 percent in 1880 to only 14 percent in 1913. More impressively, British investment abroad led the world by a huge margin, accounting for well over 40 percent of the total. But diversion of so much capital overseas, where better interest rates were available, reduced investment in domestic industry, where modernization was badly needed if the British were to compete successfully with their American and German rivals.

Russia's industrial production actually grew faster than that of any other European power during the last three decades before the outbreak of World War I. By 1913, Russia ranked fourth among the industrial powers of the world, but its achievement was less impressive when measured against the country's enormous population. In terms of per capita industrial growth, Russia ranked far below the three industrial giants and even behind Austria-Hungary and Italy. Foreign investors owned much of Russia's industry, while its foreign debt was the world's largest, and 80 percent of the population still engaged in agriculture. Russian agricultural methods were also extremely backward, and crop yield remained low. Russia also spent enormous amounts for military purposes, which at times brought the government dangerously close to bankruptcy.

Austria-Hungary and Italy both gradually increased their industrial production but trailed far behind the United States, Germany, and Britain. Even Russia had outdistanced them by 1914. Of the two, Austria-Hungary made greater strides in the last four decades before the outbreak of World War I, although its growth rate slowed down after 1900. Its economy was also out of balance, with most of the industrialization taking place in Austria and Bohemia, while Hungary remained primarily agricultural, and certain areas of the empire were extremely backward. Italy, too, represented a study in uneven economic growth. The north made considerable progress in the development of iron and steel industries in the early twentieth century, but the south remained overwhelmingly agrarian and much of it desperately poor.

IMPERIALISM

Economic rivalry among European powers coincided with a great upsurge in overseas imperialistic activity in the last two decades of the nineteenth century. Imperialism of this type was nothing new. It had been going on for centuries, but the new burst of activity was especially intense and took the form of a virtual race for colonies. When it began in the 1880s, Britain already possessed by far the world's most far-flung and extensive overseas colonial empire. It included Canada, India, the entire continent of Australia, and territory at the southern tip of Africa as well as other scattered possessions. France ranked second having already acquired the sprawling North African territory of Algeria, as well as much of Indochina in Southeast Asia. During the period from 1880 to 1900 European powers partitioned most of the remainder of Africa, and nipped at the southern and eastern peripheries of Asia. In the process, France gained most of northwestern Africa, while Britain acquired an almost continuous belt of territory in eastern Africa, extending from Egypt on the north to Cape Colony in the extreme south. Only Tanganyika on the coast of the Indian Ocean eluded them. It fell into German hands instead.

Several weaker European states also amassed substantial colonial holdings. Portugal held Angola on the west coast of Africa and Mozambique on the east, while Belgium controlled the vast Belgian Congo, with its rich mineral resources, in the heart of Africa. Spain managed to cling to its few enclaves along Africa's western coast. The Netherlands had long governed the oil-rich East Indies off the coast of Southeast Asia.

Germany and Italy also entered the race for colonies, but because they started "from scratch" after gaining unification, they had to be content largely with the leftovers. This was particularly the case with Italy, which, prior to 1900, gained only two parched and unproductive stretches of territory along the eastern coast of Africa. Russia refrained from overseas ventures, finding ample opportunities for expansion along its southern frontier in Asia, as well as in the Balkans. The Russians engaged in numerous aggressive actions in such areas as Manchuria, Persia, and Afghanistan. They also followed an ambitious policy of encroachment in the Balkans throughout the nineteenth century. Austria-Hungary limited its imperialistic activity to seeking economic and political influence in the Balkan area of southeastern Europe, most of which still remained under weak Turkish rule. The United States and Japan also joined the ranks of imperialistic powers during this period. The Americans gained control of the Philippines and Puerto Rico following their victory in the Spanish-American War of 1898 and annexed the Hawaiian Islands the same year. Japan defeated China in the Sino-Japanese War of 1894-95 and seized the island of Taiwan as its reward.

In part, the great upswing in imperialism resulted from accelerating industrialization and the desire to obtain new markets for manufactured goods as well as sources of raw materials. Once it began, the quest for economic gain in foreign lands spiraled. This became especially the case as more and more powers established tariff barriers to protect their home markets. Many businessmen viewed colonies overseas as alternative areas for economic opportunities. But the realities of imperialist ventures did not always fulfill expectations. Frequently the imperialist powers spent more on their colonies than they gained from them in profits.

European states also sought to take over certain parts of the globe because they possessed strategic importance and would be useful in protecting or enhancing national interests. Islands in the Pacific or Indian Oceans, which had no particular economic value, became naval bases or fueling stations for warships and merchant vessels. The Great Powers also coveted certain coastal territories near the entrances to narrow waterways, such as the Red Sea or the Persian Gulf. Control of Gibraltar on the southern coast of Spain, near the Strait of Gibraltar, as well as Egypt, with its Suez Canal, gave Britain key strategic positions at both ends of the Mediterranean Sea. These possessions contributed to the security of what the British called their maritime "lifeline to India." In some cases, European powers sought colonies primarily for prestige. Italy was especially interested in enhancing its dubious credentials as a Great Power in this manner.

In some cases, after encroaching economically in areas of Africa or Asia, European powers found local conditions so unstable that they considered it necessary to dominate them politically to protect their investments. Egypt provided a classic example of this type of situation. In the 1880s, the British government, more or less against its will, gradually extended its domination over Egypt. It did so in response to repeated governmental crises in that country, which appeared to endanger British access to the

Suez Canal. Christian missionary activity among the native populations of underdeveloped areas accompanied and sometimes preceded European encroachment. The colonial powers tended to look upon these efforts to convert the populations of the underdeveloped portions of the globe as providing an element of moral justification for their own imperialism.

All of this imperialistic activity bore strong racist overtones. Clearly, the colonial powers saw themselves as superior to the brown, black, or yellow-skinned peoples they were attempting either to exploit, to lead to religious salvation, or both. They also preached the "need" to extend the benefits of Western civilization to the poor, benighted peoples of Africa, Asia and elsewhere. And, indeed, there were some benefits, including the establishment of schools and hospitals. Missionaries also sincerely believed that they were performing a great service by spreading the doctrines of their respective creeds and helped their converts in various ways.

FRICTION AMONG THE IMPERIALIST NATIONS

The headlong race for colonies led to friction among some of the imperialist powers. Britain and France were especially bitter rivals in Africa and Asia and almost came to blows over the Sudan, the vast area stretching southward from the border of Egypt. In 1898, a British military force encountered a smaller French expedition near Fashoda, triggering a serious crisis. The threat of war ended, however, when the French withdrew and accepted Britain's claims to the Sudan. In return, the British recognized French control of areas to the west. Hostility developed between Britain and Russia, too, as the Russians gradually pushed southward in the direction of India. The two powers also became involved

in rivalry over Afghanistan, a primitive, mountainous country bordering India on the northwest, and over Persia (now Iran), India's neighbor to the west.

While economic and colonial rivalry clearly contributed to the growth of tension in Europe during the last few decades before 1914, certain economic factors also promoted peaceful relations. Despite their pursuit of new markets in Africa and Asia, the European powers continued to engage in far more trade among themselves than with their colonies. Although British and French business interests worried about German competition, they sometimes engaged in joint ventures with their counterparts in Germany. Investment capital also flowed from one European power to another, adding to the unmistakable signs of growing interdependence. To be sure, industrialists might implore their governments to help them surmount the economic challenge of foreign rivals through the erection of tariff barriers or other means, but they feared the economically disastrous effects of a European war on their own interests, which were so closely intertwined with those of others.

Despite a multitude of colonial squabbles over territories in Africa, Asia, and the Pacific, none of them led to war between the Great Powers. In fact, the imperialist states had settled most of their major points of contention outside the Continent before 1914. Those that remained seemed to be on their way to resolution. But within Europe itself, rivalry between Austria-Hungary and Russia, the only Great Powers that were not participants in overseas imperialism, proved less amenable to solution. Their rivalry focused on the Balkans where Russia had pursued ambitious policies ever since the days of Peter the Great in the eighteenth century. The Balkans became the single greatest source of instability in European power politics in the last decade before 1914.

GROWTH OF RIVAL ALLIANCES

The danger of war between Austria-Hungary and Russia over the Balkans increased with the development of rival alliances among the Great Powers in the late nineteenth and early twentieth centuries. This process began innocently enough as a result of Bismarck's efforts to ensure Germany's security from potential enemies and to provide a prolonged period of peace and stability during which the newly united country could develop and prosper.

Bismarck had united Germany through a combination of skillful diplomacy and war, but once he had completed this task he faced the challenge of preserving his creation through diplomacy. The chancellor feared that his recent enemies, Austria and France, might join forces in the future to destroy the new German Empire. To prevent this, he set out to cultivate the friendship of one of them. Prospects for agreement with France appeared virtually nil in view of French anger over the loss of Alsace-Lorraine. Austria was another matter. Bismarck had treated Austria leniently in the peace settlement following the Austro-Prussian War, and the Austrians shared a bond of kinship with their fellow Germans across the border. Austria also remained bitter over the failure of the French to come to its aid in the war against Prussia and had maintained neutrality when the Prussians defeated France in 1870. Bismarck had encouraged Austria to make the 1867 agreement that granted the Magyars equality with the Austrians in the dual monarchy of Austria-Hungary. The Magyars were grateful to Bismarck and looked to Germany to support this arrangement in the future.

But Bismarck wanted more than an alliance with Austria. He hoped to create a lasting bond among the three Great Powers of Eastern Europe—Germany, Austria-Hungary, and Russia. Such an arrangement, in addition to strengthening German security, would go a long way in the direction of isolating France from potential allies and possibly create greater stability on the European continent. The prospect seemed promising, even though relations between Austria and Russia had been cool in recent years. All three nations were conservative politically, remaining firmly committed to the monarchical form of government as opposed to what they viewed as French radicalism. They also shared a desire to keep Poland permanently dismembered. In 1873, Bismarck enticed Austria-Hungary and Russia into a limited agreement—the Three Emperors' League. It fell short of a military alliance but did bind the three powers to maintain benevolent neutrality, should one of them be attacked by an outside power.

Bismarck's hopes soon foundered on the problem of Austro-Russian rivalry in the Balkans. In 1877, Russia went to war with Turkey in support of revolts against Turkish rule by Slavic peoples in Bosnia in the western Balkans and Bulgaria to the east. The government in St. Petersburg was motivated partly by Pan-Slav agitation, but it also hoped to increase its influence in the Balkans and, if possible, to bring the Straits connecting the Black Sea with the Mediterranean under Russian control. Russia had cherished this goal throughout the eighteenth and nineteenth centuries. Although the Russians failed to achieve the latter ambition, they did win the war and liberated most of the Balkans from Turkish rule. The Treaty of San Stefano in early 1878 recognized three new independent countries—Serbia, Montenegro, and Rumania. It also created a large new autonomous state of Bulgaria, encompassing much of the southern Balkans and clearly intended to be a Russian satellite. This massive change in the Balkan balance of power inspired protests from both Britain and Austria-Hungary. British Prime Minister Benjamin Disraeli was especially truculent. Fearing that the large Bulgarian state would bring Russian influence into the Mediterranean, he sent a fleet to Constantinople in an effort to force St. Petersburg to back down and accept a revision of the treaty. Austria-Hungary feared that the virtual elimination of Turkey's presence from the Balkans would encourage nationalistic ambitions among its own subject ethnic groups.

For a time it appeared that Britain and Austria-Hungary might resort to war with Russia. However, at this moment Bismarck intervened to persuade all concerned to attend a conference in Berlin that would work out a compromise and preserve the peace. The ensuing Congress of Berlin later in 1878 produced a new treaty that reduced Bulgaria's size by two-thirds and maintained a considerable amount of Balkan territory under Turkish control. The Treaty of Berlin also confirmed the independence of Serbia, Montenegro, and Rumania. Moreover, in a provision that held considerable importance for the future, it granted Austria the right to administer the small provinces of Bosnia and Herzegovina, although both remained nominally under Turkish overlordship. The Russians, outraged by what they considered a betrayal by Austria-Hungary and, to a lesser extent, Germany, now abandoned the Three Emperors' League.

As consolation, Bismarck turned to an arrangement with Austria-Hungary only. This time he worked out an actual defensive military agreement—the Dual Alliance of 1879. Because of Austria's concern over a possible war with Russia, the pact was anti-Russian in character. It provided that, if Russia attacked either partner, the other would come to its aid. If either were the victim of an attack by another power, the remaining partner would follow a policy of benevolent neutrality. The Dual Alliance was destined to remain the cornerstone of Germany's foreign policy until World War I.

Russian estrangement from Germany proved short-lived, however. Soon after the creation of the Dual Alliance, Russia approached Berlin about a possible accord. To Russia's chagrin, Bismarck insisted that Austria be included and, after lengthy negotiations, the Russians agreed. The revived Three Emperors' League of 1881 went beyond the scope of the original treaty. It provided that, if any of the three partners became involved in a war with a fourth power, the other two would remain neutral.

In 1882, Italy also made an alliance with Germany. The Italians had been on especially close terms with Bismarck ever since Italy joined Prussia in the war against Austria in 1866 and acquired Venetia as its reward. The Italians had also taken advantage of the French evacuation of their garrison from Rome during the Franco-Prussian War to occupy the "Eternal City." But it was France's establishment of a protectorate over the North African territory of Tunis that provided the direct motivation for Italy's decision to seek an alliance with Germany. Rome had long coveted Tunis for itself but had failed to act. Lying across a narrow stretch of the Mediterranean from the Italian island of Sicily, Tunis would have provided Italy with an especially strong strategic position. The Italians were so enraged that they agreed to an alliance, not only with Germany but also with their old enemy Austria, despite the fact that the Austrians still possessed the Italian-populated areas of the Trentino and the city of Trieste. This new Triple Alliance provided that, if France engaged in unprovoked aggression against Italy, Germany and Austria would come to their ally's aid. If France should attack Germany, Italy would extend military support to the Germans.

The following year Bismarck concluded still another defensive military alliance, this one linking the newly independent state of Rumania to Germany and Austria-Hungary. Rumania's King Carol I, a member of a branch line of the Hohenzollern dynasty, shared a bond of kinship with William II and looked to Germany for protection against his country's powerful Russian neighbor to the northeast. He also was grateful for Austria-Hungary's support for his recent transformation of Rumania from a principality to an actual kingdom.

Germany was now allied to five powers and also enjoyed good relations with Britain. France remained totally isolated from poten-tial allies. But Bismarck questioned how reliable Italy would be once its anger toward France had cooled, especially in view of Austria's possession of the territories that Italian nationalists referred to as "unredeemed Italy." To make matters worse, Austria-Hungary and Russia quarreled again, this time over Bulgaria. St. Petersburg expected Bulgaria to conduct itself as a virtual Russian dependency. Instead, the Bulgars acted quite independently. In 1886, Russia attempted to place a puppet ruler on the Bulgarian throne but backed down when Austria-Hungary and Britain objected. Although Bismarck tried to follow a neutral course between his two allies, the Russians reacted angrily to both Austria's intervention and Bismarck's lack of support for them. The Three Emperors' League did not survive the crisis, and this time there would be no revival.

But Bismarck hoped to maintain at least a connection between Germany and Russia, and the Russians feared a hostile Austro-German combination. In 1887, Russia proposed a new relationship, and Bismarck agreed. This "Reinsurance Treaty" provided that, should either power be attacked, its partner would follow a policy of benevolent neutrality. Thus, if Austria committed aggression against Russia, Germany would remain neutral. In the eyes of some Germans, the treaty conflicted with the Dual Alliance, but in reality the two were compatible because the Dual Alliance restricted Germany's military obligation to cases of Russian aggression against Austria. It said nothing of joining in an Austrian attack on Russia.

Among those who felt uncomfortable about the Reinsurance Treaty were the men who inherited the formidable task of guiding German foreign policy when Bismarck stepped down as chancellor in 1890. Despite Bismarck's enormous prestige, the power he had exercised was not actually his but the emperor's. The constitution for the German Empire, carefully drafted under Bismarck's overall supervision, made the emperor's role the most powerful in the political system with complete control over foreign policy as well as military and naval affairs. The emperor could and did delegate much of that power to the chancellor, but the power remained his. By contrast, the German parliament, the Reichstag, was much weaker. It could not even initiate legislation, although it did control appropriations, including the military budget. This power required Bismarck to engage in skillful manipulation to obtain his goals.

CHANGES IN GERMANY

As long as William I lived, Bismarck was secure as the dominant figure in the German government. But when William died in 1888 at the age of 91, the situation began to change. His immediate successor, Frederick, was dying of throat cancer when he came to the throne and lingered only three months. Frederick's son, William II, took the throne later in 1888 and was determined to play a major policy-making role. This insistence brought him into conflict with the strong-willed chancellor on a number of issues, and in 1890 he dismissed Bismarck from office. The architect of Germany unity had become a victim of the system he himself had created.

Despite Bismarck's retirement, his system remained. It required a man of his stature to make it function properly. Unfortunately, neither William nor any of the four men who served as chancellor during the following years proved to be such a leader. Although intelligent, the new emperor had little formal education and seemed proud of it, even boasting that he never read the newspapers. William was also given to vacillating behavior, a point driven home by a German diplomat's remark that the emperor's viewpoint on any issue was "that of the last comer." Outwardly, William II was given to bombastic speeches and posturing in his grandiose military uniforms, but inwardly he suffered from great insecurity, apparently traceable to his often unhappy relationship with his parents as well as his self-consciousness over a withered left arm.

Extremely conservative in his political views, William firmly believed that the emperor must remain the focal point of the political system, and he held great contempt for parliamentary government. He clearly revealed his authoritarian outlook in a statement he once made to a group of army recruits: "When your emperor commands you to do so, you must shoot at your fathers and mothers." This comment also reflected his militaristic attitude. He loved to play at warfare and, before coming to the throne, often commanded troops during war games. Although he demonstrated little military ability, officers in control of the maneuvers always saw to it that his side won. William also had an alarming tendency to blurt out in public whatever occurred to him on the spur of the moment. This led him into embarrassing situations, especially in the delicate realm of foreign affairs.

William and Bismarck's immediate successor as chancellor, General Georg Leo von Caprivi, harbored misgivings about the Reinsurance Treaty. They feared that the Russians might reveal the existence of the secret agreement in an effort to create antagonism between Germany and its ally, Austria-Hungary. The Reinsurance Treaty, like most arrangements of its type, bound the participants for a limited number of years, in this case, three, but was renewable. If Bismarck had remained in power, he clearly would have renewed the agreement, but shortly after his dismissal, Friedrich von Holstein, an influential foreign ministry official, persuaded the emperor and Caprivi to allow the treaty to lapse. The German leaders hoped to compensate for the loss of the Russian connection by making an agreement with Britain, but unfortunately for them the British had no intention of cooperating. Thus, by casting their former ally adrift, the Germans freed the Russians to seek friends elsewhere. They soon found France waiting in the wings.

FRENCH-RUSSIAN TIES

To be sure, obstacles stood in the way of a Franco-Russian arrangement. Relations between the two countries had often been hostile during the nineteenth century, and France's democratic Third Republic contrasted dramatically with the authoritarian regime of Czarist Russia. However, the French realized that the Germans had provided them with the opportunity to emerge from their diplomatic isolation. They quickly sought closer ties with Russia. Czar Alexander III and his ministers were willing to listen. Russia clearly was now as isolated as France. Moreover, its new industrial program had already benefitted from French loans. An agreement with Paris would almost certainly lead to additional financial assistance. By 1891 the two countries had agreed to consult with one another in case either of them felt threatened by aggression.

Certain leaders in both countries were content with this achievement and did not relish the prospect of a more far-reaching agreement that might lead to a war in which their own interests were not really at stake. Most notably, Russia had no interest in helping France regain Alsace-Lorraine, while France had little sympathy for Russian designs on the Balkans or in Asia. But mutual fear of Germany and a desire to safeguard their own security led them into an actual defensive military convention in 1894. This Franco-Russian Alliance provided that, if either power were attacked by Germany, the other partner would join in its defense. The alliance would also go into effect if Italy attacked France, with German support, or if Austria-Hungary committed aggression against Russia, again with German aid.

BRITAIN SEEKS ALLIES

The creation of the Franco-Russian Alliance left Britain as the only Great Power without an ally. But this was by choice; the British had long referred to this situation as "splendid isolation." Throughout the nineteenth century the British had avoided any alliance that might involve them in a Continental war. As an island power with the world's largest navy, Britain felt secure from invasion. Although dedicated to upholding the balance of power in Europe, the British pursued economic and imperialistic interests throughout the world and devoted most of their rather meager military strength to maintaining their colonies, especially India. However, as Germany and the United States threatened Britain's industrial leadership, and as the Continental alliances took shape in the century's last few decades, the former confidence began to fade. British leaders came to question whether iso-

lation was splendid any longer. They concluded that it might benefit Britain to acquire allies or, at least, friends.

The first candidate for this role was Germany. Prospects appeared reasonably bright. The British had no long-standing tradition of hostility toward Germany as they did toward France and Russia, and certain bonds of kinship existed. Both peoples spoke Germanic languages, and Britain's Queen Victoria was the grandmother of William II. To be sure, Anglo-German relations had not always been happy. The British had brushed aside German overtures for an alliance following the dropping of the Reinsurance Treaty, and bitterness developed between the two countries as a result of developments in South Africa.

Cecil Rhodes, prime minister of Britain's Cape Colony, dreamed of British expansion that would ultimately link Capetown with Cairo, Egypt, by means of a trans-African railroad. Among the territories coveted by Rhodes were the republics of the Transvaal and the Orange Free State to the north of Cape Colony. Both were ruled by the Boers, the descendants of Dutch settlers, who had colonized the Cape of Good Hope at the southern tip of Africa, starting in the seventeenth century. The Boers had migrated northward after Britain gained control of Cape Colony during the Napoleonic Wars. In 1895, Dr. Leander Starr Jameson, one of Rhodes's associates, led a small military force in a raid against the Transvaal. Although the British disavowed any responsibility for the Jameson Raid, few Europeans believed them. On this occasion, William II sent a congratulatory telegram to Prime Minister Paul Kruger of the Transvaal, hailing his country's ability to repel the raid without aid from "friendly powers." His intemperate words implied that Germany would have been prepared to provide that aid, if necessary. The British were not amused.

This setback did not prevent efforts by British Colonial Secretary Joseph Chamberlain and German officials to secure closer relations between the two powers in 1898. Although these contacts continued intermittently until 1901, they led nowhere. Lord Salisbury, the British prime minister, did not share Chamberlain's enthusiasm, while the Germans would accept no agreement that did not bind Britain to the Triple Alliance. The British were not willing to accept such a far-reaching commitment.

Anglo-German relations took a decided turn for the worse when Britain went to war with the Boer republics in 1899. The conflict did not go well for the British for some time. They underestimated the Boer forces, which resorted to successful guerrilla tactics. The war also proved most unpopular in other countries, including Germany whose sympathy clearly lay with the Boers. Britain eventually resorted to rounding up Boers in large-scale actions and interning them in concentration camps, a policy that turned German and world opinion even more strongly against the British. When Britain finally brought the Boer War to a victorious conclusion in 1902, the benefits of seeking better relations with other powers had become quite clear to leaders in London. However, German and European hostility in general during the conflict prompted them to look elsewhere for potential friends. Britain was especially concerned over the growth of Franco-Russian naval power in East Asia as well as continued Russian encroachment on China, Persia, and Afghanistan. These fears led to a remarkable departure in British policy—the signing of an actual defensive military alliance with Japan in 1902. Britain had long avoided such agreements. The Anglo-Japanese Alliance provided that, if either partner became the victim of aggression in East Asia by two powers, the other partner could come to its assistance. If either

one was attacked by just one power, the other partner would remain neutral. The alliance not only reflected mutual fear of Russia but also concern that France would support its ally if it became involved in war in East Asia. Since Japan maintained a formidable navy, the British now felt secure in withdrawing most of their naval forces from this area for redeployment elsewhere. They also encouraged the Japanese in their ambitions against Russia in East Asia.

FRENCH INITIATIVES

If the world was surprised by Britain's alliance with Japan, it was astonished two years later when the British moved in the direction of better relations with France, a country with whom it had almost gone to war at the time of the Fashoda crisis in 1898. In part, this remarkable transformation was due to the efforts of Théophile Delcassé, who became France's foreign minister in 1898 and greatly strengthened his country's diplomatic position during the next seven years. Delcassé was very much an imperialist who looked forward to expanding France's position in the Mediterranean and Africa, but he was haunted by fear of Germany becoming a power in this area. The origin of this concern was his belief that Austria-Hungary would soon disintegrate because of its nationalities problem. If this happened, he expected Germany to acquire the German-inhabited areas of the Dual Monarchy as well as Austria's territory along the Adriatic seacoast, giving the Germans access to the Mediterranean.

Delcassé's dread of German intrusion into what he considered a French sphere of influence contributed to his efforts to strengthen the Russian alliance. In 1899, he reached agreement to extend the time limit of the alliance indefinitely and to widen its provisions to include the possibility of war with Britain as well as to preserve the balance of power in Europe. In keeping with his desire to aggrandize French influence in the Mediterranean and especially the northwestern African territory of Morocco, Delcassé also courted better relations with Italy. The anger over French occupation of Tunis, which had prompted Italian adherence to the Triple Alliance, had long since cooled. In fact, Italy had conceded France's control of that country two years before Delcassé became foreign minister and had turned its own ambitions toward Tripoli and Cyrenaica, bordering Tunis to the east. Relations improved still more with the signing of a commercial treaty in 1898, and France soon became Italy's chief source of loans.

The two powers also made progress toward a definitive agreement on colonial issues, a development that German Chancellor Bernhard von Bülow referred to as Italy's "extra dance." Their efforts culminated in Italian recognition of France's right to encroach on Morocco, while the French acknowledged a similar "free hand" to Italy in Tripoli and Cyrenaica. Even more dramatically, the two powers pledged neutrality should either of them fall victim to aggression or go to war in response to a direct provocation infringing on its honor or security. Although critics contend that this agreement brought Italy's obligations to Germany and Austria-Hungary into question, it did not actually violate the terms of the Triple Alliance, which was strictly defensive in nature.

Delcassé eventually moved in the direction of another agreement, this time with Britain. His policy toward London reflected concern over the Anglo-Japanese Alliance. The French worried about the possibility of being drawn into a war against Britain in defense of Russia's East Asian ambitions. Lord Lansdowne, the British foreign secretary, shared Delcassé's misgivings about the Far Eastern situation. These fears mounted as

rivalry increased between Russia and Japan over China's northeastern territory of Manchuria and the nominally independent state of Korea, adjoining Manchuria on the south. By early 1904 both powers were preparing for war. Japan struck first with a devastating surprise attack on the Russian naval squadron stationed at Port Arthur on the Manchurian coast in February. The outbreak of hostilities stimulated efforts by France and Britain to reach an understanding to avoid being drawn into the conflict in support of their respective allies.

BRITISH FEARS OF GERMAN NAVAL POWER

The British had grown anxious over what they viewed as an alarming increase in German naval power. The architect of this expansion was Admiral Alfred von Tirpitz, a close friend of William II and former commander of the German cruiser squadron in the Far East who became naval secretary in 1897.[1] While the emperor envied Britain's far-flung empire and saw a large battle fleet as the key to Germany achieving a similar stature as a "world power," Tirpitz preferred to keep German warships in home waters rather than scatter them around the globe. The admiral combined technical and organizational ability with a flair for public relations, which belied his rather fierce appearance, enhanced by a long forked beard. In 1898, he created the Navy League, a propaganda organization designed to agitate for the development of a large fleet. By 1908, the league boasted more than a million members. The admiral also forged close ties with German industrialists and maintained strong support for his policies among politicians in the Reichstag.

---

[1]In 1901, after passage of legislation to increase the size of the navy, Tirpitz was made a noble. Henceforth, his last name was preceded by "von."

Tirpitz dreamed of ultimately creating a fleet of capital ships two-thirds the size of Britain's Royal Navy, the world's largest. Tirpitz believed that such a navy would ensure that the British would not risk entering a war against Germany and might entice them into making an alliance with Berlin, thus linking Europe's two most formidable naval powers. Germany began to translate Tirpitz's dream into reality in 1898 when it introduced a program to construct a large number of battleships during the next two decades.

At first, British leaders did not appear overly concerned about Germany's naval program, but by 1902 their attitude had changed, in large part because of the growth of animosity between the two powers during the Boer War. Tirpitz's policy posed a direct threat to Britain's "two-power standard," which held that the key to British security was a navy stronger than the next two largest European fleets combined. Britain, as an island power, had always depended primarily on seapower for protection against potential enemies. Its growing population also required massive imports of food, while its economic prosperity rested on access to overseas markets and sources of raw materials. The British believed that their very survival depended on continued naval supremacy.

BRITAIN AND FRANCE IMPROVE RELATIONS

Despite British concern over Germany's naval construction program and Anglo-French desires to avoid involvement in the Russo-Japanese War, it was mutual willingness to resolve colonial issues that proved the catalyst for better relations between Britain and France. The key area in question was Morocco. The French hoped to transform this North African territory into a protectorate, but the British had some misgivings. While not necessarily opposed to a French protectorate there, they were determined to secure the neutralization of the northern Moroccan coast, which lay across the Mediterranean from Britain's naval base at Gibraltar.

Contacts between the two powers began as early as 1902, but they did not take the form of serious negotiations until Delcassé and Lord Lansdowne conferred personally in July 1903. King Edward VII, who was pro-French and detested William II, contributed his personal support to the process. Although progress was slow, Lansdowne and Paul Cambon, the French ambassador to London, completed an agreement in April 1904. It became known as the *Entente Cordiale* (Friendly Understanding). Under its terms, France recognized the preponderant position that the British had already attained in Egypt, and the British granted the French a "free hand" in Morocco, except for the coast along the Strait of Gibraltar. The latter area was to remain unfortified and would go to Spain if France secured a protectorate over the rest of Morocco.

At first, Germany did not appear unduly disturbed by the remarkable change in Anglo-French relations. Berlin indicated that it did not oppose French penetration of Morocco, provided that German commercial interests there were safeguarded. But Delcassé, emboldened by the entente with Britain, forged ahead with his plans to transform Morocco into a protectorate without consulting Germany. In late 1904 the French pressured the sultan of Morocco to accept a number of financial, economic, and military reforms as the prelude to this objective. France also used its influence to prevent Morocco from buying war material from Germany. All of this angered the Germans, who also realized that France was hampered by some serious weaknesses. Relations between French civilian and military leaders were at low ebb because of the republican government's efforts to purge officers with monarchist sympathies. A program introduced in 1901 to rejuvenate the French navy had also made little progress, and France's ally Russia had suffered a series of disasters in its war with Japan as well as an outbreak of revolutionary activity in early 1905.

GERMAN COUNTERMEASURES

This combination of factors encouraged Chancellor Bülow to embark on a bold course. William II had appointed Bülow to the chancellorship in 1900, boasting that he had discovered his own Bismarck. To say the least, he was guilty of overstating Bülow's talents. While superficially polished and unquestionably blessed with wit and charm as well as some ability, the chancellor was shallow and lacking in vision. His reputation for slipperiness inspired Tirpitz to remark that, compared to him, an eel was a leach. Bülow also courted William's favor by flattering him, a practice that strengthened the emperor's already inflated sense of self-importance. A diplomat with 20 years' experience in foreign capitals, Bülow had served as foreign secretary since 1897. Despite this impressive background, he often deferred to the views of Friedrich von Holstein, a shadowy but influential official in the Foreign Office since the days of Bismarck. In early 1905, Bülow and Holstein agreed that Germany would challenge France's plans for Morocco and, in the process, test the strength of the *Entente Cordiale*.

Bülow and Holstein did not believe that Britain would support France if confronted by a serious crisis. They prevailed upon William II to stop at the Moroccan port of Tangier during a Mediterranean cruise and, while there, make a declaration of Germany's position regarding Morocco. The emperor had serious misgivings about the wisdom of this approach but went along with their desires. After reaching Tangier on the last day

of March 1905, William proclaimed support for Morocco's independence and territorial integrity. Berlin followed with a demand that an international conference be convened to deal with the Moroccan situation.

After almost a year of indecision, the Germans had decided to challenge France's imperialist ambitions in Morocco. The French were divided on how to respond. Delcassé made some tentative conciliatory gestures toward Germany, but British assurances of support encouraged him to stand firm. Premier Maurice Rouvier worried about Germany's attitude, however, and feared that Delcassé's policy might lead to war. Growing pressure from both Germany and Rouvier finally forced Delcassé to resign in June.

Not content with the fall of Delcassé, the Germans rebuffed French efforts to reach a settlement that would provide Germany with compensation, either in Morocco or elsewhere in Africa. Instead, they continued to insist on an international conference in an effort to humiliate France still more. But by overplaying their hand in this fashion, the Germans aroused the fear and resentment of Britain. The British also worried about the possibility of Germany gaining a port on the Moroccan coast and becoming a Mediterranean naval power. Lord Lansdowne remained steadfastly loyal to France, and when Sir Edward Grey succeeded Lansdowne as foreign secretary in December 1905 Grey pursued a policy that was even more devoted to the *Entente Cordiale*.

ANGLO-FRENCH RESPONSE TOWARD GERMANY

Although Lansdowne was a Conservative and Grey a Liberal, their views on the prevailing European situation were remarkably similar. Both worried over Britain's isolation and saw the entente with France as a vital factor in safeguarding the country's security. A member of a prestigious and wealthy northern English family, Grey was known as a man of principle, scrupulous honesty, and great patriotism. A rather colorless and enigmatic figure, Grey was a widower who had no children and whose only passion, aside from politics and work, was fly-fishing. Remarkably uncosmopolitan for a foreign secretary, he avoided travel abroad, spoke indifferent French, and appeared to be happiest in the company of trout and ducks. Able rather than brilliant and tending to react to events rather than to anticipate them, Grey nevertheless dominated British foreign policy from 1905 until 1914. Even before he took office, he had grown highly suspicious of German intentions. Owing largely to the influence of Sir Eyre Crowe, a senior official in the Foreign Office, he viewed Germany as a danger to the balance of power and an enemy of Britain.

Britain's support strengthened France's resolve and, although the French agreed to Germany's demand for an international conference, they also worked diligently to gain the backing of other powers for their position on Morocco. Mutual fear over the belligerent German approach led in December to secret discussions between British and French military officials about joint action should the two powers became involved in war with Germany. The talks continued into 1906 and resulted in a British promise to send an expeditionary force of 100,000 men to France in the event of such a conflict, but they reached no decision on exactly where or how these troops would be deployed. Grey and British military leaders impressed upon the French that these measure were put forth on a contingency basis and did not constitute a binding pledge. Actual British intervention would depend on the government's evaluation of circumstances at the time such a crisis might arise. Despite this qualification, these conversations represented a dramatic shift in British policy. They

FIGURE 2–1 Sir Edward Grey, Britain's foreign secretary. National Archives

remained secret, however. When questioned in Parliament regarding the possibility of a commitment to France, Grey denied that any military conversations had taken place. Meanwhile, the Germans learned of them through a spy and knew that Grey was lying, deepening their suspicions of an Anglo-French commitment.

Ironically, William II and Bülow had no intention of resorting to military action over Morocco and had staked everything on gaining a diplomatic victory over France. Unfortunately for them, their heavy-handed approach had created little goodwill in other countries. It appeared that, despite their protestations of concern for Morocco's independence, the Germans were really interested in gaining the upper hand in that country for themselves. When the international conference finally convened in the Spanish city of Algeciras early in 1906, the result was a stunning diplomatic defeat for Germany, which received only the support of its ally Austria-Hungary. Even Italy deserted its partner in the Triple Alliance on this issue, a disturbing harbinger for the future. Although the Algeciras agreement provided for protection of the economic rights of other powers, it opened the way for France to extend its control over Morocco.

FORMATION OF THE TRIPLE ENTENTE

The final step in the creation of a counterweight to the Triple Alliance was the bringing together of France's ally Russia and France's partner in the *Entente Cordiale*, Britain. This had seemed an unlikely prospect in the months following formation of the entente. Although Lord Lansdowne had hoped that the agreement with France might lead to an understanding with Russia, a bizarre incident in the North Sea dashed his dream for the time being. This resulted from the Russian decision to send their Baltic Sea fleet to take part in the Russo-Japanese War. When these ships reached the North Sea, en route to the Far East in October 1904, they encountered a number of British fishing vessels near the Dogger Bank and somehow mistook them for Japanese torpedo boats. They fired on them, killing and wounding a number of fishermen.

For a few days it appeared that this unfortunate episode might lead to war between Britain, Japan's ally since 1902, and Russia. But Lord Lansdowne followed a policy of restraint and, with the help of French mediation, an international commission of inquiry worked out a peaceful solution requiring Russia to pay an indemnity to the casualties.

During the Russo-Japanese War a German agreement with Russia seemed more likely than an Anglo-Russian combination. While the Russians were engaged in their losing military effort, France had followed a completely neutral policy and had strengthened its relations with Japan's ally Britain. All of this created misgivings in St. Petersburg and provided the opportunity for William II, Bülow, and Holstein to try to lure Russia away from France. After the Dogger Bank incident, they proposed a Russo-German defensive alliance, but France learned of the overture and pressured the Russians to refuse, while pledging loyalty to its ally. William II tried again in the summer of 1905, following Delcassé's fall. On this occasion, William met with his cousin, Czar Nicholas II of Russia, off the Finnish island of Björkö while on a cruise in the Baltic and persuaded the czar to join him in signing a draft treaty for a defensive military alliance. But the two monarchs, trying in their own way to restore Russo-German friendship, had acted without the knowledge of their respective governments, and when Nicholas returned to St. Petersburg, the Foreign Ministry persuaded him to disavow the Björkö Treaty, pointing out that it would undermine the alliance with France.

The affair of the stillborn Björkö Treaty was characteristic of William's impulsiveness as well as the ease with which Nicholas could be persuaded to take a certain position and subsequently change his mind. In this respect, the czar was similar to his cousin. The two were also alike in that neither of them was well suited for the role of emperor. But while William was given to bombast and posturing, Nicholas was gentle, retiring, and well meaning. Both were devoted to their respective dynasties and determined to maintain their own power. Nicholas shared William's disdain for parliamentary government. He was convinced that he ruled by the grace of God and that the formation of policy must be in keeping with his own conscience.

Britain's concern over German naval power mounted during this same period, a trend symbolized in 1904 by the appointment of the dynamic and fiery Admiral Sir John Fisher to the position of first sea lord in command of the Royal Navy. Possessed of enormous energy and given to spouting biblical quotations, Fisher was absolutely fearless and extremely outspoken. On one occasion, he became so carried away during a conversation with King Edward VII that the monarch felt compelled to demand, "Will you kindly leave off shaking your fist in my face?" The admiral worked tirelessly to strengthen the Royal Navy and prepare Britain for what he viewed as an inevitable confrontation with Germany. Fisher warned that the Germans ultimately intended to use their growing fleet to attack Britain. To counter this danger, he speculated on a possible "Copenhagen" attack on the German navy in emulation of Lord Nelson's peacetime bombardment and seizure of the Danish fleet in 1807 to prevent it from falling into the hands of Napoleon. Such wild schemes did not endear the admiral to other British leaders, but Fisher gained a much more positive response when he insisted on the construction of a revolutionary new battleship, the *Dreadnought*.

This ship, due to join the fleet in 1906, was larger and faster than any vessel afloat and was equipped with long-range guns and turbine engines. It gained its name from Fisher's motto: "Fear God and dread nought." The *Dreadnought* made all other warships, including those of Britain itself, obsolete and opened a new dimension in not only the Anglo-German naval rivalry but also that of other powers. Despite the potential danger that such a development posed to Britain's supremacy on the high seas, the advance of naval technology clearly indicated that one power or another would soon develop such a warship. The British believed that they should take the lead. In view of Britain's financial stability and abundant shipyards, they also felt that they could maintain their lead. Admiral Tirpitz felt obliged to adopt a policy of building similar warships. In the following years all major powers laid down dreadnoughts in abundance. The British hoped to widen their lead, while the Germans attempted to narrow the gap. This naval race, more than anything else, aggravated relations between the two countries during the years before 1914.

The naval rivalry, combined with Germany's truculent behavior during the Moroccan crisis, persuaded Foreign Secretary Grey to revive Lansdowne's hope for an understanding with the Russians. Clearly, Russia now appeared less of a danger to British interests than did Germany, especially in view of the continued disastrous course of the war with Japan. The Russian Baltic fleet proceeded half-way around the world following the Dogger Bank incident, only to be annihilated in the Battle of Tsushima in May 1905. Repeated defeats, including the Japanese capture of Port Arthur, had increased discontent among Russian social classes, culminating in the outbreak of revolution in January 1905. In an effort to end the revolutionary turmoil, Nicholas II proclaimed a manifesto in October, which guaranteed civil rights, legalized political parties, and granted an elected parliament. The Russians also opened negotiations to end the war, culminating in the Treaty of Portsmouth in September 1905.

The settlement enabled Japan to gain a virtual protectorate over Korea and a dominant position in southern Manchuria.

Japan's victory had eliminated any Russian threat to British interests in the Far East and stimulated London's desire to settle the remaining sources of friction between the two countries. Grey especially wanted to safeguard the security of India by resolving differences over Persia, Afghanistan, and the Chinese territory of Tibet to the north of India. The Russians hoped that an agreement with Britain would strengthen their alliance with France and help persuade London to drop its traditional opposition to opening to Russian warships the Straits linking the Black Sea with the Mediterranean.

Negotiations began in May 1906, and although they progressed slowly, they concluded in an agreement in August 1907. Under its terms, neither country would seek a dominant position in Tibet, while Russia recognized British predominance, already well established, in Afghanistan. The two powers solemnly upheld Persia's independence and then proceeded to divide the country into three zones. Russia was to have dominant influence in the north and Britain in the south, while a "neutral zone" in the central part of the country would remain open to the commerce of both powers. As in the case of the *Entente Cordiale*, the agreement did not provide for a military alliance, but it did create another three-cornered relationship among major powers that soon became known unofficially as the "Triple Entente." Although the Anglo-Russian Agreement did not prevent friction between the two powers over Persia in the future, it did improve relations overall and strengthened the entente between Britain and France.

The Germans viewed the formation of the Triple Entente with alarm. In the following years they complained repeatedly of encirclement by the Entente powers. The new state of affairs

convinced them that they must stiffen ties with their only reliable ally, Austria-Hungary. This resolve posed the likelihood of Germany becoming embroiled in the rivalry of the Dual Monarchy and Russia over the Balkans.

MILITARY PLANNING

Despite the development of the Triple Entente, little concrete military planning marked Britain's relations with her partners until 1911. The Anglo-French staff talks, which began during the Moroccan crisis, ended in May 1906. A lull continued until Brigadier General Henry Wilson became Britain's chief of military operations in August 1910. An Anglo-Irish staff officer with a distinctly rebellious nature as well as great energy and ability, Wilson harbored extreme contempt for politicians but shared Grey's loyalty to the entente with France. He also got on well with French officers. The general was convinced that sooner or later Germany would attack France and believed that Britain must support the French. He also set out to improve the quality of Britain's army, a task already begun by Richard Haldane, a stocky Scottish lawyer who had become secretary of war in 1905. Despite having no prior experience with military affairs, Haldane proved an able and innovative minister. He shared Wilson's belief that the army's primary role should take the form of an expeditionary force that would fight on the European continent alongside the French in case of war with Germany. By the spring of 1911, General Wilson reached agreement with the French to increase the number of British troops earmarked for the British Expeditionary Force (BEF) to 150,000 men. The accord also provided for the arrival of the BEF in France within 14 days of the start of hostilities.

But there had been no corresponding progress in the direction of coordinating Anglo-

French naval forces. Admiral Fisher and Admiral A.K. Wilson, who succeeded Fisher as First Sea Lord in 1909, were determined to maintain the Royal Navy's traditional position as the premier factor in the defense of Britain. They opposed a Continental commitment that would relegate the navy to supporting army operations in France and doubted that a British military force of the proposed size could play a decisive role in a Continental conflict. Both men avoided staff talks with French naval officers and even refused to participate in a meaningful dialogue with British army leaders. This situation began to change in the following years.

In October 1908, the London *Daily Telegraph* published an account of an interview with William II of Germany in which the emperor professed both his friendship for Britain and his profound irritation with the British for their criticism of him. He even went so far as to claim that he had given them the military plan that had ultimately resulted in their victory in the Boer War. His condescending, tactless remarks created an extremely bad impression in Britain and cast doubt on the reliability of a country led by such an intemperate monarch. But they provoked an even greater uproar in Germany where all shades of political opinion found them offensive in some way. Indeed, William felt compelled to curb his public outbursts in the future.

A little over a month later, Britain's First Lord of the Admiralty, Reginald McKenna, warned his colleagues in the cabinet that the Germans were secretly collecting materials, including guns, turrets, and armor, in advance of actually laying down the keels of new dreadnoughts and were speeding up their timetable for producing these ships. He warned that this posed the danger that Germany would soon surpass Britain in dreadnoughts, predicting the possibility of a margin of 21 to 16 in the former's favor by 1912. McKenna argued that Britain should lay down six dreadnoughts in 1909 with the possibility of adding two more, if national security required it. Some cabinet members opposed this plan, and Prime Minister Herbert Asquith persuaded all concerned to accept a compromise proposal. This sought parliamentary approval for construction of four dreadnoughts as well as authorization to build four more, if it proved necessary.

When the British government revealed its fears of German cheating in dreadnought production, a "naval scare" quickly gripped the country. Conservatives in Parliament as well as a substantial segment of the public charged that Asquith's proposal was not enough and took up the cry "We want eight and we won't wait." These demands became so insistent that the government finally agreed. The scare even spread to the dominions, and New Zealand and Australia each offered to pay for construction of an additional dreadnought in 1910. Thus, the British wound up with ten new super battleships. Ironically, although the Germans had gathered additional materials and had even awarded contracts to shipyards in advance, they had no plans to increase production in 1909 beyond the four dreadnoughts authorized by the Reichstag.

British fears of German intentions mounted still more when a serious Balkan crisis arose in October 1908 following Austria's annexation of Bosnia[2] and Herzegovina in violation of the Treaty of Berlin. Turkey, Serbia, and Russia all quickly challenged this action. Germany, despite misgivings, backed its ally, while France and Britain offered more tepid support to St. Petersburg. For a time the possibility of war loomed, but Russia backed down in early 1909 and persuaded Serbia to follow its lead. Austria was able to

---

[2]See Chapter 3 for a more detailed account of the Bosnian crisis.

keep the two provinces, but the Dual Monarchy's relations with Russia and Serbia had suffered a serious setback.

The issue that brought the matter of Anglo-French naval cooperation to a head, however, was another German excursion into Moroccan politics. Germany had recognized France's special political position in Morocco during 1909 in return for a French promise to safeguard German economic interests. But France did little to implement this pledge, while increasing its own military presence in the country. In April 1911, the French revealed plans to send a relief column to Fez to protect European citizens in the Moroccan capital from an alleged threat of attack by rebellious tribes. The Germans considered such an action to be a violation of the Algeciras agreement and the prelude to establishment of a French protectorate. They warned Paris that their acceptance of such a step would be dependent on compensation for Germany, either in the form of a Moroccan port or a slice of the French Congo in west-central Africa. However, instead of pursuing negotiations, they triggered a second Moroccan crisis.

SECOND MOROCCAN CRISIS

The architect of this crisis was Alfred von Kiderlen-Wächter, who became German foreign secretary in 1910. Kiderlen remains a most controversial and paradoxical figure. Possessed of considerable ability, he was a skillful career diplomat, likened by his admirers to Bismarck. In his private life, he was light-hearted and charming, especially when in the company of a beautiful blond woman who often lived in his house but whom he never married. It would seem that he was sincerely devoted to peace and tried valiantly but unsuccessfully to reverse Tirpitz's naval policy. He clearly recognized its disastrous effect on Anglo-German relations. Nevertheless, Kiderlen often approached relations with other powers in a

ruthlessly brutal manner and appears to have assumed that by pounding his fist on the table he would get his way in a crisis. He and his German colleagues employed this strategy on July 1, 1911, when they dispatched the gunboat *Panther* to the port of Agadir on Morocco's Atlantic coast. Publicly, they claimed that this action was necessary to protect German citizens and economic interests in southern Morocco, but in reality they intended to force concessions from the French.

The brusque nature of the "*Panther*'s leap" to Agadir inspired renewed fears in Paris and London. This consternation increased still more when Kiderlen demanded a huge portion of the French Congo as Germany's compensation. The French regarded the cession of such a vast expanse of territory, larger than all of Morocco, as totally unacceptable, although they were willing to negotiate with Germany. Britain's initial reaction was one of moderation. Foreign Secretary Grey urged the French to reach an agreement, but key members of the Foreign Office were deeply suspicious of Germany and urged a show of support for France. The most notable example of this support came in a speech delivered by Chancellor of the Exchequer David Lloyd George with the authorization of both Grey and Prime Minister Asquith.

Although a Welshman known for his pacifism, Lloyd George phrased his remarks in bellicose terms. He declared that, if a situation arose which threatened Britain's interests and position as a Great Power, "then I say emphatically that peace at that price would be a humiliation intolerable for a great country like ours to endure." Although the speech clearly represented a public warning to Germany, in private Grey continued to urge the French to work for a settlement. This combination of outward resolve and inward restraint helped pave the way for a Franco-German agreement in November 1911. Under its terms, Germany received a much smaller and less important portion of the French Congo than Kiderlen had originally demanded. In return, Berlin conceded French domination of Morocco. France established the long-coveted protectorate slightly over a year later, while most of the northern coastal strip went to Spain.

WINSTON CHURCHILL: FIRST LORD OF THE ADMIRALTY

Another Moroccan crisis had ended peacefully, but once again it also led to a tightening of Anglo-French relations. A key factor in this process was the appointment in 1911

FIGURE 2–2   Winston Churchill, First Lord of the Admiralty. National Archives

of Winston Churchill to the office of First Lord of the Admiralty. Churchill, destined to become Britain's great World War II prime minister, was a descendant of the illustrious John Churchill, Duke of Marlborough. Marlborough had led Britain to victory over the French during the War of the Spanish Succession in the early eighteenth century. Winston's own father, Lord Randolph Churchill, had been one of the rising young leaders in the Conservative party during the 1880s. Lord Randolph served briefly as Lord Salisbury's chancellor of the exchequer in 1886, but a quarrel with his colleagues led to his resignation and ended his career. The young Winston served as an officer during the British campaign in the Sudan in 1898 and the following year went to South Africa to report the Boer War for a London newspaper. He gained renown by making a dramatic escape after being taken prisoner by the Boers and then turned to a career in politics, winning election to Parliament in 1900 as a Conservative. Churchill broke with his party in 1903 over a proposal to introduce a protective tariff, however, and soon found refuge in the Liberal party. He served as president of the board of trade and later as home secretary in Asquith's government.

Even before moving to the Admiralty, Churchill had become a convinced advocate of the entente with France and supported General Wilson's plan to send an expeditionary force to the Continent in case of war with Germany. He now launched a new era of cooperation between the navy and the army as well as between British and French naval leaders. But naval staff talks did not progress far until after the failure of an Anglo-German attempt to curb the naval race in early 1912. The cost of building so many battleships had grown increasingly burdensome to both countries. Theobold von Bethmann-Hollweg, who succeeded Bülow as German chancellor in 1909, was dubious about the wisdom of Tirpitz's naval program. It had failed to narrow the gap between the German and British fleets, while having a disastrous effect on relations with Britain.

SIZE OF NAVIES DEBATED

The new German chancellor contrasted sharply with the flamboyant Bülow. Not even remotely charismatic, Bethmann was quiet, hardworking, and lacking in humor. After spending most of his career in the state of Prussia's ministry of the interior, Bethmann served as German interior secretary for two years before becoming chancellor. Not surprisingly, he was much more knowledgeable about domestic affairs than about foreign policy. Although highly conscientious, he lacked imagination and possessed limited vision of the future. By nature, training, and ability, he was primarily an administrator rather than a leader. Conservative politically and devoted to the monarchy, he had little love for the Reichstag, which he referred to as "a madhouse" following a particularly turbulent debate in 1913. Bethmann was, nevertheless, willing to compromise with those political elements favoring a more democratic system. This proved most difficult, however, in view of the reactionary views of the emperor, the army, and many other influential figures.

Bethmann agreed with Foreign Secretary Kiderlen-Wächter that Germany must give first priority in foreign policy to improving relations with Britain. Accordingly, in early 1912 he invited the British to send an envoy to Berlin to discuss the naval question. They chose Haldane, the war secretary, to undertake the mission. Bethmann proposed to link naval limitations with a political understanding, but he soon encountered opposition from Tirpitz and William II, neither of whom wanted any reduction in the naval program. When Bethmann threatened to resign, however, the emperor agreed to delay construction of new ships, if necessary, to secure an arrangement with Britain. But Bethmann's political proposal was unacceptable to British Foreign Secretary Grey. It called for a British pledge to remain neutral in the event of a European war. Grey rejected this on the grounds that it would undermine the ententes with France and Russia. Because the Germans were insistent on the neutrality provision, no agreement was forthcoming. Moreover, Churchill had undermined the Haldane mission on February 9 when he publicly criticized the German fleet as a "luxury." The British also contended that the six dreadnoughts they were building for other countries should not be counted as part of their strength. The Germans objected to this, charging that the British would commandeer these ships in time of war.

The failure of the Haldane mission increased Anglo-German suspicion and acted as a spur to additional cooperation between the British and French. Naval discussions began in earnest in July 1912, and in November the two powers attempted to spell out their mutual obligations in regard to a possible war. Although the understanding did not commit either country to take military action in any future crisis, it did require consultation in case one of them felt threatened by an unprovoked attack, or if there arose a danger to the general peace. In either situation, the two powers would consider the plans of their general staffs as the basis for possible joint action. Although Grey and other British leaders clung to the belief that they would have complete freedom of action in such an eventuality, they had compromised that freedom by agreeing to what was in reality a quasi-alliance. They had also clearly encouraged both France and Russia that Britain had a definite commitment.

In early 1913, the naval talks resulted in a convention that called for France to assume primary defense of entente interests in the western Mediterranean, while Britain would be responsible for defending the Strait of Dover, which linked the North Sea with the English Channel. Since the French had to divert ships from their Channel bases to the Mediterranean, Britain had assumed a virtual moral obligation to defend France's Channel coast in case of a German attack. British leaders also faced a potentially embarrassing domestic political issue became of the complete secrecy that surrounded all of the military and naval agreements. Virtually no one outside the cabinet and the leadership of the armed forces knew of their existence. The government also continued to deny that any such arrangements had been made. If a crisis of the type specified in the November 1912 agreement should come to pass, it could lead to a serious division of British opinion over the propriety and extent of these clandestine measures.

France and Russia also agreed to a naval convention in July 1912. It bound the two allies to cooperate closely in naval planning and provided for annual staff conferences. In February 1914, Russia began to seek closer ties with Britain as well. The British were reluctant to expand their relationship with the Russians beyond that of the 1907 agreement but finally yielded to pressure, not only from St. Petersburg but from Paris. In May, they agreed to hold naval staff talks with the Russians, but only one inconclusive meeting actually took place before the outbreak of World War I that summer. This was enough to further convince the French that Britain would be on their side if it came to war with Germany.

THE "FATEFUL CHAIN REACTION"

The emergence of the Triple Entente as a counterweight to the Triple Alliance clearly created a potentially dangerous element in European power politics. A crisis involving a member of each of the two coalitions might lead to a chain reaction that could trigger a general European war. But the existence of the two rival groupings did not make war inevitable. Indeed, at times members of each coalition acted as a restraining influence on their partners. The alliances also did not prevent members of one coalition from cooperating with those of the other grouping or encouraging defection of members of the opposition. The latter tendency was clearly present in Italy's "extra dance" with France in 1902 and Germany's attempts to woo Russia at the time of the Russo-Japanese War. However, despite these inter-alliance contacts, the fateful chain reaction did eventually come to pass. It came not as a result of imperialistic bickering over Africa and Asia but because of continuing animosity between Austria-Hungary and Russia in the Balkans. Their old rivalry became dangerously intertwined with the ambitions of the small state of Serbia, which seemed to threaten the very existence of the Dual Monarchy. It was this lethal combination that ultimately led to the outbreak of World War I.

3

THE EXPLOSIVE BALKANS

The Balkans, where Europe's fate ultimately would be decided, formed an especially crucial aspect of "the Eastern Question," which had been a source of increasing friction among the Great Powers since the eighteenth century. The Eastern Question focused on the obvious fact that Turkish power was declining at a quickening pace. By the mid-nineteenth century it appeared to be only a matter of time until the entire Ottoman Empire disintegrated. The real question at the core of the Eastern Question was who would get what when this collapse finally came to pass, not only in the Balkans but also in the rest of the empire. The inability of the Great Powers to agree on a division of spoils was the major reason why "the sick man" of Europe's death was so long in coming.

RUSSIAN DESIGNS

Of all the powers involved in the Eastern Question, Russia traditionally had followed the most aggressive policy. The Russians especially coveted control of the Straits connecting the Black Sea with the Mediterranean—the Bosporus, Sea of Marmara, and the Dardanelles. As long as the Straits remained in Turkish hands, Russia could not be certain of free passage for its merchant ships to the Mediterranean. An international agreement, the Straits Settlement of 1841, also prohibited foreign warships from traversing the Straits when Turkey was at peace. This provision, updated by the Treaty of Paris in 1856, prevented the Russian Black Sea fleet from participating in the Russo-Japanese War. If Turkey were at war with

Russia, however, it could open the Straits to an allied fleet.

Britain was the country traditionally most opposed to Russian dreams of encroaching on Turkey and the Straits. The British feared that Russian control of the Straits would pose a danger to their naval power in the Mediterranean as well as their interests in the Middle East. After construction of the Suez Canal in the 1860s, London became increasingly concerned about any threat to its lifeline to India, which now passed through the Suez Canal. These factors led Britain to pursue a policy of propping up Turkey and maintaining Turkish control of the Straits.

The Austrians had opposed Russian designs in the Balkans since the late eighteenth century and shared Britain's concern over the Straits. But, as a Danubian power, Austria also worried about Russia gaining domination over the mouths of the Danube River, which bordered Russian territory along the Black Sea. The Dual Monarchy possessed economic interests in the Balkans as well, and these grew more significant as Austrian industry expanded in the late nineteenth century. But even more importantly, Austria-Hungary hoped to prevent Russia from becoming too influential among the Slavic peoples of the Balkans. The Austrians and Magyars both resented Pan-Slav agitation there as well as among the Slavic groups within the Dual Monarchy itself. Not surprisingly, they shared Britain's desire to prop up Turkey and staunchly opposed the hopes of Balkan nationalities to break away from Turkish rule. The destruction of Turkish power in the Balkans would pose an alarming example for the subject ethnic groups of Austria-Hungary.

The mutual fears of Britain and Austria-Hungary had inspired their opposition to the Russian-imposed Treaty of San Stefano in 1878, which had attempted to create a large Bulgarian state as a puppet of St.

Petersburg. Their cooperation had forced Russia to accept a much smaller Bulgaria in the Treaty of Berlin. Both were relieved when the Bulgars, far from acting as a Russian satellite, as St. Petersburg had expected, followed an independent policy during the 1880s.

THE INTRICACIES OF BALKAN POLITICS

Austria-Hungary's concern over the Balkans slackened during the 1890s as Russia's ambitions, thwarted in 1878, shifted to the Far East. In 1897, the two powers agreed to maintain the status quo in the Balkans, and relative quiet reigned in this area for the next few years. But Russia's defeat at the hands of Japan diverted its attention back to the Balkans and renewed its determination to secure the Straits through which the Black Sea Fleet had been denied passage in 1904. This unfortunate turn of events coincided with a disastrous deterioration of relations between Austria-Hungary and its neighbor to the south—Serbia, which increasingly became a Russian protégé.

Serbia had loomed as a potential problem to Austria-Hungary for many years. When the small Slavic state became independent in 1878, its borders embraced only a small portion of the territory inhabited by Serbs. Austria-Hungary contained a sizable Serbian population within its own borders, not to mention the Serbs in the Austrian-administered provinces of Bosnia and Herzegovina, while still others remained under Turkish rule. However, despite its kinship with the Serbs living under Austro-Hungarian rule, Serbia retained especially close relations with the Dual Monarchy until the early twentieth century. In fact, Milan II, the ruler of Serbia at the time of the Congress of Berlin, had virtually offered to sell his country to Austria in return for a handsome financial subsidy and a palace in Vienna. The Hapsburg government had turned down the offer, but Serbia became a virtual Austro-Hungarian protectorate under Milan and his successor, Alexander II.

The situation began to change in June 1903 when a group of nationalistic Serbian army officers shot to death Alexander and his queen and then proceeded to hack their bodies to pieces before throwing them out of a palace window. Since the slain royal couple had no children, this barbaric assassination abruptly ended the Obrenovich dynasty. Alexander's successor was Prince Peter of the rival royal house of Karageorgevich, which the Obrenovich family had supplanted on the throne over 50 years earlier. While Peter's government continued Serbia's tight links to Austria-Hungary for the time being, it also sought closer relations with Russia and tolerated the proliferation of Pan-Serb and anti-Austrian organizations. These groups worked to create unrest among the Serbian population of the Dual Monarchy. They also sought to unite, not only the Serbs still living under Austro-Hungarian and Turkish rule, but the other South Slavs—the Slovenes, Croats, Bosnians, and Macedonians—in a "Greater Serbia." Whether these groups wanted to be liberated by the Serbs was quite another matter. Although all the South Slavs were related, they also differed from one another in various ways. For example, while the Serbs and Croats both spoke Serbo-Croatian, the Serbs used the Cyrillic alphabet and were Orthodox in religion; the Croats used the Latin alphabet and were Roman Catholic.

THE PIG WAR

Relations between Austria-Hungary and Serbia plummeted with the onset of a commercial struggle, known by the curious name "the Pig War," starting in 1906 and continuing until 1910. In the decades prior to the Pig War, Serbia's economy had been almost totally tied to that of the Dual Monarchy. Under this arrangement, Austria enjoyed a convenient market for its manufactured goods, while Serbia provided its powerful neighbor with agricultural commodities, especially pigs. In 1905, the Serbs attempted to reduce their economic dependence by making a commercial agreement with Bulgaria. The Austrians responded the next year by cutting off all imports of Serbian livestock, hoping to force Serbia to drop its arrangement with Bulgaria. But this action only angered the Serbs, who found markets in other countries, most notably Germany. In fact, the Germans acquired much of the Serbian market for manufactured goods and contributed greatly to Serbia's quest for commercial independence.

RUSSIA AND AUSTRIA-HUNGARY

Russia's pursuit of closer relations with Serbia in the aftermath of the Russo-Japanese War did not prevent St. Petersburg from seeking an agreement with the Dual Monarchy as well. This process began with contacts between the new foreign ministers of the two powers—Alexander Izvolsky of Russia and Alois Lexa von Aerenthal of Austria-Hungary, both of whom took office in 1906.

Izvolsky had prepared for his role as the architect of Russian foreign policy by serving in a variety of diplomatic posts in the Balkans, Japan, and Denmark. Ambitious and vain, Izvolsky dreamed of achieving great things for his country and himself. He initially hoped to chart a middle course between France and Britain on the one hand and Germany and Austria-Hungary on the other. But rapprochement with Britain was crucial to his policy. He recognized that the British alliance with Japan had encouraged

Tokyo to attack Russia in 1904, and, of course, Britain's opposition had been the primary factor in preventing the Black Sea fleet from gaining access to the Straits. He was instrumental in the creation of the Anglo-Russian Agreement in 1907, but he tried to assure Berlin and Vienna that it was strictly a limited understanding and was in no way directed against them. At the same time, Izvolsky strove to strengthen Russia's position in the Balkans and harbored unrealistic notions of gaining international acceptance for the opening of the Straits to Russian warships.

Aerenthal assumed the direction of foreign policy in Vienna after serving eight years as ambassador to St. Petersburg. He shared Izvolsky's ambitious tendencies and pursued his policies with a determination not seen in a Hapsburg statesman in many years. He hoped to improve relations with Russia, while at the same time expanding Austria-Hungary's influence in the Balkans. Indeed, he believed that the Dual Monarchy must pursue a vigorous approach to foreign policy if it was to maintain the respect of other powers, especially Germany. Although a staunch supporter of the Triple Alliance, he disliked Berlin's view of his country as the junior partner in the relationship or, as William II put it, "Germany's brilliant second."

AUSTRIA EYES ANNEXATION OF BOSNIA AND HERZEGOVINA

Specifically, Aerenthal sought the annexation of Bosnia and Herzegovina, already under Austrian administration since 1878, to better control the increasingly militant Slavic agitation within the provinces. He also hoped that this action would enhance the Dual Monarchy's prestige in the eyes of its German ally. Finally, he saw such a policy as the best way to rally the various nationalities in support of the empire and the Hapsburg dynasty.

In 1906, the two men explored the possibility of a bargain that would provide Austrian support for the opening the Straits to Russian warships in return for Russia's endorsement of Austrian annexation of Bosnia and Herzegovina. Discussions continued in secret during the next two years and appeared on the verge of agreement in the summer of 1908 when a revolt erupted in Turkey, which still held nominal overlordship in Bosnia and Herzegovina. The rebels, nicknamed "the Young Turks," quickly gained control and forced the despotic Sultan Abdul Hamid II to grant a constitutional regime and institute a number of reforms. Since the Young Turks were ardent nationalists, Aerenthal feared that they might try to reassert direct Turkish rule over Bosnia and Herzegovina. To Aerenthal, this possibility increased the urgency for annexation of the provinces. In September, Izvolsky accepted Aerenthal's invitation to meet with him at Buchlau in Bohemia.

Exactly what transpired at this meeting is unclear because the subsequent accounts of the two participants differ, but it appears that Izvolsky agreed to Austria's annexation of the provinces, while Aerenthal gave assurance of Austrian support for opening the Straits. However, although Aerenthal contended that he had informed Izvolsky that annexation was imminent, the latter denied that he had received precise information regarding the timing of the action. Two weeks after the meeting Izvolsky set out to visit the capitals of the other powers, seeking approval for the proposed change in the status of the Straits. When he reached Paris, his first stop, he received word that the annexation would take place three days later. Although apparently not shocked by the news, he was dismayed by the negative response he received from the French and later the British in regard to the Straits. Not only that, he had not informed his own government of the

Buchlau bargain, and St. Petersburg was taken by surprise by the annexation announcement. Both Turkey and Serbia were outraged at this violation of the Treaty of Berlin.

By far the strongest reaction came from Serbia, which deeply resented the inclusion of the Serbian population of Bosnia-Herzegovina in the Dual Monarchy. Serb nationalists demanded an invasion of Bosnia, and the government in Belgrade also considered the possibility of war. But such an action would be foolhardy unless Serbia had

Russian support. Even then, with Russia weakened by the conflict with Japan and the Revolution of 1905, the outcome was not promising. Any possibility of a military solution vanished when Izvolsky informed Serbia that Russia was not in a position to go to war. He did demand an international conference to discuss compensation for Serbia and Turkey, however. Britain supported his position, but France, which did not relish the prospect of being drawn into a war over Bosnia, offered much more tepid approval. Austria-Hungary refused to consider com-

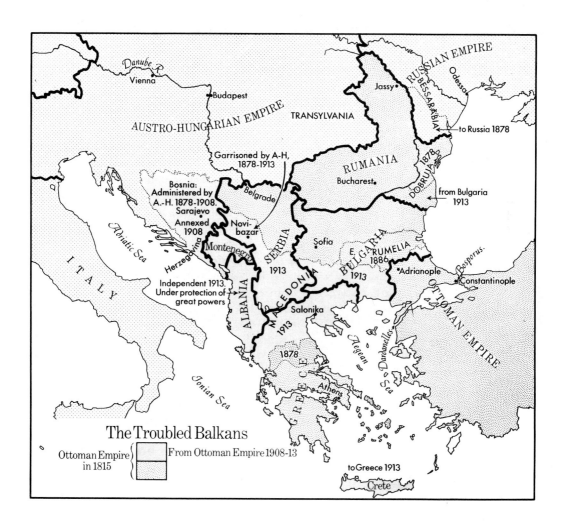

The Troubled Balkans

Ottoman Empire in 1815   From Ottoman Empire 1908-13

pensation for Serbia, however, and turned to Germany and Italy for help.

Germany's response at first was one of irritation because Austria-Hungary's decision to annex the provinces had caught Berlin as much by surprise as it had the Russians. William II, Bülow, and Kiderlen-Wächter also saw the crisis as an impediment to their pursuit of better relations with Turkey. But, since Austria-Hungary was Germany's only reliable ally, they soon adopted a strongly supportive policy and maintained it throughout the crisis. Italy, on the other hand, offered no such assurances and joined in the call for a conference.

The greatest danger came from tension between Serbia and Austria-Hungary. The ferocity of the Serbian response to the annexation only hardened the Dual Monarchy's resolve. In fact, General Franz Conrad von Hötzendorf, who had become the army's chief of staff in 1906, was all for a military solution. The son of a colonel, who had fought against Napoleon, Conrad was devoted to the Hapsburg dynasty and bitterly opposed efforts of the subject nationalities to gain greater autonomy. The general shared Aerenthal's advocacy of a vigorous foreign policy, but his views went far beyond those of the foreign minister. He frequently urged war, not only with Serbia but also with Austria-Hungary's ally Italy. Conrad thoroughly distrusted the Italians and was convinced that they would not remain loyal to the Triple Alliance. Despite his bellicose personality, Conrad was inordinately attracted to women. His first wife, who bore him four sons, died of stomach cancer in 1905. Two years later he became infatuated with a married woman, Gina von Reininghaus, the mother of six children whom he pursued relentlessly for many years, pouring out his passion in innumerable love letters.

Conrad regarded Serbia and anti-Hapsburg agitation among the Serbs of Austria-Hungary

as a menace that would only grow more serious in the future. During the Bosnian crisis, he insisted that the time had come to eliminate the Serbian "nest of vipers." Even Aerenthal briefly considered the possibility of war, but Emperor Francis Joseph opposed such drastic action.

EMPEROR FRANCIS JOSEPH

Francis Joseph was much more than emperor of Austria, king of Hungary, and head of the House of Hapsburg, Europe's oldest ruling dynasty. He was the symbolic linchpin, which to a large extent held the Dual Monarchy together. In 1908, when the Bosnian crisis began, he celebrated the 60th anniversary of his ascension to the throne. He was then 78 years old. Widely respected, even revered, he provided a grandfather figure for all the nationalities that populated his far-flung domain. Austro-Hungarian leaders worried about the fate of the empire when the emperor died. Many believed that it would surely disintegrate without his unifying presence.

Despite his crucial role and the veneration with which he was held, Francis Joseph was actually a most ordinary man. Blessed with neither brilliance nor imagination, he was relentlessly formal and cold in his personal relationships. It was said that no one really knew him well. In fact, one of his closest associates noted that "the monarch takes counsel of none save the Deity to whom alone he feels responsible." This remark clearly conveys the political outlook of the emperor. At heart an absolutist, he viewed parliaments, elections, and political parties as unpleasant nuisances forced upon monarchs by the modern world. Indeed, he found little of contemporary life to his liking. He rejected modern conveniences such as the telephone and the typewriter and insisted on using smoky and foul-smelling kerosene lamps in his palaces long after the advent of electricity. His daughter-in-law personally paid for the installation of the first modern toilets in the Hofburg, the main Hapsburg residence in central Vienna.

Frequent and violent tragedy had marred the emperor's personal life. His brother Maximilian, who briefly ruled Mexico on behalf of France, died before a firing squad when he was overthrown in 1867. The emperor's son Crown Prince Rudolf, apparently murdered his mistress and then committed suicide in 1889 at the hunting lodge of Mayerling near Vienna. And, the emperor's wife, the Empress Elizabeth, renowned for her beauty but long-estranged from her husband, fell victim to an assassin's knife in 1898.

Whatever his personal failings and misfortunes, Francis Joseph approached his responsibilities with singular dedication, habitually rising at 5 A.M. and poring over a myriad of details. However, despite his conviction that he ruled by Divine Right, the emperor usually left initiation of policy to other leaders. He did have the final say on all major decisions, however, and on occasion intervened emphatically, as when he rejected General Conrad's demand for war with Serbia during the Bosnian crisis. His heir apparent, the Archduke Francis Ferdinand, backed him strongly against the general on this issue.

GERMAN SUPPORT OF AUSTRIA

The emperor and archduke chose restraint and received support for this policy from Chancellor Bülow of Germany. Bülow, alarmed by British hostility during the naval "panic" of 1909 and the possibility of war over the provinces, threatened Russia that, unless it backed down, the Buchlau bargain would be revealed to the Serbs. This, of course, would prove highly embarrassing to

St. Petersburg. In January 1909, General Helmuth von Moltke, the German army chief of staff and nephew of the great hero of Bismarck's wars of unification, went so far as to assure General Conrad that, if the Austrians felt compelled to act against Serbia, they could count on German support. This would apply, he added, even if it meant war with Russia. Clearly, as far as Moltke was concerned, the Dual Alliance was not merely defensive, as Bismarck had intended. His pledge of military aid amounted to a "blank check" endorsement of an offensive war by Austria-Hungary although, of course, it did not obligate the German government itself.

But war did not come. Russia, realizing its weakness, yielded to pressure from Austria-Hungary and Germany and accepted the annexation. Serbia, not knowing that Izvolsky had negotiated the provinces away, followed suit as did Turkey. Once this had been accomplished, the other powers adhered to a revision of the Treaty of Berlin, recognizing the changed status of Bosnia and Herzegovina.

NEGATIVE EFFECTS OF ANNEXATION

Despite the success of Austria-Hungary's determined policy, the negative effects of the Bosnian crisis really outweighed the benefits of gaining a tighter grip on the provinces. The crisis had a disastrous effect on the Dual Monarchy's relations with Russia. Russian leaders felt humiliated by their inability to support Serbia's protests or to aid their Slavic brethren in the provinces and were determined not to back down "next time." Izvolsky lost his position as foreign minister, but his successor, Sergei Sazonov, shared his convictions. In 1910, Izvolsky became ambassador to Paris and worked to increase French support for Russia, which had been disappointing in 1908. The appointment of the rabidly Pan-Slav Nicholas Hartwig as Russia's ambassador to Belgrade soon after the conclusion of the Bosnian crisis reflected St. Petersburg's frustration. Hartwig remained relentlessly anti-Austrian until his death in July 1914. He constantly encouraged Serbia to pursue its efforts to create a Greater Serbia and even a South Slav state at the Dual Monarchy's expense.

The effect on Serbia's relations with Austria-Hungary, already aggravated by the Pig War, was far worse. The Serbs now viewed the Dual Monarchy as an implacable enemy. More anti-Austrian secret societies came into existence during the crisis, most notably *Narodna Odbrana* (National Defense). This organization urged vigorous efforts to achieve a Greater Serbia at the expense of both Turkey and Austria. Much more sinister and much more secret was the *Crna Ruka* (Union of Death, or the Black Hand), which came into being in 1911. Organized by Serbian army officers who had been involved in the assassination of Alexander II, it shared *Narodna Odbrana*'s desire for a Greater Serbia but also favored terrorist activities in Bosnia. Although such organizations were relatively small, they exerted growing pressure on the Serbian government. They also became a cause of mounting paranoia among Austro-Hungarian leaders who were aware of the existence of some of them and became obsessed by fear of "the Serbian menace."

The conclusion of the Bosnian situation in March 1909 climaxed five eventful years that had witnessed the creation of the *Entente Cordiale*, the First Moroccan Crisis, the Russo-Japanese War, and the Anglo-Russian Agreement. During the two years that followed, Europe experienced a period of calm, although both Serbia and Russia persisted in their hostile feelings toward Austria-Hungary and continued to harbor their ambitions in the Balkans. The Dual Monarchy in turn remained deeply suspicious of them. But a new series of crises arose in 1911, starting with the Second Moroccan Crisis during the summer and fall.

WAR BETWEEN ITALY AND TURKEY

Even before this dispute had reached a peaceful conclusion in November, another crisis erupted when Italy and Turkey plunged into the Tripolitanian War in September of that year. Italy had been gazing hungrily at the barren, unproductive Turkish possessions of Tripoli and Cyrenaica for some time but did not act until the other powers were preoccupied with the crisis over Morocco. Although the French had declared their disinterest in these territories, the Italians feared that the French might have a change of heart once they had consolidated their control over Morocco. Thus, Rome believed the time had come to strike.

Italy gained the reluctant support of both France and Russia for its undertaking, as well as assurances of sympathy from Britain during the summer of 1911. Austria-Hungary hovered between the desire to see Italy bogged down in a North African adventure and fear that Turkey's involvement there might lead to complications in the Balkans. Germany was torn between the desire to maintain the dubious loyalty of its Italian ally and fear of jeopardizing its friendship with Turkey, which it had carefully nurtured in recent years. Convinced of the strength of its position, Italy declared war on September 29, 1911, and sent forces to occupy five ports in Tripoli and Cyrenaica. The Italians found it difficult to advance inland, however, as fierce Arab tribesmen waged a guerrilla war that dragged on for over a year. Italy, nevertheless, announced the annexation of both territories and merged them in a new Italian colony, which they named Libya.

THE BALKAN LEAGUE

Turkey's preoccupation with the Tripolitanian War created an irresistible temptation for the small Balkan states to pool their resources in an effort to drive the Turks out of Europe. For some time Russia had been encouraging Serbia and Bulgaria to join in an alliance, which St. Petersburg hoped would further its ambitions in the Balkans, and in March 1912 the two countries concluded an agreement. During the next few months other alliances linked the Serbs and Bulgars with Greece and Montenegro in what soon became known as the Balkan League. But the intent of the Balkan League, and its Russian advisers, was anything but defensive. By October 18, all four countries were at war with Turkey and within five weeks had driven the Turks out of most of their European territory. Only Constantinople and three isolated fortresses managed to hold out. This quick and dramatic success astonished the world, and in early December, Turkey asked for an armistice. Negotiations began soon afterward.

THE "SICK MAN OF EUROPE" WEAKENS

The victory of the Balkan League was a disaster for Austria-Hungary. The "Sick Man of Europe" appeared to be at death's door, and Serbia, as one of the heirs, clearly would gain territory as well as confidence. Belgrade could then focus its attention solely on the Serbian minority in the Dual Monarchy. General Blasius Schemua had succeeded General Conrad as chief of staff of the Austro-Hungarian army in November 1911. This change had resulted from Francis Joseph's exasperation with Conrad's demand for an attack on Italy, while the Italians were preoccupied with the Tripolitanian War. Schemua shared Conrad's concern over Serbia, however, and even before the start of the war he had urged mobilization of reserves. He also favored occupation of the Sanjak of Novi Bazar, a narrow neck of land separating Serbia from Montenegro. This would prevent the creation of a common border between the two Slavic states and their potential merger. Count Leopold von Berchtold, who succeeded the dying Aerenthal as foreign minister of Austria-Hungary in February 1912, refused to accept these proposals. He hoped to avoid war and believed that such measures would only make the situation worse.

Russia, fearing that the Dual Monarchy might move into the Sanjak, ordered a trial mobilization of reserves in Poland. Schemua considered this provocative and renewed his plea for mobilization and intervention in the Sanjak, even if this led to war with Russia. But Berchtold again refused, although he did agree to a strengthening of forces opposite the Russian border. Russia responded by retaining 400,000 troops, scheduled to be discharged, on active duty. General Vladimir Sukhomlinov, the Russian war minister, even went so far as to urge mobilization of the Kiev military district and half the Warsaw military district, an action that might well have triggered war with both Austria-Hungary and Germany. Premier Vladimir Kokovtzov and Foreign Minister Sazonov both begged for restraint, and the czar followed their advice.

Clearly, at this point there were still voices of moderation in both Austria-Hungary and Russia, despite the mounting tension. It is noteworthy that among them were the two foreign ministers, each of whom would later change his approach. Until recently, historians have viewed Berchtold with contempt as weak, frivolous, and inept. They saw him as much more interested in clothes, art, and horse racing than in his duties as foreign minister. Such scathing appraisals now appear unfair. To be sure, he was something of a dandy in his appearance and certainly enjoyed racing of various kinds, including auto and air competition, and it is also undeniably true that his policies ultimately contributed tragically to the outbreak of World War I, but this was the result of miscalculation rather than incompetence or frivolity.

It is also clear that he doubted his own capacity for the all-important role he was to play and only accepted the appointment out of a sense of obligation. He would have much preferred to devote himself to his vast landed estates. Indeed, he had actually retired to them briefly in 1911 after 28 years in public service, including five years as ambassador to St. Petersburg. Russian leaders welcomed his elevation to foreign minister, while Britain viewed him suspiciously as too pro-Russian. His greatest weakness, when he took office, was his lack of experience in Balkan affairs. Nevertheless, he conducted himself capably during the recurring crises over the Balkan wars. But his refusal to follow a more aggressive policy resulted in a barrage of criticism from proponents of a hard-line approach to Serbia and Russia.

FIGURE 3–1   Count Leopold von Berchold, the Austro-Hungarian foreign minister. National Archives

Sazonov, Berchtold's counterpart in Russia, lacked Izvolsky's vanity, personal ambition and deviousness, but he also did not have the advantage of his predecessor's extensive and varied high-level background in diplomacy. He did possess ability, however, and was scrupulously honest, conscientious, and hardworking. Unfortunately, he suffered from poor health and an exceptionally nervous and indecisive temperament. Both Russian and foreign observers noted his difficulty in following a consistent policy and his susceptibility to the views of others. In particular, Prince G. N. Trubetskoy, head of the foreign ministry's department for Balkan and Turkish affairs from 1912 to 1914, appears to have wielded strong influence over Sazonov. Trubetskoy favored a policy that would further Russian interests in the Balkans and encourage the aims of Slavic peoples in the area. At the same time, he harbored intense distrust of Germany and advocated strict adherence to the Triple Entente to defend Russian interests and security as well as to preserve the balance of power in Europe. To the extent that Sazonov followed policies that were at all consistent, his approach coincided with Trubetskoy's desire for expansion of Russian influence in the Balkans and distrust of Germany.

With the victory of the Balkan League, the leaders of the Dual Monarchy realized that they could not prevent Serbia from expanding southward into the province of Macedonia. But they insisted on denying the Serbs an outlet to the Adriatic Sea in the area of Albania to the east of Macedonia and south of Montenegro. Vienna believed that this would allow Austria-Hungary to salvage something from the wreckage of the Balkan wars and would clearly demonstrate that the Dual Monarchy was still a Great Power whose interests could not be disregarded. It was hoped this would prevent Serbia from gaining greater economic independence, while eliminating the possibility of the Serbs granting Russia a naval base on the Adriatic. Other powers were also uneasy about Serbia's ambitions in Albania. Unfortunately, Serbia was determined, above all else, to secure an outlet to the sea.

ATTITUDE OF THE OTHER POWERS

While both Vienna and Belgrade staked a great deal on the question of Serbia's access to the sea, other Great Power leaders did not relish the prospect of a war over this obscure and backward area of Europe. To be sure, Italy, for once, sided with Austria-Hungary but did so primarily to pursue its own interest in Albania. Germany actually had little sympathy for Austria-Hungary's attitude and took the position that it was not obligated to offer its ally a "blank check" in the Balkans.

Both France and Britain hoped to avoid a confrontation that might drag them into war on Russia's side. France's President, Raymond Poincaré, assured St. Petersburg that France would honor its obligations under the Franco-Russian Alliance, but he emphasized the defensive nature of that agreement, while working for a peaceful solution to the crisis. Poincaré was an exception to the ceremonial role played by most presidents of the French Third Republic. He assumed office in January 1913 after serving for a year as both premier and foreign minister. With one brief interlude in early 1914, he dominated French foreign policy until the outbreak of World War I. A native of Lorraine, Poincaré was a boy of 10 when the Germans occupied his province in 1870. This experience left him permanently distrustful of Germany.

Both brilliant and exceedingly hardworking, he earned his arts and law degrees simultaneously at the age of 20. After winning election to the Chamber of Deputies in 1887, he held ministerial positions in several different cabinets. Poincaré frequently encountered difficulty in making up his mind and, as a result, developed a reputation for avoiding responsibility. When he did arrive at a decision, however, he usually adhered to it tenaciously. His cardinal principle in foreign policy was to maintain and strengthen the Triple Entente. However, he opposed the proposals of other French leaders to weaken the Triple Alliance by luring Italy or Austria-Hungary away from Germany. To him, both alliances were bulwarks of the balance of power, and he believed that any attempt to disrupt the Triple Alliance would increase the chance of war.

Britain was also determined to maintain the Triple Entente, but Sir Edward Grey, Britain's foreign secretary, strove diligently to prevent a rupture of relations between Austria-Hungary and Russia. In the months to come, he worked closely with the Germans in an attempt to resolve the Albanian quarrel peacefully. As for Russia, Sazonov, who had originally supported Serbia's ambitions, now urged the Serbs to give up their claim to the Albanian coast. Apparently the narrow escape from war, stemming from Sukhomlinov's mobilization scheme, had sobered the Russian foreign minister to the dangers of the situation.

A conference of ambassadors of the Great Powers convened in London in December and continued intermittently until August 1913. Although the powers agreed to the Dual Monarchy's position on Albania from the start, disagreement arose over the precise borders between the new Albanian state and Montenegro. Meanwhile, peace negotiations between Turkey and the Balkan League states broke down in February 1913, and fighting again erupted. Once again it did not go well for the Turks. In April, they concluded an-

other armistice and agreed to peace terms in May, which required them to give up all their European territory, except Constantinople and a small area to the west and south.

Peace lasted less than a month, however. The Balkan powers could not agree on how they should divide the territory. Bulgaria was at odds with Serbia and Greece over Macedonia and rashly attacked the forces of both countries in the disputed province at the end of June, triggering the Second Balkan War. This proved a serious mistake. Rumania soon entered the conflict to gain a slice of northeastern Bulgaria. To add to the troubles of the beleaguered Bulgars, Turkey, sensing the opportunity to win back some of its territory, also took the offensive against them. Confronted by this multitude of enemies, Bulgaria had no choice but to seek peace. In the Treaty of Bucharest, signed in the Rumanian capital on August 10, 1913, Serbia, Greece, and Rumania helped themselves to slices of Bulgarian territory. Soon afterward, in another treaty, the demoralized Bulgars accepted the loss of the major fortress city of Adrianople to the Turks.

The outcome of the Second Balkan War represented a serious setback for Austria-Hungary. The Dual Monarchy had tried to prevent hostilities between its ally Rumania and Bulgaria, realizing that a Bulgarian defeat would strengthen Serbia. But Germany had refused to cooperate and supported the ambitions of Rumania, with whom it was also allied. Once the conflict began, Austro-Hungarian leaders hoped desperately that the Bulgars would win, but they could do nothing to assist them because of their alliance with Rumania and the attitude of Germany. When the war ended, Serbia emerged roughly doubled in size, while the Rumanians, having tasted victory, began to look longingly toward Hungary's province of Transylvania where three million of their kinsmen lived under Magyar domination.

Rumania's loyalty to the Triple Alliance soon became as questionable as that of Italy, especially since the Bucharest regime was quite aware that Austria-Hungary had favored Bulgaria's cause in the war. Germany's unsympathetic behavior during the crisis added to the Dual Monarchy's sense of isolation and gloom.

To increase Austro-Hungarian dissatisfaction still more, Serbia triggered a new crisis in October by delaying the withdrawal of its troops from territory that the London conference of ambassadors had awarded to Albania. This, combined with Serbia's indication that it favored a revision of the border agreement, rekindled fear in Vienna that Serbia might attempt to obtain an outlet to the Adriatic. Conrad, who had returned to his position as chief of staff of the Austro-Hungarian army, once again demanded an attack on Serbia. But now, to his surprise, he found that he had allies. Berchtold, the Austrian foreign minister who had opposed provocative action during the Balkan wars, moved closer to Conrad's position. He agreed that conditions for a military solution were more favorable at that time than they would be when Serbia and Russia had both grown stronger. Stephen Tisza, the Hungarian premier and another former advocate of a peaceful policy, also accepted the need for vigorous measures to secure Serbia's withdrawal. On October 17, 1913, after receiving Germany's pledge of support, Berchtold issued an ultimatum to Belgrade demanding the removal of Serbian troops within eight days. If Serbia failed to do so, the Dual Monarchy would take "proper means" to secure compliance. Russia advised Serbia to agree, and the Serbs, now isolated, evacuated their troops.

This diplomatic triumph convinced Berchtold that firmness was the best policy in dealing with Serbia. Russia's failure to support the Serbs also led Austro-Hungarian leaders to believe that they could expect a similar response in the future. Their confidence in a hard-line approach increased still more when, immediately following the Serbian withdrawal, William II offered profuse assurances of German support for the Dual Monarchy, if it felt obliged to take action against Serbia. The emperor also expressed his belief that Russia would not be in a position to intervene for the next six years. Some observers have seen William's emphatic words as solidifying the Dual Alliance to such an extent that, henceforth, Austria-Hungary could count unreservedly on German support, if it decided to settle the Serbian Question by force. But, Austrian leaders recognized that, after his unhappy experience with the Björkö Treaty in 1905 and the *Daily Telegraph* interview in 1908, the emperor's views did not necessarily represent those of the German government.

Indeed, the Germans soon turned to a more peaceful approach, much to the chagrin of Vienna, and urged the Dual Monarchy to seek better relations with Serbia. Berlin also resisted Austrian proposals that the Dual Alliance seek closer ties with Bulgaria. To Berchtold and his colleagues, Bulgaria seemed a far more promising candidate for friendship than did Rumania. After all, the Bulgars harbored grudges against both Serbia and Rumania but had no grievance at all with the Dual Monarchy. But, while Austria-Hungary increasingly doubted Rumania's loyalty to its alliance obligations, Germany insisted that Bucharest could be trusted.

In reality, there was no chance at all for better relations between Austria-Hungary and Serbia, which gravitated closer to Russia in the following months. The Serbs were completely alienated from Vienna following their humiliation in the Albanian border dispute. As for the Russians, they were bitter, as they had been after the Bosnian crisis, over their inability to aid their Serbian protégés. They resolved not to back down a third time. In early February 1914, Nicholas II, although he was not one of the Russian "hard-liners," assured Serbian Premier Nicholas Pašich of Russian support in the future, adding that "for Serbia we shall do all." Russia and Serbia also tried to woo the Rumanians away from the Triple Alliance by encouraging their ambitions in Transylvania. Rumania was willing to listen.

Relations between Russia and Germany also took a turn for the worse in late 1913 and early 1914. In the aftermath of their defeat in the Balkan wars, the Turks set out to rebuild their defenses and improve the quality of their army. They requested a German military officer to supervise this process, and in December 1913, General Otto Liman von Sanders arrived in Constantinople at the head of a sizable German mission. He was to serve as inspector general of Turkish military forces as well as the commander of Turkey's First Army, based in Constantinople. News of Liman's appointment was far from welcome in St. Petersburg. Sazonov especially challenged the propriety of Liman actually commanding Turkish troops.

Germany pointed out that his role was quite similar to that of Admiral A.H. Limpus, who headed a British naval mission to Turkey and had in effect commanded the Turkish navy since 1912. Sazonov assumed, nevertheless, that Germany planned to use Liman's position to achieve dominant influence over Turkish affairs, including control of the Straits, promotion of economic interests and especially the German plan to build a rail line to connect Constantinople with the Persian Gulf—the Berlin-to-Baghdad Railroad. He pleaded to France and Britain to join Russia in an attempt to scale down Liman's power. Delcassé, the former French foreign minister who was now ambassador to St. Petersburg, assured Sazonov of French

support. Although President Poincaré appears to have opposed the Russian demand because he was trying to cultivate better relations with Germany at the time, Sazonov believed that Delcassé had given him a "blank check" and that "France would go as far as Russia may wish." The British foreign secretary, Edward Grey, thought that the affair was not "worth all the fuss that Sazonov makes about it" but felt compelled, in the interest of the Triple Entente, to apply British pressure on Berlin to reach an understanding.

The Germans, who had been pursuing more cordial relations with the British since their cooperation during the Balkan wars, were more than willing to put an end to the crisis. They devised a solution in January 1914 that provided for Liman to give up command of the Constantinople garrison, while remaining inspector general of the Turkish army. The Russians accepted the compromise, but Sazonov was not happy about the aggrandizement of Germany's influence in Turkey. The lack of vigorous British endorsement for Russia's position also troubled him. He became convinced that in future crises, the Russians must take a stronger stand to ensure firm support from their allies. In this respect, his attitude was not unlike that of Berchtold in Vienna.

Despite the growth of Germany's influence after Liman's arrival in Constantinople, Turkey followed a policy of trying to balance its relations with the various Great Powers. Although Liman had responsibility for modernizing the army, most command functions remained in Turkish hands. Germany also did not establish economic domination in Turkey. It continued to lag behind Britain, France, and even the Austrians in volume of trade with the Turks, although the latter served as middlemen for German interests to some extent, but German activity in connection with the Berlin-to-

Baghdad Railroad made their presence especially visible.

FATALISM AND HOPE

The proliferation of crises, not only in the Balkans but also in Morocco, created growing tension and a sense of fatalism among the powers of Europe during the last decade before 1914. However, there were signs of hope as well. For one thing, any of these crises seemingly could have triggered a general war, but none of them did. The cooperation between Britain and Germany in solving the delicate Albanian boundary dispute clearly demonstrated that it was possible for members of the rival alliance systems to work together. The two powers also attempted to settle some of the issues that had divided them, while Franco-German relations took a turn for the better in certain respects as well.

Much of the improvement centered on Germany's long-cherished scheme for construction of the Berlin-to-Baghdad Railroad. In 1889, a group of German investors had gained a concession from the Turkish government to build the first stage from the Straits across Anatolia in Asian Turkey. Ten years later, they obtained the right to extend the line. But by 1903, the Germans had encountered a severe shortage of capital and tried to entice British and French investors to participate. The plan fell through because of French and British skepticism over German political and economic intentions in Turkey as well as determined Russian opposition. German efforts to gain the cooperation of Britain and France continued intermittently during the following years, but it was not until Russia, in the interest of obtaining better relations with Germany, withdrew its opposition in 1911 that they began to make progress.

In June 1914, Britain and Germany initialed an agreement, providing for the Ger-

mans to complete the line to Baghdad and beyond to Basra, while the British would construct an extension from Basra to their protectorate of Kuwait on the Persian Gulf. Actually, Britain had originally established this protectorate to block the extension of the railroad to the gulf. France and Germany did not begin serious negotiations until shortly before the advent of the Liman von Sanders Affair. Paris and Berlin finally reached an accord in February 1914. It provided for French financial participation in the project, while Germany conceded France the right to construct railroads in other parts of the Ottoman Empire.

Meanwhile, Anglo-German discussions were also taking place on the future of Portugal's colonies in Africa and Southeast Asia. As early as 1898, the two powers had agreed to divide the colonies between them, if Portugal, which appeared to be facing bankruptcy, had to liquidate its overseas possessions to obtain financial assistance. However, Britain seemingly contradicted this accord the following year when it reaffirmed an obligation dating back to the seventeenth century to defend Portugal's territorial integrity, including that of its colonies. The issue of the colonies arose again during British War Secretary Haldane's mission to Berlin in 1912, and in October 1913 the two powers modified their earlier agreement. The new arrangement conceded Germany a larger share of the colonies, again providing that Portugal's continuing financial difficulties became critical. The British, nevertheless, insisted on publicizing their traditional commitment to Portugal along with the contingency agreement. The Germans balked at this, and a resolution of the matter was still pending in the summer of 1914.

The peaceful conclusion of the Liman von Sanders Affairs, as well as the improved relations between Germany and the two Western powers, ushered in a period of relative quiet in European power politics that lasted into the early summer of 1914. One veteran of the British foreign office observed that he had never seen "such calm waters" during his long career.

To be sure, there were disturbing undercurrents. It was during this period that Britain and Russia took steps to initiate their naval staff talks, much to the consternation of Berlin, which soon learned of them. Warnings also appeared in the German press that the Russians were preparing for an attack on Germany in the next few years. These unfounded accounts appeared even more ominous in view of Russia's stated intention of expanding its army to 2,300,000 men by 1917. The Russians, largely at French insistence, were also constructing strategic railroads that would greatly shorten the time required to bring reserve troops into position for use against both Germany and Austria-Hungary. These indications of Russia's military revival became a source of growing concern to German leaders. And, despite Franco-German cooperation on the Baghdad Railroad, both countries were uneasy about recent increases in their respective military strength. In 1913, France had extended its term of service from two to three years with the intention of raising its peacetime army to 770,000 men. At the same time, Germany had taken measures to boost its army to 870,000 during the next few years.

Despite these concerns in the realm of foreign affairs, the attention of many leaders focused on internal problems. The British cabinet was immersed in the affairs of Ireland where it appeared that a civil war was about to break out over the issue of Home Rule, which would grant autonomy to the island after centuries of direct British administration. The Catholic Irish, who constituted a majority of the overall population of that country, strongly favored Home Rule. The Protestants, who dominated the northern

province of Ulster, feared that they would be at a disadvantage in a united Ireland and insisted on the exclusion of Ulster from any Home Rule arrangement. During the early summer of 1914, both sides were preparing for what appeared to be an inevitable clash of arms. In France, all eyes were focused on the trial of Madame Caillaux, the wife of the French finance minister. She was charged with the murder of a prominent newspaper editor, who had waged a bitter press campaign against her husband. This scandal rocked the government, especially when reports began to circulate regarding secret negotiations Monsieur Caillaux had conducted with the Germans when he served as premier at the time of the Agadir crisis.

During the first six months of 1914, Russia experienced a wave of strikes by industrial workers seeking to improve their grossly inadequate wages. This social unrest, coupled with the hostility of opposition parties to the reactionary policies of the czar's government, sparked fears of another revolution. In the Dual Monarchy, many of the national minorities had grown more restless since the Balkan wars. Those in Hungary resented the Magyarization program of the Tisza government. Obstructionist tactics by the Czechs, demanding autonomy, and Social Democrats, seeking benefits for the working class, paralyzed the Austrian parliament. In March 1914, Austrian Prime Minister Karl Stürgkh suspended the assembly, and the government ruled by emergency decree for the next three years.

Tension also marked the internal affairs of Germany. Here it focused on the surprising gains of the Social Democratic party in the parliamentary election of 1912. Much to the alarm of the emperor and the conservatives, the Social Democrats became the largest single party in the Reichstag with almost one-third of the seats. Their concern increased still more when the Social Democrats joined with the liberals and Catholic Center party to secure passage of a capital gains tax in 1913. They feared that the conservative elite's traditional domination of Germany was in danger, as well as the future of the monarchy itself. But the brief cooperation of the middle of the road parties and the Social Democrats did not last.

By early 1914, an impasse had developed in the Reichstag, which now featured three blocs, consisting of the parties of the right, center, and left. The blocs were of relatively equal strength and increasingly hostile to one another. As a way out of this dilemma, conservatives considered the possibility of a coup by the emperor to curb or abolish the Reichstag and put an end to universal suffrage. But such a drastic action might well provoke a revolution from the left. This unhappy prospect turned the thoughts of some supporters of the traditional order toward an adventure in foreign policy as a solution to the domestic deadlock. They believed a victorious war might unite the various social groups behind the government. But, as Bethmann-Hollweg observed, war was a risky enterprise. Military defeat could lead to revolution and the overthrow of the imperial system.

ASSASSINATION OF FRANCIS FERDINAND

This pattern of outward calm and internal turmoil was shattered by the assassination of Archduke Francis Ferdinand, heir to the thrones of the Austro-Hungarian Empire, and his wife on June 28, 1914, in Sarajevo, Bosnia. Francis Ferdinand was and remains a controversial figure. The nephew of Francis Joseph, he did not get along well with the stiff-necked emperor, who did not approve of his marriage to Countess Sophie Chotek, a Czech woman of non-royal blood. In fact, Francis Joseph saw to it that their children

were barred from succession to the throne. Extremely conservative, even absolutist, in his political inclinations and devoutly Catholic, Francis Ferdinand was devoted to the dynasty and shared the emperor's view of the army as the bulwark of Hapsburg rule. Not surprisingly, he always took a keen interest in the army and even maintained his own informal military chancellery. It was due to his influence that Conrad von Hötzendorf became chief of staff, although the two men later became estranged over Conrad's constant advocacy of war.

Many contemporary observers believed that Francis Ferdinand was among those Austrian leaders who favored granting the South Slavs equality with the Austrians and Magyars in a system of trialism, but his exact intentions are obscure. It appears that he actually preferred a unitary system in which all nationalities would be subject to rule from Vienna. It is abundantly clear that he disliked the system of dualism and detested the Magyars with their independent and often uncooperative attitude. He once observed that, "It was an act of bad taste on the part of these gentlemen ever to have come to Europe." The Magyars, who were quite aware of his dislike for them, responded with similar contempt for him and did not relish the prospect of his ascension to the throne. The archduke's abrasive personality did not win him many friends in Vienna either, but he did enjoy a good relationship with William II of Germany.

Although the details of the conspiracy leading to the assassination are still vague, the Black Hand, led by Colonel Dragutin Dimitrijevich, the intelligence chief of the Serbian general staff and leader of the plot to kill King Alexander II in 1903, was deeply involved in the assassination. This organization also was in close contact with the Russian military attaché in Belgrade, Colonel V. A. Artamonov, who probably was aware of

FIGURE 3–2   Emperor Francis Joseph and his heir, the Archduke Francis Ferdinand. National Archives

the conspiracy. It also appears that Serbian Prime Minister Pašich at least knew of the plot. The instruments of the assassination itself were three young Bosnians living in Belgrade. Fanatically devoted to the creation of a Greater Serbia, which would include all South Slavs, they were determined to take the life of the archduke, whom they viewed as a symbol of Austro-Hungarian domination. They also saw him as a threat to their dreams of a Greater Serbian state because of his apparent endorsement of equality for the South Slavs within the Hapsburg empire. Dimitrijevich and the Black Hand shared this fear. The Black Hand provided the three young men with weapons, training, and assistance in crossing the Serbian border into Bosnia.

Despite the determined efforts of the conspirators, the plot probably would have failed had General Oskar Potiorek, the governor of Bosnia, provided reasonable security measures during Francis Ferdinand's visit to Sarajevo. Even without such precautions, the archduke might have emerged unscathed had his driver not taken a wrong turn and stopped to back up before proceeding. By a grim stroke of luck, the open car came to a halt at the very spot where one of the conspirators, Gavrilo Princip, was waiting. He fired two shots at close range, mortally wounding the imperial couple.

Except for a brief period at the start of the Balkan wars, Francis Ferdinand had always favored a peaceful policy for Austria-Hungary. Ironically, his death triggered a crisis, which unlike previous Balkan crises, would not end peacefully but would lead Europe into war.

4

THE JULY CRISIS
AND THE OUTBREAK
OF WAR

News of the assassination of Archduke Francis Ferdinand created shock and revulsion in the capitals of all the Great Powers of Europe. Messages of sympathy poured into Vienna, not only from Berlin and Rome, but from London, Paris, and St. Petersburg. The archduke's death was far from a source of sorrow in Budapest, however, and even in Vienna there was little authentic grief. But leaders in both parts of the Dual Monarchy expressed genuine outrage over the intolerable affront to the dignity of a Great Power. Since authorities in Sarajevo quickly arrested Gavrilo Princip and his fellow conspirators, it soon became clear that they had received their weapons and other assistance in Serbia. The complicity, if any, of the Serbian government was not clear. Indeed, the very existence of the Black Hand remained unknown to the Austro-Hungarian

leaders. But they considered the available evidence sufficient to confirm their suspicions that the plot had been engineered in Serbia, very likely with the blessing of Belgrade.

Although, with the exception of Colonel Dimitrijevich, high-ranking Serbian officials had not been involved in planning the assassination conspiracy, they had been aware of its existence. Premier Nikola Pašich had even ordered an investigation, but to officially warn Austria-Hungary of the plot would certainly make the government vulnerable to charges from Serbian nationalists of providing aid and comfort to the hated enemy. It would aggravate the already strained relations between Pašich, who considered the Black Hand dangerously irresponsible, and Dimitrijevich, who viewed the government's refusal to adopt a stronger policy toward the Dual Monarchy as tantamount to treason.

The closest thing to a warning to Vienna came in the form of a suggestion by the Serbian minister that the archduke's visit would be considered provocative by the Bosnian people and might lead to trouble. His remarks were so vague that they were disregarded, and the visit took place as scheduled. Later the Austro-Hungarian finance minister, Leon Bilinski, realized that they might have been a warning, further implicating the Serbian government. It was clear that Pašich was unable or unwilling to prevent a tragedy that might well lead to war.

AUSTRIA REACTS TO THE ASSASSINATION

Austrian outrage soon translated into determination to take drastic action against Serbia. General Conrad favored immediate mobilization, and Berchtold's chief advisers urged the foreign minister to be firm. It appears that Berchtold needed little prodding. The crisis over the Albanian border in the fall of 1913 seems to have convinced him that war eventually would be necessary to settle the Serbian question. Berchtold's success in that crisis also encouraged him to hope that Russia would remain neutral, especially in view of the sympathy that the assassination had aroused in St. Petersburg. Francis Joseph had consistently advocated restraint in past crises, but by July 3 he, too, had accepted the need for war. Only István Tisza remained dubious. The Hungarian premier feared that an attack on Serbia would trigger Russian intervention.

Tisza wielded strong influence in the Austro-Hungarian leadership. The son of Kálmán Tisza, who had dominated politics in Hungary as prime minister from 1875 to 1890, Tisza carried on many of his father's principles. Both men were strong defenders of Magyar interests but also staunch supporters of the *Ausgleich*. They could see the benefits that Hungary derived from the system of dualism and resisted efforts by extreme Magyar nationalists to reduce or sever ties with Austria. The Tiszas were members of Hungary's powerful landowning gentry, intensely Calvinist in religion and ultra-conservative politically. The younger Tisza had been prime minister from 1903 to 1905 before spending several years in opposition. He once again became the dominant figure in Hungarian politics in 1910, although he did not return as prime minister until the summer of 1913. Arrogant, stubborn, and autocratic, Tisza enjoyed the respect of his associates but inspired hatred in his opponents. He not only influenced the foreign policy of the Dual Monarchy personally, but through his representative, Stephen Buriàn, at the imperial court in Vienna as well. A close friend of Tisza, Buriàan shared most of the prime minister's political views.

All the Austro-Hungarian leaders agreed that no action could be taken without Germany's support. Assurance was forthcoming on July 5, when an angry William II pledged that Austria-Hungary could "in this case, as in all others, rely upon Germany's full support." The emperor added that this would apply even if action against Serbia led to war with Russia. Although Berchtold knew that William did not necessarily speak for the government, he found reassurance the following day when Chancellor Bethmann-Hollweg of Germany offered somewhat more cautious support. Both William and Bethmann urged immediate measures against Serbia, while European opinion was still sympathetic. The German leaders shared the Austrian belief that Russia would be unwilling to go to war in defense of a country responsible for the murder of an imperial prince. Bethmann appears to have recognized the danger of war with Russia to a greater extent than did the emperor, but he was willing to take this risk to enable Austria-Hungary to remain a great power. He also feared the growth of Russian military strength in the next few years and believed that Germany would be in a better position to fight Russia in 1914 than would be the case in 1917. To Germany, he later admitted, World War I was "in a certain sense…a preventive war."

The German assurance of support to Austria-Hungary appeared so open-ended that Vienna saw it as a "blank check." Nevertheless, the Dual Monarchy did not act quickly against Serbia, as the Germans had insisted. There were still problems to resolve. First, it

undertook a police investigation in an attempt to determine Serbian complicity in the assassination. Second, István Tisza did not agree to war until July 14, and then only with the proviso that Austria-Hungary renounce any intention of annexing Serbian territory. Tisza hoped that such restraint might persuade Russia to remain neutral. But his insistence on this point reflected his opposition to incorporating any more Slavs in Austria-Hungary. He was convinced that there were already quite enough of them within the borders of the Dual Monarchy.

FIGURE 4–1   Chancellor Theobold von Bethmann-Hollweg of Germany. National Archives

Another reason for delay was the awkward fact that many members of the army were on leave to help with the harvest in their home areas. They would not return to their units until as late as July 21. To cancel the leaves would not only interfere with the harvest but would alert other powers to the fact that military action against Serbia was imminent. Finally, French President Poincaré and Premier René Viviani would be in St. Petersburg on a state visit from July 20 to July 23. If Vienna deferred action until after their departure for home, it would be difficult for Russia and France to coordinate their response because Poincaré and Viviani would be at sea for several days.

Austro-Hungarian leaders eventually agreed to dispatch an ultimatum to Serbia, containing a number of demands. Some of them were so harsh that the Serbians would be highly unlikely to accept them. Their refusal would provide the pretext for a declaration of war on Serbia. Vienna based the ultimatum on the results of its investigation of the Sarajevo crime. Although the investigation, which was limited to the Austrian side of the border, could find no evidence of complicity on the part of the Serbian government, it was obvious that the murder plot had originated in Belgrade. It was also obvious that Serbian officials had provided weapons and other assistance to those involved in the assassination. The Austro-Hungarian minister delivered the ultimatum in Belgrade on Thursday, July 23, shortly after the departure of Poincaré and Viviani from St. Petersburg.

The ultimatum, in which Germany played no part, demanded the immediate end to anti-Austrian publications in Serbia as well as subversive activities within Austro-Hungary itself, including the smuggling of arms across the border. It also called for the suppression of *Narodna Odbrana* and other secret societies, the ouster of a number of

Serbian military and government officials to be specified by Vienna, and the arrest of two minor officials who were implicated in the assassination plot. Finally, Serbia was to accept the participation of Austro-Hungarian officials in a judicial investigation of the conspiracy. Belgrade was to notify Vienna of its unconditional acceptance of all these demands by 6 P.M. on Saturday, July 25, 1914.

REACTION OF THE OTHER POWERS

News of the ultimatum's contents reached the other Great Powers on July 24 and shattered the deceptive calm that had characterized Europe since shortly after the assassination. Sergei Sazonov, the Russian foreign minister, exclaimed that "this means a European war" but urged the Serbs to act with restraint in responding to Vienna and collaborated with them in drafting a reply to the ultimatum. At the same time, he gained the czar's consent in principle for the mobilization of four army districts for possible use against Austria-Hungary. The following day the Russian government secretly initiated a "period preparatory to war," effective on July 26. This would enable the army to undertake measures necessary for the start of actual mobilization, but it was also a dangerously provocative action and encouraged the Serbs to refuse unconditional acceptance of the ultimatum. Meanwhile, Russian diplomats denied reports in foreign capitals that such steps were in progress.

In London, British foreign secretary Sir Edward Grey described the ultimatum as "the most formidable document I have ever seen addressed by one State to another..." He promptly proposed a conference of the four Great Powers less directly involved—Britain, France, Germany, and Italy—to mediate the dispute. In the absence of Poincaré and

Viviani, who were still at sea and would not return to Paris until July 29, the French ambassador to Russia, Maurice Paleologue, assured Sazonov of France's support. In doing so, he was acting on his own, without any authorization from his government. Nevertheless, during their visit to St. Petersburg, both Poincaré and Viviani had encouraged Russia to stand firm no matter what might happen. Russian leaders appear to have viewed these words as constituting a blank check to persevere in an intransigent policy of support for Serbia.

Serbian leaders, alarmed by the harshness of the ultimatum, drew up their reply after consultation with the Russians and presented it to the Austrian minister in Belgrade two minutes before the deadline. Although they responded in generally evasive terms, the document clearly provided a basis for negotiation. The Serbs accepted all of the demands except two. Most importantly, they refused to allow Austrian officials to participate in the investigation of the conspiracy on Serbian soil. Austria-Hungary insisted on total compliance, however, and quickly broke diplomatic relations. The Serbs, anticipating this response, had already begun mobilization and were in the process of moving their government from Belgrade, dangerously close to the frontier, to the more remote city of Nish. Austria-Hungary began mobilization soon afterward.

In London, concern mounted after receiving news of the rupture of Austro-Serbian relations. The British government again invited France, Italy, and Germany to join Britain in a conference to mediate the dispute between the Dual Monarchy and Serbia. Unfortunately, Britain offered no concrete proposals for a solution to the crisis. Italy quickly agreed, as did France after some hesitation, but Germany rejected the proposal. Chancellor Bethmann-Hollweg insisted that his country could not summon its

ally before a European court of justice. Sir Edward Grey also urged Berlin to encourage Vienna to either accept the Serbian response or refer the matter to a conference of the Great Powers. Bethmann advised Austria-Hungary to reject Grey's proposal but added that he felt compelled to pass it on to Vienna, so as not to give the impression that Germany opposed all offers of mediation. Russia urged restraint on Austria-Hungary and indicated that it would advise Serbia to accept the remaining ultimatum demands, if Vienna would agree to some modification. Sazonov also proposed direct talks between Russia and the Dual Monarchy. Viviani, still on board ship, telegraphed St. Petersburg that France favored a peaceful solution but remained loyal to its alliance obligations.

WAR IS NEAR

Austria-Hungary was still in no mood to compromise, however. It was already planning to declare war on Serbia. The only question was the timing of this action. Conrad insisted that it should be delayed until mobilization was completed on August 12, but Berchtold believed that it was not possible to stall the diplomatic process that long. On July 27, the government agreed to declare war within the next two days.

Meanwhile, William II, apparently assuming that the Austro-Serbian quarrel would not escalate, had gone on a three-week cruise. As a result, he did not read the Serbian response to the ultimatum until the morning of July 28, the day after his return. He considered it so conciliatory that it represented an Austrian diplomatic triumph and removed "every reason for war." He urged Austria-Hungary to limit its actions to an occupation of Belgrade as a pledge of the Serbian promise of compliance already received and offered to mediate personally the remaining matters of contention. Although Bethmann-Hollweg delayed the emperor's appeal for 12 hours, he had been urging Vienna to negotiate and "localize" the conflict. When he relayed William's appeal, he instructed the German ambassador not to give "the impression that we wish to hold Austria back" but, at the same time, to indicate Berlin's desire to avoid a world conflict. By the time the message reached Vienna late on July 28, Austria-Hungary had already declared war on Serbia. It took this action after receiving information of Russian military measures and Serbian mobilization.

MOBILIZATION BEGINS

In Russia, where the government had already initiated a number of measures preparatory to mobilization, Sazonov responded to the Austro-Hungarian declaration of war by urging mobilization against Austria-Hungary. He soon encountered opposition from General Nikolai Yanushkevich, the chief of staff, who informed Sazonov that the army had no plan for partial mobilization. It had long assumed that the outbreak of war between Russia and Austria-Hungary would automatically trigger German intervention and, thus, had provided only for general mobilization. To be sure, it would be possible to alter the railway timetables to allow for the mobilization of only the four army districts opposite Austria-Hungary, but if it later proved necessary to order general mobilization, the result would be utter confusion. When confronted by this disturbing revelation as well as news that the Austrians had bombarded Belgrade, Sazonov agreed to general mobilization. Nicholas II at first reluctantly agreed but then refused after he received a telegram from his cousin William II expressing Germany's hope of arranging direct negotiations between Austria-Hungary and Germany. Nicholas insisted on partial mobilization only.

Meanwhile, after hearing of Russian measures preparatory to mobilization, Bethmann became increasingly pessimistic about chances of avoiding a general war involving both Russia and France. His mind now focused more and more on the need for Germany to avoid provocative measures, while waiting for Russia to order mobilization. This would put the onus for starting the war between the Great Powers on Russia in the eyes of the German people and, possibly, other powers as well. He still hoped that Britain would remain neutral. To the Germans, it did not matter whether the Russians ordered partial or general mobilization. General von Moltke, chief of the German general staff, made it abundantly clear that Germany's hope of victory in a general conflict depended on the speed of its mobilization timetable. To wait until Russia had already carried out partial mobilization would nullify that advantage, not to mention the fact that Germany was obligated to stand by its ally. Moltke shared Bethmann's belief that Germany would be in a much better position to win a general war in 1914 than would be the case in the future.

Bethmann's willingness to accept war cooled on July 29 as a result of disturbing news from London. Foreign secretary Grey informed the German ambassador that Britain could remain neutral in case of war between Austria-Hungary and Russia, but if Germany attacked France, British intervention was a distinct possibility. This revelation prompted Bethmann to appeal to Austria-Hungary to accept William II's "halt in Belgrade" proposal. But on July 30, reports of the extent of Russia's partial mobilization alarmed Moltke. The chief of staff called for immediate German mobilization and, on his own authority and contradicting Bethmann's earlier plea for restraint, he urged Austria-Hungary to undertake general mobilization as well. Berchtold was so puzzled by the

FIGURE 4–2   General Helmuth von Moltke the Younger, chief of the German general staff. National Archives

mixed signals emanating from Germany that he asked, "Who actually rules in Berlin, Bethmann or Moltke?"

Meanwhile, Sazonov's pessimism regarding the likelihood of a general war had escalated as a result of Austria-Hungary's intransigence toward Serbia and his own growing suspicion of German intentions. With the support of General Yanushkevich and A.V. Krivoschein, the minister of agriculture who was particularly influential in the government at this time, Sazonov urged

Nicholas II to abandon his opposition to general mobilization. This would help Russia overcome the disadvantage of its slower mobilization timetable. On July 30, worn down by increasing evidence that partial mobilization would lead to confusion, Czar Nicholas acquiesced.

By now, the momentum of events had placed the determination of policy largely in the hands of the generals of the various powers and what they deemed military necessity. Confronted by the swift escalation of the crisis, France ordered partial mobilization on July 30. The next day, Austria-Hungary followed the Russian lead and ordered general mobilization, while the Germans proclaimed a state of imminent war and issued ultimatums to both Russia and France. They demanded that St. Petersburg cease mobilization within 24 hours and that Paris agree to remain neutral in the event of war between Germany and Russia.

German leaders had long taken for granted that war between Germany and Russia would result in hostilities with France as well. Indeed, the German strategic plan, to be used in case of war, made this inevitable. That plan, originally devised in 1905 by General Alfred von Schlieffen, Moltke's predecessor as chief of staff, had provided for such a war to open with a quick German campaign against France, while remaining on the defensive against Russia. Once the Germans had defeated the French, within 39 days after mobilization, it was hoped, they would shift the bulk of their forces to the east for an offensive against the Russians. Neither General Schlieffen nor General Moltke had provided for a war that would involve only Russia. Thus, there was pressing need either to secure French neutrality or launch an offensive in the west. The Schlieffen Plan was designed to take advantage of the slow Russian mobilization timetable, which the Germans did not expect to be completed until after the defeat of France.

But the Schlieffen Plan did not provide for an attack directly across the Franco-German border. The French had fortified the hilly, heavily wooded terrain along the frontier, and an operation in this area did not promise a speedy victory, which the Germans considered vital to their plans. Schlieffen had something else in mind—an offensive that would swing through northeastern Belgium, avoiding the difficult Ardennes Forest to the south, and then penetrate into north-

western France. The Germans would then advance to the southwest of Paris before wheeling to the east, with the hope of sweeping the French armies back toward the German border and encircling them in a gigantic trap. Schlieffen believed that this bold plan was the only feasible way to knock France out of the war before the Russians invaded East Prussia.

Unfortunately, the plan would involve the violation of an international agreement, signed by all the Great Powers in 1839, guaranteeing Belgium's permanent neutrality. Such an operation posed the distinct likelihood of British intervention against Germany because Britain looked upon Belgium's neutrality as a sacred trust. The British were especially sensitive to the possibility of a Great Power gaining control of Belgium because it contained Antwerp, one of the largest and best ports on Europe's Atlantic coast. Antwerp would provide an ideal concentration point for a possible invasion of Britain.

GERMANY DECLARES WAR

At noon on Saturday, August 1, the deadline for Germany's ultimatums expired with no reply from either Russia or France. Moltke, now frantic, demanded immediate mobilization, but Bethmann in a last desperate effort to avoid war, postponed the deadline another five hours. France ordered general mobilization at 4:45 P.M. German time. Finally, 15 minutes later, Germany became the last of the Continental powers to mobilize. It also declared war on Russia. By waiting so long, Bethmann had badly disrupted Moltke's timetable for the invasion of Belgium. This delay probably destroyed whatever chance Germany had of winning the war. The following day, German troops occupied the Grand Duchy of Luxembourg, and Berlin issued still another ultimatum, this time to Belgium, demanding the right of free passage for German troops en route to France. If Belgium agreed, Germany would guarantee its territorial integrity after the war. When the Belgians refused to accept the ultimatum on August 3, Germany declared war on France and sent troops into Belgium the following morning.

Britain now faced its moment of decision. The British cabinet had already been wrestling with the question of whether to enter the war in defense of France but had reached no decision. Despite the close military and naval planning of the last few years and the moral obligation to defend France's Channel coast against a possible German attack, the cabinet was split. The French, especially Paul Cambon, the ambassador to London, were growing concerned that Britain would leave them in the lurch. A sizable group of cabinet ministers had long resisted Foreign Secretary Grey's policy of closer relations with France and Russia. They feared that the creation of the Triple Entente would drag Britain into a Continental war. But events were beginning to force Britain's hand. A majority of the cabinet agreed on Sunday, August 2, that the Royal Navy could not allow a German fleet to enter the English Channel, but two members resigned in protest. The British took this action in part out of loyalty to France but perhaps even more because of the threat such an action would pose to Britain's own coast. It appears, however, that Winston Churchill and certain other leaders did not really believe that the Germans would be so bold as to shell the French coast. More significantly, the German occupation of Luxembourg persuaded the British cabinet that Germany would soon violate Belgium's neutrality, an event that would provide justification for British entry into the conflict.

But despite Britain's prior commitment to send troops to the Continent, if it joined France in a war against Germany, the cabinet now refused to authorize such a step and agreed to limit involvement to naval action only. This decision evoked strong protests from General Henry Wilson, the chief of military operations, and key members of the Foreign Office, not to mention the French. On the evening of August 2, the British received news of the German ultimatum to Belgium, and on the following morning, Monday, August 3, King Albert of Belgium appealed to Britain for diplomatic intervention on behalf of his country, while two more British cabinet members resigned. That afternoon Foreign Secretary Grey informed the House of Commons of the seriousness of the situation and revealed the existence of the military and naval discussions with France during recent years. At the same time, he emphasized the nonbinding nature of these contacts and insisted that Britain was still free to act as it chose. However, despite this disclaimer, Grey also announced the cabinet's decision to provide naval assistance to the French should the German navy enter the English Channel. Finally, Grey briefed the House of Commons on Germany's ultimatum to Belgium and King Albert's appeal for British support. After outlining Britain's obligations to Belgium under the treaty of 1839, Grey asked whether the country "could run away from those obligations of honor and interest..." To do so, he insisted, would undermine its position as a Great Power. A decided majority of the House of Commons strongly supported Grey's speech, and those who had resigned rejoined the government even though some of them remained opposed to Grey's policy.

Shortly afterward, Grey and Prime Minister Asquith drafted an ultimatum, demanding that Germany respect Belgium's neutrality, although they did not actually send it until after the Germans had crossed the Belgian border. The British ambassador reported that when he had presented the ultimatum at 7 P.M. on August 4, Bethmann sadly remarked that Britain was taking a terrible step "just for a scrap of paper." These unfortunate words remained forever associated with his name. The British made adroit use of Bethmann's words in their wartime propaganda. To the people of Britain as well as those of neutral countries, such as the United States, they seemed to convey German disregard for international law. The "scrap of paper," of course, was the treaty of 1839 that guaranteed Belgium's neutrality.

BRITAIN ENTERS THE WAR

Bethmann had sounded more apologetic when he had defended the violation of Belgium's neutrality in the Reichstag earlier on August 4. The invasion was "a breach of international law," he admitted, "but the wrong—I speak openly—that we are committing we will make good as soon as our military aims have been reached." In his view, however, it was a matter of military necessity, and "necessity knows no law." Britain entered the war when the time limit on its ultimatum expired at midnight, but it was not until August 6 that the cabinet finally authorized dispatching an expeditionary force of five divisions to France.

While Grey could feel satisfaction that Britain had fulfilled its obligations, he was not without misgivings. On the night of August 4, as the time limit on the ultimatum drew toward its end, he gazed out of a Foreign Office window and sadly exclaimed to an aide, "The lights are going out all over Europe. We shall not see them lit again in our lifetime." Grey's sense of immense tragedy was shared by many others, including Nicholas II, William II, Bethmann, and members of the French and Austro-Hungarian governments. Their failure to find a diplomatic solution to the last Balkan crisis had plunged Europe into a general war that perhaps no one really wanted.

ITALY REMAINS NEUTRAL

Of the six major powers of Europe, only Italy remained neutral. Oddly enough, relations between Rome and the Triple Alliance had improved between 1910 and 1914. The Marquis di San Guiliano, the Italian foreign minister, had followed a policy of cooperation with Austria-Hungary during the crisis over the Balkan wars, although, to be sure, in keeping with his own country's interests in Albania. The chief of staff of the Italian army, General Alberto Pollio, was a strong supporter of the Triple Alliance and, starting in December 1912, pushed for closer military cooperation between his country and Austria-Hungary. He even offered to send troops to aid Italy's allies in case of war with Serbia and Russia. Franco-Italian relations had deteriorated during the Tripolitanian War, and Italy had become concerned about possible French naval domination of the Mediterranean in the wake of the Anglo-French naval agreement of 1912. This fear led to Italy signing a naval convention with Austria-Hungary in 1913, calling for a united command of the Italo-Austrian fleets in the event of war.

Conrad had long distrusted the Italians and had more than once called for an attack on them, despite the fact that they were allied with Austria. But he got on well with Pollio and appears to have grown more optimistic about Italy's reliability. Unfortunately, Pollio died on the very day of the assassination at Sarajevo, and San Guiliano was seriously ill. As a result, the premier, Antonio Salandra, who favored cooperation with the Triple Entente, played the major role in foreign policy during the July crisis.

Despite the better relations of the past few years, Austro-Hungarian leaders did not see fit to inform Italy of their plans regarding Serbia until the day after the ultimatum to Belgrade. The Italian response was not encouraging. On July 24, Rome notified Vienna that, according to the defensive nature of the Triple Alliance, Italy was not obligated to support Austria-Hungary if it attacked Serbia. The Italians also indicated that they would not agree to Austrian occupation of any Serbian territory, unless it was in accord with previous consultation with the other members of the alliance. In other words, Italy expected territorial compensation for any Austrian gains at Serbia's expense. German leaders pressed the Dual Monarchy to offer Italy the Trentino, if necessary, to secure at least Italian neutrality, a proposal that met with little enthusiasm in Vienna.

When Berchtold informed Conrad of Italy's position, the chief of staff warned that, if there were a danger of Italian intervention against Austria-Hungary, there should be no mobilization against Serbia. He added ominously, "We could not fight a war on three fronts." Nevertheless, both Conrad and Berchtold still appear to have anticipated Italian neutrality and went ahead with their plans for war. For the time being, they were correct, but Italy's permanent neutrality and loyalty to the Triple Alliance were by no means certain.

Rumania also declined to support its partners in the Triple Alliance. Although King Carol professed loyalty to them, the government of Premier Ion Bratianu favored neutrality. Rumania's obligations, like those of Italy, were strictly defensive, while Austria-Hungary and Germany were clearly the aggressors. But just as clearly, the permanence of Bucharest's neutrality was questionable, especially since the Entente powers could entice the Rumanians with the promise of gaining Transylvania if they joined them in the war.

REASONS FOR THE WAR

From the start of hostilities, each of the opposing sides blamed the other for causing the war. Historians soon joined in and have continued to this very day to argue about who or what caused the catastrophe. Although it is unlikely that complete agreement will ever be forthcoming, certain observations appear warranted.

The conspirators who carried out the assassination of Archduke Francis Ferdinand, with the active participation of Dimitrijevich's Black Hand organization, clearly ignited "the spark that set the world afire." And although the Serbian government did not authorize their action, Pašich and other officials in Belgrade were certainly aware of the plot and did little to alert Vienna to the magnitude of the danger. Their anti-Austrian policies and Greater Serb ambitions had also contributed mightily to the deterioration of relations with the Dual Monarchy. They assumed, moreover, that if it came to a showdown with Austria-Hungary, Serbia's "big brother" Russia would back them up.

As for Austria-Hungary, it is hardly surprising that its leaders, outraged by the assassination of Francis Ferdinand, were convinced that Serbia was responsible and must be punished for this terrible crime. There is no doubt that, almost from the start of the crisis, most of them were resolved to go to war with Serbia. Whether Vienna would have actually translated this intent into reality without assurance of German support is less clear. But when Germany extended its "blank check," the Dual Monarchy pursued this policy with rigid single-mindedness, even at the risk of war with Russia, assuming that its "big brother" would provide the necessary support. Foreign Minister Berchtold and the other Austro-Hungarian leaders seemed virtually to close their eyes to the possibility of Russian intervention, however. One historian has observed that Austro-Hungarian leaders conducted policy during the July crisis as though Russia did not exist. To them, all that mattered was the elimination of the Serbian menace. Conrad, of course, had long urged such action, and Berchtold appears to have been convinced by the success of his tough policy during the Albanian border dispute in 1913 that a hard-line approach would once again persuade the Russians to back down.

The leaders in Vienna took their desperate gamble to save the Hapsburg Empire from impending disintegration. If the Dual Monarchy was as weak as they feared, however, it is ironic that they believed it capable of waging war to the victorious conclusion they deemed necessary for its salvation. In reality, it does not appear that many of them felt very confident. Conrad, the arch-warmonger, confided to his mistress that the coming war would be "a hopeless struggle." Nevertheless, he was willing to accept this outcome "because such an ancient monarchy and so grand an army cannot perish ingloriously."

German leaders certainly encouraged Austria-Hungary to take firm action against Serbia, believing that this was essential if the Dual Monarchy were to retain its position as a Great Power. They assumed, however, that if it came to war, it would be possible to "localize" the conflict, especially if Vienna acted promptly while European opinion was still sympathetic to Austria-Hungary and hostile toward Serbia in the aftermath of the assassination. Indeed they were overly confident of Russian neutrality in the event of an Austro-Serbian war. Furthermore they were willing to risk Russian intervention to keep their ally in the ranks of the Great Powers. It is also certain that both Bethmann and Moltke believed that Germany was in a better position to face war in 1914 than would be the case a few years later.

Some historians have contended that Bethmann and other German leaders made the decision to provoke a war as early as 1912

out of fear that the traditional political and social structure of Germany was in danger from the growing strength of the Social Democrats and the threat of government paralysis. According to this argument, Bethmann and his associates hoped to rally the German people, including the working class, behind the government in a great wartime crusade that would save the traditional system. Although German leaders clearly worried over the threat from the left and the danger to the stability of the government, this interpretation is not convincing. It appears that Germany based its response to the July crisis primarily on an appraisal of foreign policy considerations at the time. Berlin was convinced that Austria-Hungary must deal firmly with Serbia if it was to remain a Great Power. But Bethmann did attempt to restrain Austria-Hungary when it became increasingly obvious that war with Serbia would spark a general European conflict. He also resisted Moltke's persistent demands for mobilization until the last possible moment and may have unwittingly endangered Germany's hopes for victory in the process.

Russia had long acted in an irresponsible manner by encouraging Serbia in its hostile policies toward Austria-Hungary. The machinations of Hartwig, the minister to Belgrade, were especially dangerous. Russia, of course, was also the first Great Power to order general mobilization. Critics of this action have pointed with scorn to the absence of an alternative plan for partial mobilization against Austria-Hungary only. Clearly the failure to provide for such a possibility represents a lamentable absence of flexibility. But even partial mobilization entailed serious danger. Moltke and other German generals were convinced that Germany could not wait for Russia to complete partial mobilization. Some of the military districts involved in such an operation bordered

Germany as well as the Dual Monarchy. Moreover, the Schlieffen Plan called for precise timing. Even a slight delay in putting it into effect might prove fatal. Finally, could the Germans stand idly by while the Russians brought their military strength to bear on Austria-Hungary?

Even if Russia believed that war was inevitable, as Sergei Sazonov, the Russian foreign minister, apparently did, it would have benefitted by delaying any kind of mobilization until Conrad had committed his forces against Serbia. The Russians had already initiated a period preparatory to war. This gave them several days advantage over their opponents, and by concentrating against the Serbs, Austria-Hungary would weaken its forces in Galicia opposite the Russians. In fact, the Austrians would not actually be able to start hostilities until August 12. It was conceivable, although doubtful, that the other powers might be able to work out the basis for a diplomatic settlement by then. But the leaders in St. Petersburg felt that they must take action to defend their little Serbian ally. By ordering mobilization, they enabled the chain reaction, initiated by Austria's declaration of war on Serbia, to continue its fateful course.

France also contributed to the increasingly explosive atmosphere during the July crisis. Critics have focused especially on the roles played by President Poincaré and Paleologue, the French ambassador to St. Petersburg. Poincaré unquestionably contributed to strengthening the Triple Entente well before 1914, which made it more rigid and susceptible to a chain reaction. He and Viviani also encouraged Russia to stand firm while they were in St. Petersburg in July. It appears that the Russians welcomed their words as a "blank check." They no doubt strengthened Russia's resolve to back Serbia to the limit. And although Poincaré was at sea during the most critical days of the crisis, he failed to suggest any solution after his return to Paris. Paleologue assured the Russians of strong French support in the absence of Poincaré and Viviani despite having no authorization from Paris.

There are also those who believe that Britain might have persuaded the Germans to follow a more restrained policy had Foreign Secretary Grey announced early in the crisis that Berlin could not expect the British to stand aside in case of a German attack on France. But such criticism ignores the fact that Grey was reluctant to make such a statement without the support of Parliament, which at that time still knew nothing of the Anglo-French secret military and naval planning of the previous few years. In fact, Grey himself appears to have had difficulty recognizing the extent of British commitment to France and he clung to the belief that Britain retained a free hand until late in the crisis. To be sure, Grey is liable to criticism for the deviousness of his policy, not only in regard to his own people but also to other countries. France undoubtedly counted on British support until late in the crisis and based its encouragement of Russian firmness at least in part on this confidence. When it appeared that the British might not enter the war, French leaders not surprisingly felt betrayed. Grey, it seems, had become a prisoner of his own deviousness. He could not extricate himself from this dilemma until the other powers were already at war, and violation of Belgium's neutrality was a certainty. Grey also failed to offer any definite proposals for a way out of Europe's dilemma when he suggested a conference to mediate the Austro-Serbian dispute following the rupture of relations between the two countries.

It is questionable whether any of the Great Powers actually desired a general war when the July crisis began. But Austria-Hungary, justifiably angry with Serbia and assured of German backing, definitely sought a local-

Europe before the War, 1914

ized conflict, while Germany, Russia, and France appear to have been willing to accept a general war, if conditions seemed sufficiently promising. But the extent of the general conflict that began early in August 1914 was to be far greater than any of them had anticipated. It was to lead to four years of ghastly slaughter and would profoundly change the fabric of European society as well as the predominant position which the Continent had enjoyed in the world for so long.

GREAT EXPECTATIONS: WAR PLANS AND THE SHORT WAR ILLUSION

Perhaps the most striking factor associated with the outbreak of war in the summer of 1914 was the almost universal failure of the European powers to anticipate the type of conflict they were unleashing. Most of the leaders, both military and civilian, of the belligerent countries badly underestimated the length of the struggle, its costliness in lives and wealth, and its impact on the social and political foundations of the Continent. If they had been more farsighted, it would seem logical that they would have tried harder to prevent the coming of hostilities.

THE SHORT WAR ILLUSION

By far the most serious of their miscalculations was the expectation that the conflict would be short, a belief that later became known as "the short war illusion." To be sure, they could point to most of the European wars of the nineteenth century as evidence to support their optimism. The Austro-Prussian War of 1866 lasted just seven weeks, the Franco-Prussian War of 1870–1871 a few months, even though its outcome had been determined in the first few weeks. The more recent Balkan wars were also brief.

Along with their confidence in the brevity of the conflict, European leaders believed that the outcome of the war would depend on offensive striking power rather than defensive staying power. The side that brought to bear the greatest weight of offensive might and employed it skillfully would win, according to the prevailing wisdom. Again, the examples of the Austro-Prussian, Franco-Prussian, and Balkan wars seemed to demonstrate that this was true. As further proof, the prophets of a short-war-to-be-decided-by-offensive-strength emphasized the revolutionary new weapons that had come into existence during the last few decades before 1914. These included rapid-firing rifles, which were far more efficient than any comparable previous weapons; the machine gun, which could discharge a steady stream of bullets with amazing speed; and various forms of heavy artillery, capable of firing enormous quantities of explosive shells over long distances. Clearly, no defense would be capable of resisting an overwhelming concentration of such offensive weapons for long, or so it seemed.

Somehow those who preached the doctrine of offensive striking power and its capacity to determine the conflict's outcome decisively and quickly failed to take into account certain notable exceptions to the rule of the short war. The American Civil War of 1861–1865 lasted four bloody years, killing an estimated 600,000 men for the North and South combined. This terrible struggle provided repeated examples of the capacity of defensive firepower to cut down huge numbers of attacking troops. It also introduced Americans to the horrors of trench warfare. The Crimean War of 1853–1856 essentially consisted of a long siege operation. French and British troops hammered away for almost a year before finally breaking through the formidable landward defenses of the Russian naval base of Sevastopol on the Crimean Peninsula. The Russo-Japanese War also involved trench warfare complete with heavy casualties for both sides before the Japanese captured the Russian strongholds of Port Arthur and Mukden.

A PROTRACTED WAR PREDICTED

Not all observers were dedicated to "the short war illusion," however. Both General Moltke, chief of staff of the German army since 1906, and General Joseph Joffre, who became chief of the French army's general staff in 1911, foresaw the possibility of a long war of attrition. But neither of them did anything to prepare their respective countries for such a disastrous development and conducted themselves in 1914 as though the conflict would be brief. Lord Horatio Kitchener, who succeeded Haldane as secretary of war on the day that Britain entered World War I or the Great War as it was called then, immediately predicted that the conflict would last at least three years. After brief reflection, he added, "no one living knows how long." Kitchener, unlike Moltke and Joffre, actually tried to initiate measures to fight a war of such duration. He attempted to persuade his colleagues of the need to raise a mass army to replace the inadequate British volunteer force, but no one else in the government agreed with him. In short, vision was a rare commodity in 1914 and would remain so in the years to come.

THE CENTRAL POWERS

Germany and Austria-Hungary, shorn of their former ally Italy, became known as the Central Powers soon after the fighting started. By November 1914, they had gained the support of Turkey, and Bulgaria joined their coalition almost a year later. The Central Powers especially were counting on a quick war, because a long struggle was almost certain to end badly for them. They were, to some extent, victims of their central geographic location and now were encircled militarily as they had been encircled diplomatically in the years before the war. The British Royal Navy added to the Central Powers' dilemma by resorting to a maritime blockade, a traditional British strategy, that cut off the Central Powers from the resources of the outside world.

THE ENTENTE POWERS

The Entente Powers—Britain, France and Russia, along with their newly acquired junior partners, Serbia and Belgium—ultimately became known as the Allies. They enjoyed a number of advantages in addition to the physical isolation of the Central Powers. Although none of them individually was the equal of Germany in terms of industrial or military might, together they possessed greater economic and manpower resources. Their control of the high seas also provided access to the wealth of the rest of the world. Ironically, despite the baneful effect of Admiral Tirpitz's naval construction program on Anglo-German relations in the prewar years, Germany's navy had not been able to bluff Britain into remaining neutral. It also was not strong enough to risk a full-fledged encounter with the Royal Navy.

Tirpitz had built the fleet in part on his belief that the British would initiate a close blockade that would bring their warships within a short distance of Germany's North Sea coast. This would enable German submarines and torpedo boats to engage in hit-and-run attacks on British ships and then dart back to the safety of their nearby bases. He hoped that these tactics would gradually erode the enemy's numerical advantage. Only when the Germans had gained virtual equality, along with completely favorable conditions, would their High Seas Fleet seek a showdown battle.

But the British saw no need to venture so close to German territorial waters. Instead, they adopted a distant blockade, that was just as effective as a close blockade and far less risky. This involved blocking German access to the English Channel as well as the waters between Norway and the Orkney and Shetland islands to the north of Scotland. The only offensive option for German surface ships would be to sally forth far from their bases to attack British vessels in the North Sea. But this would leave them vulnerable to an encounter battle with a more powerful enemy force, the danger of being cut off from retreat, and possible annihilation. Thus, the German High Seas Fleet remained close to its home bases during most of the war. The only other weapon available was the German submarine force. Unfortunately, there were too few U-boats (*Unterseeboote*) in the early stages of the war to pose more than a nuisance to the British.

ADVANTAGES OF THE CENTRAL POWERS

But the Central Powers did have some advantages. Not the least of these was the great strength of the German army and the superb fighting quality of its individual soldiers. Germany's military training was superior to that of any other power in the world. It also possessed outstanding reserve forces. These were able to operate with remarkable effectiveness in combination with regular divisions and they doubled German strength. The army also had an abundance of weapons of the highest quality, including heavy artillery, such as the huge and awesomely powerful 420-mm howitzer known as "Big Bertha." When the war began, the Germans had 87 infantry and 11 cavalry divisions. This gave them a considerable numerical advantage over the French and British combined. In raw numbers, Germany's forces were inferior to the huge Russian army, but they were far superior to their eastern enemy in all other respects. The Central Powers also benefitted from internal lines of communication, the one great advantage of their geographic location. Germany's exceptional railroad network made it possible to shift forces and material from one front to another for quick deployment wherever they were needed.

The Central Powers also benefitted from close coordination of German and Austro-Hungarian forces. But this did not come about immediately and involved a decidedly negative factor. It actually resulted from the Dual Monarchy's military weakness. The proud Hapsburg Empire soon clearly became the junior partner in the alliance with its army increasingly dependent on German support and subject to overall German direction. In 1914, Austria-Hungary's military spending lagged behind that of all the other major European powers, including Italy. This was in large part a product of the ongoing rivalry between Austria and Hungary. Many Magyars had desired a separate Hungarian army ever since the *Ausgleich* of 1867. But Francis Joseph had firmly resisted their efforts to achieve this additional confirmation of Hungary's separate identity within the Dual Monarchy. To the emperor and other Austrian officials, the common army remained the key to the dynasty's rule over the empire. For many years, the Hungarian Diet stubbornly refused to vote the funds necessary to enlarge and modernize the army. At times, anti-military elements in the Austrian *Reichsrat* also successfully opposed appropriations for the military.

It was not until 1912 that Hungary relented sufficiently to provide funding for a fairly substantial increase in the number of recruits. This change was due almost solely to the efforts of Premier Tisza, who recognized the deterioration of Austria-Hungary's position in the wake of the Balkan wars. Even so, the authorization came too late to be of much use in strengthening the army before the outbreak of hostilities in 1914.

As a result, the Dual Monarchy possessed a total of only 48 infantry and 11 cavalry divisions, far fewer than those of any other European Great Power, except Britain. But the British, of course, enjoyed the benefits of a secure geographic position and relied primarily on their navy for defense. Austria-Hungary entered the conflict with largely inadequate artillery, both in quantity and quality, although some newly designed modern field pieces were starting to come into mass production. Moreover, its Skoda 305-mm howitzer proved to be one of the best heavy siege mortars of the war. Ammunition was in short supply, too, and of generally poor quality. The Hapsburg army suffered from the additional drawback of its multinational composition, but for some time this proved less of a problem than many had feared. The Austro-Hungarian officer corps, primarily recruited from the Austrian and Magyar ethnic groups, consisted for the most part of capable and dedicated men. Unfortunately, the leading generals lacked vision and placed their faith in the ability of infantry attacks to overwhelm prepared defensive positions, even without artillery support.

STRENGTHS AND SHORTCOMINGS OF THE ALLIES

The forces of the Allies possessed definite strengths and many shortcomings. In terms of size, Russia's army was by far the largest of any of the belligerents. It initially put 114 divisions into the field and had the potential to expand this total many times. The sheer mass of Russian troops had inspired the nickname "the steamroller." It had provided comfort to the French in the prewar years, while alarming the Germans and Austro-Hungarians. But behind the numbers lay equally impressive weaknesses. The bulk of Russian soldiers consisted of uneducated peasants who possessed the ability to persevere despite appalling hardships but lacked initiative and needed a great deal of leadership. Unfortunately, the latter quality was conspicuously missing. The officer corps was perhaps the most inefficient of any of the major warring armies. It was woefully weak in organizational, logistic, and planning skills.

Traditionally, the man who appeared to symbolize the deplorable condition of Russian military leadership was General Sukhomlinov, the minister of war since 1908. His detractors portrayed him as lazy, deceitful, devoted to pleasure, and totally unprogressive. More recently, however, historians have revised their view of Sukhomlinov. He now appears to have actually favored reforms intended to modernize the army. Unfortunately, he encountered resistance from influential cavalry and artillery officers, who feared that his reforms would threaten or at least alter the roles of their respective branches of service. This led to a prolonged struggle for predominance between them and General Sukhomlinov's supporters and a lack of coordination of the army's efforts.

Among other things, artillery officers prevented Sukhomlinov from scrapping a number of obsolete fortresses. Not only were they able to save these useless bastions, but they succeeded in diverting much of the army's heavy artillery to their defense rather than to the forces in the field. In similar fashion, the army continued to provide for a large cavalry force, that proved of little use in modern warfare and required a disproportionate amount of railroad capacity to supply its horses with fodder.

Not surprisingly, the Russians suffered from a shortage of field guns when the war began as well as shells for those guns they did possess. They soon encountered serious shortages of other types of weapons and equipment, including rifles. Even though Russia had increased its industrial capacity and expanded the strategic railway network, it still faced the obstacles of technological backwardness, an inadequate distribution system, and administrative inefficiency. These problems took on ever greater magnitude as time passed.

Although the French army could not approach Russia's in size, it was far superior in quality. France initially fielded 62 infantry and 10 cavalry divisions, considerably fewer than the Germans. The French also had little confidence in the ability of their reserves to work effectively with regular troops and, accordingly, devoted less effort to their training than did their German counterparts. France possessed an outstanding light artillery piece in the 75-mm gun, which had exceptional range and accuracy as well as being highly mobile. Skilled 75-mm gunners could fire as many as 20 shells per minute, although the usual rate was six. Unfortunately, France's military leaders had such supreme confidence in this weapon that they failed to develop adequate heavy artillery and, unlike Germany and Austria-Hungary, had no howitzers at all. This soon proved to be a serious drawback. Even the 75-mm gun, though superior to the equivalent German 77-mm gun, was at a disadvantage of almost 2 to 1 numerically.

LORD KITCHENER AND THE BEF

Britain, of course, started the war with the smallest army of any Great Power. It consisted of only 11 infantry and five cavalry brigades. Most of it soon made its way to the Continent as the British Expeditionary Force (BEF) and took its place on the left flank of the French. The BEF totaled 160,000 men in 1914. It appeared so insignificant to William II of Germany that he dismissed it as "contemptibly small." But in terms of quality, it was the best in Europe. Lord Kitchener argued that, since this was the case, it should play the role of the vital nucleus of a greatly expanded army. He warned that it would be folly to sacrifice it in battle before a mass force had been created.

FIGURE 5–1 Field Marshal Lord Kitchener, Britain's war secretary. National Archives

Kitchener's imperious attitude and lack of diplomacy won him few friends among his fellow officers or political leaders. He received his post as war secretary, not because of his vision, but because of his popularity with the British people. Kitchener had served as a volunteer with the French Army during the Franco-Prussian War, but he became a hero to the masses by virtue of his great victory in the Battle of Omdurman during operations in the Sudan in 1898. Kitchener later directed the final stages of the difficult British campaign against Boer guerrilla forces in the South African War of 1899–1902. During the following seven years, he served as commander of the British army in India, winning promotion to the rank of field marshal. His last post before the war was as consul general of Egypt. Kitchener had become so accustomed to being the dominating presence in the Sudan, South Africa, India, and Egypt that he conducted himself in an arrogant, larger than life manner. His piercing eyes and the bushy abundance of his mustache completed the impression of determination and strength. His face soon became an obvious choice for one of the most famous recruiting posters of the war.

STRATEGY OF THE CENTRAL POWERS

Given the geographic position of the Central Powers, their strategy focused on an immediate attempt to break the Allied encirclement. They hoped that they could accomplish this swiftly and decisively. If their initial effort failed, prospects for victory would diminish sharply, and the negative aspects of their central location would increase markedly. The key to fulfillment of their expectations lay in Germany's long-prepared Schlieffen Plan.

General Alfred von Schlieffen, the initial author of this bold offensive scheme, had served as chief of the general staff from 1891 to 1906. In appearance, Schlieffen was the epitome of the monocled, aristocratic Prussian officer. He was proud to the point of arrogance, spoke in a highly sarcastic manner, and displayed a completely single-minded devotion to military matters. A famous anecdote illustrates this total absorption in his profession. It seems that, during a train trip in East Prussia, an aide drew the general's attention to a particularly scenic view of a river glistening in the sunshine. After a perfunctory glance, Schlieffen snapped, "an unimportant obstacle of no military importance."

Schlieffen believed firmly in the dictum of General Karl von Clausewitz, the renowned Prussian military theorist, that the key to victory lay in the speedy destruction of the enemy's field army. This would be accomplished by a surprise attack with overwhelming strength at the critical point. To Schlieffen, such a decisive battle could only take place in western Europe, where distances were relatively small and the encirclement of enemy forces appeared a real possibility. Accordingly, he rejected the plan of the elder Field Marshal von Moltke to concentrate on Russia in the event of a two-front war. Schlieffen believed that the vast expanse of Russia eliminated any chance of a swift victory in the east.

While Moltke had directed brilliant campaigns against Austria in 1866 and France in 1870–1871, Schlieffen lacked firsthand experience with war. He had spent his career in staff work, and his outlook was that of the professional planner. Schlieffen trusted too much in the ability of troops to carry out precise plans according to exact timetables. The general was especially fascinated with the spectacular Battle of Cannae in 216 B.C. In this famous encounter, the Carthaginian general Hannibal had destroyed a numerically superior Roman army by means of double envelopment. In other words, the two wings of Hannibal's forces had encircled and totally crushed the enemy. Schlieffen thought in terms of a variation on this classic theme. Because of the heavily fortified Franco-German border and the rugged hill country of the Ardennes Forest in southeastern Belgium and Luxembourg, he believed the only way to knock out France was to swing around these obstacles by way of northeastern Belgium and then into northern France. He hoped to destroy the French by sending an overwhelmingly powerful right wing in a swift advance along this route. This right hook would swing well to the southwest of Paris. Then it would wheel to the east, enveloping the enemy forces from the rear and

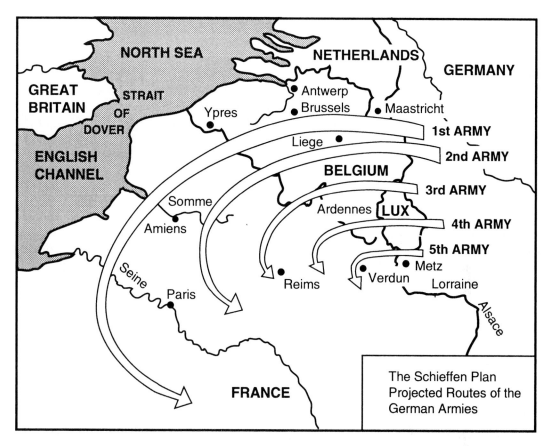

The Schieffen Plan
Projected Routes of the
German Armies

culminating either in their annihilation or surrender.

By 1905, Schlieffen had completed his final version of the plan. He believed that if the drive through Belgium were to succeed, it would be necessary to utilize the rail and road lines of the southeastern Dutch province of Limburg. This region included the Maastricht "Appendix," a narrow strip of land jutting southward from the rest of the Netherlands and separating northeastern Belgium from Germany. Schlieffen insisted that the right wing, forming the German spearhead, must have a 7 to 1 advantage in strength over the left wing, that was to assume a defensive position against a possible French attack in Lorraine. He also emphasized that the right wing should advance as close as possible to the English Channel before making its turn to the east. This would eliminate the opportunity for a French counterattack from the coastal area against the German flank. As Schlieffen put it, "The man farthest on the right should brush the Channel with his sleeve."

The Schlieffen Plan was extremely grandiose and highly inflexible. It reflected the dilemma confronting Germany. In a two-front war, Schlieffen believed that the Germans could only win by knocking out France before Russia could mobilize its huge reserves. This would require victory over the French within 39 days after mobilization. His plan provided for exceptionally large forces, moving on foot over considerable distances, according to a remarkably tight timetable. It also entailed immense logistic problems, most notably dependence on railroad lines that the Belgians were almost certain to destroy or damage as they retreated. It would be necessary to repair them before they would be of any use to the advancing armies. Furthermore, the Germans depended primarily on horse-drawn wagons to haul supplies and equipment from the railhead to the front. Trucks were in short supply, and the few that were available received the top priority assignment of transporting ammunition.

When Schlieffen devised his plan, the great city of Paris loomed as an additional obstacle. The French capital was a fortified city, with a garrison of 100,000 men, as well as the rail hub of northern France. The Germans did not have sufficient forces or the necessary logistic support to take the city without halting the forward momentum of the right wing. But unless they neutralized this powerful enemy stronghold, it would pose a threat to the German army as it made the turn to the east. Schlieffen himself later came to realize the magnitude of this problem. After his retirement, he actually predicted that the plan, that he had authored, would fail.

When Helmuth von Moltke the younger (nephew of Field Marshal von Moltke) succeeded Schlieffen in 1906, he also inherited his operational plan. Although an intelligent staff officer who had served bravely in battle during the Franco-Prussian War, Moltke lacked Schlieffen's great self-confidence. In fact, he doubted his own ability to be Germany's chief of staff, at least in wartime. Chancellor von Bülow recalled that Moltke once told him, "I lack the power of rapid decision; I am too reflective, too scrupulous, or if you like conscientious for such a post. I lack the capacity for staking all on a single throw." To be sure, Moltke labored under a formidable handicap. As the nephew of one of Germany's legendary military heroes, he

always operated in the elder Moltke's shadow. He could even see his uncle's equestrian statue from the window of his home. Moltke's interests, far wider than Schlieffen's, extended to reading philosophy, painting, and playing the cello. At 66, he suffered from kidney disease and often traveled to the health spa at Carlsbad in a vain quest for a cure. But despite his self-doubt and poor health, he was not afraid to argue strenuously with the German emperor on numerous occasions. He also followed a decidedly truculent approach to the various crises before the war.

Moltke appears to have questioned the infallibility of the Schlieffen Plan, but he made no effort to scrap it and adopt an entirely new approach. He did modify the plan, however, with the help of Colonel Erich Ludendorff, chief of the operations section of the general staff. He eliminated the provision for violation of Dutch neutrality, a change that would funnel the German drive through the bottleneck of eastern Belgium and place additional pressure on the Belgian railroads. Moltke also reduced the ratio of strength for the right wing from 7 to 1 to 3 to 1. He did this in part to defend against an anticipated French attack in Lorraine, but he also toyed with the idea of an offensive by the strengthened German left wing, that would create a two-pronged operation more reminiscent of Hannibal's Cannae maneuver. These changes certainly weakened the German right wing but probably made little real difference in the outcome of the operation. The crucial problem proved to be one of logistics. It would be increasingly difficult to supply the German troops as their advance took them farther away from their bases.

PLAN 17

France also had a strategic plan to be put into effect as soon as possible after the start of hostilities. The French general staff referred to it unimaginatively as Plan 17, the last in a long line of such schemes. It provided for an attack on German-controlled Lorraine with the main thrusts directed on either side of the strongly fortified city of Metz. The French were to leave the Franco-Belgian border to the west of the Meuse River virtually undefended. While they assumed that the Germans would violate Belgian neutrality, they did not expect them to advance farther west than the Meuse, which separated the eastern third of Belgium from the remainder of the country. And they viewed this incursion as merely supportive of the main enemy spearhead, which they expected to come in Lorraine to the west of Metz. The French did not think that the Germans had enough troops to advance beyond the Meuse in Belgium. They based this conclusion on their belief that the enemy would not employ reserve divisions on a basis of equality with regular divisions. The French failed to understand that Germany's military leaders did not share their own low regard for reserve troops.

The intention of Plan 17 was to break through the German defenders, cut behind the enemy forces attempting to penetrate to the west of Metz, defeat them, and liberate Lorraine. Beyond these aims, the plan stipulated no ultimate objective, although French officers made vague statements about an eventual thrust all the way to the Rhine River. Commanders were to exploit whatever opportunities presented themselves, once the breakthrough had been achieved.

The man who assumed primary responsibility for formulating Plan 17 was French General Joseph Joffre, chief of the general staff and, when the war began, commander-in-chief of the French army. But much of the work was actually performed by his deputy, General Noel de Castelnau, and other staff officers. General Joffre seemed a peculiar choice for his lofty position. He had no experience in planning strategy or in command-

ing troops in the field. The son of a barrel manufacturer from the Pyrenees Mountains near the Spanish border, he had served in the Franco-Prussian War but made his reputation as an engineer engaged in building fortifications and in the field of logistics. Joffre had spent most of his career carrying out assignments in various French colonies. His background was far from that of most French officers who attained the top post in the army. He actually was a compromise candidate. General Joseph Gallieni had turned down the appointment, and the republican government had ruled out General Paul Marie Pau because of his monarchist political views.

At 59, Joffre was far from the image of the ideal commanding general. Massive in size, he possessed an ample stomach and jowly face, complete with bushy white mustache and eyebrows. His manner inspired little confidence, particularly since he rarely spoke. But he did have strong organizational skills and, as a moderate republican, was politically acceptable to virtually everyone. He also displayed another noteworthy quality—his utter imperturbability. In this regard, he was the direct opposite of his German counterpart, Moltke.

Much of the inspiration for Plan 17 came from younger staff officers, who were true believers in a veritable French cult of the offensive. While other armies clearly thought in offensive terms and formed their strategy accordingly, only the French endowed the offensive with mystical overtones. At the heart of this mystique lay a belief in the concept of *elan* or spirit, as by far the most important element in war. The more enthusiastic apostles of *elan* insisted that, if an army were totally imbued with fighting spirit, it would prove invincible against any foe and any odds. To achieve the full potential of such *elan*, the army must dedicate itself totally to the offensive. It followed logically that any

FIGURE 5–2 General Joseph Joffre,

officer who favored a defensive approach to war was considered defeatist.

This irrational reverence for the offensive originated with General Ferdinand Foch, the director of the French War College from 1908 until the outbreak of war. But Foch tempered his enthusiasm for the offensive with the warning that spirit alone would not bring victory. He insisted that an offensive must also be based on strong firepower and adequate material, although his estimate of how much of each would be necessary proved seriously inadequate for the type of war unleashed in 1914. Unfortunately, Foch's disciples in the cult of the offensive neglected the practical side of his doctrine and exaggerated its mystical aspects. Most notably, Colonel Loyzeau de Grandmaison, director of the general staff's bureau of operations, preached the doctrine of "the offensive to the limit." He urged his fellow officers to abandon any thought of the defense and to "seize and retain the initiative." Revised field regulations, issued in the fall of 1913, reflected this dictum in their insistence that the French army "henceforth admits no law but the offensive."

This fervor for the offensive won out over a much more sensible proposal for France to adopt a defensive strategy. The champion of this approach was General Augustin Michel, vice president of the Supreme War Council, who was to become commander-in-chief in case of war. In 1911, Michel anticipated the Schlieffen Plan by arguing that Germany would not risk a frontal assault against France's formidable defensive positions in Lorraine but would send its forces through Belgium to the west of the Meuse. Michel proposed to stymie the German plan by moving powerful troops into Belgium, where they would defend a line extending from the great port of Antwerp on the North Sea southeastward to the fortress of Verdun in northern France. To increase this force to the size necessary to stop the German drive, he urged that regular divisions be bolstered by reserve units. To say the least, Michel's plan aroused violent opposition on two counts—its defensive character and dependence on reserves. It particularly provoked the anger of Adolphe Messimy, the minister of war, who considered the proposal "insane." Messimy and the War Council rejected it and punished Michel for his heresy by relieving him of his command. His departure opened the way for Joffre to take over as chief of staff.

Despite Messimy's unfortunate rejection of Michel's plan, he did attempt to improve the French army's equipment and tried valiantly but unsuccessfully to substitute a less conspicuous color for the vivid red trousers worn by French soldiers since 1830. His efforts aroused violent objections from officers, who viewed his proposal as an affront to French military dignity. A former war minister went so far as to proclaim, "Eliminate the red trousers? Never! The red trousers are France." Thus, the French who went into battle in 1914 made the finest targets of any soldiers in Europe.

Although Joffre and his staff had abandoned Michel's proposal to establish a defensive position in Belgium, they would have preferred to take the offensive against Germany by moving through that country. This would eliminate the need to assault the strong German defenses in Lorraine. But such an action would mean violation of Belgian neutrality, and this would certainly anger the British. Belgian officials also showed no interest in allowing French troops to pass through their territory and adhered scrupulously to their neutrality. Accordingly, the French ruled out the Belgian option and settled instead for Lorraine.

BRITAIN'S ROLE

The role, if any, that the British would play in case of war also bedeviled the French planners. Despite the close cooperation in recent years, Britain had no actual commitment to aid the French and, at best, would contribute no more than six divisions to joint military action. Even General Henry Wilson, the most enthusiastic proponent of British intervention on the Continent, insisted that London retain its right to determine how the BEF would be utilized after its arrival in France. In view of this uncertainty, Plan 17 made no provision for British participation, although Joffre hoped that it would be forthcoming. He and his staff spoke vaguely about utilizing the BEF to help defend the open left flank along the Belgian border from the Meuse to the North Sea.

RUSSIA'S STRATEGY

A crucial factor in France's planning was the role of its ally in the east, Russia. Without a firm promise of a Russian attack against Germany, a French offensive in the west would be out of the question. Prior to 1912, Russian intentions remained vague, but during that year St. Petersburg pledged to undertake an offensive, either in East Prussia or toward Berlin, with 800,000 men. The operation would start on the fifteenth day of hostilities. This Russian commitment enabled Joffre to complete work on Plan 17, which became operational in May 1914. But it also was quite unrealistic in view of the great difficulties inherent in the Russian mobilization program. The country's huge size, coupled with its inefficient rail network, made it impossible to mobilize the entire army within 15 days. If Russia were to keep its promise to France, it would have to attack before all of its forces could take the field or, in a crisis, undertake mobilization secretly to gain a head start on the Germans.

Russia based its planning for war largely on the fact that Russian Poland formed a huge salient between Germany's province of East Prussia to the north and Austria's Galicia on the south. This created both a danger and an opportunity. If Germany and Austria-Hungary directed their efforts at cutting off the salient at its eastern base by simultaneous attacks, Russian forces to the west would face potential encirclement. This would be especially threatening if the Central Powers struck before Russia had completed its mobilization. At the same time, the salient presented offensive possibilities to the Russians. East Prussia jutted along the Baltic coast far to the east of the primary mass of German territory. This made it vulnerable to an attack from Russian Poland. Berlin also lay relatively close to the Russian border. To the south, Galicia, although not as exposed as East Prussia, formed something of a salient, that the Russians might be able to exploit.

Most Russian leaders favored attacking Galicia because of their desire to liberate its Slavic population and their animosity toward the Dual Monarchy. But the French pressured them to attack East Prussia or Berlin to distract German strength away from France. These opposing tendencies culminated in a compromise plan, that diluted Russia's striking power and reduced the likelihood of a decisive success anywhere. The Russians referred to their blueprint for war as Plan 19. It provided for a two-pronged invasion of East Prussia. One army was to strike directly from the east and drive to the north of the Masurian Lakes. This force would pin down as many defenders as possible, while a second army attacked from the south, cutting around the lakes and outflanking the enemy positions in the northeast. Meanwhile, a larger concentration of four armies was to assault Galicia. Two of them would penetrate from the east, while two others drove south from Russian Poland. They were to converge on Lemberg (Lvov), the Galician capital, and the great fortress of Przemyśl. If all went well, the two arms of this pincer movement would encircle the Austro-Hungarian forces north and east of the Carpathian Mountains, which formed Galicia's southern border.

AUSTRIA-HUNGARY'S STRATEGY

Austria-Hungary's approach to the war also represented a compromise, but of a rather peculiar kind. It was largely a product of the Dual Monarchy's geographic position and its multitude of potential enemies. But it

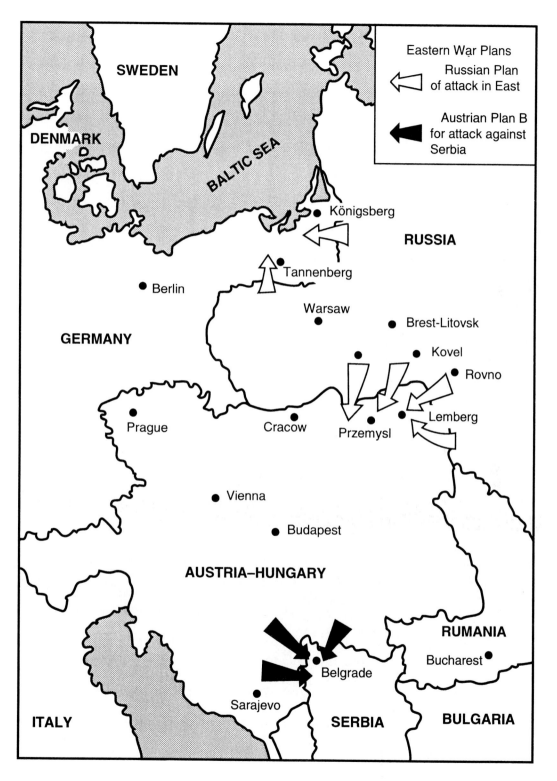

also bore the imprint of the alliance with Germany as well as a combination of confusion and deceit on the part of the two partners. Austria-Hungary not only faced the possibility of war with Serbia and Russia but never felt secure from an attack by its ally Italy. Chief of Staff Conrad von Hötzendorf devised plans, that would go into effect if the Dual Monarchy found itself at war with any of the three powers separately or a combination of them.

As time passed, the prospect of war with Serbia loomed largest in Conrad's thinking. But the entry of Russia into such a conflict in support of its little Balkan ally was also a distinct possibility, despite St. Petersburg's propensity to back down in the earlier Balkan crises. However, if the Dual Monarchy did find itself embroiled in war with both enemies, Conrad favored dealing with Serbia first, in what he hoped would be a quick campaign, before turning on Russia.

Unfortunately, Conrad's priorities were not the same as those of Germany, whose plan, of course, called for concentrating most of its strength in the west for the speedy defeat of France. Conrad's proposal would leave the Germans vulnerable to a Russian attack in the east. To provide greater security against a potential disaster there, Moltke insisted that Austria-Hungary take the offensive against Russia in Galicia before focusing on Serbia. When negotiations between the two general staffs began during the Bosnian crisis in 1909, Moltke pressed Conrad for a promise to follow such a strategy. He emphasized the crucial importance that a German victory over France would have on the fortunes of the Central Powers. Recognizing the validity of Moltke's argument, Conrad agreed to take the offensive against Russia as soon as war began. However, in return, he insisted that Germany also agree to launch an attack against the Russians in East Prussia. Moltke reluctantly consented to a limited operation but pointed out that a major offensive would have to wait until after the defeat of France.

In the years to come, and specifically in 1914, both men reneged on their promises. Moltke never had any intention of honoring his pledge. As for Conrad, he continued to plan for various contingencies by organizing his forces into three groupings. The largest of these, designated as A-*Staffel*, consisted of 28 divisions. Its basic mission was to defend Galicia from invasion. The second, *Minimalgruppe Balkan*, comprised of only eight divisions, was to defend against a possible Serbian attack. The remaining force of 12 divisions. B-*Staffel*, functioned as a separate offensive force. It would supplement one of the other groups, depending on where it was needed.

If Austria-Hungary went to war with Serbia and it appeared that Russia would not intervene, B-*Staffel* would join *Minimalgruppe Balkan* for an offensive (Plan B) designed to crush the Serbian menace. But if it became apparent that Russia would support the Serbs, this force would merge with A-*Staffel* for an attack on Russia from Galicia (Plan R). Unfortunately, if Austria-Hungary opted to take the initiative against Serbia, and Russia entered the conflict somewhat later, it would be extremely difficult to shift B-*Staffel* to Galicia in time to take part in defensive operations, much less to participate in offensive action.

Complicating this problem was Austria-Hungary's deplorable lack of an efficient system of strategic railroads. This weakness was due primarily to Hungarian obstruction. The Magyars had refused to cooperate with Austria in a plan to integrate the railroads of the two halves of the Dual Monarchy. Hungary was interested in emphasizing its role as a separate state rather than promoting the joint character of the empire. As a result of this shortsightedness, forces moving from Hungarian territory to Austrian Galicia would face roundabout routes and long delays.

Despite his provision for alternate plans, depending on relations with Russia at the outbreak of war, Conrad and other Austro-Hungarian leaders in 1914, chose to ignore obvious indications that Russia was going to intervene. Thus, Conrad dispatched B-*Staffel* to take part in an attack on Serbia. When Russia did enter the war, Conrad shifted a portion of these troops to Galicia, and all the inherent weaknesses of his planning came into play with disastrous consequences. To compound his mistake, Conrad apparently took Moltke at his word and expected a German offensive from East Prussia to take some of the pressure off his own forces. Conrad seemed genuinely surprised when Moltke shattered his illusion by informing him that Germany's commitment in the west prevented any such undertaking in the east for at least six weeks.

THE FAILURE OF WISHFUL THINKING

All of the plans devised by the Great Powers in staff rooms and on peacetime maneuvers shared certain common characteristics. They were based, in effect, on wishful thinking. Each of them assumed that everything would work out for the best, that troops would accomplish their appointed tasks according to long-prepared and often unrealistic timetables. They also anticipated that their enemies would do precisely what they wanted them to do. There was little provision for the unexpected. And, they all believed, of course, that the war would be short. Every one of the plans ultimately failed. This universal frustration of the great expectations, that the Great Powers had cherished for so long, led to a kind of war that few leaders had foreseen and none was really prepared to fight.

6

1914:
DEADLOCK
ON THE WESTERN FRONT

When war broke out in the summer of 1914, the Great Powers, in pursuit of their vision of swift offensive victory, put their long-prepared plans into operation. During the next few weeks, events of truly momentous proportions followed one another in rapid progression. Perhaps the most dramatic of all unfolded in Western Europe where Germany became locked in desperate combat with France, supported by Britain. Both sides believed that their efforts during this period would determine the outcome of the war. And so they did, but in a manner quite different from what they had anticipated. They led not to a speedy resolution of the conflict but to a bloody deadlock that continued for four years.

SCHLIEFFEN PLAN LAUNCHED

Germany launched the Schlieffen Plan first. Swift mobilization, greater efficiency, and precise advance planning contributed to its head start over the French. German units moved into defenseless Luxembourg on August 2, and other units invaded Belgium on August 4th. Three armies formed what Schlieffen had considered the all-important right wing of the invasion. On the north, General Alexander von Kluck's First Army was to skirt the Netherland's Maastricht Appendix before swinging into Belgium, using Brussels, the capital, as its pivot for a southward thrust toward the French border. Just to the south of Kluck's forces, the Second Army of General Karl von Bülow was to cross the Meuse prior to moving in a southwesterly direction. General Max von Hausen's Third Army was to penetrate through the Ardennes Forest in the southeastern corner of Belgium and then hook into France on Bülow's left flank.

Two other armies, the Fourth, commanded by Albrecht, Duke of Württemberg, and the Fifth, under William II's son, Crown Prince Frederick William, were to act as the pivot upon which the armies of the right wing would turn as they made their way into France. The Fourth army would move cautiously through the Ardennes in Luxembourg, while the Fifth army would advance into France just to the south of the Grand Duchy. Two additional armies, the Sixth and Seventh, would remain on the defensive in Lorraine and Alsace, where the Germans anticipated a French attack.

The first key defensive position confronting the Germans was the city of Liège on the steep west bank of the Meuse. A dozen forts, six on each side of the river, formed a powerful ring around the city. Liège dominated a 12-mile gap that created a bottleneck between the Maastricht Appendix on the north and the Ardennes to the south. It also was the rail hub of eastern Belgium. Until the Germans captured Liège and its forts, they could not fan out into the plain of central Belgium and execute their dash for the French border. The German High Command entrusted the taking of the city to a special force of 60,000 men commanded by the able and determined General Otto von Emmich. This elite unit had trained specifically for the task. But it proved difficult to accomplish. The Germans had not expected Belgium to resist but, even if this belief proved incorrect, they had not anticipated a garrison of more than 6,000 men to defend Liège. Instead, the defending force numbered 25,000. It also possessed a vigorous commander in General Gerard Leman, whom King Albert had ordered to defend the forts of Liège "to the end."

Emmich's initial attempt to take the city came on the night of August 5–6, but it failed to infiltrate the Belgian position because of efficient fire from the forts, and German forces suffered heavy casualties. Nevertheless, one German brigade, led by Erich Ludendorff, who had recently been promoted to general, managed to penetrate a weak point in the Belgian defenses and drove to the outskirts of Liège. Ludendorff was not actually the brigade's commander. He was serving as liaison officer between the Second Army and Emmich's forces, but he happened to be with the brigade when its commander was killed, and he assumed its leadership.

FIGURE 6–1 German forces advance during the war's opening offensive on the Western Front
National Archives

General Leman now realized that it would not be possible to hold Liège and, rather than allow its garrison to be cut off, he ordered it to withdraw to the west. Ludendorff's troops occupied the now virtually undefended city on August 7. A bizarre incident added to the drama of Ludendorff's triumph. After entering Liège, he ordered his driver to take him to the citadel overlooking the city, mistakenly assuming that it had already fallen to the advance guard. When he reached his destination, he banged on the gates. To his surprise, when they were opened, the Belgian soldiers inside surrendered to him. This episode made Ludendorff the first German hero of the war and marked the start of his meteoric rise to prominence during the next few weeks.

However, despite the fall of Liège, all of the forts were still in Belgian hands, and General Leman was determined that they would carry out King Albert's orders. Until they fell, the invading forces could not cross the Meuse. To break the impasse, the Germans resorted to a surprise weapon, the world's largest mobile artillery pieces. They included two huge 420-mm siege howitzers, fresh from the Krupp armament firm in Essen, and several 305-mm Skoda howitzers on loan from Austria-Hungary. Going into action on August 12, these monsters hurled gigantic explosive shells, equipped with solid steel heads, thousands of feet into the air. The shells struck their targets at virtually right-angle impact and penetrated the massive protective skin of the forts, killing many of the defenders. Almost worse than the shells' appalling destructiveness was the horror of anticipation. Soldiers inside the forts had to listen to the ever-increasing volume of the explosions as each successive round came closer and closer to them.

When the howitzers had destroyed the big guns of the forts, the Germans followed with infantry assaults against the remaining defenders. The first of the forts fell on August 13, and the last succumbed on August 16 after a shell penetrated into its magazine, touching off an enormous explosion. Among the survivors was General Leman, whom the victorious Germans at first believed to be dead when they discovered him lying in the ruins. He was only unconscious, however, and had clearly carried out his king's orders to fight "to the end."

Once the forts had fallen, the Germans crossed the Meuse: Kluck's First Army to the north of the city, Bülow's Second Army to the south. The valiant Belgian resistance had delayed the German timetable by two days. Now that the Germans had traversed the Liège gap, the bulk of the Belgian army withdrew into the fortress port city of Antwerp, which lay considerably to the northwest of the route of the German spearhead. Kluck's army took Brussels on August 20, while executing its southward swing toward the French border. Bülow's forces rolled toward Namur, still another fortress city, situated at the juncture of the Meuse and Sambre rivers.

THE FRENCH OFFENSIVE

While the Germans were battering away at the forts of Liège, General Joffre, now the French commander-in-chief as well as chief of staff, remained unperturbed by growing signs that the German spearhead might be coming through Belgium. He was determined to put Plan 17 into effect. As a preliminary to the main assaults on either side of Metz, he sent the Seventh Corps into southern Alsace on August 7 to capture the important city of Mulhouse and destroy the bridges over the nearby Rhine. The conquest of Mulhouse would secure the southern flank of the French armies farther north as they executed Plan 17. Unfortunately, the Seventh Corps' commander, General Joseph Bonneau, lacked the requisite *elan* for the task. Deeply pessimistic about chances for success, he directed his advance with extreme caution and did not capture Mulhouse, only 15 miles away, until August 8. The enemy garrison had already withdrawn, but German reinforcements quickly arrived and recaptured the city on August 10. As a result of this failure, Bonneau became the first of many French generals to be dismissed during the war. Joffre now reinforced the Seventh Corps with four divisions to create the new Army of Alsace, and he placed it under the command of General Paul Marie Pau.

The French launched the first phase of their two-pronged Plan 17 offensive on August 14. The thrust to the east of Metz came first. The First Army of General Auguste Dubail directed its attack into Lorraine with the town of Sarrebourg as its initial objective. It was to follow with a drive northeastward toward the Rhine. On Dubail's left, General de Castelnau's Second Army struck toward Morhange with the intention of outflanking Metz. At the same time, Pau launched an attack on Mulhouse and was to thrust northward through Alsace to protect Dubail's flank.

Dubail was an ardent champion of the prevailing French offensive doctrine and had been instrumental in the rejection of General Augustin Michel's defensive strategy. Noted for his determination and energy as well as his good looks and the rakish way he wore his cap cocked to one side, General Dubail did not get on well with Castelnau. Republican political leaders also did not care for Castelnau, Joffre's former deputy chief of staff. They resented his monarchist sympathies, aristocratic background, and ostentatiously fervent Catholicism. The latter quality had earned him the sarcastic nickname "the monk in boots." General Joffre had called Pau out of retirement in France's hour of need. A veteran of the Franco-Prussian War, in which he had lost an arm, Pau was on good terms

with Joffre despite their differing political views and the fact that he had been a contender for the chief of staff position.

Opposing Dubail's forces was General Josias von Heeringen's Seventh Army, while the Sixth Army of Prince Rupprecht, Grand Duke of Bavaria, lay in the path of Castelnau's troops. The German High Command entrusted Rupprecht with authority over both armies on August 9. Prince Rupprecht was descended from a collateral line of the ruling royal dynasty of Bavaria. In 1886, when King Ludwig II's eccentric behavior convinced other Bavarian leaders that he was insane, Rupprecht's family had provided the regent who ruled in the monarch's behalf. Fortunately, Rupprecht conducted himself in a remarkably sensible manner and maintained the correct proprieties at all times. He was also related to the Stuart dynasty that had ruled England in the seventeenth century, and his wife's sister was married to Belgium's King Albert.

Since Joffre mistakenly assumed that the largest concentration of German troops on the Western Front was poised at Metz, he and his army commanders anticipated a considerable numerical advantage along the 65-mile front selected for their offensive. In reality, the German defenders were almost equal to the attacking forces. Nevertheless, during the first few days the French advanced against only sporadic German resistance. But the Germans subjected them to heavy and almost continuous artillery fire from positions too far away for the French 75's, with their limited range, to respond. The terrain proved a greater problem. Featuring hills, heavy woods, and poor lateral roads, it tended to channel the advance into the easier country of the river valleys, making it difficult to maintain a continuous front. Gaps began to appear between the French forces. These obstacles contributed to a marked absence of *elan* and boldness on the part of the advancing troops, despite the overwhelming importance attached to these qualities in French military doctrine.

Dubail's First Army captured Sarrebourg on August 17, but enemy resistance stiffened soon afterward. When the French attempted to advance beyond the Sarre River, they encountered a powerful artillery barrage and fell back toward Sarrebourg. The German commanders, Rupprecht and Herringen, were not content merely to lure the French deeper into Lorraine to further the progress of the right wing through Belgium. They repeatedly pressed Supreme Headquarters (*Oberste Heeresleitung*, or OHL) for permission to counterattack, and finally Moltke reluctantly agreed. The Germans were able to gain a slight numerical advantage in this sector by shifting several divisions from other areas. On the afternoon of August 20, they launched their assault and, after a bloody encounter, forced the French to abandon Sarrebourg. Dubail's forces fell back to a strong position, however, and were far from defeated.

But a second German attack the same day gained greater success against Castelnau's Second Army. As the French neared the outskirts of Morhange, the first objective of their offensive, they fell victim to a powerful German assault, which created panic among some of Castelnau's troops. By August 22, Rupprecht's forces had pushed the French back to the Meurthe River. The Second Army's precipitous withdrawal had uncovered the First Army's left flank and necessitated its retreat as well, much to Dubail's disgust. This turn of events did little to ease his strained relations with Castelnau.

The first attempt to carry out Plan 17 had failed miserably. But General Joffre refused to abandon his offensive strategy. On August 22, he unleashed the Third and Fourth armies to the northwest of Metz in the second phase of his great operation. This one had even less

chance of success. The more difficult terrain of the Ardennes lay in its path as well as strong German forces. General Albert Ruffey, who commanded the Third Army, was far more imaginative than most French generals. He made enemies because of his advocacy of heavy artillery and refusal to accept the revered 75-mm gun as sufficient for France's needs. To make matters worse, he even favored a large air force. This was tantamount to heresy. Ruffey also did not win many friends when he warned Joffre's headquarters that enemy forces opposing his army appeared far larger than French intelligence had indicated. General Fernand de Langle de Cary, the Fourth Army commander on Ruffey's left, received similar reports of strong German troop concentrations but refused to let them slacken his unbridled enthusiasm for the offensive. A veteran of the Franco-Prussian War, Langle de Cary was in line for retirement in 1914 when the outbreak of hostilities gave his career new life.

There was good reason for General Ruffey's concern. At the very moment that the French began to push northeastward into the Ardennes, the Duke of Württemburg's Fourth Army and the Crown Prince's Fifth Army were advancing to the southwest as the pivot for the German right wing's wheel through Belgium. They were at least equal in size to the French forces. Heir to the throne of Germany, the Crown Prince, at 32, shared his father's unfortunate tendency to swagger and bluster but lacked the emperor's keen intelligence. Although he extolled the warlike virtues publicly and demonstrated unwarranted confidence in his own military ability, his fragile physique was anything but that of the model warrior. His appointment to command the Fifth Army was political in nature, and his authority was more apparent than real. General von Knobelsdorf, his chief of staff, made most of the important decisions.

GERMAN ADVANCES

The Germans, believing that they would not encounter any serious opposition short of the French border, pushed forward more vigorously than originally planned. Their optimism proved quite unfounded because they soon collided violently with the advancing French forces. The Germans had the better of the confused fighting that followed, however. Langle de Cary's Fourth Army suffered heavy casualties, one crack division losing 11,000 of its original 17,000 men, and was forced to fall back on August 24. Ruffey's Fourth Army, although more successful, found itself in a vulnerable position as a result of this withdrawal and also had to retreat.

To the southeast, Pau's Army of Alsace had recaptured Mulhouse against much weaker opposition. But the developments in Lorraine and the Ardennes created a pressing need for reinforcements, some of which could be siphoned from Pau's army. In view of this diversion of strength, Joffre reluctantly ordered Pau to abandon Mulhouse. The French retained only a small sliver of Alsace and continued to hold it throughout the remainder of the war.

The German successes in Lorraine and the Ardennes emboldened the army commanders in this sector to press Moltke for permission to launch a major offensive of their own. Moltke, who had long flirted with the idea of a double envelopment modeled after Cannae, agreed. The Germans launched their attack on August 24. Although they hammered away until September 9, they experienced many of the same problems that had troubled the French earlier—difficult terrain, strong defensive positions, and determined resistance. They made limited progress. There would be no double envelopment.

While the French were hammering away in their vain efforts to crown Plan 17 with success, Joffre received repeated warnings that the German forces moving through Belgium to the north of the Ardennes actually constituted the enemy spearhead. These reports had come from General Charles Lanrezac, whose Fifth Army lay to the northwest of Langle de Cary's forces. Even before the war, Lanrezac had shared Michel's concern about the possibility of a German thrust through Belgium to the north of the Ardennes and across the Meuse. His fears increased after the outbreak of the conflict when mounting evidence confirmed that strong German forces were heading for the Meuse. Joffre turned aside Lanrezac's warnings, however, insisting that the enemy planned to strike at Metz. He did authorize Lanrezac to shift one corps from his army to the Belgian town of Dinant on the Meuse, about 40 miles to the southeast of the fortress city of Namur, but he retained the remaining two corps for his Ardennes offensive. Although refusing to heed Lanrezac's advice, Joffre held the general in high regard and with good reason. Lanrezac was a brilliant planner and widely admired for both his intelligence and courage, despite his outspoken, often sarcastic manner and tendency to lecture subordinates and even superiors. Physically, Lanrezac resembled Joffre, with his ample stomach and bushy white mustache.

By August 14, intelligence reports pointed increasingly to the concentration of German strength in Belgium. Joffre responded by authorizing Lanrezac to shift his entire army into the triangle formed by the juncture of the Meuse and Sambre rivers, just to the west of the Ardennes. However, despite his apparent concern, Joffre stubbornly refused to abandon his offensive in Lorraine and the Ardennes and clung to the belief that the Germans might divert part of their force north of the Meuse and Sambre to the Ardennes.

Although Lanrezac had reduced the likelihood of disaster by persuading Joffre to shift the Fifth Army to the west, he was by no means optimistic. The British Expeditionary Force, coming up from the south, was not yet in position. Until it arrived, Lanrezac's left flank would be unprotected. He also had difficulty deciding whether to make his stand behind the Sambre or to move across the river. By the time he had overcome his doubts on August 21 in favor of the latter course, the Germans had already captured two bridges intact and were across the river between Namur and Charleroi.

While Lanrezac grappled with his indecision, Moltke ordered Bülow to besiege the Belgian garrison defending Namur and simul-

taneously attack the French position along the Sambre. Moltke also placed Kluck's First Army temporarily under Bülow's overall direction during the Sambre operation. Bülow, worried by the French concentration on the Sambre, ordered Kluck to shorten his wide wheel through Belgium and swing due south to support the Second Army's right flank. Kluck protested this departure from the Schlieffen Plan, but to no avail. Unknown to either Bülow or Kluck, this decision brought the First Army into a collision course with the BEF, which was moving northward.

Kluck and Bülow were both 68 years old and veterans of the Franco-Prussian War.

FIGURE 6–2   General Alexander von Kluck (center), commander of the German First Army, confers with two of his staff officers. National Archives

Beyond that, they had little in common. Noted for his bad temper and arrogance, Kluck was far bolder than Bülow in his approach to offensive warfare. This quality had earned him the plum role of commander of the army farthest on the right in Schlieffen's grand design. The austerely handsome and relatively youthful-looking Kluck believed that speed of execution was the key to victory and it might prove necessary to take risks to achieve success. Bülow, white-haired, heavy-set, and appearing far older than the dashing Kluck, was much more cautious and unwilling to court danger. The Second Army commander was haunted by the spectre of the Allies exploiting gaps between the armies of the right wing. He especially feared that Kluck's rapid advance to the west would expose his own army to a British flanking attack. Moltke, who harbored similar concerns, agreed that it would be best if Bülow supervised the overall direction not only of Kluck's troops on his right flank but also Hausen's Third Army to the left.

ALLIED RESPONSE

At the very time that the French Third and Fourth Armies were hammering in vain against the powerful German forces in the Ardennes, the far weaker Allied troops in the path of the massive enemy spearhead were fighting a trio of separate battles along the Meuse and Sambre—at Namur, Charleroi, and Mons.

The most spectacular of the three took place at Namur where Bülow's Second Army besieged the fortresses surrounding the city, much as they had those of Liège. They utilized the same howitzers that had wreaked such havoc earlier. Again, the helpless Belgian garrisons listened in mounting tension and horror as the enormous projectiles came ever closer and then crashed through the concrete roofs of the fortresses. On August 23, the surviving defenders abandoned Namur, and the Germans occupied the strongest position of the triangular defensive front formed by the river barrier.

The Belgian withdrawal was only one problem confronting Lanrezac and the French Fifth Army to the south. The French failed to force the Germans out of their bridgeheads on the right bank of the Sambre near Charleroi and were falling back, while Hausen's forces had crossed the Meuse south of Dinant. Even worse, Lanrezac learned of the disastrous end of Langle de Cary's offensive in the Ardennes and the Fourth Army's subsequent retreat. This combination of misfortunes uncovered the Fifth Army's right flank. Visions of the French disaster at nearby Sedan in 1870 now filled Lanrezac's thoughts. On August 23, he decided that only an immediate retreat could save France from another catastrophe. In announcing his intention, he also contended, quite maliciously, that his left flank was also vulnerable because of the failure of the British Expeditionary Force to reach its designated position.

In reality, on the same day that Lanrezac made his decision, the BEF was heavily engaged with the Germans along the Mons-Condé Canal, that intersected with the Sambre at Charleroi. Clearly, Lanrezac was attempting to deflect some of the blame on the British for his inability to hold the Meuse-Sambre line. To be sure, coordination between the British and French was less than close. This was due largely to the fact that Lanrezac and the BEF commander, Field Marshal Sir John French, detested each other.

French, a gentleman cavalry officer who cut quite a figure in British society, looked down upon both Lanrezac and Joffre because of their humble social origins. The imperious Lanrezac was equally dubious about French's lack of intellectual distinction.

Short, stocky, highly emotional, and hot-tempered, French had won fame for his dashing cavalry exploits during the South African War. He became chief of the Imperial General Staff in 1912, despite his lack of experience in staff work and disdain for the study of military strategy and tactics. A Liberal in politics, he resigned in protest when a number of Conservative generals announced their refusal to enforce Home Rule in Ireland. The outbreak of war rescued him from his self-imposed limbo. French owed his appointment as commander of the BEF to his connections with the Liberal government and his popularity as a war hero. He certainly would not have been the choice of the commanders of the two corps that comprised the BEF, General Sir Douglas Haig and General Sir Horace Smith-Dorrien. Both questioned his fitness for command.

The Germans could have avoided fighting the Battle of Mons. It was a product of Bülow's decision to divert Kluck's First Army to cover his right flank. Had he allowed Kluck to carry out his original intention, the German First Army would have passed well to the west of the BEF and been in position to outflank the entire Allied line. Instead, his forces collided head-on with the enemy along the Mons-Condé Canal. It was the first actual battle that Kluck's forces had fought during their drive through Belgium, as well as a baptism of fire for the BEF. French's troops enjoyed the benefit of the 64-foot-wide canal barrier. The gloomy, somewhat surrealistic landscape of the coal-mining area around Mons provided additional cover in the form of numerous slag heaps and villages containing the homes of the miners. But the Germans held a big advantage in numbers—170,000 troops to 70,000 for the BEF.

The battle began at nine in the morning as church bells called unsuspecting Belgian villagers in their Sunday best to attend Mass. Expert British riflemen laid down such a swift and murderous hail of fire that the advancing Germans believed they were being victimized by massed machine guns. The attacking forces suffered heavy casualties, but powerful German artillery raked the British defenders, steadily reducing their already relatively small numbers. The fighting raged until mid-afternoon when the Germans broke off their assault. Kluck planned to shift his efforts to the west of the British the next morning in an attempt to outflank them, but Field Marshal French had already ordered his BEF troops to fall back during the night. News of Lanrezac's withdrawal on his right gave French no other choice.

FRENCH ARMY RETREATS

The Battle of Mons and Lanrezac's decision to retreat signaled the end of the initial series of encounters, that had begun with the French attacks in Lorraine. All of these engagements, collectively referred to as the Battle of the Frontiers, were a grim portent of even greater horrors to come. Both sides had suffered greatly, but especially the French, who had lost 300,000 killed, wounded, and missing.

As the Battle of the Frontiers drew to a close, the scales finally fell from Joffre's eyes. He realized now that he had been wrong. The German right wing, crashing through Belgium, was indeed the enemy spearhead. Much weaker Allied forces lay in its path, while a vast open flank yawned on its right. Only the most determined action could save France. Although his devotion to Plan 17 and wishful thinking about the intention of the Germans had been responsible for this dilemma, Joffre's remarkable calm in the face of impending doom would lead, not to catastrophe, but to salvation.

Joffre now ordered a general retreat by the French Fourth and Fifth armies to the southwest to establish a stronger front in the path of the German advance. He also formed a new army, the Sixth, commanded by General Michel-Joseph Maunoury. It consisted primarily of seven divisions that had supported Castelnau's forces in their resistance to the German counterattack in Lorraine. Maunoury, who had been wounded as a young officer in the Franco-Prussian War, came out of retirement at age 67 to take command. Joffre had the utmost respect for Maunoury, a former military governor of Paris. Maunoury's troops, strengthened by reinforcements from Algeria and Morocco, moved by rail from Lorraine to take positions along the Somme River near the city of Amiens to the left of the BEF. The Sixth Army's primary mission was to prevent

Kluck's forces from moving around the Allied left flank and, secondarily, to protect Paris. Its stay at Amiens was short, however. Almost immediately after arriving, it joined in the general retreat. A vital factor in this redeployment was the availability of excellent lateral railroads, that enabled Joffre to shift his forces quickly and efficiently.

Conversely, on the German side of the line, Moltke lacked adequate lateral railroads, while the Belgian rail network required extensive repair. All of this made it much more difficult for the Germans to supply and reinforce their advancing troops. To add to their problems, Moltke, whose nerves were growing increasingly frayed, had established his headquarters too far to the rear of the front.

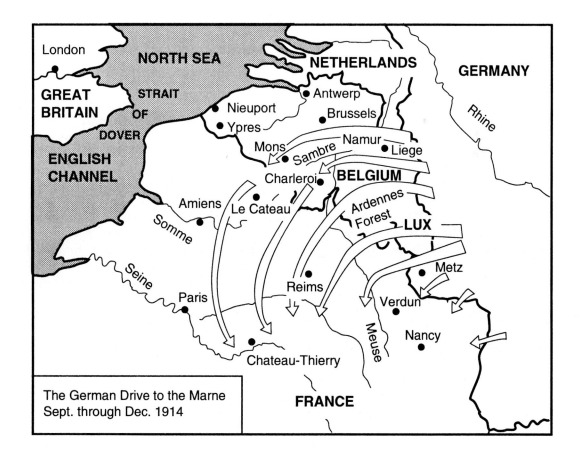

The German Drive to the Marne
Sept. through Dec. 1914

He remained at Koblenz well inside Germany until August 30 when he moved to Luxembourg city. As the German spearhead moved steadily to the southwest, he found it difficult to keep abreast of developments. Inadequate German telephone and radio communications contributed to his troubles. The sheer scope of the Schlieffen Plan created additional strain. Gaps began to appear between the armies of the right wing as the breadth of the front expanded. To compound the difficulty, the Germans had dwindled in number due to the need to detach troops to seal off the fortress of Antwerp, garrison Brussels, and contend with two pockets of French resistance well behind the front. Moltke also shifted two corps from the right wing to defend East Prussia against a Russian offensive, that had developed much faster than OHL had expected. By the end of August, the strength of the advancing German forces had actually declined to less than that of the Allies—67 divisions to 79.

Despite his concerns, Moltke sensed that victory was tantalizingly close, if his forces continued to exert unrelenting pressure on the Allies. But his soldiers were nearing exhaustion from the feverish pace of advance and the repeated fighting against a still not beaten enemy. On August 27, Moltke ordered the First Army to advance to the west of Paris along the Oise River. He added, nevertheless, that it might prove necessary to swing to the east of the city in an effort to destroy the French forces in that area.

ALLIES CONTINUE TO RETREAT

Regardless of Moltke's indecision and the mounting obstacles confronting the Germans, the initiative still lay with them. The Allied forces found themselves extremely hard-pressed as they fell back. Field Marshal French added another problem. The BEF operated as an independent force, over which

Joffre exercised no jurisdiction. After Mons and a subsequent hard-fought battle at Le Cateau to the south, the mercurial British commander became more and more pessimistic. Repelled by his association with Lanrezac, he quite irrationally lost all confidence in French commanders. On August 31, he informed Kitchener that he considered it necessary to retreat to the southwest of Paris, apparently preliminary to embarking his forces for home. It proved necessary for Kitchener to hurry to France to persuade French to return to the Allied line.

As the Germans pushed southward, the defense of Paris became of paramount importance to the French government, if not to Joffre. The commander in chief wielded virtually absolute authority in both military and civil matters in the so-called Zone of the Armies, the general area where the fighting was taking place, but Paris lay beyond his jurisdiction. In reality, the great fortress of Paris, that Schlieffen had feared as the Achilles' heel of his plan, had fallen into neglect. Its defenses were of no consequence and its garrison virtually nonexistent. War Minister Messimy, growing steadily more concerned about the threat to the capital, appointed the vigorous General Joseph Simon Gallieni military governor of Paris.

Gallieni, at 65, shared certain things in common with General Maunoury, the commander of the new Sixth Army. He, too, emerged from retirement to take his command and had served as a youthful lieutenant in the Franco-Prussian War, having been taken prisoner at Sedan. Like Joffre, he had spent his career in the colonial army, rather than in staff work. However, unlike the commander-in-chief, he had become a hero as a result of his conquest of the huge island of Madagascar, off the southeastern coast of Africa. A recent widower and afflicted with prostate disease, that would kill him within two years, Gallieni was tall, slender, and forbidding in manner. His pince-nez glasses gave him a professorial air in keeping with his brilliant and studious nature. Paris soon came within the Zone of the Armies, and Gallieni received reinforcements. As Maunoury's Sixth Army fell back toward the French capital, it also came under Gallieni's overall control.

While the Germans pushed relentlessly forward, Joffre reluctantly concluded that he must relieve Lanrezac as commander of Fifth Army. Lanrezac, who had been so right in predicting the route of the enemy spearhead, had proved an ineffective leader in the field and had grown ever more defeatist. He had resisted Joffre's order of August 26 for a counterattack along the Oise River between St. Quentin and Guise and, after reluctantly agreeing, carried out the assault in a lackluster manner. Only the spirited intervention of General Louis Franchet d'Esperey's First Corps prevented a complete failure and resulted in a tactical victory. In the aftermath, it came as no surprise that Joffre selected Franchet d'Esperey as Lanrezac's successor on September 3.

Absolutely determined and overwhelmingly confident, the new commander was 58, short and stocky, and possessed piercing eyes as well as a dominating voice. A devout Catholic with monarchist connections, his father had been the godson of King Louis XVIII who had ruled France from 1814 to 1824. While always a disciplinarian, he had also been good-natured, but now he pushed his officers with cold-blooded fury. Victory was all that mattered, and his motto, in effect, became "march or die." The British later referred to him as "Desperate Frankie."

Joffre also had to deal with the problem of a dangerous and widening gap between the Fifth Army and Langle de Cary's Fourth Army to the right. It was a product of the latter's successful defensive stand along the Meuse near Sedan at the same time that

the Fifth Army was falling back. To plug the gap, Joffre scraped together a new army, soon to be designated the Ninth, from forces shifted from both the Fourth and Third armies. As its commander, Joffre selected General Foch, who had previously led the 20th Corps during the fighting in Lorraine. The father of the doctrine of the offensive to the limit, Foch remained devoted to his belief in this approach, despite the bloody failure of the Plan 17 offensives.

As the German right wing converged on the Marne River to the northeast of Paris, Bülow sensed the possibility of destroying the French Fifth Army as it retreated to the south. But he also grew increasingly alarmed by the gap between his own army and Kluck's forces on his right. To satisfy both his desire for success and his cautious nature, he asked Kluck to wheel to the southeast of Paris to cover his flank. Kluck, who appears to have believed that victory was near, agreed. On August 31, Moltke approved the change in direction, that effectively scrapped the Schlieffen Plan and its grandiose vision of the great wheel to the west of Paris. It also rendered Kluck's right flank vulnerable to an attack by Maunoury's Sixth Army, operating from the Paris area, especially since Kluck continued to push boldly southeastward in an attempt to encircle the French troops in his path.

ALLIES PLAN COUNTERATTACK

When Joffre became aware of the change in German strategy, he consulted his general staff officers as well as Gallieni, Maunoury, Franchet d'Esperey, and Foch to determine if and when they would be able to mount a counterattack. They all agreed that they would be ready by September 6. But Joffre had no control over the British Expeditionary Force, and BEF Field Marshal French had again succumbed to doubts. He refused to commit his troops to the offensive, and indeed some British units were falling back toward the Seine River. Joffre, stunned by this turn of events, visited French on September 5 and begged him to change his mind. Abandoning his usual quiet manner, he appealed to French in the most emotional terms, stressing the gravity of the situation and the vital necessity of British participation in the offensive. It was a matter of life or death for France. In conclusion, Joffre insisted that "I cannot believe the British army will refuse to do its share in this supreme crisis...the honor of England is at stake!" To which, French, with tears in his eyes, assured Joffre that "we will do all we possibly can."

Joffre's plan called for an attack by Maunoury's Sixth Army against Kluck's right flank, while Franchet d'Esperey's Fifth Army struck Bülow's forces. Foch's Ninth Army was to cover Franchet d'Esperey's right flank against the threat of attack from Hausen's Third Army. The BEF was to penetrate into the gap between the forces of Kluck and Bülow. The great counterstroke was to begin on September 6.

BATTLE OF THE MARNE

The ensuing Battle of the Marne actually began the day before Joffre had intended, when elements of the Sixth Army clashed with units of Kluck's forces. Kluck shifted troops from his left flank to strengthen his position against Maunoury. As a result, the gap between himself and Bülow widened to over 20 miles, creating the potential for disaster. The way was now open for the BEF to move into the void. But this required speed, and French, the BEF commander, advanced much too slowly to take advantage of his opportunity. Meanwhile, Franchet d'Esperey attacked Bülow's advance troops and forced them to pull back. It appeared as though the Fifth Army would now be able to assist

the BEF in exploiting the gap between the German armies.

Unfortunately, Franchet d'Esperey soon faced a more urgent need to shift forces to the east to aid Foch whose newly formed Ninth Army was not yet accustomed to working as a unit. Foch's troops found themselves subject to great pressure on both flanks from Hausen's Third Army and had to give ground. But Foch refused to be discouraged. Assuming that Hausen had weakened his center to increase striking power on the flanks, Foch ordered an all-out attack against the enemy's center. In his order before the assault, he urged his men to "Attack, whatever happens! The Germans are at the extreme limit of their efforts....Victory will come to the side that outlasts the other!" This time his obsession with the offense paid dividends. Hausen had to fall back.

While these developments were taking place on the eastern extreme of the Marne front, the struggle between the forces of Maunoury and Kluck was still raging on the western edge. On September 8, the French tried to swing around the rear of the German defenders but found two enemy corps blocking their path. For a time, it appeared as if Kluck would prevail. Maunoury was thinking of retreating toward Paris, but Gallieni sent reinforcements, newly arrived from the Third Army. To facilitate this relief effort, he collected 1,200 Parisian taxicabs that transported 6,000 of the soldiers to the front. The dramatic intervention of this "taxicab army" soon created a legend that, as legends usually do, greatly exaggerated its actual contribution to victory. Yet it symbolized the French spirit of determination.

As all of these dramatic encounters unfolded near the Marne, far away at his headquarters in Luxembourg, Moltke neared the verge of nervous collapse. Victimized by his poor communications and isolation, he vainly tried to gain a clear picture of the situation at the front. On September 8, he sent Lieutenant Colonel Richard Hentsch, OHL's senior intelligence officer, to visit the commanders of the five armies on the right of the German line. Although he gave his emissary no written instructions, Hentsch contended afterward that he had received oral authorization to order a retreat northward to the Aisne and Vesle rivers should conditions required such action.

The commanders of the Fifth, Fourth, and Third armies all assured Hentsch that they were ready and able to pursue the offensive, but Bülow considered a withdrawal inevitable in view of the gap on his right flank. When Hentsch arrived at First Army headquarters, he found that preparations were already underway for the first phase of a retreat. Hentsch now concluded that a general withdrawal was necessary and issued the order on September 9. German writers later argued that he had exceeded his instructions, but a court of inquiry found no substance to those charges.

Although Joffre hoped that his forces could take advantage of the German retreat by swift pursuit and outflanking maneuvers, the Germans were able to fall back in good order. The Allies were exhausted by the long retreat and the desperate fighting of the past few days, and their commanders were cautious in their approach. Wet weather added to their troubles. By September 14, the Germans had stabilized the front along a line extending from north of the Aisne River near Soissons all the way to the Swiss border. They had yielded considerable territory and no longer directly menaced Paris, but they were still in possession of much of northern France.

AFTERMATH OF THE MARNE BATTLE

In looking back on the Battle of the Marne at a later date, General Foch described the desperate conditions on his sector of the front: "The first day, I was beaten. The last day, it was a question of holding out. Yet I advanced six kilometers. Why? I don't know. Largely, because of my men; a little, because I had the will. And then,—God was there."[1] If, indeed, God was with Foch at the Marne, the aftermath of the battle was a cruel joke played by the Deity, not only on the Allies but also on the Germans.

The Battle of the Marne proved to be one of the most decisive in history, but in a curious way. It was decisive because it was indecisive. The Allies had won a strategic victory because they had forced the Germans to break off their offensive and retreat. But they had not defeated the Germans tactically. Joffre had won at the Marne because, for the first time since the campaign began, he had gained numerical superiority at the crucial point and because the Germans were not able to prevent gaps from developing in their line. But henceforth the two sides possessed virtual equality in numbers, and the war developed into a bloody stalemate. Moreover, the terrible new weapons, which were viewed as the key to a quick offensive victory, proved admirably suited for defense. The Battle of the Marne had determined that the war would not be short. This was not readily apparent to either the Allies or the Germans at first, but it gradually dawned on them that they had become embroiled in a war of attrition in which the two sides tried to wear each other down at the expense of appalling casualties. It would not end for more than four horrible years.

One noteworthy casualty of the Battle of the Marne and the subsequent retreat was General Moltke. On September 14, William II

---

[1]Stefan T. Possony and Etienne Mantoux, "DuPicq and Foch: The French School," in Edward Mead Earle, ed., *Makers of Modern Strategy: Military Thought from Machiavelli to Hitler* (New York: Antheneum, 1970), p. 230.

informed Moltke that, owing to the general's deteriorating health, he was relieved of command. As his successor, the emperor chose the Prussian state minister of war, General Erich von Falkenhayn. In the aftermath of the Marne, many professional military men and, later, historians blamed Moltke for the failure of the Schlieffen Plan. Their charges focused both on his departures from Schlieffen's grand design before the war and his direction of the offensive in 1914. It is now clear that much of this criticism was based on faulty assumptions.

Among these was the importance they attached to Moltke's reduction in the size of the right wing. Moltke cut the number of corps allotted to Kluck and Bülow from 16 to 12 but, as historian Martin van Creveld has pointed out, this reduction was more apparent than real. Moltke's decision to respect the neutrality of the Netherlands eliminated the need for at least two corps for use against the Dutch army. Moltke also reduced the number of corps earmarked for the siege of Antwerp from five, as prescribed by Schlieffen, to only two. Thus, Moltke actually increased the forces allotted to the sweep through Belgium by one corps. He also had to be concerned about a French offensive in Lorraine.

WEAKNESS OF THE SCHLIEFFEN PLAN

The real problem was the scope of the plan as envisaged by Schlieffen. The troops that he had provided for the vast wheel well to the west of Paris were far too few for such an ambitious task. Indeed, the gaps that developed in the German front in 1914 were minor compared to those that would have appeared had the Schlieffen Plan been carried out in unmodified form. It seems likely that the last man on the right would have been a very lonely figure. Moltke had recognized this problem before the war and had provided for

a much shorter wheel to take place considerably closer to Paris. But even this proved too ambitious.

The logistic weaknesses inherent in the Schlieffen Plan also contributed significantly to its failure. The need to repair the damage, that retreating Allied troops inflicted on Belgian and French railroads, posed a severe and continuing problem. The Germans performed this task remarkably well, but as they penetrated deeper into France, the advancing troops widened the gap between themselves and the nearest railheads. They also depended primarily on horsedrawn transport from the railheads to the front. The Germans used their limited number of trucks chiefly to transport vital ammunition. Although the supply service kept the fighting forces reasonably well provisioned even during the Battle of the Marne, its efforts were nearing the breaking point. If the Germans had won the battle, it is highly likely that serious supply problems, coupled with the exhaustion of the troops, would have required breaking off their offensive. To be sure, Moltke's decision to respect the Netherlands' neutrality deprived the Germans of the Dutch rail facilities, but the problem of transporting supplies from the railheads to the front would have remained.

Critics of Moltke also attacked two other departures from the Schlieffen Plan. The first involved Schlieffen's intention to shift two corps from Lorraine to the right wing after the Germans had stopped the anticipated French offensive. In 1914, Moltke chose to retain them in Lorraine for the German counteroffensive there. It now appears that the logistic obstacles involved in transferring these forces to the right wing were so great that they would not have arrived until after the Battle of the Marne. This transfer would also have compounded the supply problem for the troops of the right wing. Moltke's other departure, even more soundly criticized, was his decision to transfer two corps from the right wing to the Eastern Front. Clearly, this diminished the striking power of the German spearhead, but whether it was crucial in the outcome of the Battle of the Marne is not at all certain. Furthermore, the availability of these troops would have created even greater logistic difficulties and might well have led to a breakdown of the supply system before or during the battle.[2] The primary significance of the Russian offensive proved to be psychological, as it, together with the pressures of command, brought Moltke to the point of nervous collapse.

Certainly, Moltke's conduct of the campaign left much to be desired but, in view of the shortcomings of the Schlieffen Plan, either in its original or modified version, it does not appear that Moltke's performance was the determining factor. The basic fault lay with the grandiose character of the plan, its inadequate provision of troops for the task involved, and the insufficient logistic means to carry it to a successful conclusion.

THE "RACE TO THE SEA"

Despite the German setback in the Battle of the Marne, the war of movement did not immediately come to an end. A vast open flank still lay to the west of both armies. If one of them could outflank the other, it might still be possible to follow a successful offensive strategy, or so it seemed. During the next two months both sides attempted to carry out such a maneuver, but all their efforts failed. In the course of these operations, instead of extending the front directly westward, the belligerents veered sharply northward and

eventually reached the North Sea in extreme southwestern Belgium. This process soon became known by the misleading term "the race to the sea." In reality, it was not a race, and the sea was not the initial goal.

The first offensive action after the Germans reached the Aisne was not a flanking effort at all. It took the form of an ill-advised frontal attack, that Joffre launched on September 15 in an attempt to break through the new enemy defenses along the ridge known as the Chemin de Dames. Unfortunately for Joffre, this position proved remarkably strong. The Germans had dug trenches there, and their rifle, machine gun, and artillery fire took a heavy toll of the attackers. This First Battle of the Aisne proved a brief preview of the future course of war on the Western Front.

When it became apparent that battering-ram tactics had not succeeded, Joffre switched to an end run. The Germans sidestepped to their right and stymied this effort as well. Joffre's maneuver and the German response launched "the race to the sea." They also began the process through which the front hooked northward, first into the province of Picardy, where additional fighting took place in late September. Next, the armies lurched across the Somme River into the province of Artois, the site of a 10-day struggle early in October.

The last laps of the "race" occurred in the area of Flanders in southwestern Belgium. The architect of these final attempts to break the deadlock in 1914 was the new German chief of staff, General Falkenhayn, who, at 53, was much younger than Moltke. An able soldier, later destined to serve with distinction as a commander in the field, Falkenhayn has remained highly controversial in his role as head of OHL. Most appraisals have been negative. Aristocratic and dashing in appearance, his youthful face contrasted sharply with his gray hair. Falkenhayn soon encountered intense opposition to his conduct of the

---

[2]See Marvin van Creveld, *Supplying War: Logistics from Wallenstein to Patton* (Cambridge: Cambridge University Press, 1977), for a concise and convincing account of the logistic and other problems inherent in the Schlieffen Plan.

war from other leading military figures, and most of his two years as chief of staff were to be stormy.

THE FLANDERS OFFENSIVE

As a vital preliminary to his offensive in Flanders, Falkenhayn planned to settle the unfinished business of the great port of Antwerp, that the Germans had sealed off in August. Following the collapse of the Schlieffen Plan, Antwerp remained a thorn in the German side as well as a potential anchor for the Allied line, if it could be extended that far north. A ring fortress, comparable to Liège and Namur, it experienced a similar ordeal when huge siege howitzers launched another deadly tattoo on September 27. King Albert begged the British for aid, and Winston Churchill responded by dispatching three poorly equipped marine brigades to the city. Preparations were also underway to send an army corps, but on October 6 the Belgians decided to abandon Antwerp. They made their way to the southwestern corner of Flanders where they took a position on the far left of the Allied line near the coast.

The fall of Antwerp also freed the besieging German forces to take part in Falkenhayn's Flanders offensive, that began on October 20. In this case, there was no possibility of outflanking the Allies, who had already reached the sea. Falkenhayn intended to break through the enemy line and drive to the ports of Dunkirk, Calais, and Boulogne on the English Channel. He struck first at the weakest link in the Allied line, the Belgian position along the meager obstacle created by the narrow Yser River between Diximude and Nieuport, where the stream emptied into the sea. German heavy artillery decimated the Belgian defenders who, despite gallant resistance, could not prevent the enemy from crossing the Yser. But the Belgians had one trump left to play.

They held the highest ground in the area, while most of the remainder lay below sea level. By opening the sluices in the dikes that held back the sea on October 29, they flooded the land between their position and the Germans all along the 20-mile stretch from Diximude to Nieuport. This new two-mile wide water barrier saved them from being overrun and protected them from the Germans for the remainder of the war.

Falkenhayn unleashed a much more powerful series of attacks against the city of Ypres, that controlled the lateral roads leading to the Channel ports. No stranger to warfare, Ypres had been a leading commercial center during the Middle Ages. Its wealth came from the manufacture of cloth and was symbolized by the Gothic grandeur of its cathedral and cloth hall, both dating from the thirteenth century. But, starting in the sixteenth century, the city went into eclipse, due largely to the frequent battles fought in the area during innumerable wars. Although pronounced *Ee-pruh*, to the Tommies, as the British soldiers were nicknamed and who came to know it well, it was "Wipers."

The Allied position took the form of a small salient or bulge in the line because of the fact that Ypres could be best defended from the high ground extending to the east of the city. French forces manned the flanks, and the BEF held the center. During the earlier stages of the "race to the sea," the British had gradually moved to the northwest until they had reached Flanders, which brought them closer to their supply ports. Unfortunately, the compact nature of the salient made it vulnerable to German artillery fire, a problem compounded by the failure of the Allied troops to dig trenches of sufficient depth.

Falkenhayn's forces included the newly reconstituted Fourth Army, under the Duke of Württemberg's command, as well as a cavalry corps. The Fourth Army contained the

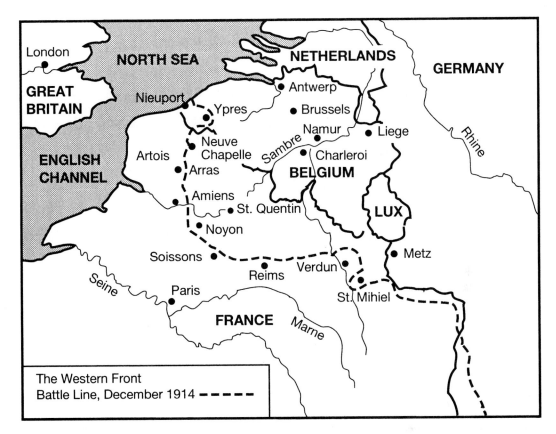

The Western Front
Battle Line, December 1914 ▬ ▬ ▬ ▬

units that had taken part in the siege of Antwerp as well as eight new divisions, largely composed of underage volunteers. Falkenhayn also shifted the Sixth Army, still commanded by Prince Rupprecht of Bavaria, from Lorraine, to the Ypres front. All of these forces gave the Germans a considerable numerical advantage.

The assault began on October 31 with cavalry attacks, which forced a much smaller British cavalry unit to abandon the Messines Ridge at the southern edge of the salient. Shortly afterward, other German forces struck General Haig's First Corps farther north and for a time broke through, only to be thrown back by a British counterattack. During the fighting in this sector, youthful German volunteers hurled themselves with reckless abandon on the British defenders,

while singing patriotic songs. However, despite their fervor, they failed to dislodge the enemy, while suffering horrendous casualties.

Two crack regular German divisions made a second attempt, starting on November 11. Focusing their thrust along the Menin Road, they also attacked in waves and scored a clean breakthrough, but they were too slow in exploiting this success. Their hesitation enabled the British to scrape together a rag-tag force, including medical orderlies, office personnel, cooks, and engineers. It managed to close the gap. This dramatic encounter proved crucial, even though fighting continued until November 22. At that point, the onset of winter weather, if not the fearful carnage, led to the breaking off of hostilities.

THE HIGH COST OF WAR

The First Battle of Ypres—there were to be two others—more than any other engagement of 1914 foreshadowed the war of the future on the Western Front. Although the trenches in this sector were primitive by later standards, the intensity, length, costliness, and futility of the struggle were all prophetic. It is difficult to determine actual total casualties for the fighting at Ypres, because the French did not release specific figures for individual battles in 1914, while the Germans published none at all for this early stage of the war. But British casualties were in excess of 50,000. French losses may have reached 65,000, and estimates for the Germans range from as low as 100,000 to as high as 130,000. In terms of the effect on overall strength, the British suffered most. The battle decimated the BEF. Its survivors now came to refer to themselves as "the Old Contemptibles," an ironic reference to William II's disparaging remark about the BEF's small size.

But the First Battle of Ypres was not the last offensive action of 1914 on the Western Front.

Joffre insisted on two more attacks in December, one in Artois, the other well to the east in the famous wine-producing province of Champagne. Neither accomplished anything. Both squandered many lives.

BEGINNINGS OF TRENCH WARFARE

By the end of the year, two lines of trenches, stretching 300 miles from the North Sea to the Swiss frontier, had confirmed the stalemate on the Western Front. The entrenchments had not yet taken final form in regard to depth of the defensive belts, or the potential of their firepower. But, seemingly, it should not have been difficult to foresee that additional mass offensives would lead to an ever more abundant harvest of death and futility. Unfortunately, the commanders, especially those of the Allied armies, were not yet convinced. They were still blinded by visions of the conflict they had thought they were going to fight. Many months, even years, would pass before they realized that they were indeed only visions.

7

1914:
DEADLOCK
ON THE EASTERN FRONT

While the Schlieffen Plan and Plan 17 both came to grief, and the German and Allied armies engaged in their unprecedented bloodletting on the Western Front, fierce fighting also erupted in Eastern Europe. It, too, led to frustration of the belligerent powers' high expectations as well as casualties of similar proportions. But the extent of the Eastern Front was much greater than that in the West, stretching from near the shores of the Baltic to the Carpathian Mountains of Galicia. As such, it offered much greater room for maneuver, but the net result was the same—another deadlock.

EVENTS IN EASTERN EUROPE

Germany had no choice but to assume a defensive posture in the east, while pursuing its plan for quick victory in the west. Its 135,000-man Eighth Army had sole responsibility for defending East Prussia. This meager force consisted of a single cavalry and 11 infantry divisions and was especially weak in heavy artillery. It faced a Russian army group of 650,000 men, including 8 cavalry and 30 infantry divisions, placing it at a numerical disadvantage of almost 5 to 1. Russia and Austria-Hungary both readily accepted the role of initiating offensive operations but not exactly as either would have preferred. Russia, if left to its own devices, would have attacked the Dual Monarchy in Galicia, while avoiding action against Germany for the time being. But the entreaties of the French to divert German strength away from the Western Front precluded such an approach. Instead, the Russians would stage offensives against both enemies. This division of resources made it unlikely that both would achieve decisive success. Nevertheless, the Russians were in a position to invade East Prussia, which, with the bulk of the German army committed against France, was almost defenseless. This highly promising situation was the fruit of the mobilization measures that Russia had undertaken early in the July crisis. While this head start on mobilization had helped to precipitate the war, it now appeared to have provided Russia with the opportunity to win the conflict.

Austria-Hungary had hoped to settle its score with Serbia in a rapid campaign before turning its full strength against Russia. But, in response to German pleas, Conrad committed himself to an offensive against Russian Poland. Despite his pledge, however, he refused to abandon his plan for an attack on Serbia. Indeed, he still intended to remain on the defensive in Galicia until disposing of the Serbs. Such a strategy seemed possible because of his expectation that the Germans would launch at least a minor assault on the Russians in keeping with Moltke's promise. Conrad had already sent B-*Staffel*'s 12 divisions, which formed the Second Army, southward when Moltke informed him that Germany would stage no offensive in the east until the successful resolution of the Schlieffen Plan. Now, rather than persevere in his original approach, Conrad shifted half of the Second Army to Galicia, while retaining the remainder for use against Serbia. This dilution of strength proved a recipe for disaster on both fronts.

THE RUSSIAN COMMAND

In keeping with Plan 19, the Russians prepared to move against Germany by sending the Northwest Army Group, commanded by General Yakov Jilinsky and consisting of two armies, into East Prussia. General Paul Rennenkampf's First Army was to strike from the east, moving to the north of the Masurian Lakes. It was to lure the bulk of German forces into this area before driving in a southwesterly direction to link up with General Alexander Samsonov's Second Army pushing northward from the Polish salient. If all went well, Samsonov's forces would swing behind the enemy defenders, cutting off their retreat to the west. The czar's cousin, Grand Duke Nicholas, received the assignment of supervising the entire operation as commander-in-chief, a position he had attained in the last days of the July crisis. In reality, he acted in the capacity of a figurehead, and real power resided with Jilinsky and other army group commanders. Organized just as the war was starting, Stavka, the grand duke's High Command headquarters, exercised only limited control over the army groups. As a result, it encountered great difficulty in attempting to coordinate their operations.

The grand duke had earned a seemingly undeserved reputation as a military reformer before the war. Indeed, he appears to have been more interested in opposing General Sukhomlinov's reforms and safeguarding the importance of the cavalry. An imposing figure physically, Nicholas stood 6 feet 6 inches and was one of the few high commanders on either side who had remained slender. He possessed dashing good looks, complete with a well-trimmed pointed beard, as well as a somewhat excitable and arrogant temperament. As a young officer, Nicholas served in his father's victorious army in the Russo-Turkish War of 1877–1878. He held the post of inspector-general of cavalry during the disastrous Russo-Japanese War and, afterward, became chairman of the State Defense Council, which attempted to rejuvenate the army following its defeat.

Noted for his hostility to both Germany and Austria, the grand duke had been instrumental in persuading the czar to abandon the Björkö Treaty and had vigorously supported the alliance with France. His wife and sister-in-law were both daughters of Montenegro's King Nikita, which may have contributed somewhat to his strongly pro-

FIGURE 7-1 The Grand Duke Nicholas, Russia's commander in chief, towers over Czar Nicholas II as they confer in the field. National Archives

Slav views. During the Revolution of 1905, he had won the animosity of reactionary figures at court when he urged the czar to grant a constitution. The Czarina Alexandra also hated him for his opposition to Gregori Rasputin, her spiritual and political adviser of highly dubious qualifications. She even suspected the grand duke of conspiring to force her husband to abdicate so that he could take the throne for himself.

Jiliniski's appointment to command the army group proved highly unfortunate. He had served as chief of staff to the commander-in-chief during the Russo-Japanese War. Like the grand duke, he had emerged from the defeat without serious damage to his reputation and went on to become chief of staff. It was Jilinsky who had promised the French that Russia would launch an offensive against Germany within 15 days of the start of mobilization. Yet, during maneuvers in 1913, he became deeply pessimistic about the chances for success of such an operation. Now, having stepped down as chief of staff three months before the outbreak of war, he found himself obligated to put the plan into effect, despite his lingering doubts.

Rennenkampf and Samsonov were both cavalry officers but, while the former had revealed a flair for boldness and speed in peacetime maneuvers, the latter had demonstrated a notable absence of these qualities. Indeed, Rennenkampf, 61, had tended to move too quickly and, since the Russian plan required both armies to advance at roughly the same pace, this clearly posed a potential danger. Sukhomlinov, who had served as commander during these exercises had chosen to ignore the problem, however. Rennenkampf was a somewhat shadowy figure of German ancestry who was reputed to have been guilty in the past of some unrevealed moral misconduct. Samsonov, 55, the leader of a cavalry division during the Russo-Japanese War, had no such clouded past, but his qualifications to command such a large force in the impending operation became the source of some concern. According to the German staff officer Colonel Max Hoffmann, the two generals had been on bad terms ever since the war with Japan and had even come to blows on one occasion. But, despite the intriguing notion of an ongoing feud and its possible effect on the fate of the Russian offensive, no such altercation ever took place, although Samsonov was a supporter of Sukhomlinov, while Rennenkampf was a member of the opposing faction.

Colonel Hoffmann served as deputy chief of operations for the German Eighth Army, which was responsible for the defense of East Prussia. As its ranking expert on Russian affairs, he received the task of divining enemy intentions for an offensive and planning German countermeasures. At 45, Hoffmann had long devoted himself to the consumption of almost legendary amounts of food and wine. He had paid for his pleasures by amassing great weight but managed to carry it fairly well on his tall frame. Despite these weaknesses, as well as a tendency to laziness, Hoffmann was extremely bright, shrewd, and cynical, qualities that were to carry him far during the war. His vitriolic memoirs provide ample evidence of his lack of respect for virtually everyone.

THE GERMAN COMMAND

The actual commander of the German Eighth Army was the 67-year-old General Max von Prittwitz und Gaffron, who shared Hoffmann's fondness for gluttony but not his brilliance. His prodigious girth had earned him the unhappy nickname "der Dicke," the moral equivalent to "fatso" in English. Prittwitz had received his post because of his friendship with the emperor, who enjoyed his gossip and humorous stories. Moltke considered him unfit for command, especially one so critical in nature, and had tried in vain to replace him on at least two occasions.

Hoffmann took advantage of the fact that the Russian plan contained one great weakness. The geography of East Prussia made it obvious that the Russians must attack in two narrowly constricted areas to the north and west of the Masurian Lakes. The Russians had to contend not only with lakes but with forests, rolling hills, and marshland. They also suffered from poor communications, consisting largely of dirt roads. This posed the possibility that the Germans could repel the enemy with numerically inferior forces. Many years earlier, Schlieffen had visualized the general approach that the Russians would employ. He had urged that the German defenders "strike with all possible strength at the first Russian army that comes within reach." This dictum became the key to Hoffmann's strategy.

But there were two other alternatives. The first involved a withdrawal to the Vistula River, which formed the western boundary of East Prussia and represented a much less exposed position. Whether such a maneuver made sense militarily, the sacrifice of "sacred" German territory was politically unacceptable. The second option provided for the Germans to fall back on the fortress port city of Königsberg in northeastern East

Prussia but, in this case, the retreating force would find itself cut off in an isolated position. Moltke suspected that General Prittwitz might have the latter solution in mind and specifically ordered him to abandon such thoughts. Unfortunately, Moltke left him the opportunity to take advantage of the first alternative by adding that, if his army found itself in danger of being overwhelmed by vastly superior numbers, it was to pull back to the Vistula. Hoffmann feared that the temptation of this loophole might prove too great for Prittwitz to resist.

Hoffmann's defensive plan provided for primary concentration of German strength in the northeast against Rennenkampf, whose army he correctly assumed would strike first. The German First and 17th Corps, along with the First Reserve Corps, were to take up positions along the Angerapp River. Initially, General Friedrich von Scholtz's 20th Corps would have sole responsibility for resisting Samsonov in the south.

RUSSIAN CONCERNS

The Russians suffered from concerns other than the predictability of their plan. Although they would have a substantial numerical advantage, the haste with which they would put the operation into effect and the inefficiency of their logistic system assured problems. Compounding them were the absence of lateral railroads in the staging areas of Poland and the fact that Russian rail gauge was wider than that utilized in Germany. This meant that the advancing troops would be unable to use the East Prussian railroads unless they captured German locomotives and rolling stock intact and in abundance, a most unlikely prospect. The Russians also had no work teams available to lay new track. As a result, they would be completely dependent on horse-drawn transport. The invading troops also faced monumental communication

problems. They would rely primarily on German telegraph lines because their supply of wire was too meager for them to lay their own. The only other recourse was to communicate by radio. This, too, posed serious difficulties because of the primitive nature of Russian codes and inadequate methods for decoding messages. Indeed, when the invasion actually began, orders were often sent in the clear without any attempt to use code, much to the glee of the Germans.

Elements of the Russian First Army penetrated East Prussia as early as August 12 and seized a small village, but Rennenkampf launched his main invasion on August 17. Hoffmann intended to allow the Russians to advance without opposition during the first two days. He hoped to lure them into overextending themselves, making them more vulnerable to a counterattack. If the Germans could defeat Rennenkampf's army quickly, they could then shift forces to the south in time to strike against Samsonov.

Hoffman's carefully laid plan soon ran into difficulty, not from the Russians but owing to the actions of the commander of the Eighth Army's own First Corps, General Hermann von François. An officer of skill and boldness, François made an art of disregarding orders with which he did not agree. In defiance of Prittwitz's insistence on standing fast along the Angerapp, François sallied forth to defend German territory to the east of the river. He soon became embroiled in a battle with two Russian brigades, which his forces caught off guard near the village of Stallupönen. When Prittwitz ordered François to fall back, the corps commander responded impudently that he would do so after defeating the Russian forces. And defeat them he did. Afterward, he did retreat toward the village of Gumbinnen. Rennenkampf apparently assumed that the Germans were carrying out a general withdrawal. He feared that

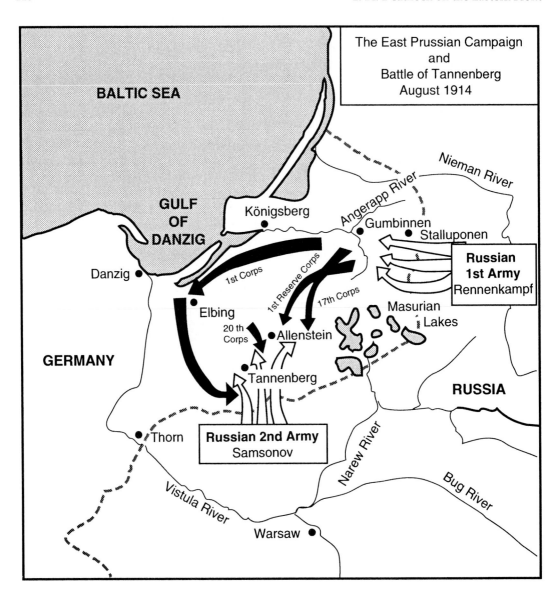

this would wreck the Russian plan because Samsonov was not yet in position to attack the enemy from the rear. In an effort to entice the Germans to linger, he broke off his advance, a decision to which supply problems also contributed. By refusing to push on, he unwittingly upset Hoffmann's plan to attack the Russians from the prepared positions along the Angerapp.

THE BATTLE OF GUMBINNEN

As Hoffmann and Prittwitz weighed their options, they received news that Samsonov's Second Army had penetrated into southern East Prussia. This settled the issue. The Germans must strike quickly at Rennenkampf to the east of the Angerapp and to do so without a coordinated plan, if they were to have time to shift forces afterward to counter Samsonov. In this muddled manner, the Battle of Gumbinnen unfolded on August 20, 1914. François's forces attacked first because of their advance position and made good progress, virtually annihilating one Russian division and swinging around Rennenkampf's right flank.

Unfortunately for the Germans, their other two corps did not fare nearly as well, especially General August von Mackensen's 17th Corps on François' right flank. Large numbers of refugees streaming westward slowed Mackensen's advance, and his troops suffered heavy casualties from Russian artillery fire before they came into direct contact with the enemy. When they did collide with Rennenkampf's forces, a vigorous Russian assault sent two German divisions reeling back in panic. By the time that General Otto von Below's First Reserve Corps came into action, Mackensen's rout was already underway, and Below's forces could do little more than join in the retreat. The flight of the 17th Corps also uncovered François's right flank, and his troops, despite their success in the north, had no choice but to fall back as well. The attempt to defeat Rennenkampf's army had failed, and during the struggle the threat from Samsonov had increased still more in the south. But Rennenkampf did not pursue the retreating Germans. He paused to rest his Russian troops and bring up supplies.

Prittwitz, badly shaken by the deteriorating situation, now insisted that only a general retreat beyond the Vistula could save his army, and he called Moltke to inform him of his decision. Later, however, he changed his mind when Hoffmann pointed out that Samsonov's army was closer to the Vistula than were the Germans, making a withdrawal of this magnitude out of the question. Hoffmann now outlined a plan to transfer most of the troops from the north to reinforce the 20th Corps in the south and launch a surprise attack against Samsonov. He intended to carry out this bold stroke, however, only after striking once again against Rennenkampf. Prittwitz agreed to the transfer of forces for the operation in the south but wisely insisted that the projected second attack in the north be abandoned. He believed that the only chance of success lay in the immediate transfer of troops southward. Time would not allow any other approach. The Germans would have to hope that Rennenkampf remained inactive.

CHANGES IN THE GERMAN HIGH COMMAND

Unfortunately, no one saw fit to inform Moltke that Prittwitz had abandoned his plan to withdraw to the Vistula, and the supreme commander, whose own nerves were growing taut because of problems on the Western Front, decided that he must replace the obviously rattled Eighth Army commander. As the official successor to Prittwitz, Moltke chose a retired 67-year-old veteran of both the Austro-Prussian and Franco-Prussian wars, General Paul von Hindenburg, who was Prittwitz's brother-in-law. He selected him because of his aristocratic heritage, which remained a prerequisite for high command in Imperial Germany, and not because of any perceived intellectual ability. But, more importantly, he designated Ludendorff, the hero of Liège and newly promoted to major general, as Hindenburg's chief of staff. Ludendorff was a far better planner than Hindenburg, but his humble birth as the son of a small businessman made him unacceptable as army commander.

Hindenburg provided more than the proper social credentials, however. He shared Joffre's quality of imperturbability. This was of no small importance because Ludendorff possessed a mercurial personality, making him prey to nervousness, rage, and even panic in crisis situations. The placid Hindenburg proved a steadying influence in these difficult times. The senior member of this new and soon to be famous partnership traced his lineage back to the Teutonic Knights who had battled the Slavs for possession of East Prussia during the Middle Ages. He had won the Iron Cross, Second Class, for bravery at Sedan in 1870 and had served on the general staff under Schlieffen. Deeply patriotic, ultra-conservative politically, and devoted to the emperor, Hindenburg had retired in 1911 but welcomed the opportunity to return to wartime duty.

Equally conservative and nationalistic, as well as ambitious, determined, and ruthless, Ludendorff had earned his appointment to the general staff by virtue of enormous dedication to work and considerable ability. His reverence for Schlieffen intruded into the realm of hero worship. He had labored as chief of the mobilization section of the general staff from 1904 to 1913 to perfect the Schlieffen Plan under both the original author and Moltke. Undistinguished in appearance with a lumpish body, bull neck, double chin, and harsh, downturned mouth, Ludendorff was personally cold and distant. He had no real friends and approached life in a painfully serious and rigid manner, at least partially in emulation of Schlieffen.

Soon after Hindenburg and Ludendorff arrived in East Prussia, Moltke made his controversial decision to transfer the two corps from the right wing of the forces executing the Schlieffen Plan in the West to bolster the Eighth Army. This action was the result of a variety of factors. Moltke had long feared the weakness of German forces in the east, and Prittwitz's initial panic after Gumbinnen had increased his concern. Influential East Prussian leaders also urged OHL to defend their homeland against "the Russian hordes." Finally, Moltke was optimistic about chances

for success in the west at that point, and General Bülow assured him that the right wing could spare the troops. When Ludendorff received the news on August 26, he pointed out that these forces would arrive too late to be of any use in defeating the Russians. But he did not make a determined stand to prevent their transfer, even though he was one of the foremost experts on the workings of the Schlieffen Plan.

GERMANS PLAN STRATEGY

Even before their arrival in East Prussia, Ludendorff and Hindenburg had agreed on a plan that was essentially the same as that devised by Hoffmann and approved by Prittwitz. Indeed, Hoffmann had already taken the initial steps to transfer all three corps from the Angerapp to Samsonov's front. Only a cavalry division was to remain as a thin shield in the north. The plan called for François's First Corps to make a wide swing by railroad to the west and then to the south prior to striking at Samsonov's left flank. Below's First Reserve Corps would march southward to bolster Scholtz's 20th Corps in the center of the German line. Mackensen's 17th Corps was to pivot southeast to be in position for an attack on the Russian right flank. The latter two units had to cover 90 miles by road.

While the Germans shifted their forces, starting on August 23, Samsonov continued his advance with surprising speed. But Jilinsky, the army group commander, pressed him repeatedly to push forward even faster. Samsonov insisted that his troops were exhausted and suffering from a variety of shortages, including food, while the extremely sandy terrain made progress most difficult. He pointed out that, under the circumstances, his men were incapable of a swifter pace. None of this was of any consequence to Jilinsky, who distrusted Samsonov because of his reputation for slowness during peace-time "war games." Ironically, while mercilessly prodding Samsonov, Jilinsky made no effort to force Rennenkampf to resume his advance. When Rennenkampf finally did so on August 23, he moved due west toward Königsberg instead of southwest to link up with Samsonov, a change that Jilinsky did not oppose. The fact was that Jilinsky, with his headquarters far from the front, had become completely confused as to the true state of affairs. When Samsonov realized that the Germans were building up strength opposite his flanks, he asked permission to adjust his advance accordingly. Jilinsky accused him of cowardice and urged him forward in the face of what he termed nonexistent enemy forces.

But the Germans were far from imaginary. François's corps came into position on August 23, although his artillery had not yet caught up with the bulk of his infantry. Ludendorff ordered him to attack on August 25, but the maverick commander refused until his artillery was in place. Meanwhile, Samsonov continued to advance with two of his best corps arrayed in the center as a powerful spearhead. Although they succeeded in capturing the major communications center of Allenstein, they were now dangerously overextended. On August 26, Mackensen and Below launched the first attacks against the Russian Sixth Corps, which was guarding Samsonov's right flank. They caught the enemy unit with its forces thinly stretched and drove it back in confusion. The following day, François finally struck the Russian left flank and gained a similar success against the First Corps. It came largely as a result of a furious artillery bombardment, clearly vindicating François's refusal to be hurried.

RUSSIAN FORCES ROUTED

Both Russian flanks had given way, and Samsonov ordered a general retreat in an ef-

fort to extricate his advance forces. It was too late. François's troops were wheeling eastward to prevent their flight. The exhausted Russians had no recourse but to surrender or face death in a rapidly shrinking pocket that soon became a killing ground. An estimated 30,000 Russians died in the battle, while the Germans took another 92,000 prisoner. But the encirclement was not complete. Two Russian corps on the right wing managed to elude the trap and escaped back across the border. They were able to do so largely because Ludendorff, fearful that Rennenkampf might attack his rear, was reluctant to allow Mackensen and Below to swing too far west in an attempt to cut off their retreat. Toward the end of the Russian debacle, Samsonov said farewell to his staff and disappeared into a wooded area. Soon after a single shot rang out, the general apparently having taken his own life, although his body was never discovered.

During the initial attack on Samsonov's right wing on August 26, some Russian soldiers in their haste to get away blundered into a lake and drowned. A German eyewitness account of this incident later became exaggerated and provided the basis for a myth that the Germans had forced thousands of others into swamps and lakes where they, too, perished. In reality, the number who suffered this fate was quite small.

The battle soon became known by the name of one of the small villages in the general area of the fighting—Tannenberg. Leaders of the German Eighth Army chose to call it that because Tannenberg had been the scene of the defeat of the Teutonic Knights at the hands of the Poles in 1410. The Germans hailed their great victory as fitting revenge for that centuries-old humiliation.

Historians generally consider the battle the single most brilliantly conducted operation of the entire war. The Germans had demonstrated skilled planning, swift movement, and considerable daring. They had destroyed Russia's bid for a quick victory in East Prussia and the possibility of a follow-up offensive against Berlin. Their triumph also made both Ludendorff and Hindenburg larger-than-life heroes and launched them on the path that eventually was to carry them to positions of great power in Germany. But it was Hindenburg, as the official commander, who became the towering symbol of German military might as well as the savior of East Prussia. He was to retain a special place in German hearts for the remainder of the war and well beyond. Moltke actually suppressed news of the triumph for reasons of security until after the German setback on the Marne. The announcement at that time did much to offset the impact of the far more significant failure in the West on the morale of the German people.

REASONS BEHIND THE GERMAN VICTORY

Clearly, the victory was not due solely or even primarily to H-L, as Hindenburg and Ludendorff soon became known. The original plan was Hoffmann's, and the much-ridiculed Prittwitz had insisted on the crucial provision for the immediate transfer of forces to the south rather than after a second assault against Rennenkampf. François's stubborn refusal to attack until his artillery had arrived also contributed greatly to the extent of the German victory. Ludendorff's nerves actually tightened on two occasions during the battle. Most notably, after the initial attack on Samsonov's right flank, he put too much credence in reports that Rennenkampf was about to fall on Mackensen's rear, at the same time that a cavalry force was supposedly threatening François's flank. Ludendorff actually proposed calling off the latter's attack against the First Corps, which would have imperiled the entire operation. Luckily, the

cooler Hindenburg and Hoffmann intervened to persuade Ludendorff to change his mind.

Russian blunders also contributed fundamentally to the German victory. General Jilinsky loomed as the chief culprit. His refusal to believe reports of the Second Army's remarkable progress and his constant demands for greater speed led to Samsonov's headlong rush into the German trap. At the same time, his failure to apply any pressure on the First Army to cease its dawdling, along with Rennenkampf's reluctance to move forward to link up with Samsonov, enabled the Germans to shift their forces with impunity. Finally, there was the slipshod nature of Russian communications, the total failure of which came to be symbolized by the desperate recourse to sending messages in the clear. As Hoffmann later admitted, "We had an ally, the enemy. We knew all about the enemy's plans."

Now that the Russian Second Army was no more, Ludendorff and Hindenburg shifted their forces northward against Rennenkampf. Bolstered by the troops that Moltke had transferred from the west, the two German commanders positioned four corps in the north to pin down enemy forces there, while two other corps attempted to break through the weaker Russian concentration around the Masurian Lakes to the south. When the offensive began on September 8, it made no progress, but François's corps broke through in the south the following day. Rennenkampf, fearful of a disaster similar to Tannenberg, called for a general retreat by most of his army. To slow the German pursuit and save as many men as possible, he decided to sacrifice two divisions by ordering them to attack the German center. This desperate expedient allowed the remainder of his troops to reach the sanctuary of Russian soil by September 13. Nevertheless, this First Battle of the Masurian Lakes cost the

Russians another 125,000 casualties. It also led to the dismissal of General Jilinsky.

The victories at Tannenberg and the Masurian Lakes were the result of brilliantly executed operations against a numerically superior enemy. They demoralized the Russians and left them with feelings of inferiority relative to the Germans, which were to haunt them throughout the remainder of the war.

THE WAR IN THE SOUTH

While these dramatic events unfolded in East Prussia, far to the south Austria-Hungary set out to end "the Serbian menace" and meet the

FIGURE 7–2 Marshal Franz Conrad von Hötzendorf, chief of staff of the Austro-Hungarian army. National Archives

challenge of its long-time Balkan rival Russia. Neither quest was destined to end happily for the Dual Monarchy. Austria-Hungary's military operations during the war were under the overall supervision of the Army High Command (*Armee Oberkommando*, or AOK). Although AOK's nominal leader was the venerable Archduke Frederick, the real command functions lay in the hands of the chief of staff, Count Franz Conrad von Hötzendorf. AOK's authority came to be very great indeed. Conrad ran the war with virtually no civilian control and often left government leaders in the dark as to both his plans and their results. The only person, who could have secured civilian jurisdiction was the emperor, but Francis Joseph was too old and tired to act with any vigor.

After the war some observers praised Conrad as a brilliant strategist, but there appears to be little basis for this claim. His conduct of operations demonstrated both boldness and lack of foresight, a combination that usually translates as rashness and often results in disaster. Although Winston Churchill later insisted that "Conrad made his headquarters at Przemysl in a barrack-room with straw as his bed and an oil lamp for light,"[1] the field marshal actually operated from Teschen in Austrian Silesia far from the front and made few visits to his troops. Instead, he and his staff lived in luxury, almost as if the war were an unpleasant and remote abstraction.

THE SERBIAN CAMPAIGN

Before the Dual Monarchy came to grips with Russia, it attempted to win a quick victory over Serbia. Determined, as he had been for years, to crush the "Serbian menace," Conrad initially sent the Second Army to bolster the Fifth and Sixth armies already in position

opposite Serbia. He assumed that this combined force would certainly be sufficient to defeat the little Balkan power. In this, he and other Austro-Hungarian leaders gravely underestimated their enemy and Serbia's mountainous topography. The Serbian army had the potential to mobilize 450,000 men and, though short of equipment, it did possess some modern artillery. Well-trained and willing to accept hardship, it had gained valuable experience in the recent Balkan wars. In their commander, General Radomir Putnik, the Serbs possessed an outstanding and dedicated soldier. Although elderly and in appallingly poor health, Putnik had served with distinction in the Balkan wars. He proved especially skillful in defense and demonstrated remarkable ability to outmaneuver his opponents. Putnik had been in Budapest for medical treatment when the war began and could well have been taken into genteel captivity. Instead, Francis Joseph chivalrously granted him safe conduct home, a decision the emperor may well have come to regret.

Despite Conrad's otherwise dominant position in the conduct of the war, he played a most limited role in the Serbian campaign. General Potiorek, the powerful governor of Bosnia-Herzegovina, conducted operations against the Serbs with little supervision by AOK. He maintained this remarkable independence despite the fact that his lax security measures at Sarajevo had contributed in no small way to the death of Archduke Francis Ferdinand. His strong connections at court allowed him to overcome this woeful demonstration of his incompetence. They also enabled him to gain virtual freedom to carry on his own little war. But Potiorek proved to be a mediocre military commander. Even after Conrad belatedly ordered the Second Army to Galicia for operations against the Russians, Potiorek managed to retain four of its divisions in the Serbian theater of operations,

---

[1]Winston Churchill, *The Unknown War: The Eastern Front* (New York: Charles Scribner's Sons, 1931), p. 139.

instead of shifting the entire force to Galicia. Unfortunately, they proved insufficient to gain victory for Potiorek but were sorely missed in Galicia. In all, Potiorek's forces numbered close to half a million men, but many of his units consisted of badly trained and equipped militia.

Potiorek stationed the Fifth Army along the Sava River and its tributary, the Drina. Together, these substantial streams formed the northwest angle of Serbia's border with Austria-Hungary. The Sixth Army took up a position farther south on the Drina in Bosnia. Potiorek launched his offensive on August 12, 1914 when the Fifth Army crossed both rivers. Soon after the Sixth Army pushed across the Drina. The Serbs resorted to a fighting withdrawal to the Jadar River where Putnik counterattacked on August 16. He caught the Austro-Hungarians by surprise and drove them back across the border by the end of the month. In early September, Putnik actually sent a force across the Sava into Hungary, but it fell victim to a counterattack and retired to the Serbian side of the river. Potiorek opened a second offensive on October 8 but was no more successful as the Serbs once again put up fierce resistance. To make matters worse, Putnik sent troops into Bosnia in an effort to raise its Serbian population in revolt against the Dual Monarchy. This phase of the struggle continued indecisively until late October.

In early November, Potiorek staged his third offensive. This one produced far better results, at first. His armies defeated the Serbs in a battle near the Kolubara River and occupied Belgrade on December 2. Potiorek now pressed his soldiers on for what he sensed would be the kill. It was not to be. The wily Putnik believed that the enemy would soon encounter difficulties from the rugged terrain and growing exhaustion. He proved to be a prophet. When he counterattacked with his last reserves on the day after the fall of the

capital, the Austro-Hungarians were not able to withstand the shock. They ended their short stay in Belgrade and, by December 15, were streaming back across the border.

Austria-Hungary's last attempt to crush Serbia without help had failed. All of its efforts had accomplished nothing. They had cost 28,000 dead, 120,000 wounded and 75,000 men taken prisoner. And there were two other casualties—Potiorek, who joined the war's growing ranks of dismissed generals, and the Dual Monarchy's reputation as a great power. It was now quite clear that the objective which had led Austria-Hungary into war was beyond its ability to accomplish, at least with the forces available for the task. The "Serbian menace" remained alive, but not well, because the Serbs also had suffered greatly, their casualties totaling close to 170,000. Both sides had also fought in a most ruthless, barbaric manner and had committed many atrocities. Mutual hatred grew accordingly.

RUSSIAN VICTORIES AGAINST THE DUAL MONARCHY

Long before the final frustration of Austria-Hungary's dream of victory over Serbia, the Dual Monarchy suffered a far worse setback against the Russians in Galicia. In part, this failure was the result of Russian numerical superiority, which turned out to be greater than Conrad had expected. But it was also due to Conrad's excursion into wishful thinking by dispatching the Second Army to participate in the invasion of Serbia. This seriously weakened his forces on the Galician front in a series of clashes collectively referred to as the Battles of Lemberg. Finally, Conrad's strategy proved quite unrealistic and reckless.

When it became obvious that he could no longer ignore Russia, Conrad proceeded to make good on his promise to Moltke by putting Plan R into effect. This provided for an offensive into Russian Poland from Galicia with four armies. Unfortunately, one of them, the Second, which Conrad had planned to use as a strategic reserve, would not be available until it made its way laboriously from the southwest and then only at half strength. The plan called for General Viktor von Dankl's First Army to thrust northward between Lublin and Chelm to cut the main railroad from Kiev, the capital of the Ukraine, to Warsaw. On Dankl's right, the Fourth Army, commanded by Field Marshal Moritz von Auffenberg was to strike northeastward toward Lutsk, while General Rudolf von Brudermann's Third Army would move eastward toward Rovno.

All of the Austrian army commanders shared Conrad's devotion to the offensive, although Dankl was more restrained and probably the best commander in the field. Auffenberg was the most notable personality among them, having served as war minister from the fall of 1911 until December 1912, largely because of support from Francis Ferdinand. He shared the archduke's dislike of the Magyars, and in 1904 he had even drafted a plan for armed intervention in Hungary if the Magyars attempted to dissolve the *Ausgleich*. While war minister, he had succeeded in increasing the size of the army and had ordered 12 siege mortars from the Skoda works without the authorization of the parliaments of the Dual Monarchy.

Unfortunately, Conrad deployed his three armies in such a way that their routes of advance would disperse them much too widely. As a result, gaps were almost certain to develop between them. To compound this problem, the commander of the Russian Southwest Army Group, General Nicholas Ivanov, had situated his strongest forces to the east where they would be in position to strike against the Austrian flank. This was not by design, however. Ivanov had actually expected the enemy to attack eastward and had massed his troops to stage a frontal assault

against them. Ivanov's group consisted of four armies. The weakest of them, General Ivan Salza's Fourth Army, lay directly in the path of Dankl's forces. To his left, the Fifth Army of General Sergei Plehve stood somewhat to the northwest of the projected route of Auffenberg's advance, while General Nicholas Ruszky's Third Army blocked Brudermann's progress toward Rovno. General Alexei Brusilov's Eighth Army took up a position along the eastern border of Galicia, where it would be able to attack Brudermann's vulnerable right flank and threaten Lemberg, the provincial capital.

Although a dedicated professional, Ivanov possessed little imagination and was both hesitant and pessimistic. His army commanders showed greater initiative, especially Brusilov and Ruszky. Brusilov proved to be the most energetic and most able Russian commander of the war. Unlike the majority of his colleagues, he was innovative and devoted to the element of surprise as the vital factor in warfare. Hot-tempered and forceful to a fault in his personal relations, Brusilov often argued with his superiors and earned their enmity as a result.

Despite his numerical inferiority, Conrad, on August 22, 1914, sent his armies thrusting deeply into Russian Poland. Both sides were virtually ignorant regarding the intentions of their opponents. Ivanov used his cavalry to fill gaps between his armies rather than in reconnaissance. Conrad sent his cavalry on a wide sweep, but it failed to gather much information. Instead, it suffered many casualties. At first, all went well for Conrad's advancing troops. Dankl's forces collided head on with those of Salza at Krasnik south of Lublin on August 23. During the ensuing three-day battle, both sides sustained numerous casualties, but the Russians finally fell back toward Lublin. To the east, Auffenberg outmaneuvered Plehve at Komarov and came close to encircling the entire Russian Fifth Army. But, just as a great victory appeared within his grasp, Auffenberg received an urgent plea for help from Brudermann's Third Army to the east. Ruszky and Brusilov were simultaneously assaulting the flanks of Brudermann's badly overextended and outnumbered troops along the Gnila Lipa River. Auffenberg im-

The Eastern Front
August-December 1914

Front Line, Dec. 31, 1914
Attacks by Central Powers
Attacks by Allies

mediately shifted forces to apply pressure on Ruszky's army, but they were insufficient to reverse Brudermann's fortunes. Unfortunately, the diversion prevented Auffenberg from closing the trap on Plehve's army, which managed to escape.

The situation had become so serious that even the offensive-minded Conrad had no choice but to order Brudermann to retreat back to Lemberg on August 28. Conrad had not abandoned hope for resuming his attacks, but events were moving too quickly for him. Brusilov isolated Lemberg and continued to threaten Brudermann's rear. At the same time, Ruszky's Third Army and Plehve's revitalized Fifth Army turned against Auffenberg's flanks at Rava-Russkaya and Russian cavalry threatened to envelop Auffenberg's entire army. The entire eastern wing of the Austrian force was giving way, but Conrad still did not realize the extent of his predicament. He ordered both Auffenberg and Brudermann to stand fast, while Dankl attacked toward Lublin in the west, but when it became apparent that Plehve's forces were also threatening Dankl's seriously exposed right flank, Conrad realized that he was confronted by the spectre of total disaster. He ordered a general withdrawal to the San River on September 11. Three days later, he changed the destination of the retreat to the Dunajec River, 140 miles west of Lemberg. He did so after receiving intercepted enemy messages indicating that the Russians were threatening to outflank the San River position. Again, as in East Prussia, the Russians sent these messages in the clear. By doing so, they denied themselves the opportunity of completely destroying the Austro-Hungarian forces.

Conrad's ambitious offensive had degenerated into a rout with panic-stricken remnants of his three armies fleeing for their lives, while Cossack cavalry nipped at their heels. Ironically, elements of the Second Army, which had arrived from the Serbian front too late to participate in the offensive, now became caught up in the disastrous retreat and suffered many casualties. Nevertheless, the Austro-Hungarians were able to consolidate a new front extending southward along the Dunajec to the Carpathian Mountains, but most of Galicia lay in Russian hands. In an effort to prevent the enemy from penetrating the Dukla Pass through the Carpathians into Hungary, Conrad left 150,000 men to hold out in the powerful fortress city of Przemyśl.

The catastrophic campaign cost the Dual Monarchy at least a quarter of a million casualties as well as another 100,000 men taken as prisoners. In all, the army lost roughly one-third of its combat strength, including many of its vital junior officers and non-commissioned officers who had held the multilingual units together. The Hapsburg Empire had suffered a reverse from which it would never completely recover. And, far from safeguarding Germany's rear, as Moltke had hoped, the offensive left the entire German flank from East Prussia to Silesia open to a possible Russian attack. Certainly a defensive strategy would have made more sense. It would have preserved the Austro-Hungarian army's strength while inflicting severe casualties on any attacking Russian force.

AFTERMATH OF THE DUAL MONARCHY'S LOSSES

The disaster also inflicted another crippling blow to Austria-Hungary's reputation as a Great Power. Clearly the Germans had lost all respect for their partner. As their ambassador to Vienna, Heinrich von Tschirschky, ascerbically remarked, "God preserve my poor fatherland from ever again making war with Austria as an ally." The expression "We are shackled to a corpse" soon became a form of gallows humor among German officers. But the leaders of the Dual Monarchy were also bitter over the failure of their German allies to provide any assistance in the east. After all, Conrad had undertaken his ill-fated offensive in response to Moltke's plea for help, while Germany settled accounts with France. It had, indeed, drawn Russian reserves away from East Prussia and contributed to the German victory at Tannenberg, but at a fearful price to Austria-Hungary.

The Dual Monarchy's defeat led to growing dependence on German support. Both Conrad and the government appealed to General von Falkenhayn, the new German chief of staff, for help soon after the front had stabilized. They warned that, without such aid, they would be forced to consider a separate peace. In effect, Austria-Hungary now put itself under the protection of its ally. The price it paid was increasing subordination of its military and foreign policies to German domination. Economically, too, it became more and more an appendage of its powerful partner. Not surprisingly, Conrad came to refer to the Germans as "our secret enemies." But humiliating submission did not save the Dual Monarchy from ultimate defeat and dismemberment. It merely postponed this fate for four horrible years.

RUSSIA AND GERMANY PLAN NEW OFFENSIVES

Russia's victory in Galicia had done much to relieve the gloom caused by the defeat at Tannenberg. It inspired the Russians to plan another offensive against the Germans, this time in the direction of Silesia. French pleas for an additional Russian operation to take the pressure off them also contributed to the decision. By late September, 1914, Russian mobilization was nearly complete, while equipment and other supplies in the forward areas were much more abundant than they had been earlier. Stavka, Grand Duke

Nicholas's High Command headquarters, had now assembled no fewer than seven armies, stretching from the border of East Prussia to Galicia.

Ludendorff and Hindenburg both realized the danger to Silesia as well as the need to come to the aid of their reeling allies to the south. With Falkenhayn's approval, they scraped together a new army, the Ninth, from the two corps that Moltke had sent from the Western Front as well as other units scattered elsewhere in the east. Hindenburg and Ludendorff assumed its command, and, utilizing the railroads, rapidly shifted it to the south, while General von Schubert took over the Eighth Army in East Prussia. The Ninth Army positioned itself to the north of Dankl's Austrian First Army. Despite German efforts, the Russians still outnumbered them by at least 60 divisions to 18. Ludendorff and Hindenburg urged Falkenhayn to send more troops to the Eastern Front, but the chief of staff was engaged in the first stages of "the race to the sea" and could not spare them from the Western Front.

In view of this overwhelming numerical inferiority, Ludendorff believed that his best option was to mount a spoiling attack by the Ninth Army northeastward to the Vistula, while Dankl's forces protected his right flank. If he could strike swiftly before the enemy was ready to launch his offensive, it might be possible to disrupt his plans and, if all went well, to capture Warsaw. The defensive nature of the operation was apparent in Ludendorff's order that all bridges along the way be prepared with explosives for detonation should a hasty exit be required.

The operation began on September 28, 1914, and by October 9 the German Ninth Army had reached the Vistula south of Warsaw, while Dankl's troops had also advanced to the river. Meanwhile, the Austrian Fourth Army had moved south of the great bend of the Vistula and had reached the San River at the point where it flowed into the Vistula. To the south, both the Austrian Third and Second armies reached the San as well and relieved the besieged fortress of Przemysl. At the same time, the main Russian force had taken up positions on the east bank of the two rivers. Unfortunately for the Germans, the forward movement of the Ninth Army had greatly extended its left flank, leaving it wide open to an attack by Plehve's Russian Fifth Army to the northeast. In mid-October, Stavka ordered Plehve to swing behind the Germans in an effort to encircle them. In the ensuing heavy fighting, Ludendorff soon realized that he had no choice but to abandon his offensive. He managed to elude the impending envelopment, and by the end of the month all of the forces of the Central Powers had returned to their original positions.

Ludendorff also learned from intercepted Russian messages, again sent in the clear, that the enemy was planning to open an offensive against Silesia soon. He decided to launch a second spoiling attack to upset this threat to the Fatherland. It became apparent that Plehve's attempt to cut off the Ninth Army had opened a gap between his forces and the reconstituted Russian Second Army to the north. Ludendorff decided to exploit this opportunity with an audaciously bold action. Taking advantage of the excellent rail network in eastern Germany, again he sent the bulk of his forces westward to Breslau in Silesia, then northward to Posen and finally to the east. Ten days later, they were in position to strike into the gap between the two Russian armies. This bold and skillful shifting of forces badly confused the numerically superior Russian armies. Again, the German troops, under the command of General von Mackensen, broke through to the Vistula, just to the south of Warsaw. The Germans were too few to maintain this forward position for long, as Ludendorff had realized all along. However, by repeatedly taking the initiative

during the previous two months, he had prevented the enemy from launching its offensive against Silesia. When the Russians finally brought their superior strength to bear, the German Ninth Army fell back. By the end of November it had returned a second time to its original position. The Austrians had also withdrawn, leaving Przemyśl once again an isolated fortress, which would surrender after a four-month siege. Nevertheless, it was now clear that the Dual Monarchy had survived its first disasters and, though badly weakened, would remain in the war.

POWER STRUGGLE IN THE GERMAN MILITARY

In Germany, the campaign had spawned disagreement and the beginning of a power struggle among military leaders. Ludendorff and Hindenburg were unhappy with the resources at their disposal, especially in view of the enormous size of Russia's army and the deplorable condition of Austria-Hungary. They tried again, just before launching their second offensive toward Warsaw, to obtain reinforcements, but Falkenhayn refused. At that time, he was concentrating all his energy on the First Battle of Ypres, which he viewed as Germany's last chance to win a decisive victory in 1914. The emperor found himself caught in the middle of this dispute. While feeling obligated to support Falkenhayn, he could not estrange Hindenburg and Ludendorff, because of their growing popularity. On November 1, the emperor granted the two officers a significant concession by creating a combined High Command structure for all German forces on the Eastern Front—*Oberkommando Ost (Oberost)*—with Hindenburg as commander in chief in this theater and Ludendorff as his chief of staff. This decision increased the independence of the two eastern generals from OHL The German spoiling offensives in October and

November, fleeting though they may have been, were classic military campaigns. Not surprisingly, they increased still more the popular adulation of Hindenburg and Ludendorff. Friction between H-L and Falkenhayn was to increase during 1915 and came to focus on the question of whether an eastern or western strategy held out the best prospect for victory.

One thing was abundantly clear: Despite their brilliance, the German operations on the Eastern Front had led to another stalemate. The three empires of Eastern Europe, once allied in their common defense of conservatism and monarchy, were now locked in a desperate struggle for supremacy. Clearly there would be no swift decision. Instead, another chapter of war by attrition had barely begun. This one differed from that unfolding in the west, however. The vast distances involved made it possible for much greater expanses of territory to change hands, but the overall result was the same—massive loss of life, horrible suffering, tremendous strain on the socioeconomic systems of the belligerents, and no resolution in sight.

8

1915:
THE WESTERN FRONT
AND GALLIPOLI

If 1914 had dashed the hopes of both sides for quick victory, it had not extinguished the belief that the war could still be won in the relatively near future. The members of each alliance could and did explain the failures of the first five months of the conflict in terms of mistakes, missed opportunities, and too many commitments. Despite their frustrated hopes, the leaders of the belligerent powers believed that they had learned valuable lessons from the horrible carnage of 1914. However, they often disagreed on what those lessons were.

BOTH SIDES PLAN STRATEGY

After the German failure in the First Battle of Ypres, General Falkenhayn became convinced that further offensives would not produce a decisive victory on the Western Front. They would only deplete Germany's strength through meaningless bloodshed. The two adversaries were too evenly matched and the Allied defenses too formidable, but Falkenhayn also did not expect to win the war by concentrating primary strength on the Eastern Front. It might be possible to push the Russians back, relieve the threat to Austria-Hungary, and inflict heavy casualties on the enemy, but the vast distances in this theater of operations offered endless opportunity to retreat. This posed the danger that the Germans would overextend their forces and become vulnerable to counterattacks far from their supply bases. Such a strategy would also do nothing to eliminate the more advanced members of the Allied coalition, Britain and France. As a result of all these considerations, Falkenhayn accepted the inevitability of a long war of attrition. Since a lengthy conflict was likely to go against the Central Powers, he may have already

FIGURE 8–1 Austro-Hungarian troops defend the Eastern Front. National Archives

concluded that Germany could not win. But if this was his conviction, he could not admit it to the emperor, his fellow generals, or the German people, all of whom remained confident of ultimate victory.

In dramatic contrast, Hindenburg and Ludendorff staunchly clung to visions of victory. They saw it coming on the Eastern Front where, of course, they were in command and would reap the benefits of such a triumph. They agreed with Falkenhayn that it would be best to switch to a defensive position in the west, but the two generals favored a massive offensive in the east aimed at forcing Russia out of the war. With the eastern enemy defeated, it would be possible to focus on a great operation in the west, very likely with themselves again in command. Perhaps the defeat of Russia would in itself be sufficient to induce Russia's allies, France and Britain, to make peace as well.

This difference of opinion between "Westerners" and "Easterners" had been gradually developing ever since Hindenburg and Ludendorff took command in East Prussia. It reached major proportions by the end of 1914. The short-term resolution to this question proved to be something of a compromise. Falkenhayn agreed to shift substantial forces to take part in a major offensive in Russian Poland in 1915, but since he did not expect this offensive to prove decisive, he had no intention of making the Eastern Front the key to his future plans. Thus, the debate would continue. It would also take the form of a power struggle as it became increasingly intertwined with the personal ambitions and growing animosity of Falkenhayn and his eastern rivals.

A similar difference of opinion existed among British leaders. Both David Lloyd George and Winston Churchill feared that victory could not be attained on the Western Front. Appalled by the ghastly death toll of 1914, they looked elsewhere for the key to winning the war. Although often referred to as "Easterners," they thought more in terms of attacking along the periphery of the Central Powers, specifically against Turkey or Austria-Hungary. However, their arguments made little headway with most British military leaders, who were wedded to the idea that victory must be achieved on the Western Front against the major opponent—Germany. The generals opposed "sideshows" that would deflect badly needed resources.

Lord Kitchener, at the war office, was also a "Westerner," but he opposed additional offensives until the BEF was much larger. To help achieve this condition, he issued a call for 300,000 volunteers in October 1914. The response of British youth was astonishing. Filled with patriotic enthusiasm and a strong belief that Britain's cause was just, they flocked to the recruiting offices, creating a "new army" in the process. Of course, it would take time to train all of these eager young recruits. Meanwhile, regular troops recalled from the colonial army would fill the gaps in the BEF created by the terrible losses of 1914. The "Territorials," second-line troops created by War Secretary Haldane early in the century for the defense of Britain itself, and militia units took their place in the colonies. The self-governing dominions also loyally and voluntarily sent forces to fight alongside the British. Canada led the way, dispatching 33,000 men to Britain in October 1914. These troops soon took up positions on the Western Front. Australia and New Zealand also sent military contingents. They went, not to Europe, but to Egypt where they helped defend the Suez Canal against the Turks. South African forces relieved British regulars in that country and had their hands full repressing a revolt by anti-British irregular bands, largely composed of veterans of the South African War. These rebels resisted until January 1915.

Field Marshal Sir John French, who had overcome the recurring inclination to pull his troops out of the line during 1914, favored resuming the offensive before Kitchener's new army was ready. His attitude and that of other British commanders on the Western Front dovetailed with the absolute dedication of all French leaders to win the war on the Western Front. To General Joffre and other French patriots, no other strategy was acceptable or even thinkable. The Germans had occupied a large portion of France's "sacred" soil. They must be driven out. In view of the much greater French contribution to the ground fighting, it would be difficult for the British not to leave the primary role in determining strategy to the French.

EVENTS OF 1915: TRENCH WARFARE

The redeployment of German strength to the east meant that the Western Allies would have the advantage in numbers on the Western Front in 1915. To Joffre and French, this offered the opportunity to score the breakthrough in the enemy line that had proven so elusive in the opening months of

the war. Joffre visualized an offensive, featuring attacks at opposite ends of the German salient in northern France that still bulged menacingly toward Paris. As in his unsuccessful offensive at the end of 1914, he would strike in Artois and Champagne, but this time with more strength and the benefits of experience. He hoped to cut off the salient and then stage a third attack from Verdun to sever the only enemy rail line south of the Ardennes. If he could accomplish this, he believed that the Germans would be forced to abandon France and much of Belgium because their remaining railroads to the north would be inadequate to supply their troops.

Neither Joffre nor French realized that the nature of trench warfare had made their dreams of a breakthrough virtually impossible to achieve. Although the opposing defensive positions had not yet assumed their final complexity and strength, these positions were already formidable. The entrenchments varied, depending on the nature of the terrain and other factors, but they usually featured two lines of trenches, separated by 200 yards or more and connected by communications trenches. All of them featured zig-zag construction to minimize the impact of shells and prevent enemy flanking fire, which could cut down an entire row of soldiers. About 700 yards or more behind the second trench line, a belt of machine gun nests provided additional problems for advancing forces. Barbed-wire entanglements of considerable depth protected each successive line. Support trenches in the rear supplied the needs of troops in the forward trenches. Still farther back were the artillery positions.

The attacking Allied armies prepared the way for an offensive with artillery fire, designed to destroy enemy barbed wire as well as troops in the forward trenches. But the Germans held their front trenches lightly and maintained supporting forces in the rear for counterattacks. They also dug deep, and elaborate bunkers that were impervious to shelling. As the war progressed, the length and intensity of this "softening up" shelling increased prodigiously. Unfortunately, it also warned the opposing forces as to where the offensive would take place. As troops pushed forward across "no-man's land," they fell victim to defensive artillery fire. Then, as they neared the enemy trenches, machine guns took their toll. To increase their killing power, it became common practice to place machine guns so that they could fire diagonally. This enabled them to intersect with the guns of the next nest, creating a deadly crossfire.

Among the formidable obstacles confronting the Allied armies in their offensives during 1915 was the fact that the Germans had gained control of most of the ridges on the Western Front in 1914. While many of these ridges were not terribly high, they enabled the Germans to look down on the enemy and gave them a clear field of fire. The Allies also continued to suffer from a considerable numerical disadvantage in artillery, especially heavy guns. The French worked diligently to bring their 1913 model howitzer into mass production, however, and also diverted old cannon as well as guns from fortresses in "safe areas" to the front. The British were especially short of artillery of all kinds and suffered from a severe shell shortage in 1915. These weaknesses seriously reduced the length and velocity of the bombardments preceding their offensives.

The Germans also maintained a big lead in number of machine guns. Allied commanders proved inordinately slow to realize the importance of this weapon, despite the losses it inflicted on their troops. Britain's General Sir Douglas Haig remarked as late as April 1915 that "the machine gun is a much overrated weapon, and two per battalion is more than sufficient." Belt-fed machine guns, such as the British Vickers or German Maxim-type Spandau, had a deadly rate of fire of 500 rounds per minute. But they had heavy water-filled jackets for cooling the barrels and were only suitable for defense. Light air-cooled machine guns, such as the French Chauchat and British Lewis gun, could be carried by assault troops but had limited magazines and could only be fired in short bursts. Development of light automatic weapons later would restore the initiative to the attacker.

Joffre originally intended to launch his offensive in March 1915 with attacks in both Champagne and Artois. As a part of his plan, he asked the British to relieve French forces in the Ypres salient to enable them to participate. However, reinforcements were slow in reaching the BEF. As a result, Field Marshal French was unable to fulfill Joffre's request, and this delayed the start of the offensive. But French did feel strong enough to strike with British troops at a weakly held sector of the German line near the village of Neuve Chapelle in Artois and to do so before the main offensive began.

French entrusted the assault to Haig, who had actually been thinking in terms of such an operation for some time. Haig's First Corps, augmented by reinforcements, was now designated as the First Army. It attacked along a narrow front of only 3,500 yards on March 10 and had an advantage of four divisions to only one for the Germans. Haig opened with a heavy bombardment, although it lasted just 35 minutes. It proved effective. The British moved rapidly forward and appeared to be on the verge of a breakthrough, but they were too few in number and their penetration was too narrow. The Germans on their flanks subjected them to heavy fire, and enemy reinforcements soon closed the gap. Before the three-day Battle of Neuve Chapelle ended, it cost both sides about 13,000 casualties. The British had also consumed about one-third of their supply of artillery shells.

THE SECOND BATTLE OF YPRES: THE HORRORS OF GAS WARFARE

Although Falkenhayn planned to remain on the defensive in the west in 1915, he carried out one memorable offensive in April—the Second Battle of Ypres. Falkenhayn intended this operation to accomplish four things. Most importantly, (1) he wanted to divert attention away from the Eastern Front where he was planning his major effort. But he also hoped to (2) disrupt Franco-British plans for their own assault and to (3) straighten his own line in the process. Finally, (4) he had agreed to test a hideous new weapon—poison gas—even though he had little faith in its potential. According to his technical advisers, the Ypres salient offered the best wind conditions for such an experiment. The Germans had first used gas— nonlethal tear gas—in a demonstration at Bolimov, west of Warsaw on the Eastern Front, on January 31, 1915. But cold weather had negated its effects.

Falkenhayn opened his attack on April 20 with a massive two-day bombardment, utilizing the same siege howitzers that had torn apart the forts of Liège, Namur, and Antwerp. They now reduced the town of Ypres, with its cathedral and cloth hall, to rubble. Then, after a brief lull on April 22, the mortars began to fire again, and almost simultaneously the Germans released chlorine gas from canisters in their own trenches. As the gas drifted toward the Allied line, it caught the defenders completely by surprise, even though a German deserter had warned them that such an attack was coming. The Allied commanders had either refused to believe it or could not make up their minds how to deal with it. At any rate, they failed to alert the troops.

Taking the form of a yellowish-green cloud, the gas drifted along the ground and into the trenches held by colonial troops from Algeria and overage French Territorials.

Chlorine was a choking agent that silently attacked the lungs and respiratory systems. Many soldiers died in agony. Others survived to face a horrible epilogue to their lives. Those who managed to escape fled in blind panic, while others not directly affected joined the hasty exodus. They left a four-mile wide gap in their wake. Falkenhayn had been so skeptical about the results of the gas experiment that he did not provide sufficient reserves to exploit the opportunity for a breakthrough. The German forces that were available halted when they caught up with the residue of their own gas and also met fierce resistance from Canadian forces on their left. Many of the Canadians became engulfed in the lethal gas cloud but drenched rags in canteen water and tried to cover their mouths to filter out the gas. They fought valiantly until the British were able to scrape together reinforcements. This combination of factors stalled the German advance. But the Allied position remained precarious.

General Foch, now in command of the French Northern Army Group, nevertheless ordered an immediate counterattack. However, since the French forces were in disarray and the British too weak, General Smith-Dorrien, commander of the recently created British Second Army, argued that it would be more sensible to fall back to a shorter line just to the east of Ypres. To say the least, this suggestion did not please British Field Marshal French, who disliked Smith-Dorrien and promptly dismissed him from his command. But General Sir Herbert Plumer, who replaced him, was no fool. He promptly endorsed his predecessor's proposal for a withdrawal. French now felt that he had no choice but to agree, and the British managed to hold their new position, despite heavy fighting.

Falkenhayn tried a larger-scale gas attack on May 24, but this time it lacked the element of surprise. The British did not panic and repulsed the infantry assaults that followed.

Although the Germans had reduced the salient to a slight bulge during the course of the five-week battle, Falkenhayn's lack of faith in the new weapon and his refusal to allot the necessary reserves denied the Germans the chance for a breakthrough. The cost was high, almost 70,000 casualties for the Allies, over 35,000 for the Germans.

The Second Battle of Ypres had introduced the world to the horrors of gas warfare; but not only had the experiment failed, it also provided the British with another propaganda windfall. Once again, it appeared as though the Germans were inhuman brutes who would resort to any device, no matter how terrible, to achieve victory. Despite the new dimension of terror, that it introduced, gas did not prove to be a war-winning weapon. It was too unpredictable. A shift in wind could and frequently did sweep a deadly gas cloud back on those who had unleashed it. More effective gas masks also came into use. The Allies were soon to adopt the use of gas themselves and, since the prevailing winds on the Western Front were westerly, the diabolical weapon ultimately worked to the disadvantage of the Germans. As the war progressed, even more horrible forms of poison gas came into use. By 1916, artillery shells could deliver gas, eliminating the former dependence on wind for propulsion. Both sides fired gas shells during artillery barrages. The defenders' chief dilemma was to decide when to put on gas masks because their charcoal filters were limited in the amount they could absorb.

THE ARTOIS OFFENSIVE

Even before the end of the Second Battle of Ypres, General Joffre opened his long-delayed offensive in Artois. He did so despite the absence of seven divisions, which were tied down in defense of Ypres. According to his plan, French and British troops attacking simultaneously were to break through and link up along the Vimy and Aubers ridges behind the enemy lines. General Victor d'Urbal's French Tenth Army launched its assault toward 400-foot Vimy Ridge on May 9, following a six-day artillery barrage. A corps, commanded by General Henri Pétain, penetrated the center of the German position and pushed forward almost three miles. But just as his forces were nearing the top of the ridge, the Germans rained down artillery fire on them, while machine gun nests directly in their path forced the troops back from the crest. Instead of breaking through, the French became locked in another bloody struggle, lasting more than a month.

Meanwhile, Haig's army unleashed its attack toward the lower-lying Aubers Ridge to the north. Although delivered with considerably more strength than the earlier assault at Neuve Chapelle, it enjoyed little success. The British lacked shells for more than a 40-minute preliminary barrage, but even those they did fire lacked sufficient impact to do serious damage to the enemy position. The advancing troops encountered formidable defenses and fierce resistance. Although they did capture the first trench line, murderous artillery fire inflicted heavy casualties.

THE FATAL FLAW IN ALLIED TACTICS

The failure of the Artois offensive demonstrated clearly the fatal flaw in Allied methods. Although attacking forces could, with sufficient preparatory bombardment, penetrate both lines of enemy trenches, they inevitably came to grief from artillery and machine gun fire when they attempted to move beyond them. At this point, they had also usually advanced beyond the range of their own supporting artillery and it was difficult to move the batteries forward because the bombardment had badly churned up the ground. The Germans were able to bring in reserves and counterattack just as the advancing forces were becoming exhausted. This scenario was to unfold again and again. But the clarity of the dilemma somehow eluded the Allied generals. They consistently underestimated the strength of enemy defenses and took refuge in the contention that larger numbers and greater firepower would secure victory. But increasingly they came to place emphasis on the need to wear down the Germans through attrition before they could achieve their elusive triumph. Such an approach had one major failing. Attrition was almost certain to take a greater toll on attacking forces than on defenders, and France, with its smaller population, was in a poor position to pursue such a strategy.

Undeterred by these failures, Joffre prepared to strike again as soon as possible. This time his main thrust would come in Champagne with a secondary attack in Artois. A variety of delays, due largely to the need to build roads and other facilities in Champagne, pushed the starting date back to late September. Meanwhile, it was not difficult for the Germans to recognize what was afoot, and Falkenhayn made lavish preparations to meet the attack. Most importantly, he ordered construction of a second defensive system located two to four miles behind the first. This decision was a major step forward in the development of defense in depth. Falkenhayn also returned four divisions from the Eastern Front where the German summer offensive had already gained a sweeping victory over the Russians.

Joffre's plan for the Champagne operation provided for the Eastern Army Group, led by General Castelnau, former commander of Second Army, to strike midway between Verdun on the east and Reims to the west. Castelnau's forces included two armies under Generals Langle de Cary and Pétain.

The latter had risen dramatically from the rank of colonel at the start of the war to command successively a brigade, division, corps, and now an army in a year's time.

A massive three-day bombardment preceded the offensive, which got underway on September 25 in pouring rain. Hopes were high. Once again, there was much talk about the *elan* of the troops, and bands even played the *Marseillaise*, the French national anthem, when the advance began. And once again, the initial results were encouraging. The French overran the enemy's first position but then came under heavy artillery fire. It soon became apparent that the second line of defense was far too strong, and this time Joffre called a halt. Unfortunately, Falkenhayn, not content with a defensive victory clearly consistent with his strategy, insisted on a counterattack to regain the lost territory. As a result, the battle dragged on until early November. The cost: 145,000 French casualties, 75,000 German.

The offensive in Artois was no more rewarding. Here General d'Urbal's Tenth Army again struck toward Vimy Ridge. To the north, Haig's First Army attacked in the direction of the coal-mining town of Loos. After breaking through the enemy line, the two forces were to converge on the town of Lens and cut the lateral railroad serving the Germans. Unfortunately, the defenses in the path of the French were so strong and complex that they earned the nickname "the Labyrinth." The struggle became essentially a repetition of the bloodletting of May. Once again, the French reached the crest of Vimy Ridge, only to be driven off by a hurricane of German artillery fire.

The British fared even worse. Both Field Marshal French and General Haig were uncharacteristically pessimistic, largely because the sector allotted to them consisted of difficult terrain, dotted with slag heaps, mine pits, and villages. Now, ironically, Lord Kitchener, who had opposed the earlier offensives, insisted that they undertake the attack according to Joffre's plan. Despite the myriad of obstacles, Haig's forces did penetrate the first line of trenches and reached the second, but further progress depended on prompt intervention by reserves under French's control. The field marshal kept them too far back, however, and by the time they reached the front, they were exhausted from their long march. When Haig finally resumed the advance, his men soon collided with the powerful second German defensive system. Instead of breaking off what was clearly a hopeless enterprise, the British kept attacking in waves with reckless bravery. The Germans cut them down in such numbers that they later referred to the site of the battle as the "corpsefield of Loos."

The Allied efforts in Artois added another 190,000 French casualties along with 60,000 British to the distressing toll on the Western Front. German losses have been estimated at approximately 213,000. The British failure at Loos also led to the ouster of French as commander of the BEF. Although losing support with the government for some time, his poor handling of reserves in the Loos operation provided the final blow to his prestige. Haig took his place. All of the appalling slaughter of the 1915 offensives had barely changed the contours of the front. The Germans had pushed the line a few miles westward in the Ypres salient. The Allies had achieved two small dents in the German line in Artois and another in Champagne.

But the senseless events along the Western Front were far from the only disastrous failure suffered by the Allies in this lamentable year. Another unfolded near the northeastern end of the Mediterranean area—the Dardanelles or Gallipoli campaign. It, too, started with high hopes and ended in disillusionment. This operation had its origin in Turkey's decision to enter the war on the side of the Central Powers.

TURKEY ENTERS THE WAR

In the immediate prewar period neither side had shown any great interest in luring the Turks into closer relations. On the contrary, between May and mid-July 1914, Turkey tried in vain to entice Russia into an alliance and Britain and France into better relations. Shortly before Austria-Hungary delivered its ultimatum to Serbia, Turkey approached Germany with a proposal for an alliance, but German leaders pursued the matter hesitantly and were highly skeptical of Turkish military strength. The Liman von Sanders mission, which had caused such a hostile response from Russia when the Germans sent it to Constantinople in December, 1913, had made only limited progress in modernizing the Turkish army. Nevertheless, the two countries signed a treaty of alliance on August 2, 1914.

General Enver Pasha, the 32-year-old Turkish minister of war and one of the leaders of the Young Turk movement, was the chief architect of this pact. He and his allies in the Turkish cabinet had conducted the negotiations in secret without consulting other members of the government. When those who had been left out learned of the agreement, they were not pleased. Some of them favored neutrality, others an arrangement with the Allies. They argued against implementation of the alliance, and three months of wrangling followed. An immediate entry into the conflict was out of the question under any circumstances, however, because of Turkish financial difficulties, slowness in mobilizing reserves, and concern over the intentions of Turkey's neighbors—Greece, Bulgaria, and Rumania.

Many observers have portrayed the pro-alliance Turkish faction as being rabidly pro-German, but this does not appear to have been the case. Enver Pasha was the only one among them with marked pro-German sympathies. He had served as military attaché in Berlin for two years and had come to admire German military power and efficiency. For a time he had developed a friendship with William II and even adopted the upward-turned style of mustache worn by the German emperor. But their relationship had cooled long before the summer of 1914. It appears that Enver and his colleagues chose alliance with Germany because they expected the Central Powers to win and because they feared that Russia would precipitate a partition of the Ottoman Empire should the Entente prevail.

Once the war began, Germany abandoned its former indifference toward Turkey and pressed Constantinople to take action against Russia. Germany became increasingly exasperated by what it considered the dilatory approach of the Turks. Meanwhile, the Turkish government tried to maintain its outwardly neutral status so as not to provoke the Allies. But relations deteriorated when, on August 3, Winston Churchill, the First Lord of the Admiralty, suddenly commandeered two dreadnoughts, which Turkey had ordered from a British shipyard, for the Royal Navy. This action raised loud protests in Turkey and strengthened Enver and his clique.

The plot thickened still more when the German battle cruiser *Goeben* and light cruiser *Breslau* arrived in Turkish waters on August 11. These ships, under Admiral Wilhelm Souchon's command, had been operating in the Mediterranean during the summer of 1914. After the outbreak of war they left the Austrian naval base at Pola on the Adriatic and bombarded French ports on the Algerian coast on August 4. During the following week, Souchon outmaneuvered the French navy and 11 British cruisers, which expected him to head for Gibraltar or return to the Adriatic. Instead, he moved eastward toward the Aegean Sea and the Straits. When Souchon reached the Dardanelles on August 10, he proceeded to sail up the Straits toward Constantinople. In return for Turkish approval of this action, Germany supported the Turkish demand for an end to "capitulations," the far-reaching economic concessions that the European Great Powers had long enjoyed in Turkey.

To disguise what was clearly not a neutral act, Turkey announced that it had purchased the cruisers from Germany to take the place of the undelivered dreadnoughts. The Germans went along with this fiction. When Souchon's ships arrived at Constantinople, German sailors even donned red fezzes and Turkish uniforms. The Turks also officially appointed Souchon commander of their own navy. On September 8, Turkey terminated all capitulations. But to its surprise, the Allies indicated that they might be willing to accept the arrangement, if Turkey remained neutral. This response strengthened those Turkish leaders who opposed implementation of the German alliance.

However, Enver's position improved when Germany agreed to grant Turkey a loan of one million Turkish pounds to prosecute the war. On October 21, Enver and his naval minister, Ahmet Cemal Pasha, set out to provoke Russia into declaring war by authorizing Souchon to attack Russian targets in the Black Sea. They did so without informing the full Turkish cabinet. Eight days later Souchon's fleet bombarded Odessa and other ports, destroying several ships. Russia responded with a declaration of war on October 31, 1914, and Britain and France followed suit three days later.

Once in the war, Turkey quickly revealed its weakness as it became involved in fighting on three fronts—Egypt, Mesopotamia, and the Caucasus Mountains along its northeastern frontier with Russia. On November 14, the Turks proclaimed a *jihad* (holy war) against the Allies, hoping to arouse their fellow Muslims in Egypt and Central Asia to revolt against the British and Russians, respectively. Their appeal had little effect, especially among Arabs, whose hatred of the Turks was as great or greater than their dislike of the Allies. When Turkey completed mobilization, it was able to field an army of 800,000 men, but they were poorly equipped and victimized by a rudimentary communications system. The Turks possessed little in the way of industry and were cut off from German aid when Rumania, succumbing to Russian pressure, blocked the only rail link from Austria-Hungary to Turkey.

Djemal Pasha (or Kemal Pasha) took control of military operations in Syria and, with German encouragement, sent 20,000 men to attack Britain's vital Suez Canal. But this proved no easy task. It required a 150-mile march across the desolate wastes of the Sinai Desert. Djemal's forces were already exhausted and suffering from hunger when they arrived at the canal in early February 1915. Although they surprised the British, and a few men actually crossed the canal, the Turks encountered strong resistance from Indian troops supported by the Australian New Zealand Army Corps (Anzac). Turkish forces soon retreated back across the Sinai. The attack did have one major effect, however. It frightened the British into maintaining troop strength in defense of the Suez canal out of all proportion to the extent of the Turkish threat.

The British took the initiative themselves in Mesopotamia, which corresponded roughly to present-day Iraq. They landed Indian troops near the estuary of the Tigris and Euphrates rivers in November 1914. Britain carried out this operation primarily to protect the pipeline and oil refining installations of the Anglo-Persian Oil Company on the nearby island of Abadan in the Persian Gulf. It also hoped to raise the Arab population of Mesopotamia against the Turks. The Indians captured the port of Basra on November 23, and by December 9 they had pushed as far north as Qurna at the juncture of the Tigris and Euphrates.

By far the bloodiest of the three fronts was that in the Caucasus where Enver Pasha took command of operations. Enver fancied himself a great general, although he actually possessed limited ability. He had led troops against the Senussi tribesmen in the interior of Libya during the Tripolitanian War and later served in the Balkan wars. Although he took great pride in the capture of Adrianople in the latter conflict, in reality his troops merely marched into the city after the Bulgarian garrison had evacuated. Enver visualized campaigns of Napoleonic scope, while ignoring both the difficulties involved and the basic requirements necessary for success. This proved particularly dangerous in the Caucasus where the mountainous terrain and poor communications made it a formidable theater of operations. The Turks started off well enough as they halted a Russian offensive aimed at the Turkish fortress city of Erzerum in November. But Enver decided to follow this defensive victory with an offensive of his own, hoping to inspire an uprising of Turkic peoples in Russia's Central Asian territories to the east.

Enver moved forward with about 95,000 men on December 24, seeking to outflank the Russians and cut their road link to the supply base at Kars across the border. His plan totally disregarded the horrors of a winter campaign in this mountainous country. Temperatures plummeted well below zero, and snow clogged the mountain passes, while howling gales lashed the Turkish troops, who were not dressed for this type of weather. Although they managed to capture the border town of Sarikamis to the southwest of Kars on December 26, the Russians drove them out soon afterward.

In January 1915 the Russian commander, General Nikolai Yudenich, mounted a brilliant counteroffensive and soon encircled the

Turkish forces. Enver and 18,000 men escaped, but thousands of others were killed or froze to death, while many more were taken prisoner. Yudenich's troops drove southward toward Lake Van before their drive stalled. The Turks had suffered a bitter and costly defeat, but the net effect was the creation of still another deadlock.

The Turkish failures in Egypt, Mesopotamia, and the Caucasus had a profound effect on the thinking of those British leaders who were searching for an alternative to the bloodbath on the Western Front. Perhaps it would be possible to force the weakest of the Central Powers out of the war. This would open the way for other operations against the enemy's southeastern flank, what Winston Churchill was to refer to during World War II as the "soft underbelly" of Europe. By now, British leaders also feared a long war and realized that Russia would need munitions from the Western powers. The German navy denied access to the Baltic, while the port of Murmansk in the far north lacked rail connections, and Vladivostok on the Pacific coast was much too distant. This left only the Black Sea Straits. If the British could wrest control of them from the Turks, they would be able to open an ideal supply route to the Russians. All of these considerations soon led to the Dardanelles, or Gallipoli campaign.

BEGINNINGS OF THE GALLIPOLI CAMPAIGN

British attention had focused to some extent on the possibility of an operation in this area of Turkey as early as August 1, 1914, well before the Turks had officially entered the war. This interest originated with an offer from the pro-Allied but neutral Greek government of Premier Eleutherios Venizelos to cooperate militarily with the Allies. Soon afterward, British leaders began to speculate on a potential combined action to seize control of the Straits. But the project fell afoul of opposition from Greece's King Constantine, who was married to the sister of William II and favored the German cause. Russia also objected to the prospect of Greek domination of Constantinople. Nevertheless, the British continued to hope for Greek and even Bulgarian cooperation.

When Turkey finally became an active belligerent, Churchill wasted no time in staging a naval "demonstration." It took the form of a brief shelling of the outer forts of the Dardanelles on November 3. Although inflicting little damage, it served as a warning to the Turks to strengthen their defenses, especially minefields inside the Dardanelles and artillery along the coast. In late November, Churchill suggested a combined military and naval action against the Dardanelles but gained little support. Kitchener voiced the loudest objection, noting that there were no troops available for such an undertaking. Nevertheless, Lt. Colonel Maurice Hankey, the secretary of the Committee of Imperial Defense, suggested in late December that the Allies seize the Dardanelles as a prelude to knocking Turkey out of the war. On the first day of January 1915, Lloyd George urged a landing along the Syrian coast.

Clearly a number of British leaders were thinking in terms of operations against Turkey as the new year dawned. But it was an appeal from the Grand Duke Nicholas of Russia that provided the catalyst. On January 2, he implored the British to make a "demonstration" against the Turks. His plea came when the Russians were worried about the early success of Enver's winter offensive in the Caucasus. The following day, Admiral Sir John Fisher, Britain's First Sea Lord, proposed a British and Indian landing on the Asian coast of the Dardanelles along with a Greek attack against the Gallipoli Peninsula on the opposite shore. He also urged a naval expe-

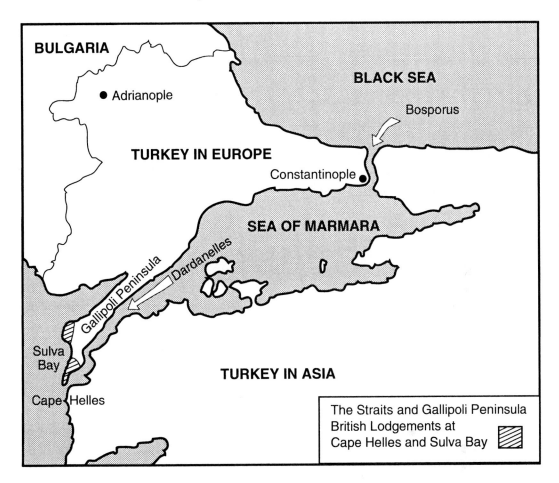

BULGARIA

● Adrianople

BLACK SEA

Bosporus

TURKEY IN EUROPE

Constantinople ●

SEA OF MARMARA

Gallipoli Peninsula

Dardanelles

Sulva Bay

Cape Helles

TURKEY IN ASIA

The Straits and Gallipoli Peninsula
British Lodgements at
Cape Helles and Sulva Bay

dition to force its way through the Dardanelles. Churchill enthusiastically endorsed Fisher's proposal to attack the Straits. Unfortunately he deleted the provision for a land campaign, apparently because, remembering Kitchener's earlier opposition, he did not expect sufficient troops to be available.

Churchill received lukewarm support from naval officers, but he did not bother to consult the army general staff. Fisher opposed such an operation without a corresponding landing but was reluctant to bring his objections before the War Council, apparently because he did "not think it seemly." Kitchener believed that something must be done to satisfy the Russian request but still

insisted that he had no troops to spare for a land operation. On January 11, Admiral Sir Sackville Carden, the commander of a squadron in the Aegean Sea near the Straits, responding to an inquiry from Churchill, concluded that a naval force could neutralize the Dardanelles forts. But it would take time, at least a month. It would also require a large force of a dozen battleships, three battle cruisers, and numerous smaller craft. Armed with this appraisal, Churchill won over the War Council to the concept of gaining control of the Straits through naval action alone. The council agreed on January 28 that the expedition should take place in February and would "bombard and take the Gallipoli Peninsula with Constantinople as its chief objective." The whole enterprise had a vague quality about it, especially the reference to a naval expedition "taking the Gallipoli Peninsula." Apparently the British leaders expected the Turks to collapse once the British navy had broken through the Straits.

Despite endorsing the principle of seizing the Straits by naval action only, British leaders continued to toy vaguely with the idea of using troops. On February 6, two battalions of British marines sailed from Britain to the Greek island of Lemnos 50 miles west of the mouth of the Dardanelles. France also agreed to send a division, and hope for the intervention of Greek troops persisted as well. But the likelihood of the latter diminished as the Greeks became increasingly worried about the possibility that Bulgaria might join the Central Powers. Kitchener finally agreed on February 16 to release the British 29th Division for possible use against the Dardanelles, but this decision aroused so much opposition from the generals in France that he reversed it three days later. The Anzac troops in Egypt would go to Lemnos instead.

Confusion still prevailed regarding the actual mission of a military expedition. While some leaders believed that it must undertake a landing, most saw it as an occupying force after the navy had somehow ended the possibility of resistance on the Gallipoli Peninsula. In this strange manner, Britain drifted into the Dardanelles operation. Ironically, the Russians had crushed the Turkish threat to the Caucasus well before the British agreed to undertake the campaign, eliminating the need for any "demonstration" in this area.

The naval assault began, under Admiral Carden's command, on February 19, 1915. A capable officer but neither brilliant nor innovative, Carden had been in charge of the dockyard on the island of Malta when the war began. After the *Goeben* incident, he took command of the squadron patrolling the Aegean. Carden received this important position despite the fact he had never commanded a fleet at sea. A far better choice would have been Admiral Limpus, the head of the British naval mission to Constantinople, which left Turkey shortly after the *Goeben*'s arrival. Limpus was highly knowledgeable about the defenses of the Straits since, ironically, he had helped the Turks plan them.

On February 19, Carden bombarded the outer forts of the Dardanelles with 12 of his 22 battleships; the result was a conspicuous lack of success. With the exception of the battle cruiser *Inflexible* and dreadnought *Queen Elizabeth*, these were generally older ships not suited for fleet action in the North Sea. The task proved far more difficult than the British had expected. Naval gunfire lacked both the accuracy and the pulverizing power of the howitzers that had devastated the forts of Liège, Namur, and Antwerp. Howitzers were siege guns, designed to be used at relatively close range with their targets clearly visible. Their shells also had an exceptionally high trajectory, giving them maximum impact as they plunged downward. Naval guns were fired from long range with their targets often obscured, and the low trajectory of their shells greatly lessened striking power. Bad weather delayed further attacks until February 25.

When the shelling resumed, it produced better results, neutralizing the outer forts within two days with the help of landing parties that blew up some of the guns. Next, Carden hoped to clear the 12-mile intermediate stretch of coastal batteries and minefields before attacking the guns guarding the Narrows, a mile-wide bottleneck of water extending four miles in length whose defenses had been recently upgraded. But the fleet soon encountered difficulties from mobile batteries, which the Turks moved about so quickly that they did not remain targets for long. Poor British shooting also contributed to less than satisfactory progress. But most vexing of all were the minefields. It was difficult for the British minesweepers to eliminate the mines until they silenced the guns on shore, but the ships could not move close enough to the coast to be effective as long as the minefields remained in place. The British used North Sea fishing trawlers, modified for minesweeping and manned by civilian crews, which had been pressed into reserve duty. Progress proved disappointingly slow.

Admiral Carden, already suffering from an ulcer, could not cope with the strain and teetered on the verge of a nervous collapse. He resigned on March 16, and his second in command, Admiral John de Robeck, took his place. At 52, Robeck was five years younger than Carden and much more stable. He was an extremely conservative officer who always "went by the book," however, and displayed little daring or imagination. Carden had intended to execute an all-out effort to destroy the Turkish batteries protecting the minefields as well as the forts defending the Narrows. With the coastal defenses silenced, the minesweepers could then remove the mines without fear of attack. Once beyond the Narrows, there would be little to prevent the Allied fleet from proceeding into the Sea of Marmara and on to Constantinople. Now, even though Carden was gone, de Robeck adopted his predecessor's plan.

FAILURE OF ALLIED NAVAL POWER

On March 18, sixteen Allied battleships subjected the Turkish fortifications to a fearful pounding for four and a half hours. Unfortunately, the ships penetrated into an undetected minefield, which the Turks had only recently laid. There were only 20 mines, but they paid handsome dividends. Just before 2 P.M. the old French battleship *Bouvet* struck one of them. It blew up and went down with most of its 640 men. About two hours later the British battle cruiser *Inflexible* and battleship *Irresistible* both collided with mines, as did another British battleship, the *Ocean*, soon afterward. The *Irresistible* and *Ocean* both eventually sank, while the *Inflexible* was badly damaged. Confronted by this disaster, de Robeck broke off the operation and withdrew his forces. Despite the prolonged shelling of the coast, the British had knocked out only a handful of Turkish guns. The loss of three capital ships and the crippling of three others was a heavy price to pay for such meager results.

Although de Robeck insisted that he was prepared to launch another attack, British leaders were coming to the conclusion that the fleet alone was not capable of forcing open the Straits. They were not yet convinced that the whole enterprise should be abandoned. British prestige was now so deeply committed that it was difficult to admit defeat. Opinion both within the army and navy had been moving in the direction of a military campaign even before the fleet started to bombard the outer forts. The subsequent naval failures only served to strengthen the trend. Earlier, on March 10, Kitchener had once again reversed himself and ordered the British 29th Division to Lemnos, increasing the force there to 70,000 men. Two days later, he appointed General Sir Ian Hamilton to command this new army.

Hamilton, who had served as Kitchener's chief of staff during the South African War, represented a strange blend of qualities. At 62, he was tall, willowy, and possessed a sensitive and quite unwarlike face. His demeanor did not inspire confidence, and the fact that he was extremely intelligent and cultivated made some of his fellow officers doubt his military ability. In reality, he had enjoyed a distinguished and varied career as a soldier, having seen action on the northwest frontier of India and gaining a reputation for bravery, even suffering a wound to his foot, that left it partially paralyzed. His experience as an observer in the Russo-Japanese War had led him to predict the likelihood of trench warfare in future conflicts. Hamilton believed in delegating authority to his subordinate commanders, a tendency that unfortunately made him reluctant to overrule them, even when such action was necessary.

USE OF LAND FORCES PLANNED

The actual mission of Hamilton's army did not become clear until he met with Admiral de Robeck on Lemnos five days after the naval disaster of March 18. The two commanders agreed that the Allied fleet should abandon its attempt to force its way through the Straits, while the army landed on the Gallipoli Peninsula to destroy the forces defending the Dardanelles. This decision led to lingering controversy. Some observers contend that, in view of the negligible damage inflicted on the Turkish defenses, the failure to clear the minefields, and the losses in Allied ships, the only sensible decision was to halt the naval assault. Others insist that it would have been far wiser to persist. They point especially to the fact that the Turks were nearing the end of their ammunition supply. We shall never know the answer with certainty. But, in view of the remarkable record of muddled thinking, poor management, mistakes, and outright blunders that were part and parcel of the Dardanelles-Gallipoli campaign, it seems highly questionable that continuation of the attacks would have provided the magical key to victory.

Although Churchill much preferred another naval attack, he encountered opposition from Fisher and other top officers at the Admiralty. Prime Minister Herbert Asquith shared Churchill's view but believed that he could not resist the mounting support for a

military campaign. Landings could not take place until late April, however, because of the need to wait for the 29th Division's arrival and a number of supply problems. Hamilton and his staff had to plan the invasion from scratch and in a hurry. There was an abysmal lack of information about the terrain of the peninsula, its roads, and its water supply, if any. Those maps that did exist were inaccurate.

The plan called for landings at two sites along the peninsula. General Sir Aylmer Hunter-Weston's 29th Division was to land at Cape Helles at its tip, with the objective of capturing Achi Baba, a 700-foot ridge six miles inland, which dominated the surrounding area. The Anzacs, under the command of General Sir William Birdwood, were to go ashore near the cliffs of Gaba Tepe on the western side of the peninsula near its narrowest point. They were to take the commanding heights of 850-foot Chunuk Bair before driving across to the Dardanelles. This thrust would cut off the enemy forces to the south and enable the Anzacs to assault the forts overlooking the Narrows from the rear. Meanwhile, to mislead the Turks, the French were to land on the Asian mainland at Kum Kale near the entrance to the Dardanelles. Once they had lured enemy troops to that area, they would evacuate. In another feint, the Royal Naval Division was to sail in the direction of the northern neck of the peninsula, giving the impression that it was going to land at Bulair on the Aegean coast.

The Turks had just one division available for defense of the entire Dardanelles area when the naval assault began in February. However, by the time of the actual Allied landings, they had gathered six divisions, grouped in the new Fifth Army. Enver Pasha had appointed General Liman von Sanders, the head of the German military mission in Turkey, to command these forces. A narrowly professional but highly able soldier who lacked diplomacy and was extremely stubborn, Liman had clashed frequently with Turkish leaders. He had been especially critical of Enver's ill-starred Caucasus offensive. Whatever his shortcomings, Liman did an excellent job of organizing the Turkish defense of the Dardanelles. He placed two divisions on the Asian side and four others on the peninsula—two at Bulair, one near Cape Helles and the remaining one as a reserve. Not the least of Liman's services to Turkey was his appointment of Lieutenant Colonel Mustapha Kemal to command the latter unit.

Mustapha Kemal was destined for great things. He was to turn apparent Turkish defeat into victory on several occasions during the struggle for the Gallipoli Peninsula, and after the war he was to lead a revolution that created a new Turkish republic. Although a brilliant soldier, he was also grim, arrogant, bad-tempered, and introverted, qualities that had contributed to a less than flourishing career prior to the war. Kemal had thrown himself passionately into the Young Turk movement but was constantly overshadowed by the dynamic and charismatic Enver. The two men did not get along, and by 1914 it appeared as though Kemal's star had set, while Enver's was at its zenith. An ardent nationalist, Kemal was violently opposed to foreign influence in Turkey and harbored anti-German feelings.

The Allied landings finally took place early on April 25. The diversionary operations at Kum Kale and Bulair both drew Turkish forces away from the real landing areas. Liman von Sanders himself rushed to Bulair, convinced that it was the site of the main enemy thrust. The French even captured the fortress of Kum Kale before withdrawing to reinforce the troops at Cape Helles. The beaches at Cape Helles were not extensive enough to allow concentration at any one point. Instead, the 29th Division landed at five different locations.

Two of them were on the Dardanelles side of the peninsula, at opposite ends of Morto Bay, and were designated as S beach on the northeast and V beach to the southwest. The other three were on the Aegean side, extending from W beach near the tip of the peninsula to Y beach about four miles to the northeast, with X beach between them. The landings at S and X beaches took place with little difficulty against light resistance, while the one at Y beach encountered no enemy defenders at all. But none of the forces at these three outer beaches made any attempt to move inland. Later, when the Turks attacked those at Y beach, fierce fighting broke out, and when the engagement ended, each side believed it had been beaten. The British were so convinced of this that they evacuated altogether, abandoning the beach that might have proved the key to a successful operation.

Unfortunately, the largest British troop contingents, landing at V and W beaches, both received rude receptions. Those coming ashore at W beach ran into extensive barbed wire, both in the water and on the shore. The Turks also greeted the attackers with withering machine gun fire. Nevertheless, some of the British troops made it beyond the beach and reached the top of the cliff where they consolidated their position. The First Battalion of the Lancaster Fusiliers Regiment paid bitterly for this small lodgement. Of its original strength of 957 officers and men, only 316 managed to avoid becoming casualties.

The situation was even worse on V beach. Here the British tried an experiment. To say the least, it did not succeed. The main landing force of 2,000 men boarded the coaltender *River Clyde*, which was to beach itself on the enemy shore. Two holes called "sallyports," cut in the bow of the ship, were to serve as exits for the men as they stormed ashore. Once the *River Clyde* ran aground, naval personnel maneuvered two barges into position ahead of the ship and lashed them together to serve as a sort of primitive landing ramp. Unfortunately, Turkish machine gunners mowed down the men as they emerged from the sallyports. Casualties ran into the hundreds, and the sea around the ship literally turned red from the blood gushing and oozing into it from the dead, the dying, and those who were merely wounded. The remaining 1,000 British soldiers approached the shore in rowboats. They, too, felt the lash of the machine guns and died in large numbers. Nevertheless, when this bloody day ended, the British had gained a precarious foothold on the beaches.

Ironically, had the forces that landed unscathed at S, Y, and X beaches moved inland, they could have taken the outnumbered Turkish defenders from the rear. However, owing to confusion, overly rigid adherence to orders, and a lack of direction from General Hamilton and the divisional commander, Hunter-Weston, the troops did nothing. On this occasion, Hamilton's reluctance to overrule his subordinate had unfortunate results. Hamilton broached the possibility of sending reinforcements to exploit the situation at Y beach, but Hunter-Weston, who resented suggestions from his superior, rejected the proposal. Whether these reinforcements would have made any difference at Y beach is not clear, but at least they would have provided greater strength for a possible advance inland, rather than an evacuation.

Meanwhile, to the north, at Gaba Tepe, an uncooperative current washed the Anzacs a mile above their intended destination. They landed unopposed, however, along the narrow beach, soon to be known as Anzac Cove; they brushed aside weak defending forces and scrambled through rough terrain toward Chunuk Bair. But when Mustapha Kemal received word of the landing, he led a single battalion to Chunuk Bair and, though outnumbered three to one, his forces beat back repeated Anzac attempts to capture the heights.

By the next day, a total of 30,000 Allied troops had landed on the Gallipoli Peninsula, but the Turks still held the dominating high ground everywhere. The struggle was already taking on the form of a miniature battle of attrition similar to that on the Western Front, complete with the digging of trenches. Allied forces continued to try to break through the Turkish defenses and repeatedly failed. The Anzacs launched a major effort on May 2, but the reinforced Turks fought with a bravery close to frenzy. The Turks counterattacked with suicidal charges on May 19, resulting in 10,000 casualties. Neither side was able to break through, and the stalemate continued. The Allies tried several more times during May and June, but victory remained elusive. Meanwhile, Admiral Souchon, in the battle cruiser *Goeben*, discouraged any Russian action against the Bosporus, the northernmost part of the Straits, and, indeed, almost paralyzed the Black Sea Fleet for the rest of the war.

THE POLITICAL REPERCUSSIONS OF THE GALLIPOLI DEFEAT

The Gallipoli failure, following the Dardanelles fiasco, led almost inevitably to political repercussions. The Conservatives in the British Parliament denounced the Liberal government's handling of the war in general and Gallipoli in particular. They demanded formation of a coalition government as well as measures to remedy the persistent munitions shortage. On May 26, the Conservatives got their way. Although Asquith continued as prime minister, four Conservatives and one member of the Labour party entered the cabinet. Lloyd George took over the newly created post of minister of munitions. His dramatic success in remedying the munitions shortage in the months to come greatly increased his stature as a war leader. More and more, he loomed as a potential replacement for Asquith. Admiral Fisher, now totally estranged from Churchill, resigned as First Sea Lord, and Churchill lost his title as First Lord of the Admiralty.

CONTINUATION OF THE GALLIPOLI OFFENSIVE

The coalition government refused to end the Gallipoli campaign, however. Instead, Kitchener sent three more divisions to strengthen the troops there. Ironically, the war secretary, who had originally opposed the operation, now became its chief spokesman, staking his reputation and influence on finding a way to secure victory. He and General Hamilton intended to use the enlarged forces in a major offensive. It would feature a landing by two divisions at a new site—Suvla Bay about five miles to the north of Anzac Cove. Suvla Bay offered both relatively easy terrain and an absence of a strong defensive force. Hamilton hoped to catch the Turks by surprise and move quickly inland. But the offensive's main thrust was to come at Anzac Cove. Three divisions, under General Birdwood, would attempt once more to capture Chunuk Bair and the adjacent heights. Both attacks were to take place simultaneously at night. The two forces were to link up and push across to the Dardanelles at the Narrows. Troops at Cape Helles would also mount an attack to freeze the Turkish troops on that front.

The Suvla Bay operation seemed to offer a real chance of victory, but the forces involved consisted of raw recruits who had not seen previous action. Conversely, seniority was the long suit of their commander, General Sir Frederick Stopford. In fact, Kitchener had chosen him specifically because he had greater seniority than did General B.T. Mahon, commander of the 10th Division,

who would be serving under him. Stopford had retired in 1909 because of poor health and had never held a combat command. Hamilton harbored serious misgivings over his selection, and Stopford proved the worst possible choice. To compound the problem, most of Stopford's subordinate generals and colonels had also returned from retirement to active duty and lacked both vigor and initiative.

Prepared in great secrecy, the offensive began on August 6. The landings at Suvla Bay took place successfully with the help of new armored landing barges called "Beetles." Designed by Admiral Fisher, they were the forerunners of World War II landing craft. The beach was virtually undefended, and reinforcements quickly moved in after the original landing. Speed was now the key to victory. A rapid thrust inland might have won the day, but speed was conspicuously absent. Confusion and inertia took its place. In short, there was no effort, from Stopford or anyone else, to move forward. Stopford was filled with pessimism and could think of nothing but digging in to consolidate his position. Hamilton, as usual, was slow to prod his commander into action, but even when he finally did insist on an advance on August 8, it took place at an incredibly slow pace. Meanwhile, the Anzac forces at Anzac Cove pushed forward and on August 9 actually dislodged the Turks from Chunuk Bair.

Once again, Mustapha Kemal responded to the Allied threat with unbelievable vigor, driving himself without sleep for days at a time. He brought reinforcements to bear at both trouble spots and succeeded in occupying the hills overlooking Suvla Bay virtually by default. The task of regaining Chunuk Bair and the neighboring heights proved much more difficult. Fighting there was the most intense, heroic, and bloody of the entire campaign. It dragged on for three days until both sides were exhausted, but in the end Kemal and the Turks prevailed. Not surprisingly, the Anzacs felt betrayed by the inactivity at Suvla Bay.

ALLIED WITHDRAWAL

Although the battle continued for some time, the Turkish resistance during the first few days had really sounded the death knell, not only for this offensive, but the entire Gallipoli campaign. In late August, inactivity settled in as both sides suffered from heat, dust, flies, lice, and, most of all, dysentery attributable to inadequate food and contaminated water. During September and October, cold winds and rain dispelled the heat but heralded the arrival of a new form of discomfort, a series of storms in November. General Sir Charles Monro replaced General Hamilton as Allied commander in mid-October. Monro had no illusions. He urged an evacuation, and his superiors accepted his advice. The withdrawal began in mid-December with the removal of 83,000 men from Anzac Cove and Suvla Bay. It concluded on January 9, 1916, when 35,000 troops left Cape Helles. In contrast to the tragic manner in which the campaign had unfolded, the British skillfully carried out the evacuation at night, even using

timing devices to fire off rifles after the men had silently filed down to the boats. They demonstrated such a flair for deception that the Turks scarcely knew what was taking place.

The dismal Gallipoli campaign had cost each side over 250,000 casualties and reflected badly on British leadership. In addition to the ouster of Churchill and the weakening of Asquith's position, it seriously undermined Kitchener's prestige and influence. The Gallipoli operation has remained one of the most controversial campaigns of the entire war. Unlike the hopeless offensives on the Western Front, it seemed to offer a real chance of success on more than one occasion. Some observers have referred to it as the campaign of missed opportunities. The entire enterprise, both at sea and on land, with the notable exception of the evacuation, was a model of flawed management, poor coordination, and shoddy execution. Those who directed it lacked the ability to move quickly once they had achieved initial surprise or to alter their plans to take advantage of unexpectedly promising developments. Too often, generals received their appointments on the basis of seniority, rather than skill, imagination, and boldness, and the intellectual

FIGURE 8–2 Anzac troops charge a Turkish trench on the Gallipoli Peninsula. National Archives

Hamilton was not the commander to provide dynamic leadership.

However, even if the Gallipoli campaign had been a complete triumph, it is difficult to believe that it would have proved decisive. Certainly control of the Straits would have opened an excellent supply route to Russia, but in view of the shortages confronting Britain as well as French insistence on concentrating strength on the Western Front, it is questionable that enough supplies would have reached Russia to make any major difference. Moreover, shortages of arms and munitions represented only a part of the multitude of problems confronting the Russians. It is also unlikely that the Allies could have used their control of the Straits as a springboard to a decisive campaign in the Balkans. No matter how grim its prospects, the Western Front remained the decisive theater, and Germany by far the most important enemy. Knocking Turkey out of the war and nibbling at the southeastern periphery of Europe would not change that.

Clearly, meat-grinder offensives were not going to bring victory on the Western Front either. The only alternatives that appear to have made sense were a negotiated settlement or simply remaining on the defensive. But the chances of attaining the former were remote and the latter hardly appealing. Unfortunately, the brutal nature of modern warfare offered no real prospect for breaking the deadlock, either on the main front or elsewhere.

CHAPTER
9

1915:
STALEMATE IN THE SOUTH, ALLIED DISASTER IN THE EAST

While the Allies hammered away fruitlessly in Artois and Champagne and executed their futile attempts to break through at the Dardanelles, the war also went badly for them in other parts of Europe during 1915. Their only lasting success during this mournful year came not on the battlefield but in the diplomatic arena—the entry of Italy into the conflict on their side in May. But this proved far less of a boon than they had hoped, as the Italians soon became bogged down in another bloody stalemate along their mountainous frontier with Austria-Hungary. And, on the Eastern Front, disaster followed disaster throughout the summer as German and Austro-Hungarian forces rolled back the Russians in Galicia and Poland. Catastrophe also overtook the gallant Serbs as they finally succumbed to an all-out offensive by the Central Powers. Bulgaria joined Germany and Austria-Hungary in this enter-

prise, and its adherence to their side went a long way toward offsetting the Italian presence in the Allied coalition.

ITALY JOINS THE ALLIES

Italy's decision to become a belligerent ended nine months of competition for its affections. The Italians, of course, had refused to side with their partners in the Triple Alliance when war broke out in 1914. Italy pointed to the defensive nature of the alliance, and however Austria-Hungary and Germany might base their actions on what they considered necessity, clearly they had attacked their neighbors. However, Italy implied that its services were available at the right price. As it turned out, the Allies could offer the best deal because much of the territory coveted by the Italians consisted of portions of the Dual Monarchy. Austria-Hungary, not surprisingly, was reluctant to part with them, especially since it had gone to war to preserve its empire. Germany could be more generous with Austrian territory and urged Vienna to grant Italy the Trentino, if this would be sufficient to purchase Italian neutrality. But this was far less than Italy could obtain by joining the Allies.

The conservative Premier Antonio Salandra favored the latter approach, which he justified on the basis of *sacro egoismo d'Italia* (the sacred egoism of Italy). Foreign Minister Sidney Sonnino, who was part English and had served briefly as Italian premier on three different occasions since 1906, agreed. But strong support existed for continued neutrality, both within parliament and among the people. The champion of this policy was Giovanni Giolitti, who had served as premier four times since 1892 and as recently as March 1914. Giolitti believed that Italy could gain its primary aims from Austria in return for neutrality and at no cost in blood or money. Salandra and Sonnino brushed aside such pleas for prudence and pushed hard for major territorial concessions as the price for joining the Allies.

THE TREATY OF LONDON

These demands proved embarrassing to Russia because, in addition to the Trentino and Trieste, a predominantly Italian port on the Adriatic, Italy also insisted on possession of Istria to the southeast as well as most of the Dalmatian coast along the Adriatic. Although the Italians referred to these territories as "unredeemed Italy," both Istria and the Dalmatian coast were predominantly South Slav in population. Russia, of course, felt obligated to defend the interests of its little Slavic brethren. Britain and France felt no such moral compunction, however, and persuaded St. Petersburg to agree to most of the Italian demands. The result was the Treaty of

London, signed on April 26, 1915. It yielded to Italy's desires on the Trentino, Trieste, and Istria, while also granting about one-third of the Dalmatian coast as well as many of the offshore islands and a free hand in Albania. If the Allies partitioned Turkey and the German colonies in Africa after a victorious conclusion to the war, Italy would also receive a share of these spoils.

Salandra and Sonnino made the agreement without referring the matter to parliament, much to the anger of Giolitti and a majority of the parliamentary parties. Confronted by this opposition, Salandra's government resigned. But Salandra refused to leave it at that. He appealed to Italian nationalists, who responded with widespread demonstrations and mob violence. These strongarm tactics, in part inspired by the former Socialist and future Fascist Benito Mussolini and the poet and superpatriot Gabriele D'Annunzio, effectively cowed the opposition to Salandra. He and his cabinet returned to office. The Treaty of London went into effect on May 23 when Italy declared war on Austria-Hungary, but Rome promptly violated the treaty by refusing to take similar action against Germany until August 1916. Italy's quarrel was with Vienna, not Berlin. The Germans also refused to declare war on Italy, preferring not to add to their list of opponents. Austria-Hungary viewed Germany's actions both before and after the Italian declaration as more in keeping with those of an enemy rather than an ally.

SHORTCOMINGS OF THE ITALIAN MILITARY

For the Dual Monarchy, Italy's entry into the conflict came as another in the series of disastrous blows that had rocked the country since it provoked war with Serbia in 1914. But the shortcomings of the Italian armed forces, industry, and natural resources helped reduce

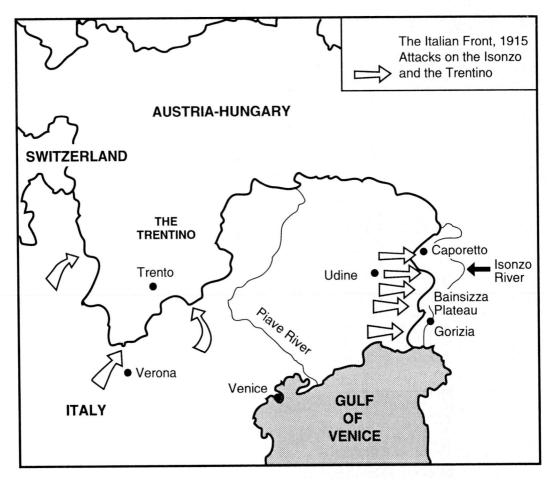

The Italian Front, 1915
Attacks on the Isonzo
and the Trentino

AUSTRIA-HUNGARY

SWITZERLAND

THE
TRENTINO

Trento

Caporetto

Isonzo
River

Udine

Bainsizza
Plateau

Piave River

Gorizia

Verona

Venice

ITALY

GULF
OF
VENICE

the impact. Italy could field an army of 875,000, but it was in some respects similar to that of Austria-Hungary. It was poorly equipped and short of both machine guns and artillery, especially heavy guns. Much of its leadership was also of dubious quality. Austria-Hungary could muster only 100,000 men against this new threat and, in view of its obligations against Russia and Serbia, had to accept a defensive role, despite Conrad von Hötzendorf's intense desire to attack the "perfidious Italians."

But the Dual Monarchy enjoyed one major advantage—the mountainous nature of the terrain along its 410-mile border with Italy. Various ranges of the Alps rose precipitously

around the large Austrian salient formed by the Trentino, which jutted deeply between northwestern Italy and an Italian salient on the east. Along the eastern edge of the latter salient, the Isonzo River flowed southward, before reaching the Adriatic. Mountains flanked it along much of its length before blending into a 20-mile-long plateau, varying from four to six miles in width. Known as the Carso, this plateau consisted of eroded limestone, wooded near its southern end but exceedingly barren to the north. Many extensive sink holes pitted its surface, making ideal defensive positions. Underground caves and natural passageways often connected them, creating a veritable honeycomb of shellproof quarters, supply dumps, and other facilities. Peaks and razor-sharp rocks festooned the moonlike landscape. The Carso was such a forbidding area that one observer referred to it as "a howling wilderness of stone sharp as knives."[1] The terrain to the north around the city of Gorizia was no better. A series of Austrian-dominated peaks overlooked the Isonzo from the east, making it devilishly difficult for the Italians to cross the river.

Uninviting as the Isonzo was, the Italians deemed it more promising than the deep Alpine ranges of the Trentino. The border also favored the Austrians because they held the highest ground all along its length as well as a large slice of the southern slope of the Alps. This made it far easier for them to menace northern Italy than it was for the Italians to move into Austrian territory. Since the Austrians had never trusted the Italians, they had fortified their marvelous natural positions to make them even stronger.

THE ITALIAN STRATEGY

The author of Italian strategy was 65-year-old General Luigi Cadorna, an ascetically handsome man, with a deeply-lined face. The son of a Piedmontese nobleman and general who had led Italian troops in the seizure of Rome in 1870, Cadorna was an artilleryman by training and an excellent organizer. He became chief of the general staff when General Pollio died in July 1914. A stern disciplinarian, he drove his men relentlessly with little consideration for their welfare. Although noted for his brilliantly analytical military mind, Cadorna persisted in repeated offensives on the Isonzo Front. In all, he was to fight 11 Battles of the Isonzo. The first four were spawned in 1915.

The objectives of each of them were to cross the river and capture the heights to the north and south of Gorizia before taking the city itself and opening the way to Trieste to the southeast. From there, Cadorna hoped to push through the pass known as the Ljubljana Gap into the plain of the Danube River. The Archduke Eugene commanded the Austrian troops in this theater, but the actual field commander on the Isonzo Front was General Svetozar Boroevich von Bojna. Boroevich ably organized his forces to make the most of their powerful natural defensive position.

The battles on the Isonzo Front had a grimly monotonous similarity. They required the Italians to force their way up steep heights against murderous enemy fire. In the Carso, among the dangers to the advancing troops were jagged shards of limestone, which flew like shrapnel when artillery shells exploded. These lethal fragments killed men in large numbers, while blinding many others. The First Battle of the Isonzo began on June 23, 1915, and lasted until July 7. The second battle followed as soon as July 18 and continued until August 3. Neither resulted in any appreciable gains. The third and fourth battles in October and November, though utilizing a much greater concentration of artillery, were no more successful. The Italian soldiers fought with a gallantry often unappreciated in the West, while the outnumbered Austro-Hungarian forces demonstrated considerable skill in defense. Troops of Slavic origin fought far more spiritedly against the Italians than they did against the Russians or Serbs. The cost of the four battles was on a par with the going rate on the Western Front and Gallipoli. The Italians suffered a quarter of a million casualties in the four battles, the Austrians 165,000. Only the onset of winter put an end to the bloodshed. But seven more battles of the Isonzo lay ahead.

---

[1] Sir James E. Edmonds, *A Short History of World War I* (London: Oxford University Press, 1951), p. 11.

AUSTRIA-HUNGARY
AND THE GALICIAN FRONT

The year 1915 started off far less auspiciously for Austria-Hungary on the Galician Front. Conrad von Hötzendorf was determined to stage an offensive there to push the Russians away from the crest of the Carpathians and to do so during the winter. But he needed German forces to bolster his own battered armies. His request for this aid led to a quarrel between General von Falkenhayn and the German general's rivals at *Oberost*, Hindenburg and Ludendorff. Falkenhayn did not want to part with the necessary troops, whereas Hindenburg and Ludendorff strongly supported Conrad. The German emperor eventually sided with the eastern generals and also agreed to their proposal for a second thrust to be made by their forces in East Prussia. They visualized a pincers movement that would drive deeply behind the Russian forward positions.

Unfortunately, their dreams of another Cannae fell far short of realization. In the north, they did gain a local victory in the Second Battle of the Masurian Lakes, but Conrad's operation in the south proved a dismal failure. The offensive in East Prussia featured attacks by the German Tenth and Eighth armies, which in early February 1915, succeeded in encircling the Russian Tenth Army in the Augustów Forest, just across the Polish border to the east of the Masurian Lakes. Almost 100,000 Russians were killed and at least 90,000 taken prisoner. Fought in swirling blizzards and intense cold, this "Winter Battle" was a brilliant tactical triumph for the Germans but, strategically, it failed to attain the ambitious hopes of Hindenburg and Ludendorff. They simply lacked the strength to continue the offensive in the face of Russian superiority in manpower. As a preliminary to the battle, elements of the Eighth Army had carried out

a diversionary assault in the direction of Warsaw on January 31. This attack was noteworthy because the Germans used gas for the first time at Bolimov, but it was nonlethal tear gas and the intense cold negated its effect.

Conrad's offensive in the Carpathians also unfolded in appalling winter conditions, which were even more severe in the higher elevations of the Carpathians. His chief instrument was the newly established South Army, consisting of both Austrian and German units and commanded by the German General Alexander von Linsingen. But Conrad also used the Third Army, headed by General Boroevich before Boroevich's transfer to the Italian front. Conrad's forces attempted to push the Russians out of the central Carpathians and relieve the besieged fortress of Przemyśl but failed totally. Instead of a great victory, Conrad had to settle for another demoralizing defeat as the Russians mounted a counterattack that captured Przemyśl and its 120,000-man garrison on March 23. Augmenting their strength with troops that had been engaged in the siege of Przemyśl, the Russians took the initiative. Russian General Radko Dimitriev's Third Army pushed the Austrians out of the Dukla Pass in April and appeared poised to break into the grain-rich Hungarian Plain. Farther west, they threatened Cracow, the major city of western Galicia. But the savage winter weather also took its toll on the Russian forces, which were near exhaustion and plagued by a severe shortage of both weapons and ammunition as well as reserves.

Despite Conrad's conspicuous lack of success in his operations since the start of the conflict, he maintained his enormous power over the conduct of the war. The chief of staff continued to make little effort to cooperate with the government and succeeded in designating more and more of the Austrian half of the empire as war zones under military control. Conrad even extended the army's

FIGURE 9–1 Russian supply personnel issue bread rations to troops on the Galician Front. National Archives

jurisdiction over major Austrian war industries. Conrad was less successful in Hungary where Hungarian Prime Minister István Tisza continued to wield great authority. Tisza also enjoyed extensive influence over the joint government's foreign policy and grew increasingly skeptical of Foreign Minister Leopold von Berchtold's ability to resist German pressure for Austro-Hungarian concessions to Italy and Rumania.

When Berchtold urged a negotiated peace in late 1914, Tisza played the decisive role in forcing him from office in January 1915. He also secured the appointment of his own close associate, Baron Burián, as Berchtold's successor. Tisza, Burián and Austrian Prime Minister Count Strürgkh, dominated the Dual Monarchy's foreign policy until late 1916,

but Tisza's influence was always strongest. The three men stood for both continuation of the war and resistance to German domination of the alliance. But in view of Austria-Hungary's dismal performance on the battlefield and the entry of Italy into the conflict, there was no disguising the Dual Monarchy's growing dependence on Germany.

GERMANY ACTS TO SAVE AUSTRIA-HUNGARY

The disastrous failure of Conrad's Carpathian offensive and the dangerous Russian counteroffensive that followed convinced General von Falkenhayn that Germany must save its ally from collapse. He proposed a major operation in Galicia to eliminate the

Russian threat to the Dual Monarchy once and for all. But, Falkenhayn was still not interested in becoming too deeply committed in the east. He was also concerned about the British naval assault on the Dardanelles, which took place at almost the same time as the fall of Przemyśl. This new development focused his attention on the need to open a supply route to the Turks. If this were to be accomplished, it would be necessary to crush Serbia and entice Bulgaria into an alliance. Falkenhayn also hoped to shift forces back to the Western Front in time to parry the next Allied offensive.

Hindenburg and Ludendorff did not agree with Falkenhayn's appraisal. They still visualized a giant Cannae operation with major attacks from the north as well as the south. Its objective would be the sealing off of the entire Polish Salient and, they hoped, the encirclement of huge numbers of Russian troops. To Falkenhayn, their scheme was far too grandiose. He doubted that success would be as easy or as sweeping as they believed, considering that the two arms of the proposed pincers movement were separated by 600 miles. Falkenhayn won out, and the German emperor approved his plan, providing for a major effort in the south with only a minor supporting operation by Hindenburg's forces in the north.

The plan had actually originated in Conrad's fertile mind. It provided for an attack in the foothills at the edge of the Carpathians in northwestern Galicia. In Falkenhayn's version, General August Mackensen's new 11th Army would deliver the primary blow with a frontal attack between the towns of Tarnow to the north and Gorlice on the south. The Eleventh Army consisted of eight German and four Austrian divisions. Germany's leaders had become convinced that Austro-Hungarian troops fought better when stiffened or "corseted" by German forces. Results seemed to

confirm their argument. Archduke Joseph Ferdinand's Austrian Fourth Army guarded Mackensen's left flank. Falkenhayn intended to break through the weak Russian Third Army and swing eastward behind three other Russian armies in the Carpathians.

Although nominally subject to the overall jurisdiction of Conrad and the AOK, Falkenhayn, who had moved his headquarters to the east, actually supervised the entire campaign. To say the least, dealings between the two chiefs of staff did not improve Austro-German relations. Falkenhayn did nothing to conceal his contempt for Austrian military prowess and treated the proud and highly sensitive Conrad as a subordinate in the most arrogant manner. He also saw to it that his eastern rivals Hindenburg and Ludendorff, already smarting over his rejection of their plan, played no part in the offensive. This widened the rift between OHL and *Oberost*.

Mackensen had recovered from the rout of his 17th Corps in the opening stages of the Russian offensive in East Prussia to lead his forces in the great victory at Tannenberg. He had also commanded the Ninth Army in the various German offensives in Poland during the last few months of 1914. Like so many other German generals, he had fought as a young officer in the Franco-Prussian War. Said to be a descendant of the chief of a Scottish Highland clan named Mackenzie, he played down this claim during the war. Now 66 and with a mane of white hair and white flowing moustache, he was strikingly handsome. He also got on well with the Austrians in marked contrast to both Falkenhayn and Hindenburg. Although he became one of the most successful generals of the entire war, many of his achievements were due in large part to his brilliant staff officers, most notably Colonel Hans von Seeckt, soon to become a general. Seeckt admirably performed his duties as chief of staff in the forthcoming campaign, but did so out of the limelight. He became the leading military figure in Germany during the early postwar era.

RUSSIANS CAUGHT BY SURPRISE

Falkenhayn moved the 11th Army into position with great secrecy, and Russian intelligence failed to discover the concentration. As a result, the offensive caught General Dimitriev's Third Army completely by surprise. Of Bulgarian birth, Dimitriev was one of Russia's better generals and had performed well in the fighting of 1914 and early 1915. But his forces held a considerable breadth of front, and the Central Powers enjoyed a marked numerical superiority at the point of attack with 11 divisions to only six for Dimitriev. The Russians were also woefully short of artillery, while the Germans unleashed a pulverizing bombardment by 250 heavy and more than 700 light guns on May 2, 1915. It was the most ferocious artillery assault the Eastern Front had experienced, and it created panic among the Russians. Many of them abandoned their positions, and when Mackensen's forces advanced, they made rapid progress. By the third day, they had virtually wiped out the Russian Third Army and had torn a gaping hole in the Russian line between Tarnow and Gorlice. German troops were soon over the border and into the Polish salient south of Lublin.

An even greater disaster now threatened the Russian Eighth, Ninth and 11th armies to the southeast in the Carpathians. Only an immediate withdrawal would save them from being outflanked. By the end of May, they and the fleeing remnants of the Third Army had fallen back to a line along the San and Dniester rivers, while three Austrian armies and the Austro-German South Army pursued them from their positions in the Carpathians. The Austrian Third Army recaptured the fortress of Przemyśl in early June. By the middle of the month, the Central Powers had retaken Lemberg and had pushed the Russians back to the Bug River.

The Russians had suffered a serious setback, and Austria-Hungary was free from the prospect of invasion, at least for the time being. Nevertheless, the extreme northeastern portion of Galicia remained in Russian hands. The offensive clearly had not resulted in total Russian defeat, but to Falkenhayn it had served its purpose, and his other goals beckoned. Austria-Hungary also had to face a new enemy on its southern flank since Italy's entry into the war in May. Conrad favored an all-out offensive against the Italians and urged Falkenhayn to shift German troops to the Southern Front for this purpose. However, Hindenburg and Ludendorff argued vehemently that this was no time to slacken the pressure on Russia and continued to visualize an operation that would culminate in a Cannae battle of encirclement. William II, enthused by the triumphs in the east that contrasted so vividly with the frustration in the west, supported them. The offensive would continue.

FIGHTING IN THE EAST CONTINUES

Hindenburg and Ludendorff urged an operation far to the east with the major thrust coming from East Prussia, utilizing forces under their control. They proposed to drive to Vilna in Lithuania and then swing south to Minsk, well beyond the Polish salient. They also called for the Austro-German forces in Galicia to drive northeastward toward the same goal. Falkenhayn again protested that this plan was far too ambitious and invited logistic problems. He preferred a more mod-

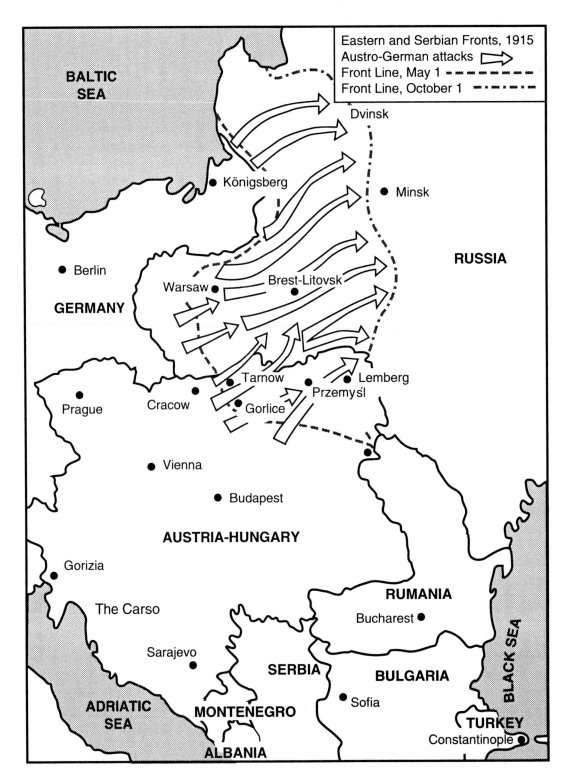

est operation farther to the west. It provided for the 11th Army to execute the main thrust from Galicia northeastward between the Vistula and the Bug rivers. The ultimate goal was Brest-Litovsk 125 miles east of Warsaw. Meanwhile, the German Ninth Army would attack eastward toward the Vistula, while the 12th Army would advance from East Prussia toward the Narew to the northeast of Warsaw.

Although Hindenburg and Ludendorff insisted that only their plan offered the prospect of a decisive victory that would force Russia out of the war, Emperor William supported Falkenhayn. While this debate over strategy was taking place, Falkenhayn took the lead in proposing a separate peace, which supposedly would not provide for the transfer of any Russian territory. The czar flatly refused the offer, remaining faithful to Russia's allies and the dream of eventual victory.

Falkenhayn's offensive began in mid-July and made progress everywhere but at a slower rate of advance than that following the Gorlice-Tarnow breakthrough. Stavka and General Mikhail Alexeyev, commander of the Russian Northwestern Army Group, realized that Russia must abandon the Polish salient and ordered a retreat. They left a garrison of 90,000 overage reserve troops to hold the old fortress of Novogeorgievsk on the Vistula to the northwest of Warsaw in an effort to slow the pursuit. The Germans simply bypassed it and took Warsaw on August 5. Like Liége, Namur, and Antwerp, Novogeorgievsk fell victim to the merciless pounding of siege howitzers. It fell on August 19. By the end of the month, the Germans had taken Brest-Litovsk, and the Polish salient had ceased to exist. But the Russians had avoided encirclement.

As far as Falkenhayn was concerned, the offensive had fulfilled his objective. It had eliminated the likelihood of a Russian threat to Austria-Hungary for the foreseeable future.

In fact, he had already begun to shift forces back to the Western Front and to the south for operations against Serbia. But Hindenburg and Ludendorff won Falkenhayn's reluctant agreement to continue attacks by their troops in the north and the Austrians in the south. The latter made little headway, except for the capture of the fortress city of Luck, but they suffered such heavy casualties from Russian counterattacks that they had to call for German reinforcements. Despite Conrad's efforts, the Russians continued to hold the extreme eastern angle of Galicia.

Hindenburg and Ludendorff were more successful, but their results again fell short of their hopes. They visualized a pincers movement by General Hermann von Eichhorn's Tenth Army attacking toward Vilna on the north and General Otto von Below's Eighth Army thrusting toward Grodno on the south. If all went well, they would cut off two Russian armies to the east of the Nieman River. Although Below's forces took Vilna in late September, the trap was slow in closing, and the Russians escaped. Nevertheless, by the end of September, the Germans had advanced to the Dvina River in Latvia near the Baltic port of Riga. They had also consolidated the front along a line running southward from there and passing 100 miles east of Brest-Litovsk before continuing on to the Carpathians.

It had been a long, disastrous summer for the Russians. The Germans had pushed them back 300 miles at the farthest point, clearing Poland, and creating a relatively straight front devoid of major salients. The campaign ranks as Germany's greatest triumph of the war. The Germans and their Austro-Hungarian allies had taken an estimated one million Russians prisoner and had killed or wounded almost as many. To be sure, the victory had not been cheap. The Central Powers had suffered approximately 650,000 casualties among them.

CZAR NICHOLAS ASSUMES MILITARY CONTROL

The magnitude of Russia's disaster fairly cried out for a scapegoat, and Czar Nicholas II's court circle found one in the Grand Duke Nicholas. The czar dismissed his cousin as commander in chief on September 5, 1915, relegating him to the position of military governor of the Caucasus region. The grand duke's fall was due less to the czar than to the efforts of the Czarina Alexandra and her adviser Rasputin. Nicholas II now left for the front to assume personal command of the army despite the fact that he had neither experience nor ability in military matters. He hoped to rally the Russian people to himself as leader of Holy Mother Russia in her time of desperate crisis. But by taking command, he tied himself and his dynasty directly to the direction of the war. When the next military failure came, the Russian people would not have far to look for another scapegoat. Clearly the grand duke had not been a gifted military leader, and his direction of the war had been far from inspired or consistent, but he was at least a professional soldier.

As his new chief of staff, the czar chose General Alexeyev, former commander of the Northwestern Army Group. Although a capable and hardworking officer who had been more responsible than the grand duke for managing the retreat during the summer, he was not a powerful personality or a great soldier. Like the czar, he tended to be indecisive and overly embroiled in minor details. Even more ominous than the czar's assumption of military command was the effect of his departure from the political scene in Petrograd.[2] While far from a strong or able

ruler, Nicholas did conduct himself with good intentions and a certain amount of common sense. In his absence, direction of the government fell more and more into the hands of Czarina Alexandra and Rasputin, much to the chagrin of the progressive political elements in Russia, who distrusted both of them and were especially contemptuous of Rasputin.

The causes of Russia's disaster in the summer of 1915, of course, ran far deeper than the questionable leadership of the grand duke. It is doubtful that anyone else would have been able to salvage the situation. The basic inefficiency, incompetence, and corruption present in both the political and military systems lay at the root of the problem. Woeful shortages of arms, including artillery, munitions, and even rifles as well as food and clothing plagued the army from start to finish. Ironically, weapons and supplies were often available but, for various reasons, officials tended to hoard them in depots and fortresses and were reluctant to issue them to the troops at the front. Many soldiers actually went into battle without rifles. They had to wait until their comrades were killed, freeing weapons for their use, providing, of course, that they did not meet death first. Russian military leadership was capable of dealing with the Austro-Hungarians on a basis of equality or even superiority, but it was markedly inferior to the Germans. Although outnumbering the Germans by close to half a million men, the Russians were unable to take advantage of this superiority because of poor organization, the inadequacy of the transportation network, and the vast expanses of the front and Russia itself.

But distance was also Russia's chief asset, along with a seemingly inexhaustible supply of manpower for use as cannon fodder. It provided endless room for retreat. Some of the Germans, most notably the eastern gener-

---

[2]Soon after the outbreak of the war, Nicholas II had changed the name of St. Petersburg, which was actually of German derivation, to the Russian Petrograd.

als—Hindenburg, Ludendorff, and Hoffmann—were sorely tempted to lunge into this vast void in pursuit of the victory they thought was so near. These men heaped scorn on Falkenhayn both during the war and afterward for not concentrating Germany's war effort on Russia. But there is no reason to believe that the adoption of their grandiose dreams of an eastern Cannae would have led to an earlier departure of Russia from the war. It almost certainly would have resulted in enormous logistic problems and an ever-expanding front.

CENTRAL POWERS EYE SERBIA

Falkenhayn was to claim one more victory for the Central Powers before the end of 1915—the conquest of Serbia. This, of course, had been one of his objectives all along, but the need to dispel the Russian threat to Austria-Hungary had taken precedence. An Austro-German invasion certainly would have been sufficient to overrun Serbia, but Falkenhayn hoped to encircle and destroy the Serbian army. This would be unlikely unless Bulgaria joined the Central Powers and attacked the Serbs from the southeast.

Bulgaria, like Italy, waited on the sidelines for months after the outbreak of the war, weighing offers for territorial gains from the two coalitions and attempting to divine which side would win. The Bulgars certainly had no love for Serbia, a sentiment that also held true for their other neighbors. Most of them had helped themselves to territory that the Bulgars had hoped to gain from the Balkan wars, while Rumania had acquired a portion of Bulgaria's own territory. Unlike the case of Italy, the Central Powers were in a better bargaining position than the Allies this time. They were able to offer large slices of Serbian as well as Greek territory, should Greece enter the war on the side of the Allies.

Despite the fact that King Ferdinand of Bulgaria was a member of the German family of Saxe-Coburg-Gotha and devoutly hated Russia, he was reluctant to enter the conflict until he felt certain which side would emerge victorious. The resounding success of the German summer offensive against Russia and the growing signs of Allied failure in the Gallipoli campaign finally persuaded him to join the Central Powers. On September 6, a month after the Allied landings at Suvla Bay, he signed an alliance with Germany and Austria-Hungary. As its reward, Bulgaria was to receive a free hand in Serbian Macedonia as well as a substantial portion of northeastern Serbia and a slice of Turkish Thrace to the southeast. In addition, the Bulgars would gain a part of Greece's Aegean coast and the return of the territory lost to Rumania, if those countries sided with the Allies. Germany and the Dual Monarchy agreed to attack Serbia within a month, while Bulgaria promised to strike five days later.

Meanwhile, the Allies had made arrangements to come to Serbia's rescue should the Central Powers attack their little Balkan ally. This would involve the landing of an expeditionary force at the Greek Aegean port of Salonika and an advance through the Vardar River valley into southern Serbia. Their ambitious plan soon became mired in the morass of Greece's domestic politics. The same tug of war between pro-Allied Premier Eleutherios Venizelos and pro-German King Constantine that had bedeviled Allied plans for operations against the Dardanelles and Gallipoli now cast doubt on the validity of this scheme.

The French took the lead in preparing to intervene as it became increasingly clear during the late summer that the Central Powers were massing troops along Serbia's borders. They convinced Britain to agree to the transfer of two divisions—one British and one French—from Gallipoli to Salonika. This decision also enabled General Joffre to remove the troublesome General Maurice Sarrail from France by placing him in command of the French force. Sarrail, who had started the war as a corps commander, had replaced General Albert Ruffey as head of the Third Army during the retreat prior to the Battle of the Marne. He had defied Joffre's order to abandon the fortress of Verdun, and his troops had maintained control of a salient around the city during the 1914 fighting. In fact, Verdun became the anchor point for the successful French stand on the Marne. Sarrail was a staunch republican in politics and soon became the darling of French leftist and anti-clerical groups, which became highly critical of Joffre's conduct of the war. Their opposition grew more intense when Joffre dismissed Sarrail from his army command in July 1916.

When news of Bulgaria's adherence to the Central Powers leaked out, Serbia asked Greece to honor its obligations under a defensive treaty signed in 1913. This agreement required the Greeks to come to the aid of the Serbs, if they were attacked by the Bulgars. Premier Venizelos readily accepted this commitment and asked for Allied troops to land at Salonika to take part in the common defense. But King Constantine pointed out that the Serbs had failed to mass 150,000 troops in the field opposite Bulgaria, as stipulated in the treaty. Since Serbian General Radomir Putnik had only been able to scrape together a total of 200,000 men and was facing an imminent Austro-German invasion, this was hardly surprising. King Constantine refused to honor Greece's commitment, however, and dismissed Premier Venizelos for good measure. Despite turning his back on Serbia, Constantine felt constrained to allow the Allied troops to land at Salonika. Venizelos had already lodged a diplomatic protest to give the impression that the Allies were acting

alone. Constantine continued this fiction, while maintaining a strange sort of neutrality. He informed Germany that he had no choice but to allow the landing in view of British naval power in the Aegean.

ALLIED TROOPS NO HELP FOR SERBS

The arrival of the Allied troops provided no help for the Serbs, however. They were far too few to be of much use under any circumstances, but the swift overrunning of Serbia by the Central Powers precluded any kind of cooperation. Austro-German forces with a combined strength of 250,000 men, under the overall command of General von Mackensen, the victor of the Gorlice-Tarnow offensive, crossed the Danube and Sava rivers into northern Serbia on October 7. Brilliantly planned by Colonel Richard Hentsch, who had ordered the German retreat from the Marne in 1914, and preceded by a vicious bombardment, the offensive made rapid progress. Belgrade fell within three days, and the Bulgars struck from the southeast with another 250,000 men the following day. General Putnik, realizing that his best hope lay in avoiding encirclement, retreated southward. But the Bulgarian Second Army cut the vital rail connection to Salonika, severing his escape route to Greece, while at the same time blocking the advance of the Allied forces from the south.

It soon became clear that Putnik would have to fall back toward the mountainous wasteland of Montenegro and Albania to the southwest. He fought a skillful retreat and managed to escape encirclement. By the end of November, his Serbian army had crossed into Albania, but its flight through the snow-clogged and frigid mountain passes turned into a nightmare. When this epic retreat finally ended at the Adriatic, only about 125,000 men had survived. Once there, Italian

FIGURE 9–2 Austro-Hungarian troops shoot blindfolded prisoners in Serbia. National Archives

and British ships took them to the nearby Greek island of Corfu. The French had seized Corfu in January, violating Greek sovereignty as well as an international treaty, dating back to 1863, that guaranteed Greek neutrality. The Serbs eventually took their place alongside the other Allied troops at Salonika. Pursuing Austrian troops conquered Montenegro and went on to occupy half of Albania, primarily to prevent additional expansion there by the Italians, who had already taken the Albanian ports of Valona and Durazzo and later moved into the southern part of that backward country.

Meanwhile, Sarrail's French forces, now consisting of three divisions, had penetrated beyond the Greek border. They reached a point 40 miles into the Vardar valley of Serbia before numerically superior Bulgarian troops forced them back. The British had refused to cross into Serbia but became involved in fighting along the border. Both Bulgaria and Austria-Hungary urged an operation to drive the Allies from Salonika. But Falkenhayn had once again accomplished his objectives—

elimination of Serbia and the opening of a supply route to Turkey. Seeing no strategic value in an advance into Greece and eager to turn his attention to the Western Front, he wisely refused to embark upon an additional distraction.

Logic would seem to have dictated an Allied withdrawal from Salonika. The British certainly favored this course, but the French refused to leave and indicated that they would view any British evacuation with distaste. Thus, the Allies established an entrenched camp around Salonika, nicknamed the "Bird Cage." They actually increased the size of its garrison during the following months. By 1917, it reached a total of 600,000 men, but its mission remained shrouded in uncertainty. The Germans contemptuously referred to this bloated, unproductive force in its entrenched position as the "largest Allied internment camp." It remained essentially inactive until the last few months of the war, while its troops were badly needed elsewhere. In view of France's insistence on the primacy of the Western Front, the decision to hold on at Salonika was one of the strangest of the entire conflict.

A DISMAL YEAR FOR THE ALLIES

As the fighting wound down in the Balkans, 1915 drew to its dismal end. For the Allies, it had been a year of almost unrelieved failure and disillusionment. For the Central Powers, it had been one of almost continuous success. The Germans had administered a series of defeats to the Russians. The much-humiliated Dual Monarchy had fought Italy to a standstill along the Isonzo, and the Turks had repelled the British attempt to force their way through the Straits. Bulgaria had joined the Central Powers and had participated in the destruction of Serbia. But despite their achievements, the Central Powers were no closer to victory. They had paid a high price in men, material, and wealth, while all their triumphs had been local ones in the last analysis. Stalemate continued on the Western Front, and despite the pummeling that Russia had experienced, it refused to make peace. Austria-Hungary, while finally rid of "the Serbian menace," and saved from any imminent Russian threat, now faced a bloody ongoing struggle with Italy. Worse yet, the tensions between its ethnic groups had grown more severe, and the morale of the army continued to decline, while its obvious dependence on Germany had increased.

Despite the indecisive nature of 1915, both sides looked to the new year with optimism, a quality that never seemed to be in short supply. Both were planning offensives on the Western Front, which they thought would surely win the war in 1916. Even Russia proved capable of one last throw of the dice. Again, all their hopes were doomed to frustration. The most dreadful year of the entire war was about to begin.

10

1916:
THE HELL OF VERDUN
AND THE SOMME

As hideous as 1915 had been, it paled by comparison to the ghastly events of 1916. It was during 1916 that the war reached new depths of horror, frustration, and desperation. Most notably, the Western Front witnessed two massive battles—Verdun and the Somme—that for concentrated slaughter were unmatched in history. But the Eastern Front also experienced a new and bloody paroxysm as Russia unleashed one last attack—the Brusilov offensive. Moreover, no fewer than six indecisive encounters unfolded along the rugged border between Italy and Austria-Hungary. When the year ended, Europe would never be quite the same again.

ALLIES PLAN WESTERN STRATEGY

On the Western Front, both sides planned offensives, which they hoped would bring them the victory that had proved so elusive.

French General Joffre believed that the Allied offensives of 1915 had failed because of a lack of coordination. What was needed, he thought, was for all the members of the alliance to undertake powerful offensives more or less simultaneously as part of an integrated process. In pursuit of this objective, he convened in December 1915 a conference of Allied military representatives at his headquarters in the Palace of Chantilly, 26 miles north of Paris. All accepted Joffre's plan and agreed to delay the start of their attacks until the summer of 1916 when Britain and Russia would be better prepared.

The British recognized that, despite the exceptionally enthusiastic response to Lord Kitchener's appeal for British volunteers, the new force needed to be trained and equipped before it could go into action. The British also finally concluded that it would be necessary to resort to conscription for the first time in the country's history to create an army large enough to make a massive contribution to winning the war. Many months would elapse before this force would be ready for combat. In addition, the Russians needed time to recover from the effects of their defeats in 1915. They also had to fit their army with the help of Western aid sent to the Arctic ports of Archangel and Murmansk. Moreover, the intervening months would enable the French and especially the British to strengthen their artillery in an effort to reduce the superiority that the Germans had so long enjoyed in these weapons of destruction. On February 14, 1916, General Joffre and British General Douglas Haig agreed that they would launch a joint offensive near the Somme River about 20 miles to the east of the city of Amiens in June.

GERMAN STRATEGY: STARVE BRITAIN, "BLEED" FRANCE

But Germany upset their hopes by launching an offensive of its own long before the summer arrived. The genesis of this plan lay in Falkenhayn's gloomy interpretation of the war and the prospect for continued deadlock. He had long ago discarded hope of achieving the breakthrough that other generals still clung to with increasing unreality. He had grown especially concerned about Britain. As an island power with the world's strongest navy, it was immune from invasion. Falkenhayn believed that two factors held the key to forcing the British to abandon the conflict. One was the adoption of unrestricted submarine warfare to inflict such heavy losses on British shipping that they would be starved into submission. The other was to deprive Britain of its "best sword" on the Continent—the French army. If Germany could destroy France's army, Falkenhayn felt that the British would not fight on alone.

But how could Germany eliminate the French sword? Falkenhayn grimly concluded that the only way to accomplish this was to kill so many French soldiers that France would be "bled white" and would have no choice but to make peace. At the same time, it would be necessary to carry out this mission without bleeding Germany white.

The next question was to determine the best way to accomplish this bleeding process. During 1915, Falkenhayn had made a good start by standing on the defensive and allowing the French to throw away their soldiers in huge numbers in Joffre's futile offensives. Would it not make sense to continue this approach? Unfortunately, two factors worked against it. Such a strategy meant a lengthy war of attrition. Falkenhayn feared that Germany could not win a long conflict. Perhaps even more pressing was the insistence of the emperor and the eastern generals as well as many other German leaders that Falkenhayn undertake an offensive in 1916. If it did not take place on the Western Front, the alternative seemed to lie on the Eastern Front. Falkenhayn, of course, did not believe that final victory could be won on that front. Also, the return to such a strategy would represent a triumph for the ideas of Hindenburg and Ludendorff and perhaps the loss of control over operations to them.

Falkenhayn finally arrived at an ingenious and cold-blooded solution. Germany must attack an objective, which was so important symbolically to the French that they would commit more and more troops to holding it. He visualized an attack on a narrow front to channel French defenders into an area where they could be destroyed by an unprecedented concentration of artillery. This huge display of firepower would enable Germany to conserve its own manpower. Weapons would do the work of men in Falkenhayn's view.

VERDUN CHOSEN AS TARGET OF GERMAN OFFENSIVE

Falkenhayn chose the salient around the fortified city of Verdun as the target for the German offensive. Verdun, lying astride the Meuse River, had been an important place in history ever since the Romans established a fortified camp there. Attila the Hun had sacked it in the fifth century when it was known as Verodunum. It gained its greatest fame in A.D.843 as the site of the signing of the treaty that divided Charlemagne's empire into three parts, two of which ultimately became the basis for France and Germany. Verdun was the scene of a tenacious but unsuccessful resistance to an invading Prussian army during the French Revolution. It was also the last major French bastion to fall in the Franco-Prussian War. After the loss of Alsace-Lorraine, following that conflict, the French created a powerful line of fortresses along their new border with Germany. Verdun, at its northeastern extremity, became the strongest position of the entire system. It had also anchored the French line at the time of

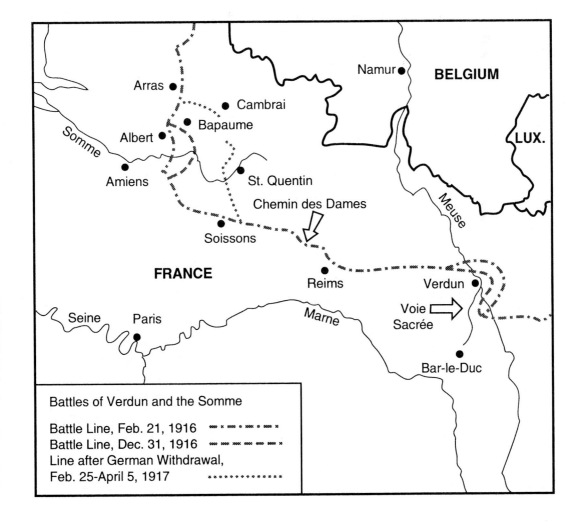

Battles of Verdun and the Somme

Battle Line, Feb. 21, 1916

Battle Line, Dec. 31, 1916

Line after German Withdrawal,
Feb. 25-April 5, 1917

the Battle of the Marne. Falkenhayn believed that both tradition and more recent events would entice the French to commit themselves unreservedly to the defense of the city.

In December 1915, Falkenhayn persuaded the German emperor to approve his plan. The assignment of luring the French into the killing ground of the Verdun salient went to the German Fifth Army, commanded by the Crown Prince William. But the operational planning as well as much of the authority over the army lay in the hands of General von Knobelsdorf, the tenacious, ruthless, and highly capable chief of staff to the crown prince. Knobelsdorf proposed to attack on both sides of the Meuse, which flowed northward from Verdun. He believed that this offered the best chance of capturing the city as quickly as possible.

Falkenhayn, however, was not interested in a swift conquest of Verdun or perhaps even taking the city at all. He wanted to limit the number of German troops committed to the operation and to keep the front narrow in order to channel French troops into the deadly fire of his artillery. Thus, he ordered the Fifth Army to attack only along the east bank of the Meuse. The object, of course, was to kill Frenchmen. Verdun could wait. It appears, however, that he never made this clear to either the crown prince or Knobelsdorf and certainly not to the German troops involved. It seemed likely that the soldiers would fight better if they thought that the capture of Verdun was their goal. The operation received the ominous code name *Gericht*, a German word meaning, among other things, a place of execution.

The Germans carried out preparations for the offensive with exceptional speed, efficiency, and secrecy. The latter quality contributed to the complacency of the French High Command, which persisted in viewing the Verdun salient as a quiet sector as it had been since shortly after the Battle of the Marne.

This was not the impression of French officers in the salient. They had received intelligence reports indicating a major German buildup in the area and warned that their position was not strong enough to withstand an attack. A special army delegation visited the salient in December and agreed completely with their appraisal. But General Joffre angrily insisted that the defenses of the salient were adequate. To say the least, he was wrong.

The position of Verdun was one of great natural strength, based on steep hills along the east bank of the Meuse and lower hills dissected by ravines on the west bank. It also boasted no fewer than 60 forts, 20 of them of major importance, arranged in three concentric rings around the city. Unfortunately, Joffre had reduced Verdun to a fortress in name only. The fate of Liége, Namur, and Antwerp convinced him that such bastions were death traps. He proceeded to strip Verdun's forts of most of their guns, and transferred them to strengthen his artillery during the 1915 Champagne offensive. After that, the defending forces essentially deserted the forts in favor of poorly prepared positions in the open. The French had only three divisions to defend the salient, two of which did not arrive until February 12, 1916, in belated recognition that something might actually be brewing opposite Verdun. They had only 270 artillery pieces of various kinds and quality.

On the German side of the line, six divisions, grouped in three corps, were to make the attack, with two more corps in reserve. But the key to Falkenhayn's plan was artillery. He had provided the greatest concentration of guns yet arrayed on such a narrow front—1,100 pieces, including 542 heavy guns and 152 mine-throwers. Among the awesome "heavies" were 13 "Big Bertha" siege howitzers, 17 Austrian 305-mm mortars and two 15-inch naval guns. The mine-throwers were particularly fearsome because they hurled huge containers of high explosives with immense destructive power. To assemble this vast mass of firepower as well as the troops and supplies for the operation, the Germans quickly and efficiently constructed ten new railroad lines and many supply depots.

BATTLE OF VERDUN BEGINS

Falkenhayn had planned to open his attack on February 12, the very day that the two new French divisions arrived in the salient. But a blizzard accompanied by fog forced postponement until February 21. The artillery bombardment began at dawn with unbelievable fury. It destroyed the poorly constructed French trenches, killed many of the defenders and shredded forests in the projected breakthrough area, yet despite this hurricane of steel and high explosives, not all the French in its path were killed. When the German infantry moved forward, they did not employ mass assaults. Instead, they sent patrols to occupy ground, which Falkenhayn believed the artillery would have already won. Much to their surprise, they encountered heavy resistance from the vastly outnumbered survivors, many of whom had to dig their way out after being buried alive by the shelling. As the Germans advanced, they unveiled a new and especially hideous weapon—the flamethrower. It created much panic among the French, until eventually they discovered that the men operating these awkward devices were terribly vulnerable. Any bullet puncturing a flamethrower's fuel tank immediately sent the operator to his reward.

German progress was disappointingly slow and casualties alarmingly heavy. Nevertheless, by February 24, the Germans appeared on the brink of a breakthrough at Verdun. Falkenhayn did not want a breakthrough, however, but the commitment of more French troops, which could then be destroyed. Joffre and his chief of staff, General de Castelnau, former commander of the Eastern Army Group, obliged. Castelnau visited the front and came away convinced that the French could hold the salient. Joffre agreed and dispatched enough reinforcements to create a new army, the Second. He also sent General Henri Pétain to command this force.

Pétain was a 60-year-old bachelor with far more than a passing interest in the opposite sex. In fact, the officer who brought the news of Pétain's appointment, had to interrupt the general during an amorous dalliance in a Paris hotel. Although of peasant stock, Pétain was elegant and aristocratic in appearance, with a trim athletic body and handsome face. Despite his love of women, he impressed his fellow officers as coldly austere and aloof. Politically, he hated the Third Republic with all its intrigue and self-seeking politicians. Refusing to cultivate friends in high places, he had even insulted President Raymond Poincaré on one occasion.

Seemingly lacking any ambition for promotion, Pétain had risen slowly in rank before the war and had fashioned an undistinguished record. He had particularly retarded his career by opposing the "offensive" mania that gripped the bulk of the officer corps. In fact, he had developed a counter-doctrine based on the killing power of artillery, correctly predicting that it would decimate attacking formations. With the outbreak of war, Pétain clearly demonstrated his ability during the fighting of 1914–1915 and rose rapidly in rank and responsibility. Despite his icy personality, Pétain retained a deep and sincere concern for his soldiers. He never looked upon them as mere cannon fodder, and their suffering moved him deeply. His attitude earned him their undying devotion in return.

When Pétain arrived at the front, he immediately received the shattering news that Fort Douaumont, the strongest fortress in the entire Verdun defensive system, had fallen to the Germans without firing a shot. The fort had become a mere skeleton of its former self. Only a fixed 155-mm gun in a revolving turret remained from its once formidable firepower. Its only defensive force was the small crew that manned this still powerful weapon. Unfortunately, a lone German company man-aged to infiltrate the fort, caught the garrison by surprise, and forced its surrender. This humiliatingly easy conquest of the symbol of Verdun's former strength spread deep gloom among the French and great elation among the Germans. The way to Verdun now appeared open.

Despite this inauspicious start to Pétain's new assignment, all was not lost. The French 20th ("Iron") Corps reached Verdun almost simultaneously with his arrival, and other

FIGURE 10–1   A French truck convoy transports reinforcements and supplies along the Voie Sacrée enroute to Verdun. Photo courtesy of Roger Sherman

reinforcements soon followed. Pétain quickly instilled new hope in the *poilu* (the hairy ones), as the French soldiers were called. The general also reorganized and increased the size and power of the artillery. And, of special importance, he ordered the widening and improvement of the road stretching northward from Bar-le-Duc to Verdun and requisitioned an enormous number of trucks. In the following weeks and months, a steady stream of troops and supplies moved along this route. It became the sole lifeline to Verdun, since German shelling prevented use of the only railroad. The road soon became known as *la Voie Sacrée* (the Sacred Way). Pétain also instituted a policy of relieving troops from the salient at regular intervals, replacing them with fresh forces. He hoped in this way to keep morale as high as possible.

The revitalized French halted the enemy advance on February 28 as German troops reached the point of exhaustion and fell victim to artillery fire from the west bank of the Meuse. Falkenhayn had previously refused to allow an attack against the west bank, but now he agreed to requests from the crown prince and General Knobelsdorf to undertake such an assault to eliminate the offending artillery. The new offensive began on March 6. Its primary objective was the capture of a barren hill ominously and prophetically known as *le Mort Homme* (Dead Man's Hill). Some of the strongest French field batteries were located there. If the Germans could capture the hill, they would not only eliminate these guns but would look down upon the neighboring ridge to the southeast, the Bois Bourrus, which sheltered a large concentration of heavy artillery.

FRENCH RESISTANCE STIFFENS

After another enormous bombardment, the Germans moved forward swiftly at first, aided by the surrender of over 3,000 French soldiers, whose morale had collapsed from the shelling. But the French stiffened their resistance when the Germans reached *le Mort Homme*, and the struggle for the hill dragged on for almost three months. It became perhaps the single most horrible encounter of the entire campaign, featuring almost constant shelling and bloody hand-to-hand combat. French batteries on Hill 304 to the west subjected the attacking Germans to such punishment that Knobelsdorf ordered its capture. On May 3, Hill 304 became the target of the most intensive barrage thus far. It lasted more than two days, causing unbelievable destruction and chaos. When it ended, the elevation of the hill had been lowered by 25 feet. However, despite this pounding, the Germans needed three days of close-quarter fighting to finish the job. The fall of Hill 304 contributed greatly to the operation against *le Mort Homme*, which the Germans finally captured late in May, ending their offensive on the west bank. The Germans had inflicted 89,000 casualties on the French, but their toll was almost as high—82,000. Both sides were clearly bleeding profusely.

Despite Pétain's resolute direction of the defense of Verdun, General Joffre grew increasingly irritated by Pétain's frequent demands for reinforcements to enable him to rotate troops from the salient. This approach diverted forces away from Joffre's pet scheme for an offensive on the Somme, set to begin in the early summer. Joffre decided to remedy this problem by promoting Pétain to succeed Langle de Cary as commander of Army Group Center, on April 19. He also chose General Robert Nivelle, who had commanded the Third Corps at Verdun, to take over leadership of the Second Army. Even though Nivelle remained subordinate to Pétain, he now had direct control over the forces in the salient and rallied them with the stirring cry, "They shall not pass!"

Two years younger than Pétain, Nivelle was also handsome and elegant in manner. His career had paralleled Pétain's to a considerable extent since the start of the war. He, too, had been a colonel in 1914 and had served with distinction as leader of an artillery regiment during the Battle of the Marne. Rapid promotion followed as he became commander of a division before taking over the Third Corps. However, in most respects, he was the direct opposite of Pétain. He was both a consummate politician, who loved the limelight, and a staunch believer in the *offensive á outrance* school of General Foch and Colonel Grandmaison. In his pursuit of victory, he was willing to accept heavy casualties without the qualms that troubled Pétain. He also abandoned his predecessor's rotation policy. Nivelle possessed both unlimited ambition and self-confidence as well as the ability to captivate politicians. He soon overshadowed Pétain as the rising star of the French army.

Nivelle quickly put his offensive philosophy into action, in part at the urging of General Charles Mangin, commander of the Fifth Division. A 49-year-old veteran of the colonial army, Mangin had grown hard and ruthless during various campaigns in Africa, being wounded three times in the process. Forbidding in appearance with a cruel mouth and a square jaw, he provided a sharp contrast to Nivelle physically, but shared his dedication to the offensive and was even less concerned about casualties. His men referred to him as "the Butcher." Nivelle agreed that Mangin should lead an attack to recapture Fort Douaumont on May 22, but the Germans repulsed this hasty and ill-conceived assault and decimated Mangin's troops. It was not a happy start to the new partnership, and Mangin went into eclipse for the time being.

As the Battle of Verdun dragged on from one bloody month to another, it took on a momentum of its own. Verdun became a sym-

bol to the French, which, as Falkenhayn had foreseen, they would not abandon. Yet, while Falkenhayn was bleeding the French, he was also bleeding his own forces, and as the battle dragged on he considered calling off the offensive. The crown prince had long since favored an end to the carnage, but General Knobelsdorf remained a true believer. He persuaded both men to try again with an all-out effort to capture the last ring of forts to the south of Fort Douaumont.

The Germans launched their attack on June 1 with Fort Vaux to the southeast of Fort Douaumont as its first objective. They reached the fort on the following day, but for the next five days the small garrison of 600 French defenders put up an incredible resistance under the inspiring leadership of Major Sylvain-Eugéne Raynal. The major had been seriously wounded three times during the war and walked with the aid of a cane. Forced down into the interior of the fort, Raynal and his men fought the Germans in narrow underground corridors, which were only five feet high. The action unfolded in stifling heat as well as total darkness, broken only by flashes from grenade explosions and the glow of flamethrowers. At times, dense smoke added to the discomfort. Worse yet, the French suffered from a severe shortage of water, which eventually ran out entirely, and from the stench of both rotting bodies and human excrement. The latter became an increasing problem after the Germans captured the last latrine. Finally, on June 7, Raynal realized that his men could resist no longer and surrendered. The crown prince later chivalrously received Raynal, treating him with the honor worthy of such a gallant warrior.

GERMANS PREPARE NEW ATTACK

Following the fall of Fort Vaux, the Germans prepared to attack Fort Souville, the final major position blocking them from the last ridge overlooking Verdun. Morale appeared near the breaking point in some French units. But on June 12, Falkenhayn received alarming news of a Russian offensive, led by General Brusilov, that threatened disaster for the Austro-Hungarian forces in its path. He decided to break off the offensive at Verdun for the time being and shifted three divisions to the Eastern Front. However, the Russian menace ultimately proved less serious than originally believed, and later in the month Knobelsdorf persuaded Falkenhayn to resume the assault against Fort Souville.

This time, the Germans had a trump card to play, a new and especially lethal form of poison gas—phosgene—which they called "Green Cross" gas because of the markings on the shell cases. On the night of June 22, the Germans launched a gas attack against the French artillery and at first knocked out many of the gun crews. But, like Falkenhayn at Ypres in 1915, General Knobelsdorf had limited faith in the new weapon and early the next morning switched to a high-explosive barrage. The German infantry swarmed forward and drove to within 1,200 yards of the last ridge above Verdun, but they were able to advance no farther.

FAILURE OF THE GERMAN ASSAULT

The failure of the German assault on June 23 proved to be the turning point in the epic of Verdun. The Allies opened their offensive along the Somme on July 1, and although Knobelsdorf resumed his assault on July 10, it bogged down within two days. A few Germans occupied part of Fort Souville on July 12 and briefly glimpsed the city of Verdun two and a half miles away. But French counterattacks beat them back. Knobelsdorf still harbored hopes for another attack, but the crown prince had clearly

had enough. He persuaded the emperor to transfer Knobelsdorf to the Russian front on August 23. Five days later, William also dismissed Falkenhayn and replaced him with Hindenburg as chief of the German general staff. The indispensable Ludendorff remained at the right hand of Hindenburg. The emperor offered him the title of second chief of staff, but Ludendorff refused and chose instead to become first quartermaster general. In practice, Hindenburg and Ludendorff shared authority over operational decisions. Falkenhayn's departure technically came as a result of his inability to foresee Rumania's entry into the war on the side of the Allies in late August 1916. But clearly his failure at Verdun had prepared the way. He had lost his long struggle for supremacy with the eastern generals.

Hindenburg and Ludendorff visited the Verdun battlefield soon after taking command. They were shocked by what they saw and immediately ordered an end to offensive operations there. Pétain also ordered General Nivelle to refrain from further piecemeal counterattacks and to conserve his men for a major counteroffensive later in the year. Pétain insisted that the French must have superiority in manpower and especially artillery at the point of attack. In the following weeks, he amassed 650 guns, more than half of them heavy pieces. They included two new Schneider-Creusot 400 mm railway guns of great range and penetrating power. These behemoths were even more lethal than the German Big Berthas.

FRENCH COUNTERATTACK PLANNED

While Pétain carried out the overall planning, Nivelle took charge of detailed preparations and perfected the concept of the "rolling" or "creeping" barrage. In this approach, advancing troops were to "hug" a churning curtain of artillery shell explosions that "rolled" forward at a walking pace of 100 yards every four minutes as the gunners changed elevation on their pieces and the fuse settings on shells. This tactic avoided the need to lift artillery fire to the next objective, which in the past had often resulted in the barrage "running away" from the infantry if they were held up by uncut barbed wire or other obstacles, and had allowed the defenders to regain their firing positions. The offensive's main objective was the recapture of Fort Douaumont.

The French Second Army began its preliminary bombardment on October 19 and continued intermittently until the start of the ground attack on October 24. In the process, French guns knocked out well over half the German artillery, while the monster shells of the railway guns so devastated Fort Douaumont that the Germans had to abandon it. The French began their advance in thick fog and were on top of the enemy defenders before they realized what had happened. By the end of the day, Fort Douaumont was back in French hands. On November 2, General Mangin's forces recaptured Fort Vaux after the Germans had evacuated. A second French counterstroke on December 15 succeeded in pushing the Germans back to a line two miles beyond Fort Douaumont. This action finally brought the Battle of Verdun to a close.

Soon after it ended, the battle claimed one more victim—General Joffre. Despite his remarkable domination of the French war effort since 1914, he could not survive the swelling chorus of criticism over his direction of the war, especially the carnage of Verdun and the undeniable fact that he had neglected its defenses. In late December, he received a promotion to marshal in recognition of his contributions, becoming the first man to receive this honor since 1870. But shortly afterward, he joined the many generals that he

had relegated to the sidelines. His successor was not Pétain, the chief architect of France's gallant defensive stand and eventual successful offensive at Verdun. Instead, the vibrant Nivelle, who had been more visible in the final victory, took Joffre's place, completing his spectacular rise from obscurity.

THE HIGH COST OF VICTORY

During the ten months of savage fighting, the French suffered at least 377,000 casualties, of which more than 162,000 were killed or missing. German casualties totaled at least 337,000, including more than 100,000 killed and missing. Other estimates are considerably higher for both sides. But these enormous numbers do not capture the utter horror of the many engagements that made up the Battle of Verdun.

Certainly horror was never in short supply in any of the battles of World War I, but Verdun holds a special place in this respect. The ingredients, which gained it this dubious distinction, included the concentrated area of the front, the incessant artillery duels, and the great length of the struggle. The constant deafening roar of the guns and the appalling effects of the shells on both men and nature virtually defy description. Nowhere else during the war did so small an area suffer such extraordinary devastation. Shells reduced forests to fields of tangled splinters and then obliterated them altogether as one crater replaced another. Eventually, no vegetation remained at all. Rain turned the tortured clay of the salient into a gelatinous mud clogged with corpses and parts of bodies. In some areas, the ground was composed more of human flesh and bone than of earth. Shell craters filled with a liquid ooze, and their slopes became so slippery that men who took cover in them or fell into them literally drowned. Many of the troops on both sides never saw the enemy. All they experienced was the dreadful crescendo of the artillery and the sickening impact of shells on their comrades and themselves.

To both French and German survivors, life in the Verdun salient was equivalent to being condemned to hell. Few of them ever got over the experience. But the impact was perhaps greatest on the French. To be sure, Pétain's system of frequent relief of troops spared them prolonged periods in the salient, until Nivelle abandoned this humane approach. But it also meant that most of the French army spent time in this inferno. The Germans refused to adopt such a policy, and their troops who survived had suffered a much longer term in hell, being removed only when they were totally exhausted. But the number of German soldiers with memories of Verdun were far fewer, and the effect on German morale overall was not as great. Firsthand accounts of Verdun abound. One that is especially poignant is to be found in the May 23, 1916, diary entry of a French lieutenant, who was later killed by an artillery shell:

Humanity is mad. It must be mad to do what it is doing. What a massacre! What scenes of horror and carnage! I cannot find words to translate my impressions. Hell cannot be so terrible. Men are mad![1]

EVENTS LEADING UP TO THE SOMME BATTLE

And then there was the Somme. It was to the British what Verdun was to the French, a struggle of grotesque horror. Generals Joffre and Haig had intended the Somme offensive to be a joint operation in which both countries would contribute massive forces. But the German offensive at Verdun diverted more and more French troops to defend the salient, transforming the Somme into a primarily British operation. This was ironic because General Haig had not been happy with the choice of the site for the battle. He had much preferred Flanders but went along with the Somme out of deference to Joffre. The area selected was certainly not ideal. The Germans not only dominated the high ground there, as they did over most of the front, but had established an exceptionally powerful defensive position in the chalk ridges. It included two main systems, each consisting of several lines of trenches complete with deep underground shelters. Thick belts of especially heavy barbed wire 40 yards deep protected the approach to each system. The Germans had also fortified the villages and wooded areas as well as the chalk quarries and pits scattered between the two systems. They had begun construction of a third system, which was almost completed, and in some areas a fourth system had been started. Churchill later described the overall effect as "undoubtedly the strongest and most perfectly defended position in the world."[2]

When the British began their great offensive, they were operating under new leadership. General Haig, of course, had succeeded General French as commander of the BEF in December 1915, but a change had taken place at the War Office as well. Kitchener had perished while on his way to Russia aboard the cruiser *Hampshire* to visit the Eastern Front. *Hampshire* struck a mine off the Orkney Islands north of Scotland on June 5, and Kitchener was never seen again. Lloyd George took his place, much to the disgust of General Sir William Robertson, Chief of the Imperial General Staff. Robertson, who had managed to diminish Kitchener's influence in the aftermath of the Gallipoli fiasco, did not relish the prospect of another strong personality in the War Office, much less a civilian such as Lloyd

---

[1]Quoted in Alistair Horne, *The Price of Glory: Verdun 1916* (Harmondsworth: Penguin Books, 1964), p. 236.

[2]Winston Churchill, *The World Crisis*, Vol. III (New York: Charles Scribner's Sons, 1927), p. 171.

George. Relations between the two men were strained from the start and grew steadily worse.

But Robertson got on very well with Haig. Both men were Scottish and had served in the army in India, but they differed greatly in background. While Haig traced his descent from an old family that had made a fortune by distilling whiskey, "Wully" Robertson was of working-class origin and had made his way up through the ranks. Robertson was exceptionally determined and a most able administrator. He admired Haig and agreed with him on most things, including the belief that civilians should be kept from interfering in military matters as much as possible. The two men also shared the conviction that the Western Front was all-important.

Haig had few close friends, although he had cultivated good relations with King George V. Extremely serious and utterly humorless, Haig's personality was as cold as Pétain's, but unlike the French general, he had no rapport with his troops. One of the most handsome leaders of the war, he looked extremely dashing with his well-trimmed mustache, penetrating gray eyes, and well-tailored uniform. Although he was painfully inarticulate in speech, he had a flair for writing. Unfortunately, he used this gift to express such obsolete views as the "role of Cavalry on the battlefield will always go on increasing." His contention that bullets had "little stopping power on a horse" was even less inspired. Intensely religious, he attended the Presbyterian services of the Church of Scotland every Sunday.

His high degree of self-confidence and self-righteousness has prompted some observers to compare him to the great general of the English civil wars of the seventeenth century, Oliver Cromwell. Like Cromwell, Haig seems to have believed that he was carrying out God's work on the battlefield. In other respects, he was quite unlike Cromwell.

Although a capable corps and army commander under General French, especially in the defense of Ypres, Haig was unimaginative in his approach to offensive warfare. An old cavalryman, he thought only in terms of massive attacks aimed at achieving the elusive breakthrough, after which cavalry would exploit the opportunity and bring victory. Haig was willing to accept heavy casualties as the price of this success.

There was no immediate strategic objective to be gained in the area around the Somme River that General Joffre had selected for the great 1916 offensive. The nearest point of any real significance was the key railroad junction of Busigny, but it lay 60 miles away. In terms of World War I distances, it might just as well have been on the moon. The site's only notable advantage was its location at the hinge between the British and French forces. This provided the opportunity for both nations to participate in the operation. It does not appear that Joffre really expected a major breakthrough. To him, the offensive would be just another opportunity to wear down the enemy through the war of attrition, which by now he had accepted as being in the nature of things. But Haig did not share Joffre's pessimism. He aimed at nothing less than a breakthrough. To accomplish this, Haig would rely upon General Sir Henry Rawlinson's Fourth Army to make the main attack on either side of the road between Albert and Bapaume. Albert lay about a mile and a half west of the front line on the British side, and Bapaume 10 miles east on the German side.

General Sir Edmund Allenby's Third Army would make a diversionary attack to the north of Rawlinson's forces in an effort to lure German defenders away from the primary thrust. To the south of Rawlinson, the French Sixth Army of General Marie Émile Fayolle would attack on both sides of the Somme. The area chosen for the offensive extended for 25 miles in a southerly direction with a small salient jutting eastward near the juncture of the British and French positions. Once the attacking troops had scored a breakthrough, General Sir Hubert Gough's Reserve Army, consisting of three cavalry and two infantry divisions, would dash into the gap and attack the enemy's rear.

Opposing this formidable Allied host was the German Second Army, commanded by General Fritz von Below. The Allies enjoyed a considerable initial advantage in numbers with 18 British and five French divisions to only six German. But Below's forces could take comfort in the tremendous strength of their defensive position. They also had the benefit of superior training and long experience in the bloody business of trench warfare. While the French troops could match the Germans in their knowledge and skill in battle, the British forces were green for the most part. Eleven of the 14 British divisions that were to participate in the initial assault were composed either of volunteers who had answered Kitchener's call in 1915 or territorials. The conscript army, still in process of formation, would not take part in the offensive.

Unfortunately, despite the lapse of time since the volunteers had entered the army, they had received inadequate training. This was the result of both poor organization and facilities as well as the tendency to rush recruits into the trenches to guard against the possibility of a German attack, such as the one at Verdun. The British regular officers also doubted the volunteers' capacity to master the art of war, feeling that only years of experience would suffice for this. As a result, they instructed the troops to advance across no-man's-land almost shoulder to shoulder in waves, assuming that the recruits were incapable of anything more sophisticated. They also burdened the soldiers with packs and equipment weighing 66 pounds, making

a slow rate of advance virtually inevitable. In effect, the men would walk upright toward the German positions, almost as if they were marching on the parade ground.

The British had devised a bombardment scheme that they believed would make this leisurely stroll relatively safe. First would come the usual heavy shelling, lasting several days. It would demolish the enemy trenches and tear huge holes in the vast fields of barbed wire blocking access to them. Then, as the troops left their own trenches to begin their advance, the artillery would switch to a barrage that formed a curtain in front of them. This supposedly would allow them to approach close to the enemy positions without heavy casualties. Then, according to a pre-programmed interval, the barrage would lift to the next objective, providing the opportunity for the infantry to reach the first trenches before the defenders could emerge from their shelters. The attacking forces would overwhelm the Germans and enable the troops following them to move on to the second trench line, again preceded by the curtain barrage. Obviously, the entire advance had to unfold according to a precise time schedule with close coordination between artillery and infantry.

SOMME OFFENSIVE BEGINS

Haig chose June 29, 1916, as the date for the start of the Somme offensive. He also planned a preliminary bombardment of five days' duration. It began on June 24, but heavy rains forced postponement of the ground attack until July 1. In the meantime, the bombardment continued. The Allies employed the largest array of artillery utilized up to that time. The British concentrated over 1,500 guns on their front of 18 miles, but only 46 were heavy pieces. The French used 2,000 on their front of only seven miles, including 900 heavy guns, firing high-explosive shells.

British gunners alone fired over a million and a half rounds. Unfortunately, approximately a million of them were shrapnel, which had little effect on the German barbed wire. The British munitions industry, despite Lloyd George's efforts, was not yet able to produce sufficient high-explosive shells with instantaneous fuses, which were really needed for this task. Those that were available had limited destructive power. Many shells also proved defective. Despite severe damage to their first line of trenches, the bulk of the Germans opposite the British had survived in their deep shelters. When the bombardment lifted, the German troops scurried up the shafts with their machine guns and took up positions in shell craters in plenty of time to intercept the British as they moved across no-man's-land.

The French enjoyed far greater success with their bombardment. In addition to their advantage in heavy guns and howitzers, their gunners possessed much more experience and skill than their British counterparts. This combination resulted in the destruction of the enemy barbed wire and defensive positions in the path of their advancing troops. The new super-heavy 400-mm guns smashed most of the deep dugouts as well. French infantry also employed far more sophisticated tactics than those of the British. Unlike their allies, they avoided advancing in straight lines and in tightly bunched masses. Instead, they darted forward in small groups and in short bounds. As they pushed across no-man's-land, the French utilized whatever terrain features offered protection and provided covering fire for each other.

French forces to the north of the Somme launched their attack at the same time as the British and easily captured the first enemy position. Their comrades to the south of the river, who started two hours later, caught the Germans completely by surprise and were even more successful, pushing beyond the second line in several places. British troops just to the north of the French also achieved good results, in part because they benefited from the heavy French bombardment. At the northern end of the front, General Allenby launched his diversionary attack with considerable caution. He did not relish the role that Haig had assigned to his forces; it deliberately aimed at diverting the attention of the Germans to his sector. Although some of his troops reached their objectives, others did not. Even those that had scored initial gains were eventually forced to fall back with heavy losses.

BRITISH SUFFER HEAVY CASUALTIES

A far worse fate befell the main British attack in the center of the front, where three corps clambered out of their trenches promptly at 7:30 A.M. on July 1. They moved forward with great enthusiasm in intense heat and under a vivid blue sky, confident that the bombardment had obliterated the enemy and that their officers would lead them to victory. Their optimism proved short-lived. Advancing at a slow walk in four successive lines at intervals ranging from 50 to 100 yards, the British troops soon ran into trouble. Some encountered heavy fire shortly after emerging from their trenches. Others moved forward without incident until within 100 yards of the enemy line, when they fell victim to lethal machine gun fire. Still others made it as far as the enemy barbed wire, only to find it intact or only slightly damaged. The British soldiers made excellent targets for German machine guns while searching frantically for a way through this vicious wilderness of tangled metal. The slow-moving infantry also failed to keep pace with the curtain barrage, and the barrage itself failed to destroy the enemy machine gun nests.

A German participant in the struggle recalled the carnage on his portion of the front in these words:

...a series of extended lines of British infantry were seen moving forward from the British trenches. The first line appeared to continue without end to right and left. It was quickly followed by a second line, then a third and fourth. They came on at a steady easy pace as if expecting to find nothing alive in our front trenches....A few minutes later, when the leading British line was within 100 yards, the rattle of machine gun and rifle fire broke out from along the whole line of craters....and immediately afterwards a mass of shells from the German batteries in rear tore through the air and burst among the advancing lines. Whole sections seemed to fall, and the rear formations, moving in closer order, quickly scattered. The advance rapidly crumpled under this hail of shells and bullets. All along the line men could be seen throwing their arms into the air and collapsing never to move again. Badly wounded rolled about in their agony, and others less severely injured crawled to the nearest shell-hole for shelter....Again and again the extended lines of British infantry broke against the German defence like waves against a cliff, only to be beaten back.[3]

Here and there, some of the British troops were more successful and actually captured portions of the enemy's first trenches. Some even reached the second line but could not hold out in their exposed forward positions. Of the 100,000 British troops who took part in the attack on July 1, over 57,000 became casualties before the day ended. Of these, almost 20,000 died. Not even the inferno of Verdun had witnessed such slaughter. But despite this fearful bloodletting, news of the disaster was slow to filter back to Generals Haig and Rawlinson. Assuming that the shelling had destroyed the German wire and that the attack was proceeding according to plan, they remained optimistic for some time. The advancing units, pinned down by withering fire, found themselves cut off from communications with the rear. Without radio contact, they were dependent on runners, but few of them could make it back across bullet-swept no-man's-land.

Those who suffered most in this holocaust were the wounded. Many of them lay where they fell or managed to crawl into shell holes and remained there until after dark or much later. Some did not escape the horror until as late as July 4. During their long wait for rescue, many were hit again and again by bullets raking the battlefield. One observer has estimated that as many as a third of the fatalities on the first day died as a result of wounds from which they might possibly have recovered had they received medical attention within the first few hours.[4]

Even after it became apparent that the assault had failed, Haig was not aware of the full extent of the catastrophe. He thought that his forces had suffered only 40,000 casualties and considered this toll acceptable. He refused to abandon the offensive, but now it was clear that available manpower would not allow attacks all along the line. Instead, he decided to strike in the south where the greatest progress had been made.

General Rawlinson, who had been appalled by the carnage of July 1, chose a new approach, an attack at dawn rather than in full daylight, hoping to surprise the enemy. He directed it against the German positions on Longueval Ridge on July 14, preceded by a heavy bombardment but one lasting only five minutes. The British dashed forward rapidly and did achieve surprise. They quickly captured the German first and second positions along a front of over three miles. For a time, it appeared as though an even greater breakthrough was in the offing on the left flank at the Bois des Foureau, or what the British called the "High Wood." But the cav-

---

[3]Ibid. pp. 177-178.

[4]John Keegan, *The Face of Battle* (New York: Vintage Books, 1977), p. 269.

FIGURE 10–2 Canadian forces go over the top on the Somme Front in October 1916. National Archives

alry, which was to exploit this opportunity, was slow in moving up, and the Germans, as usual, rushed reinforcements to plug the gap. Fierce resistance in Delville Wood also halted progress on the right flank. Whatever chance there might have been for a major gain was now gone. The struggle soon deteriorated into a prolonged battle of attrition as the Allies inched forward in the following weeks.

TANK WARFARE PLANNED

Despite the grinding nature of the fighting and continued heavy casualties, Haig persisted in his dream of a breakthrough. To achieve this, he planned another major as-

sault in mid-September. But this time he would employ a secret weapon—the tank. The idea of creating an armored vehicle operating on treads, such as those of American-made caterpillar tractors, had been in the air for some time. Colonel Ernest Swinton had actually proposed a weapon of this type as early as October 1914, but the British War Office had shown no interest, considering it impractical. Winston Churchill, then at the Admiralty, recognized its potential, however, and diverted naval funds to the development of a "landship." In the summer of 1915, the depressing stalemate prompted the army to reconsider the matter, and a joint service committee began work on such a vehicle, using

Swinton's specifications. By February 1916, a working model had come into existence, and the War Office ordered 150 of them. The work went on in remarkable secrecy throughout this period.

The creators of the tank had urged that it not be used until available in large enough numbers to assure a major breakthrough in the enemy line. Lloyd George and other cabinet ministers agreed. But Haig insisted that he be allowed to use those available in his September offensive. Supported as usual by Robertson, he got his way. "Tank" was actually a cover name to maintain secrecy. Since the first model, the ungainly Mark I, resembled a large water cistern, or reservoir, the British ultimately agreed to call it a "tank." It came in both a "male" model with cannon in side positions and a "female" version mounting machine guns.

Haig's insistence on using tanks in his offensive proved unfortunate. Not only did it destroy the secrecy that had shrouded development of the weapon, but the tanks were too few to be decisive and also proved quite unreliable. Only 32 of them reached the assembly point for the offensive. Of these, 23 either broke down or foundered in the shell holes and mud of the battlefield. The nine tanks that did see action created panic among some Germans. One tank attacked a trench and forced the surrender of 300 men. Four others helped capture a village. But it was a case of too little, too soon. Once again, there would be no breakthrough.

There also would be no end to the battle. It continued until November when it finally wound down in the snow and mud of early winter. The five months of the Battle of the Somme had enabled the Allies to create a bulge in the German line 30 miles long and seven miles deep at its farthest extent. The long struggle had cost the British at least 420,000 casualties, the French almost 200,000, and the Germans about 450,000. To be sure,

along with Verdun, it had sapped German strength on the Western Front, but at a staggering price. And, to add a crowning irony, Hindenburg and Ludendorff, who had replaced Falkenhayn shortly before the September offensive, decided to shorten their line by abandoning the area fought over throughout the Battle of the Somme. They worried about German losses, a shortage of reserves, and the fact that only their third defensive system remained intact. Ludendorff immediately began construction of a powerful new position 25 miles to the rear.

STALEMATE IN THE WEST

When completed, the Germans called the new system the Siegfried Line, while the Allies referred to it as the Hindenburg Line. The Germans began to pull back to the new position in February 1917 and completed the operation in April. By withdrawing from the tormented earth of the Somme battlefield, they shortened their front by 27 miles, enabling them to make better use of their manpower and confronting the Allies with an even more formidable defensive barrier.

As British casualties mounted during the Battle of the Somme, Lloyd George, the war secretary, grew more skeptical of Haig's direction of the war and concluded that the general should be replaced. But Robertson staunchly defended Haig, who also retained his influence with King George and other cabinet ministers and was even promoted to the rank of field marshal early in 1917. Haig remained in charge on the Western Front, but relations between him and Lloyd George continued to deteriorate. Lloyd George was more successful in getting rid of Prime Minister Asquith, whose position had weakened steadily since the creation of the coalition government in 1915.

CHANGES IN BRITISH LEADERSHIP

While in many respects an able peacetime minister, Asquith's temperament did not suit him for the role of war leader. Colorless and remarkably unwarlike, he had often been indecisive in foreign policy even before the war and had allowed Sir Edward Grey to run the Foreign Office virtually without interference. After the war began, Asquith failed to capture the imagination and devotion of the people. Instead of acting as a vigorous leader with clear ideas on how to achieve victory, he served as more of a mediator between opposing viewpoints. His critics accused him of having no real policy at all.

Among those critics, Lloyd George grew more and more dubious about Asquith's ability to manage the war effort. And since he himself possessed both unlimited self-confidence and great ambition, Lloyd George saw himself as Asquith's logical successor. He moved steadily closer to the Conservative leaders in the coalition, most notably Andrew Bonar Law, Sir Edward Carson, and Sir Max Aitken, all of whom shared Lloyd George's concern about Asquith. In the fall of 1916, Lloyd George proposed the establishment of a four-man war cabinet, with himself in charge, to direct the conflict. Asquith would remain prime minister but with jurisdiction over domestic affairs only. Asquith angrily rejected the proposal, and Lloyd George as well as the Conservative ministers resigned. Now confronted by a major cabinet crisis, Asquith had no choice but to resign as well. On December 7, Lloyd George became prime minister, and both Asquith and Grey found themselves relegated to the sidelines. Arthur Balfour, a Conservative who had served as prime minister from 1902 to 1905, took Grey's place. Although Asquith

vowed to support the new government, he felt betrayed by Lloyd George. The split between the former Liberal colleagues did not heal and actually widened in the following years.

HEAVY LOSSES, FEW TANGIBLE GAINS

As the fighting subsided on the Western Front in the waning days of 1916, the peoples of France, Britain, and Germany, as well as their soldiers, were bewildered and horrified by the stupefying sacrifice of lives at Verdun and the Somme. Not only had hundreds of thousands of men died or suffered terrible wounds, but the meat-grinder nature of these operations and the almost total absence of any tangible gains weighed heavily on the human spirit.

Elements of the French army at Verdun had demonstrated that they could take no more and had surrendered. In the later stages of the Battle of the Somme, some German units had shown a similar weakening of morale. The British volunteer army betrayed fewer of these symptoms, perhaps because it was still too new to life in the trenches and no-man's-land. On the home front, there were few families in any of the belligerent nations that had not experienced the loss of loved ones. War weariness had clearly set in and a desire for peace grew steadily. Even some political leaders questioned the sanity of continuing the war. But those who controlled the governments and led the armies could not abandon hope that somehow they could find a way to defeat the enemy and prove that the slaughter had not been in vain. Although they might toy with the idea of a negotiated peace, they prepared their plans for the campaigns of 1917. Death clearly had not abandoned center stage in the ongoing drama on the Western Front.

11

1916: ATTRITION IN THE SOUTH AND EAST

A year and a half of fighting had brought a combination of success and defeat to both Austria-Hungary and Russia as 1916 began. But the bloody failures weighed much more heavily in each country and weakened the two governments. War weariness, repeated evidence of gross inefficiency, and massive casualties had increased dissatisfaction with the czarist regime in Russia. Criticism of the czar, the czarina, and Rasputin mounted, and relations between the Duma and the government steadily worsened. In Austria-Hungary, the grievances of the subject nationalities had grown more pronounced, and some army units had proved unreliable. Czech, Rumanian, and Ruthene troops in some cases had refused to fight or had gone over to the enemy during the operations of 1915.

A serious food shortage had developed in Austrian-governed areas of the Dual Monarchy from the very start of hostilities due to a disappointing harvest in 1914. The problem grew even more serious in 1915. Agriculturally rich Hungary had fared much better. But in an amazing demonstration of narrow-minded selfishness, the Magyars refused to share more than a small portion of their grain supply with the Austrians. Vienna, of necessity, turned to Germany for help, increasing its dependence on its ally. But the Germans had food problems of their own and provided only limited aid. Food shortages persisted in the Austrian half of the empire and, indeed, grew steadily worse.

THE POLITICAL SITUATION IN THE EAST

Austrian political leaders looked increasingly to the possibility of a negotiated peace as the only way to avoid both military and economic collapse. But the foreign minister,

Stephan von Burián, remained adamantly in favor of a policy of no compromise, believing that the victories over Russia and Serbia would lead to peace overtures from the Allies. By the end of 1915, István Tisza, once as strong a supporter of the war as Burián, was entertaining second thoughts. He, too, feared that the Dual Monarchy could not stand the strain much longer and believed that Burián's position was too rigid. More and more he came to favor a negotiated settlement. However, despite his insistence on the eve of the war that the empire must not absorb any more Slavs, he now looked forward to the partition of Serbia between Austria-Hungary and Bulgaria. Even Conrad advocated a separate peace with Russia, while continuing to fight "perfidious Italy." But he was even more hostile toward Serbia and insisted that the Dual Monarchy annex the entire country.

Despite the conversion of Tisza and Conrad theoretically to the cause of a settlement, in practice their position was essentially the same as that of the foreign minister. They, too, made no effort to initiate negotiations. Like Burián, they hoped that the triumphs over Russia and Serbia would prompt the Allies to seek a negotiated peace. An initiative from the enemy would place the Central Powers in a better position to seek territorial compensation. But however the leaders of Austria-Hungary might speculate about the achievement of war aims, the Russians had no intention of sacrificing their Serbian ally or making other concessions. Instead, Petrograd was determined to pursue the war to a victorious conclusion. Certainly no peace overture would be forthcoming from the Western Allies at this time. Since no diplomatic solution came to pass, Conrad took steps to convert his long-cherished dream of an attack against Italy into reality. He visualized an offensive that would punish the Italians for their desertion of the Triple Alliance.

AUSTRIA-HUNGARY PLANS CAMPAIGN AGAINST ITALY

Conrad hoped to deliver a staggering blow to Italy by thrusting out of the Trentino toward the all-important rail center of Padua 25 miles to the southeast. If his forces could take Padua, they would sever rail communications to the Italian troops along the Isonzo. Another 20-mile advance would bring them to the sea, completely cutting off the northeastern Italian salient. Conrad's optimism, somewhat shaken earlier, had returned in full bloom by the end of 1915. One reason for this was his army's remarkable recovery from its disastrous early defeats. It had found replacements for the heavy losses of 1914-1915, although at the price of reducing physical requirements for new recruits. Officers remained in short supply, however, largely due to continued insistence that they be drawn primarily from the Austrian and, to a lesser extent, Magyar and Czech populations. By early 1916, the army had added 20 new divisions. Improved artillery, including both field guns and howitzers, had also become available in large numbers, although there were still shortages of some weapons, most notably light machine guns and trench mortars.

Despite this marked improvement, Conrad needed German cooperation to carry out his ambitious plans for the Trentino offensive. In December 1915, he asked Falkenhayn to provide replacements for nine Austrian divisions that he wished to shift from the Eastern Front to Italy, but Falkenhayn refused. The German chief of staff had no faith in Conrad's scheme. He insisted that at least 25 divisions would be necessary to execute it properly, far more than were available. Falkenhayn also argued that even a successful offensive in northern Italy would not result in that country's exit from the war. But most importantly, he had no intention of diverting strength away from his attack at Verdun, scheduled to begin in February 1916.

Although angry at this rebuff, Conrad remained determined to carry out his plan. Without informing Falkenhayn, he shifted the nine Austro-Hungarian divisions and considerable heavy artillery from the Russian front to the Trentino to help create a striking force of 15 divisions and various other detachments. He planned to attack in early March 1916, oblivious to the fact that the front in the Trentino ran along the peaks and glaciers of the Alps where suitable weather could hardly be expected so early. It should not have come as any surprise when heavy snow prevented the start of the offensive until the middle of May.

Meanwhile, General Luigi Cadorna had launched another assault along the Isonzo River. Although he had been planning this operation for the summer in keeping with a pledge given at the Chantilly Conference in December 1915, he speeded up his timetable in response to General Joffre's plea for help to relieve German pressure at Verdun. Accordingly, he launched his attack on March 11, despite the persistence of winter conditions. He struck to the north and south of Gorizia, but after making two small penetrations in the enemy line, his operation bogged down. This Fifth Battle of the Isonzo lasted until March 29, although the main fighting occurred during the first week.

Even before the battle had ended, Cadorna had received ample warning of Conrad's impending assault from the Trentino. It was difficult to disguise such a large concentration of troops and material. Utilizing his internal lines of communication, Cadorna shifted forces to meet this threat. He also alerted General Roberto Brusati, commander of the Italian First Army on the Trentino front, to prepare his forces to meet the enemy assault. But Brusati resented Cadorna's interference and refused to believe that Conrad would actually stage a major operation in this rugged area. As a result, he and his troops were surprised when the attack came. Conrad opened his offensive on May 15 with General Dankl's 11th Army in the vanguard and the Third Army of General Hermann Kövess von Kövessháza in reserve to exploit the anticipated breakthrough. This disposition proved a mistake because the assaulting troops of the 11th Army were spread too thinly over too wide a front.

AUSTRO-HUNGARIAN DRIVE HALTED

The short but devastating bombardment preceding the attack dislodged huge segments of rock from the lofty peaks, creating avalanches that obliterated large sections of the first enemy positions. Aided by Brusati's lax preparations and despite the appallingly difficult terrain, the Austro-Hungarian troops pushed forward. By the end of the month, they had captured the town of Asiago in the valley of the Adige River, and only one more ridge of mountains blocked their access to the plains of northern Italy. But it proved enough. Tenacious Italian resistance, along with the rigors of advancing in the mountains, slowed the drive. As the front widened, it also proved necessary to move the Third Army into the line. This created a problem of coordination and disrupted the offensive's momentum. During the first few days of June 1916, it became apparent that there would be no breakthrough. To add to Conrad's difficulties, General Aleksei Brusilov opened a major Russian offensive on June 4 that threatened to destroy the entire Austro-Hungarian position on the Eastern Front. Although Conrad persisted in continuing operations in the Trentino, on June 17 he had no choice but to officially terminate his offensive and transfer eight divisions to deal with the danger from Brusilov.

Cadorna had already mounted a counter-attack on June 16, and ten days later Conrad ordered a general retreat to a more easily defensible position. The withdrawal required abandoning about half the Austro-Hungarian gains, but the new line held. Conrad's great plan died amid mutual recriminations. He criticized General Dankl for bungling the operation, while General Kövess took the chief of staff to task for a faulty plan of attack. Falkenhayn had been right all along. Conrad lacked the strength to carry out his offensive successfully and had so depleted his forces on the Eastern Front that they proved terribly vulnerable to Brusilov's assault. Casualties as usual were heavy for both sides in the Trentino campaign—147,000 for the Italians, 81,000 for the Dual Monarchy.

ITALIANS MOUNT ISONZO OFFENSIVE

General Cadorna was eager to take advantage of the Austro-Hungarian concentration in the Trentino by undertaking another offensive along the Isonzo River. To provide as great a chance of success as possible, he halted his attack in the Trentino in mid-July and began to shift forces from there to the Isonzo soon afterward. Again capitalizing on his internal lines of communication, he quickly massed 22 divisions in two armies, the Second and Third, against the Austrian Fifth Army's nine divisions. He also built up a great advantage in artillery. Cadorna opened his attack on August 6 with the intention of capturing Gorizia. He gained complete surprise since the Austro-Hungarians did not think that the Italians could transfer their forces from the Trentino so rapidly. The Italian Second Army seized the formidable Monte Sabotino to the north of Gorizia and the Third Army took Monte San Michele to the south on the edge of the Carso. By August 9, Gorizia itself was in Italian hands. But the

drive soon foundered along the rugged slopes just to the east of the town and in the rocky desolation of the Carso. This Sixth Battle of the Isonzo drew to a close on August 17. It had created a bulge three miles deep along a 15-mile front.

But Cadorna was far from finished. He unleashed a Seventh Battle of the Isonzo on September 14 with the purpose of widening the salient around Gorizia, which was vulnerable to artillery fire. But by now the Austrians had reinforced their positions, and Cadorna's offensive accomplished nothing. Instead, it became the prelude to the Eighth and Ninth Battles of the Isonzo in October and November, respectively. These relatively minor engagements extended the salient into the Carso slightly, but the gains were hardly worth the human cost. In the four battles from August to November, the Italians suffered over 126,000 casualties, the Austro-Hungarians more than 103,000.

POLITICAL REPERCUSSIONS IN ITALY

The shock of the Austrian offensive in the Trentino resulted in the fall of Premier Antonio Salandra. His government had experienced increasing internal and external strains since it forced Italy's entry into the war in May 1915. Salandra depended on the support of a coalition of interventionists in and outside of the Italian Parliament. All of the interventionist groups saw the war as necessary, if Italy were to gain territory, but they differed sharply on other matters. Salandra, Foreign Minister Sonnino, and their supporters favored the maintenance of the European balance of power after the war and hoped to avoid hostilities with Germany. But other interventionists believed that Italy should approach the conflict as a crusade for the establishment of democracy in Europe and favored war with Germany as a step in that direction. They also desired the creation of a widely based coalition government. But Salandra and his followers were opposed to this and favored a virtual wartime dictatorship with little parliamentary participation.

For the first year, Salandra had his way, despite the fact that the interventionists actually represented a minority in the Italian Parliament. Italy's declaration of war had resulted from the violent demonstrations in the streets and the intimidation that they had created. Once the country had entered the conflict, however, the former neutralist parties in Parliament either rallied to support the war effort or at least refused to oppose the government.

When Italy took up arms in May 1915, Salandra and his followers had expected the war to be short. They believed that Austria-Hungary was near collapse and would soon make a separate peace with Russia. Instead, the disastrous Russian defeats that summer, coupled with the bloody and inconclusive Italian offensives on the Isonzo, led to increasing criticism of Salandra's conduct of the war. To make matters worse, Salandra and Cadorna clashed over the respective powers of the military and the government in regard to overall direction of the conflict. The Austrian offensive in the Trentino during 1916 aggravated their disagreement, especially since shortly before the start of the attack, Cadorna had promised Salandra that the Trentino posed no danger. The issue came to a head in June, just as the offensive was winding down, when the premier openly criticized the general's defensive measures in the Trentino as inadequate.

The whole affair weakened Salandra, and on June 10, 1916, he lost a vote of confidence in Parliament, leading to his resignation two days later. His successor, the 78-year-old Paolo Boselli, was a political nonentity who was acceptable because he seemed to threaten none of the other leaders. Boselli formed a coalition government representing all political parties except the revolutionary Socialists. Despite his effort to create greater national unity, his government proved badly divided throughout its 16 months of existence.

Although the Trentino offensive led to the downfall of Salandra, the Italian army had at least prevented the Austro-Hungarians from breaking into the plain of northern Italy. Some have attributed the failure of Conrad's operation to the success of the Brusilov offensive on the Eastern Front. But it is clear that the combination of insufficient Austrian forces, difficult terrain, and tenacious Italian resistance had dashed Conrad's hopes even before General Brusilov began his assault. The spectacular Russian breakthrough on the Eastern Front ended any possibility of resuming the attack in Italy, however, and plunged the Dual Monarchy into a serious crisis.

ORIGINS OF THE BRUSILOV OFFENSIVE

The Brusilov offensive had its origin in the Russian promise, given at the Chantilly Conference in December 1915, to undertake a military operation in June 1916. It was to precede the Anglo-French assault along the Somme by a few days to prevent the Germans from shifting troops to the Western Front. However, the German offensive at Verdun prompted Joffre to beg for at least a limited offensive at an earlier date. In keeping with his usual chivalrous response to such pleas, Czar Nicholas II agreed. The Russian attack came to the east of Vilna (Vilnius) on March 18 near the point where General Alexei Kuropatkin's Northern Army Group and the Western Army Group of General Alexei Evert came together. Elements of each army struck along a 90-mile front to the north and south of Lake Naroch.

FIGURE 11–1   A supply cart provides ammunition for Russian machine guns. National Archives

The Russians enjoyed a big superiority in numbers over General Eichhorn's German Tenth Army and unleashed their heaviest bombardment to date against enemy positions. But the Germans had constructed strong fortifications and resisted ferociously. Although the Russians succeeded in overrunning the first two enemy positions, their subsequent attacks were poorly coordinated, and a sudden thaw turned the ground into a morass of mud. The Germans, as usual, rushed in reinforcements as well as a heavy concentration of artillery. They subjected the Russians to a severe bombardment before counterattacking in late April and pushing them back to their original line. The hastily planned offensive had accomplished nothing. It had cost the Russians 110,000 casualties to only 20,000 for the Germans and cast doubt on the possibility of carrying out the major operation in June which Russia had promised at the Chantilly conference.

This disastrous failure also convinced both Generals Kuropatkin and Evert that further Russian attacks against the Germans would be futile. Both men were cautious and unimaginative, and Kuropatkin was no stranger to defeat, having commanded the Russian forces in Manchuria during the Russo-Japanese War. The two military leaders insisted that the best strategy was to remain on the defensive. But General Brusilov, who had recently succeeded General Ivanov as commander of the Southwestern Army Group, did not share their reluctance.

When the czar convened a conference of his army group commanders in April, Brusilov urged a major offensive by all three army groups more or less simultaneously. He argued that only such a joint operation would prevent the habitual German practice of shifting forces to meet isolated Russian attacks, as had happened in the Battle of Lake Naroch.

Brusilov proposed that his own army group deliver the main thrust against the weaker Austrians in the south. But Kuropatkin protested that he could not possibly attack before fall, and Evert clearly was reluctant to pin down Germans, while Brusilov carried out a far easier task against the forces of the Dual Monarchy. Sensing the collapse of his entire plan, Brusilov now suggested that Evert carry out the major attack after his own forces struck the Austrians in a diversionary thrust to lure German reserves to his front. Czar Nicholas, overcoming his initial uncertainty, agreed, and Evert also reluctantly went along with the proposal. The French, who were eager for the major attack to come against the Germans, enthusiastically concurred.

RUSSIANS REVISE THEIR STRATEGY

Brusilov had been one of the few bright lights among Russian commanding generals during the first 20 months of the war. He and his staff officers believed that Russian offensives had been too obvious, too ponderous, and too slow. This combination had led to repeated disasters. They decided to take a different approach in their new offensive, emphasizing surprise and speed of execution. Instead of the usual prolonged bombardment that eliminated any chance of surprise, and an advance by huge masses of tightly bunched men who offered perfect targets, they chose a shorter but intense period of shelling, followed by the rapid advance of smaller numbers of shock troops. The latter would infiltrate as quickly as possible into the enemy's first position. A second echelon would then move up to strengthen the initial attacking force, while two additional waves of troops would pass through the first line to fall upon the second and third positions.

Conducting his preparations in great secrecy, Brusilov provided intensive training to the troops engaged in each step of the operation. To confuse the enemy, he planned to attack all along his front of over 200 miles. This would stretch his forces rather thinly, but it would also keep the enemy guessing about where the main thrust would come and make it difficult for him to concentrate his reserves.

The Russian army, like the Austro-Hungarian, had made a remarkable recovery from earlier disasters. It had found replacements for the huge number of men lost in the great summer defeats of 1915. Factories had greatly increased production and were now turning out 100,000 rifles a month. Western Allied aid had also reached the front by way of the ports of Archangel and Murmansk in Russia's Arctic north as well as Vladivostok in the Far East. Machine guns and artillery were now plentiful. However, despite these obvious signs of improvement, many of the old weaknesses persisted. The Russian army was still top-heavy with generals of little ability, daring, or imagination. The fighting of 1915 had also inflicted dreadful punishment on the lower ranks of the officer corps as well as noncommissioned officers. Russia's old standbys—inefficiency, corruption, indifference, poor planning, and clumsy execution on the battlefield—all remained. So did the shortcomings of the country's communications network, although the retreat of 1915 had brought the army closer to its sources of supply.

The Brusilov offensive originally was to start in mid-June, but the initial success of Conrad's Trentino campaign prompted General Cadorna to request a Russian attack as soon as possible to reduce the pressure on his Italian forces. Moreover, Joffre again appealed for Russian help to distract German attention away from Verdun where the drive on Fort Vaux was underway. Once again, the czar agreed to act according to the dictates of chivalry. Brusilov would attack on June 4 and Evert supposedly would strike ten days later.

RUSSIANS MAKE LIGHTNING GAINS

Although Brusilov had stressed secrecy, he did not catch the Austro-Hungarians by surprise. They were aware of his preparations and had even intercepted a message on June 3, ordering the start of the attack, but they did not seem alarmed. Their attitude quickly changed when the Russian Eighth Army smashed through all three positions of the Austrian Fourth Army on the first day of the assault. They unwittingly contributed to the Russian success by massing too many troops in the first line and not enough in reserve. The Russians soon opened a gap 20 miles wide in the enemy front. The Russian Ninth Army also scored remarkable progress against the Austro-Hungarian Seventh Army at the extreme southern end of the front. Only the Southern Army, consisting of nine Austrian and one German division for stiffening, held its ground. Panic gripped many units, and some Czech and Ruthene troops gave up without resistance. In other cases, artillery units fled the battlefield, leaving the infantry, which they had been supporting, in the lurch. By the end of the first week, the Austro-Hungarian front had dissolved, and the Russians had pushed forward as much as 25 miles. They captured 200,000 prisoners by June 23.

As news of the disaster became ever more ominous, Conrad and the AOK teetered on the verge of panic. Having transferred nine divisions to the Trentino, Conrad had no reserves to employ in an effort to stem the Russian flood. He had no choice but to appeal to Falkenhayn for help. Although the German chief of staff was most reluctant to do so and was thoroughly disgusted with Conrad's behavior, he felt obliged to comply.

Five divisions from Hindenburg's reserve as well as four divisions from the Western Front made their way to bolster the Austrians. Conrad also recalled eight of his own divisions from the Trentino.

The continued success of Brusilov's offensive depended on prompt action by Evert to the north, but Evert repeatedly delayed the start of his assault. Despite the fact that he had great numerical superiority, he insisted that he was not ready. His dilatory behavior allowed the Germans to shift forces from opposite his front to help stall Brusilov's advance. When Evert did finally attack on July 3, he did so half-heartedly and made little progress. Fierce fighting again developed near Lake Naroch, and the Russians, advancing in the traditional mass formations, absorbed heavy losses. Evert's assault came much too late and was much too ineffective to provide any real help for Brusilov. The combination of stiffening resistance and growing logistic problems slowed the latter's momentum. By the end of July, it was clear that the offensive had essentially run its course.

THE TIDE SHIFTS

But Brusilov refused to accept the fact that the situation had changed. He insisted on continuing his attacks, and General Mikhail Alexeyev, the chief of staff, shifted reserves from Evert's front to increase Brusilov's striking power. Unfortunately, now that he had the luxury of greater resources, Brusilov resorted to the battering-ram tactics he had originally rejected. His casualties soared accordingly. The logistic situation also worsened as the inadequate Russian rail lines behind the front became overtaxed, while the Germans had the advantage of better rail facilities, including lateral lines that enabled the speedy transfer of troops and supplies. Brusilov scored his final success at the ex-

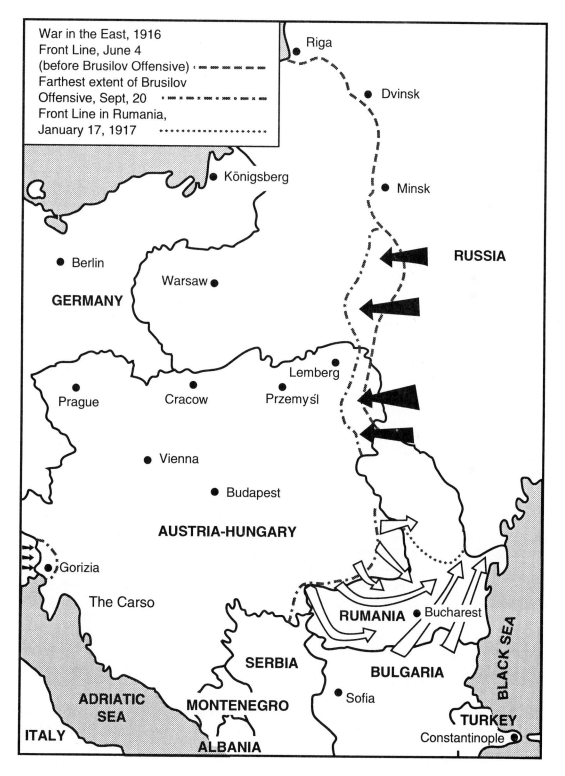

War in the East, 1916
Front Line, June 4
(before Brusilov Offensive)
Farthest extent of Brusilov
Offensive, Sept, 20
Front Line in Rumania,
January 17, 1917

Riga

Dvinsk

Minsk

Königsberg

RUSSIA

Berlin

Warsaw

GERMANY

Lemberg

Prague

Cracow

Przemyśl

Vienna

Budapest

AUSTRIA-HUNGARY

Gorizia

The Carso

RUMANIA

Bucharest

SERBIA

BULGARIA

ADRIATIC
SEA

MONTENEGRO

Sofia

BLACK SEA

ITALY

TURKEY

ALBANIA

Constantinople

treme southern end of the front as his forces conquered all of Bukovina, the Austrian province wedged between the southeastern end of Galicia and the northernmost tip of Rumania. Once again the Russians menaced the Carpathian passes. However, the Central Powers were soon able to stabilize the front. Although Brusilov tried anew in September, he had little success. By October, his great offensive had ended. Its later stages represented a definite return to the war of attrition. In all, the Brusilov campaign had cost Austria-Hungary 750,000 casualties, almost 400,000 of them prisoners. The Germans had suffered 350,000 killed, wounded, and missing. But Russia's victory had been as expensive as the great defeat of 1915. Its losses numbered about one million men.

RUMANIA ENTERS WAR ON ALLIED SIDE

The Brusilov offensive also played a role in Rumania's entry into the conflict on the side of the Allies. It is usually contended that, since 1914, Rumania had been playing the Allies and Central Powers against each other, while striving to gain the best possible territorial deal as the price of its participation in the conflict. Actually, it appears that Ion Bratianu, the Rumanian prime minister, had concluded that the Allies would win the war at least as early as the German failure in the Battle of the Marne. The long delay in Rumania's decision to intervene was the result of Bratianu's cautious policy of preparing his country both diplomatically and militarily for this crucial step. Among other problems confronting him was the attitude of King Carol, who was willing to accept neutrality but was opposed to going to war with Rumania's former allies, in part because of the fact that he was related to William II of Germany. After Carol's death in

October 1914, his nephew Ferdinand, who succeeded him, was more than willing to allow Bratianu to determine foreign policy. Ferdinand's wife, a granddaughter of both Queen Victoria of Britain and Russia's Alexander II, staunchly supported the Allies.

During 1915, Bratianu concentrated on gaining Allied approval of Rumanian territorial demands. If it had not been for the spectacular German success over Russia during the summer and the Allied failure at Gallipoli, he almost certainly would have brought Rumania into the war that year. During 1916, Bratianu focused on improving Rumania's military prospects. He insisted on Allied offensives, both in the East and West, to coincide with his country's intervention. The Brusilov offensive and the Somme operation satisfied this demand. He also gained Allied promises to supply Rumania with 300 tons of war material per day until the end of the conflict. In addition, Russia agreed to send 200,000 men to help Rumania against a possible Bulgarian attack from the south. Finally, Bratianu sought assurance of an Allied offensive from their entrenched camp at Salonika against the forces of the Central Powers in Serbia and Bulgaria. Negotiations over the latter issue actually delayed final agreement for several weeks.

The Rumanians signed a political and military alliance on August 17 in Bucharest. Under its terms, they were to receive not only Transylvania but also the large area of the Banat to the south. On August 27, Rumania declared war against the Central Powers. It was not an auspicious time. The Brusilov campaign had clearly bogged down, and the Central Powers had intercepted diplomatic messages indicating that Rumania's intervention was imminent. Falkenhayn had failed to foresee this Balkan complication, an oversight that resulted in his ouster as chief of staff, but the indecisive bloodbath at Verdun and the Allied offensives at the

Somme and in Russia had clearly paved the way for this decision.

German and Austro-Hungarian forces quickly responded to the new challenge. The Allies had urged Rumania to concentrate most of its strength against Bulgaria, while using the powerful natural position of the Carpathian Mountains and Transylvanian Alps to remain on the defensive against Austria-Hungary. But the Rumanians could not resist the lure of Transylvania, which they had coveted for so long. They launched a hasty and poorly conceived offensive through the mountain passes but made little progress against Austro-Hungarian forces under the command of General Arthur Arz von Straussenburg. The Central Powers now set out to eliminate the Rumanian problem. Falkenhayn, immediately following his dismissal as chief of staff, received the task of organizing the combined German-Austro-Hungarian Ninth Army in Transylvania. In Bulgaria, General von Mackensen took command of the Third Army, a predominantly Bulgarian force but also containing German and even Turkish units. The Rumanians hoped for Allied aid to offset this combination of enemies. But Russia had already reneged on its original agreement because of the Brusilov offensive and initially could spare only 50,000 men. The Allied offensive from Salonika also proved ineffective.

Rumania had to confront the forces of the Central Powers virtually alone on two fronts. Mackensen's Bulgarian troops crossed the border and struck toward the Black Sea port of Constanta. On September 30, Falkenhayn began to infiltrate through the Transylvanian mountain passes and skillfully drove the Rumanians back into their own country. By the end of November, his troops had broken into the Rumanian Plain, while Mackensen crossed the Danube from the south. Both armies converged on Bucharest, and the capital fell on December 5. Falkenhayn then pursued the retreating enemy northeastward. With the help of Russian reinforcements, the Rumanians finally managed to stabilize the front along the Sereth River in the northern province of Moldavia. Rumania had seen its dreams of aggrandizement cruelly shattered at the expense of 200,000 casualties and another 150,000 men taken prisoner. The Central Powers suffered much lighter losses.

Although the victory came against a weak, poorly organized and badly led army, the Rumanian campaign once again demonstrated German organizational and tactical brilliance. Their performance contrasted vividly with the lackluster results of the offensive undertaken by General Maurice Sarrail's Allied force at Salonika. The Bulgars had actually launched a spoiling attack on August 17, delaying the start of the Allied operation until September 10. Sarrail's effort took the form of a limited offensive in which Serbian troops, with French and Italian assistance, scored the only success. They drove through exceptionally difficult mountainous terrain and pushed the Bulgars out of the town of Monastir in southern Serbia on November 19. This local victory did nothing to help Rumania, although it provided the Serbs with some solace by enabling them to reestablish a slender foothold in their own country.

GREECE JOINS ALLIES

Greece's neutrality, already badly infringed by the Allies, suffered escalating indignities as the fighting continued along that country's northern border. King Constantine grew more antagonistic to the Allies the longer they remained in his kingdom and as the size of their force increased. General Sarrail, whose arrogant behavior did not improve relations, became more and more fearful that the Greek army might attack the Allies from the rear. When the Bulgars occupied a Greek border fortress, the Allies charged Greece with complicity in the seizure. They imposed a limited naval blockade of the coast and forced the Greek army to demobilize. Sarrail also promoted an uprising by supporters of dismissed Premier Venizelos. The rebels set up a provisional government on August 30, which renounced allegiance to the king and declared its adherence to the Allies. But King Constantine refused to buckle under, and many Greeks remained loyal to him. They were especially outraged by the imposition of a full Allied blockade as well as the seizure of a number of small Greek ships. Sporadic outbreaks of civil war soon followed.

Despite the growing chaos in Greece, Sarrail shied away from actually deposing Constantine, in part because both Britain and Russia opposed the overthrow of a monarch. Italy also did not relish the prospect of a Venizelist government in Greece because Rome suspected that it would challenge Italian claims to Greek-populated Turkish territory in Asia Minor. Finally, the French feared the possible impact of such an action on American public opinion. Thus, Constantine clung to his shaky throne until after the United States entered the war in the spring of 1917. Premier Venizelos finally returned to office in June of that year, and Greece officially joined the Allies.

PROBLEMS PLAGUE THE DUAL MONARCHY

None of the belligerent powers could find anything to be optimistic about in the aftermath of the terrible events of the summer and fall of 1916 on the Eastern Front. To be sure, the Germans had managed to halt Brusilov's offensive and had once again saved Austria-Hungary from apparent catastrophe. But despite the improvement in the Dual Monarchy's army during the winter of 1915-1916, Brusilov's offensive had dramatically

revealed that the old defects of poor leadership, bad morale, and ethnic diversity were still present. After the humiliating disasters of June and the bloody fighting of the following months, the Austro-Hungarian army, while not yet finished as a factor in the war, would never really recover. Morale continued to deteriorate, and the reliability of many Slavic units remained problematical.

The civilian population, oppressed by the dreary catalogue of defeats and mounting casualties, fell victim to ever mounting war weariness. The food shortage in Austria's half of the empire reached alarming proportions by the end of the year, making the outlook gloomier still. Despite the plight of Austria, the Magyars remained unwilling to make any sacrifices to help alleviate the problem. This made the Austrians even more dependent on Germany for aid, but the Germans, with increasing food problems of their own, were less than sympathetic. They pressured Austria and Hungary to reach an accord, but to no avail. The conquest of much of Rumania opened a new source of grain to exploitation by the Central Powers. But Germany assumed responsibility for administration there and gave first priority to its own needs, leaving little for Austria. Industrial production in the Dual Monarchy, which had improved during 1915 and 1916, started to fall off drastically by the end of the year and continued downward. Coal shortages became a problem during the winter of 1916-1917, and the transportation system began to break down as rolling stock deteriorated under the strain of wartime demands.

In view of these depressing internal conditions and the Dual Monarchy's woeful military performance against the Russians, Germany exerted growing influence over Austria-Hungary. In September 1916, Hindenburg and Ludendorff succeeded in establishing the unified "Supreme

Command Central Powers" (*Oberste Kriegsleitung*, or OKL) on the Eastern Front. Conrad had resisted earlier German overtures for such an organization but now had no choice but to agree. OKL placed Hindenburg and Ludendorff in a position to dominate Austro-Hungarian military policy.

THE DEATH OF FRANCIS JOSEPH

If all the military disasters and accumulating internal problems were not sufficient, the Dual Monarchy suffered what may have been a mortal blow when Emperor Francis Joseph died at the age of 86 on November 21, 1916. Despite his personal shortcomings as a leader, Francis Joseph had been an enormously important symbol of unity during his nearly 68 years as emperor of Austria and king of Hungary. Even before the war Austro-Hungarian leaders had feared that the empire might not hold together after Francis Joseph's death. Now, with the army's fortunes at low ebb and the bonds uniting the various ethnic groups already loosening, these fears appeared close to realization.

Francis Joseph's successor was the Archduke Charles, the 29-year-old son of Francis Ferdinand's brother Otto. Although Charles had no political experience, he set out to play a much more active role in policy-making than had been the case with Francis Joseph during the last few years of his life. The young emperor firmly believed that Austria-Hungary must seek a negotiated peace. He also favored transforming the system of dualism into a democratic federal system, even before the war ended. Charles shared his uncle's animosity toward the Magyars but also detested the Germans and their increasing domination over his country. Clearly a man of good instincts, Charles unfortunately lacked the strength of character to fulfill his aims. He had difficulty persevering in one course of action and naively ignored the immense stumbling blocks in the path either to peace or a reformation of the political system.

German opposition to a negotiated settlement proved critical in wrecking his hopes for peace, along with the reluctance of both Austrian and Magyar leaders to act without German agreement. István Tisza, Hungary's prime minister, feared Charles's anti-Magyar attitude and his desire to end the *Augsleich* of 1867. He cleverly outmaneuvered the new emperor by immediately assuring him of Hungary's allegiance and arranging an early date for Charles's coronation as king of Hungary. Once crowned, it proved difficult for Charles to alter the political structure of the Dual Monarchy, which he had essentially confirmed by accepting the crown.

Charles also planned to impose his control over military matters. Despite having little previous experience, he had commanded a corps during the Trentino offensive, and in its aftermath bitterly criticized Conrad's plan as being unrealistic. He later commanded an army group on the Eastern Front during the Brusilov campaign, although German General Hans von Seeckt served as his chief of staff and made the critical decisions. Charles especially wanted to dismiss Conrad, whose stock had fallen dramatically since the Trentino and Brusilov offensives. He moved in this direction by assuming personal command over all armed forces and renegotiating the OKL agreement on terms more favorable to Austria-Hungary.

Finally, on February 27, 1917, he dismissed Conrad as chief of staff. His choice as Conrad's replacement was General Artur Arz von Straussenburg, a relatively junior but highly regarded commander who had performed well in defense of Transylvania against the Rumanians. General Arz von Straussenburg was much less assertive and ambitious than Conrad and in effect became a personal adviser to Charles. He left much of

FIGURE 11–2 Emperor Charles, the last of the Hapsburg monarchs. National Archives

the operational planning to his staff, which unfortunately led to considerable confusion. Conrad now took command of the army group in the Trentino and soon began to dream of renewed offensives against "perfidious Italy."

Long disenchanted with Stephan von Burián, whose hard-line policy contrasted so sharply with his own longing for peace, Charles also dismissed Burián as foreign min-

ister in December 1916. Count Ottokar Czernin von und zu Chudenitz, a former close associate of Francis Ferdinand, succeeded to this critical position and held it almost until the end of the war. Arrogant, ambitious, and opinionated, Czernin has remained one of the conflict's most controversial figures. He shared the emperor's desire for peace and his dislike of both dualism and the Magyars, whom he once referred to as "a plague boil on the body of the Monarchy." But Czernin differed from Charles by remaining steadfastly loyal to Germany, believing that German support was crucial for maintaining the existence of the empire. He insisted that Austria-Hungary could not leave the war without its ally's approval.

Highly reactionary in his political views, Czernin also had long opposed any thought of a democratic federation of nationalities, such as Charles proposed, and actually favored a centralized state dominated by the Austrian and Czech nobility. Once in power, however, Czernin bowed to wartime expediency and embraced the idea of dualism to appease the Magyars. The divergence in views of Charles and Czernin, combined with the former's indecisiveness and the latter's assertiveness, virtually assured that there would be no negotiated settlement and no meaningful internal political change. Charles did succeed in dismissing István Tisza as Hungarian prime minister, but his successor Count Móric Esterházy proved ineffective. Sandor Wekerle, a politician notable primarily for his avoidance of serious issues, soon took his place. Under him, the Magyars remained adamantly opposed to any concessions to other nationalities within the Dual Monarchy.

Austrian Prime Minister Karl von Stürgkh, the third member of the triumvirate that had ruled Austria-Hungary since early 1915, fell victim to an assassin's bullets on October 21, 1916, while dining in a Viennese restaurant. His assailant, Friedrich Adler, the son of Social Democratic leader Viktor Adler, resorted to this act to protest the continued suppression of the Austrian parliament, the Reichsrat, and Stürgkh's unpopular rule by imperial decree. A series of ineffectual men succeeded to Stürgkh's position for the remainder of the war. The Reichsrat reconvened in late May 1917, but its sessions became increasingly chaotic as Czech and South Slav delegates insisted on autonomy within a federal system, while Polish representatives called for outright independence. The Austrian government as well as the Magyars opposed these demands, and nothing was accomplished, but divisions between the nationalities grew more intense.

RUSSIA DEMORALIZED

If the aftermath of the Brusilov offensive was bleak for Austria-Hungary, it was no happier for Russia. This operation was destined to be the last major effort of the Russian army. Although able to bounce back from the defeats of 1915, it proved incapable of recovery from the effects of the Pyrrhic victory of 1916. In addition to the ruinous losses, all of the old problems remained, and the morale of large numbers of soldiers had been virtually destroyed. Desertions, a problem since 1914, now increased alarmingly. The old officer corps, badly decimated by two and a half years of fighting, received replacements in the form of university students who had gained their commissions after losing their exemptions from military service in 1915. Many of them were somewhat radical in their political views.

On the home front, shortages of food and other necessities, which had plagued the cities since the start of the war, grew steadily worse. Hope for victory had faded, while longing for peace mounted. Faith in the czar and his government had virtually vanished. The potential for revolution was clearly present within a demoralized Russia.

CHAPTER
12

THE WAR
AT SEA
AND IN THE AIR

It is obvious that the war's first two and a half years had demonstrated that technology had progressed much faster than the ability of military minds to cope with the revolutionary changes it had brought to the battlefield. Blessed with an unprecedented abundance of material, the generals on both sides persisted in assuming that, if they could amass enough military hardware at the critical place, they could achieve the long-coveted breakthrough and win the war. By the end of 1916, it should have become painfully clear that this approach had not worked and was not likely to work, but unfortunately this lesson still remained to be learned. Surprisingly, military leaders underestimated the value of the tank, the weapon most likely to achieve the goal that had tantalized them for so long. Perhaps the tank was too new. Certainly, the performance of its early models left much to be desired. Technology had also made revo-

lutionary changes in the navies of the belligerent powers, and the advent of the airplane, as recently as 1903, had opened a completely new approach to warfare. Again the leaders of the powers were slow to appreciate the significance of at least some of these changes.

The transition from sail to steam power in warships had come to pass during the second half of the nineteenth century. The all-big-gun dreadnought with its superior armor and exceptional speed had made all previous battleships obsolete in the first decade of the twentieth century. Moreover, the development of the submarine posed startling new possibilities. But in August 1914, the commanders of the navies of the rival powers had no experience with these ships in war. They still thought in terms of battles of annihilation. The British Admiral Horatio Nelson's great victory over the French and Spanish in the Battle of Trafalgar in 1805 remained the model to be emulated. More recently, there was the example of Japanese Admiral Heihachiro Togo's destruction of the Russian fleet in the Battle of Tshushima in 1905. Naval leaders looked upon the submarine as almost exclusively a defensive weapon, ignoring its offensive potential. In fact, when the war started, there was a tendency not to take submarines seriously and to look upon them as unsporting. Admiral Sir Arthur Wilson, one of the prewar British first sea lords, observed that they were "Underhand, unfair and damned un-English."

Experience with airplanes was so novel that there was no tradition to interfere with the development of theories on how to use them effectively. Airpower was in its infancy, and realization of its full potential lay in the period long after the end of World War I. As with all innovations in warfare, the airplane was subject to a great deal of trial and error, but amazing progress did take place. By the end of the conflict, its more enthusiastic champions saw airpower as capable of winning the next war virtually by itself. But to many others, it would never be anything more than a useful auxiliary to ground troops.

BRITISH AND GERMAN NAVAL STRENGTH

As foreshadowed in their fierce prewar rivalry, the key combatants in the struggle for supremacy at sea were Britain and Germany. Britain enjoyed its traditional advantages—the world's largest navy, a highly favorable geographic location, access to the resources of the rest of the world, and a long history of predominance at sea. To be sure, the German naval construction program had reduced the British margin of superiority but, nevertheless, the navy it had created was still second best. Germany's geographic position was also much less favorable. With its main bases

concentrated along the North Sea coast, the High Seas Fleet could only break into the Atlantic by way of either the 20-mile wide Strait of Dover between England and France or the 200-mile wide gap between Scotland and Norway. The chief aim of British naval strategy was to prevent this by means of a blockade. With its greater strength, it could easily deprive Germany of seaborne access to the resources of the world beyond Europe. The Germans also lacked Britain's long history of supremacy at sea and the sense of self-assurance that this tradition had nurtured. But they had some advantages, too.

While Germany's naval tradition was of exceedingly short duration, Admiral Alfred von Tirpitz and his staff had created their navy with the usual German flair for efficiency and precision. They had based construction of their dreadnoughts on British models but were able to avoid some of the mistakes in design of these earlier ships, while incorporating improvements of their own. By 1914, the original *Dreadnought*, the world's finest ship in 1906, was already obsolete. Admiral Sir John Fisher had stressed the importance of heavy armament, and the latest British "super-dreadnoughts" possessed 13.5-inch guns. Their German counterparts had only 12-inch guns but greater muzzle velocity, giving their shells more penetrating power. British dreadnoughts were generally faster, but not as well armored as their opponents. German gunnery also proved more accurate.

The British, at Admiral's Fisher's instigation, had begun to develop submarines before the Germans did. They based their first models on an early American design and by 1907 had created a class of oceangoing underwater vessels. Admiral von Tirpitz did not authorize experimental submarine construction until 1905, and the first oceangoing U-boats appeared during the period 1908-1910. When the war began, Germany had far too few submarines to be a decisive weapon. Although by May 1914 the German navy had prepared a study on the use of large numbers of submarines against British shipping, its leaders persisted in viewing the U-boat as primarily a defensive weapon against surface attacks on German bases. Even after the war began, they initially failed to foresee its potential impact on enemy commerce, despite Britain's dependence on imports of food and other resources.

The Germans also worried about the restrictions of international law. These stipulated that commerce raiders must halt merchant ships, search them for contraband, and look after the safety of their crews before capturing or sinking the ships. Such time-consuming measures put submarines, with their thin skins, at special risk to enemy countermeasures. It was not until 1915 that Germany decided that expediency required its U-boats to violate the law of the sea and sink merchant ships without warning, as did British submarines in the Baltic Sea and the Sea of Marmara, which links the Bosporus with the Aegean Sea through the Dardanelles. Until then, they limited the submarine's offensive role to attacks on enemy warships.

Britain faced the additional problem of having to parcel out its naval strength to protect its interests in various parts of the world. Germany, except for a few ships scattered about the globe when the war began, could concentrate its striking power primarily in the North Sea. It stationed its older, weaker vessels in the Baltic for use against Russia. The Royal Navy's chief striking force, the Grand Fleet, distributed its ships among three bases in Scotland. These included the great open anchorage of Scapa Flow in the midst of the barren Orkney Islands to the north, Cromarty Firth on the northeast coast, and Rosyth farther south on the Firth of Forth. None of them had permanent defenses or adequate protection against submarine

attack. Together they sheltered 21 dreadnoughts, eight pre-dreadnought battleships, and four battle cruisers as well as 80 cruisers of various types and destroyers. A battle cruiser was faster than a dreadnought battleship and almost as well armed but more poorly armored. To defend the English Channel against the unlikely prospect of a German attack, the British maintained the Channel Fleet at a number of older bases on England's southern coast. It consisted of 19 pre-dreadnoughts and an array of smaller supporting craft. A final force of light cruisers, destroyers, and submarines operated from Harwich on the eastern English coast.

Germany's High Seas Fleet, under the command of Friedrich von Ingenohl, utilized bases along the arm of the North Sea, known as the Heligoland Bight, between the German coast and the island of Heligoland. The naval base at Wilhelmshaven on Jade Bay provided a well-protected haven for the largest concentration of ships. In all, the High Seas Fleet included 13 dreadnoughts, 16 pre-dreadnoughts, five battle cruisers, and 40 cruisers and destroyers.

The Royal Navy had also assumed the task of defending Allied interests in the eastern Mediterranean. Its strength there included three battle cruisers, a number of other cruisers of various types, and 16 destroyers. France, as stipulated in the 1912 agreement, took responsibility for the western Mediterranean and maintained a large fleet of pre-dreadnought battleships along with one dreadnought at its naval base of Toulon for this purpose. The French navy's primary missions were to transport troops from North Africa to France and to guard against the possibility of sorties by the Austro-Hungarian navy out of the Adriatic into the Mediterranean. But Austria's geographic position was even less favorable than that of Germany unless Italy became an ally. The French were able to keep the Dual

Monarchy's fleet of six battleships and supporting craft bottled up by blockading the narrow Strait of Otranto at the Adriatic's southern outlet. Until the spring of 1915, the French also had to remain on the alert to combat Italy's navy should that country enter the war on the side of its former partners in the Triple Alliance.

Russia's navy faced a similar geographical dilemma to that confronting the Dual Monarchy. Its two primary fleets, concentrated in the Baltic and the Black Sea, were unable to venture into either the Atlantic or Mediterranean. German naval domination of the outlet from the Baltic and Turkish control of the Straits prevented any ambitious Russian operations on the high seas, although Russia could have been more aggressive within the Baltic itself. In addition, the Russians had lost 17 battleships during the Russo-Japanese War, and their four dreadnoughts in the Baltic and three in the Black Sea were still under construction when the war began. The four Baltic vessels went into service between November 1914 and January 1915. Two of the three in the Black Sea were commissioned in July and October 1915.

BRITISH NAVAL LEADERS

Britain's long tradition of naval predominance was not without its negative aspects. Many officers were more noteworthy for smug complacency than for ability, imagination, or willingness to accept modern methods and weapons. Before the war, the commanders of some ships had even thrown overboard their allotment of shells intended for gunnery practice, rather than risk the accumulating grime that would mar the luster of their ships should they actually fire this ammunition. To be sure, there were some fine officers, but they were in relatively short supply.

Among them was Admiral Prince Louis of Battenburg, a grandson of Queen Victoria and a member of the ruling family of the German state of Hesse. Battenberg had become a British citizen and demonstrated great administrative ability, which enabled him to assume the title First Sea Lord in 1912. His keen mind made him suspect in the eyes of many far less intellectually gifted officers. He contributed greatly to preparing the British fleet for war, but he never overcame the burden of his German heritage, and on October 30, 1914, he was replaced by Admiral Fisher. Other highly regarded admirals included Sir John Jellicoe and Sir David Beatty.

Jellicoe became commander in chief of the Grand Fleet at the age of 54 immediately following the outbreak of the war. A protégé of both Fisher and Churchill, Jellicoe had won renown for his ability as a gunnery officer and an outstanding commander of ships at sea. He had risen rapidly in the Admiralty's hierarchy. Highly intelligent and exceptionally conscientious, Jellicoe won the admiration and, indeed, the love of his fellow officers as well as ordinary seamen. Standing only 5 feet 6 inches, his large, kindly eyes redeemed the otherwise undistinguished features of his face, which included an ample nose and slit-like mouth. In most respects an excellent administrator, he suffered from an inability to delegate authority and agonized over a myriad of minor, time-consuming details. Unlike most British naval officers, Jellicoe recognized the navy's weaknesses, including flaws in dreadnought design, and did not underestimate the Germans. He pursued a policy of caution and insisted on avoiding risks that might reduce the fleet's numerical superiority over the enemy.

In dramatic contrast to Jellicoe, Beatty, the commander of the Grand Fleet's battle cruiser squadron, was flamboyant in appearance and manner. A member of the Anglo-Irish gentry, Beatty married the daughter of

American department store tycoon Marshall Field. Her wealth was far greater than Beatty's and enabled him to indulge in his love of yachting, hunting, and polo. Unfortunately, she proved emotionally unstable, and their marriage was far from happy. Beatty attracted attention by virtue of his rugged good looks and the rakish angle of his cap. He liked to strike a jaunty pose with his hands thrust into the pockets of his nonregulation jacket. Only 43 years old when the war began, Beatty had enjoyed a meteoric rise to prominence. Although quick-witted and blessed with a good sense of humor, he was high-strung and somewhat lacking in imagination in tense situations. Beatty disliked Jellicoe's cautious, defensive policy and preferred a bolder, offensive approach in the swashbuckling tradition of British seapower. He dreamed of luring the German High Seas Fleet into a battle of annihilation.

THE GERMAN NAVAL COMMAND

William II and the German naval staff followed a cautious policy similar to Jellicoe's. The emperor and Admiral von Ingenohl both feared the loss of their precious fleet and believed that Germany must keep its ships close to their home bases. Admiral Tirpitz, the architect of the German navy, disagreed. He believed that Germany must seek an offensive victory over the British. Ingenohl had expected the Royal Navy to impose a close blockade. This would have enabled the Germans to exploit the proximity of their bases to engage in hit-and-run attacks without undue danger to their own ships. When Britain employed a distant blockade instead, it confronted the Germans with the prospect of venturing much farther from their bases, if they were to attack British ships. This greatly increased the risks to the German High Seas Fleet. To Tirpitz, they were risks worth tak-

ing. But, while Emperor William played a passive role in the land war, he took a proprietary interest in the navy and essentially determined how it would operate. The emperor made sure that the German High Seas Fleet remained close to port. Germany's offensive action would depend primarily on U-boat attacks, occasional surface raids, and laying of mines.

This policy saved the German surface fleet from heavy losses but at the price of immobilizing it during much of the war. It was possible that a skillfully executed surprise attack by the High Seas Fleet soon after the outbreak of hostilities might have succeeded in dramatically reducing the Royal Navy's numerical advantage. The Germans at that time possessed superiority in the number of battle cruisers available for action in the North Sea as well as better gunnery, shells, and torpedoes. Of course, there was also the chance that such a daring undertaking might have ended disastrously. But would this have been any worse for Germany's prospects than self-imposed inactivity? Considering the expenditures lavished on the fleet before the war, it is clear that Germany did not receive an adequate return on its investment, although domination of the Baltic did guarantee vital iron ore shipments from Sweden and did contribute to the collapse of Russia.

OPENING SKIRMISHES AT SEA

In the war's initial stages, however, German cruisers and armed merchant ships, already at sea or in ports around the world, did try to inflict damage on Allied commercial shipping and bases. The Royal Navy set out to hunt down these raiders. The most famous of the German cruisers were the *Goeben* and *Breslau*, under Admiral Wilhelm Souchon's command, in the Mediterranean. They, of course, managed to elude stronger British forces and escaped to safety at Constantinople in August 1914. Their success was due largely to the timing of Britain's entry into the war and confusion over the intent of orders issued by the Admiralty to British forces. Timidity and lack of initiative by commanders on the scene also played an important role. The cruisers' escape and the subsequent Turkish entry into the conflict brought humiliation to both the Admiralty and British commanders in the Mediterranean.

The shadowboxing between the German cruisers and the British in the Mediterranean hardly constituted a real engagement. However, the next encounter involving German cruisers and a British intercepting force led to disaster for Britain. Among Germany's naval forces scattered about the oceans, the East Asian naval squadron of Admiral Graf (Count) Maximilian von Spee was destined to be the most successful for a time. Spee ranked among the most able German naval leaders. Noted for the exceptional gunnery of his ships, Spee's approach to war was one of boldness and great efficiency. His squadron, consisting of the armored cruisers *Gneisenau* and *Scharnhorst*, left its base at Tsingtao, a German-leased enclave along China's coast, shortly before the war. It sailed to the Caroline Islands, a German possession in the western Pacific, where the light cruiser *Nurnberg* joined it. On August 6, 1914, Spee set sail for South American waters where he intended to prey on Allied merchant shipping even though he realized his ships would never reach Germany again.

By mid-October, he had reached Easter Island, about 2,300 miles west of the coast of Chile. There the light cruisers *Leipzig* and *Dresden* joined his squadron before it headed for Chilean waters. *Leipzig* had been operating off Mexico's west coast and *Dresden* in the West Indies. The Admiralty in London ordered Admiral Sir Christopher Craddock's South American squadron to guard the Straits of Magellan near South America's

southern tip against the possibility that Spee might move into the Atlantic. Unfortunately, "Kit" Craddock, a daring and well-liked officer who was famous for his fox-hunting exploits, possessed a much weaker force than Spee. It consisted of two old armored cruisers, his flagship *Good Hope*, and the *Monmouth*, both inferior to *Gneisenau* and *Scharnhorst*, and the poorly armed converted liner *Otranto* as well as one modern light cruiser, the *Glasgow*. Churchill also dispatched the battleship *Canopus* from the Mediterranean to reinforce Craddock. However, *Canopus* was so old, slow, and poorly armed that Craddock viewed it as more of a liability than an asset.

NAVAL ENCOUNTERS IN SOUTH AMERICAN WATERS

Despite his weakness, Craddock chose to seek out Spee without waiting for *Canopus* to arrive. He sailed through the Straits of Magellan into the Pacific, and on November 1 he made contact with the German squadron 50 miles off Coronel on the coast of Chile. Spee arranged his ships so that the British would have to maneuver to the west of them where they would be silhouetted against the glowing sky after the sun had set. German gunnery proved shatteringly effective, quickly sending both *Good Hope* and *Monmouth* to the bottom. All hands, including Craddock were lost. *Glasgow*, though slightly damaged, and *Otranto* managed to escape. Spee's ships emerged virtually unscathed. Although undoubtedly a gallant effort, Craddock's action had amounted to virtually a blood sacrifice.

While Spee's squadron put in at Valparaiso on the Chilean coast to refuel, the British Admiralty took measures to ensure that Spee would soon share a fate similar to that of Craddock. London dispatched the battle cruisers *Invincible* and *Inflexible* along with two light cruisers for this purpose. Under the command of Admiral Sir Doveton Sturdee, they made for the Falkland Islands off the southeastern coast of Argentina. Sturdee, who had commanded a cruiser squadron before the war, had spent several months as chief of the naval staff, a position for which he was ill-suited, in large part because he disliked the staff system. The admiral had acted in a high-handed fashion and ignored the advice of his subordinates. He was much more at home on the high seas and set out enthusiastically to track down Spee's squadron.

Spee made it easy for him. He rounded Cape Horn in early December, planning to cross the South Atlantic. But before doing so, he decided to attack installations at Port Stanley in the Falklands on December 8. To his surprise, Sturdee's squadron was already there and was in the midst of taking on coal. Had Spee opted to open fire on the British while they were in this awkward position, he might have subjected them to severe damage and perhaps saved his own command. Instead, he chose to flee, but unfortunately his ships were not fast enough to outrun the swift British battle cruisers.

When Sturdee caught up to Spee, the two fleets maneuvered for position. For a time, the Germans were able to hold their own through superior gunnery, but the British finally began to score hits on the enemy. With their heavier guns and bigger shells, they sank the *Gneisenau*, *Scharnhorst*, *Nurnberg*, and *Leipzig*. The *Dresden* escaped, but its reprieve ended in March 1915 when fittingly it fell victim to the *Glasgow* off the coast of Chile. The British victory in the Battle of the Falkland Islands avenged the defeat at Coronel and restored the luster to Britain's reputation as the world's premier naval power.

Destiny had overtaken two other German light cruisers, *Karlsruhe* and *Emden*, even before the disaster that befell Spee's squadron. Spee had detached *Emden* from his command while in the Carolines. It headed for the Indian Ocean where it raided successfully for three months, sinking 17 merchantmen as well as a Russian cruiser and a French destroyer. Its luck ran out on November 9 when the heavier and faster Australian cruiser *Sydney* overwhelmed it with its superior firepower. The *Karlsruhe* preyed on Allied shipping in the central Atlantic before accidentally blowing up, also in November. Still another light cruiser, the *Königsberg*, operated in East African waters. It blew up a British cruiser off Zanzibar and then took refuge up the Rufiji River until it was discovered and destroyed in July 1915. The British hunted down and destroyed other commerce raiders and, by the end of 1914, German surface ships had virtually vanished from the high seas.

FIRST NORTH SEA BATTLE

Long before the dramatic encounters in South American waters, the naval war in the North Sea also got off to a relatively active start. The first action, involving elements of the two surface fleets, took place on August 28, 1914. This minor encounter, remembered as the Battle of the Heligoland Bight, came about through the inspiration of two relatively young British naval officers. Commodore Reginald Tyrwhitt commanded the cruiser force at Harwich, and his friend Commodore Roger Keyes led the submarines stationed at the same base. These two men reflected the fighting tradition of the British navy and chafed at the defensive posture struck by the Admiralty and Admiral Jellicoe. They observed that German destroyer patrols in the Heligoland Bight followed a recurring pattern and proposed to lure them and their supporting forces into action. Two light cruisers supported by destroyers would carry out the operation. The Admiralty approved their scheme over Jellicoe's objections, but once the decision had been made, Jellicoe granted Beatty's request that his battle cruiser squadron also be allowed to participate. Owing to a communications breakdown, Tyrwhitt and Keyes never received word of Beatty's involvement. This resulted in a great deal of confusion and several incidents of mistaken identity that almost led to British ships firing on each other. But fortune favored the enterprise and, instead of a disaster, the British sank three German light cruisers and a destroyer while suffering serious damage to only one of their own light cruisers.

GERMANS PLAN HIT-AND-RUN RAIDS

Despite poor staff work and abysmal communication, the victory provided a much-needed boost to British morale after the *Goeben* fiasco and the depressing news from the Western Front prior to the Battle of the Marne. It also reinforced the German navy's sense of inferiority and prompted the emperor to insist on more caution in the future. Nevertheless, German battle cruisers did undertake a series of hit-and-run raids during the following months in an attempt to goad the British into action. The man in charge of these operations, Admiral Franz von Hipper, was one of the finest commanders in the German navy. In dramatic contrast to the naval staff's conservative approach, Hipper believed in taking the battle to the enemy and agreed with Admiral Tirpitz that the longer Germany waited to do this, the less chance there would be for success. Thoroughly professional and possessing exceptional skill in handling large numbers of ships at sea, he shared Admiral Sturdee's aversion to staff work. Although strict and brusque, he forged a bond of mutual devotion with his officers and men.

In his first raid on November 3, 1914, Hipper attempted to lure the British into dividing their forces by enticing the eager Beatty and his battle cruisers away from the cautious Jellicoe and the rest of the Grand Fleet. If Beatty took the bait and chased Hipper's squadron, perhaps he could be drawn into a trap and destroyed by the remainder of the German fleet under Admiral Ingenohl. Hipper's squadron caught the British by surprise as it shelled the English coast and laid mines in adjacent waters. Although the raid did little damage and failed to lure Beatty to his doom, it did force Jellicoe to divide his fleet. With the outraged British press screaming about German "baby-busters," Jellicoe felt obliged to split his forces to provide better protection for the coast. Beatty's battle cruisers moved to Invergordon on Cromarty Firth, while Admiral Sir Edward Bradford's old *King Edward VII*-class battleships took up residence farther south at Rosyth on the Firth of Forth. The rest of the Grand Fleet remained at Scapa Flow.

Admiral Hipper did not achieve surprise with his second raid in December. British intelligence had deciphered German messages pertaining to the raid. Their ability to accomplish this was due to two strokes of good fortune. Russian divers had recovered German cipher books from the cruiser *Magdeburg* after it was sunk in the Baltic in late August. They passed them on to the British two months later. The British had also discovered charts, indicating ship dispositions, among the wreckage of a German destroyer on October 17. Armed with these advantages, a secret department in the Admiralty, referred to as "Room 40," soon began to decipher enemy fleet messages on a regular basis.

Emboldened by news of the departure of two British battle cruisers to the South Atlantic to intercept Spee's squadron, Admiral Ingenohl again ordered the German High Seas Fleet to support Hipper's battle cruisers in a raid on December 16. Alerted by Room 40 to the impending action, the British dispatched Beatty's remaining battle cruisers as well as six dreadnoughts to intercept Hipper's force. But deciphered messages had not revealed that the High Seas Fleet had also set sail. Thus, the Germans had a marked numerical superiority and might have inflicted a serious defeat on the British, but when the High Seas Fleet came into contact with the enemy destroyer screen, Ingenohl ordered it to withdraw, fearing that the entire British Grand Fleet might be lurking in the gloom behind the destroyers. He failed to inform Hipper, however, who proceeded on to shell three coastal towns, killing 137 persons and injuring 592. Despite his now vulnerable position, Hipper managed to escape. Beatty's light cruisers did make contact with Hipper's squadron but, because of confused signals, soon lost him. Thus, both sides escaped what might have been a disaster.

The Germans were not so fortunate in their next sortie into the North Sea, although they did avoid what might have been a far worse defeat. Ingenohl ordered Hipper to sail to the Dogger Bank, about 60 miles east of the English coast, on January 19, 1915, with three battle cruisers and the smaller and less-well armored cruiser *Blücher*. Hipper was to destroy any light British forces in the area. This time, however, Ingenohl would not risk the High Seas Fleet. British intelligence again alerted the Admiralty of the impending action, and Beatty's five battle cruisers set out to intercept the Germans. When Hipper became aware of the approach of this superior British squadron, he wheeled about to return home. But Beatty's battle cruisers, built for speed and demonstrating exceptional engineering skill, caught up with the Germans. Unfortunately, their gunnery was not of the same quality, although they did manage to mortally wound the *Blücher* and seriously damage the battle cruiser *Seydlitz*. The Germans crippled Beatty's

flagship *Lion*, however, forcing it to fall out of line.

With his wireless (radio) knocked out, Beatty signalled the other ships to continue pursuing the main enemy force. But Beatty's second in command, Admiral Archibald Moore aboard the *New Zealand*, interpreted the signals as an order to finish off the already doomed *Blücher*. Accordingly, he instructed the squadron to carry out this task, a diversion that allowed the enemy battle cruisers to escape.

The world viewed the Battle of Dogger Bank as a victory for the Royal Navy. And, while technically it was, Beatty and other British leaders were haunted by their failure to achieve what appeared to be the certain annihilation of the enemy battle cruisers. The Germans, though relieved that they had not suffered a catastrophe, were shaken by the experience. William II reacted by dismissing Admiral Ingenohl because he felt that he had acted rashly in sending out Hipper's ships. He replaced him as commander of the High Seas Fleet with Admiral Hugo von Pohl. Under Pohl's ultra-cautious leadership, Germany's great ships were shifted to operations in the Baltic.

THE BATTLE OF JUTLAND

During the spring of 1916, however, the focus of naval warfare once again returned to the North Sea as the most dramatic surface encounter of the entire conflict unfolded. It was to be the last great clash between capital ships that the world would ever experience—the Battle of Jutland. This struggle had its origin in the fighting character of Admiral Reinhard Scheer, who became commander of the German High Seas Fleet early in 1916, succeeding Admiral von Pohl, who died of cancer shortly afterward. Unlike most German admirals, Scheer had risen to his lofty position despite a middle-class background. He had accomplished this remarkable feat by virtue of both tactical skill and administrative brilliance. Like Admiral Hipper, he realized that Pohl's policy of avoiding action in the North Sea had undermined morale and was making the German navy the butt of insulting jokes from military and civilian sources alike.

Scheer persuaded the German emperor to allow him to pursue a more active approach. Far from blind to the Royal Navy's numerical superiority, which was now considerably greater than at the start of the war, Scheer did not contemplate waging a pitched battle between dreadnoughts. This would be suicidal. Instead, Scheer returned to the strategy utilized by Hipper and Ingenohl in 1914. He hoped to lure elements of the British Grand Fleet into a trap and, using swift destroyers and submarines armed with torpedoes, to destroy as many British capital ships as possible. Scheer sent Hipper on a sortie to shell the British coast on April 24, 1916. It caused some damage but failed to result in any action between the two fleets. He planned a follow-up raid in late May against the northeast English coast, hoping to lure Beatty's battle cruisers from their base at relatively nearby Rosyth, with the help of Zeppelins used for observation and early warning of Beatty's actions.

Bad weather forced cancellation of this raid, however, and Scheer decided instead to send Hipper northward. His destination was the Skagerrak, the strait separating the southern coast of Norway from Denmark's Jutland Peninsula. Scheer would follow Hipper at a distance with the High Seas Fleet. Together these forces would seek to destroy any enemy merchant ships in the area and, it was hoped, entice the British to dispatch warships to the Skagerrak. If all went well, submarines positioned near enemy ports would take a heavy toll of them, and German dreadnoughts and battle cruisers would ambush those that made it through the U-boat screen.

Oddly enough, Admiral Jellicoe had planned a similar operation. He had ordered a sweep by light cruisers in the Skagerrak, with both Beatty's Battle Cruiser Fleet and the Grand Fleet following behind. They would lurk off the western edge of the Skagerrak in position to intercept any elements of the High Seas Fleet that might attack the cruisers. Jellicoe was especially pleased when he learned from deciphered German messages that Scheer was going to carry out an operation in the same waters on May 31, 1916. Thus, it was not by mere chance that both fleets steamed into the Skagerrak that day. Beatty's scouting force, forming the British vanguard, had the support of four dreadnoughts under the command of Admiral Hugh Evan-Thomas, in addition to its six battle cruisers, 14 light cruisers, and 27 destroyers. Jellicoe's Grand Fleet included 24 dreadnoughts, three battle cruisers, 11 light cruisers, and 53 destroyers as well as eight obsolete armored cruisers. Hipper commanded a scouting force of five battle cruisers, five light cruisers, and 30 destroyers. Scheer's High Seas Fleet consisted of 16 dreadnoughts, six old battleships, six light cruisers, and 31 destroyers. Britain enjoyed crushing superiority, at least in numbers.

The British managed to elude the U-boat screen, which Scheer had hoped would inflict serious damage. By 2:15 in the afternoon of May 31, 1916, Beatty's force was within 50 miles of Hipper's squadron. It was just starting to wheel to the north when two of his scouting light cruisers spotted a pair of German destroyers. Beatty now swung southward to try to cut off any enemy forces to the east but, due to confusion in signalling, Evan-Thomas' dreadnoughts continued to steam northward for eight crucial minutes. By the time they finally turned to the south, Beatty's battle cruisers were well ahead of them. Thus, Beatty was unable to coordinate his full strength against Hipper's squadron. Hipper, now aware of Beatty's approach, turned his ships southward to lure the British into a collision course with Scheer's dreadnoughts.

As the two battle cruiser forces raced toward the High Seas Fleet, they engaged in a long-range duel with their heavy guns. Both sides inflicted punishment, but the Germans had the better of it. This was due in part to the fact that mist shrouded their ships, while the British were silhouetted against the lighter sky to the west. Beatty's unlucky flagship *Lion*, severely damaged at Dogger Bank in 1915, took several direct hits. Worse yet, a shell from the German battle cruiser *von der Tann* penetrated one of *Indefatigable*'s gun turrets, touching off a tremendous explosion. The great ship capsized with the loss of almost all of its 1,000-man crew. Soon afterward, *Derfflinger* and *Seydlitz* scored numerous hits on the *Queen Mary*, setting off still another huge magazine explosion. The ship quickly vanished from sight along with virtually its entire complement of over 1,200 men. After the loss of the *Queen Mary*, Beatty turned to the captain of the *Lion* and muttered, "There seems to be something wrong with our bloody ships today." Indeed there was. The battle cruiser gun turret trunks lacked adequate internal flash protection, coupled with the tendency of British cordite powder to ignite flash explosions down to the powder magazines.

When Evan-Thomas's dreadnoughts caught up with Beatty's squadron, the shells from their 15-inch guns began to rake Hipper's ships. But now the British spotted the vanguard of Scheer's High Seas Fleet. Beatty quickly reversed his course and proceeded to lure the enemy toward Jellicoe and the Grand Fleet to the north. Another running fight ensued with both sides scoring hits. Despite the confusion of the battle and the poor visibility, Jellicoe managed to deploy his dreadnoughts in the classic naval maneuver known as "crossing the T." In other words, they were stretched out in a line to intercept

the German column moving northward toward them. They were now in position to train all guns against the enemy, while only the forward guns of the advance German ships were in satisfactory firing position.

In the ensuing melee, starting at 6:15 P.M., the Germans scored still another lethal hit on a British battle cruiser whose powder magazine exploded. This time the victim was the inappropriately named *Invincible*, which had been Admiral Sturdee's flagship in the Battle of the Falkland Islands. Another shattering explosion blew the stricken ship apart, killing over 1,000 men. The British also inflicted serious damage on the German battle cruisers. They disabled the *Lützow*, which later sank, but the others, though damaged, remained in action. Scheer's fleet found itself in danger of being completely destroyed. But at 6:35, he ordered his column to make an abrupt and extremely difficult about face and, with the help of a torpedo boat attack and an effective smoke screen, his capital ships fled. Jellicoe, fearing the torpedoes, did not pursue immediately and the Germans disappeared.

Shortly afterward, as Admiral Scheer turned eastward again, for a second time he found Jellicoe "crossing his T." It appeared as though his luck had run out but, while the British rained down shellfire on both his battleships and battle cruisers, Scheer once again ordered the abrupt turnabout maneuver covered by a torpedo boat attack and a "death-ride"charge by the battle cruisers. This time Jellicoe veered away 45 degrees and the Germans escaped again. Before long, darkness masked the two fleets and, although a series of confused engagements followed, Jellicoe proceeded with great caution.

It was still possible that Jellicoe might be able to cut off the German fleet, but he assumed that Scheer would proceed southward to his home bases. He positioned his dreadnoughts to prevent this, hoping for another engagement at dawn. Instead, Scheer made for the channel through Horns Reef off the coast of the Jutland Peninsula. In Jellicoe's defense, he received inadequate and sometimes conflicting intelligence on Scheer's whereabouts, but he also ignored other factors pointing to Scheer's intentions. Most notably, he disregarded the flashes from guns to the northeast where the High Seas Fleet had encountered the British destroyer screen. He also took no notice of a transmission from the Admiralty indicating that Scheer was sailing in the direction of Horns Reef. As a result, Scheer made good his retreat by following a course that took him behind the Grand Fleet. His ships reached safety by 3 A.M. on June 1 after more than 12 hours of hectic action.

Critics of Jellicoe have contended that his caution and stubbornness robbed the British of the chance to annihilate the enemy. His defenders insist that his chief responsibility was to prevent a disaster from befalling his own fleet and maintain Britain's numerical superiority. This he accomplished. It is also questionable whether he would have been able to destroy Scheer's naval force. The German ships had proven remarkably tough despite the punishment inflicted on them by British guns. Unquestionably, the British could have caused greater damage had Jellicoe chosen a bolder course, but he might also have lost more of his own ships. Even today, the "what might have been" factor remains tantalizing and the answers equally elusive.

In terms of losses in the battle, the British had little reason to celebrate. Three of their battle cruisers, along with three armored cruisers and eight destroyers, were resting on the bottom of the North Sea. More disturbing was the fact that the three battle cruisers had literally exploded, while British shells had detonated on impact instead of penetrating to the vitals of German ships. Until anti-flash baffles could be installed on Royal Navy vessels and the flaws in armor-piercing shells and fuses corrected, the fleet would refuse

another engagement. The Germans had lost one battle cruiser, one old battleship, four modern light cruisers, and five destroyers. But they had also suffered much greater damage to their remaining ships, especially the battle cruisers. Strategically, the battle was indecisive. The Germans had tried to lure the Grand Fleet into an ambush and deliver a crippling blow. Not only had they failed but they also had to beat a hasty retreat to avoid their own destruction. Nevertheless, the stalemate continued. The Royal Navy maintained its blockade, but the German fleet continued to dominate the Baltic.

Admiral Scheer had not yet given up hope of successful surface action. He attempted another raid on the British coast on August 19, hoping to engage and destroy a portion of the British navy, but "Room 40" alerted Jellicoe, who put to sea with the Grand Fleet. Both commanders, with memories of Jutland still fresh, approached each other cautiously and did not make contact. Scheer did not want to run into the entire Grand Fleet again, while Jellicoe remained determined not to split his forces and allow any part of them to fall victim to the Germans. In October, Scheer ventured out once more, but the Grand Fleet remained in port and the Germans returned to base.

SMALLER SHIPS BEGIN TO DOMINATE

From that point, the German surface fleet pursued less ambitious goals. It maintained control of the Baltic, ensuring continuation of vital iron ore shipments to Germany, while denying Western aid to Russia. By traversing the Kiel Canal, linking the North Sea with the Baltic, the battle fleet kept Russian dreadnoughts bottled up in their base at Kronstadt on the Gulf of Finland. German surface ships also protected U-boats on their departure and return from missions against enemy commerce, while

Germany's great dreadnoughts and battle cruisers stayed idle for the remainder of the conflict. But the British Grand Fleet also lay idle at Scapa Flow even after the fiery Beatty succeeded Jellicoe as its commander in chief on November 28, 1916. Beatty, aware of the defects of his ships and shells, now shared Jellicoe's caution. Destroyers, in their role as convoy escorts and U-boat hunters, had become the key ships in the Royal Navy.

GERMAN SUBMARINE WARFARE

Despite the overwhelming importance of dreadnoughts and battle cruisers in the thinking of both British and German naval leaders in the prewar years, the crucial struggle in the conflict on the high seas did not involve these large ships. Instead, it took the form of German submarine attacks, which attempted to strangle Britain's seaborne commerce and force the British out of the war, and the efforts of Royal Navy destroyers and other craft to prevent this. Once the war began, German leaders gradually came to recognize that the submarine's real value was in an offensive role. Some even began to see it as a potential war-winning weapon. But it would take time for it to assume a task of this magnitude. Unfortunately for the Germans, they possessed only 18 U-boats when the war began. They were small, slow, and carried a limited supply of torpedoes and mines. Only a few of them were ever at sea at the same time. The submarine U-21 scored the first kill of the naval war when it torpedoed the British light cruiser *Pathfinder* on September 5, 1914, in Scotland's Firth of Forth.

A far greater success awaited submarine U-9 on September 22 when it encountered three old British armored cruisers—*Aboukir*, *Hogue*, and *Cressy*—leisurely patrolling off the Dutch coast. It torpedoed *Aboukir* and, when *Hogue*

and *Cressy* attempted to rescue survivors, they too fell victim to torpedoes. All three vessels sank with heavy loss of life. German mines also became a source of growing concern to the British after one of their most modern superdreadnoughts struck a mine off the northern coast of Ireland on October 27, 1914. This great ship, the *Audacious*, commissioned as recently as 1912, later exploded and sank while an ocean liner was attempting to tow it to port.

Two days after the sinking of the *Audacious*, Prince Louis of Battenburg asked to be relieved as First Sea Lord. He had suffered from a growing torrent of vicious criticism for the navy's failures during the first three months of the war, most of it inspired by his German birth. Sensational newspapers even accused him of what amounted to treason. It was on this occasion that Admiral Fisher returned to his former position in the Admiralty after four years in retirement.

The disappointing results achieved by German surface raiders and their subsequent destruction contributed greatly to Germany's decision to pursue unrestricted submarine warfare against Allied merchant shipping. During the previous three and a half months, U-boats had been active against Allied merchantmen but had sunk a total of only ten ships. Most of these had gone to the bottom after being stopped, searched, and having their crews removed, all according to international law. The first victim of this type of humane naval warfare was the British merchant ship *Glitra*, dispatched by submarine U-17 on October 20, 1914. This approach was too slow, too risky, and too ineffective for Admiral Tirpitz and other German naval leaders.

GERMANS ANNOUNCE POLICY OF UNRESTRICTED WARFARE AT SEA

Tirpitz became the chief proponent of a policy of unrestricted submarine warfare. To gain support, he followed the same tactic that he had employed while creating his "risk fleet" in the prewar period—an all-out propaganda campaign. Again it paid dividends. Both public opinion and a majority in the Reichstag fell into line behind his plan. General von Falkenhayn, shaken by the failure of the First Battle of Ypres to produce a decisive victory in late 1914 and increasingly concerned about Britain's role in the Allied coalition, became another convert. The German emperor also gave his blessing. Chancellor Bethmann-Hollweg and Foreign Secretary Gottlieb von Jagow both opposed the policy, fearing its negative effects on the United States and Italy, but virtually their only backing came from the Social Democrats.

On February 4, 1915, Germany announced that, henceforth, it would consider all the waters approaching the British Isles to constitute a "war zone." Any enemy ship discovered within this area would be subject to submarine attack without warning. Although the Germans indicated that they would try to avoid sinking neutral ships, they warned that it would be difficult to distin-guish them from Allied vessels. They also pointed out that Allied ships sometimes flew neutral flags to avoid attack, compounding the problem of identification. The fears of Bethmann and Jagow regarding American action proved well-founded. President Woodrow Wilson declared that the United States would hold Germany accountable for the loss of American lives and property as a result of submarine attacks. The chance of such loss was highly likely because American business interests were engaged in a lucrative trade with the Allies in war material, food, and other commodities.

On May 1, 1915, the tanker *Gulflight*, plying the waters off the Scilly Isles southwest of England, became the first American victim of a German torpedo. It managed to make it to port with the help of a tow, but its captain lost his life. On May 7, a much greater disaster occurred when submarine U-20, knowing that the British were using passenger ships to transport troops from Canada, torpedoed the huge Cunard liner *Lusitania* off the coast of Ireland. The *Lusitania* was carrying civilians and sank rapidly in 20 minutes, with the loss

FIGURE 12–1 A German submarine moves along the surface in high seas. National Archives

of 1,198 lives, including 128 Americans. This incident created an angry reaction in the United States. It was never officially admitted that the liner was secretly transporting 173 tons of ammunition, which it had taken on board in New York. President Wilson protested in strong terms, but he shied away from threatening to enter the war. The closest he came was his declaration that any additional infringement of neutral rights would be considered "deliberately unfriendly." Wilson was keenly aware that public opinion, despite its outrage over the *Lusitania*, favored staying aloof from the European conflict. He, too, was reluctant to take any action that would increase the danger of such a development. As he put it, "There is such a thing as being too proud to fight."

Relations between the United States and Germany worsened when submarine U-24 torpedoed the British White Star liner *Arabic* on August 19, again off the Irish coast. Two Americans were among the numerous victims this time, and Wilson again protested. The Germans now feared that persistence in unrestricted submarine warfare would provoke a rupture of relations with the United States. On September 1, they declared that their submarines would not sink liners without warning and without looking after the safety of the passengers. Soon afterward, they pulled their U-boats from the waters west of the British Isles and shifted the focus of their operations to the Mediterranean where fewer American ships were present.

By early 1916, German naval leaders were again clamoring for renewal of an all-out policy of submarine warfare. Germany was feeling the effects of the British blockade to a much greater extent than earlier, and Falkenhayn was pleading for ruthless action on the high seas to accompany his forthcoming offensive at Verdun. In February, Chancellor Bethmann and the emperor yielded to the extent of authorizing attacks on

enemy merchant ships without warning, while remaining faithful to the ban on such action against neutral craft and avoiding passenger liners altogether. The half-hearted and virtually unworkable nature of this decision so enraged Admiral Tirpitz that he resigned as naval secretary. The cautious policy proved difficult to enforce and, on March 24, German Submarine U-29 torpedoed the French passenger steamer *Sussex* in the English Channel. Although the vessel did not sink, a number of passengers were killed and many others injured, including several Americans.

Wilson's response took the form of an ultimatum without a time limit. Either Germany must refrain from such attacks against passenger and merchant ships or the United States would break diplomatic relations. Once again, a concerned German government ordered a halt to submarine warfare, except in keeping with international law. An outward calm characterized relations between the two countries for the remainder of 1916, while Wilson attempted to mediate a negotiated peace. Behind the scenes in Germany, however, the debate regarding warfare on the high seas continued as did the construction of submarines.

By the end of the year, Hindenburg and Ludendorff, the new power brokers at OKL, allied themselves with Admiral Henning von Holtzendorff, chief of the naval staff, and Admiral Scheer in demanding resumption of all-out submarine warfare. This new and formidable group believed that the submarine was a miracle weapon that would win the war. Admiral von Holtzendorff predicted that it would force Britain to make peace within five months. By this time, the Germans had assembled 154 U-boats, all vastly improved over the models used early in the conflict, although only about 70 of them could be at sea at any one time because of the need for periodic maintenance and rest for the crews. The German submarine lobby believed that this number would be sufficient. Early in January of 1917, they won William II to their cause, leaving Bethmann as the sole opponent in the political and military hierarchy. Rather than provoke a cabinet crisis by resigning, he surrendered to the inevitable.

On the last day of January, Germany announced that it would resume unrestricted submarine warfare the following day. The most critical German action since the invasion of Belgium, this decision virtually assured American entry into the war. Certainly the Germans were not blind to this, but they considered it a risk worth taking. At this time, in view of the stalemate on both land and sea, they believed their only chance for victory was to try to cripple Britain. They did not realize how close Russia was to collapse or that the French army, demoralized by the carnage of Verdun, was on the verge of mutiny. To be sure, they recognized that if they provoked the United States into entering the war, they would be faced with a race against time. But it would take the Americans a year to create an army large enough to play a major role in the conflict. They hoped to force Britain to make peace before then. Their approach was a calculated risk, one that would prove to be a mistake.

THE AIR WAR

The war in the air did not provide anything as dramatic as the Battle of Jutland or as threatening to the Allied cause as unrestricted submarine warfare, but it did lead to remarkable strides in aircraft design and the manner in which airpower was employed. Airplanes were a minor consideration in the plans of all the belligerent powers when the war began. Most military leaders did not take them seriously at first. Only a few planes were available for action in 1914, and none were armed.

At first, Germany focused to a large extent on lighter-than-air ships, called dirigibles. The Germans referred to them, however, as zeppelins in honor of Count Ferdinand Zeppelin, a retired army officer who had pioneered their development as early as 1900. In 1914, Germany possessed 11 zeppelins. They featured a fabric covering over a rigid cylindrical frame of aluminum construction, housing 17 hydrogen gas cells. Propeller-driven by two engines, these airships were controlled by a crew operating from gondolas suspended below the frame of the airships. Although the most obvious role of the dirigible, or zeppelin, was in observation of enemy troop and ship movements, the Germans increasingly employed them as bombers to be sent over British cities. They carried out their first raids on England in January 1915 and continued them periodically until November 1917. Attacking at night and initially flying at altitudes that airplanes could not attain, the zeppelins were able to reach their targets without great difficulty, but their bombing proved dismally inaccurate. They caused little damage and relatively few casualties but did spread terror. As British fighter planes improved in quality, however, they were able to reach the same altitudes as the highly inflammable zeppelins, which proved terribly vulnerable to machine gun fire, using explosive bullets. Improved anti-aircraft guns, coupled with more effective use of searchlights, also contributed to their problems. Both sides also used balloons for observation once the stalemate of trench warfare began.

Observation was also the chief mission for airplanes in the early stages of the war, and they soon proved their value in this role. In September 1914, Allied observation planes reported General von Kluck's turning movement to the east of Paris, information that contributed significantly to the subsequent Allied victory in the Battle of the Marne. Both sides used planes as artillery spotters, too, although airships, tethered to the ground by cables and connected with telephone lines, continued to be useful in this respect. Techniques of aerial photography developed rapidly and ultimately enabled both sides to plan their ground operations with the benefit of detailed large-scale maps.

Inevitably, as airplanes demonstrated their usefulness, aerial combat ensued. The earliest planes to see action of this type were primitive contraptions, biplanes of wood construction with fabric covering, which could reach a speed of about 50 miles per hour. Most of them came to be referred to as "pushers," because of the location of their engines and propellers at the rear. The first air-to-air combat took the form of inaccurate exchanges of shots from pistols, rifles, and even shotguns. Before long, machine guns took the place of these weapons, and "tractor" planes, with the engines and propellers in front, replaced the pushers.

In October 1915, the Germans introduced a dramatically better aircraft, the Fokker Eindecker, the creation of Dutch engineer Anthony Fokker who operated a factory near Berlin. It was a tractor monoplane, but its best feature was an "interrupter gear" that synchronized machine gun fire between the revolving propeller blades. This innovation gave the Germans mastery of the air for the next eight months. Nevertheless, in 1916 the Allies effectively challenged the Fokker with the introduction of the French Nieuport and Spad fighters. The pendulum swung back in favor of the Germans in the fall of 1916 when they unveiled an improved version of an earlier plane, the D-3 Albatros. These aircraft enabled Germany to dominate the skies until well into early 1917. In April of that year the Royal Flying Corps lost so many planes that the British nicknamed the month "Bloody April."

During the summer of 1916, Oswald Boelcke, a former schoolteacher who had earned fame as a Fokker Eindecker pilot, de-

vised new tactics featuring the formation of units called *Jagdstaffeln*. These were elite squadrons, staffed by top-notch pilots, whose only purpose was to seek combat and dominate Allied fighters. Boelcke's squadrons proved highly efficient and inflicted heavy losses on British planes during the Battle of the Somme. His innovation represented a major step forward in the development of aerial tactics. Unfortunately, Boelcke, who personally commanded one of these elite units, was killed when the plane of one of his own pilots collided with his aircraft.

The number of *Jagdstaffeln* increased steadily, and in June 1917 the German High Command grouped four of them in a mass unit called a wing (*Jagdgeschwader* 1). Baron Manfred von Richtofen, who had already won fame as a member of Boelcke's elite squadron and later as leader of *Jagdstaffel* 1, became the wing commander. Richtofen refined the tactics originated by Boelcke and shifted his forces as needed to maintain air supremacy in strategically important sectors of the front. *Geschwader* 1 soon became known as "the Flying Circus," in part because of its practice of shifting rapidly from sector to sector, but also because of the use of a wide variety of colors in decorating its aircraft. Red was the dominant color, however, and Richtofen flew an all-scarlet plane, which led to him being nicknamed "the Red Baron."

NEW AIRCRAFT INTRODUCED

During the spring and summer of 1917 the Allies introduced a series of new fighters, most notably the British Sopwith Camel and an upscaled version of the French Spad. With their help, they were again able to contest for control of the air. By 1917, both Sopwith and Fokker were producing triplanes. The three stubby wings of these aircraft gave them maximum lift and tight turning capability. In September of that year, the Germans intro-

FIGURE 12–2 "The Red Baron," Manfred von Richtofen, Germany's greatest flying ace. National Archives

duced the two-seater Halberstadt CL-2, which proved to be an excellent fighter, and in April 1918 they added the Fokker D VII biplane. These aircraft, along with the AEG armored "Flying Tank," assured that Germany would be able to contest the skies until the end of the war.

Early in the conflict, aerial combat took on some of the trappings of a bygone age. Pilots on both sides looked upon their opponents as respected rivals rather than hated enemies. They often made chivalrous gestures at the same time that they were trying to shoot each other down. Life expectancy for pilots was incredibly short, especially for the Allies who were reluctant to use parachutes! This was reflected in their behavior while off duty, which often took the form of roistering good fellowship and ample consumption of alcoholic beverages, complete with toasts to the dead and those next to die. Popular films such as "Dawn Patrol," made long after the war, captured something of the flavor of this precarious lifestyle.

Each country had its aces, a pilot who downed five enemy planes, including the Canadian Billy Bishop, credited with shooting down 72 enemy planes, and the Frenchman René Fonck with 75 "kills", both of whom survived the conflict. Most famous of all was Baron von Richtofen, who was responsible for 80 kills. Richtofen lost his life in April 1918 when his plane was shot down behind enemy lines. Allied flyers saw to it that he received a funeral worthy of his exploits with British pallbearers and an Australian honor guard. Richtofen's successor as commander of *Geschwader* 1 was none other than Hermann Goering, an ace in his own right with 21 kills who was destined to lead the German *Luftwaffe* during World War II. Numerous Americans enlisted in the Allied air forces well before the United States entered the war. Among the combat groups in the French air force was the all-American Lafayette Escadrille. After the United States became a belligerent, Edward (Eddie) Rickenbacker, a former race car driver, became the country's leading ace, shooting down 22 planes and four balloons, although American-designed planes never saw combat.

The character of aerial combat had changed significantly by 1917 as a result of the innovations of Boelcke, Richtofen, and others. Larger and larger concentrations of aircraft had superseded the old one-on-one "dogfights." By the fall of 1918, the Allies were able to put as many as 1,500 planes into the sky during an American offensive.

AERIAL BOMBING LAUNCHED

Both sides adapted some of their aircraft for the purpose of bombing military objectives early in the conflict. The French established the first squadron of planes specifically assigned to bombing missions in September 1914. Techniques were most primitive at first. Crew members simply dropped bombs out of their open cockpits by hand, often while on scouting operations. Before long, bomb racks began to appear on the undersides of planes. Germany was the first to utilize bombers in a fairly consistent early form of strategic bombing. They experimented with attacks on Britain in December 1914, but zeppelin raids continued to be the favored method until late 1916. The first squadron, especially designed to carry out air raids on British cities, took to the air in May 1917. It consisted of two-engine Gotha bombers. Later, four-engine "Giant" bombers joined the Gothas in this assault. The raids continued intermittently until June 1918.

Although their accuracy was poor and the damage inflicted negligible, these raids did kill 788 persons and wounded over 1,800. They also created terror far beyond that warranted by their results. Absenteeism among workers in British defense plants mounted alarmingly with a corresponding drop in armament production. As many as 300,000 people crowded into London subways to spend nights sleeping on station platforms, even when raids did not occur. The Germans eventually developed incendiary bombs, but the war ended before they were able to use them in "fire raids" on British cities. The development of these weapons, nevertheless, foreshadowed the incendiary attacks on British cities and, most notably, the fire-bombing raids on German and Japanese cities during World War II.

The British organized civil defense measures to combat German attacks, including searchlights, anti-aircraft guns, and barrage balloons, designed to interfere with enemy aircraft, as well as damage-control measures. Aircraft spotters warned of the approach of bombers, while fighter squadrons attempted to shoot them down. All of this again anticipated similar actions that would be taken during German air raids launched in the Battle of Britain in 1940.

THE RAF CREATED

Inevitably, the German attacks led to retaliation. In 1917, the British perfected the outstanding long-range Handley Page bomber and in April 1918 created the Royal Air Force (RAF), the first air service independent from both the army and navy. The RAF directed a bombing offensive against German cities in the last few months of the war. French bombers also engaged in raids on cities in western Germany in retaliation for occasional German attacks on Paris and other French towns. By the summer of 1918, American-manned planes took part in such raids as well. Again, the damage and casualties inflicted were minimal.

Although the results of their bombing of British cities deeply disappointed the Germans, the British were distressed by the end of virtual immunity from direct enemy attack, something they had always enjoyed because of their insular position. The impact of these contrasting attitudes lingered long after World War I. In the future, the RAF became enthusiastic about the potential of strategic airpower. Its more extreme champions believed that long-range bombers might be able to win the next war almost without help from ground or naval forces. The British

ultimately developed long-range four-engine bombers that devastated one German city after another during World War II. They also created first-rate fighter planes to defend Britain against bombing raids. Germany neglected strategic airpower and instead concentrated on the development of a tactical air force, which ably assisted the army in its spectacular victories during the early phase of World War II. But it proved quite inadequate in its attempt to bomb Britain into submission in 1940.

THE FIRST AIRCRAFT CARRIER

Still another innovation, combining both air and naval power, gradually evolved during World War I—the aircraft carrier. Actually, both Britain and the United States had experimented with landing airplanes on improvised flight decks aboard warships before 1914. When the conflict began, Britain converted a tramp steamer into the first aircraft carrier, the *Ark Royal*, although it carried only seaplanes. The British later converted several passenger ships into seaplane carriers. Vessels of this type played minor roles in both the Gallipoli operation and Jutland. Development of carriers for aircraft other than seaplanes progressed much more slowly. It was not until July 1918 that the British completed conversion of the light battle cruiser *Furious* into a carrier. Its role in the remaining few months of the war was of little importance. Few could foresee at the time that the aircraft carrier was destined to supersede the dreadnought and the battle cruiser as the primary surface warship within a little over two decades.

13

WAR AIMS
AND TOTAL WAR

When the Great War began in the summer of 1914, many civilians in the various belligerent countries greeted the news with jubilation as though they were embarking on a glorious new adventure. Huge throngs filled the squares of European cities to show rapturous support for their governments. Thousands of others lined the streets to cheer wildly and throw flowers to marching troops as they left for the front. Men flocked to the recruiting stations to volunteer for the army. They, too, looked forward to the conflict as a thrilling departure from the drab routine of civilian life. As one young German recruit enthusiastically observed when he received his uniform and weapons, "War is like Christmas." This early romantic acceptance of war amazed those who later reflected on the horrors that followed. It also led to a tendency to exaggerate the degree to which the European peoples welcomed the conflict.

Certainly not everyone eagerly embraced the strange new world that had dawned. Pacifists, those who distrusted the military, some union members, and socialists were hardly thrilled by the outbreak of war. And, the loved ones of those who set out to fight looked to the future with misgivings.

APPEALS TO PATRIOTISM

Many of those who did greet the war with enthusiasm found themselves caught up in patriotic appeals and a well-nigh universal belief that their own countries were the victims of aggression. In Germany, Chancellor Bethmann-Hollweg's hope that the people would accept Russian mobilization as irrefutable evidence of aggressive intent bore fruit. Even the Social Democrats, former champions of internationalism and peace, rallied to the support of the Fatherland in its hour of need. The political parties speedily agreed to submerge their differences in a political truce known as the *Burgfrieden* (Truce of the Fortress). This bound them to abstain from opposition to the government in the interest of the war effort. Similar responses occurred elsewhere. In France, President Raymond Poincaré appealed for a *Union Sacrée* (Sacred Union), and the political parties stifled their animosities to embrace the cause of *la Patrie* (the Nation). Russian political parties also put aside their disagreements to rally to the defense of Holy Mother Russia against Germany and Austria-Hungary. Even in the Dual Monarchy, various nationalities initially submerged their rivalries in declarations of unity and patriotism, although this spirit of a common bond did not last as long as elsewhere. The violation of Belgium's neutrality led to the conversion of the British Labour party and dissident Liberals—who had opposed the war only the day before—to the righteousness of Britain's cause.

The allure of war soon faded as the appalling casualty lists brought home its terrible reality, but in most countries the spirit of unity and dedication persisted for a long time to come. As the losses mounted and neither side was able to secure the expected knockout blow, leaders and important groups in society concluded that their countries must secure territorial and economic gains that would help justify the slaughter. Despite prewar tension and antagonism, the conflict had erupted so suddenly that the major powers at first had few, if any, clear-cut war aims. But they quickly developed them. During the remainder of the fighting, these goals varied according to the fortunes of war at any given time, but their basic outlines remained consistent.

AN APPETITE FOR TERRITORY

On the Allied side, Russia possessed the most robust appetite for European territory. It dreamed of acquiring gains at the expense of all the Central Powers with the exception of Bulgaria. A greatly augmented Russian-dominated Poland loomed especially large in Petrograd's plans. This would include Austrian Galicia as well as Germany's Polish territory, along with the industrial area of Upper Silesia, which had never been a part of Poland but contained a population that was one-third Polish. In addition, the Russians coveted a slice of East Prussia. Perhaps most important of all, the Russians sought to satisfy their age-old hunger for control of the Straits and Constantinople. They also desired portions of Turkish territory in Asia Minor.

The extent of Russia's war aims proved embarrassing to France and Britain. But the Western Allies felt that they must take a sympathetic approach, fearing the possibility of Petrograd making a separate peace if they did not. At the same time, they worried over the prospect of Russian power increasing to such an extent that it would upset the postwar equilibrium in Eastern Europe and the Near East. Despite these fears, in March 1915, the Western Allies agreed specifically to approve Russia's claim to the Straits and Constantinople, abandoning their long-standing opposition to Russian expansion into that region.

Russia also supported the aspirations of the Serbs to acquire the South Slav–populated areas of Austria-Hungary as well as Rumania's claim to Transylvania and the Banat, west of the Transylvanian Alps. Later, they also looked sympathetically at the prospect of independence for the Czechs. If all the ambitions of these various ethnic groups were satisfied, along with Russia's aims in Galicia, it would clearly mean the end of the Dual Monarchy.

FRENCH DESIGNS

Despite their misgivings, the French felt obliged to encourage Russian greed in order to secure their ally's support for their own aims in Western Europe. France's wishing list was not nearly as lengthy as Russia's, at least in regard to its own aggrandizement. Its centerpiece was the restoration of the lost provinces of Alsace and Lorraine. Beyond this, France's designs were less clear. They centered on what the French called security guarantees and involved four areas—Belgium, Luxembourg, the Saar, and the remainder of German territory on the west bank of the Rhine, usually referred to as the Rhineland.

The French were determined to restore the independence of Belgium, but based on close economic and political cooperation with France. Luxembourg, which had been closely associated economically with Germany before the war, was also of special interest to the French. They favored the Grand Duchy's annexation either by Belgium or preferably France. The Saar, a small area just to the north of Lorraine, was completely German in population, but the French hoped to annex it so that they could exploit its rich coal and iron ore deposits. As for the Rhineland, the more extreme among the French hoped to absorb it as well, but most leaders aspired to the more moderate goal of detaching it from German rule in the form of one or more separate states. They also looked forward to a close economic relationship with this area and a French military presence there for at least a number of years. Paris viewed the separation of the Rhineland as the key to France's security against the possibility of a future German attack. In their most imaginative flights of fancy, some Frenchmen speculated on breaking up all of Germany into a number of small states and the drastic reduction of Prussian influence. Especially dear to French hearts was the destruction of "Prussian militarism" by enforcing definite limits on German armed forces. French leaders also desired colonial compensation in the form of a share of Germany's West African colonies of Togoland

and the Cameroons as well as portions of the Ottoman Empire, most notably Syria.

To be sure, not everyone in the government agreed on the extent of the war aims, and French society, as in regard to so many other issues, was divided on this matter. Industrial and commercial organizations as well as various patriotic leagues tended to favor the more extreme goals. Socialists, labor unions, and pacifist groups preferred a peace that would not antagonize the Germans and make them eager for revenge. Socialist leaders opposed annexations and even favored a plebiscite in which the people of Alsace-Lorraine could determine their own fate. French ambitions also came under the restraining influence of Britain, which did not relish an excessive growth of French power in the postwar era. When the United States entered the war in 1917, Washington also opposed many of France's war aims. In fact, before America became a belligerent, President Wilson tried to mediate a negotiated settlement, which would have restored Europe essentially to its prewar status quo. Given these internal and external restraints, French leaders always aspired to more in private than they admitted publicly.

BRITISH AIMS

Britain possessed no ambitions in Europe other than a desire to preserve the balance of power that London believed Germany threatened, the destruction of German naval and maritime commercial power, and relatively free access to European markets. But the British did maintain their traditional interest in colonial compensation. They especially coveted the German African colonies of Southwest Africa on the Atlantic and Tanganyika (German East Africa) on the Indian Ocean. Acquisition of the latter would provide the final link in a chain of British possessions extending from the Cape of Good Hope to Egypt. Britain, like other Allied powers, was interested in Turkish territory as well, but the British also hoped to gain the active cooperation of millions of Arabs living under Turkish rule. In addition, London sought the support of Jews in the worldwide Zionist movement that desired establishment of a Jewish homeland in Palestine.

To obtain these varied and conflicting goals, the British were extremely free with promises. In early 1916, they agreed to the establishment of an independent Arab state after the war, although they were rather vague about its borders. This pledge contributed to the outbreak of an Arab revolt against the Turks in 1916, coordinated by Captain T. E. Lawrence who negotiated in good faith with King Hussein, one of the Arab leaders. But contrary to the spirit of its promise to the Arabs, Foreign Secretary Arthur Balfour declared in November 1917 that Britain would "view with favor the establishment in Palestine of a national home for the Jewish people" and would work "to facilitate the achievement of this object."

Worse yet, Britain and France had already agreed to partition much of the northern Arab-populated areas between themselves. This understanding, worked out by Sir Mark Sykes, representing Britain, and Georges Picot of France in May 1916, recognized Britain's predominant interest in Palestine and Mesopotamia and France's in Syria. The conflicting obligations to the Arabs and Jews as well as the Sykes-Picot Agreement became the source of controversy and conflict that lingered long after World War I.

Italy, of course, specifically stipulated its price for intervening on the Allied side in the 1915 Treaty of London—the Trentino, Trieste, Istria, and much of the Adriatic coast as well as portions of Asia Minor. However, Serbia would accept nothing less than annexation of all South Slav–populated territory in Austria-Hungary, an aspiration that came into conflict with those of Italy in Istria and the Adriatic. Even little Belgium harbored dreams of annexing both Luxembourg and the Maastrict Appendix of the neutral Netherlands' province of Limburg.

GOALS OF THE CENTRAL POWERS

Members of the Central Powers also became embroiled in conflicts over various territories. Bulgaria and Turkey each had designs on Thrace, which stretched along the northern coast of the Aegean Sea. The Turks agitated for the return of those portions that Bulgaria and Greece had gained at Turkish expense in the Balkan wars. They also wanted to regain their former Macedonian territory from both Greece and Serbia as well as Transcaucasian provinces along their northeastern border with Russia. The latter area had been lost in the Russo-Turkish War of 1877–1878. Not content with this, the Turks also hoped to acquire additional land beyond the 1877 frontier. Some leaders dreamed of regaining Egypt and Libya as well as expanding into parts of Persia and Russia's Central Asian provinces. Bulgaria expected to regain the land it had lost to both Rumania and Serbia in the Balkan wars, while retaining the territory it had gained from Turkey in the same conflict.

Austria-Hungary had entered the war under István Tisza's prohibition against annexation of any additional Slavic territory. However, before long, various leaders began to speak in terms of partitioning Serbia among the Dual Monarchy, Bulgaria, and Albania. Conrad, true to form, urged that Austria-Hungary absorb, not only all of Serbia but also Montenegro. Policy toward Serbia remained vague, however, and Austro-Hungarian leaders actually devoted more attention to the fate of Poland. This interest originated with an upsurge of Polish nationalism after the outbreak of the war and the desire of Polish leaders to create a restored Poland from territory that the Central Powers wrested from Russia in 1915. To the Austrians, such a development posed a threat to the Polish population in Galicia. They came to believe that the best solution would be to unite Russian Poland and Galicia within the borders of the Dual Monarchy. One possible way to accomplish this would be to grant the new Polish state equality with Austria and Hungary on the basis of trialism. This would supersede the traditional system of dualism in effect since the *Augsleich* of 1867 and was quite unacceptable to Tisza, Foreign Minister Stephan Burián, and other Magyar leaders. They preferred that Poland be annexed to the Austrian portion of the monarchy and that Hungary receive compensation in the form of Bosnia and probably the Dalmatian coast along the Adriatic.

Austrian ambitions toward Poland also encountered firm opposition from the Germans, who were sensitive to such a solution because it might act as a magnet to the Poles within the borders of eastern Germany. In addition, Poland became a major item on Germany's own list of war aims, by all odds the most extensive of any of the warring powers. This area became one of the chief bones of contention between the two major Central Powers. As Germany's stature in the coalition grew ever more dominant, it became increasingly obvious that Poland would be drawn permanently into its orbit, if the Central Powers won the war.

Not only that, the Germans visualized a new *Mitteleuropa* (Central Europe), which would link the Dual Monarchy and Germany in a customs union. Such a development would lead to German economic domination of its partner because Austria-Hungary's less well-developed industries would be unable to compete with those of Germany in a free-market situation. It also would promote

closer political and military ties. While the Dual Monarchy managed to resist this proposal, it did concede Russian Poland to Germany in July 1916, following the disastrous Brusilov offensive. As the war dragged on, Austria-Hungary's chief war aims became the preservation of its own existence and resistance to German domination.

As for Poland, Germany planned to annex a strip of territory along its border for strategic purposes. In November 1916, the Germans actually established an "independent" Poland, in which they would exercise strong influence. Germany's war aims in the east went well beyond Poland, however. Berlin envisaged the creation of separate states in Lithuania, Courland (Kurland), and Livonia as well as the Ukraine. Some leaders preferred annexation of Lithuania and Courland. Eventually, Germany extended its focus to include creation of new states in Estonia, Finland, and even Transcaucasia. Its interest in the latter area, which it viewed as a bridge to Central Asia, conflicted with those of its Turkish ally. The Germans also contemplated increasing their economic influence in Russia and extending their *Mitteleuropa* scheme to include much of Eastern Europe as well as the Scandinavian states.

In the west, German aims were not as grandiose. They included annexation of Luxembourg and perhaps parts of Belgium and strong German influence in the remainder. The Pan-German League favored absorption of France's iron-rich area of Longwy-Briey adjacent to Lorraine and French membership in an economic union linked to *Mitteleuropa*. The Pan-German League also looked forward to expansion in Africa. This would include appropriation of the Belgian Congo in the heart of the continent and an assortment of French colonies bordering the Congo, creating a vast German *Mittelafrika*, as well as the Portuguese possessions of Angola along the Atlantic coast and Mozambique on the Indian

Ocean. The Pan-German League sent a petition to Chancellor Bethmann-Hollweg in May 1915, urging him to adopt their program; the petition also appeared in the press. The government, however, attempted to suppress this annexationist agitation. In January of that same year it had even ordered the searching of homes, confiscation of annexationist materials, and the placing of some league members under surveillance. League leaders had protested all of this as a violation of civil rights.

Although German military leaders were most insistent on extreme war aims and the most favorably inclined toward actual annexation of territory, some civilian leaders shared much of their expansionist ardor as did large elements of German society. Indeed, German industrialists often saw eye to eye with the generals and admirals. In recent decades, specialists in this period of German history have argued vehemently over the question of Bethmann-Hollweg's support for expansionist war aims. While his defenders contend that he tried to moderate them as much as possible in the face of intense pressure, critics accuse him of being only slightly less expansionist. This argument is likely to continue as long as the debate over the question of responsibility for the war itself.

RATIONALIZING THE WAR

As the conflict persisted, not only did the death toll mount to absurd levels but the pressure on the economies of the belligerent powers grew ever more intense. Logic seemed to dictate a negotiated peace to stop the bleeding and the drain on resources. Indeed, all the warring powers recognized the need to end the conflict as quickly as possible. But their war aims defied logic and took on a momentum of their own. And, since the aims of the rival alliances were so diametrically opposed, there was no real basis for peace.

Although the powers played at negotiation from time to time, they did so in an atmosphere of total unreality. Most notably, in the fall of 1916, the Central Powers explored the possibility of a peace overture to the Allies. But both Germany and Austria-Hungary sought extensive territorial gains in the process, none of which would have been acceptable to the Allies. Indeed, Germany's were so grandiose that Chancellor Bethmann-Hollweg insisted on mentioning no specific terms. When the Central Powers dispatched their peace note on December 12, it simply announced that they were willing to discuss peace. The Allies turned down the proposal on the grounds that it lacked any concrete terms.

Six days later, President Woodrow Wilson, operating independently, offered to act as mediator to secure a settlement and requested specific proposals of war aims from both sides. Germany again refused to be pinned down and indicated that Wilson's efforts undercut Berlin's own peace initiative. The Allies were much more forthcoming. On January 10, 1917, they frankly stated many of their major war aims as the basis for any consideration of a settlement. Although thoroughly discouraged by this mutual intransigence, on January 22, Wilson called for a "peace without victory," adding that only a settlement "between equals can last." Obviously, neither side was interested in such an approach and chose to continue the conflict.

THE DESIRE FOR PEACE, THE THREAT OF REVOLUTION

The desire for peace became more pronounced after the unfolding of the horrors of 1916. Weakening French morale had been evident during the Battle of Verdun. The same held true of the Germans in the later stages of the Battle of the Somme. The Brusilov campaign and its lingering after-

math had brought both the Russian and Austro-Hungarian armies near the breaking
point. The futility of war and the passage of
time had also eroded the unity of the civilian
populations. Agitation for peace, hardly dis-
cernible in the early stages of the conflict,
became more evident by the end of 1916 and
increased sharply during 1917.

The chief impetus for peace came from the
Left. But for some time it was a feeble and
disjointed one. The patriotic fervor with
which European society greeted the war shattered the supposed unity of socialism and
sounded the death knell for the Second International organization. Most socialists had
rallied to the defense of their own country
and loyally supported its war effort, but
the more radical elements had remained
aloof and viewed the conflict as an imperialist struggle engineered by the capitalist-
dominated governments on both sides.
The Bolshevik or Orthodox Marxist wing of
Russian socialism was the most militant.
Vladimir Lenin and other Bolshevik leaders
were living in exile in Switzerland when the
war began. To them, the conflict offered an
ideal opportunity for the socialist cause. They
believed it would spawn widespread dissatisfaction and sap the strength of the capitalist
regimes, creating the conditions necessary for
a successful revolution.

Other left-wing socialists viewed such
cynicism as immoral. They reacted to the
war's massive carnage with horror and believed that their first duty was to win back the
working class to the cause of peace. It was a
tricky undertaking, requiring a delicate bal-
ancing act that avoided offending the patriotic workers, who might look upon such an
approach as defeatist and possibly treason-
ous. For a long time, it did not produce any
significant results.

In September 1915, Italian and Swiss socialist leaders attempted to bring together
representatives from the various countries in
a secret conference at Zimmerwald, Switzerland, but only 38 delegates attended. The
conference unanimously approved a declaration calling upon the workers of Europe "to
reorganize and begin a struggle for peace."
This Zimmerwald Manifesto advocated "a
peace without annexations and war indemnities." The delegates also organized a new
International Socialist Committee with headquarters in the Swiss capital of Bern to further
the cause of peace.

Lenin wanted to go far beyond this. He
urged his fellow socialist leaders to transform
the war into a class conflict. The majority of
the delegates refused to adopt such a policy,
but a minority group rallied around Lenin
and formed what soon became known as the
Zimmerwald Left movement. When a second
socialist conference convened in Kienthal,
also in Switzerland, in April 1916, Lenin's
group increased its representation but still
failed to gain general acceptance of its radical
program.

Not all opponents of the war were on the
Left. Lord Lansdowne, the former Conservative British foreign secretary who had helped
create the *Entente Cordiale* in 1904, circulated
a memorandum to members of the cabinet
favoring a negotiated peace in November
1916. A year later, he publicly advocated such
a settlement. Lansdowne quickly became the
target of a vicious campaign of vilification by
the more rabidly patriotic press. In France,
Joseph Caillaux, who had served as premier
at the time of the Second Moroccan Crisis,
feared the impact of the war on France with
its smaller population as well as the danger
of a socialist revolution. He proposed a negotiated peace as early as 1915, and in
1917 the French government actually
charged him with treason, although he won
acquittal. During the second half of 1917,
former French Premier Aristide Briand engaged in contacts with German intermedi-
aries, mistakenly believing that Germany

would agree to return Alsace-Lorraine to France. Not surprisingly, his efforts accomplished nothing. In Italy, Giovanni Giolitti, who had opposed his country's entry into the war in 1915, shared Caillaux's concern about the threat of revolution and also favored a negotiated settlement.

THE CONCEPT OF TOTAL WAR

All of these sources of opposition continued for some time to be voices crying in the wilderness. The governments of the warring powers remained committed to winning the conflict and attaining their war aims. As it became obvious that the struggle would be long, arduous, and expensive, they turned to the task of harnessing their countries' efforts to achieve this monumental task. A new concept of "total war" gradually took shape. It focused on the interrelationship among war and politics, technology, the economy, and the morale of both the armed forces and the civilian population. The extent to which the belligerent governments succeeded in approaching a total mobilization of their resources varied considerably from country to country. But, unlike other wars, there were few people who did not feel the impact of the struggle on their lives. In the past, innumerable areas overrun or besieged by invading armies had experienced the horrors of war. But World War I was the first conflict in which zeppelins and airplanes rained death from the skies, an innovation that had special meaning for the British in their once virtually impregnable island home. These attacks, nevertheless, were still relatively isolated occurrences.

A much more general development came in the form of the gradual regimentation of the civilian population for the purpose of winning the war. Again, this was not without precedent. During the war that was triggered by the French Revolution in the 1790s, the government in Paris had created a mass conscript army and attempted to instill a revolutionary spirit in the French people. In this case, however, the revolutionary regime faced not only external enemies but also substantial numbers of internal foes who opposed many of the revolutionary changes as much too radical. It never achieved such an all-inclusive unity as that of the *Union Sacrée* of 1914.

THE POWER OF PROPAGANDA

The creation of national unity, combined with the war's great length and the high degree of sacrifice required of servicemen and civilians alike, imbued the conflict with ideological overtones unmatched since the wars of religion in the sixteenth and seventeenth centuries. In this desperate struggle, governments on both sides portrayed the enemy as the personification of evil, capable of the most heinous atrocities and harboring the most diabolical war aims. Propaganda created a new dimension in warfare, one that was especially effective because of the speed and breadth of communications. The warring powers sought to mobilize the popular press and film in the cause of victory and fulfillment of their war aims through the use of censorship and managed news. One way to accomplish this was to foster hatred of the enemy. Publications that were less than enthusiastic about the conflict could expect government hostility and perhaps suppression.

ATTITUDES OF TROOPS

Ironically, the opposing soldiers who were engaged in the daily occupation of killing their fellow men frequently harbored less hatred toward the enemy than did civilians on the home front. Soldiers shared a bond of suffering that transcended the reality of artillery, machine guns, and barbed wire. On quiet sectors of the front or during lulls in the fighting, troops from both sides at times observed informal truces. In 1914, some Allied and German soldiers even exchanged gifts at Christmas. To the civilian populations, however, the enemy was far less tangible. He became an abstraction, a symbol to be hated and, if possible, destroyed.

Indeed, fighting men frequently bore greater animosity toward their own countrymen living secure lives in Paris or Berlin than toward the "poor bastards" on the other side of "no-man's-land." They were particularly bitter toward those who profited shamelessly from the war, government officials who were responsible for shortages, and staff officers who ordered suicidal offensives while living in comfort far from the battlefield. Workers in war industries also became objects of their scorn because they had escaped combat, were relatively well paid, and, of course, were living at home. To the men at the front, the complaints of workers regarding wartime privations were little more than whining about minor inconveniences. Soldiers home on leave often found it difficult to adjust to a routine devoid of danger, dirt, and death. They frequently felt a certain relief when they left this strange world behind and returned to their comrades and the reality of the front. This sense of the comradeship of the front would linger long after the shooting stopped in 1918. As the novelist Erich Maria Remarque, who served in the German army during the war, later wrote:

It is a great brotherhood, which to a condition of life arising out of the midst of danger, out of the tension and forlornness of death, adds something of the good-fellowship of the folk-song, of the feeling of solidarity of convicts, and of the desperate loyalty to one another of men condemned to death...[1]

---

[1]Erich Maria Remarque, *All Quiet on the Western Front* (Greenwich, Conn.: Fawcett Publications, Inc., 1958), p. 162.

While the great economic progress of the nineteenth century and early twentieth century created the potential for total war, it also made the belligerent powers extremely vulnerable. Their economies were geared to the intricate worldwide network of peacetime industry and trade. The voracious demands of war dislocated this pattern of relationships and created great strain on the economies of individual nations. This pressure effected the warring powers in different ways.

EFFECTS OF THE WAR ON FRANCE

France quickly found its ability to produce war material sharply curtailed by German occupation of the northeastern region of the country. Unfortunately, this area contained many of its coal deposits and much of its iron and steel production as well as major textile centers. To compensate for this, the French developed new industries in the suburbs of Paris and the central and southern parts of the country, while expanding the size and capacity of existing factories. The mobilization of millions of men into the army also created a serious industrial manpower shortage. To fill this void, women assumed jobs in war industries even before the government began to encourage employment of females in such positions during 1915. The number of women engaged in production of war materiel grew steadily until late 1917 or early 1918. Women found employment in many areas of industry, although they were unable to gain access to most skilled positions, which remained a male monopoly. While their wages remained lower than those of male workers, the gap between them appears to have narrowed during the war.

All of these unprecedented efforts resulted in an amazing increase in war production. France, nevertheless, had no choice but to look to Britain and the United States for raw materials and other forms of aid. By 1916, it depended on the United States for 30 percent of its imports and was the beneficiary of American loans totaling well over three billion francs. This growing economic dependence on America acted as a restraining influence on French war aims.

Despite the proliferation of wartime problems, France's standard of living did not decline markedly for some time, and the value of the currency remained relatively stable. France, unlike Britain, Germany, and Austria, had been self-sufficient in agriculture before the war. Unfortunately, the army's demand for manpower drained away agricultural workers, creating a labor shortage in the countryside. In 1917, a bad harvest confronted France with a food shortage for the first time in many years. Inflation also gradually worsened and by early 1917 had created unrest among French workers, who resorted to a rapidly accelerating series of strikes. Real wages for French workers dropped by 20 percent, owing largely to the impact of inflation. These factors, combined with the impact of the dreadful casualties and the indecisiveness of the war, gradually eroded morale and weakened the Union Sacrée.

Until 1917, the French military rather than the civilian government dominated France's war effort. Under both Generals Joffre and Robert Nivelle, the army determined strategy as well as allocation of resources. The government essentially went along with its demands in the interest of victory. In the Zone of the Armies, the military ruled as a law unto itself and only released information as it saw fit to both the government and the people. It persisted in putting the best possible face on its bloody and futile offensives.

The government of Premier René Viviani, which had come to power in June 1914, transformed itself into a national coalition in August of that year. Viviani dedicated himself to maintaining the Union Sacrée and winning the war. To help achieve these goals, his government imposed censorship of the press and banned all publications favoring peace or even discussing the possibility of a negotiated settlement. The Chamber of Deputies met in frequent sessions but for a long time staunchly backed the war effort and abandoned its chronic political infighting. Viviani and his cabinet were unable to survive the combined military disasters of 1915, however, and resigned in October.

His successor Aristide Briand, who later became a leading advocate of a negotiated peace, took the opposite approach during his 16 months as French premier and championed the cause of war to a victorious conclusion. His government was even more insistent on censorship of any publications preaching the need for peace. Briand held office throughout the Battle of Verdun and was instrumental, along with Poincaré, in the dismissal of Joffre as commander-in-chief of the army and the choice of Robert Nivelle as his replacement in December 1916. The premier himself felt compelled to resign in March 1917, amidst growing criticism of Nivelle from both military and civilian sources.

When Nivelle launched a disastrously unsuccessful offensive in April 1917, the Chamber of Deputies was so outraged that it began to take a more active role. This resulted in a brief return to instability as two men, Alexander Ribot and Paul Painlevé, served in turn as premier during the next eight months. The Nivelle offensive led to widespread mutinies in the army as well as demands from socialists and pacifists for an end to the fighting. In November, President Poincaré called upon his old political enemy, the fiery Georges Clemenceau, to form a new government. Poincaré recognized that Clemenceau, a former radical in the tradition of the French Revolution, shared his all-consuming fervor for victory and would accept nothing less. Clemenceau proved true to his nickname, "the Tiger," and turned ferociously on anyone whom he considered guilty of defeatism. To him, those who favored a negotiated peace were guilty of treason. Under Clemenceau, the French government gained control of the direction of the war for the first time. Clemenceau introduced measures to mobilize the economy totally for the purpose of achieving victory and pressed successfully for the pooling of the economic resources of the Allies in this common cause.

But the events of 1916–1917 had destroyed the *Union Sacrée*. While the bulk of the population no doubt supported Clemenceau, opponents of the war, though stifled by the government, remained sullenly opposed to Clemenceau's policies.

EFFECTS OF THE WAR ON BRITAIN

When the war began, Britain devoted only a small amount of its industry to the production of war materiel. As it became clear that the British would contribute far more man-

FIGURE 13–1 "The Tiger," Premier Georges Clemenceau of France. National Archives

power to the land war than originally believed, war industries expanded dramatically as did governmental expenditures on armament and munitions. By 1918, they accounted for 52 percent of the country's gross national product and 80 percent of government spending. This vast expansion created a demand for manpower but, as more and more men became members of the armed forces, women moved into the work force in greater numbers. This influx did not begin immediately, however. Initially, many women already employed in industry found themselves thrown out of work as peacetime production declined, especially in textile industries. The greatest increase in employment of women in war production took place after June 1916. By June of the following year, women constituted almost half the work force. Again, as in France, many of the most skilled jobs in such areas as shipbuilding and the manufacture of heavy artillery remained in the hands of men. Women's wages also lagged behind those of males. Overall, workers improved their position during the war as a result of full employment and overtime work. The union movement also flourished, its membership almost doubling between 1914 and 1918. But working-class grievances remained, and strikes increased in number in the last years of the war.

Few people anticipated the tremendous impact that the war would have on the British economy and the free enterprise system. Many expected to do "business as usual" and even anticipated the advantage of acquiring Germany's overseas markets. These happy illusions soon faded as it became clear that Britain did not have the capacity to continue normal peacetime production and trade at the same time that it vastly increased the output of war materiel. Far from expanding their share of world markets, the British quickly lost most of their existing ones to American and Japanese competition.

The government soon encroached on the operation of various industries, most notably railroads and shipping. Parliament also enacted the first of a series of Defence of the Realm Acts, nicknamed DORA, within four days of Britain's entry into the war. DORA initially granted the government extensive powers to take action against any activities that might threaten national security. As amended during the next two years, it authorized extensive controls over the economy. The government used this power to regulate industry and extract from labor unions an agreement to abandon strikes for the duration of the conflict and to accept arbitration in disputes. It eventually gained control over the management of coal mines and introduced food rationing in early 1918. Many liberal-minded people viewed all of this as a dangerous interference with individual freedom.

Britain also resorted to censorship of the news, establishing an official bureau that issued press releases and checked other stories not originating from the government. Censorship tightened as the deadlock at the front continued. The government shielded the population from the full horror of war in the trenches as well as the extent of German bombing raids on British cities. At times, the government suppressed pacifist publications as well as newspapers critical of the conduct of the war. British authorities also made skillful use of propaganda. They emphasized accounts of German atrocities, often in an exaggerated form. These focused on such things as the shooting of Belgian hostages and submarine attacks on merchant ships and passenger liners, most glaringly the sinking of the *Lusitania*. Propaganda proved useful both in increasing anti-German feeling among the British people and in helping create pro-British sympathies in neutral countries, especially the United States.

Inflation became an increasing problem, and during 1917 the government sought a remedy through price and wage controls and increased taxes. Britain paid for its war expenditures from taxation to a much greater degree than did most other powers. The British also played their traditional role of financing their allies, who soon found it impossible to pay for the enormous cost of imported war materiel through their own resources. Eventually, however, the task became too much, and Britain as well as its allies had to turn to the United States for loans.

When Lloyd George became prime minister at the end of 1916, most of the controls on manpower, economic resources, and public opinion were already in place. But he approached the war with a dedication similar to that of Clemenceau, and the former pacifist would accept nothing short of complete victory. His government resorted to increased censorship and the overstating or outright fabrication of German atrocities as it attempted to counteract the growth of war weariness and support for a negotiated peace. While British military leaders never gained the degree of independence from civilian control that their French counterparts enjoyed, Generals Robertson and Haig had maintained strong influence over strategy under Asquith. Lloyd George strove to bring them to heel and even tried to oust Haig from his command. But Haig maintained such tenacious support from Robertson and other civilian leaders that the prime minister was never able to remove him. Almost immediately after coming to power, Lloyd George also had to grapple with the new and, for a time, extremely serious menace posed by Germany's policy of unrestricted submarine warfare.

CONDITIONS IN GERMANY

Despite its industrial leadership and vaunted reputation for efficiency, Germany entered the conflict with no more economic planning for a long war than did either France or Britain. It had approached the struggle with confidence that the Schlieffen Plan would bring a speedy victory. The government had made no provisions for dealing with the food shortage certain to result from a British naval blockade. Like Britain, Germany was dependent upon large-scale food imports from overseas and from Russia. All of these sources quickly dried up, forcing the Germans to fall back on their own limited agriculture and imports from the Netherlands and Scandinavian countries. To meet this challenge, the government quickly introduced food rationing and before long developed *ersatz* (substitute) foods, such as nonmeat sausages and "war bread," consisting of a mixture of 80 percent flour and 20 percent potato or turnip. Shortages of other resources soon added to Germany's problems, although certain developments such as the invention by the chemist Fritz Haber of synthetic nitrates—crucial for munitions and for agricultural fertilizers—demonstrated the tremendous resilience of a modern industrialized nation. Despite such efforts, shortages of food and many other items grew steadily worse. The government's only other early major regulatory measure was the establishment in late 1914 of a section in the War Office for the allocation of raw materials. No full-scale attempt at economic mobilization came until 1916.

Germany's financial situation never had been as strong as that of Britain or France, and the country did not possess the reserves necessary to deal with the staggering cost of modern war. But the Germans proved most reluctant to finance the conflict through increased taxation and resorted to massive borrowing instead. As a result, the national debt rose rapidly, and inflation increased throughout the war. By October 1918, the German mark had lost 60 percent of its prewar value, creating great hardship for many people, especially those living on fixed incomes, pensions, and savings.

At the same time, the government failed to establish industrial price and wage controls until early 1918 and then only in a half-hearted way. Industrialists producing war materiel reaped large profits in the process. With the usual wartime labor shortage confronting them, they offered high wages to workers in an attempt to lure them away from agriculture and from industries producing consumer goods. The influx of women into the labor force was not as extensive in Germany as it was in France and Britain. Those who did replace men in war industries tended to shift from prewar manufacturing jobs in the consumer-goods sector of the economy. Despite its reluctance to establish controls on industry, the government's concern about the food supply led to the imposition of stringent price controls on food, which hurt agricultural interests.

The combination of the relentless carnage on the battlefield, persistent shortages, and other hardships among the civilian population gradually undermined the *Burgfrieden*. The worsening of the food supply during the terrible winter of 1916, referred to as the "turnip winter" because of growing dependence on the turnip for food during this period, also took its toll on civilian morale. The first opposition to the war came from the left-wing socialists, who were a minority within the Social Democratic party. They never had much confidence in the government's insistence on the defensive nature of the conflict. But they initially voted for war credits in the Reichstag to maintain party unity. As time passed, however, they voted against additional credits. This action brought them into conflict with the majority of the party, who remained loyal to the war effort. In 1917, they broke away and established the Independent Social Democratic party. However, the Independent Socialists were badly split between

moderates, who merely opposed the war, and radicals, who believed the party should pave the way for revolution. Starting in mid-1916, the radicals helped inspire a series of naval mutinies and strikes that continued into 1918.

POLITICAL CHANGES IN GERMANY

Despite the Social Democratic split, both parties continued to work for reform of the undemocratic electorate in the state of Prussia. The majority Social Democrats also cooperated with the liberal Progressive party in an attempt to make the German chancellor and state secretaries responsible to the Reichstag. By 1917, the leaders of the Catholic Center party and some of the National Liberals had joined in this effort. Together they constituted a majority in the Reichstag, but conservatives, including Hindenburg and Ludendorff, remained totally opposed to any change in either the Prussian franchise or the role of the Reichstag.

For a long time, Chancellor Bethmann-Hollweg tried to steer a tortuous course between the two extremes. In the process, he lost the support of both. Early in July 1917, the Social Democrats, Progressives, and Catholic Center all cooperated in an effort to gain passage of a resolution stating that Germany held only defensive war aims. Bethmann-Hollweg urged the parties not to push such a peace resolution and, to appease them, he took the desperate step of pressuring William II to issue a declaration supporting a democratic suffrage for Prussia. This was too much for Hindenburg and Ludendorff, who already distrusted the chancellor because of his opposition to unrestricted submarine warfare. They threatened to resign unless the emperor dismissed Bethmann-Hollweg. Confronted by their ultimatum, the chancellor decided that he had no choice but to resign. After suggesting

Tirpitz and former chancellor Bülow, both of whom were unacceptable to the emperor, as Bethmann's successor, Hindenburg and Ludendorff finally insisted on the appointment of Georg Michaelis as chancellor. William agreed without consulting the party leaders in the Reichstag.

Angered by this insult, the reform parties refused to abandon their intention to push for a negotiated settlement, and the Reichstag passed a peace resolution on July 25. It stated somewhat vaguely that the Reichstag sought a peace of understanding and reconciliation but fell short of an outright rejection of all territorial annexations. Michaelis simply accepted the resolution but added the qualification "as I understand it." In effect, he understood it as leaving the way open to the pursuit of ambitious war aims.

The ouster of Bethmann-Hollweg as German chancellor represented a serious military encroachment on the government. From this point, Germany increasingly took on the character of a military dictatorship. Hindenburg and Ludendorff remained dominant in the decision-making process until late in the war as William II gradually faded into the role of a virtual figurehead. Michaelis was little more than a front man for them. A narrow Prussian conservative, he had spent his entire career in secondary roles in the Prussian government and lacked political experience. He had done an able job of administering the rationing of grain and

FIGURE 13–2 Field Marshal Paul von Hindenburg (left) and General Erich Ludendorff (right) brief Emperor William II at their military headquarters. National Archives

bread in Prussia but was completely out of his depth in trying to deal with the parties in the Reichstag. Michaelis lasted less than three months and was succeeded by the 78-year-old Bavarian Count Georg von Hertling. Although a man of liberal tendencies who favored Prussian suffrage reform, Hertling was well past his prime and determined to avoid antagonizing the all-powerful generals at OKL. He also opposed any additional peace proposals in the Reichstag.

Ludendorff became the dominant figure in the emerging dictatorship, but he operated behind the imposing facade of the fatherly Hindenburg, who had become the symbol of Germany's war effort. Ludendorff set out to instill a militaristic spirit and all-consuming will to victory in the German people. To help accomplish this, he promoted the image of Hindenburg as a larger-than-life hero who would lead Germany to inevitable triumph. He received aid from Admiral Tirpitz and the Pan-German extremist Wolfgang Kapp, who organized the ultrapatriotic Fatherland party. They viewed the party as a mechanism to unite the people behind Hindenburg and the war effort as well as a peace that would secure maximum territorial gains. Always the master of propaganda, Tirpitz was able to recruit well over one million members to the party, but they came almost exclusively from the landowning and upper middle classes.

Despite their assumption of virtual dictatorial power, Hindenburg and Ludendorff proved remarkably ineffective in their efforts to carry out a massive increase in war production. Too many shortages confronted them, while German industrial firms remained amazingly independent from government controls and pursued their own interests. Ironically, Britain and France, where civilian authorities had retained overall control of the war effort, proved much more efficient in organizing and directing a total war economy.

CONDITIONS IN ITALY

The task of pursuing a total war policy proved far more difficult for Italy, Austria-Hungary, and Russia. Their economies were far less well developed than those of Britain, France, and Germany, and their governmental structures were poorly suited for shouldering this burden. They did what they could to increase production and make efficient use of resources but quickly became dependent on their allies for aid.

Italy had a particular problem in its almost total lack of natural resources. This required it to import vast amounts of raw materials. It also needed large-scale loans to finance its war effort. For some time, the Western Allies were so hampered by shortages of weapons and munitions themselves that material aid was slight, but financial assistance was more readily available. More than most of the other major powers, Italy faced the additional problem of disunity on the basic question of the wisdom of entering the conflict. There was no Italian *Union Sacrée*, because Italy could hardly contend that it was waging a defensive war.

Although the former neutralists supported the war effort once the conflict began, they did so without enthusiasm. As the casualties mounted and the fighting along the Isonzo and in the Trentino brought no gains worth mentioning, this support weakened, and the neutralists became increasingly critical of the government. Shortages quickly hamstrung efforts to boost war production and created hardships among the civilian population. The Italian government also proved incapable of introducing effective economic controls. Prices rose, the food supply contracted, and the standard of living declined. By the summer of 1917, food riots broke out in the northern city of Turin.

The interventionists, who vigorously supported the war, deeply distrusted the neutralists. Some of them urged measures to crack down on dissidents and were angry when the government failed to take action. General Luigi Cadorna became insistent on such a policy. After the fall of the government of Antonio Salandra and the establishment of Paolo Boselli's government in 1916, he violently criticized Minister of the Interior, Vittorio Orlando for his refusal to deal with what the chief of staff referred to as "the enemy within." As time passed, the socialists became steadily more insistent on the need for peace, and many Catholics also criticized the continuation of the war. In the summer of 1917, Pope Benedict XV called for an end to the "useless carnage" and sent notes to all the warring powers offering his mediation in a quest for peace. Prowar enthusiasts urged Cadorna to combat "defeatism" from leftist and Catholic circles by creating a military dictatorship. By the fall of 1917, both civilian and military morale had reached a low ebb.

CONFLICTS IN THE DUAL MONARCHY

Austria-Hungary, of course, suffered from the unique problems of its multitude of ethnic groups and the system of dualism. Effective economic mobilization was impossible in the face of Hungary's insistence on its separate identity and reluctance to share its food supply with Austria. As in the case of other powers, the Dual Monarchy had not undertaken any advance economic planning for a long war. It had provided no reserves of food or raw materials, and its industrial sector, while stronger than Italy's, was clearly inadequate for the enormous pressure of total war. Despite all these problems, Austria-Hungary did make remarkable progress in industrial production until late 1916 when a coal shortage and wear and tear on the rail system reversed this trend. Women freed many male workers for service

in the army. In fact, by 1916, women provided 78 percent of the work force in some munitions plants. For the entire war, females in the labor force increased by about 40 percent. As in other countries, however, their wages lagged well behind those of men.

Austria-Hungary suffered from a weak financial base and resorted to large-scale borrowing and printing of paper money. Inflation rapidly caused difficulty for both government and society, making the Dual Monarchy dependent on its ally for financial support, even though Germany was also wrestling with financial problems. Hungary's continued refusal to release grain made Austria's dependence on Germany even greater. The Austrian agricultural dilemma was due in large part to a labor shortage attributable to the army's manpower demands, but inefficient government direction, a shortage of fertilizer, and hoarding of agricultural commodities also played roles.

Despite obvious signs of economic deterioration, growing estrangement of various ethnic groups and weakening of morale in the army, Austria-Hungary made no effort to secure a separate peace and remained steadfastly loyal to the German alliance. It also continued to cherish exaggerated war aims long after they were even remotely feasible. Until 1917, it might have been possible to secure a separate peace on reasonable terms by taking advantage of the Western Allies' desire to isolate Germany. Neither Britain nor France had any real quarrel with the Dual Monarchy. To achieve such a goal, the Western Allies might have been willing to strike a deal that would have kept Austria-Hungary largely intact, while sacrificing Italian, Serbian, and Rumanian ambitions. But the Dual Monarchy refused to abandon its commitment to Germany. By early 1917, the Allies had hardened their position. On January 10 of that year, in response to President Wilson's mediation overture of December 1916, they called for the liberation of the subject nationalities from foreign domination. Henceforth, they began to cooperate with the exile groups representing the various nationalities in the Dual Monarchy. The longer the empire waited to seek peace, the more certain became its ultimate disintegration.

RUSSIA: DISILLUSIONMENT AND UNREST

Russia proved the least able to withstand the rigors of total war. It faced many of the same problems that bedeviled Italy and Austria-Hungary and added the unique dilemma of its own enormous size, which created special obstacles to communication. Russia's geographic location largely isolated the country from its allies, making it difficult but not impossible to receive material aid from them. Despite its backwardness, Russia did succeed in increasing the output of weapons substantially, but its rail network proved incapable of adequately supplying both the army and the civilian population. The cities increasingly fell victim to shortages of food, fuel, and other supplies. As the Western Allies increased their own production, they were able to ship large amounts of aid to the Russians, but these supplies unfortunately tended to pile up in the Arctic ports of Archangel and Murmansk, while the Central Powers continued to control the Baltic and Black Sea approaches to Russia.

Women increasingly replaced male workers in industrial jobs as the Russian army relentlessly conscripted men to fill the void left by the huge casualties. They found employment in industries ranging from textiles to coal mining as well as in farm production. Agricultural output declined, however, largely because of a continuing shortage of both manpower and horses.

War profiteering, government corruption, and gross inefficiency as well as Russia's ap-

pallingly weak financial position added to the dismal situation. Rather than raise taxes, the government resorted to massive borrowing and issuing a flood of paper money. Inflation soared out of control. Although wages kept rising, they could not keep up with the increase in prices. By the end of 1916, prices had risen by almost 300 percent above the 1914 base. Labor unrest increased and led to waves of strikes during 1915 and 1916, while morale at the front grew steadily worse. Deep-set war weariness prevailed and disillusionment with the government became more widespread and intense.

THE "SINISTER PRESENCE" OF RASPUTIN

Symbolizing the decadence of the Russian system more than anything else was the sinister presence of Grigori Rasputin. One of the most bizarre figures of the war, Rasputin was of Siberian peasant stock. Like many Russian peasants, he actually had no surname. Rasputin means "the dissolute," and Grigori apparently came by the name because of his lifestyle. He gained notoriety for his sexual orgies as well as his fondness for alcoholic beverages. Despite his obvious human frailties, he found himself attracted to religious life. He became a sort of weird holy man, not uncommon in Russia, and wandered for many years throughout the country and as far away as Mesopotamia. In 1905, this dirty, scraggly-haired, and bearded man with piercing—almost hypnotic—eyes gained the attention of the Czarina Alexandra because of his reputation for curing hemophilia, a blood disease.

This terrible disease afflicted Alexis, the only son of Czar Nicholas and Czarina Alexandra. It is characterized by the failure of the blood to clot properly. As a result, a minor scratch or bruise can lead to uncontrollable bleeding and death. Rasputin possessed the ability to stop the bleeding, possibly through hypnotism. This gift endeared him to Alexandra, who referred to him devotedly as "Our Friend." Although Nicholas was not altogether taken with Rasputin, Alexandra's strong influence over the czar assured the monk's continued presence in the imperial court. After Nicholas left Petrograd for the front in 1915, Rasputin's power increased over the appointment of government ministers and other important decisions. As conditions deteriorated in Russia, the government resorted to growing repression to put down unrest. This approach made sense to Alexandra, who wrote to her husband that "Russia loves to feel the whip."

Hostility toward Rasputin, Alexandra, and Nicholas continued to accelerate. Finally, some loyal supporters of the czar, fearing the possibility of revolution, decided to end Rasputin's evil influence. The ringleader was Prince Felix Yusupov, who had married the czar's niece. He recruited several associates, including Nicholas's favorite cousin, to join a conspiracy to assassinate Rasputin. On December 31, 1916, Yusupov lured Rasputin to his home and plied him with poisoned wine and cakes. Despite consuming copious quantities of both, Rasputin appeared to feel no effect. The conspirators now resorted to shooting him at least twice and beating him repeatedly on the head before dumping his body into the Neva River. An autopsy later revealed that he had apparently drowned. But Rasputin's death only removed a symptom of the malaise that gripped Russia. Matters continued much as they had before his murder, and the country moved inexorably toward revolution.

14

THE RUSSIAN REVOLUTIONS

When revolution erupted in Russia in March 1917, it was not altogether unexpected. Responsible political figures had warned the czar for some time that an insurrection was likely unless he appointed a government more acceptable to the people, one that would take a more enlightened approach to the war and attempt to alleviate the suffering of the citizenry. But Nicholas II, with astonishing blindness and subject to the growing influence of Alexandra and, indirectly, Rasputin, refused to heed this advice. The revolution also was not the result of a conspiracy. No individuals or groups planned it. It merely happened. But it did not erupt by accident either. It was the fruit of the terrible slaughter and mounting privations spawned by the interminable and unsuccessful war. This melancholy drama had created the opportunity for the latent grievances of various classes in Russian society to boil to the surface. All that was needed was the right set of immediate circumstances to trigger a chain reaction.

ORIGINS OF THE REVOLUTION

Actually, the origins of the revolution predated the war by many years. They had their roots in the failure of the czarist regime to come to terms with the modern world politically and socially as well as the failure of the Russian economy to modernize sufficiently. These serious shortcomings had made the Russian people increasingly dissatisfied, although actual grievances differed greatly from one class to another. When the war began, it aggravated these tensions and also created new ones. It also glaringly demonstrated the weakness of the Russian political and economic systems. As the war progressed, the problems confronting Russia mushroomed and ultimately overwhelmed the inefficient and unpopular regime. When the revolution finally came, the government proved helpless to resist.

THE REVOLUTION OF 1905

Russia, of course, had experienced an earlier and far more moderate revolution in 1905, also the product of an unpopular and unsuccessful conflict—the Russo-Japanese War. That revolution had demonstrated both the extent of disenchantment with the czarist government and the lack of unity within Russian society. It had also resulted in the decision of Nicholas II to grant concessions in the form of a document issued in October. This October Manifesto guaranteed the civil liberties of the Russian people for the first time, legalized political parties, and granted a parliament, called the Duma, to be chosen by an electorate that came close to universal manhood suffrage. However, the October Manifesto did not provide ministerial responsibility.

It appeared at first as though these concessions had set Russia on course to become a constitutional monarchy. Unfortunately, these hopes proved deceptive. The October Manifesto had the effect of splitting the revolutionaries. One group of liberals, drawn from the upper middle class, accepted it as essentially satisfying their demands and became known as the Octobrists. Another group of liberals, representing the middle and lower ranks of the bourgeoisie and called the Constitutional Democrats (Cadets), were not satisfied. The Cadets demanded ministerial responsibility and a truly democratic system. The socialists were also not impressed, and most of them insisted on the election of a constituent assembly that would draft a constitution for a new form of

government. In Russia, socialism was even more divided than in most countries. The Social Democratic party suffered from the usual split between the revisionist majority, the Mensheviks, and the orthodox Marxist minority, the Bolsheviks under Lenin's leadership. Still another party, the Socialist Revolutionaries, was non-Marxist, although influenced by the teachings of Karl Marx to some extent. Unlike the Social Democrats, the Socialist Revolutionaries championed the interests of the peasantry, still by far the largest Russian social class, rather than those of the working class.

The conservatives wanted no change at all in the system but begrudgingly supported the October Manifesto. The czar also hoped to keep changes to a minimum. In May 1906, he issued another document, the Fundamental Laws, which removed any doubt that the czar still retained great power, including complete control over foreign policy, the army, and the navy. Nicholas even revised the electoral law granted by the October Manifesto to give an advantage to the conservatives and Octobrists who supported the system.

The Revolution of 1905 had satisfied only a small portion of the original high expectations that it had unleashed. The Duma, as formulated, proved an extremely passive body, and the czarist regime remained much as it had been before. But its policies were not completely reactionary. Peter Stolypin, the premier between 1907 and 1911, was a loyal supporter of the czarist system but believed that the government must widen its base of support by gaining the allegiance of the peasantry. To achieve this, he sponsored a land reform program that enabled peasants to purchase land with the help of government loans. In this manner, roughly half of the peasantry became small independent landowners by the outbreak of World War I, but unfortunately those who did not remained dissatisfied. Even peasants who had acquired land often did not have enough to be prosperous. Thus, much of the peasantry continued to be "land hungry" and far from reconciled to the system.

Beyond this, however, the czarist regime resisted all efforts to modify the system and cracked down on dissent, driving a number of socialist leaders, including Lenin, into exile. Much of the population remained disaffected and potentially revolutionary. In fact, fear of revolution gripped the government during the first half of 1914 as a wave of strikes disrupted industrial production and demonstrated the deeset unhappiness of the working class over low wages and bad conditions, especially overcrowded housing. The euphoria, created by the outbreak of war, kindled the patriotism of the workers for some time, but as the fighting and civilian hardships went from bad to worse, morale deteriorated and hostility toward the government returned in a stronger form than ever before.

EVENTS LEADING TO REVOLUTION

The Duma, waking from its long torpor, became a source of opposition following the military disasters of 1915. The Cadets, under the leadership of the noted historian Paul Miliukov, joined with the Octobrists and the Progressives, another liberal party somewhat to the left of the Octobrists, to form the Progressive Bloc. This grouping represented a majority in the Duma and pressured the czar to oust his incompetent ministers and establish a liberal government that would be acceptable to the people and provide capable leadership. Nicholas II refused, and the bloc returned to well-behaved opposition. However, in November 1916, Miliukov delivered a forceful speech in which he accused the government of being guilty of either folly or treason in its conduct of the war.

Following the murder of Rasputin and the failure of that act to change the course of the government, conspiracies to remove Nicholas II from power proliferated. Among those who considered such action were members of the Progressive Bloc as well as conservatives, even including relatives of the czar. However, none of them actually took any action. When the revolution came, it was the common man and woman in the streets who were responsible.

The Russian Revolution of 1917 actually consisted of two revolutions. The first began in March, or February according to the old-style calendar in use in Russia at that time. It involved the overthrow of the czarist regime and the establishment of a provisional government. The second revolution in November, or October under the old style calendar, featured the ouster of the provisional government and the establishment of a Bolshevik dictatorship.

The first revolution began with demonstrations in Petrograd on March 8, 1917, protesting the shortage of food and coal. Before long, these protests had turned into riots. Striking workers joined in, and during the next three days the crowds swelled to perhaps 300,000 people, while disorders accelerated. The government ordered troops to assist the police in dispersing the crowds, but they refused to do so and some actually fraternized with the demonstrators. Mobs began to chant "down with the German woman," an obvious reference to the czarina. On March 11, soldiers did fire into a crowd, killing about 60 persons, but soon afterward, military units began to mutiny and go over to the side of revolution.

FIGURE 14–1 Czarist troops disperse demonstrators in Petrograd early in the March Revolution. UPI/Bettmann Archives

COLLAPSE OF THE CZARIST GOVERNMENT

Confronted by this growing threat to its existence, the czarist government virtually collapsed. It proved incapable of taking any effective action. Instead, political authority shifted by default to the Duma, on the one hand, and a new revolutionary council, or *soviet*, on the other. The soviet consisted of representatives of the revolutionary workers and soldiers. At first, the Duma had looked on the turmoil in the streets with uncertainty, but when it became apparent that the government had lost control, the Progressive Bloc, with the assistance of representatives from the Socialist Revolutionaries and Mensheviks, established a provisional council. On March 12, after consultation with the Petrograd Soviet, the council established a provisional government. The soviet intended to pressure the Provisional Government to follow essentially its policies, while refusing to allow any

of its own members to participate in this bourgeois-dominated regime. It essentially looked upon the Provisional Government as the mechanism for guiding Russia through the bourgeois stage of the revolution. Later, the soviet itself would preside over the transition to an actual socialist revolution. The prominent liberal Prince Georgi Lvov became premier in the new government with Miliukov as foreign minister and the influential Alexander Kerensky as minister of justice.

Born in the small town of Simbirsk on the Volga River about 400 miles southeast of Moscow, Kerensky was only 36 years old. He had acquired fame as a successful attorney, defending persons accused of political crimes. After gaining election to the Duma in 1912, he won still more renown when he went to Siberia on behalf of the Duma to investigate a massacre of striking miners in the Lena gold fields. Known for his flamboyant and spellbinding oratory, Kerensky was a member of the moderate wing of the Socialist Revolutionary party. When the revolution began, he became one of two deputy chairmen of the Petrograd Soviet. His great prestige enabled him to defy the soviet's edict against participation in the Provisional Government. As a result, he enjoyed the distinction of being the only person who was a member of both. He rapidly became the most influential government minister and provided a link between the two revolutionary bodies.

Initially, Nicholas II had expected the army to crush the revolution, but when it became clear that this was not going to happen, he hoped at least to keep his throne. General Alexeyev, the chief of staff, and other generals realized that this was impossible and urged the czar to abdicate. Still aspiring to retain the monarchy, Nicholas followed their advice. In view of his son's health, he also renounced Alexis's claim to the throne and designated his brother, the Grand Duke Michael, as his successor. The grand duke had few illusions, however, and also abdicated. Soon afterward, revolutionary authorities placed Nicholas and his family under arrest at his palace at Tsarskoye Selo near Petrograd.

SHORTCOMINGS OF THE PROVISIONAL GOVERNMENT

Despite the Provisional Government's acquisition of power, it never held the political stage by itself. It always had to contend with the Petrograd Soviet, which for some time to come was under the domination of the Socialist Revolutionaries and Mensheviks. In fact, a whole network of soviets sprang up all over Russia during the next few months, both in the cities and the countryside. They looked to the Petrograd Soviet for leadership. The soviets and particularly the Petrograd Soviet continued to control the revolutionary elements in society. If they

should withdraw support from the Provisional Government, it could not expect to remain in power. The Petrograd Soviet also acted under its own authority at times, most notably on March 14, when it proclaimed that, henceforth, elected committees would control military and naval units, while officers would command only during actual operations. Although, the Soviet later qualified the order by stating that the committees' authority extended only to political matters, the damage had been done. This decision contributed greatly to the army's deteriorating discipline.

At first, both the Provisional Government and the Petrograd Soviet followed a moderate course. They cooperated in the enactment of a number of political and economic reforms. These included the guarantee of basic civil rights and equality of rights for all men and women. The government abolished the hated secret police (the Okhrana) and the notorious special courts previously used to stifle dissent, while granting the right to trial by jury. Workers in many industries received the eight-hour day, and labor unions gained full freedom of action. The government also attempted to satisfy the grievances of national minorities. It granted independence to the Poles, all of whom by this time were living under enemy occupation, and extended autonomy to the Ukraine and certain other areas.

While these reforms won widespread approval, the government failed to solve Russia's multitude of economic problems, including inflation, which grew worse by leaps and bounds. And, while stating its support for the principle of land reform, it took no action to distribute additional land to the peasantry. The Provisional Government, as the name indicated, was a temporary regime, designed to hold power only until a constituent assembly could convene to draft a constitution for the permanent political system. In view of this, it believed that the best course was to leave the question of land reform to the constituent assembly. However, it repeatedly delayed elections to choose members of this assembly. In the meantime, the peasants blamed the Provisional Government for its failure to act on land reform and joined with other groups in society to criticize its failure to hold elections for the assembly.

Most critical of all, the Provisional Government insisted on continuing the war, clearly underestimating the enormous longing for peace in Russian society. Government ministers believed that, if they provided stronger, more efficient and inspiring leadership, the people would rally once again behind the war effort. Unfortunately for their hopes, it was much too late for another appeal to patriotism. Moreover, the reliability of the army was highly questionable. Many of the common soldiers had become infected with radical political ideas and had no desire to fight. The question of continuing the conflict also became intertwined with the matter of war aims. The Provisional Government, especially Foreign Minister Miliukov, favored fulfillment of those aims, but the Petrograd Soviet staunchly supported a peace without annexations or indemnities. It pressured Miliukov to publicly endorse its position on April 9. Behind the scenes, however, he continued to assure the Western Allies of Russia's loyalty to its treaty commitments.

LENIN AND REVOLUTION

If the government did not face enough problems, it soon had to contend with the return of Vladimir Lenin from exile. Although destined to be the great revolutionary leader, Lenin came from a comfortable middle class background. He was born Vladimir Ilych Ulyanov, ironically in Kerensky's hometown of Simbirsk. His father was a teacher who eventually rose to the position of provincial superintendent of schools. At the age of 17, Vladimir immersed himself in revolutionary activity after his brother Alexander was hanged for his involvement in an unsuccessful attempt to assassinate Czar Alexander III in 1887. Lenin became a dedicated Marxist and in 1895 was sentenced to 14 months in prison, followed by three years of exile in Siberia.

While in Siberia, he acquired his pen name "Lenin," apparently derived from the Lena River, and a wife, Nadezhda Krupskaya, whom he had met several years before. Lenin's wife shared her husband's devotion to Marxism, and she had also been banished to Siberia for her revolutionary activities. Soon after completing his term, Lenin moved to Switzerland. There, in collaboration with several other Marxist leaders, he launched the revolutionary newspaper *Iskra* (the Spark). He returned to Russia toward the end of the revolutionary year of 1905 and remained there until early 1907, before once again resuming a rootless life in exile in various parts of Europe.

Lenin fell out with many of his Marxist colleagues over his rejection of a democratic organization for the Russian Social Democratic party. He insisted that the key to success lay in the domination of the party by a core of dedicated professional revolutionaries. In his view, if left to itself, the working class would abandon the cause of revolution and seek respectability as part of the lower middle class. He believed that the party leadership must become the vanguard of the revolution and direct the rank-and-file members toward the cherished goal. His approach troubled party moderates, who favored an organization that would allow all members to be involved in party decisions. Departing somewhat from Marxist doctrine, Lenin also insisted that the party must adjust to the realities of Russia's economic and social conditions. Thus, it must appeal not only to the workers but also to the peasantry, the largest social class, for support.

In 1903, Lenin had precipitated the division of the party into two factions, when he forced through a number of resolutions favorable to his position. From that point, he referred to his group as the Bolsheviks (majority men), while the rival faction became known as the Mensheviks (minority men). In reality, the majority status of his faction lasted for only a brief interlude, but the names of the two groupings persisted. In 1912, they parted company altogether and became separate parties.

When World War I began, Lenin was residing in Austria-Hungary but shortly afterward returned to Switzerland where he remained until 1917. During 1916, he completed work on *Imperialism: The Last Stage of Capitalism*, in which he charged that the war was the product of imperialistic rivalry between the Great Powers. In keeping with the view that characterized the Zimmerwald Left movement, he contended that the struggle offered an unparalleled opportunity for revolution. The length and ferocity of the struggle had weakened the warring powers to such an extent, he insisted, that the stage was set for revolution. But his position remained in the minority within the Marxist movement. Even his fellow Bolsheviks in Russia did not share his optimism.

When the revolution began, the Bolsheviks were a much smaller group than either the Mensheviks or Socialist Revolutionaries and exerted little influence. They believed that the time for a socialist revolution had not yet arrived. Remaining faithful to the Marxist model, they visualized the need for a transitional period of bourgeois rule. Accordingly, they cooperated with the Mensheviks and Socialist Revolutionaries in support of a moderate approach, including endorsement of the bourgeois-dominated Provisional Government. Until Lenin returned to his homeland, there was little chance that this situation would change.

LENIN RETURNS TO RUSSIA

The German general staff saw an advantage in helping Lenin to return to Russia. To them, such a revolutionary firebrand would add immeasurably to the growth of chaos in Russia and weaken the country as a factor in the war. The Germans did not expect him to actually lead the Bolsheviks to victory over the Provisional Government and create the world's first Marxist (Communist) regime. To facilitate their scheme, they provided a sealed train to transport Lenin and his associates across Germany. After reaching the Baltic coast, they took a ship to Sweden and from there proceeded once again by train, arriving at Petrograd's Finland Station on April 16.

Soon after his arrival in Russia, Lenin declared in unmistakable terms, both in speeches and in writing, that the Bolsheviks must sever all relations with the Provisional Government as well as other political parties and strive for a working-class revolution. He demanded "all power to the soviets" and spoke out against the war as one between rival gangs of imperialist exploiters. Finally, he called for the expropriation of the land of the aristocracy. The "April Theses" laid down by Lenin in these pronouncements astonished even the members of his own party, many of whom thought that he had lost touch with reality. Undeterred by the less than rousing reception of his ideas, Lenin continued to hammer away at the government's war policy and won growing support for this aspect of his position. Matters came to a head early in May 1917 when Miliukov announced Russia's continued loyalty to the Allied cause in the quest for a "decisive victory." He also indicated that this would include fulfillment of the country's treaty obligations, contradicting his earlier endorsement of a peace without annexations. This prompted widespread demonstrations by workers and soldiers in the streets of Petrograd, demanding an end to the Provisional Government and "all power to the soviets."

Miliukov had no choice but to resign, and a new coalition government came into being, containing representatives of the Mensheviks for the first time. Although Georgi Lvov remained premier, the moderate socialists were in the majority, and Kerensky, now war minister, was more than ever the dominant figure. The cabinet shuffle represented a victory for the Petrograd Soviet, and the Provisional Government adopted the soviet's foreign policy, complete with a renunciation of annexations and war indemnities.

FAILURE OF THE KERENSKY OFFENSIVE

Despite this change in policy, Kerensky still dreamed of winning the war. Together with the Russian Army High Command, he planned another military offensive. Kerensky hoped that the abandonment of expansionist war aims would instill new fervor and a sense of fighting for a just cause in Russian soldiery. He won approval for his scheme from the Petrograd Soviet as well as the First All-Russian Congress of Soviets. This congress, consisting of representatives of 350 local soviets, convened in Petrograd on June 16. Unfortunately, the army was far from the ideal instrument to carry out Kerensky's offensive. With the utmost effort, General Brusilov, who had taken over for General Mikhail Alexeyev as Russian chief of staff, assembled the best and most loyal units to act as the spearhead of the operation. These included a brigade of Czech soldiers, who had deserted from the Austro-Hungarian Army or had been taken prisoner

by the Russians earlier in the war. However, much of the army was in no mood to resume the fighting.

Brusilov preceded his attack with a massive artillery bombardment on June 29, followed by a thrust toward Lemberg in Galicia on July 1. For the first few days, the Russians moved forward against Austrian troops that also were in no mood to fight. However, once again German forces came to the rescue and opened a major counterattack on July 19. By the end of the month, they had hurled the Russians back well beyond their original jumping-off point. The Kerensky offensive had completed the destruction of the Russian army as a fighting force, and war-weary soldiers deserted in droves.

Anger over the Kerensky offensive, along with worsening economic conditions, helped ignite an uprising in Petrograd on July 16. Large numbers of soldiers, sailors, and workers took to the streets and denounced the government, while demanding "all power to the soviets." Violence followed, leading eventually to the loss of about 400 lives. Although Lenin appears to have considered the timing premature, the Bolsheviks quickly assumed leadership of the uprising, and their own party militia, the Red Guards, took part in the street fighting. It was indeed too soon for such an attempt. Some military units remained loyal to the government and, most importantly, the Petrograd Soviet refused to endorse the violence. The government also accused Lenin of treason because of his dealings with the Germans. By July 19, the "July Days" had ended.

The government now moved somewhat tentatively against the Bolsheviks, arresting some leaders and suppressing the Red Guards and Bolshevik party newspapers. It fell short of outlawing the Bolshevik party itself, however, fearing a backlash from the moderate socialists, if such action were taken. Lenin went into hiding in Finland, from where he continued to direct the party. It appeared as though the Bolsheviks had suffered a serious defeat, but it proved only a temporary setback. They continued to win supporters among the workers and their membership in the soviets increased steadily. Lenin believed that the soviets held the key to eventual victory. If the Bolsheviks could gain a majority in the soviets, especially in Petrograd, they could use them as the mechanism for seizing power.

COUNTERREVOLUTIONARY MOVEMENT FORMED

The Bolsheviks soon received help from an unexpected source. The growing signs of radicalism and chaos alarmed many members of the liberal middle class as well as conservative landowners and led to the development of a counterrevolutionary movement. In the wake of the July Days, Kerensky became premier in a new coalition government, but he and his colleagues inspired little confidence. The counterrevolutionary movement found a leader in General Lavr Kornilov, who had shown to good advantage while commanding troops in the Kerensky offensive. As a reward, Kerensky appointed Kornilov commander-in-chief of the army in place of Brusilov. Although General Alexeyev described Kornilov as a man possessing "the heart of a lion and the brains of a sheep," Kornilov had risen from peasant origins to fashion an excellent military record. Actually a man of democratic instincts, he worried over the deterioration of law and order as well as the threat from the Bolsheviks and believed that firm action was necessary.

At first, Kerensky and Kornilov cooperated in attempting to restore discipline to the army and agreed that troops should be sent to the capital, Petrograd, to protect the Provisional Government. However, Kerensky soon suspected that Kornilov in- tended to overthrow the government and establish a military dictatorship. He dismissed the general and ordered the troops intended for Petrograd to remain where they were. Kornilov refused to step down and in September he directed his forces to proceed to the capital. Kerensky, now desperate, appealed to the Soviet and the people of Petrograd to resist. He also allowed the Bolshevik Red Guards to take up arms again and later released the imprisoned party leaders. Kornilov's advance soon turned into a fiasco. Striking railroad workers refused to transport his troops and equipment, while telegraph workers balked at sending his messages, and Soviet agents sowed dissension among his soldiers. The whole enterprise collapsed without ever reaching Petrograd, and Kornilov was soon under arrest.

SUPPORT FOR PROVISIONAL GOVERNMENT COLLAPSES

Although Kerensky tried to take credit for stopping the attempted takeover, the Kornilov Affair placed him and his government in an exceedingly weak position. Since he had appointed Kornilov to his command, at the very least Kerensky's judgment was suspect. From that point, popular support for the Provisional Government soon dwindled to almost nothing. The Russian armies continued to disintegrate as the Germans advanced deeply into the Baltic provinces. On September 3, General Oskar von Hutier's Eighth Army captured Riga, and on October 12, the German navy landed the 42nd Infantry Division on the Baltic islands of Oesel (Sarema) and Dagö (Hiiumaa), opening the Gulf of Riga and threatening an advance on Petrograd itself. During the next two months, unrest grew rapidly among the peasants, who increasingly seized the landed estates of the aristocracy. Workers and soldiers turned in droves to the Bolsheviks, who gained a majority in both the Petrograd and Moscow soviets soon after the Kornilov Affair. They also made marked gains in other soviets. Lenin now urged the party to take the final step and seize power. He received invaluable assistance toward achieving this goal from the former Menshevik Leon Trotsky.

LEON TROTSKY

Trotsky, whose real name was Bronstein, had been born into a wealthy Jewish family in the Ukraine. Like Lenin, he joined the revolutionary movement at the age of 17 and spent time in prison and in exile in Siberia. He took the name of one of his jailers, Trotsky, as his pseudonym. Unlike Lenin, he escaped from Siberia before making his way to Western Europe. Trotsky later served as a contributor to *Iskra* but broke with Lenin in 1903 and joined the Mensheviks. Returning to Russia during the Revolution of 1905, he led the first short-lived workers' soviet in St. Petersburg. In 1907, he found himself exiled to Siberia a second time. Once again he escaped and spent the next ten years abroad. When the revolution began, he was living in New York but returned to Russia in May 1917. He joined the Bolsheviks during the July Days and quickly moved into a position of leadership, displaying both ruthlessness and exceptional administrative ability. The equal of Lenin intellectually, Trotsky was a much better orator. He was able to inspire both Bolsheviks and other socialists by his stirring outpouring of words. Although arrogant and not well liked by many of his associates, he remained devoted to Lenin for the remainder of his life.

THE BOLSHEVIK REVOLUTION

Lenin returned secretly to Petrograd for a crucial meeting on October 23, 1917, and overcame the objections of some of the other Bolshevik party leaders to his proposal for a coup. However, immediately afterward he went back into hiding, leaving Trotsky to organize the actual mechanics of the takeover. Trotsky had become chairman of the Petrograd Soviet soon after the Kornilov Affair. He also masterminded the creation of a Soviet Military Revolutionary Committee in October, ostensibly to defend Petrograd against a possible German offensive, and he became its leader. The committee soon gained control over the Petrograd garrison and the arms depots in the capital, giving the Bolsheviks the means to carry out the coup successfully.

During the night of November 6–7, 1917, the light cruiser *Aurora* switched on its searchlights as the signal for elements of the Petrograd garrison and Bolshevik Red Guards to go into action. They occupied key points throughout the capital and stormed the Winter Palace where the Provisional Government maintained its headquarters. This November (October in the old-style Russian calendar) Revolution easily toppled the thoroughly discredited Provisional Government, which fell with hardly a hand being raised in its defense; however, Kerensky managed to escape. For a few days he took refuge with a military unit to the southwest of Petrograd and tried to lead it on an expedition to the capital. Following a brief skirmish, his force fell under the spell of Bolshevik agitators and began to disintegrate. Kerensky fled and soon afterward left Russia, making his way to the United States where he spent the remainder of his life.

Lenin moved quickly to create a Bolshevik-dominated regime, but he recognized the value of associating it with the revolutionary soviets. The Second All-Russian Congress of Soviets convened on November 7. Refusing to follow Lenin's lead, the Mensheviks and many Social Revolutionaries stormed out of the session in protest. Trotsky, chairman of the congress, dismissed them as "so much refuse that will be swept into the rubbish heap of history." Those who remained issued a decree establishing a provisional executive council, the Soviet of People's Commissars, to govern the country. Although, responsible to the Soviet Congress, the new government as well as the congress were clearly under the control of the Bolsheviks. Lenin became chairman of the new executive body and now headed both the Bolshevik party and the government. Trotsky became commissar for foreign affairs.

The Bolsheviks had more difficulty gaining control of Moscow, where it was necessary to battle troops loyal to the Provisional Government for a week before they consolidated their power. In the following weeks and months, the Bolsheviks used the soviets and other Bolshevik-dominated organizations to extend their control throughout much of Russia. However, resistance developed among the trade unions, postal employees, government workers, and some of the ethnic groups as well as business and other middle class elements, all of which opposed the Bolshevik coup. Counterrevolutionary forces soon began to organize in areas where the Bolsheviks were weak. The Bolsheviks, aware that they remained a minority, fell back on their greatest strength—centralized leadership—and moved quickly to introduce numerous reforms, including establishing the principle of state control over industry and confiscation of the landed estates of the aristocracy.

BEGINNINGS OF THE BOLSHEVIK DICTATORSHIP

Lenin, bowing to tremendous pressure from the opposition groups to hold the long-delayed elections for the constituent assembly, announced that they would be held on November 25. The Bolsheviks allowed the elections to take place in complete freedom,

despite Lenin's misgivings about their outcome. His concern proved warranted as the Socialist Revolutionaries were the big winners, gaining 370 of the assembly's 707 seats, which gave them an absolute majority and seemingly the right to form a new government. The best the Bolsheviks could do was to win 24 percent of the vote and 170 seats. When the assembly met on January 18, 1918, the Bolsheviks subjected it to all sorts of disruptive tactics. Nevertheless, a majority of the delegates voted in favor of a democratic republic. Lenin now decided to put an end to this experiment in democracy. He ordered troops to prevent any additional sessions and dissolved the assembly. These actions confirmed that Russia was now a Bolshevik dictatorship.

Shortly afterward, a Third All-Russian Congress of Soviets, again dominated by Bolsheviks, made the dictatorship official. It transformed the provisional soviet regime into a permanent form of government, officially designated as the Soviet Russian Socialist Republic. The congress also proclaimed that the new regime consisted of a "federation of national Soviet republics." This step disguised the fact that, although the various nationalities were declared to be free, they were in reality still subject to the rule of the central government in Moscow through the mechanism of Bolshevik party domination.

In July, 1918, the Fifth All-Russian Congress of Soviets adopted an actual constitution. This document created an elaborate governing system of soviets, forming a pyramid of authority extending from local soviets up through the levels of district, county, and provincial soviets to the All-Russian Soviet at the apex. The system gave the illusion of democracy. In reality, it was a façade for the dictatorship of the Bolshevik, or Communist, party, as it had been officially renamed in March 1918. The Communist party dominated each level of the hierarchy, with overall control being wielded by the executive committee of the Russian soviet.

REVIVAL OF SECRET POLICE

Lenin also resorted to a policy of terror to root out and destroy enemies of the Bolshevik revolution. To accomplish this, in December 1917 he revived one of the most hated of czarist institutions—the secret police. Officially named the Extraordinary Commission to Combat Counterrevolution and Sabotage, this new organization became better known as *Cheka*, an acronym derived from the initials of the key words in the longer and more unwieldy title. Under the direction of Felix Dzerzhinsky, one of the most sinister, fanatical, and cold-blooded Bolshevik leaders, it proved far more efficient than the old czarist Okhrana.

LENIN SEEKS END TO WAR

Meanwhile, Lenin had attempted to carry out his promise to the Russian people to make peace. He considered fulfillment of this pledge absolutely essential for the survival of his government. It proved a far more difficult task than he or anyone else had expected. It was an easy enough matter to arrange an armistice, but when negotiations for a peace treaty began in late December 1917 at Brest-Litovsk in Poland, the Germans attempted to achieve their extreme war aims. Trotsky, as foreign commissar, was the chief Russian negotiator. He was so taken aback by the draconian nature of the German demands that he turned them down and adopted a novel policy of "no war, no peace!" That is, he declared the war over but refused to accept the peace terms. In doing so, he hoped that this approach would promote revolt among German and Austro-Hungarian soldiers. Unfortunately, this strategy proved useless. The Germans merely took advantage of the ab-

sence of resistance to send their troops steadily eastward. Lenin believed that Trotsky's policy was a mistake and would only cause Germany to increase its demands. His fears were well founded.

As the Germans moved relentlessly forward against no opposition and without any sign of crumbling discipline in their own ranks, Lenin resorted to his formidable persuasive powers to argue for a resumption of peace talks. He had to overcome the resistance of most of the other Bolshevik leaders but finally prevailed. When the soviet delegates returned to Brest-Litovsk in March, they found that the Germans had indeed increased their demands. Although Count Czernin, Austria-Hungary's foreign minister was present, Germany's delegation, headed by Foreign Minister Richard von Kühlmann and General Hoffmann, the architect of the victory at Tannenberg, clearly dictated the peace. On March 3, 1918, the Bolsheviks reluctantly accepted the Treaty of Brest-Litovsk.

THE TREATY OF BREST-LITOVSK

Under its terms and those of subsequent agreements, Russia surrendered Poland, the Ukraine, its Baltic provinces, and Finland, essentially into Germany's safekeeping, although a government in Kiev had already proclaimed the Ukraine's independence. The Russians also gave up much of their Transcaucasian territory. The exact fate of this area remained particularly vague, but both Germany and Turkey cherished ambitions there, not to mention the dreams of independence harbored by the various peoples inhabiting this region. In the remaining months of the war, it became a source of growing tension between the Germans and the Turks. For Russia and the Bolshevik government, the treaty was a humiliating settlement. In addition to the huge loss of territory, the Russians parted with 50 million people as well as one-third of their agricultural land, 90 percent of their coal, and almost all of their oil. Although Germany presided over the partitioning of these territories, Russia's subject nationalities were already breaking away. The Germans obviously wanted to set up governments in the new states that were friendly to them.

Despite the end of hostilities, Lenin worried about the presence of German troops in Estonia, within easy striking distance of Petrograd. He feared that they might move on the capital in an attempt to crush his regime. Thus, soon after the signing of the peace treaty, the Bolshevik government, again on the insistence of Lenin, moved from Petrograd to Moscow. Before long, however, a far more real danger threatened the existence of the government. It came from counterrevolutionary forces in southern, eastern, and northern Russia as well as Siberia. Various generals from the old czarist army organized military units, and by the summer of 1918 plunged Russia into civil war.

THE RUSSIAN CIVIL WAR

For a time, it appeared as though the Whites, as these counterrevolutionary forces were called, would destroy the fledgling Bolshevik (Communist) regime. They cut off Moscow and Petrograd from contact with the Ukraine, much of central Russia, and Siberia. But the Bolsheviks raised a new military force, the Red Army, from scratch. Under Trotsky's direction, it gradually grew into a formidable fighting organization. To a large extent it had to depend on former czarist officers and "noncoms" for leadership. Among the victims of the Civil War were Nicholas II, Alexandra, and their family. The Provisional Government had sent them from Tsarskoye Selo to Tobolsk, Siberia, in July 1917, and in April of the following year,

the Bolsheviks transferred them to Ekaterinburg (later renamed Sverdlovsk) in the Ural Mountains. When Czech troops, allied with the Whites, threatened the city in mid-July, Bolshevik officials made their fatal decision. On July 16, the czar and czarina, their son, Alexis, and their four daughters were all shot, together with their doctor, servants, and even the family spaniel, although the idea would persist that one of their daughters, Anastasia, somehow managed to escape to the West.

To complicate the mounting tribulations of the Bolshevik cause, various Allied powers, including Britain, France, the United States, and Japan, sent troops to Russia during 1918. The Western Allies sought the restoration of a democratic regime and hoped to prevent arms and munitions, which they had sent to such ports as Archangel and Murmansk, from falling into the hands of the Germans. The Japanese intervened to exploit opportunities created by Russian weakness in the Far East. Allied sympathies clearly lay with the Whites, and they frequently provided them with military equipment and supplies. When the European War drew to a close in November 1918, Allied forces were still on Russian soil and the Civil War continued to rage with no resolution in sight.

Meanwhile, the end of Russia's role in the European War relieved Germany of the need to pursue additional military operations in the east. The chaotic conditions that prevailed, nevertheless, required them to maintain a substantial number of troops to control the areas ceded by Russia at Brest-Litovsk. But the German High Command had begun to shift forces to the Western Front long before conclusion of the eastern peace settlement. There was reason for haste. The United States had entered the war on the Allied side less than a month after the start of the March Revolution. Although, in early 1917, America was a negligible military

FIGURE 14–2   Czar Nicholas II poses for the camera while in confinement following his abdication. National Archives

power with a small volunteer army, it had the potential to create huge armed forces. But this would take time. In fact, the United States would not become a factor of any importance on the Western Front until the summer of 1918. This left the Germans a window of opportunity in the spring, a last chance to defeat France and Britain before fresh American manpower entered the Allied line in strength. Ludendorff was eager to strike.

AMERICA
ENTERS THE WAR

The Western Allies greeted the March Revolution in Russia with mixed emotions. Their initial response was one of concern, but before long it became intertwined with hope that the new Russian government might be able to establish true democracy, provide stronger direction for the war, and lead a united people in quest of victory. In short, they tended to share the attitude of Kerensky and the Provisional Government. They also tried to stiffen Russian resolve and urged another offensive, heedless of the obvious indications that the Russian army was incapable of carrying it out successfully. Less than a month after the start of the first Russian revolution, the Allies also drew hope from another source—the entry of the United States into the European War.

AMERICAN ATTITUDES

Germany's policy of unrestricted submarine warfare, of course, precipitated America's decision. But many other factors contributed to this not altogether unexpected development. At first, most Americans viewed the war as not much more than a curiosity that had little to do with them. They accepted American aloofness from European wars as being in the nature of things. The government in Washington realized, however, that in the world of the early twentieth century, this was not as easy to ensure as it once had been. World trade patterns and the revolution in communications and weaponry combined to make it impossible for a major neutral power to be unaffected by a conflict involving all the other leading powers. But all American leaders were determined that the country would remain on the sidelines. They would, of course, be willing to offer their good offices to help secure a peace settlement.

Despite their determination to maintain neutrality, the sympathies of most Americans lay with the Allies from the start. They felt much closer to the democratic Western Allies than to the authoritarian Central Powers. To be sure, Russia, with its far-from-democratic regime, was an exception to this, but even the Russians had entered the war to protect their little Serbian ally from the bullying of Austria-Hungary. It was even more obvious that Belgium and France were victims of German aggression, made worse by Chancellor Bethmann-Hollweg's cavalier remark about Belgium's neutrality as "a scrap of paper." This unfortunate comment reinforced American dislike of Prussian militarism and German navalism. Before long, references to William II as "the beast of Berlin" became familiar in the United States. A common language and similar cultural traditions also contributed to a pro-British mind-set, as did the country's generally good relations and close economic connections with Britain in recent years. America also felt a lingering debt of gratitude to France for its contribution to the winning of independence in the Revolutionary War. In fact, sympathy for France probably ran deeper than it did for Britain.

Certainly, German-Americans did not share this pro-Allied attitude, particularly in the early stages of the war. They tended to accept Bethmann-Hollweg's contention that the Allies had forced Germany into the conflict. As time passed, however, many German-Americans questioned the propriety of Germany's actions, especially unrestricted submarine warfare. Irish-Americans, traditionally anti-British and in favor of Irish independence from Britain, also found it difficult to support the Allies. Many of them thought that a German victory would facilitate Ireland's quest for freedom. This attitude became more pronounced when members of an independence movement in Ireland itself succeeded in gaining German agreement to send weapons and munitions to be used against British rule in an uprising during Easter Week of 1916. Unfortunately for their plans, a British warship intercepted the vessel carrying the arms, and the German captain scuttled his ship, sending its cargo to the bottom. A small band of Irish nationalists insisted on carrying out the revolt, nevertheless, as a "blood sacrifice" aimed at rallying the people of Ireland in favor of independence. Although on a small scale and hopeless from the start, the Easter Rebellion led to severe British reprisals, including the execution of 15 rebel leaders. The harshness of Britain's response proved a major public relations blunder. It alienated many in Ireland, who previously had little sympathy for what they considered a foolhardy revolt. It also created revulsion in the United States, particularly among Irish-Americans.

ANTI-GERMAN PROPAGANDA

The clumsy handling of the aftermath of the rebellion contrasted sharply with the otherwise generally skillful British use of propaganda. To be sure, the Germans contributed greatly to this effort by some of their actions, including the shooting of Belgian hostages in reprisal for alleged sniping attacks by civilians against German soldiers. The accidental burning of much of the medieval center of the Belgian university city of Louvain, with its library dating back to 1426, also aroused widespread disgust, although German soldiers actually helped fight the fire. References to the Germans as "Huns" soon appeared in newspapers. An even more spectacular case of German "barbarism" involved the shelling of the glorious Gothic cathedral of Reims shortly after the Battle of the Marne. In October 1915, the Germans committed still another insensitive deed when a firing squad executed the British nurse Edith Cavell, who had helped Allied soldiers escape from occupied Belgium.

With such raw material, the British were able to weave ghastly details of German excesses and even to create stories about atrocities that never took place, such as the cutting off of the hands of babies and the crucifixion of a Canadian soldier. The British also portrayed the Allies as defenders of Western civilization against the Hunnish hordes thirsting to destroy it. Germany countered with propaganda of its own, but these efforts lacked the skill of the British and proved far less believable. The Germans also could not compete with the British, who controlled the trans-Atlantic cables, in providing up-to-date news information.

EFFECT OF THE WAR ON AMERICAN COMMERCE

American business and government leaders expected the outbreak of war to increase American trade, but at first they were disappointed. Exports actually declined for some time as the British blockade cut off much of the Continent from the outside world, while the Allies fell back on their own resources. By the summer of 1915, however, the demand for American goods increased steadily, and production escalated in many industries, especially iron and steel and those that manufactured munitions and other war material. The Allies also imported much more wheat and other foodstuffs from America. Prices for agricultural commodities moved sharply upward, bringing sudden prosperity to American farmers. American exports to the Allied powers rose from about $825 million in 1914 to over $3 billion in 1916.

The war also resulted in a remarkable change in America's financial position. In 1914, the United States was still a debtor nation, but it soon became a creditor nation on an increasingly large scale. As the war progressed, the Allies resorted to more and more loans from American institutions to finance their purchases. Despite the development of opposition to extending credit to belligerent powers, especially from Secretary of State William Jennings Bryan, the practice continued. By 1917, the Allies had borrowed over $2 billion from U.S. financial firms. Bryan warned in vain that loans to the Allies violated the spirit of neutrality.

Germany, cut off from trade with the United States by the British blockade, also protested American commercial and financial dealings with the Allies as a breach of neutrality because of its one-sided nature. It urged an embargo on arms shipments to the Allies. The United States argued that its trade was in keeping with the laws of neutrality. It also contended that America was not to blame for Germany's inability to purchase munitions and supplies. Washington refused to take the alternative course of simply cutting off trade with all belligerents. Its commercial dealings with Britain and France gave the United States an economic stake in an Allied victory. However, this did not mean that American business interests favored entry into the conflict. It was much more profitable to reap the benefits of wartime trade without assuming the expense and uncertainty of actual belligerency. Unfortunately, it proved exceedingly difficult to maintain trade with the Allies while at the same time insisting on neutrality. Although these two objectives were understandable and desirable, they proved increasingly incompatible.

Another source of American animosity toward the Central Powers came in response to their efforts to interfere with American industry and transportation through espionage and sabotage. Since the British blockade prevented German access to American resources, the German embassy in Washington accepted the task of doing what it could to deny the same benefit to the Allies. It coordinated efforts of German agents seeking to foment unrest among American industrial workers and plotting to carry out actual acts of sabotage. Although most of these attempts came to nothing because of the vigilance of American authorities, a dock explosion in Jersey City during July 1916 did result in two deaths and extensive property damage. This policy actually proved counterproductive because it led to growing anti-German sentiment. The ringleaders behind these efforts were the German ambassador, Johann von Bernstorff, and his Austrian counterpart, Constantin Dumba. The activities of Dumba as well as the German military and naval attachés led to their ouster from the United States during 1915.

FACTORS BEHIND AMERICA'S ENTRY INTO THE WAR

Despite sympathy for the Allied cause, growing hostility toward Germany, and the increasing importance of American economic relations with the Allies, the determining factor in America's entry into the war was the German policy of unrestricted submarine warfare. However, Germany was not the only power to pose a threat to America's neutral rights on the high seas. In fact, the first problem in this respect stemmed from the British naval blockade. The United States upheld the Declaration of London of 1909, the most recent attempt to spell out the rights of neutrals on the high seas. Britain, however, had never ratified this document, recognizing that to do so would hamstring its navy, clearly its primary means of waging war.

Before long, the United States and Britain became involved in a dispute over what constituted contraband, that is, goods which a neutral may not furnish to a belligerent power and which are subject to seizure. At first, the British drew up a modest list of commodities that they considered contraband. As time passed, however, they lengthened the list to include such things as gasoline, rubber, and even food. Britain also took liberties with the customary procedure of halting and searching neutral ships for contraband. It insisted on diverting many ships to British ports for search, a practice that proved most time-consuming for American shipping interests. The British did this in part because of the danger that submarines posed to warships engaged in the searching process at sea. They did reimburse shippers for any cargoes that they actually confiscated, as well as for time lost.

Another source of irritation to Americans resulted from the British interpretation of the doctrine of "continuous voyage." This involved stopping U.S. ships headed for neutral countries near Germany on the grounds that their cargoes were destined ultimately for reshipment to Germany. Britain was able to make particularly effective use of this approach by virtue of its distant blockade. Since this involved blocking access to the North Sea, it enabled the British to intercept ships headed for Scandinavian countries and the Netherlands. The British also aroused anger by opening American mail, both in Britain and on the high seas, ostensibly in search of contraband. American businessmen charged that, in the process, the British sometimes acquired trade information that proved useful to their own firms. Finally, in July 1916, Britain released a "blacklist" of over 400 neutral firms, including 85 American companies, suspected of trading with the enemy; the British government barred its citizens from dealing with them.

Although many American business interests protested British interference with neutral rights, the government in Washington followed a cautious policy. To be sure, it dispatched frequent protests to London but refused to push matters to a diplomatic showdown. The British countered with a series of delaying tactics, sometimes waiting as long as six months to reply to American objections. When they did respond, they generally conceded nothing. They believed that their survival depended on control of the sea and enforcement of an efficient and rigorous blockade. The loudest official American protest followed the announcement of the blacklist. On this occasion, the British, realizing that they had blundered, did back down and began to remove the names of American firms from the list.

However angry Britain's high-handed approach to neutral rights might make American leaders, their sympathy for the Allied cause always tempered their outrage. President Wilson, while sincerely dedicated to following a neutral policy, could not overcome his growing tendency to identify American interests with those of the Allied cause. Of Scotch-Irish and English stock, he greatly admired Britain's culture and political institutions as well as the type of liberalism practiced by the great nineteenth-century British prime minister William Ewart Gladstone. Wilson's most trusted adviser, Colonel Edward M. House, was staunchly pro-Ally. Although Colonel House held no official position, he maintained strong influence with the president. The American ambassador to London, Walter Hines Page, was far more favorably inclined toward the Allies than either Wilson or House. He often softened the impact of American protests in private contacts with British officials.

GERMAN SUBMARINE WARFARE

The greatest antidote to anti-British feeling in the United States came in the form of Germany's death-dealing submarine policy. However exasperating British infringements of neutral rights might be, they at least did not take any American lives. From the start, Washington took a much stronger line against Germany's policy on the high seas than it did with Britain's. In November 1914, when Britain announced that, henceforth, it considered the North Sea a military area, the United States made no protest. However, when Germany proclaimed the waters surrounding the British Isles a war zone, Washington emphatically denounced this action and indicated that Berlin would be held accountable for the loss of American lives and ships. The sinking of the U.S. tanker *Gulflight* and, most notably, the British liner *Lusitania* greatly increased American hostility toward Germany. In response to the *Lusitania* tragedy, the *New York Times* likened German conduct of war on the high seas to that of "savages drunk with blood."

Although Wilson limited his reaction to the sinking of the *Lusitania* to protests, his choice of words was too strong for Secretary Bryan, who considered it tantamount to an ultimatum that would lead to war. Bryan, a dedicated pacifist and the only totally neutral member of the cabinet, felt obliged by his conscience to resign. He devoted himself afterward to warning the country of the danger of stumbling into war and became the target of charges of disloyalty in the process. His successor, Robert Lansing, had no such qualms. An avid supporter of the Allies, Lansing had served as a high official in the State Department. He worked steadfastly to avoid a rupture of relations with Britain over its violations of neutral rights, while favoring a vigorous policy toward Germany's submarine warfare. After the sinking of the British liner *Arabic* in June 1915, Lansing considered breaking diplomatic relations with Germany but recognized that public opinion did not favor such drastic action.

He and Wilson received verification of this early in 1916 when Senator Thomas Gore of Oklahoma and Representative Jeff McLemore of Texas, both Democrats, offered resolutions to deny passports to American citizens planning to sail on ships of belligerent powers. Wilson opposed the resolutions because they limited the rights of the United States as a neutral country and would also weaken his own leadership. He managed to rally enough Democrats to defeat these resolutions in both houses of Congress, but the incident clearly demonstrated the depth of antiwar feeling in the country.

THE WAR'S IMPACT ON AMERICAN POLITICS

As the war progressed and the likelihood of the belligerents agreeing to peace on their own grew more unlikely, Wilson also attempted to play the role of mediator. In January 1915 and again in December of that year, he sent Colonel House to Europe as a special envoy, despite House's complete lack of diplomatic experience, to try to arrange a possible peace conference. Both attempts failed because of the refusal of either side to abandon hopes of fulfilling its war aims.

The various incidents in the North Atlantic during 1915, along with the torpedoing of the French Channel steamer Sussex in March 1916, convinced many Americans that, while pursuing neutrality, the United States should at least prepare itself for the possibility of war. Critics, such as Representative Augustus Gardner of Massachusetts, former president Theodore Roosevelt, and General Leonard Wood, who had led the famous "Rough Riders" volunteer unit in Cuba during the Spanish-American War, warned that America was unprepared for war. They urged measures to remedy this situation.

At first, Wilson opposed efforts to increase American preparedness as contrary to his hope of acting as a mediator between the warring powers. But as the threat to American rights increased, he gradually changed his mind. The president began to speak in favor of measures to strengthen national defense as early as May 1915, and at the end of that year he asked Congress to increase appropriations for both the army and navy. In June 1916, Congress passed the National Defense Act, which provided for an increase in the size of the army from 90,000 men to 175,000, with the possibility of an additional increase to 220,000. This legislation also called for the National Guard to be brought under federal control and its size boosted eventually to 400,000 men, as well as the establishment of a Reserve Officers Training Corps (ROTC). In August, Congress passed another act, authorizing the construction of at least five battle cruisers and other ships during the next three years. Other legislation a little later in the year provided funds for the acquisition of merchant ships and established a Council of National Defense to coordinate industry and resources.

American neutrality and national preparedness loomed as major issues in the presidential election campaign of 1916. The Republicans nominated Justice Charles Evans Hughes of the Supreme Court to challenge Wilson for the presidency, but he proved a weak campaigner. While the Republicans attacked Wilson's foreign policy as not tough enough on Germany, they also tried to court the German-American vote by accusing Wilson of being pro-British. It was not difficult to detect the contradictory nature of these arguments. Hughes confused matters even more with vague statements that did little to explain where he stood on the issues and earned him the nickname Charles "Evasive" Hughes. In contrast, Wilson benefitted immensely from the slogan "He kept us out of war," which implied, but did not promise, that he would continue to do so if reelected.

The voting proved extremely close, nevertheless, and early returns prompted some newspapers to declare Hughes the winner by virtue of his victories in all of the large eastern states as well as most of the key midwestern states. However, the "Solid South" and a majority of the states west of the Mississippi shifted the election in Wilson's favor. He won reelection by 600,000 popular votes, although his margin in the electoral college was only 23 votes.

U.S. BREAKS OFF DIPLOMATIC RELATIONS WITH GERMANY

Wilson tried to satisfy those who had voted for him in expectation that he would continue to keep the country out of war. It was at this time that he made his last attempt to mediate between the warring powers, which, of course, failed and led to his call for a "peace without victory" in January 1917. Less than ten days later, Germany announced its intention to resume unrestricted submarine warfare. Ironically, America's relations with Germany had been more cordial than those with the Allies during the period since Berlin abandoned its attacks on neutral ships in May 1916. This was the period of anger over the British blacklist. But the Germans had only made their pledge to halt submarine attacks in response to Wilson's threat to sever diplomatic relations following the *Sussex* incident. Now, confronted by Germany's new challenge, the president felt that he had no choice but to break off relations, and he did so on February 3, 1917. Public opinion rallied behind him, despite a lingering hope of avoiding war.

THE ZIMMERMANN TELEGRAM

This support increased still more as the result of another major German blunder. In mid-January, Foreign Secretary Arthur Zimmermann had cabled Germany's minister in Mexico to seek an alliance with the Mexican government should the United States enter the war. In return for Mexico's participation in hostilities, a highly unlikely possibility, Germany would provide financial aid to facilitate the reconquest of "the lost territory of New Mexico, Texas and Arizona." British intelligence intercepted and deciphered the telegram but refrained from passing the information to Washington until after the rupture of relations between the United States and Germany. A groundswell of revulsion greeted the news throughout America, especially after Zimmermann admitted to an incredulous Reichstag that the offer had been made. Relations between the United States and Mexico had indeed been strained, most notably after Wilson sent a punitive expedition across the border during 1916 in quest of the rebel leader Pancho Villa, but it was inconceivable that Mexico would go to war with America. Shortly after receiving news of "the Zimmermann Telegram," Wilson requested congressional approval to arm U.S. merchant ships. However, despite overwhelming approval in the House of Representatives, a group of antiwar senators delayed the bill in the Senate until Congress adjourned on March 4. Reluctantly, Wilson ordered the arming of the ships by executive action.

It was now only a matter of time until incidents in the North Atlantic plunged the United States into war. The first American merchant ship to fall victim to the new German U-boat offensive was the *Algonquin* on March 12. Three more vessels suffered the same fate soon afterward, one of them with the loss of 15 crew members. Meanwhile, the March Revolution had begun in Russia, and the establishment of the Provisional Government on March 12 ended the czarist autocracy and promised democracy. This made participation in the war more acceptable to both Wilson and the American people. On

March 20, the cabinet agreed that the country must enter the conflict, and on April 2, 1917, Wilson went before a joint session of Congress to seek a declaration of war. In his speech, the president proclaimed that "the world must be made safe for democracy" and promised that:

... we shall fight for the things which we have always carried nearest our hearts—for democracy, for the right of those who submit to authority to have a voice in their own Government, for the rights and liberties of small nations, for a universal dominion of right by such a concert of free peoples as shall bring peace and safety to all nations and make the world itself at last free.

Enthusiastic applause repeatedly interrupted his speech. On April 6, 1917, the Senate voted 82–6 in favor of war. The House followed suit four days later, 373–50.

AMERICA ENTERS THE EUROPEAN WAR

Now that war had come to the United States, Wilson, the would-be peacemaker, approached the new task with all the fervor of a crusader. His choice of words in asking Congress for a declaration of war reflected this change. To him, the conflict was not merely a reaction to German submarine attacks but an opportunity, almost a sacred calling, to set the world on the path to a bright new future in keeping with the traditional values of America. Wilson's new course also reflected his own background and cherished beliefs.

Born Thomas Woodrow Wilson, he was the son of a Presbyterian minister. Strongly influenced by his Calvinist upbringing, he remained deeply religious and filled with a sense of moral righteousness throughout his life. He also could be extremely stubborn and had a tendency to make bitter enemies of his political opponents. A graduate of Princeton, Wilson went on to study law at the University of Virginia and earn a doctorate in history and government from Johns Hopkins. He later became president of Princeton and served briefly as governor of New Jersey before winning election to the presidency on the Democratic ticket in 1912.

As president, Wilson embarked on an ambitious reform program designed to reduce the power of big industrial corporations and financial institutions, while attempting to free organized labor from many of the restrictions that had hampered the growth of unions. In foreign policy, much against his will, he found himself drawn into the affairs of Mexico where revolution had been raging since 1910. In March 1916, when Pancho Villa's forces raided the U.S. border town of Columbus, New Mexico, killing 17 Americans, the president ordered a cavalry expedition, commanded by General John J. Pershing, to apprehend the rebel leader. But Villa remained highly elusive and, in view of worsening relations with Germany, Wilson recalled Pershing's troops in January 1917.

In keeping with his idealistic view of the conflict, Wilson looked with dismay at Allied war aims. To him, they clearly reflected European imperialism and the traditional balance-of-power system, both of which he detested. Rather than risk tainting America by becoming too closely linked to the European powers, he chose to designate the United States as an "associated power" instead of an actual member of the Allies. American war aims would remain pure, limited to such things as ensuring the right of all peoples to determine their own future free from the domination of others, promotion of democratic government, securing freedom of the seas and of international trade, and abolishing war as a means of settling disputes. In keeping with the last of these goals, Wilson had for some time cherished the idea of a League of Nations to act as a peacekeeping organization. It was Wilson's task to instill the same idealistic attitude in the American people and lead them to victory.

But idealism was not enough. Realism was also required if America were to become a real force in the war and if Wilson were to achieve his dream. His preparedness measures had done little more than provide a meager beginning to the process of transforming the United States into a major military power. It would be necessary to raise a much larger army than Wilson had originally envisaged. It would also be necessary to harness the country's vast industrial power to the production of war materiel on a massive scale. Moreover, if the job was not done quickly, it might be too late. In its first few months, Germany's submarine offensive proved even more successful than German leaders had expected. A real danger existed that the U-boats might starve Britain into submission. French morale was dreadfully low after the failure of General Robert Nivelle's spring offensive, and it was questionable how long Russia could remain in the war.

ROLE OF THE NAVY

The navy assumed the first real American combat role. Britain needed its help to fight the U-boat menace. Admiral William Sims became the architect of America's naval effort. An exceptionally able and clear-minded officer of Canadian birth, Sims had acquired valuable experience both at sea and as naval attaché in Paris and St. Petersburg. A critic of naval practices before the war, he had done much to improve the quality of gunnery on U.S. warships. Sims had gone to London shortly before the outbreak of hostilities and began to plan joint operations with the Royal Navy. The admiral disagreed with the Navy Department's opposition to the use of the convoy system to protect merchant ships. He sided instead with the British in their

belated recognition that convoys represented the best hope to defeat the submarine offensive. Sims also urged the dispatch of destroyers and torpedo boats to Britain for convoy escort duty. Henceforth, the navy emphasized construction of destroyers and smaller "sub-chasers."

It soon became apparent that the Western Allies needed much more than naval, material, and financial aid. The United States would have to create a mass army, train it, and then transport it across the Atlantic. Obviously this would take time, but the French appealed to Washington to send at least a token force as quickly as possible to strengthen morale. American leaders were thinking along the same lines, and in May 1917 Wilson appointed General Pershing to command an American Expeditionary Force (AEF), initially numbering 14,500 men. The newly formed First Infantry Division landed in France on June 26. Nicknamed "the Big Red One," it was destined to become one of the army's most famous combat divisions. Other troops followed, but only 200,000 men had arrived by the end of the year, and only a few of these saw any action. Most of them took their place alongside British and French units on quiet sectors of the front. Pershing insisted that the United States must send an army of a million men to France by the spring of 1918 to enable the Allies to undertake a war-winning offensive.

BUILDING UP THE MILITARY

General Hugh Scott, the army's chief of staff, had already urged adoption of conscription to provide the manpower. Secretary of War Newton Baker agreed and persuaded Wilson to seek passage of the necessary legislation. Both Baker and Wilson had to overcome their own personal objections to conscription as well as those of opponents both in and out of Congress. Many disliked the compulsory na-

FIGURE 15–1   General John J. Pershing, commander of the American Expeditionary Force. National Archives

ture of conscription and feared that it would create a permanent militaristic spirit in the country. Despite this resistance, Congress passed the Selective Service Act on May 18; the act required all males, 21 to 30, to register for the draft. The first draftees actually went into uniform in September. During the following months, the number of conscripts steadily increased until it reached more than 2,810,000 by the end of the war. Many men did not wait to be drafted but enlisted in the army, navy, or marines. When the conflict

drew to a close in 1918, almost five million men were serving in the armed forces.

Increasing the size of the army was only one problem. It also proved necessary to construct 16 army camps, complete with a variety of facilities, and to provide instructors, often borrowed from the French and British, to train troops in the methods of modern warfare. A pressing need for officers and noncommissioned officers soon developed, requiring additional training programs. The government also faced the huge challenge of transforming American industry from peacetime to wartime production. This proved particularly difficult and again entailed the need to overcome widespread opposition, this time by those who objected to the government's intrusion into the realm of private enterprise. Such intervention clearly was unavoidable if the transition was to be made successfully. Indeed, during the next year and a half, government regulation of industry, agriculture and transportation reached unprecedented heights, a process denounced by some as war socialism.

ECONOMIC MOBILIZATION

A great deal of trial and error went into the process of economic mobilization. At first, Wilson entrusted overall coordination of the economy to the Council of National Defense, which was one of the fruits of his preparedness legislation. Consisting of six key cabinet members, the council worked with an advisory commission of experts from various fields of industry and communication. An array of new administrative agencies also rapidly came into existence and soon dominated various aspects of the war effort. These included the Shipping Board, with power to purchase, lease, and construct merchant ships; and the Food Administration, designed to control food production and distribution. Other important administrative bodies controlled the nation's coal and petroleum supply and nationalized the railroads. The Council of National Defense encountered growing problems in attempting to coordinate the proliferating boards.

In its quest for solutions to these difficulties, the council created a War Industries Board (WIB) in July 1917, but it, too, lacked sufficient power to get the job done properly. It was not until Bernard Baruch became its chairman in March 1918 that the situation changed. Baruch, a white-haired Wall Street investment broker who had served earlier as a member of the Council of National Defense advisory commission, received such enormous powers that he became a virtual dictator over the nation's economy. Before long, the WIB became completely free from the jurisdiction of the Council of National Defense, and Baruch reported directly to the president. Under Baruch's direction, the WIB regulated all industries involved in the war effort, screened the requirements of various agencies as well as those submitted by Allied powers, and determined their order of priority. The WIB also controlled the allocation of resources as well as the conversion and expansion of industry, and it even fixed prices.

The war opened many opportunities for workers. The demand for labor suddenly created full employment. As in European countries, many women found jobs in war industries, but they usually worked in occupations that traditionally had been earmarked for females. The number of working women actually remained essentially stationary from the start of the war to its conclusion. Some women did replace men in industrial jobs, but more frequently males from minority groups filled this role. Nevertheless, the war did enable some women to experience greater independence by finding employment in industry or government. It also provided an impetus to the crusade of the women's suffrage movement to obtain the vote for females. During 1918, Congress passed a constitutional amendment providing for women's suffrage; the amendment became effective after completion of the ratification process in 1920.

Although some Afro-American radicals argued that blacks had no stake in what they viewed as a "white man's war," most black-Americans supported the conflict. Some hoped that black participation in the armed forces and war industries would lead to reduced discrimination. They were sadly disappointed. The army and navy limited most of their Afro-American personnel to menial noncombat service, while the marines and AEF air service refused to allow blacks to enter their "elite" ranks. The army grouped its small number of black combat troops in segregated units commanded by white officers. Few blacks became officers, and those who did faced the same type of discrimination experienced by black enlisted men. Half a million blacks emigrated from the South to the industrial cities of the Northeast and Midwest, a trend that continued long after the war. Whites did not welcome their arrival, and racial tensions mounted, sometimes flaring into violence. Thousands of Mexican-Americans also moved north and also found both opportunity and discrimination.

Wages for industrial workers rose sharply, but from a generally low base, and with the steady increase in prices, the cost of living soared. Samuel Gompers, president of the American Federation of Labor (AFL), was a dedicated patriot who strove to maintain close cooperation between workers and government. Gompers resisted criticism of the war from left-wing socialists and tried to prevent strikes. His efforts received strong support from the administration, which followed a policy generally sympathetic to labor. Union membership grew by over a million workers during the war.

Despite all of this cooperation, workers' grievances did continue and strikes did occur. In an attempt to create greater harmony and efficiency, Wilson established a National Labor Relations Board (NLRB) in April 1918. Under the leadership of former president William Howard Taft and of Frank Walsh, a highly successful attorney, this organization worked to settle labor disputes fairly. It also supported the right of workers to organize unions as well as to engage in collective bargaining and even ordered equal pay for women doing equal work in war industries. Another agency, the War Labor Policies Board, headed by Professor Felix Frankfurter of the Harvard Law School, regulated hours and wages in the most important industries.

THE FOOD PROGRAM

Remarkable progress also rewarded efforts to provide food for the armed forces and the American people as well as the country's Allies despite poor grain crops in 1916 and 1917. The Council of National Defense created the Food Administration as early as April 1917 to increase production and decrease consumption of food in the United States. Its chairman, Herbert Hoover, had enjoyed an exceptionally successful career as a mining engineer and won worldwide fame for his dazzlingly effective role as head of the Belgian Relief Commission during the years of American neutrality. Hoover worked out arrangements with both Germany and the Allies to enable his organization to provide large-scale shipments of food to save the people of occupied Belgium from starvation. The U.S. ambassador to Great Britain, Walter Hines Page, described this orphaned son of an Iowa blacksmith as "a simple, modest, energetic man who began his career in California and will end it in Heaven ...."

An outstanding administrator, Hoover wielded great power delegated to him by Wilson. This authority came as a result of passage of the Lever Act in August 1917, which granted the president extensive powers over food and fuel. Hoover fixed a high price of $2.20 per bushel for wheat to encourage farmers to increase production and worked to stimulate the output of other foodstuffs. Although this approach worked well, wheat farmers soon bemoaned the fact that their price remained fixed at $2.20, while prices of commodities such as cotton continued to rise freely. In 1918, Congress responded to this complaint by passing legislation to raise the price of wheat to $2.40 per bushel. But Wilson feared that this would aggravate the country's inflationary trend, which had already reached serious proportions. The British also expressed concern over the prospect of paying more for imported wheat and warned that this would force them to seek increased financial aid from the United States. The president finally vetoed the bill, an action that alienated the farmers of the midwestern wheat belt and contributed to the defeat of many Democratic candidates in the November congressional campaign.

To encourage conservation of food, Hoover appealed to the patriotism of the American people and instituted wheatless Mondays and Wednesdays, meatless Tuesdays, and porkless Thursdays and Saturdays. A variety of food substitutes also came into use, including such delicacies as wheatless bread, vegetable lamb chops, and sugarless candy. The results of Hoover's efforts were remarkable. In 1918, the country increased its food production by one-quarter and its exports by one-third, and Hoover accomplished all of this without resorting to the European practice of rationing. He believed that voluntary action would have a much better effect on morale.

FUEL AND TRANSPORTATION

Impressive results also were forthcoming in the realms of fuel and transportation. The Fuel Administration, headed by Harry Garfield, the son of former president James Garfield who had been assassinated in 1881, increased coal production by approximately two-fifths. Garfield also stressed voluntary conservation, utilizing such devices as "heatless Mondays." He took other measures to conserve petroleum, including a ban on nonessential driving on "gasless Sundays." The Railroads War Board tackled the job of coordinating operation of the nation's many independent rail lines, which had been short of

funds and badly in need of new equipment as well as repair of existing facilities even before the war. The sudden dramatic increase in traffic due to the requirements of transporting troops and materials for war industries threatened to overwhelm the system. These problems persisted until Wilson appointed his son-in-law, Secretary of the Treasury William McAdoo, to the position of director general of railroads in December 1917. McAdoo took over the direction of all the country's nationalized rail lines as a single consolidated system. His efforts transformed the railroad network into a smooth-running operation. The government also eventually assumed control over the telegraph, cable, and telephone systems.

America faced still another pressing task in providing enough ships to transport both troops and materiel across the Atlantic. The Shipping Board, already in existence when the war began, along with the Emergency Fleet Corporation, assumed this responsibility. Although they eventually succeeded in constructing vast numbers of ships, 533 of them in 1918 alone, many vessels did not come into service until after the war ended. Of more importance were the 105 enemy ships interned in American ports when the war began and 400 ships under construction in the United States for foreign buyers, all of which the government simply commandeered.

The government gained the cooperation of business leaders in its ambitious effort to mobilize the nation's resources in part because many of them were motivated by patriotism, but other factors were even more important. In some cases, the government used its power over allocation of resources to persuade reluctant businesses to cooperate. Generally it could secure compliance by merely threatening to cut off access to scarce materials or rail transport, although at times it had to resort to actual punitive measures, including commandeering facilities. But, most significant, the administration allowed businesses to enjoy profits that were far greater than those of peacetime. This incentive proved far more effective then coercion. Business executives also filled the leadership positions on wartime boards and agencies, thus creating a situation in which business in effect regulated itself within the framework of a managed economy under government auspices.

PAYING FOR THE WAR

Obviously, the process of creating a powerful military force and the transition to a wartime economy cost a great deal of money, in all about $33.5 billion. This figure did not include lingering postwar expenses, such as veterans' pensions. About one-third of the funds needed to pay this immense bill came from taxation in the form of a steeply graduated income tax—ultimately ranging from a

FIGURE 15–2 Hollywood film star Douglas Fairbanks urges a crowd to buy war bonds during a Liberty Loan rally in New York City. National Archives

low of 2 percent to a high of 77 percent—from corporation and excess profits taxes, and from inheritance and excise taxes. The other two-thirds came from borrowing. The American people provided most of it by purchasing bonds at low-interest rates in a series of four great "Liberty Loan" drives during the war and a final "Victory Loan" campaign immediately following the end of hostilities. These manifestations of patriotism produced a rich harvest, amounting to $21.5 billion.

Despite the government's remarkable achievements in mobilizing the country's resources, the conflict ended before the full effects of the transformation could be felt. As a result, American-produced artillery did not reach the troops at the front in time to be used in the fighting. American machine guns were only available in quantity during the last three months of the war and, although the United States turned out 1,100 aircraft, only 200 of them ever reached France. Thus U.S. forces had to depend on their hard-pressed allies for many of their weapons.

MOBILIZING PUBLIC OPINION

Increasing the size of the armed forces and mobilizing economic resources represented only a part of the task confronting the administration in Washington. As soon as the nation entered the conflict, Wilson and his advisers recognized the need to ensure that the American people were united behind the war effort. Unfortunately, there were discouraging signs that many persons were at best apathetic, while others actually opposed the war. Citizens of German heritage also did not look forward to hostilities with their kinsmen in Germany, and Irish-Americans did not relish the prospect of an alliance with Britain. It became obvious that something must be done to imbue the population with a sense of emotional involvement in the war.

The question of censorship of the news soon became intertwined with this goal. Both the army and navy favored a rigid system of censorship similar to that used in European countries. Obviously this did not go over well with the press, which strongly opposed such an approach. Wilson decided to try a different strategy. Within ten days of America's declaration of war, he had created a Committee of Public Information (CPI) and appointed 40-year old George Creel as its director. A native of Missouri, and largely self-educated, Creel had worked as a crusading journalist in Kansas City, New York, and Denver. He had also served briefly as police commissioner in Denver. An ardent reformer, Creel believed strongly in American institutions and values as well as in the wisdom of the average American citizen. Although he had an acid tongue and made many enemies, he possessed great energy and abundant imagination. Under his domination, the CPI served two main functions: to disseminate the news as widely as possible and to "sell America."

Instead of resorting to direct censorship, the CPI flooded newspaper offices with a vast number of press releases and kept the public well informed about the war. Creel also engaged in propaganda to encourage patriotism and win over those who were critical of the war. He and his associates had the advantage of the purity of America's war aims. The absence of territorial ambitions facilitated their work of portraying the conflict as a crusade for all that was good in the world, in keeping with Wilson's own professed ideals. Of course, it said nothing about the much more ambitious aims of America's allies.

The committee used all available propaganda devices, including no fewer than 75,000 speakers, who held forth during the screening of movies as well as in schools, churches, and virtually every other type of public forum. They kept their speeches short, giving rise to the nickname "Four-Minute Men." Pamphlets, leaflets, and films appeared everywhere, often graphically portraying the savagery of "the Hun." Creel also tried to influence the enemy with literature dropped from planes over German lines. This material contained explanations of America's noble war aims, supported by excerpts from Wilson's stirring speeches, as well as warnings of the irresistible power that the United States would unleash unless Germany made peace.

Creel's efforts were highly successful, but they had the unfortunate effect of fostering hatred, not only of the enemy but also of Americans who did not demonstrate sufficient fervor for the war. They also created such an aura of idealism around Wilson's war aims that they inspired unrealistic expectations about the kind of peace that would follow the conflict. Despite Creel's protestations to the contrary, he and his committee did engage in censorship, although of a less overt type than existed in European countries. The Post Office Department participated in censorship as well, by denying use of the mail to radical and foreign-language newspapers. State and local officials also took part in varying degrees of censorship. Creel's propaganda became one factor in the growing mood of intolerance to any form of dissent regarding the war and its noble purposes, but there were many others.

ANTI-GERMAN PROPAGANDA TURNS SHRILL

Ultra-patriotic groups warned in increasingly shrill tones of the threat of subversion from within. German-Americans became their primary target, despite the fact that most of them were steadfastly loyal and many served in the armed forces. Fear of sabotage, already present during the days of neutrality, now mushroomed. Before long,

anti-German hysteria reached absurd levels. Some high schools stopped teaching the German language, and terms using the word "German" were Anglicized. Thus, German measles became, of all things "liberty measles," while hamburger became known as "liberty steak" and sauerkraut "liberty cabbage." Even dachshunds soon became another breed—"liberty pups." Symphony orchestras discontinued playing the works of such illustrious German composers as Beethoven, Brahms, and Wagner. German-born musicians also became unpopular. Frederick Stock lost his position as conductor of the Chicago Symphony Orchestra, and the famous Austrian violinist Fritz Kreisler was barred from performing a concert in Jersey City. When the Bolsheviks overthrew the Provisional Government in Russia and especially when they made a separate peace, fear of bolshevism also became prominent.

THE HUNT FOR SUBVERSIVES

Government shared the rising concern about disloyal activities. The Justice Department organized the American Protective League (APL), consisting of a quarter of a million volunteers, to help ferret out opponents of the war and anyone who might be guilty of subversive activities. Members of the APL often impersonated Secret Service agents and broke into offices, opened mail, and wiretapped telephones in their relentless quest for such culprits. State and local governments authorized the formation of voluntary councils of defense, which were grouped under the federal Council of National Defense and diligently investigated persons suspected of dissent. In June 1917, Congress passed the Espionage Act, which provided terms of imprisonment ranging up to 20 years and stiff fines for various kinds of subversive activity. The even more stringent Sedition Act of May

1918 made it a crime to speak or publish anything that could be construed as disloyal to the government or the war effort. It, too, provided for long prison terms and heavy fines. Wilson, deserting his liberal principles, supported both acts. Socialists who refused to embrace the war suffered most from this legislation. Their opposition to "the capitalist war" led to charges of subversion.

Eugene V. Debs, the outspoken leader of the American Socialist party who had run four times for the presidency, received a ten-year prison sentence in 1918, although he gained a pardon in 1920. William ("Big Bill") Haywood, leader of the left-wing Industrial Workers of the World (IWW), and 14 other IWW officials were even more unfortunate. A court in Chicago sentenced them to 20 years in prison, while 85 others drew shorter terms. Hysteria over subversion reached a ludicrous extreme in the case of the Hollywood producer Robert Goldstein, whose film *The Spirit of '76* portrayed British soldiers bayoneting women and children during the Revolutionary War. Goldstein received a sentence of ten years' imprisonment for fomenting animosity between the United States and its ally. Again, Wilson, a proponent of a just and humane peace, failed to raise his voice in protest over such repressive actions. In all, the U.S. Justice Department prosecuted 2,200 persons for opposition to the war, and 1,055 of these were convicted.

Self-appointed superpatriots also sometimes resorted to violence against antiwar radicals. Frank Little, an IWW official in the Montana mining town of Butte, was one notable victim of such vigilante action. He lost his knee caps while being dragged through the streets from the back of a car and then lost his life when his assailants hanged him. Ironically, hysteria over disloyalty reached far greater proportions in the United States, obviously much farther removed from the German threat, than it did in either Britain or France.

AMERICA BECOMES MAJOR MILITARY POWER

At times, Wilson criticized mob violence and attempted to relax censorship, but his efforts in this respect were few and muted; actually he often took an active role in the offensive against dissent. In part, his administration provided a stimulus to wartime hysteria over real and imaginary threats to the country and the war effort, but its actions were also in part a response to the views of the extremist groups, which favored even more severe measures and accused Wilson of being soft on treason.

However, despite the depressing nature of this wartime hysteria and all the excesses that went along with it, the American achievement during the country's relatively brief tenure as a belligerent was amazing. To be sure, much of its economic planning had been haphazard and, even with all its mighty striving, the United States failed to produce many of the sinews of war in time to be of any use in determining the outcome of the struggle. But America had transformed itself into a major military power with startling speed. It had done so by resorting to measures that challenged its long-standing traditions of isolation from European power politics, the pursuit of peace, and the sanctity of the free enterprise system. In the process, the United States, like democratic Britain and France, made the transition to total war much more completely than did Germany with its authoritarian government and strong, military tradition. Although it entered the war late and never brought its full strength to bear, America played a vital role in securing the eventual Allied victory.

1917:
CRISIS
FOR THE ALLIES

Although the United States entered the war in April 1917, little else went well for the Allies during that dismal year. Of course, it featured the Russian Revolution and the eventual triumph of the Bolsheviks, the prelude to Russia's eventual defection from the Allied coalition, but it also witnessed events in the North Atlantic, on the Western Front, and in Italy that brought the Allies perilously close to catastrophe. To be sure, the Central Powers also faced serious problems, especially the growing privations caused by the Allied blockade, but the most obvious calamities befell the Allies. Indeed, for a time it appeared as though America's presence in the conflict might have come too late to prevent the collapse of Britain, France, and Italy.

SUBMARINE WARFARE RESUMED

Disaster beckoned first on the high seas with the resumption of unrestricted submarine warfare in February 1917. Actually, British losses to German U-boats had risen alarmingly even before this, despite the return to "cruiser warfare" in which submarines did not attack merchant ships without warning. During the period from October to December 1916, U-boat attacks accounted for a monthly average of over 175,000 tons of shipping. Still, despite all Germany's efforts since 1914, total British merchant tonnage had dropped by only 5 percent. This figure was deceptive, however, because Britain had captured or requisitioned approximately one million tons of enemy shipping to add considerably to its own total. Unfortunately, this windfall was not renewable. Moreover, British construction of new merchant shipping during 1916 had declined to little more than 500,000 tons because of other priorities and poor planning. Losses to German submarines did decline to 110,000 tons in January 1917 but rose sharply during the first few months of un-restricted submarine warfare. Allied shipping losses during February and March averaged just under half a million tons and reached the disastrous total of 869,000 tons for April, including 516,000 tons of British shipping. U-boats also disabled many other ships. The number of merchant vessels bringing supplies into Britain fell from 1,149 in February and March 1916 to under 300 during the same period in 1917.

Even before the start of the new German U-boat offensive, British concern over mounting losses had led to the decision to shift Admiral John Jellicoe to the office of First Sea Lord in December 1916, a position for which he unfortunately proved poorly suited. Jellicoe's health, never robust, had deteriorated under the strain of wartime command and overwork due largely to his refusal to delegate authority. He also shared the rigid opposition of most senior British naval leaders to the use of the convoy system, despite its proven success in maritime war, dating back to the thirteenth century. They considered the convoy a defensive approach to war that ran counter to the navy's prevailing offensive doctrine. Ever since the start of the conflict, they had refused to adopt the convoy, preferring to go on the offensive against the German U-boat menace. This involved patrols that attempted to track down and destroy U-boats, something akin to seeking the proverbial needle in the haystack. Not surprisingly, it brought few positive results.

Jellicoe and other senior admirals resisted the efforts of junior officers, who strongly believed in the potential of the convoy. The "old guard" considered the convoy to be unsuited for modern warfare with its emphasis on speed and firepower. Fearing that the concentration of large numbers of merchant ships would offer ideal targets to submarines, they held little hope that escorting warships could prevent large-scale losses. They also pointed to the difficulty of coordinating the movements of merchant ships not accustomed to operating in this manner and warned that a convoy could only sail as fast as its slowest ship. These men clung to their opposition as an article of faith, despite the recent success gained by convoys protecting British coal shipments to France as well as the convoying of troop transports early in the war.

After Germany resumed its unrestricted submarine offensive in February 1917, Jellicoe became increasingly depressed about the possibility of doing anything to reverse the ominous rise in losses. When American Admiral William Sims, who arrived in Britain in April, asked if there were any solution to the problem, Jellicoe responded, "Absolutely none that we can see now." By the end of April, Britain's supply of wheat had dwindled to only enough to feed the country for six weeks. Some British leaders expressed fear that if the losses continued, the country could not hold out beyond November. Despite these growing signs of despair, junior officers, such as Captain Herbert Richmond and Commander Reginald Henderson, continued to clamor for the adoption of the convoy system. Their insistence, coupled with the growing losses, led Admiral David Beatty to establish a committee to seek a solution. On April 20, it recommended that the navy adopt convoys on an experimental basis. Soon afterward, Lloyd George also endorsed the principle. Confronted by this increasing pressure, Jellicoe reluctantly agreed.

SUPERIORITY OF THE CONVOY SYSTEM

The convoy system soon proved its value. Although it took time to organize the system properly and still more to perfect its methods, convoys succeeded dramatically in reducing shipping losses. The U-boat, nevertheless, remained a serious menace. In May, while Allied losses declined by almost 300,000 tons, they still topped the half million mark and rose to 633,000 tons in June. But after that, they never again reached 500,000 tons. There were ups and downs in the process, but by November, the total had dropped to 260,000 and during 1918, losses dipped to a little over 100,000 tons a month.

Contrary to the fears of Jellicoe and others, the massing of merchant ships in convoys actually made them more difficult for submarines to find. A multitude of ships sailing separately created many more opportunities for chance encounters. Moreover, those U-boats that did come across convoys provided far more targets for escorting destroyers and smaller sub-chasers than would have been the case with anti-submarine patrols ranging over thousands of square miles of ocean. The use of the hydrophone, a listening device that detected the presence of submarines and was the primitive ancestor of the much more sophisticated sonar of World War II, helped tremendously. So did depth charges filled with high explosives. These devices enabled destroyers and other escorting vessels to increase their toll of U-boats from a low of two in April to a high of ten in September. The introduction of this kind of warfare increased the demand for these small, fast, maneuverable ships. New construction now concentrated on them instead of giant dreadnoughts and battle cruisers, neither of which was of any use in the type of naval warfare now taking place.

The U.S. Navy also provided large numbers of warships for escort duty. Indeed, naval cooperation between America and Britain became increasingly close. Admiral Sims proved a highly able and diplomatic officer who immediately won the respect and trust of British leaders. Admiral Sir Lewis Bagly, the British commander in the Western Approaches to the British Isles, developed a warm working relationship with the Ameri-

cans. This harmony ran counter to his reputation for being distant and demanding as well as his nickname "Old Frozen Face." American ships also participated in another aspect of the anti-submarine campaign—mine laying. During 1918, the Allied navies laid three mine barrages in an effort to deny submarines access to the open seas by way of the English Channel, North Sea, and Strait of Otranto. The North Sea operation, an American inspiration, required the laying of more than 70,000 mines, all but 13,000 of them by U.S. ships, across the 250-mile wide expanse between the Orkney Islands and Norway. Planes, dirigibles, and kite balloons also played an increasing role in Allied efforts to detect submarines and proved highly useful.

GERMAN NAVAL STRATEGY: A FAILURE

Although the submarine menace remained a serious problem until the second quarter of 1918, it had failed to fulfill the hopes of German leaders that it would starve Britain into submission within five months. They had taken their desperate gamble without giving sufficient consideration to Britain's ability to adjust to the new threat or the impact of America's intervention. The convoy system and the new methods of detection and destruction of U-boats, along with increased British ship production and U.S. resources, made it increasingly apparent that the submarine offensive would not prevail. Germany's inability to force Britain to make peace, coupled with growing pressure on the Central Powers from the Allied blockade, now made even more stringent by American participation, virtually assured that the Germans would lose the economic struggle. The Allied success in the waters around the British Isles enabled American military forces to cross the ocean and take their place in the Allied line in strength during 1918. This achievement virtually assured that Germany would also lose the war on land.

THE LAND WAR

When America became a belligerent in April 1917, a decision on the Western Front remained as distant as ever. However, despite the bloodbaths of Verdun and the Somme, the French and British were determined to take the offensive once more. The Germans, seemingly more impressed by the effects of this fearful slaughter on their manpower reserves, would remain on the defensive. In November 1916, shortly before his fall from power, General Joffre convened another conference of Allied military and political leaders at Chantilly to consider strategy for 1917. They devised a plan much like that agreed upon at the same site almost a year earlier. Offensives would take place on the Western and Eastern fronts as well as in Italy.

Joffre informed the British that France was no longer able to bear the brunt of Allied efforts on the Western Front. Thus, Britain would have to shoulder the major part of the burden. He proposed another effort to pinch off the great German salient extending from south of Arras to just east of Soissons, with the British attacking in the north and the French in the south. The operation would start on February 1. British forces would follow with a major assault in Flanders with the intention of capturing the U-boat bases at Ostend and Zeebrugge.

Britain's new prime minister, Lloyd George, still favored an "eastern strategy" and vigorously opposed Joffre's plan, considering it the prelude to a repetition of the bloody Battle of the Somme. In another conference at Rome in early January 1917, he proposed an attack in Italy featuring British, French, and Italian forces. He envisaged breaking through the Austrian position on the forbidding Isonzo front and driving northeastward toward Vienna. If the Allies could force Austria-Hungary out of the war, Lloyd George believed that Germany would abandon the struggle.

FRENCH GENERAL NIVELLE'S PLAN

Neither British nor French military leaders had any faith in this highly questionable proposal. They preferred to undertake the equally questionable scheme agreed upon at Chantilly. But Joffre had lost his command in December 1916, and his successor as commander-in-chief, General Robert Nivelle, had revamped the original plan. One of the heroes of France's gallant stand at Verdun, Nivelle had not attended the conference in Rome but had already won his government's support. Premier Aristide Briand, nevertheless, had strong misgivings, and French General Pétain warned that Nivelle's plan would end in disaster. Nivelle met Lloyd George in Paris on the prime minister's return trip to London and apprised him of his intentions. Nivelle's mother had been English, and he spoke her native tongue without trace of accent. In his warm, charming manner, Nivelle quickly captivated Lloyd George as he had French politicians. Shortly afterward, he visited London and explained his plan to the British War Cabinet.

Nivelle insisted that he visualized not another Somme but a quick, powerful blow to win the war. The main outline was similar to Joffre's but, in his version, the French would deliver the main attack along the Aisne River between Soissons and Reims. The British would merely carry out a diversionary assault near Arras. The key to victory would be the same tactics that Nivelle had used in his dramatic reconquest of Fort Douaumont in 1916—a preliminary bombardment of shattering impact, followed by a precise creeping barrage in front of the advancing troops.

The French general exuded unbridled confidence, boasting that "we have the formula" and predicting that the issue would be settled by an attack of "violence, brutality and rapidity" within 24 hours or 48 at the most. He promised nothing less than the rupture of the German front followed by hot pursuit of the beaten enemy. If the impossible did come to pass and the plan failed, he would immediately call off the operation. The British War Cabinet endorsed Nivelle's proposal and accepted the target date of April 1, 1917, for the start of the offensive. General Robertson and Field Marshal Haig did not share the prevailing optimism. Haig, in particular, believed that the plan would fail and feared that the relatively late starting date might imperil his own pet scheme for an offensive in Flanders.

Preparations for the great war-winning assault proceeded in an atmosphere of growing unreality. Nivelle intended his attack to take place at least partially in the area, where General Ludendorff had decided to evacuate after the Battle of the Somme in order to straighten and strengthen the German line. By shortening their front, the Germans added 13 formerly front-line divisions to their strategic reserve. Their new position, the Siegfried Line, or the "Hindenburg Line" as the Allies called it, was the last word in powerful fortifications.

Under Ludendorff's orders, the Germans carried out their evacuation with unprecedented ruthlessness, adopting a policy of almost total destruction of most of the towns and villages in the salient. They also cut down many trees to block roads, blew huge holes in road intersections, poisoned wells, and even ruined apple orchards by toppling trees or stripping bark off their trunks. At the same time they herded most of the population eastward as refugees. In the process, Ludendorff intended to impede the Allied pursuit and leave nothing that would be of any use to them. Those buildings that did

survive this orgy of devastation often contained booby-traps, which killed unsuspecting Allied soldiers. Prince Rupprecht of Bavaria, the German army group commander for this sector of the front, protested vehemently to Ludendorff about these savage measures, but to no avail.

The German withdrawal began in February and soon became obvious to the Allies, but Nivelle insisted that this action did not necessitate any change in his plan. The salient was not important. The only thing that mattered was the rupture of the front. Victory was assured. But Nivelle's position within France weakened steadily. In March, Briand's government fell, and the octogenarian Alexandre Ribot became premier with Paul Painlevé as his minister of war. Painlevé had absolutely no confidence in either Nivelle or his plan. Unfortunately, he felt that at this late date it would undermine morale to terminate the proposed offensive. Nivelle had stirred up remarkable enthusiasm among his troops by promising that this time they would not be undertaking another meat-grinder offensive but a quick, relatively painless surgical strike that would end the war and their suffering. He proved as persuasive with the *poilu* (the enlisted ranks) as he had with the politicians. The general also spoke dramatically of the importance of *élan* and determination in winning the battle. It was as though the ghosts of 1914 had returned to preside over French military planning.

Nivelle was amazingly careless in his willingness to inform politicians and even the press of his plans. Before long, the Germans had gained a general idea of what was coming. During March, they carried out trench raids that resulted in the capture of documents providing detailed information on the forthcoming attack. Ludendorff shifted reserves and strengthened his defenses accordingly. As time passed, more and more French generals expressed doubts, including General Alfred Micheler, whom Nivelle had personally selected as his army group commander for the offensive. But the plan had taken on a momentum of its own. Nothing would stop it—except the Germans.

BRITISH SUCCESS IN THE BATTLE OF ARRAS

The British launched their attack first in the Arras sector. It came on April 9 after a week-long bombardment, their heaviest and most effective to date. The development of much more dependable shells proved especially helpful as did a reliable new fuse that enabled high-explosive shells to do a far better job of destroying barbed wire. Artillery shells also proved more effective in delivering gas into enemy trenches. The British handled their forces much more efficiently than they had at the Somme and used underground tunnels to bring troops to the front without detection and in safety from shell fire.

The attacking forces consisted of General Allenby's Third Army, striking to the north and south of Arras, and the Canadian Corps of General Sir Henry Horne's First Army farther north. All units moved forward behind a highly effective creeping barrage. The Canadians were especially impressive as they stormed and captured the formidable heights of Vimy Ridge. The Third Army's Fourth Division broke through to the enemy's last position east of Arras and just to the north of the Hindenburg Line. This advance of three and a half miles was the largest one-day gain since the start of trench warfare on the Western Front. On April 11, General Sir Hubert Gough's Fifth Army on Allenby's right also moved forward, and two Australian brigades penetrated the Hindenburg Line itself. They could not hold their position without reinforcements, however, and when a German

counterattack inflicted severe casualties on them, they had to withdraw. By April 12, the British offensive had pretty well run its course, but it continued until May 23 because of the need to aid the French operation well to the southeast. It was Britain's most successful effort thus far, but it did not come cheaply. The British suffered 84,000 casualties to 75,000 for the Germans. Although the Battle of Arras was a minor operation, it was important because of the conquest of Vimy Ridge. This powerful position served the British well in March 1918 when it prevented the Germans from taking Arras.

THE NIVELLE OFFENSIVE

Meanwhile, Nivelle's much-heralded offensive got under way on April 16 after numerous delays because of bad weather. The preliminary bombardment had actually started on April 5 and was scheduled to last for a week, but because of the repeated postponements, it continued for ten days. Although over 7,000 guns took part and rained down 11 million shells, the results were disappointing. The artillery had to fire over a 30-mile-wide front, consisting of rugged terrain, all of which lessened its impact. Nivelle could not have chosen a more challenging portion of the front. His forces had to advance up the slopes of the large ridge known as the Chemin des Dames. The Germans had constructed their defenses in depth but had left the advance trenches lightly manned. As a result, the French moved forward rapidly and occupied the first line, but when they attempted to move on, they encountered difficulties.

German planes won control of the air over the battlefield and prevented French aerial reconnaissance from directing the artillery. As a result, the creeping barrage moved forward too rapidly for the infantry to keep

FIGURE 16–1 French infantry assault a German position in Champagne during the 1917 offensive. National Archives

pace. Once the shelling had moved beyond them, German machine gunners emerged from their dugouts and decimated the advancing troops. Despite much slower progress and far heavier casualties than predicted, the French continued to push on doggedly for two days. Although Nivelle had promised to call off the attack if it did not produce the promised breakthrough, he now refused to do so. When his offensive finally came to an end on May 9, it had actually gained more ground than any of Joffre's operations during 1915–1916, including a substantial portion of the Chemin des Dames. However, after Nivelle's tumultuous promises, it was not nearly enough.

MUTINY IN THE FRENCH RANKS

There had been no breakthrough, only another pointless slaughter. Although French casualty figures for this operation are especially controversial, they appear to have reached at least 120,000. This was too much for the *poilu* to bear. Mutinies began to break out among troops in the rear, and reinforcements moving up to the front bleated like sheep going to the slaughter. The main acts of "collective undiscipline," as the French called them, began on May 3 when the 21st Division, a veteran unit that had seen prolonged action at Verdun, refused to go into battle. A chain reaction followed, with unit after unit defying orders. Before this process ended, mutinies had afflicted 54 divisions, half the French army.

Although over 20,000 men actually deserted, most of the other mutinous soldiers agreed to defend the trenches but balked at participating in any more suicidal attacks. Some of the units elected councils, much like the soviets at the start of the Russian Revolution. This sent shivers down the spines of French military and political leaders alike and led to charges that pacifist and defeatist agitators were to blame for the mutinies. To be sure, some agitation did take place, but the disorders occurred spontaneously and were due to real grievances, not political propaganda. Even before the mutinies attained full flower, it had become obvious that Nivelle's days were numbered. General Pétain, the other and greater hero of Verdun, replaced Nivelle as commander-in-chief on May 15. Nivelle, after an unsuccessful quest for scapegoats, including General Micheler, his army group commander, and his own favorite army commander, General Charles Mangin, found himself trundled off to command forces in North Africa.

PÉTAIN ASSUMES COMMAND

General Pétain, always a friend to the *poilu*, realized that Nivelle's ill-conceived offensive was not the only cause of the mutiny. It was also the result of the disgraceful way in which the French army treated its brave soldiers. Discipline was more severe, living conditions much worse, and benefits far more limited than in either the British or German armies. Pétain now set out not only to restore discipline but to redress the soldiers' grievances. He knew he must punish the mutiny's ringleaders if he were to quell its rebellious spirit, but he kept death sentences to a minimum. Although details remain sketchy, it appears that only 55 men were executed. Many others were sent to penal colonies. The reverse side of Pétain's policy took the form of a sincere effort to improve the soldier's quality of life. This involved provision for better facilities, including lavatories, showers, sleeping quarters, and recreational centers for the men when off duty. He also took steps to improve the quality of food and the manner in which it was prepared. Perhaps his most well-received reform was the introduction of a vastly enhanced system of leave.

Even more important, Pétain visited a total of a hundred French divisions and impressed them all with his sincerity and simplicity. He spoke to the soldiers on a man-to-man basis and assured them that they had seen the last of battering-ram operations. The only offensive actions that he contemplated were limited attacks with limited objectives. Otherwise, the army "must wait for the Americans and the tanks." By this, he meant that he would pursue a defensive strategy until the Americans arrived in strength and France possessed a vast supply not only of tanks but also heavy artillery and planes. When the French finally returned to the offensive, Pétain intended to emphasize greater mobility and firepower to overwhelm the enemy, while conserving the lives of his men as much as possible.

Pétain's methods proved amazingly successful. Although the army never recaptured the qualities that enabled it to make its tragically heroic defense of Verdun, it did recover from its collapse in the wake of Nivelle's ill-conceived offensive. It would also contribute significantly to the Allied victory in 1918. This transformation was Pétain's finest achievement, greater even than his contribution to the salvation of Verdun. It is highly unlikely that any other French general would have been capable of this remarkable feat.

Miraculously, the Germans did not realize the severity of France's dilemma. The French imposed rigid censorship, suppressing all news of the mutiny, while French troops, disaffected though they were, continued to man the front lines. Even deserters refused to divulge the terrible secret to the enemy. Although the Germans heard rumors, they did not discover the full extent of the trouble until long after the situation had stabilized. Had they known earlier, the outcome of the war might have been much different.

BURDEN SHIFTS TO THE BRITISH

For the remainder of 1917, however, the French army could not play a major role. In fact, Pétain feared that it would not even be able to withstand a German attack of any magnitude. With France so seriously weakened, it fell to the British to assume the major burden on the Western Front. Field Marshal Haig was only too happy to oblige. He could now turn to the Flanders offensive, which he had been eager to launch for some time. Haig visualized breaking out of the narrow confines of the Ypres salient and dashing to the Belgian U-boat bases at Ostend and Zeebrugge. He also dreamed of outflanking the whole German position on the Western Front in the process. To accomplish this, he essentially revived the approach he had used in planning the Somme operation— an infantry breakthrough preceded by an enormous artillery barrage and followed by exploitation in the form of a cavalry charge, hardly a novel conception.

Before such an ambitious plan could go into effect it would be necessary to reduce the enormous vulnerability of the salient itself. Ever since the Second Battle of Ypres in 1915, the Germans had held the crescent-shaped high ground encompassing the salient. Extending from Messines Ridge on the south to Passchendaele Ridge on the northeast, this obstacle averaged only 150 feet in height, but it gave the Germans a perfect position from which to observe and shell the salient below. Even without any kind of offensive action, German guns accounted for 7,000 casualties a year within the salient. Messines Ridge posed an especially critical problem because it curled menacingly around the salient's southern flank. Before Haig could attempt his ambitious operation, he would need to capture Messines Ridge.

General Sir Herbert Plumer's Second Army drew this assignment. In appearance, Plumer gave the impression of being better suited for the role of a general in a Gilbert and Sullivan operetta. A pot-bellied, spindly-legged man with a walrus mustache, apple cheeks, bulbous eyes, and a weak chin, Plumer was, nevertheless, a meticulous planner and perhaps Haig's best commander. Ever since the Second Battle of Ypres, he had transformed the salient into an extremely well-defended position, despite its obvious physical liabilities. Plumer shared Pétain's simplicity and devotion to his men, and, like the French general, he had won their respect and affection. In fact, they had given him the nickname "Daddy." Plumer knew the salient and its surroundings exceedingly well and recognized the formidable obstacle posed by Messines Ridge. His staff devised an ingenious scheme to solve this problem.

BRITISH PLAN TO BLOW UP GERMAN-HELD FORTRESS

Starting early in 1916, Plumer's engineers undertook the laborious and dangerous process of digging 20 tunnels under the ridge, some almost a half-mile long, and packing the chamber at the end of each with high explosives. The British dug these shafts so deep that the enemy, who possessed inadequate listening devices, never detected the full extent of the project. To be sure, the Germans knew that the British were engaged in mining operations. In fact, they had undertaken some of their own on a much smaller scale. One of them actually came within 18 inches of a British tunnel before veering off in another direction. The Germans also stumbled across another British shaft and destroyed it.

Plumer began his preliminary bombardment on May 30 and continued it until a half-hour before the start of the attack on June 7, 1917. Then, at 3:10 in the morning, the British detonated the carefully laid mines in their remaining 19 tunnels, almost a million pounds of explosives in all. As the mines blew up more or less simultaneously, they lifted the rim of the ridge into the sky in an immense eruption, accompanied by towering columns of flame that illuminated the entire region. The deafening roar could be heard clearly as far away as London. As the surface of the ridge disintegrated, it swallowed up the powerful enemy defenses and buried thousands of German soldiers. Those who survived staggered about, totally dazed and in no condition to fight.

British, Australian, and New Zealand infantry dashed into the void created by the blast, protected by a creeping artillery barrage. As they swept up the slope of the ridge, demoralized Germans surrendered en masse. However, as the Allied forces approached the crest, enemy machine guns and counterattacks began to take their toll. Fighting continued for a week, but all German attempts to dislodge the British failed. Plumer's forces had eliminated Messines Ridge as a threat to the Ypres salient and had created the essential prerequisite for Field Marshal Haig's major Flanders offensive. They had inflicted 20,000 casualties and captured 7,300 German prisoners. Yet despite their stunning success, the victors had suffered almost 24,000 casualties themselves, most of them after reaching the summit of Messines Ridge.

LLOYD GEORGE: BRITAIN'S NEW PRIME MINISTER

While David Lloyd George was pleased with the Messines Ridge triumph, he still opposed Field Marshal Haig's more ambitious offensive plan. Indeed, later in June, Lloyd George renewed his proposal for an Italian operation. Although the British prime minister found little support for this project, other members of the War Cabinet clearly shared his misgivings about "another Somme" in Flanders. Even General Robertson, Haig's

most consistent champion, wavered. The chief of staff worried that without large-scale French aid, Britain might find itself engaged in another prolonged blood bath. Pétain flatly predicted that Haig's offensive would fail, just as Haig had foreseen the ruin of Nivelle's dream.

Haig enlisted Admiral Jellicoe, who warned of the dire peril from the U-boat menace, insisting that Britain would lose the war on the high seas unless the German submarine bases at Ostend and Zeebrugge were captured. He took this position even though only a small number of U-boats were actually based at these ports. The debate raged for several weeks, and it was not until shortly before the offensive's projected starting date that the War Cabinet finally gave its approval. In the end, Lloyd George did not feel strong enough politically to veto the commander-in-chief's plan because Haig had too many friends in high places, including King George V, who disliked the prime minister.

Lloyd George had made many enemies during his often turbulent career. This was almost inevitable, given his burning ambition and strong personality as well as his outspoken and often mercurial manner. Brought up by his uncle, who earned his living as a cobbler in a small Welsh village, Lloyd George overcame his humble origins to become a lawyer and soon entered local politics. In 1890, at the age of 27, he won election to Parliament as a radical member of the Liberal Party, who supported Welsh nationalism. Lloyd George became prominent as a self-proclaimed man of the people as well as for his opposition to the South African War. While serving as Herbert Asquith's chancellor of the exchequer, Lloyd George gained the animosity of the Conservatives because his budget of 1909 levied heavy taxation on the wealthy. He also led a successful campaign to reduce the power of the House of Lords and championed the creation of a system of national medical insurance, unemployment compensation, and old-age pensions for workers.

Although originally a pacifist, Lloyd George became increasingly hostile to Germany during the Second Moroccan Crisis and, once the European War began, he became one of its most militant supporters. His success as minister of munitions, paved the way for his rise to the office of secretary of state for war and finally prime minister, replacing Herbert Asquith. Although he cooperated with the Conservatives to bring down Asquith, they still looked upon him with suspicion, while many Liberals never forgave his disloyalty to his long-time colleague. To many in both parties, he was an opportunist completely devoid of political principle. However, few could doubt the sincerity of his devotion to victory.

Lloyd George's relations with Haig (who was promoted to field marshal in 1917) had been stormy even before he became prime minister and grew especially tense in early 1917 when Lloyd George tried briefly to subordinate Haig to Nivelle's overall supervision prior to the Nivelle offensive. The field marshal and General Robertson rebelled at this, and Haig possessed such strong political influence that he was able to hamstring these efforts. Their quarrel over the Flanders offensive and the subsequent course of that operation increased their mutual contempt still more.

THE BRITISH PLAN OF ACTION

The repeated offensives from 1914 to 1917 had clearly demonstrated that there were no "easy" sectors on the Western Front. However, Haig had chosen probably the least promising area of all as the site for his new offensive. It was not that the Ypres salient was particularly rugged. The remaining

ridges to the east were no more formidable than Messines Ridge and certainly not as forbidding as many other parts of the front. The root of the problem lay in the soil of the salient and the surrounding area. It consisted of clay of such fine grain that it was impervious to water. As a result, rain collected on the surface, creating large puddles and even swamps. In addition, the water table was extremely high. Ypres had actually been a seaport during the Middle Ages, and the peasants of Flanders had only succeeded in making the area suitable for agriculture by creating innumerable drainage ditches and dikes. However, the frequent heavy shelling during the past three years had completely demolished the drainage system. As a result, rainfall of any duration would turn the entire area into a virtually impassable quagmire. To compound the problem, Haig's great offensive would not start until July 31, 1917, and, as his chief of intelligence had discovered, during the previous 80 years or more, Flanders received heavy rains early in August "with the regularity of the Indian monsoon."

The chief factor responsible for this late starting date was Haig's decision to entrust the operation to General Gough's Fifth Army rather than Plumer's Second. Despite Plumer's outstanding performance at Messines Ridge, Haig feared that Plumer was too methodical and lacking in the requisite dash for the breakthrough-type operation that he had in mind. He considered his fellow cavalry officer, Gough, much better suited for this task. At 46, the youngest of the British commanders, Hubert Gough had a reputation for being impetuous and dedicated to the attack. During the Battle of the Somme, he had shown to good advantage in terms of ground taken, while keeping casualties relatively low. Unfortunately, he had little knowledge of the Ypres salient, and his army was a considerably less cohe-

Ypres — Ruines Eglise St-Martin   Ruins — St-Martin's church.

FIGURE 16–2 The ruins of Ypres' once beautiful St. Martin's Cathedral, a victim of intense German shelling. National Archives

sive force than Plumer's. It had not been together as a unit for long owing to frequent transfers of both men and officers. Perhaps most crucial of all, it had to move north to change places with Plumer's army. This took time, and time was at a premium because of the impending onslaught of the "monsoon" in August. If Haig had retained Plumer, it is likely that he could have launched the assault several weeks earlier when the weather was ideal.

By late July, the Kerensky offensive had collapsed in Russia, ending Germany's concern about any real threat in the East and enabling the OHL to shift forces to the West. After the Messines Ridge battle, German leaders had no illusions as to where the next blow would fall, a conclusion made more obvious by the lack of activity along most of the French sectors of the Western Front and signs of a growing British buildup

in Flanders. Under the overall supervision of Prince Rupprecht, the German army group commander, the Fourth Army of General Friedrich Sixt von Arnim greatly strengthened its defenses around the perimeter of the salient.

Gough began his preliminary bombardment on July 18 and continued it until the attack got underway almost two weeks later. In the process, the shelling tore the prospective battlefield to pieces, creating enormous craters. Even during this period, rain fell at times and began to collect in the craters as well as making the footing treacherous. After the troops went over the top at dawn on July 31, they made good progress, advancing as much as two miles, but when the Germans counterattacked, they had to yield about one-third of their gains. On August 1, the rains came in earnest and persisted for the next two weeks, turning the battlefield into an appalling morass, with water and liquid mud overflowing trenches and craters alike. The rainfall during the month reached 6.76 inches, more than twice the total for the average August.

When the rains stopped, Gough renewed his attack but made depressingly meager gains. The stubborn German defense utilized strongpoints in a checkerboard pattern, featuring concrete-covered machine gun nests called pillboxes because of their shape. Gough's failure convinced Haig that Plumer was the man for the job after all. He shifted the Second Army somewhat to the north and placed the main responsibility for the offensive in Plumer's hands. Plumer reverted to his usual meticulous, cautious approach, planning to move forward in a series of short bounds along narrow portions of the front and closely supported by artillery.

Starting on September 20, Plumer achieved considerably better results in a series of three separate engagements utilizing British, Australian, and New Zealand troops. By early October, his forces had reached the crest of the ridge overlooking Ypres from the east. Unfortunately, on October 3, the rain returned and continued to fall incessantly, but Haig was in no mood to quit, despite the advice of both Plumer and Gough to do just that. He coveted the remaining high ground near the village of Passchendaele and ordered the attack to resume on October 26.

BOTH SIDES SUSTAIN HEAVY LOSSES

It was the ensuing portion of the operation that became most closely associated with the offensive, which is often referred to as the Battle of Passchendaele rather than by its official name, the Third Battle of Ypres. The British slogged forward in the most appalling conditions of the war, sometimes barely able to walk because of the ooze through which

they had to struggle. Some men fell into shell craters and, unable to escape because of the slippery slopes, drowned in the muddy waters. The plight of the wounded was especially poignant. Many of them lay in the mud or in captured pillboxes for days, while stretcher bearers, slithering through the mud and slime, were unable to reach them. Despite these horrors, British and Canadian forces secured the top of much of the ridge by November 10. Haig now reluctantly terminated the offensive because of a disastrous Italian defeat at Caporetto that required the transfer of five of his divisions to help stabilize the front in Italy.

Although less costly than the Somme or Verdun, the Third Battle of Ypres clearly challenged the others for the dubious honor of being the most hideous campaign of the war. Officially, the British suffered almost 245,000 casualties, but some observers contend that the number was closer to 400,000. Estimates of German losses also vary from 200,000 to 400,000 men. Despite great bravery on both sides, this horrible battle not surprisingly led to definite signs of weakening morale among British and German soldiers alike.

The failure of the Third Battle of Ypres to produce the glowing results promised by Haig did nothing to enhance relations between the commander-in-chief and the British prime minister. This time, Lloyd George was able to oust Robertson as chief of staff, due in part to the fact that relations between Robertson and Haig had cooled because of their disagreement over the offensive. General Sir Henry Wilson, who had opposed the Ypres operation, replaced Robertson, but the irrepressible Haig still had too many friends in high places and survived to fight another day. Wilson had helped forge the military bond between Britain and France during the prewar years. He had no more respect for politicians than did Haig, but his relations with the commander-in-chief could scarcely have been worse.

THE ITALIAN CAMPAIGN

The disaster in Italy, which required the diversion of the five divisions from Haig's command, had been in the making for some time. The Italians, never as united in support of the war as the peoples of other Allied countries, shared the universal war-weariness of European belligerents. The repeated bloody offensives along the Isonzo River had created deep gloom. To make matters worse, Germany's U-boat offensive compounded the problems of Italy's economy with its dependence on imports of food, natural resources, and war material. Italian soldiers had fought bravely in conditions often far worse than those on the Western Front, but during 1917 the effects of two years of death and suffering were beginning to erode their spirit. Widespread antiwar agitation among the civilian population also contributed to weakening the resolve of the troops.

Despite these growing signs of strain, Italy continued to hammer away at the enemy during 1917. In keeping with the Chantilly agreement of December 1916, General Cadorna planned another offensive along the Isonzo. However, because of numerous problems, especially bad weather, the attack did not begin until after Nivelle's offensive had already come to grief. Cadorna launched his Tenth Battle of the Isonzo on May 12 with the help of a hundred guns borrowed from the Western Allies. His forces attacked both in the Gorizia area and in the Carso. The struggle lasted until June 6, and although the Italians achieved some minor gains, they suffered their usual heavy casualties. They also showed increasing signs of flagging morale.

Even though much distressed by the weakening of fighting spirit in his troops, Cadorna was determined to try again and opened the Eleventh Battle of the Isonzo on August 18. His main assault aimed at the capture of the Bainsizza Plateau, stretching along the east bank of the Isonzo to the north of Gorizia. This time, the Second Army of General Luigi Capello succeeded in crossing the Isonzo and scaling the steep face of the plateau, pushing the Austrians back an unprecedented five miles. The Austro-Hungarian high command feared that its forces could not withstand another attack in this area. However, the Italians, who had advanced beyond range of their own artillery and were encountering supply problems, had to break off their operation on September 15. As usual, Italian casualties ran much higher than those of the enemy.

Although Italy's success in the Bainsizza Plateau alarmed Austro-Hungarian leaders, they found encouragement in the failure of the Kerensky offensive in July. The Russian collapse convinced the Emperor Charles and his military advisers that they could now shift forces from the Eastern Front for an offensive in Italy. Charles hoped to carry out this operation with Austro-Hungarian troops only, but he needed Germany's approval for the transfer of the necessary manpower. He also asked for the loan of German artillery to support the assault. This placed Ludendorff in an awkward position. On the one hand, he was highly dubious of the Dual Monarchy's ability to handle such an ambitious undertaking. He also feared that an Austro-Hungarian victory over Italy, unlikely though it might be, would place Vienna in a favorable position to seek a separate peace with the Western Allies. On the other hand, he worried about the possibility that the Italians might actually defeat Austria-Hungary.

To preclude such a development, Ludendorff countered Charles's request with an offer the emperor could hardly refuse—the transfer of seven German divisions to join the Dual Monarchy in an offensive against Italy. Ludendorff also insisted that General Otto von Below, a veteran of the war on the

Eastern Front and one of the corps commanders in the Battle of Tannenberg, lead the new 14th Army, to be comprised of both German and Austrian troops. This force would provide the spearhead for the offensive. The German units included special forces trained in a new tactical approach to position warfare.

The origins of this innovation lay in some of the tactics used by both the Germans and French in the Battle of Verdun as well as the British at the Somme and, most notably, by General Brusilov in his famous 1916 offensive. By the summer of 1917, the Germans had developed the use of small groups of highly trained shock troops. These units were to move quickly forward, probing for weak spots in the enemy defenses, which they could exploit. Their chief function was to keep advancing and leave the elimination of strong defensive positions to other troops following at a distance. The shock troops would have the support of specialists armed with light machine guns, portable mortars, and flamethrowers.

In September 1917, General Oskar von Hutier, commander of the German Eighth Army on the Eastern Front, adopted these tactics, while adding innovations of his own in an attack on the Russian Baltic Sea port of Riga. The Germans had tried several times to capture Riga since 1915 but to no avail. Hutier's assault relied on surprise. To accomplish this, he abandoned the usual long bombardment in favor of a short and intensive barrage. He also relied on close coordination between his advancing shock troops and artillery. This combination proved startlingly effective. Hutier's forces broke through the Russian line on September 1 and two days later seized Riga.

General Below was to utilize these "Hutier tactics" with even more spectacular results against the Italians. He massed his assault force to the north of Capello's Second Army

in the Bainsizza Plateau. His initial objective was to cross the Isonzo near the village of Caporetto, and his final destination was the Tagliamento River, 25 miles beyond the starting point. Ludendorff did not plan to advance beyond the Tagliamento because he did not want to become bogged down in a lengthy Italian operation. Below's forces would have to make their way through the difficult terrain of the Julian Alps. His shock troops were to seek weak points in the mountain valleys and infiltrate as quickly as possible to the rear of the enemy. Other units would deal with the bypassed Italian defenders in the mountains.

Despite efforts to maintain secrecy, the Italians detected a sizable Austro-German buildup during September and also acquired detailed plans of the attack from deserters two days before it was to be launched. Although the Italians outnumbered the enemy by 41 divisions to 33 over the entire Isonzo front, the Austro-German forces had a 14 to 4 advantage in the area of the projected assault. Indeed, General Capello, who hoped to attack the enemy flank, placed his weakest troops in the path of Below's spearhead. Among them were former munitions workers who had been punished for engaging in strikes by being forced into the army. Their fighting spirit left much to be desired.

Below's carefully prepared plan went into operation on October 24 in fog and rain as well as snow in the higher elevations, all of which helped to conceal his attacking troops. His forces easily crossed the Isonzo and captured Caporetto. Although some of the vastly outnumbered Italians resisted tenaciously, large numbers surrendered or fled. By nightfall, the Austro-German forces had torn open the enemy front, advancing more than ten miles. General Cadorna ordered the Italian Second Army to withdraw to the Tagliamento, but it soon became obvious that the rapidity of the enemy advance had al-

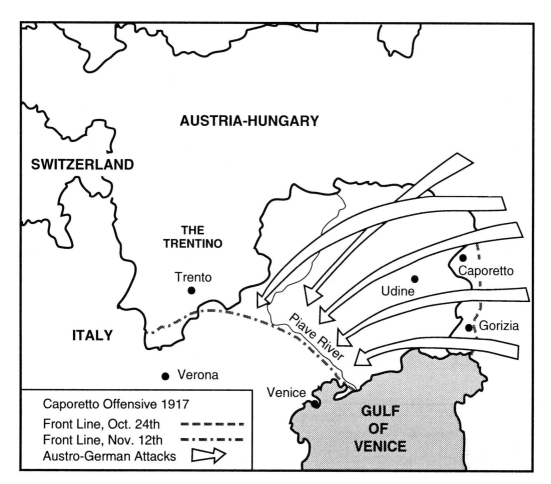

Caporetto Offensive 1917
Front Line, Oct. 24th
Front Line, Nov. 12th
Austro-German Attacks

ready outflanked that position. Accordingly, he ordered an additional retreat to the Piave River, some 70 miles from the jumping off point of the offensive and less than 20 miles from the great port city of Venice.

ITALIANS ROUTED AT CAPORETTO

The collapse of the Italian Second Army in the face of the enemy spearhead uncovered the flanks of the adjoining Third Army on the south and the Army of the Carnia to the north, forcing both to retreat as well. By November 9, the Italians had taken refuge behind the broad barrier of the Piave, where

they managed to stabilize their line. But Ludendorff had no intention of pursuing the operation any farther. He was eager to shift his forces to the Western Front preparatory to his spring offensive in 1918. Italian defenders did fight off Austrian attempts to break through until the end of January. Italy's losses had totaled 40,000 killed and wounded, 265,000 men taken prisoner, and another 300,000 deserters.

The Italian rout and retreat from Caporetto became one of the most famous episodes of the entire war, immortalized by Ernest Hemingway in his novel *A Farewell to Arms*. The collapse of Cadorna's forces was due in part to the brilliance of the German plan and its flawless execution. But it also owed much to faulty troop dispositions and the breakdown of morale on the Italian side. The latter had much in common with the French mutinies at the time of the Nivelle campaign. Not only was it a reaction to the German assault but it also owed much to the cumulative effect of the poor treatment that Italian soldiers had received for so long. Subjected to severe discipline and, like the French, rewarded for their bravery with poor pay and wretched living conditions, many of the Italian soldiers were deeply resentful. To be sure, antiwar propaganda had played a role in the collapse of morale, but the root of the problem lay in these much more personal grievances.

CHANGES IN THE ITALIAN GOVERNMENT

Caporetto led to many changes in the Italian approach to the war. Actually, one of these was not a result of the disaster but occurred almost simultaneously with the start of the offensive. This was the fall of the Boselli government and the rise of Vittorio Orlando to the office of premier. While minister of the interior under Boselli, Orlando had become the target of vicious attacks from the Right for his refusal to punish antiwar dissent. However, once he became premier, Orlando provided Italy with much stronger leadership and dedicated himself to the task of winning the war. His brilliant flair for oratory proved a valuable asset in this endeavor. Soon after taking power, Orlando relieved General Cadorna as commander-in-chief. He chose General Armando Diaz, previously a corps commander in the Third Army and once Cadorna's chief of operations, to succeed him. Eleven years younger than Cadorna, Diaz adopted an approach similar to that of General Pétain. He sincerely cared about his men and took measures to improve their dreary existence as much as possible. His

efforts greatly enhanced the Italian army's morale in the months to come and made it an effective fighting force once again.

It was not only the army's morale that improved in the aftermath of Caporetto. Now that the enemy had occupied Italy's northeastern provinces, a remarkable change also took place in the Italian people. Their first reaction had been one of shock but, once the front had stabilized, they steeled themselves for a fight to the finish. It appeared that Italy's very existence was at stake, and they rallied to Orlando's plea to "resist, resist, resist." All of the political parties, except the left wing socialists, responded to Orlando's appeal, and a belated form of *Union Sacrée* came into being.

Confronted by the Italian debacle, coming so soon after the Russian collapse, the Western Allies reacted quickly by sending six French and five British divisions to Italy, under Generals Marie Fayolle and Herbert Plumer, respectively. By the time they arrived, however, the Italians had consolidated their position on the Piave. While the retreat was in its final stages, representatives of the Allied powers met in the northern Italian city of Rapallo and, acting on Lloyd George's suggestion, established a Supreme War Council. This body was to determine strategy, distribution of forces, and all other important measures necessary to bring the war to a victorious conclusion.

THE BATTLE OF CAMBRAI

Before 1917 expired and joined its three equally misbegotten brothers of the recent past, one last drama unfolded on the rolling farmland of northern France. It is remembered as the Battle of Cambrai and, although it ended as inconclusively as any of the other clashes of arms on the Western Front between 1914 and 1917, it served as a kind of dress rehearsal for 1918. The genesis of the battle lay in the proposal of General Sir Hugh Elles, commander of the British Tank Corps, and his chief of staff, Lt. Colonel J.F.C. Fuller, for a large-scale raid using tanks and infantry to pierce a portion of the Hindenburg Line. Nothing came of this suggestion until after the Third Ypres offensive had become hopelessly bogged down. During the fall, Field Marshal Haig agreed to carry out such an operation following the end of fighting in Flanders. He chose the British Third Army, which held the line between Arras and St. Quentin to undertake the attack. General Sir Julian Byng, who had commanded the Canadian Corps in the capture of Vimy Ridge, had assumed leadership of this force in June 1917 when General Allenby took over command of the British troops fighting the Turks in Palestine.

Elles and Fuller had urged that the raid be undertaken in the area just to the southwest of the city of Cambrai, which lay 25 miles southeast of Arras. This region consisted of a plain resting on a bed of chalk, ideal for tank operations. No major military action had yet taken place on this "quiet sector" of the front. Only a few shell craters marred its surface and most of its wooded areas retained their trees intact. The prospective battlefield stretched between the Nord Canal to the west and the St. Quentin Canal on the east, a distance of about seven miles. While Elles and Fuller thought only in terms of a raid, Haig hoped to follow up the initial success by outflanking the enemy defenses between Cambrai and Arras. General Byng was even more ambitious and speculated about a drive all the way to Valenciennes, 25 miles northeast of Cambrai and almost on the Belgian border. Unfortunately, the resources available were insufficient for anything beyond the more modest goal. Byng possessed six infantry divisions and over 300 tanks. Although the tanks were still slow and ponderous, they had improved in quality and

reliability over those used at the Somme in 1916. The sturdy Mark IV came in two models, the "male" which carried two six-pounder (57 mm) guns and four Lewis machine guns, and the "female" with six Lewis machine guns. The Mark IV weighed 28 tons and had a crew of eight. Although capable of a road speed of only 3.7 miles an hour, it could span a ten-foot trench and clamber over a 4-1/2 foot obstacle. This time there also would be enough of them to make a difference.

Surprise was to be the key ingredient in the attack. Byng decided against a preliminary bombardment because prolonged shelling would alert the enemy of the impending offensive. The artillery would remain silent until the assault actually began. It would then execute a rolling barrage at a safe distance ahead of the advancing tanks. The tanks were to take the place of artillery in flattening the barbed wire protecting the German line. As they moved forward, they would create paths through the wire for the infantry following behind in columns. The British hoped that the element of surprise, coupled with the shock of such a large concentration of tanks, would result in a rupture of the Hindenburg Line. Byng massed cavalry near the front to exploit the anticipated breakthrough. The British carried out their preparations with remarkable secrecy. They brought the tanks into position in a wooded area by night and concealed the roar of their engines and the clatter of their treads by the use of low-flying aircraft in large numbers.

The attack began on the morning of November 20, 1917, and scored an immediate success. The tanks not only flattened the wire but sowed such terror among the German defenders that most of them fled for their lives. The tanks also were able to cross the wide German trenches by dropping large bundles of brushwood into them. Each tank carried two such bundles and was equipped with a device that lowered them into position ahead of the vehicle. Before nightfall, the British were in possession of the third enemy position and had sustained few casualties.

Unfortunately, all did not go well for the 51st Scottish Highland Division, ironically the highest-rated unit in the operation. Its mission was to seize the village of Flesquiéres before pushing on to capture the strategically vital Bourlon Wood, which crowned a small ridge overlooking Cambrai. Bourlon Wood held the key to victory and was scheduled to be taken on the first day. The 51st Highlanders did not follow the prescribed new column formation for infantry, however, and instead stretched out in the traditional line. This made it difficult for them to penetrate quickly through the relatively narrow paths that the tanks had created in the fields of barbed wire. As a result, they fell behind and could not support the tanks when they came under artillery fire near Flesquiéres. The tenacious German resistance at Flesquiéres delayed the capture of Bourlon Wood until November 23. By then, the offensive had lost its momentum, and the Germans had transferred reserves to stiffen their defense.

The British advance had created an awkward salient, and prudence now required a withdrawal. Unfortunately, Field Marshal Haig and General Byng were reluctant to admit failure after such a spectacular beginning, but when the Germans staged a surprise counterattack on November 30, they had no choice. Once again using infiltration tactics, the Germans scored a rapid penetration on the enemy's right flank and actually forced the British to evacuate some of the territory they had held before their offensive began. By December 5, the German drive had also sputtered to a halt, and quiet once again reclaimed the front.

VALUE OF TANK WARFARE RECOGNIZED

The Battle of Cambrai had ended in another British failure, but this time with a difference. The struggle had demonstrated the potential of tanks when used effectively in concentration and on suitable ground unchurned by prolonged artillery bombardment. In the future, not only the British but the Allies in general would rely on armor as the key to their offensive doctrine. Colonel Baptiste Estienne, France's leading advocate of armed warfare, now found more support for French tank development. By the spring of 1917, he would employ the Schneider and St. Chamond models, each mounting a 75-mm gun. These tanks also had the advantage of hull armor, which protected the tracks, although its overhang limited cross-country capability. The Germans belatedly produced the A7V tank but would employ only 20 of these clumsy, underpowered vehicles in 1918. German leaders, though impressed by the early gains scored by the tanks at Cambrai, did not see them as a war-winning weapon. Ludendorff noted that many of the armored monsters had broken down, while German artillery had destroyed still more. He placed his faith in the new infiltration tactics that had proven so successful at Riga, Caporetto, and now Cambrai. The Allies were no quicker to grasp the potential of this type of warfare than were the Germans to visualize the future impact of the tank. Cambrai foreshadowed the shape of war on the Western Front in 1918, but both sides saw its lessons as if through a glass darkly.

17

THE WAR OUTSIDE EUROPE

Although Europe remained the epicenter of the great chain reaction of violence that began in 1914, the conflict was, nevertheless, a "world" war. From beginning to end, it featured hostilities in other areas of the globe. These were campaigns of minor importance, but they often involved numbers far in excess of their significance as well as intense fighting. They lent an exotic aspect to the war and a change of pace from the meat-grinder nature of the conflict in Europe. Among the far-flung theaters of operations were the Far East and the islands of the Central Pacific, Africa, and, of course, the Middle East.

THE FAR EAST AND THE PACIFIC

The struggle in the Far East and Pacific proved brief and relatively cheap in human lives. Germany had acquired an empire of sorts in this vast area in the decades before

1914. It included the port of Tsingtao on the Shantung Peninsula along the coast of China, the northeastern quarter of the large island of New Guinea in the East Indies, and the islands of the Bismarck Archipelago and the northern Solomon Islands to the northeast. Finally, Germany controlled three vast groups of islands and atolls scattered over thousands of square miles of the Pacific—the Marianas, Carolines, and Marshalls—along with two of the Samoan Islands. Most of these colonies were more important strategically than economically, but none of them contained any strong military forces. Because Admiral Tirpitz had designed the High Seas Fleet for operations in home waters, he had no intention of using the fleet to protect the colonies. As a result, they were completely isolated and represented temptingly easy prizes for Allied forces in the area. Both Japan and Australia looked upon these possessions covetously.

Because Britain had entered the European War voluntarily rather than as the result of a direct German attack on its own territory, Japan, an ally of Britain, had no obligation under the Anglo-Japanese Alliance of 1902 to enter the conflict. However, when Britain, with some misgivings, requested Japanese aid against Germany, the Japanese were more than eager to comply. They entered the war on August 23, 1914.

Operations in the Far East and Pacific took the form of a race for German territory, most of which was virtually defenseless. Australian troops quickly occupied German New Guinea as well as the islands of the Bismarck Archipelago and the northern Solomons, while New Zealand forces took over Germany's holdings in Samoa. The Japanese, with equal rapidity, seized the Marianas, Carolines, and Marshalls. Tsingtao was the only German possession with permanent fortifications of any strength and a garrison of any size—4,000 men. Japanese troops laid siege to the port, and Britain sent forces from its colony of Hong Kong on the southern China coast to help. This combined force outnumbered the Germans by over six to one and, with the aid of naval and air bombardment, secured the surrender of the enemy on November 7, 1914. These operations ended Japan's military participation in the war against Germany, but Japanese warships did escort British convoys transferring troops from the Far East to Europe.

THE FIGHTING IN AFRICA

Germany also possessed colonies in Africa, four to be exact. On the southern coast of the great westward bulge of the continent lay the narrow corridor of territory known as Togoland. Farther to the east was the considerably larger area of the Cameroons, and well to the south stretched German South-West Africa (later Namibia). All of them bordered the

Atlantic. On the opposite side of the continent along the Indian Ocean lay German East Africa, by far the most valuable of the four colonies. These possessions all faced problems similar to those of Germany's outposts in the Far East and Pacific—inadequate military forces and complete isolation from any hope of reinforcement.

Togoland was the first to succumb to the Allies. It fell victim to an attack by Butisi tribesmen under British and French command. They converged from Britain's neighboring Gold Coast colony on the west and French Dahomey to the east soon after the war began. By August 26, 1914, the small enemy garrison had surrendered. It took much longer to subdue the Cameroons. After an abortive invasion by British-led Askari native troops from Nigeria to the west, the campaign became very much an Allied effort. Led by French military officers, native forces from Equatorial Africa on the east and even Belgian colonial units from the Congo to the southeast joined the British in the second assault. This time, they drove the enemy out of the port city of Duala and back to the capital of Yaoundé in the highlands 200 miles inland. The Allies had to struggle through insect-infested swamps, forests, and thick grassland. Intense heat and humidity as well as malaria, dysentery, and other tropical diseases caused even greater hardship. It was not until January 1916 that they reached Yaoundé, only to find that the garrison had fled, eventually interning itself in the neighboring Spanish enclave of Rio Muni on the Atlantic coast. The campaign, marked by little in the way of heavy fighting, lasted 18 months.

The British left the conquest of South-West Africa to the new dominion of the Union of South Africa. Under the command of Prime Minister Louis Botha, who had fought against the British during the South African War, Union of South African forces landed on the coast of South-West Africa and captured the German port of Lüderitz in September 1914. However, soon afterward, a revolt broke out in South Africa among anti-British Boers, who still resented their defeat in the South African War. The rebels cooperated with the Germans, and the situation remained serious for some time. It was not until January 1915 that loyal South African and British troops succeeded in putting an end to the insurrection. With order restored, Botha began converging drives into South-West Africa from the coast and across the border from the Union of South Africa.

Again, the invading forces had to battle exceedingly difficult terrain, this time semi-desert in nature. They suffered especially from a serious water shortage. Botha made skillful use of cavalry to outmaneuver the enemy, while utilizing the railroads to supply his forces. A native uprising against German rule also helped his cause. By July 1915, the Germans realized that their position was hopeless and surrendered.

The struggle for German East Africa proved by far the lengthiest and most difficult of the African operations. Lt. Colonel (later General) Paul von Lettow-Vorbeck commanded the small German forces in the colony, mostly comprised of Askari soldiers. A remarkable officer, Lettow-Vorbeck was to win fame far beyond that which a commander in such an insignificant theater of war would be expected to attain. By skillful use of his internal lines of communication, he was to outmaneuver his ultimately far more numerous enemies and prolong resistance until after the end of hostilities in Europe.

Once the war began, Lettow-Vorbeck took the initiative and sent forces into British East Africa and Uganda, both of which bordered German East Africa on the north. Initially, he enjoyed a numerical advantage, but his troops were unable to overcome British resistance and had to withdraw everywhere by the end of the year. Meanwhile, Indian troops had landed near the German port of Tanga on the coast of German East Africa. Unfortunately, they went ashore in an especially swampy and jungle-infested area and, after being repulsed by a smaller enemy force, evacuated without taking Tanga.

Nothing of consequence occurred on this front during 1915, except some minor naval clashes involving small craft on the three large lakes bordering East Africa to the west and north. This rather unusual combat ended with the British in control of these waters. In the case of Lake Tanganyika, victory came as a result of an epic journey by two armed launches that sailed from South Africa to the Congo and then made their way by rivers, swamps, and even overland portage, a distance of 2,300 miles. Two old British iron-clad monitors also penetrated up the Rufiji River from the Indian Ocean to destroy the German light cruiser *Königsberg*, which had taken refuge well upstream to escape larger enemy warships off the coast. These bizarre operations later inspired novelist C.S. Forester to write his popular adventure tale *The African Queen*, which in turn provided the inspiration for the even more well-known film of the same name.

SOUTH AFRICA AIDS THE ALLIED CAUSE

During the spring of 1916, South African troops, now available after the conquest of German South-West Africa, reinforced the British garrison to the north of German East Africa. They were under the command of General Jan Christian Smuts, who, like Botha, had fought against Britain in the South African War. Afterward, he and Botha had both joined the moderates in accepting dominion status for South Africa and continued close ties to London. Smuts hoped to encircle the enemy with the help of an Anglo-Belgian column moving southeastward from the Congo and another British force moving northeastward from Lake Nyasa. The operation proved too ambitious. As in the Cameroons, the invading troops fell victim to disease, heat, and strangling humidity as well as the sheer size of the country and its difficult terrain. Lettow-Vorbeck, using primarily Askari soldiers, succeeded in avoiding the trap, although he had to retreat into the southern part of the colony. Finally, Smuts decided that European and Indian soldiers were simply not suited for these conditions and began to recruit native forces on a large scale. This proved a wise decision.

Smuts left Africa to attend an imperial defense conference in London in early 1917 and was eventually succeeded by another South African, General Jacob Louis van Deventer, who staged an offensive in July. By late November, his troops had captured 5,000 enemy soldiers and had forced Lettow-Vorbeck and his remaining units southward into the Portuguese colony of Mozambique. Lettow-Vorbeck continued to elude pursuing British and Portuguese troops for nine months before crossing into British Rhodesia to the west. He held out there until news of the end of the war reached him on November 13, 1918. His remarkable exploits had tied down a total of 130,000 Allied troops for a period of more than four years. He had led them on a chase of close to 3,500 miles through the wilds of Africa, even though his own forces never totaled much more than 15,000 men at one time. When the campaign ended, he had only a little over 4,000 men left.

THE CAMPAIGN IN MESOPOTAMIA

Of all the war's godforsaken theaters, Mesopotamia (modern Iraq) was perhaps the most forlorn. Operations there soon took on some of the aspects of comic opera, but it was tragicomedy, a sort of grim joke that the British played on themselves and those associated with their efforts. After they had advanced as far as Qurna at the confluence of the Tigris and Euphrates rivers in December 1914, it appeared as though that would be the extent of British operations in Mesopotamia. They were in a good position to protect the Anglo-Persian oil installations on Abadan Island, and no worthwhile military objectives lay beyond this point. It would have been far better for all concerned had they remained content to stay where they were.

However, the prospect of a long defensive vigil in the desert of southern Mesopotamia did not appeal to those in charge of the operation—the British political and military authorities in India. It also was not to the liking of the offensively minded commander in Mesopotamia, General Sir John Nixon. The result was an unfortunate series of additional advances up the Tigris and Euphrates toward Baghdad, the Mesopotamian capital. These insatiable longings to be on the move had no strategic justification and did not take sufficient account of the slender resources available. Even with reinforcements from India, Nixon had only two divisions and a cavalry brigade. He also lacked adequate medical personnel, facilities, and supplies. This proved an especially serious shortcoming in a country noted for its unhealthy climate, which enabled a host of diseases to thrive.

The total lack of roads and railroads left the British completely dependent on river transport. A shortage of suitable river craft and the meandering nature of the streams assured that shipment of supplies would be meager and slow. In addition, during winter, the rivers usually overflowed their banks, causing widespread flooding, while in summer they dried up to such an extent that they were barely navigable. Intense heat, often

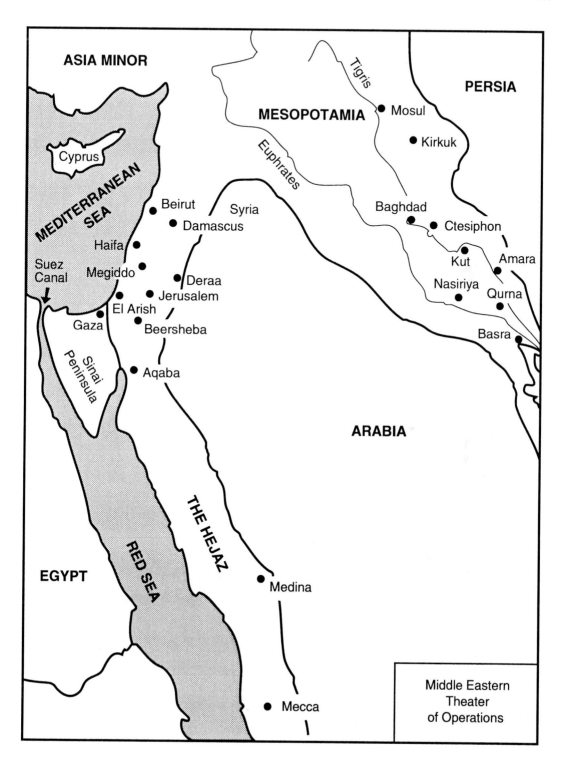

ASIA MINOR

MESOPOTAMIA

PERSIA

Tigris

● Mosul

● Kirkuk

Cyprus

MEDITERRANEAN SEA

Euphrates

Baghdad ●

● Beirut

Syria

● Ctesiphon

● Damascus

Haifa ●

Kut ● Amara

Suez Canal

Megiddo ●

● Deraa

Nasiriya ● Qurna

● Jerusalem

El Arish ●

Basra ●

Gaza ●

● Beersheba

Sinai Peninsula

● Aqaba

ARABIA

THE HEJAZ

RED SEA

EGYPT

● Medina

● Mecca

Middle Eastern
Theater
of Operations

reaching 122 degrees Fahrenheit for many days at a time, added to the unpleasant conditions.

None of this seemed to matter to those in charge. In March 1915, General Nixon received orders to advance about 70 miles to Nasiriya on the Euphrates and Amara on the Tigris, separated from each other by a distance of 100 miles. The drive on Amara proved relatively easy, although the Turks put up a strong resistance in defense of Nasiriya. By July 22, both towns were in British hands.

But now Nixon decided that he would prefer to take up positions at Kut-el-Amara 90 miles farther up the Tigris, apparently preliminary to a move toward Baghdad. Nixon was remarkably optimistic, considering his meager forces, and badly underestimated the fighting ability of the Turks. He sent General Charles Townshend northeastward toward Kut with the Sixth Indian Division and the cavalry brigade. On September 26, Townshend, a clever, bold, and ambitious commander, captured the town after a three-day battle. By now, politics, never completely absent from this theater of war, became dominant. In October, the British cabinet, embroiled in the disastrous Gallipoli campaign, was desperate for a success. It cast its eyes on Baghdad and authorized, but did not specifically order, resumption of the offensive.

Nixon needed little prodding and sent the reluctant Townshend toward the Mesopotamian capital on November 11 with a force of 12,000 men. Townshend had argued against a further advance, fearing that he had too few troops as well as a vulnerable communications line to the south. The Turkish defenders of Baghdad numbered 20,000. They chose to make their stand near the ruins of the ancient city of Ctesiphon on the Tigris, 16 miles to the south of the capital. The battle raged there for two days and, although the Turks finally fell back toward Baghdad, Townshend had suffered such heavy casualties that he felt obliged to retreat to Kut. The Turks soon followed and during December surrounded the British and besieged Kut for the next five months.

In January 1916, with the help of two Indian divisions shifted from France, Nixon dispatched a relief force to break the siege. But the Turks, now under the command of German General Kolmar von der Goltz, had created strong defensive positions around Kut and repulsed the British. Two additional relief efforts in March and April also misfired. When Townshend began the defense of Kut, his Anglo-Indian forces possessed food sufficient for only two months. Although they received some provisions dropped by airplanes, this was not nearly enough, and the garrison suffered terribly from hunger. Although the men resorted to killing horses and mules, many Indian soldiers because of their religious convictions refused to eat horseflesh. On April 29, Townshend surrendered along with his remaining 10,000 men. General von der Goltz had died of typhus ten days earlier, and Halil Pasha, uncle of Enver Pasha, succeeded to his command.

Halil Pasha had pledged to treat the starving defenders of Kut as "honored guests," but their journey into captivity proved a death march for many of the prisoners. The Turks herded the hunger-weakened men across the desert in searing heat and subjected them to savage treatment. Many others died after arriving at the wretched prison camps. Only about 3,000 survived to the end of the war. In dramatic contrast, Townshend did become the honored guest of the Turks for the duration of the conflict and even received permission to go hunting. His officers, while not that fortunate, did find themselves in tolerable internment camps.

Townshend's surrender sent shock waves through the British army and government and did nothing to increase Britain's prestige in the eyes of the Middle East Arabs. Never before had so large a British force laid down its arms. Coming so soon after the Gallipoli fiasco, it created great gloom, unrelieved by the desperate drama unfolding at Verdun. It also led to the dismissal of General Nixon from his command. In August 1916, General Sir Stanley Maude, a veteran of the Western Front as well as Gallipoli, succeeded to this post. Maude proved a much more able and far wiser leader than Nixon, despite a personality described as cold and high-strung. An outstanding organizer, if overly devoted to minute administrative detail, Maude greatly expanded the logistic capabilities of his command and saw to it that his men had plenty of everything they needed. Maude's austere devotion to duty included a deep concern for the welfare of his soldiers.

General Robertson, the British chief of staff, favored a strictly defensive strategy in Mesopotamia and perhaps even a complete withdrawal. To him, all of these strange developments in the desert represented an unfortunate diversion of strength from the main theater in the West. Maude argued against such an inactive policy and eventually won the approval of the War Cabinet for a resumption of offensive operations. He also gained reinforcements, much to Robertson's chagrin. By the time Maude was ready to advance on December 13, he enjoyed a roughly four to one advantage in manpower over the Turks and possessed far more artillery.

The British moved up the Tigris, outflanked Kut, and, after a heavy bombardment, forced a hasty Turkish retreat toward Baghdad in late February 1917. After a pause to bring up additional supplies, Maude resumed his advance on March 5 and outmaneuvered the Turkish defenders along the Diyala River, a tributary of the Tigris, ten miles to the southeast of Baghdad. The way to the capital was now clear, and the city fell on March 11. The Turks, in a badly mauled condition, withdrew some 60 miles to the north.

With the capture of Baghdad, the outcome of the war in Mesopotamia was no longer in doubt. But operations continued until the end of the conflict despite the absence of any important military objective. After the Sykes-Picot Agreement of 1916 placed Mesopotamia in Britain's postwar orbit, London sought to occupy as much of the country as possible. Anglo-Indian forces continued to push northward in an additional series of bounds. After Maude died of cholera in November 1917, General W.R. Marshall, one of his corps commanders, took his place. When Turkey agreed to an armistice on October 30, 1918, Marshall's troops were nearing the great oil center of Mosul about 225 miles northwest of Baghdad. They occupied the city on November 14.

The Mesopotamian campaign cost the British and Indians 92,000 casualties, including over 15,000 killed. Perhaps the most unnecessary campaign of the entire war, it deflected substantial manpower, almost 450,000 troops by November 1918, and other resources that might have been more productively employed elsewhere. It also caused much needless suffering. If its worth is measured in political terms, however, the occupation of most of Mesopotamia clearly strengthened Britain's claim to this oil-rich territory as part of its Middle Eastern war aims.

EGYPT, PALESTINE, AND SYRIA

Mesopotamia was not the only theater in which the British began the war in a strictly defensive stance and then gradually shifted to an offensive mode of action. Fighting in Egypt, and later Palestine and Syria, also took on this character. Again, the pattern involved a series of bounds from one position to another. In this case, the original design took the form of an effort to protect the Suez Canal against the Turks. However, the original British defensive position ran along the west bank of the canal, prompting critics to question whether the troops were there to defend the canal or to be protected by its broad 200-yard expanse. After the British had repulsed the Turkish effort to capture the canal in early 1915, General Archibald Murray set out to transform the area just to the east into a strongly fortified position.

While this work was underway, the Turks, led by the German Colonel Friedrich Kress von Kressenstein, made a series of nuisance raids on the canal and the railroad extending to the west. An uprising by Senussi tribes-men in western Egypt also proved a distrac-tion. The only Arab tribe to actually respond to the Turkish call for a holy war, the Senussi revolted first against the Italians in Libya, whom they had fought during the Tripolitanian War. They began their attacks even before Italy joined the Allies in May 1915. Later in the year, they extended their operations to raids against the British. The Senussi continued to be a problem for both Allied powers until the spring of 1917 when they agreed to a truce.

By the time that the British completed work on their defensive position east of the Suez Canal, it became abundantly clear that the Turks were far too weak to attack in any strength. General Murray now began to think in terms of pushing the British perimeter out into the Sinai Peninsula, as far east as El Arish, 90 miles from the canal and only 25 miles from the border of Palestine. But the Sinai Desert is a forbiddingly arid and hos-tile land. The British advance had to take place in stages with engineers gradually extending a pipeline for water, a railroad, and a road across vast open spaces. This task consumed almost all of 1916 as the British bested the enemy in a series of small engage-ments. El Arish did not fall until December 21, 1916.

As in Mesopotamia, the war in this theater took on strong political overtones. Lloyd George, who had become prime minister shortly before the capture of El Arish, was thirsting for a victory after the bleak events at Verdun and the Somme. His gaze fell on the Holy City of Jerusalem to the northeast of El Arish. But before any serious drive on Jerusalem could take place, it would be nec-essary to break through the Turkish position in southern Palestine between Gaza on the Mediterranean and Beersheba 20 miles inland.

Meanwhile, the Turks had encountered a new problem during 1916—a revolt among the Arabs of the Arabian Peninsula. Hussein ibn-Ali, the grand sharif of Mecca who ruled this Holy City of the Arabs as an autonomous vassal of the Turkish sultan, had made feelers for a closer relationship with Britain as early as February 1914. At that time, however, the British had shown little interest. Hussein headed one line of the ancient Hashemite family, which claimed direct descent from the prophet Muhammad. Hashemite sharifs had ruled the Hejaz, the long, narrow strip of territory stretching along the Red Sea on the western side of the vast Arabian Peninsula, since the tenth century. They had also held the title "Protector of the Two Holy Cities"— Mecca and Medina. Since the Turkish con-quest, however, they had been subject to Constantinople's overlordship in the form of a governor and military garrison in Medina. Although involved in Arab independence schemes for some time, Hussein continued to harbor a certain sense of allegiance to the sultan of Turkey. When Turkey joined the Central Powers and called for a Moslem holy war against the Allies, Hussein followed an eva-sive policy, suspecting that this was a Turkish ploy to increase their control over the Arabs.

On the day after Turkey entered the war, Lord Kitchener appealed to Hussein to join the fight against the Turks. Hussein hesitated because of his residual loyalty to the sultan. However, when Djemal Pasha, the Turkish military commander of operations against the British, began to arrest Arab nationalist leaders in Syria, Lebanon, and Palestine in early 1915, Hussein turned to the British, fearing a similar Turkish action against himself. Negotiations proceeded in a painfully slow manner until 1916. In February of that year, Sir Henry McMahon, the British High Commissioner in Egypt, pledged his country's support for the independence of the "purely Arab" areas of the Ottoman Empire. He excluded Lebanon and the coast of Syria, contending that they were not purely Arab in population. The real reason, however, was the fact that France had definite ambitions there. Hussein refrained from taking any action until April 1916 when a Turkish force of 3,500 men left Damascus, Syria, bound for Medina, 220 miles north of Mecca. The Turks came ostensibly to strengthen the Medina garrison, but Hussein interpreted this action as a threat to his rule and on June 5 initiated the Arab Revolt. By September, the Arabs controlled much of the Hejaz, but, the large Turkish garrison in Medina maintained control over that city.

Hussein and his Arab tribesmen were poorly armed, however, and after appealing to the British for aid, they received some artillery and machine guns, although much of this ordnance was obsolete. General Murray, the British commander in Egypt, was actually dubious about the political complications of the Arab Revolt and disliked diverting material, which he needed in Sinai. For a time, the Turks advanced from Medina toward Mecca, but Bedouin tribesmen harassed Turkish supply lines to such an extent that they had to withdraw. Late in 1916, the Arabs laid siege to Medina, and the British and French recognized Hussein as King of the Hejaz. An Arab army, under the leadership of Hussein's son, the Emir Faisel, also moved northward in January 1917 and captured Wejh on the Red Sea, 260 miles northwest of Medina. With the help of British

ships, Faisel's forces now were in position to strike against Turkish troops in northern Arabia.

Educated in Constantinople shortly before the war, Faisel had acquired a taste for Western clothes and Turkish manners. This apparently did not please his father, who sent him off for some tough Arab-style service in his camel corps. When the Turks tried to gain the support of Arab leaders for the holy war against the Allies, Hussein dispatched Faisel to Damascus as his deputy to discuss the Turkish proposal. After his arrival, Faisel found himself a virtual prisoner of the Turkish governor. When he finally escaped and returned to the Hejaz in the summer of 1916, Faisel had become an ardent Arab nationalist. Just before his conquest of Wejh, he was joined by one of the most flamboyant and controversial figures of the war—the 29-year-old Captain T.E. Lawrence. Soon to be known to the world as "Lawrence of Arabia," he served as liaison officer between the British and Faisel.

LAWRENCE OF ARABIA

Thomas Edward Lawrence's father, a member of the Irish landowning gentry, deserted his wife and four daughters and ran off with their governess. An illegitimate son of this alliance, which never resulted in marriage, T. E. Lawrence was a precocious child who developed an early and continuing passion for Middle Eastern archaeology and customs. In 1909, he traveled widely through Syria and Palestine on foot, while gathering material for his B.A. thesis at Oxford University. He became fluent in Arabic, although he always spoke the language with an accent, as is characteristic of Westerners. When the war broke out, he obtained a position in the geographical section of the War Office but soon entered the army as a lieutenant. After Turkey joined the Central

FIGURE 17–1   Prince Faisel (foreground) poses with Lawrence of Arabia (to the right of Faisel) and other Allied leaders. National Archives

Powers, Lawrence went to Egypt as a member of the intelligence service because of his knowledge of the Middle East. For the next two years he performed routine duties, but once he joined forces with Faisel, his life became anything but routine. Lawrence soon created his own legend and added to it after the war when he wrote a famous work on his exploits in the desert, *The Seven Pillars of Wisdom*.

A man of exceedingly complex and conflicting motivation, Lawrence combined an urge to fame and self-advertisement with apparent feelings of shame for these excesses. Although he claimed to have inspired the Arab Revolt, this clearly was not true. He also presented himself as the champion of the cause of Arab independence but appears to have been motivated primarily by his desire to promote British interests in the Middle East. Always a nonconformist, Lawrence took

to wearing Arab robes and sandals and became adept at camel riding and desert fighting. Although short of stature, he had a powerful build and remarkable powers of endurance.

Especially important for the cause of the Arab Revolt, Faisel and Lawrence, with the assistance of British subsidies, won the allegiance of the tribes of northern Arabia, most notably the Howeitat, led by its great warrior Sheik Auda abu-Tayi. During the summer of 1917, Lawrence accompanied Auda and Nasir, the sharif of Medina, on an epic march through tractless desert in searing heat to attack the small port of Aqaba. Lying at the head of the narrow Gulf of Aqaba, separating the Sinai Peninsula from Arabia, Aqaba possessed strong defensive positions, but they faced the sea. The Arabs, approaching from the landward side, caught the Turkish garrison by surprise and captured the town on

July 6, 1917. Possession of Aqaba provided the Arabs with a base from which they could attack the Hejaz Railroad, linking Damascus with Medina, as well as the left flank of the Turkish forces in Palestine. The spectacular victory also transformed Lawrence into a British national hero, despite the fact that he played a little role in the actual battle. Just as the climactic charge began, he accidentally shot his camel in the head with his revolver and was himself knocked unconscious when he fell to the ground.

THE WAR IN PALESTINE

Meanwhile, in Palestine, General Murray had launched an attack against Gaza on March 26, 1917, and his field commander, General Sir Charles Dobell, scored an initial success. Cavalry, primarily Anzac, swung around from the east to break into Gaza's northern suburbs, while an infantry division penetrated into the town from the south. However, owing to a communications breakdown, Dobell ordered his forces to withdraw at the crucial moment, and the chance for victory was lost. A second attempt to capture Gaza three weeks later failed completely and led to the decision to replace Murray with General Sir Edmund Henry Allenby. Lloyd George, still thirsting for a victory, sent the new commander off with the admonition to capture Jerusalem as a Christmas present for the British people.

An aggressive cavalryman, the 56-year-old Allenby was a veteran of the Second Battle of Ypres, the Somme, and Arras as well as the South African War. A tall man with a large, powerful frame and a face of remarkably strong, even heroic, features, Allenby also possessed a formidable temper. Known as "the Bull," he had not gotten on well with General Haig and welcomed the opportunity to assume an independent command. Despite his rather forbidding manner, he easily gained the admiration of his troops and earned a reputation as a fighting general who stayed close to the front. During the forthcoming campaign in Palestine and Syria, he won fame for his brilliant use of cavalry.

Before Allenby could move toward Jerusalem he had to confront the unfinished business of Gaza. Once he arrived in the Middle East in June 1917, he persuaded Lloyd George to transfer three divisions to his command and embarked on meticulous planning for an attack on the Gaza-Beersheba line. Allenby intended to avoid throwing away his strength in a direct assault on heavily defended Gaza. Instead, he quietly diverted forces to the east for an attack on Beersheba, while using various deceptions to convince the enemy that Gaza would be the target. These included an artillery bombardment of the Gaza defenses three days before the assault on Beersheba began. When Allenby launched his operation on October 31, his troops outnumbered the Turks by roughly two to one and had a much greater advantage in cavalry. Although he did not catch the enemy completely by surprise, they did not expect a blow of such magnitude. An Australian cavalry brigade, forming the Allied spearhead, stormed into Beersheba on the first day and captured its vital water wells. Following this breakthrough, Allenby turned his forces toward the sea in an effort to cut off Gaza, while also assaulting it from the south. After a fierce four-day struggle, the Turks abandoned the town and fell back to another defensive position anchored on the Judean Hills 20 miles south of Jerusalem and stretching northwestward to the sea.

Ludendorff had sent General von Falkenhayn to Palestine to organize the defense of the Gaza-Beersheba line, but he did not arrive until after the fall of Beersheba and could do little more than supervise the retreat. He was also unable to prevent Allenby from driving a wedge between the Turkish forces along the coast and those de-

FIGURE 17–2   The King of Montenegro visits General Sir
Edmund Allenby, the British commander in the Middle East.
National Archives

fending Jerusalem. Allenby now directed his
main effort to clambering over the rugged
Judean Hills toward the Holy City. Despite
heavy rains and tenacious enemy resistance,
his forces closed in from the west. The Turks
could not hold out any longer and abandoned
Jerusalem on December 9, 1917. Allenby entered the holy city on foot the same day, pre-
senting Lloyd George with the promised
Christmas present some two weeks early.

While Allenby's troops pursued the
Turks northward from Gaza and Beersheba,
the Arab forces of Faisel and Lawrence oper-

ated farther inland along the Hejaz Railroad.
The Arabs protected Allenby's right flank,
while harassing the Turks with hit-and-run
tactics and specializing in demolition raids on
the rail line. By 1918, they were tying down
an entire Turkish army. Far to the south, another Arab force continued the long siege of
Medina.

THE CAMPAIGN AGAINST SYRIA

Allenby hoped to continue his offensive
northward to clear the rest of Palestine and

drive on toward Damascus, Syria, as soon as possible. Lloyd George also favored such an operation, believing that it might knock Turkey out of the war. But a dangerous German offensive on the Western Front in March 1918 required the British to shift two divisions from Palestine to France. Although Allenby later received reinforcements from India, many of the newcomers needed additional training. These problems forced him to postpone any major undertaking until September. In the meantime, he engaged in lesser actions to the east of the Jordan River, intending to capture Amman, the capital of Transjordan, and cut the Hejaz Railroad. His efforts failed, but they did convince the Turks that his major attack would come in this area, and they positioned one-third of their forces there.

Actually, Allenby intended to strike northward along the coastal plain, punch a hole in the enemy line, and then send cavalry dashing through the breach to outflank the defenders to the east. He also planned to cut the lateral rail line extending from Deraa to the port of Haifa. Deraa was a vital rail junction in eastern Palestine where the Haifa line connected with the Hejaz Railway. Allenby entrusted the capture of Deraa itself to the Arabs. In the forthcoming engagement, Allenby would be matched against a new German commander of the Turkish forces—Liman von Sanders, one of the heroes of the Gallipoli campaign who had succeeded General Falkenhayn in March.

Allenby's plan worked to perfection. He unleashed his attack on September 19, 1918, to the accompaniment of a brief, intense bombardment. His forces quickly broke through, and the cavalry began its wild dash into the void. The Fourth Cavalry Division actually covered 70 miles in 34 hours. The frenzied pace of the advance completely disrupted General Liman von Sanders's position and led to the encirclement of thousands of Turks, while the remainder fled for their lives.

Within two days, the battle had become a rout. Royal Air Force planes had gained complete control of the air well before the start of the offensive and now subjected the beleaguered Turkish enemy to incessant aerial attacks. The Arabs, under Faisel and Lawrence, encountered greater difficulty at Deraa where the Turks resisted valiantly. They did not take the town until September 27. After his great victory, Allenby christened this operation the Battle of Megiddo. Although Megiddo was only one of a number of small towns and villages in the general area, it was believed to be the site of Armageddon, described in the biblical Book of Revelation as the scene of the predicted final struggle between good and evil.

The way to Damascus now lay open, and Allenby moved briskly northward. The Turks were in no position to defend the Syrian capital, and it fell on October 2. The victorious forces had taken a total of 75,000 prisoners, while suffering only 5,600 casualties. In the process, they had shattered three Turkish armies and brought about the total collapse of the enemy front. With little to block their progress, Allied troops continued to sweep northward, reaching Aleppo 200 miles beyond Damascus on October 26.

Despite the great triumph, all was not well within the Allied camp. The Sykes-Picot Agreement of May 1916 had increased Hussein's suspicion of British intentions. His fears grew more intense when he learned of the Balfour Declaration of November 1917, proposing a national homeland for the Jewish people in Palestine. After the occupation of Damascus, it became apparent that the Sykes-Picot Agreement would take precedence over the pledge that McMahon, the British High Commissioner in Egypt, had given to Hussein in February 1916. The extent to which it would prevail only became completely clear during the peace conference following the war. The future of Palestine also did not come into sharp focus until then.

While the operations in Palestine and Syria ultimately brought disappointment to the Arabs, Allenby emerged from them with perhaps the most illustrious reputation of any British commander in the war. One eminent historian contends that "it may be well held that his strategic handling of cavalry is unrivalled in British military history."[1] Other observers have belittled his achievement by pointing out that he won his victory over the Turks rather than the Germans. Certainly the Turks, although capable of great defensive heroism, were several cuts below the Germans in their overall capabilities. They also lacked the leadership and wealth of war materiel that their allies enjoyed. But perhaps even more important was the difference in conditions in the Middle East compared to those of the Western Front. Palestine boasted nothing comparable to the impregnable defenses that blunted offensive after offensive in the West during 1914–1917. And unlike the shell-torn no-man's-land of the Western Front, cavalry could actually operate effectively in Palestine, as Allenby clearly and brilliantly demonstrated in the Battle of Megiddo.

The fact remains, however, that Allenby's victory, like those won in the other campaigns that unfolded in all the far-flung lesser theaters of operations, really played no great role in the outcome of the war. But it did contribute to the political evolution of the Middle East in the postwar era. The real verdict in the conflict came in 1918 on the battlefields of Western Europe, where first the Germans and then the Allies made their final bids for the triumph that had eluded them for so long.

---

[1] C.R.M.F. Cruttwell, *A History of the Great War* (Oxford: Clarendon Press, 1934), p. 610.

CHAPTER

18

1918:
GERMANY'S LAST BID
FOR VICTORY

If 1917 had been a grim year for the Allies, it also had done little to improve the condition of the Central Powers. To be sure, Russia was in total disarray as a result of the revolution, but Germany's extensive demands at Brest-Litovsk had delayed Russia's departure from the war until March 1918. The German U-boat offensive had failed to force Britain to make peace, and no one in the German high command any longer clung to hope that it would. Unrestricted submarine warfare's inevitable by-product had also come to pass in the form of America's entry into the conflict, even though it would not bring its full strength to bear on the Western Front until the summer of 1918. Meanwhile, the Allied blockade tightened its awful grip on Germany and Austria-Hungary and cast serious doubt on how much longer they could continue to fight.

SIGNS OF UNREST

Despite overrunning the grain-rich Ukraine in reprisal for Leon Trotsky's "no war, no peace" policy, Germany's food supply grew steadily worse. The civilian population's suffering became a matter of increasing concern, and General Ludendorff worried about securing sufficient provisions for his troops. Yet, Germany was in far better shape than Austria, where the food shortage reached the level of near starvation by the end of 1917. In January 1918, when the government again lowered the flour ration, strikes broke out in Vienna and other cities. Ominous signs also posed the specter of the possible dissolution of the empire. The Czechs issued a declaration insisting on their right to determine their own future. Sándor Wekerle, the Hungarian prime minister, renewed the old Magyar call for a separate army, seemingly oblivious to the growing threat to the dualist system, which had benefitted the Magyars for so long. It became necessary to divert more and more troops from the front in an attempt to coerce the population into remaining loyal. Austro-Hungarian leaders grew ever more insistent on the need for peace, but Germany, firmly in the grip of Ludendorff, refused to seek a negotiated settlement.

Ludendorff had other plans. He was not oblivious to the critical condition of either Germany or its ally, but he was determined to try one last desperate attempt to secure victory before American forces reached the Western Front in strength. He also recognized that the French and British, after three and a half years of war and especially following their unhappy experiences at the Chemin des Dames and Ypres in 1917, were also feeling the strain. Not all German leaders agreed with him. Prince Max, heir to the throne of the Grand Duchy of Baden, as well as both the German Crown Prince and Prince Rupprecht of Bavaria believed that the omens for a military victory were not good. To them, it made more sense to seek a negotiated peace. In view of Russia's defection from the Allied cause and the notable lack of success of Anglo-French operations during 1917, they saw the possibility of a settlement that would not be unfavorable to Germany. The key, they thought, was the renunciation of any German claim to Belgium. But Ludendorff would not have it.

LUDENDORFF PLANS WESTERN OFFENSIVE

On November 11, 1917, one year to the day before Germany would accept an armistice ending the war on Allied terms, Ludendorff convened a staff conference at Mons, Belgium, and announced his intention to launch an offensive no later than March 1918. In preparation for this eleventh-hour effort, Ludendorff began to shift divisions from the east to France that same month. This newly arrived manpower would provide Germany with a substantial numerical advantage for the first time since 1914. Ludendorff chose to direct his offensive against the British, believing that, at this stage of the conflict, they were more determined to fight on than were the French. If he could defeat them, he thought that France would not persevere for long.

Once having determined his victim, Ludendorff wrestled with the question of where to strike. His first choice would have been Flanders. A breakthrough there could possibly lead to a thrust to the sea, isolating the Channel ports. Unfortunately, the infamous Flanders mud would be a problem until at least mid-April. Ludendorff believed he could not wait that long. Once again, time had become the arbiter of strategy on the Western Front, much as it had been in August 1914. Germany must achieve victory before American manpower shifted the balance irretrievably in favor of the Allies. Thus, he chose the old Somme battlefield that he had abandoned in favor of the Hindenburg Line during 1917. Although riddled with shell craters, it provided much more solid ground than did Flanders. Unfortunately, it did not offer any immediate strategic objective such as the Channel ports. This made it questionable whether even a substantial success would destroy Britain's ability to recover and stabilize the front along a new defensive line.

Ludendorff planned to unleash three armies—General Otto von Below's Seventeenth Army, General Georg von der Marwitz's Second, and General Oskar von Hutier's eighteenth—along a 70-mile front from Vimy Ridge in the north to La Fère on the south. This force totaled 78 divisions. Thirty-two of these would make the initial attack. General von Hutier, of course, was the author of the famous tactics that bore his name and had led to the capture of Riga. General von Below had employed the same tactics in an even more spectacular manner in the Caporetto operation in Italy. Ludendorff's offensive would feature the infiltration method on a much broader scale than ever before.

This formidable German host would strike at a point where the British were weakest. In their path lay General Hubert Gough's Fifth Army, consisting of only 14 divisions stretching along a front of 42 miles, and General Julian Byng's Third Army of 17 divisions, defending the 28 miles to the north. Responsibility for the shortage of British troops resided with Lloyd George, who kept

300,000 men and 600 aircraft in Britain. He did so in part because of his fear of an insurrection in Ireland, but even more so to prevent Field Marshal Haig from embarking on any additional suicidal offensives. Lloyd George had also contributed to Gough's predicament by agreeing to the request of Pétain and Clemenceau that the Fifth Army take over 30 miles of front formerly defended by the French. Not only did this decision stretch Gough's meager forces even more thinly, but they soon discovered that the positions they inherited were poorly prepared, especially in the rear areas. The French, with their greater preponderance of artillery, placed less emphasis on strong defensive positions for infantry than did the British.

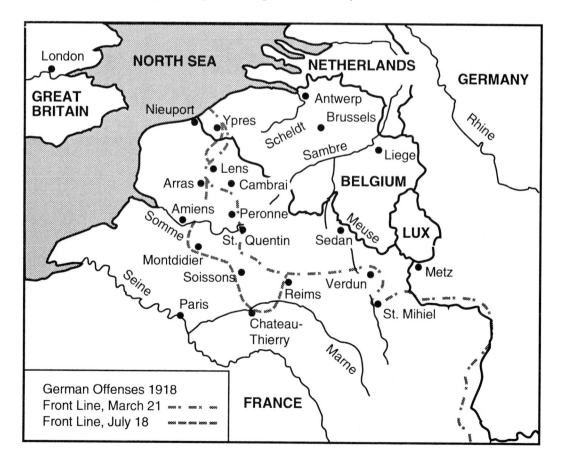

Although the Germans took special precautions to conceal their plans, the British detected mounting signs of a major enemy buildup. Gough grew especially insistent on the need for reinforcements, but Haig could do little to help, other than beseech Pétain to provide French reserves, if needed. But Pétain, while willing to shift reserves closer to the British sector of the front, was reluctant to commit them because of his fear that the Germans might actually strike against Verdun.

GERMANS RUPTURE BRITISH FRONT

Ludendorff's offensive, which received the code name "Michael," began with an enormous artillery bombardment just before 5 A.M. on March 21, 1918. Featuring trench mortar shelling of forward areas and a combination of gas and high-explosive attacks on positions in the rear, this relentless cascade of firepower continued for over five hours. It proved highly effective. Colonel Georg Bruchmüller, who had orchestrated the artillery preparation for General von Hutier's breakthrough at Riga, now played the role of maestro in another symphony of destruction and disorientation. His main objective was not to obliterate the enemy, as so many previous bombardments had tried to do without success. Instead, he hoped to disrupt the British defensive positions to such an extent that skilled German shock troops could infiltrate between them and penetrate rapidly into the rear areas. Larger forces, following in their wake, would neutralize the by-passed defenders. If all went according to plan, the entire enemy position would collapse.

For some time, all did go according to plan. At 9:40 A.M. the shock troops moved forward in dense fog, made worse by the lingering gas. As with so many other aspects of World War I, experts argue over whether the fog actually benefitted the Germans or the British. Obviously, confusion reigned on both sides, but it appears that the highly trained Germans, intent on finding the path of least resistance, were the chief beneficiaries. Certainly they achieved rapid progress, and by noon, when the fog lifted, they had advanced as much as three miles. By nightfall, they had pushed through Gough's front all the way to the Crozat Canal, a distance of seven miles.

Ludendorff's plan had provided for Hutier's army to play a subordinate role in the offensive, essentially to push forward to establish a defensive position between the British and French. It would then provide an anchor on the south for the main thrust by the two northern armies toward Arras and the key rail center of Amiens. If they achieved their objectives, it might be possible to thrust to the sea, cutting off the British forces in Flanders to the north. But Hutier's forces made by far the deepest initial penetration, and Ludendorff altered his plan accordingly. Hutier was now to thrust southwestward in an attempt to drive a deep wedge between the British and French. Ludendorff shifted six reserve divisions to bolster his advance. On March 22, Gough pulled his Fifth Army all the way back to the Somme. His retreat left the right flank of Byng's Third Army hanging in the air and forced it to give ground as well. But Byng's left flank continued to hold Vimy Ridge and other high ground, preventing General Below's forces from taking Arras or moving on to Amiens.

Opportunism had superseded strategy in Ludendorff's approach. His armies were now fanning out in such a way as to create a large salient rather than concentrating for a decisive thrust on the right. Although for a time this paid dividends in the form of captured territory, in the end it dispersed the German effort and contributed to the eventual success of the British in stabilizing a new line. For the time being this was not apparent to either side. By nightfall of the second day of the offensive, Hutier's troops had overrun the entire battle zone of the Fifth Army. On March 23 the British began to withdraw all along the front. Pétain sent reserves to cover Gough's right flank but made no attempt to counterattack, much to Haig's anger. The French general feared that Haig would pull back to protect the Channel ports, opening the road to Paris, and he was determined to use his forces to block the approaches to the French capital.

The rupture of the British front and growing disagreement on the role of French reserves led to the convening of a high-level conference at Doullens, located about midway between Arras and Amiens, on March 26. Despite the establishment of the Allied Supreme Council following the Caporetto debacle, this organization had accomplished little in the way of coordinating Anglo-French efforts. It had failed most notably to create a general reserve force, largely because of resistance from both Haig and Pétain, neither of whom wanted to surrender control over their own reserves. However, the German breakthrough had shaken Haig, who not only worried about the vulnerability of his own troops but had lost confidence in Pétain and considered him defeatist. Indeed, Pétain had grown increasingly pessimistic.

ALLIES FORM A UNIFIED COMMAND

During the Doullens Conference, Haig offered to follow the advice of General Ferdinand Foch, the French chief of staff, in regard to overall defense against the German offensive. This remarkable concession led to the appointment of Foch to coordinate all the Allied armies on the Western Front, while Haig and Pétain remained commanders of their respective armies. On April 14, with American concurrence, Foch became Supreme Allied Commander. For the first time, the Allies were to operate under a unified command.

Foch, who had served as French chief of staff since the aftermath of the Nivelle offensive, had reached the summit of his career. The former high priest of the offensive had lost his original overwhelming faith in the potential of *elan* to bring victory. The war of attrition had sobered him. But he had not lost his confidence that the Allies would prevail and was dedicated to taking the offensive, once they regained the initiative. He began immediately to prepare for that day and started to gather reserves, which he could commit to a counterattack. While the horrors of Verdun and the rigors of restoring the discipline and morale of the army after the Nivelle offensive had taken its toll on the increasingly morose Pétain, Foch still exuded optimism and martial spirit. He demonstrated this clearly during the Doullens Conference when, in response to a query about the defense of Amiens, he proclaimed: "I would fight in front of Amiens. I would fight in Amiens. I would fight behind Amiens. I would fight all the time. I would never surrender."

CLEMENCEAU GUIDES FRANCE

If Foch became the personification of the will to victory in the French army, Premier Georges Clemenceau assumed the same role in the French government. Despite his 76 years, Clemenceau remained far more vigorous than many much younger men. He was a member of an old family of somewhat threadbare country gentlemen, who were known for their democratic and republican ideals, as well as their intensely anti-clerical attitude. Following in the tradition of his father, grandfather, and great-grandfather, the young Clemenceau became a doctor but soon turned to a career in journalism, serving as a correspondent for a Paris newspaper during the American Civil War. Over the course of time he founded and edited two newspapers as well as a weekly magazine.

Clemenceau won election to the Chamber of Deputies in 1876 and later became a member of the French Senate. As leader of the Radical Party, he gained a reputation as an habitual critic of the Third Republic's many short-lived cabinets. When Clemenceau became premier in 1906, he pushed for closer relations with Britain, and even after his government collapsed three years later, he continued to urge vigorous defense measures against what he referred to as the growing threat of Germany. Noted for his independence of mind, Clemenceau had few close friends and seemed intent on avoiding any intimate relationships. Physically imposing, his dark eyes possessed a hard quality and his firm mouth was virtually concealed by his ample white moustache, which matched his bushy eyebrows. He and Foch made a formidable pair for the remainder of the war, even though little love was lost between them.

In keeping with the new vigorous approach to the war, Foch ordered General Pétain to transfer reserves to help stabilize the British line, but the Germans continued to roll forward. On March 27, Hutier's forces captured Montdidier, the main rail center for French reinforcements, and for a time opened a ten-mile gap between the British and their allies. However, the Germans could not exploit their opportunity because of a lack of cavalry. Meanwhile, a hastily assembled nondescript British force fought heroically in defense of Amiens and blocked General von der Marwitz's advance on this vital communications center. On March 28, General von Below opened an all-out assault toward Arras with nine divisions, but four of Byng's finest divisions stopped their progress along the Scarpe River.

GERMAN OFFENSIVE LOSES MOMENTUM

The German offensive was losing its momentum. The armies of Generals Hutier and Marwitz encountered the old problem of overextended supply lines. They also found it difficult to bring trucks and artillery across the badly cratered old Somme battlefield as well as the area that the Germans had devastated in their 1917 retreat to the Hindenburg Line. The French managed to link up with the British and patched together the semblance of a new defensive line by April 1. The German drive sputtered to a halt soon afterward. Operation Michael had pushed the battle line 40 miles forward at its deepest penetration. By the standards of World War I, this represented a spectacular tactical victory, but, strategically, it had accomplished nothing. The Germans had merely created another salient. They were no closer to winning the war and had squandered precious time and equally valuable manpower in the process. Casualties on each side approached 250,000, although the Germans had taken at least 70,000 British prisoners. They had also seized huge quantities of supplies, including an estimated two million bottles of whiskey!

While Operation Michael was in full flower, the Germans unveiled an awesome new weapon—the Paris gun. Ever since 1916, they had been working on an artillery weapon that could shell Paris from extremely long range. To accomplish this, the Germans modified a 15-inch naval gun and attached it to a smaller barrel 50 feet in length as well as an additional extension of 28 feet. The completed weapon, pointing upward at a 55-degree angle, resembled a huge fishing rod. It achieved a muzzle velocity of 5,400 feet per second, enabling small shells to be fired for a distance of almost 75 miles. Enroute to their targets, the missiles reached an altitude of 24 miles before plunging silently downward.

The first of these guns were fired on Paris on March 23; ten people were killed. The Germans eventually put six of the guns into service. The Paris guns shelled the French capital intermittently for the next 140 days. Although the product of a remarkable engineering feat, the guns possessed only enough accuracy to hit a target the size of a city. Obviously, these were terror weapons, designed to undermine Parisian morale, a goal the weapons never achieved. Eventually the Paris guns killed a total of 256 people; however, all but 100 of their victims died when a shell hit the church of St. Gervais on Good Friday, March 29, 1918.

Despite his failure to win a decisive victory in Operation Michael, Ludendorff was determined to try again. This time, he shifted his focus northward to Flanders for a second assault on the British. He planned to attack in the Lys River valley between the two small French towns of Armentieres and La Bassée to the south of Ypres. Once again, Ludendorff's strategic goal remained unclear. His initial objective was the rail center of Hazebrouck, but he also appears to have cherished hope of breaking through to the English Channel. Ludendorff's forces included General Friedrich Sixt von Arnim's Fourth Army north of the Lys and General Ferdinand von Quast's Sixth Army to the south of the river. Quast was to deliver the main blow against General Henry Horne's undermanned British First Army, while General von Arnim supported his left flank. The

FIGURE 18–1   A German railroad battery fires during an offensive in 1918. National Archives

area chosen for the assault, unlike the site of Operation Michael, had not been the scene of any fighting since 1915 and was relatively free of shell craters.

When General von Quast opened his attack on April 9, he had the good fortune to find a tired Portuguese division of low quality directly in its path. This was one of two divisions that Portugal had sent to the Western Front when it entered the war in 1916. After another brief hurricane bombardment, again directed by Colonel Bruchmüller, German shock troops moved forward, utilizing their patented infiltration tactics. They immediately struck terror into the hearts of the Portuguese, who broke and ran. The Germans poured through the gap in their wake, advancing more than three miles. Fortunately for the British, their troops were able to hold more firmly on the flanks, mitigating the enemy success to some extent.

The following day, German forces struck General Herbert Plumer's Second British Army north of the Lys. They quickly overran Armentieres and much of the high ground to the southeast of Ypres, including most of Messines Ridge, which the British had seized following the brilliant success of their mining operation in 1917. That evening, General Foch visited Haig and informed him that he was massing French reserves near Amiens for use, if needed, but when Haig asked for their immediate commitment, Foch refused. Foch believed that the British could hold out without them and was reluctant to squander the reserves that he was husbanding for the day when he could take the offensive. By April 11, the situation appeared so critical to Haig that he issued an uncharacteristically emotional appeal to his troops:

There is no other course open to us but to fight it out! Every position must be held to the last man: there must be no retirement. With our backs to the wall, and believing in the justice of our cause, each one of us must fight on to the end. The safety of our homes and the freedom of mankind alike depend on the conduct of each one of us at this critical moment.

The following day brought no improvement as the Germans captured the remainder of Messines Ridge. Other German forces drove to within eight miles of Hazebrouck. However, on that same day, one Australian and two British divisions, returning from Italy, moved into the line. Nevertheless, Plumer felt that he had no choice but to abandon Passchendaele Ridge, the object of so much agony in the ghastly mud of 1917. This action enabled him to shorten his line and conserve manpower. On April 17, General von Quast struck the British defenders on Mount Kemmel to the southwest of Ypres. Simultaneously, General von Arnim's forces assaulted the Belgians—who had not fought a major engagement since 1914—to the north of the Ypres salient. Both attacks failed.

Soon afterward, Foch finally agreed to commit four French divisions to the line. On April 21, they relieved the exhausted British defenders on Mount Kemmel. Unfortunately, when the Germans stormed the height again on April 25, the French put up a feeble resistance and promptly abandoned this key position, much to Haig's anger. Ludendorff made his last try for victory in Flanders on April 29. Again he attacked the French, but this time they resisted much more spiritedly and blunted the assault, in part because Foch had committed more reinforcements. The Germans also failed to dislodge the British directly south of Ypres.

Once again, Ludendorff had won a tactical victory, although not as impressive as that of March. However, a strategic breakthrough still eluded him. Instead, he had created another salient. This one was not as large as that of Operation Michael but was much more vulnerable to Allied shell fire. He had also lost another month in addition to more precious manpower, and the Americans kept arriving in ever greater numbers. Yet, although the Allies felt relief that they had been able to halt the first two German offensives, they also had suffered grievously in the process and clearly recognized that the initiative still lay with the enemy.

ALLIED RANKS BECOME STRAINED

Relations between the Allies had grown increasingly strained during this offensive. The controversy over French reserves had made Haig as bitter toward Foch as he had previously been toward Pétain. For his part, Foch believed that Haig was much too quick to call for reinforcements and failed to recognize the pressing need for a strategic reserve to undertake the eventual war-winning offensive. American relations with the European Allies had also taken a turn for the worse. This deterioration focused on General John J. Pershing's insistence on keeping his forces together in an independent American army. Both Foch and Haig preferred using American units as replacements for their own hard-pressed armies. During Operation Michael, Pershing had willingly committed his American First Division to aid the French in reestablishing the front near Montdidier, but he did this to help avert the threat of a disaster. In a conference of the Supreme War Council at Abbeville on May 1–2, Pershing made it abundantly clear that he would not yield in his determination to create a separate American army.

A native of rural Missouri, Pershing graduated from West Point in 1886 at the age of 26. He went on to serve in the last campaigns of the Indian Wars, against the Apaches in 1886 and the Sioux in 1890–1891. He fought in the Philippine Insurrection between 1899 and 1902. His fellow officers gave him the nickname "Black Jack" because he served at one

time with a black cavalry regiment. Pershing rose rapidly in rank, becoming a major general in 1906, even though 800 other officers were senior to him. After his wife and children died in a fire in their home, Pershing turned to his army career with single-minded intensity. He became famous for his expedition to apprehend Pancho Villa in Mexico, despite its failure to carry out this mission successfully. At 57, Pershing was tall, erect, and exceptionally distinguished in appearance with gray hair and a smartly trimmed mustache. Outwardly austere, he resembled Haig in his lack of charisma. In personal relations, however, he could be charming and managed to cultivate good relations with Foch and especially Haig, despite their frequent quarrels over disposition of American troops.

ROYAL NAVY ATTACKS U-BOAT BASE

While the British army engaged in its desperate struggle to repel Ludendorff's Flanders offensive, the Royal Navy carried out a daring raid on the submarine base at Zeebrugge, Belgium. Roger Keyes, the commander of the Dover patrol who had risen to the rank of vice admiral, devised a plan to block the narrow entrance to Zeebrugge and bottle up the German U-boats and light surface craft stationed there. Three obsolete cruisers, laden with cement, were to move into the harbor at night and sink themselves. A fourth old cruiser was to put a force of sailors and marines ashore along the harbor's breakwater. These troops would attack German coastal batteries to prevent them from firing on the sacrificial cruisers. But, as so often happened in this war, the operation did not work according to plan. On April 23, the feast day of England's patron St. George, as the British flotilla neared its objective, brutal German artillery fire raked the ships. The landing took place but was repulsed with heavy losses and could do little to prevent the shelling of the cruisers. Although two of the three vessels sank themselves in the harbor entrance, they were only able to block it partially. This proved just a temporary inconvenience to the Germans. A similar operation against Ostend the same night misfired completely.

GERMAN ARMY PRESSES ON

The failure of his March and April offensives persuaded Ludendorff that the root of his problem was the ability of the French to shift forces to reinforce the British. He was still convinced that the elusive final victory would only be gained by defeating the British, but he reluctantly concluded that, as a vital preliminary to a third attack on them, he must strike against the French northeast of Paris to give the impression of a threat to the capital. He believed that this would compel Foch to divert troops from the British front. With this accomplished, Ludendorff could try again to score a decisive triumph against Haig's forces. In all of this, Ludendorff seemed to overlook the fact that such a diversion would take time, and time more and more was becoming the critical factor. Moreover, it would cost him additional manpower, another finite commodity.

Ludendorff decided to attack the French on the Chemin des Dames, the ridge along which the Nivelle offensive had foundered. Although this was one of the most formidable defensive positions on the entire front, Ludendorff planned to employ the utmost secrecy to catch the enemy by surprise. He also would enjoy an additional advantage. The French were absolutely convinced that there would be no attack on the Chemin des Dames. As evidence of this, Foch ordered Pétain to defend the sector with a weak force of only 16 divisions under General Denis Duchêne, commander of the French Sixth Army. Duchêne compounded this error by

disregarding Pétain's instructions to conduct an elastic defense, if attacked. Instead, Duchêne chose an extremely rigid approach. He placed the great majority of his men in the forward positions with little strength in reserve. Although Duchêne had performed admirably as a staff officer during the 1914 retreat and the Battle of the Marne, he acted contrary to well-established wisdom on this occasion and left his troops terribly vulnerable to bombardment. To weaken the French position still more, Foch asked Haig to transfer five battered British divisions to this sector to recuperate from their recent ordeal in Flanders. This would enable larger French forces to remain near Amiens to strengthen the hinge between the two Allied armies.

The Germans were prepared to unleash 41 divisions against the weak Allied force along the Chemin des Dames. To avoid becoming bogged down in this operation, Ludendorff decreed that, once his troops had penetrated 12 miles beyond the original front line, the offensive would cease. He would then transfer forces back to Flanders for his last attempt to destroy the British and win the war. The Germans took the most meticulous measures to keep preparations for the offensive secret. They moved units into position at night and even covered the wheels of artillery pieces with bags of sawdust as they were towed to the front. Colonel Bruchmüller, again in charge of the bombardment, adeptly concealed his 4,000 guns in wooded country. It was not until the very eve of the operation that the French received warning of the attack from a German prisoner. By then, it was too late to take any major steps to improve their defensive position.

Soon after midnight on May 27, 1918, Bruchmüller began his bombardment. Its usual hurricane intensity continued for four hours, taking an exceptionally heavy toll of the Allied defenders concentrated in the forward positions. When the infantry of General

Max von Boehn's German Seventh Army moved forward, the stunned survivors were badly outnumbered and could offer little resistance. By noon, the Germans had overrun the ridge and seized the bridges over the Aisne River to the south before the French could destroy them. They had scored a clean breakthrough, and by the end of the day had crossed the Vesle River, 13 miles beyond their starting point, creating a breach 25 miles wide. Their astonishing progress continued the following day as they captured the important city of Soissons and moved to within two miles of the even more significant rail center of Reims. By May 30, the Germans had reached the Marne for the first time since September 1914 and were within 55 miles of Paris.

As usually happened, however, the German spearhead in the center penetrated much more rapidly than did the forces advancing on the flanks, creating another narrow salient. Although Ludendorff had intended the offensive as merely a feint to divert French forces away from Flanders, his amazing tactical success led him to continue the operation in a southwesterly direction toward Paris. By June 2, however, the drive had bogged down as inevitable logistic difficulties and exhaustion caught up with the Germans.

Meanwhile, Pétain had no reserves to seal the gaping hole in his front and appealed to Foch for help. Again, as in the case of Haig's earlier pleas, Foch refused, insisting that the attack at the Chemin des Dames was only a diversion. He had divined Ludendorff's original plan to shift his forces back to Flanders but failed to recognize that the German commander had altered his original intention. Pétain, accordingly, had to fall back on his only option—counterattacks by available forces on the enemy flank. French units on the Allied right and British troops on the left had been holding firm. Pétain also appealed for aid to General Pershing, who responded with

two divisions, despite his desire to maintain the integrity of the American army. Elements of the U.S. Third Division helped the French repulse the Germans near Château-Thierry on the west bank of the Marne and drive them back across the river. The American Second Division later counterattacked at Belleau Wood to the west. By June 3, the German advance had stalled and came to an end officially on June 6.

The stunning success of the German breakthrough had created alarm in Paris. Once again it seemed the capital was threatened. Officials prepared measures to defend the city and evacuate both the government and the civilian population. Criticism of Foch and Pétain mounted, but Clemenceau refused to remove either general, although General Duchêne paid the price of his folly. In an attempt to rouse the country to meet the new challenge, Clemenceau delivered a fiery speech in which he paraphrased Foch's words at the Doullens Conference: "I will fight before Paris, I will fight in Paris; I will fight behind Paris; we shall be victorious if the public authorities are equal to their task."

In reality, the threat to Paris was always more apparent than real, and the days of German ascendancy were numbered. By continuing the offensive beyond his own prescribed 12-mile limit, Ludendorff had doomed his original plan for another assault on the British in Flanders. His decision had led not to victory but to the formation of still another salient, this one 40 miles deep at its apex but invitingly vulnerable on its narrower flanks. Logic called for an evacuation to a more easily defensible line. However, the Germans had publicized the breakthrough as such a monumental triumph that Ludendorff feared a withdrawal would have a devastating effect on morale in Germany. He decided that his only option was to embark on another offensive to the northwest of the new salient in an effort to widen it and straighten his line. If he could accomplish this, he might still have time to attack the British, or so it seemed.

ANOTHER LUDENDORFF OFFENSIVE PLANNED

Ludendorff entrusted the task once again to Hutier's 18th Army. It was to attack along a 20-mile front between Montdidier on the west and Noyon to the east. The objective was the railroad center of Compiègne, about 50 miles northeast of Paris. If General von Hutier succeeded, General von Boehn's Seventh Army to the east was to attack later with the objective of taking the railroad linking Montdidier with Soissons. Ludendorff hoped that together the two assaults would greatly reduce the Allied bulge between his salients, enabling him to shorten his front and conserve manpower.

Unlike his earlier offensives, Ludendorff organized this one hastily, and it lacked the elaborate deceptive measures of its predecessors. Foch expected an enemy attack toward Compiègne, and German deserters supplied proof that his assumption was correct. Armed with this information, including the exact timing for the offensive, the French unleashed a counterbarrage against German artillery and assault troops shortly before Hutier's bombardment was about to start. Despite these advantages as well as possessing a supply of troops almost equal to those of the attackers, the French were unable to hold their forward positions. By the night of June 10, they had retreated six miles. But, on the following day, General Charles Mangin, temporarily discredited after the failure of the Nivelle offensive but now commander of the French Tenth Army, delivered a counterstroke against the German right flank and drove forward two miles. His attack employed 144 tanks, a harbinger of things to come. Mangin's effort proved sufficient to blunt the German offensive. By June 14, Ludendorff concluded that he could achieve nothing more in this sector and shifted his gaze eastward to Champagne.

More than a month elapsed before Ludendorff could put his next operation into effect. This period has been referred to as the last lull of the war, but it certainly was not free from combat. This time it was the Allies who initiated the engagements. Although minor in scope, they revealed a new aggressiveness and pointed to the tactics of the future. On June 28, General Mangin's Tenth Army launched an attack on the high ground above Soissons on the western edge of the Marne salient created by Ludendorff's third offensive. Using tanks and infantry supported by aircraft, Mangin scored a brilliant triumph. His success made him eager to extend these tactics to a major offensive aimed at eliminating the salient altogether.

Shortly afterward, General Sir John Monash's Australian Corps, with the assistance of American units, captured the village of Le Hamel and the adjacent woods near Amiens. Born of German-Jewish parents who had emigrated to Australia, Monash proved a brilliant military planner even though he was an engineer by profession rather than a soldier. He believed devoutly in harmonious teamwork among infantry, machine gunners, tanks, artillery, and planes. To Monash, a battle plan should be as precise as an orchestral composition. On this occasion, his men executed his operation so flawlessly that one historian has referred to it as "a little masterpiece."[1] This type of meticulous planning, providing for systematic cooperation among combined arms, proved to be the blueprint for British offensive operations in the near future.

---

[1] John Terraine, *To Win a War: 1918, the Year of Victory* (Garden City, N.Y.: Doubleday, 1981), p. 67.

AMERICANS WIN ANOTHER VICTORY

Marines and soldiers of the U.S. Second Division won another victory during the period of lull, but this encounter was a throwback to the slaughter of the Somme on a minor scale rather than a preview of the future. The Americans had counterattacked the Germans at Belleau Wood on June 2 during the last stages of the third German offensive. Attacking in waves with reckless heroism, they kept hammering away for 20 days and finally cleared the enemy from the wood. Before the battle ended, they needed the help of elements of the U.S. Third Division. The Second Division alone sustained 8,400 casualties, almost two-thirds of them being suffered by the attached marine brigade.

FLU EPIDEMIC MORE LETHAL THAN WAR

While the Allies pecked away at the Germans in these small operations, another enemy assaulted both sides. This was the virulent pandemic (a widely spread epidemic) known to the Allies as the "Spanish influenza" and to the Germans as "Flanders fever." The June outbreak proved to be only the first serious manifestation of what was to become the most deadly pandemic in modern times. Recurring periodically until 1919, influenza ultimately killed an estimated 20 million people worldwide, making it more than twice as lethal as the war itself. The disease hit the Germans—soldiers and civilians alike—especially hard. Weakened by malnutrition as a result of the food shortage created largely by the Allied blockade, 186,000 German troops and 400,000 civilians perished from this twentieth-century plague. Coming in the fourth year of a war of unprecedented horror, the pandemic lowered morale on both sides but again had its greatest

impact on the Germans and their partners in the Central Powers.

GERMANS REFUSE TO GIVE UP

By the time that Ludendorff was ready to embark on still another offensive, the outlook had grown increasingly bleak for Germany and Austria-Hungary. Not only did the food shortage continue to worsen but drought in Germany and eastern Europe also promised a poor harvest. Unrest became increasingly evident among the German civilian population and was far worse in the Dual Monarchy. Longing for peace rose progressively higher as each of Ludendorff's offensives failed to produce victory. Even Germany's foreign minister, Richard von Kühlmann, who had replaced Arthur Zimmermann in 1917, admitted to the Reichstag on June 24, 1918, that "an end to the war can hardly be expected by means of purely military decisions alone without diplomatic negotiations." Ludendorff was not amused by Kühlmann's frankness and pressured him to resign on July 12. Admiral Paul von Hintze now assumed the thankless task of guiding German foreign policy.

Ludendorff also faced a losing battle in the vital realm of manpower. His forces had suffered almost 700,000 casualties during the four offensives. While the Allies had also sustained grievous losses, they possessed a trump card. Their fears of a German breakthrough led to an acceleration of the transportation of U.S. troops across the Atlantic. With the help of massive amounts of British shipping, 246,000 more Americans arrived in France during May, and almost 280,000 followed in June. By the end of that month ten American divisions were in the line. Although British strength on the Western Front had fallen alarmingly during the first five months of 1918, London made vigorous, if belated, efforts to reinforce the BEF's battered

FIGURE 18–2 The ruins of the Church tower in Béthune, France, following the German offensives of 1918. National Archives

divisions after June 1. When his fifth offensive began, Ludendorff still outnumbered the Allies in divisions by 207 to 203. Unfortunately, for him, many of his units were understrength, while the fresh U.S. divisions each numbered 20,000 men, much larger than those of any of the European armies.

Despite his spiraling problems, Ludendorff would enjoy an advantage of 52 divisions to 34 in the area designated for his offensive. He planned to deliver his attack on both sides of the rail center of Reims, giving the impression of a direct threat to Paris. But his objective this time was to draw British reserves southward from Flanders, weakening their front in the north. When he was satisfied that he had accomplished his mission in Champagne, Ludendorff intended to unleash the long-delayed war-winning blow against the British in Flanders. He planned to carry out the operation in Champagne without shifting German reserves from the north. This would enable him to carry out his primary of-

fensive immediately after securing victory in Champagne. Although impressive in scope, his entire plan had an air of desperation about it.

Once again, deception was conspicuously absent as the Germans made their preparations. Allied intelligence soon became aware that Ludendorff was planning operations in both Champagne and Flanders. Although not certain where the first blow would fall, Foch believed that it would come against the French. Accordingly, he asked Haig to transfer four divisions to Champagne, and the British commander complied despite misgivings. As the date of the offensive approached, the French learned exact details of the attack from deserters and prisoners as well as Allied aerial reconnaissance. Pétain insisted on an elastic defense in depth with relatively few troops in the forward positions. But while Pétain was thinking in terms of defense, Foch prepared for a counterattack, once the enemy drive bogged down. The Germans soon learned of his intention from French deserters.

Ludendorff's plan called for Boehn's Seventh Army to cross the Marne east of Château-Thierry and then swing eastward through the river valley to Epernay. General Bruno von Mudra's First Army would attack at the opposite end of the sector with one column driving southwestward toward Châlons-sur-Marne and another more directly to the west, heading for Epernay. When the two armies linked up, they would cut off Reims to the north.

Colonel Brüchmuller was again to orchestrate the German artillery bombardment, but the French opened a counterbarrage an hour before the German guns began to fire. When Brüchmuller did unleash his bombardment just after midnight on July 15, the bulk of his shells fell on the lightly defended French forward positions. The French Fourth Army, under the command of General Henri Gouraud, lay in the path of Mudra's forces. While leading French troops in the Gallipoli Campaign, Gouraud lost an arm and suffered two broken legs when an artillery shell exploded. This high-spirited officer had carried out Pétain's elastic defensive concept with great skill, despite his own misgivings about abandoning forward positions along the Marne. As a result, when the Germans moved forward, they quickly captured the French first line but ran into heavy fire from Gouraud's well-positioned infantry and artillery in the second position. By noon, General von Mudra's drive had stalled.

On the western end of the front, the French had only established their positions following the German breakthrough in June, and they proved less formidable. The French commanders in this area also did not commit themselves to Pétain's defensive philosophy to the same extent as did Gouraud. Boehn's forces crossed the Marne and drove forward near the hinge between General Jean Marie Degoutte's French Sixth Army on the west and General Henri Berthelot's French Fifth

Army to the east. Although Degoutte's forces held firmly, Berthelot's gave way, and the Germans poured through. After an advance of six miles, however, the French were able to stabilize their front, while Allied planes administered savage punishment to the temporary German bridges across the Marne. Allied counterattacks even drove the enemy back at various points.

Ludendorff had left his commanders in Champagne to shift for themselves while he went north to prepare his offensive in Flanders. However, on the morning of July 18, he received word of an Allied counterattack in strength against the Marne salient. Ludendorff promptly called off the offensive in Champagne and postponed his Flanders operation. Neither would ever be resumed.

Foch had planned all along to deliver a counterstroke once the German offensive began to run down. Although he intended to attack both sides of the Marne salient, Mangin's Tenth Army would strike the main blow on July 18 against its western base, with Degoutte's Sixth Army providing support on the right flank. Berthelot's Fifth Army would attack from the east the following day. Foch's plan provided for the application of the lessons learned in recent minor Allied operations: a short, intensive bombardment, followed by an advance utilizing large numbers of tanks working closely with infantry and preceded by a creeping barrage. At the same time, Allied planes would attack enemy communications as well as troop concentrations. Foch also intended to employ the German practice of infiltration, probing for weak points, but with tanks rather than men in the vanguard.

When the attack began on July 18, General Mangin used the American First and Second divisions, with the crack Moroccan Division between them, as his spearhead. Although the Germans knew an attack was coming, Mangin concealed his tanks effectively and the weight of the assault surprised the enemy. The Tenth Army pushed ahead four miles on the first day, but its progress slowed significantly on July 19 as the Allied forces encountered heavy fire from German field artillery.

GERMAN ARMY IN RETREAT

Confronted by an offensive in much greater strength than he had considered possible at this point, Ludendorff experienced another attack of nerves similar to the one he had suffered during the Battle of Tannenberg in 1914. For some time he proved unable to decide what to do. He did order a withdrawal behind the Marne but was reluctant to authorize a further retreat because he feared the political impact of such a decision in Germany. But, as the French Fifth and Ninth armies joined in the counterstroke on July 19 and 20, respectively, and Mangin and Degoutte continued to move forward on the west, it became clear that he had no choice. On July 22, Ludendorff ordered his troops to fall back to the base of the salient along a line formed by the Aisne and its tributary, the Vesle. By August 4, the Marne salient no longer existed.

The Allied victory of July 1918 soon became known as the Second Battle of the Marne. It resembled its namesake of 1914 in two respects. The Allied success had not resulted in the destruction of the enemy and had featured a voluntary German withdrawal from an exposed position. But it also proved as decisive as the First Battle of the Marne because it destroyed any remaining German hope of winning the war. The initiative had passed irretrievably to the Allies, and the slaughter that had lasted for so long would come to an end in little more than three months.

CHAPTER
19

1918:
COLLAPSE
OF THE CENTRAL POWERS

Although the tide of war had turned on the Western Front as a result of the Allied victory in the Second Battle of the Marne, the Germans still managed to prevent a major break-through during the remaining brief life of the conflict. Their ability to accomplish this probably owed less to the Germans themselves than to the shortcomings of Allied technology. The Allies employed large numbers of tanks in their operations but, while the armor available at this stage of the war proved sufficient to secure repeated deep penetrations of the enemy front, it lacked the speed and range to exploit a breakthrough thoroughly. Tanks, nevertheless, played a major role in gaining the ultimate victory, along with efficient use of growing numbers of aircraft. Allied leaders sensed the dramatic potential of tanks, and the Germans now also recognized their significance, while infantrymen clamored for armor to support any attack.

In addition to heavy tanks designed to break through enemy defenses, the Allies had also developed lighter, faster models for exploitation. The British could now employ the 14-ton Whippet with a road speed of eight miles per hour, and the French would utilize over 2,000 two-man Renaults, weighing seven tons. Many of the latter featured a turret with a 360 degree traverse and mounted a 37-mm gun.

AMERICA'S PRESENCE
IN THE WAR INVALUABLE

More than anything else, the rapidly expanding American presence made the outcome of the war increasingly apparent to the Allies and Central Powers alike. The French and British had played the primary role in halting Ludendorff's offensives between March and July, but it is highly questionable that they alone could have pursued the war to a victorious conclusion. It was far more likely that the long deadlock would have continued and eventually led to mutual exhaustion and a negotiated settlement. The arrival of fresh American troops in vast numbers changed all that, making an Allied victory virtually inevitable. Not only did this infusion of new strength give the Allies a growing and insurmountable advantage in manpower, but it was largely responsible for the upward surge of British and French morale as well as the deterioration of German fighting spirit. Indeed, the promise of American participation proved even more important in speeding the end of the conflict than did the actual U.S. role in the fighting.

Since there would be no great breakthrough leading to a spectacular Allied triumph on the order of that envisaged by the Germans in 1914, the remainder of the war on the Western Front took the form of a series of Allied offensives from August until November and repeated German withdrawals in the face of the accumulating pressure. Throughout this period, Foch presided over the coordination of Allied efforts, but Field Marshal Haig and, to a certain extent, General Pershing became increasingly influential in determining objectives and the commitment of forces.

Victory in the Second Battle of the Marne had saved Foch from possible dismissal. In the early stages of Ludendorff's last offensive, Clemenceau had been so dismayed by the German success against General Berthelot's army that he had considered replacing Foch. The dramatic change in fortune created by the French counterstroke earned Foch a marshal's baton instead. The outcome of the battle clearly vindicated his persistence in hoarding reserves, despite the pleas of both Haig and Pétain for reinforcements. It had also justified Pétain's policy of avoiding large-scale offensives while waiting "for the tanks and the Americans." Foch and Haig now looked to the future with confidence. While most Allied leaders still thought in terms of the war lasting until 1919, Foch held out at least the hope of "decisive victory within a few months." Haig appears to have believed that the Germans could not continue the war through another winter.

THE AMIENS CAMPAIGN

The next Allied offensive followed within days of the triumph on the Marne. It took place near Amiens in the area of the hinge between the British and French sectors of the Western Front. Both Haig and General Henry Rawlinson, commander of the British Fourth Army, had been contemplating an offensive there ever since General John Monash's Australian Corps had scored its "little masterpiece" at Le Hamel. They envisioned a carefully planned, precisely executed operation of this type but on a much larger scale.

The appalling losses suffered by Rawlinson's Fourth Army on the first day of the Battle of the Somme had damaged his reputation. Although this disaster was by no means attributable solely to Rawlinson, and despite the fact that Rawlinson had shown to better advantage in the later stages of that offensive, Haig apparently lost confidence in him for a time. But when General Gough ran into difficulties during the Third Battle of Ypres, Haig called on Rawlinson to replace him. A member of a wealthy English gentry family, the 54-year-old Rawlinson was ambitious as well as charming and outgoing. "Rawly," as he was known to his friends, had served in India and as a staff officer in both the Sudanese and South African wars. He had also commanded a cavalry unit in the closing stages of the latter conflict. Rawlinson's army had been spared from attack during Ludendorff's offensives. As a result, it was in the best condition of any of Haig's forces.

On July 16, the day after Ludendorff began his final offensive on the Marne, Haig and

Rawlinson agreed to launch an attack on the western side of the Amiens salient. Its primary objective was to eliminate the German threat to Amiens and the railroad linking that city with Paris. Marshal Foch approved the plan and also ordered General Marie Eugéne Debeney's French First Army to join in the operation. Debeney was to attack against Hutier's 18th Army in the direction of Montdidier to the right of Rawlinson, whose army would deliver the main thrust against General von der Marwitz's Second Army.

Rawlinson's forces consisted of General Sir Richard Butler's British Third Corps on the left, Monash's Australian Corps in the center, and General Sir Arthur Currie's Canadian Corps on the right, with a cavalry corps in reserve. The addition of Debeney's army gave the Allies a total of 27 divisions, while the Germans could field only 20 understrength divisions. The British also possessed over 400 tanks and 800 planes. Since Marshal Foch had concentrated most of the French armor on the Marne front, Debeney had few tanks but contributed 1,100 aircraft. The Germans could muster fewer than 400 planes to challenge Allied domination of the sky.

The British carried out exceptional deceptive measures to keep the enemy in the dark. These included an elaborate scheme to conceal the transfer of the Canadian Corps southward from Flanders. False radio signals gave the impression that the British were really planning an attack in Flanders, and some small Canadian units actually moved into the area held by Plumer's Second Army. All of this proved remarkably effective. When the offensive began at 4:20 A.M. on August 8, it caught the enemy totally by surprise.

In emulation of Cambrai and Le Hamel, Rawlinson chose to forego a preliminary bombardment in favor of a creeping barrage that began just as his troops left their trenches. As in the German March offensive, the attacking forces moved forward in ground fog, causing confusion on both sides. However, the offensive formations again appear to have benefitted from these conditions. The sudden emergence of the tanks from the fog caused panic among many of the defenders, and the battle soon developed into a rout. By 1:30 that afternoon, the Australians and Canadians had captured all their objectives for the first day, opening a gap of 11 miles in the enemy line. The Canadians advanced as much as eight miles.

French forces produced much less spectacular results. Because of his shortage of tanks, Debeney preceded his attack with the usual bombardment, eliminating the element of surprise. When his infantry moved forward, it showed little enthusiasm and did not catch up to the Canadian advance on its left until early evening. The British Third Corps on the extreme left flank also encountered difficulty in trying to take its primary objective, Chapilly Spur, a key height above the Somme that exposed the Australians on the right to heavy fire. This failure was due at least in part to the fact that Third Corps was already weary after fighting off a German assault during the two days preceding the Allied offensive. Chapilly Spur did not fall until August 9.

Despite their considerable success, Allied forces now encountered the same old problem that had bedeviled all operations on the Western Front since 1914. It proved impossible to maintain the momentum of the initial thrust. The armor had done its job but had sustained heavy losses. Many of the crews in the surviving tanks also suffered from fumes and heat caused by the tanks' inadequate ventilating systems. When the offensive resumed the following day, few tanks were available, and the assaulting troops made much slower progress. This trend continued until Haig terminated the offensive on August 12. The British commander made his decision over the objections of Foch, who insisted that Haig continue the operation re-

FIGURE 19–1   Armed with machine guns, the French troops drive back a German attack near the Marne in 1918. National Archives

gardless of casualties. However, Haig held firm, and Foch backed down. Clearly the architect of the Somme and Third Ypres had finally learned the folly of squandering men when conditions did not promise results worthy of such sacrifice.

Although the Battle of Amiens did not prove decisive, it did shatter whatever optimism had remained in the German High Command following the defeat on the Marne. Ludendorff later referred to August 8 as the "black day of the German Army." His pessimism was not due to the Allied advance as such but to the poor German resistance. More than on any previous occasion, many of his troops had demonstrated unmistakable signs of weakening morale.

Fleeing German soldiers had shouted insults as they passed reinforcements on their way to try to seal the ruptured front, accusing them of being "war-prolongers" and "strikebreakers." Others rebuked a reserve unit moving up to the line with the cry, "We thought we had set the thing going, now you asses are corking up the hole again."

LUDENDORFF OFFERS TO RESIGN

During a high-level conference on August 11, Ludendorff blamed the breakdown of morale on agitators who had been infected with bolshevism while serving on the Eastern Front after the end of hostilities there. Now, nine months to the day after he had announced his intention to mount what he hoped would be a war-winning offensive in early 1918, Ludendorff insisted that there was no longer any possibility of victory. He urged efforts to secure a negotiated peace and offered his resignation. Both Hindenburg and William II refused to accept it, but the emperor, visibly shaken, also concluded that "the war must be ended."

Even though it appeared that the scales had finally been removed from Ludendorff's eyes, he continued to demand that Germany hold out for both Belgium and strong influence in the territory wrested from Russia at Brest-Litovsk. Such a position clearly made a settlement out of the question. He also believed that the army must continue to resist as tenaciously as possible so as not to give the impression of weakness. To him, this meant defending every inch of soil under German occupation. When calmer staff officers urged a withdrawal to the Hindenburg Line to shorten the front and conserve troops, he flatly refused.

FIGHTING CONTINUES

In addition to yielding to Haig's demand for an end to the Amiens offensive, Marshal Foch approved the BEF commander's plan for a follow-up operation to the north in the general direction of Bapaume. He also ordered French General Mangin's Tenth Army to strike at the southern edge of the Amiens salient. Mangin began his attack on August 18 and by August 22 had driven the Germans back to the juncture of the Oise and Ailette rivers, gaining as much as ten miles and menacing the enemy to the north of the Oise.

General Julian Byng's Third Army delivered the initial British thrust on August 21, striking on relatively unscathed terrain between the tortured ground of the old Somme battlefield to the south and the cratered site of the 1917 Battle of Arras on the north. After making limited gains at first, Byng resumed the attack with greater vigor on August 23, assisted by General Henry Horne's First Army on his left and Rawlinson's Fourth Army to the right. The French First and Third armies also moved forward between the BEF and Mangin's forces. By August 29, Byng's troops had captured Bapaume and had reached the Somme at the point where the river made an abrupt turn to the west near the town of Peronne.

On August 31, the Australians carried out the most remarkable feat of the battle by storming Mont St. Quentin on the east bank of the Somme. This formidable hill dominated Peronne and the entire surrounding area. With the help of an overpowering artillery barrage, a meager force of two understrength battalions, about 700 men, swept up the hill just as dawn was breaking. They overran the startled defenders, who had orders to hold their position at all costs. This spectacular coup eliminated the possibility of a German stand along the upper Somme. By the end of the month, the Allies had pushed the enemy back on an 80-mile front extending southward from Arras to Soissons. It was now clear even to Ludendorff that he had no recourse but to withdraw to the Hindenburg Line. He also abandoned the Lys salient created by his April offensive in Flanders. By September 8, his forces had reached their new positions. As they had done in their 1917 withdrawal to the Hindenburg Line, the Germans thoroughly devastated the area that they abandoned, giving special attention to rail and road communications.

The Allied counteroffensive that began on the Marne on July 18 almost by necessity had taken the form of a series of operations to reduce three major German salients. By early September, two of these, the Marne and Amiens salients, no longer existed. Neither did the minor one in Flanders. However, a third, important salient remained. This was the Saint-Mihiel salient to the southeast of Verdun. It had taken form in 1914 when the Germans tried to cut off Verdun during their execution of the Schlieffen Plan.

The French had tried twice to eliminate the salient during 1915, but in keeping with the nature of offensives on the Western Front at that time, both had failed. Protruding between the Meuse River on the west and the Moselle River to the east, the salient took its name from a small town near its southwestern extremity. Curving menacingly around Verdun's right flank, the salient had also cut direct rail communication between Nancy and Paris. It now became a source of great interest to General Pershing and the Americans. Pershing won his long struggle to create an independent American force on July 26 when he received approval to form the American First Army. It became operational on August 10, although it depended almost totally on the French for tanks, artillery, ammunition, and aircraft.

GENERAL PERSHING PLANS AMERICAN OFFENSIVE

Pershing had definite ideas about how to use his new army. For its first operation as a consolidated force, he planned to eliminate the Saint-Mihiel salient. Once his troops had accomplished this, he proposed to undertake an exceedingly ambitious offensive to capture Metz, followed by a drive to take the Briey iron ore mines of Lorraine, which were vital to Germany's war effort. On August 17, he received Marshal Foch's blessing along with a promise of six French divisions to help in the offensive.

Unfortunately for Pershing's hopes, Haig had developed other plans. He proposed a major British offensive in the Cambrai–St. Quentin area and urged a simultaneous

Franco-American converging operation aimed at Mézières near the Belgian border. Foch agreed and broke the news to Pershing at a meeting on August 30. The American commander was not pleased. Not only did this mean the end to his plan for a drive on Metz, but Foch proposed to split his forces. Half were to join the French in an attack against the Argonne Forest to the west of Verdun. The remainder would assist in another French assault farther west in Champagne. This threatened the hard-earned integrity of the U.S. First Army.

Pershing flatly refused to allow his forces to be split again, but he did indicate his willingness to accept a change of sectors for his offensive after he eliminated the Saint-Mihiel salient. The discussion became heated, and Foch, contrary to his usual diplomatic approach, directed what appeared to be a "take it or leave it" demand to the American commander before departing in a bad temper. But, with Pétain acting as a restraining influence, Foch relented two days later and agreed that Pershing could keep his army intact and choose either Champagne or the Argonne as his sector. Pershing selected the latter because of its greater proximity to his supply depots and communications.

The American assault on the Saint-Mihiel salient began on September 12, according to a plan developed in part by Colonel George C. Marshall, Pershing's chief of operations who was destined to be army chief of staff during World War II. It provided for converging attacks by American troops on both sides of the salient in an effort to cut off the enemy defenders. At the same time, French colonial troops would apply pressure against the salient's tip. Ludendorff had actually ordered the evacuation of the salient as early as September 8, but General Max von Gallwitz, the German Army Group commander responsible for the area, had been slow to comply. As a result, the withdrawal began just the day before Pershing's forces struck. The battle became a race between the retreating Germans and the Americans seeking to block their flight. The Germans fought a delaying action that enabled many of them to escape, but the Americans took 15,000 prisoners and captured 450 guns, while suffering 7,000 casualties. Marshal Foch warmly applauded the American performance, and both French President Poincaré and Premier Clemenceau made personal visits to extend their congratulations.

The Allied operations since July 18 had set the stage for the final series of offensives that would bring victory at long last. Foch referred to them collectively as "the greatest of all battles." Although the Allies had liquidated the salients created by Ludendorff's 1918 operations, the greatest of all salients remained. This was the vast bulge formed by the German invasion in 1914. It extended southward from Flanders before swinging more or less due east to Verdun. Behind it lay the all-important lateral railroad line running from Strasbourg in Alsace through the key junctions of Metz, Mézières, Aulnoye, and Lille before moving on into Flanders. If the Allies could cut this line, they would create a logistic crisis that might force the enemy to withdraw back into Belgium as far east as the Meuse.

ALLIES PLAN JOINT CAMPAIGN

Allied leaders reached agreement on a plan for a general offensive during a conference at Foch's headquarters on September 23. It essentially confirmed arrangements, that Foch had made earlier with both Haig and Pershing and strongly reflected the British commander's influence. The plan provided for almost simultaneous attacks at a number of points along the enemy salient. Pershing's U.S. First Army and General Gouraud's French Fourth Army would deliver the first

blow on September 26, with Pershing striking in the area bounded by the Meuse on his right and the Aisne to the left. Gouraud was to advance to the west of the Aisne. Both were to move in the direction of Sedan and Mézières. On September 27, Horne's First and Byng's Third British armies would strike toward Cambrai. The following day, the Belgian army and Plumer's British Second Army would attack in Flanders between the Lys and the sea. Finally, on September 29, Rawlinson's Fourth British Army and Debeney's First French Army were to move toward St. Quentin.

The Allies now possessed 220 divisions to 197 for the enemy, but many of the German units were understrength, and only about 50 of them were really fit for combat. Of the Allied divisions, 102 were French, 60 British, and 42 American, although the latter were equivalent to 84 European divisions. Twelve Belgian, two Italian, and the two discredited Portuguese formations completed the Allied array. The Allies also enjoyed a marked superiority in artillery, tanks, and aircraft. To resist this formidable aggregation, the Germans depended largely on the strength of their defensive positions, both natural and artificial.

THE ARGONNE OPERATION

The American operation became known as the Meuse-Argonne offensive because it took place along a front stretching eastward from the Meuse River to the Argonne Forest. Bordered on the west by the Aisne River and on the east by the Aire River, the Argonne was a perpetually gloomy and virtually impenetrable wilderness of trees and thick underbrush. Between the Aire and the Meuse lay a central upland criss-crossed by a series of heavily wooded ridges. The entire area was so forbidding that it had remained a lightly manned and quiet sector of the front since

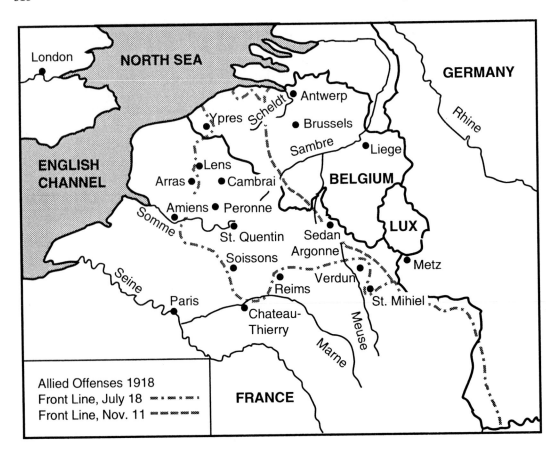

Allied Offenses 1918
Front Line, July 18 ▬·▬·▬·
Front Line, Nov. 11 ▬▬▬▬

1914. Its grim geography necessitated that the Americans make their primary thrusts through the narrow Aire and Meuse valleys on the two sides of the upland. The Germans had established their defensive system to take full advantage of this natural fortress.

Colonel George C. Marshall assumed responsibility for the monumental task of shifting over half a million men from the Saint-Mihiel salient to the jumping-off positions for the new offensive within ten days. Although the distance was not great, only three badly maintained roads led into the area of deployment. Despite the magnitude of the job, Marshall completed the transfer with exceptional efficiency. However, a myriad of logistic problems arose once the offensive began, and it proved extremely difficult to keep the troops in the field supplied with food and other essentials. Notable traffic jams developed, one lasting as long as 12 hours. Because of the short turn-around time between the two offensives, many of the units that had seen action in the Saint-Mihiel salient did not arrive in time for the start of the new operation. Four of the nine divisions in the opening assault had no previous combat experience and came to be known as "the thin green line."

Although enjoying marked numerical superiority, the Americans soon encountered difficulties with the terrain and the skillfully placed German strong points. Nevertheless, on the opening day of the offensive they moved forward as much as three miles and added another four miles the following day.

But the Americans glaringly demonstrated their inexperience, and their tactics recalled the bad old days that the Allies went through during 1915 and 1916. Advancing in waves and seemingly oblivious to the killing power of machine guns, they suffered heavy casualties. Their progress failed to fulfill the overly optimistic expectations of Pershing and Foch. French forces also made disappointing gains against strong German defensive positions. The war of attrition was not yet dead.

On September 28, Pershing decided to call a brief halt and brought up more combat-ready divisions, including "the Big Red One." When the advance resumed on October 4, it again ground slowly forward. The terrain was so wild that units had difficulty maintaining contact with one another, a problem made worse by poor overall coordination by Pershing and his staff. To add to the misery, the weather turned cold and rain mixed with sleet pelted the disheartened soldiers. The 1st Battalion of the 77th Division's 308th Regiment actually became lost in this dismal wilderness and found itself surrounded by enemy troops. It held out for five days against repeated attacks until elements of two other divisions came to its aid on October 7. Only 194 of its original 600 men survived the ordeal. This dramatic episode became a part of American folklore along with another incident involving the heroism and superb marksmanship of Alvin York, a corporal from the mountains of Tennessee. On October 8, York's platoon captured a large number of prisoners but shortly afterward many of its members fell victim to deadly German machine gun fire. Using his rifle with remarkable skill, York avenged his fallen comrades by killing 25 enemy soldiers, including the machine gunners. He also accounted for 132 prisoners and soon won acclaim as the greatest American hero of the conflict. Over 20 years later, he gained new renown when Hollywood

dramatized his heroics in the film *Sergeant York* with Gary Cooper in the title role.

By October 12, the Americans had cleared the Argonne and were gaining ground on the commanding heights along the Meuse. They had also crossed the river, expanding their front to 90 miles. That same day, Pershing formed the U.S. Second Army under General Robert Lee Bullard, who had previously served as a corps commander. Pershing also appointed another former corps commander, General Hunter Liggett, to lead the First Army, while he assumed the title of army group commander. Clemenceau had become highly dissatisfied with the slow pace of the American advance and in late October suggested to Foch that he approach President Wilson about replacing Pershing. Foch, showing a greater grasp of diplomacy than the premier, persuaded him not to push the matter.

Early in November, German resistance began to weaken, and both the Americans and the French on their left moved forward more swiftly. By November 6, the American First Army had pushed to within ten miles of Sedan. Two days later, it captured the heights overlooking the city and started to shell the enemy's lateral railroad. On November 10, the American Second Army began an attack toward the Briey iron ore fields. At the same time, Gouraud's forces closed in on Mézières.

ALLIES BATTER THE HINDENBURG LINE

While the Americans persisted in their version of a meat-grinder offensive, Haig unleashed his final assault against the Hindenburg Line. Again, the ensuing battle proved far from easy, but ultimately it produced much more dramatic results than did the struggle in the Meuse-Argonne area. Haig made his decision to assault this powerful position with the full knowledge that neither the British War Cabinet nor General Henry

Wilson, the British chief of staff, had much confidence in his scheme. Britain had suffered 600,000 casualties since March, and memories of the Somme and Third Ypres remained fresh. Leaders in London did not share Haig's optimism that the war would be over before the end of the year and feared the possibility of another hideous battle of attrition.

Although the terrain in the area of the Hindenburg Line was much less formidable than that confronting Pershing, the defenses were by far the strongest on the entire Western Front. Their toughness necessitated a departure from recent practice and a return to the prolonged bombardments of previous years. The huge fields of barbed wire required special attention before any advance was feasible. The first major obstacles confronting the British were the Canal du Nord, which lay in the path of Horne's First Army, and the St. Quentin Canal, directly in front of Rawlinson's Fourth Army. Both formed integral parts of the Hindenburg Line.

When the offensive began on September 27, General Currie's Canadian Corps formed the vanguard of Horne's attack. Currie sent two divisions against the southern and weakest portion of the Canal du Nord, where it was practically dry. The soldiers stormed across and then fanned out, with the help of reinforcements. Advancing six miles the first day, they captured the Bourlon Wood, which had proved such a difficult obstacle during the Battle of Cambrai in 1917. Byng's Third Army, supporting the First Army on the north, made slower progress, and German resistance continued to be strong everywhere. On October 1, it proved necessary to call a brief halt.

Meanwhile, by September 29, the attack of Rawlinson's Fourth Army was underway. Its objectives were the St. Quentin Canal and the main system of the Hindenburg Line looming menacingly behind it. Men of the British 46th Territorial Division secured the crucial crossing of the canal in an audacious attack under heavy fire. They used collapsible boats, rafts, and portable bridges, while others swam across with the aid of lifebelts. After this daring feat, they continued to push on another three and a half miles and penetrated the first two positions of the Hindenburg Line. Another assault, utilizing two U.S. divisions under Australian command, was less fortunate. Although the Americans made it across the top of a tunnel, through which the canal flowed at this point, they ran into withering machine gun fire from enemy outposts on the other side and suffered heavy losses. Australian reinforcements also found themselves pinned down as they tried to come to the aid of the beleaguered spearhead.

Rawlinson continued to hammer away at the Hindenburg Line, and on October 4, his troops broke through its final position. This penetration threatened the entire enemy line to the north and necessitated the withdrawal of German forces facing all three British armies. Rawlinson had achieved a great triumph, but it was due in large part to sagging enemy fighting spirit. As he quickly admitted, if German morale had "not shown marked signs of deterioration during the past month, I should never have contemplated attacking the Hindenburg Line. Had it been defended by the Germans of two years ago, it would certainly have been impregnable...."[1]

Although Rawlinson's victory proved decisive for the future course of the war, Haig's offensive in Flanders also produced a surprising success. On September 28, the Belgian army, led by King Albert, attacked on the left with the support of six French divisions,

---

[1]Gregory Blaxland, *Amiens: 1918* (Letchworth, England: Frederick Muller, 1968), p. 243.

while Plumer's Second Army moved forward on the right. The British force contained many veterans with grim memories of Third Ypres. This time, however, there was no repetition of that prolonged horror. The German defenders were far fewer and lacked the tenacity of those of 1917. By evening of the first day, the Allies held much of the ridge around the city and took the remainder on September 29 as they advanced as much as nine miles beyond the initial line. For a time it appeared as though they might be able to outflank the entire German position on the Western Front as Haig had dreamed of doing in 1917.

Unfortunately, a number of old enemies returned. Rain, which had been falling throughout the operation, gradually turned the area into the familiar morass that had plagued the British the year before. The Allies also outran their supply lines and fell victim to exhaustion, while the Germans brought in reinforcements and formed a new line. By October 2, a lull had set in, but at long last the Ypres Salient was no more.

During the remainder of October and into November, the campaign on the Western Front took the form of continued Allied attacks, followed by periods of heavy fighting and eventual enemy withdrawals to a new

FIGURE 19–2 Shattered trees and a wrecked French tank bear witness to savage fighting in Belgium during the Allied offensive in 1918. National Archives

line and then another. As they retreated, the Germans resorted once again to wholesale destruction in the areas being abandoned. All of the Allied armies gradually moved forward and, by early November, most of France was free from German occupation as well as roughly the western fifth of Belgium. While men fought and died in this fashion, the focus of attention shifted increasingly to diplomacy as Germany and its partners sought a way out of the war, which they could no longer win.

THE DIPLOMATIC WAR

Although Ludendorff, Hindenburg, and the German emperor had agreed soon after "the black day of the German army" that Germany must seek peace negotiations, nothing concrete had come of this decision. On September 27, however, Ludendorff came to the conclusion that Berlin must take immediate steps to end the war. Already discouraged by the course of events on the Western Front, he now received depressing news from the Balkans. An offensive by the Allied army in Greece had suddenly forced Bulgaria to seek an armistice. Ludendorff visualized an Allied drive against Austria-Hungary, which also showed definite signs of crumbling. These developments posed a threat to Germany itself from the southeast. Bulgaria's defection also opened the danger of the loss of Rumania and its vital oil supply to the Allies.

On September 29, German Foreign Secretary Paul von Hintze informed Hindenburg and Ludendorff that, in view of the prevailing domestic situation in Germany, it would be necessary to change the government into a democratic parliamentary regime as quickly as possible. He warned of the possibility of revolution if this transformation did not take place. Although both men were shocked by Hintze's revelation, they quickly agreed that drastic measures were mandatory. These three leaders, bulwarks of the old

authoritarian order and totally opposed to the whole idea of democracy, now confronted William II with what they all considered a most distasteful dilemma. There must be an immediate armistice as well as a "revolution from above" that would turn over direction of political affairs to a parliamentary government. William had no choice but to comply and hoped to save the monarchy in the process. Ludendorff viewed this decision in part as a way of placing blame for Germany's defeat on a democratic government.

Upon hearing of the plan for government reform, Chancellor Georg von Hertling promptly resigned. He disliked the fact that a parliamentary system would mean a more centralized form of government and lessen the power of the individual states, including his own Bavaria. Prince Max of Baden succeeded Hertling as chancellor. Although William's second cousin and heir to the ducal throne of Baden, Max held political views that differed considerably from those of the emperor. Much more of a liberal than most German noblemen, Max had urged William for some time to take steps to secure a negotiated peace. He did not really favor a democratic system in which the Reichstag would dominate, however, and found it difficult to preside over this transition. The prince also feared that the military leaders, after refusing any thought of a negotiated settlement for so long, were pursuing an armistice with a haste bordering on panic. To him, this was tantamount to a confession of abject weakness and would result in the imposition of harsh terms by the Allies. He believed it would make more sense to complete renovation of the German political system before seeking peace. This, in his opinion, would create an atmosphere more conducive to leniency.

Ludendorff insisted on an armistice, however, and the emperor informed Prince Max that "you have not been brought here to make difficulties for the High Command," a graphic admission of the shotgun nature of Germany's hasty marriage to democracy. The chancellor now bowed to the inevitable, and on the night of October 3–4, he and his government drafted a note to President Wilson requesting an armistice and the start of peace negotiations. The note also specified German acceptance of a number of provisions laid down by Wilson during the course of 1918.

WILSON'S FOURTEEN POINTS

Wilson's basic statement on peace terms came to be known as the Fourteen Points, which he first proclaimed in an address to Congress on January 8, 1918. This was a highly idealistic and largely unselfish declaration of war aims, including a call for an end to secret diplomatic agreements, such as those that Wilson believed had plunged Europe into war in 1914. It also provided for complete freedom of the seas, reduction of trade barriers and armaments, guarantee of the rights of all peoples to govern themselves, and the establishment of an international peacekeeping organization. Other points included adjustment of all colonial claims, taking into consideration the interests of the colonial peoples, restoration of Belgium, Serbia, Montenegro, and Rumania as well as rectification of Italy's border with Austria-Hungary and the evacuation of troops from Russia.

Two particularly far-reaching points stipulated "autonomous development" for the various ethnic groups in Austria-Hungary and "self-determination" for the peoples of the Ottoman Empire. Of more specific interest to Germany, Wilson called for restoration of Alsace-Lorraine to France and the creation of an independent Poland with access to the sea. The latter provisions obviously would mean the loss of German territory to the new Polish state, including a corridor to the Baltic

that would divide Germany into two parts. During the time when Wilson first announced his Fourteen Points, the Germans felt that they might win the war, while the Allies were outraged that Wilson should unilaterally state such far-reaching war aims. The Fourteen Points especially raised awkward questions about Britain's control of the seas as well as its role in Ireland. As a result, Wilson initially gained little support from either side. Yet the Fourteen Points were based in large part on the principle of nationality, and by October 1918, it appeared that a generally homogeneous Germany had relatively little to lose by accepting them as the basis for peace.

In the face of Ludendorff's insistence on the Fourteen Points as the basis for negotiations, Prince Max inquired whether the German High Command realized that the Fourteen Points would probably lead to the loss not only of German overseas colonies but also Alsace-Lorraine and Germany's Polish-inhabited areas. Ludendorff responded that the military leaders were willing to consider giving up "some small French-speaking parts of Alsace-Lorraine, if that is unavoidable. The cession of German territory on the eastern frontier is for them out of the question." This attitude cast serious doubt on the likelihood of obtaining a settlement based on the Fourteen Points. But while the Germans had accepted Wilson's peace proposal at least in principle, the president continued to encounter strong opposition to many of his Fourteen Points from the British and French. Over a month of often-heated discussion among the Allies and between the Allies and the Central Powers ensued before hostilities finally ended.

DISASTER IN THE BALKANS

In the meantime, dramatic events unfolded in other parts of Europe as, one by one, the

Central Powers collapsed. Lloyd George had long believed that the key to defeating Germany was not to hammer away in suicidal offensives on the Western Front but to concentrate on "knocking away the props" from under Germany by defeating its allies. During the course of 1918, it became increasingly clear that in reality Germany was the prop that kept the other Central Powers in the conflict. When the Germans lost the initiative on the Western Front, it shattered the last hopes of their partners for a victorious conclusion to the war.

Bulgaria was the first of Germany's allies to crack. After almost three years of bloodshed and suffering, coming so soon after the Balkan wars, both the Bulgarian army and people were sick of war. A quarter of a million casualties represented an exceptionally high price for such a small nation and, despite the occupation of Serbian and Rumanian territory, nothing of any permanence had been achieved. Bulgaria suffered from chronic shortages of virtually everything, and the army went into battle in an undernourished condition. The Bulgars also had grown increasingly anti-German and blamed Berlin for its failure to contribute sufficient troops to defeat the Allied army on Bulgaria's southern border.

Despite the fact that this Allied army had done little of consequence during its almost three years in "the greatest Allied internment camp," it still numbered well over half a million men in the fall of 1918. During late 1917, Clemenceau had sent General Louis Guillaumat to replace the controversial General Maurice Sarrail, who had spent more time intriguing in politics than in fighting since his arrival in Greece in 1915. Guillaumat vigorously set out to rejuvenate his army and planned to take the offensive in 1918 as soon as he received authorization. However, in July of that year, when the Germans were carrying out their last offensive, Clemenceau

recalled Guillaumat to replace Marshal Foch. Unfortunately for Guillaumat, Foch's victory in the Battle of the Marne robbed him of the chance to become Supreme Allied Commander. And, soon afterward, Guillaumat's successor, General Franchet d'Esperey, won fame in the Balkans.

After helping stop the German invasion in 1914, when he replaced General Charles Lanrezac as commander of the Fifth Army, Franchet d'Esperey had become an army group commander, but he lost favor as a result of the German breakthrough at the Chemin des Dames in May 1918. Now presented with a second chance, he made the most of it. Demonstrating incredible energy, he prepared for an offensive based on a Serbian plan to storm a particularly difficult mountain position in southern Macedonia. His success proved astonishing. After a heavy bombardment on September 14, two French divisions broke through the Bulgarian line, and Serbian forces moved quickly to exploit the gap. Although the Bulgars fought with their usual ferocity at first, their morale soon collapsed. Allied forces rolled northeastward and on September 19 cut the Bulgarian army in two. British and Greek troops also attacked to the east and drove into southern Bulgaria itself. On September 26, the Bulgars asked for an armistice on the basis of the Fourteen Points, and fighting ceased on September 30. The terms of the armistice gave the Allies the right to continue their advance through Bulgaria into Turkey on the east and northward toward Rumania.

Bulgaria's collapse completely isolated Turkey from its allies and plunged the Turks into despair. By this time, the British had penetrated into northern Mesopotamia and were approaching Damascus. Following the Bulgarian armistice, British troops also pushed toward Constantinople itself. On October 8, this rapidly rising crescendo of disaster led to the fall of the "Young Turk" regime, which had brought Turkey into the war. In the mounting chaos, it proved impossible to form a new government until October 14, but once in office it begged for an armistice. The British, who along with their dominions and Arab allies had carried the major burden of the war against Turkey, dictated terms on board the battleship *Agamemnon* on October 30, 1918. However, British failure to consult with their partners led to a strong protest from the French and did little to promote Allied harmony.

Once Bulgaria left the war, Allied troops began to move up Serbia's Vardar River valley toward Hungary, with only a handful of Austrian and German forces to block their progress. This growing threat from the south accelerated the process of disintegration that had been assailing the Dual Monarchy with ever-greater intensity since the failure of its last offensive against Italy in June.

Emperor Charles of Austria-Hungary had agreed to undertake this operation in response to German pressure and as a result of his own embarrassment over revelations of secret Austrian contacts with the Allies during the spring of 1917. Charles had used his brother-in-law, Prince Sixtus of Bourbon-Parma, as an emissary to feel out the French on the possibility of a negotiated settlement. Nothing came of this effort, but at one point Charles had written a letter to Sixtus in which he indicated his support for "France's just claims to Alsace-Lorraine." In April 1918, the French published this letter. The Germans were not amused, and Charles felt obligated to prove his loyalty to the alliance.

The offensive was doomed from the start. Not only was the reliability of the Austro-Hungarian troops highly questionable but they also lacked numerical superiority and suffered from a severe food shortage as well as other deficiencies. Any hope of success vanished when a disagreement arose over strategy. Field Marshal Conrad von Hötzendorf, commander of the army group in the Trentino, urged an attack in force from there, while Baron Borojevich von Bojna proposed that his army group strike across the Piave River instead. Charles finally mediated the dispute and decided on the worst possible solution, an attack by both groups in about equal strength. This decision denied either assault sufficient striking power to achieve any chance of success.

Italian intelligence learned of the attack, including the time of the preliminary bombardment. Despite the total lack of surprise, when the offensive began on June 15, it made early gains on both fronts. But the Italians, reinforced by British and French troops, limited their progress. By June 20, Emperor Charles ordered his armies back to their starting positions. They had suffered 140,000 casualties. In the search for a scapegoat that followed, Charles dismissed Conrad von Hötzendorf, who ended his military career a broken man.

This defeat proved one too many. From that point, the army's morale skidded to a new low, while mutinies and desertions became more frequent. Hunger, already a major problem, grew worse for both soldiers and civilians. In June, the Austrian government again cut the bread ration, this time by half. Demands for independence mounted steadily among the various ethnic groups. In early August, the German defeat in the Battle of Amiens deprived the Austro-Hungarian leaders of their last faint glimmer of hope. In a meeting at German army headquarters in Belgium on September 14, Charles and Stephan Burián, who had returned as Austro-Hungarian foreign minister after Count Ottokar Czernin resigned as a result of the Sixtus Affair, pleaded with the Germans to seek an immediate armistice. When Germany did not act, despite Ludendorff's admission that the war was lost, Vienna abandoned its policy of opposition to a separate peace, which it had followed for so long. On September 14, Burián appealed to the Allies for an armistice without consulting Germany. The Allied response was far from encouraging, while the Germans expressed outrage at this act of betrayal. However, when Berlin finally decided to seek peace on October 4, Austria-Hungary submitted a simultaneous request for an end to hostilities.

THE DUAL MONARCHY DISSOLVES

Following Bulgaria's defection in late September, the collapse of the Dual Monarchy, so often predicted and so often deferred, came to pass with startling speed and terrible finality. A Czech national committee had already virtually taken power in Bohemia, and the Serbs, Croats, and Slovenes established a Yugoslav national council in Zagreb on October 6. The Allies officially recognized the Czechoslovak National Council, an exile organization in Paris, as the provisional government of the new state of Czechoslovakia on October 14.

Confronted by these obvious signs of disintegration, Emperor Charles made an eleventh-hour effort to hold the empire together, more or less. On October 16, 1918, he issued a proclamation that transformed the Austrian half of the Dual Monarchy into a federal state with self-government for all nationalities. He even granted the Poles the right to break away altogether. However, he made no attempt to extend his declaration to Hungary, realizing that the Magyars would reject any interference in their internal affairs. Charles was much too late. On October 21, President Wilson finally replied to the Austrian peace note. He pointed out that in view of American recognition of Czechoslovak independence and sympathy for South Slav claims, he could no longer accept mere "autonomy" as a sufficient basis for peace.

Hungary also fell victim to dissolution. The Croats took measures to join their kinsmen in the new Yugoslav state that was taking shape across the border. On October 12, the Rumanians established a national council, while Slovak activists demanded union with the Czechs. That same day, Hungary severed all ties with Austria, except for the personal union with Charles and the Hapsburg dynasty. But even this feeble link was not to last for long. Count Mihály Károlyi, a Magyar nationalist who had long opposed dualism, demanded a democratic Hungarian republic and gained rapidly growing support for his position.

Just as the Dual Monarchy was splitting apart at the seams, the Italian army struck against Hapsburg forces in Italy. Despite the slide into chaos on the home front, the Hapsburg army had continued to hold the line, but it had little stomach for additional fighting. General Armando Diaz and the Italian government had resisted Allied pressure to undertake an offensive during the summer, but now they decided that the time had come to strengthen their territorial claims at the peace conference by an all-out assault.

On October 24, a year to the day since the start of the Caporetto offensive, General Diaz unleashed 57 divisions in an attack on three fronts—at two points in the mountains and along the Piave River to the south. His forces included three French, two British, and even one Czech division, that was composed of prisoners from the Hapsburg army. The Allies attacked 58 understrength, hungry and demoralized Austro-Hungarian divisions. At first, the defenders resisted valiantly, but General Diaz's forces crossed the Piave and, on October 29, they drove a wedge between the Austro-Hungarian Fifth and Sixth armies near the village of Vittorio Veneto. The Italians also advanced on the Trentino front. Confronted by these mounting disasters, the

Hapsburg forces melted away in a wave of mutinies and desertions.

This catastrophe, combined with the unchecked advance of Franchet d'Esperey's army northward through Serbia, provided the final impetus to the collapse of the Dual Monarchy. On October 28, the national committee in Prague proclaimed an independent Czechoslovak republic, and a Yugoslav state officially came into existence the same day. The Poles joined with their kinsmen under German domination to form an independent Poland, which included the Ruthenian-populated areas of eastern Galicia. October 30 witnessed the end of the Hapsburg dynasty in both Austria and Hungary. In Vienna, a provisional assembly, under the leadership of Dr. Karl Renner, proclaimed a republic. In Budapest, followers of Count Mihály Károlyi seized control of the city and proclaimed a Hungarian republic. The following day, four Hungarian soldiers burst into the home of Count István Tisza. Blaming the former premier for the decision to enter the war, they shot him to death in front of his family.

On November 3, the Austro-Hungarian High Command agreed to an armistice in the name of the now nonexistent empire. Charles renounced any part in the administration of Austria on November 11 and two days later terminated his connection with the Hungarian government. However, he stubbornly refused to abdicate, a decision that soon forced him into exile in Switzerland. The war to save the Dual Monarchy from "the Serbian menace" had ended with the complete destruction of both Austria-Hungary and the Hapsburg dynasty.

ALLIES CONTINUE TO PRESS GERMANY

While Turkey and Austria-Hungary were falling into chaos and seeking a way out of the war, Germany also experienced accelerating internal strains as well as the continued pressure of Allied attacks on the Western Front. At the same time, President Wilson and the German government exchanged a series of messages, and the Allied powers debated to what extent the Fourteen Points should constitute the basis for peace. Wilson had initially made the mistake of conducting a dialogue with the Germans without consulting his partners. Not surprisingly, differences soon developed within the alliance, and Wilson felt compelled to stall for time in his continuing discussions with German leaders by increasing his demands. When the president responded to Germany's peace note on October 8, far from agreeing to an immediate armistice, he expressed suspicion of German intentions. Wilson questioned whether Germany really accepted the Fourteen Points as the basis for peace. He also called for a German evacuation of all Allied territory as a prerequisite for a cease-fire. Finally, he inquired if the German chancellor actually spoke for the German people or merely in behalf of the emperor and the military leaders.

Although Clemenceau appeared satisfied with Wilson's reply, Lloyd George still voiced strong reservations about the Fourteen Points. He objected especially to the provision for complete freedom of the seas, considering this quite unacceptable to Britain with its dependence on a naval blockade during wartime. The prime minister also criticized Wilson for his failure to mention the matter of reparations for war damages.

Wilson had also framed his reply to the German peace note without consulting Allied military leaders. On October 8, Marshal Foch insisted that the Germans evacuate Alsace-Lorraine and that they agree to a temporary Allied occupation of the Rhineland as well as bridgeheads on the east bank of the Rhine. He desired all of this as security for German payment of reparations. In a joint response to Wilson, Britain, France, and Italy insisted that no specific armistice terms could be formulated without consultation with Allied military leaders.

If the president's messages created concern in the Allied camp, his stalling did not please the Germans. They found the tone of his reply disturbing. For some, it was tantamount to a demand for unconditional surrender. Nevertheless, on October 12, Berlin informed President Wilson that it did indeed accept the Fourteen Points as the basis for peace and agreed to the principle of evacuating occupied territories. The German note also assured the American president that the chancellor enjoyed the support of the Reichstag and spoke in the name of the German people. Despite the conciliatory nature of this reply, much of its effect was lost when, in a stroke of particularly bad timing, German U-boats sank a Japanese liner on October 4 and a British mail packet on October 10. Together, the two disasters took a total of over 800 lives.

When Wilson responded in his second note on October 14, he added the stipulation of the European Allies that the specific armistice terms be left to the military leaders and insisted on safeguards to assure continuation of the existing Allied military supremacy. He also demanded that Germany abandon its U-boat attacks and "wanton destruction" of areas being evacuated by its troops. Finally, he hinted strongly that he considered an end to the monarchical regime as still another prerequisite for peace.

On October 17, the German War Cabinet met to consider the president's note. Ludendorff, realizing that Wilson was unwilling or unable to negotiate on the basis of his Fourteen Points, attacked it as a demand for unconditional surrender. He called upon the government to rally the German people for a last-ditch stand rather than accept a humiliating peace. Prince Max and his gov-

ernment refused to adopt such a suicidal policy and drafted a third note on October 20, accepting Wilson's latest terms and agreeing to abandon unrestricted submarine warfare. They assured the president that meaningful constitutional reforms were underway and that the German government was "now free from all arbitrariness and irresponsible influence, and is supported by the approval of the overwhelming majority of the German people."

Wilson replied a third time on October 23, informing Berlin that the United States would consult with its Allies regarding the actual terms of the armistice. Despite German assurances, he reiterated his distrust of the professed governmental reform. Two days later, Marshal Foch and the three Allied commanders-in-chief conferred on the specifics of the armistice. Haig argued against demanding such harsh terms that Germany might feel compelled to continue the war. However, Foch, Pétain, and Pershing disagreed and demanded what amounted to unconditional surrender.

Meanwhile, in Germany, Ludendorff denounced Wilson's third note as unacceptable and vowed to continue the struggle. He even sent an order to the German troops exhorting them to continue resistance with all their strength. This proved too much for both the Reichstag and the government. Prince Max informed the emperor that he must dismiss Ludendorff or the government would resign. On October 26, William rose to the occasion and, after taking the general to task for his order to the army, accepted Ludendorff's resignation. Afterward, he remarked, "The operation is over. I have separated the Siamese twins."[2] Hindenburg, the other "Siamese twin," offered his resignation as well, but the emperor refused to accept it, fearing the negative effect of such a step on the country's already grievously weakened morale.

---

[2]Michael Balfour, *The Kaiser and His Times* (New York: W.W. Norton & Co., Inc., 1972), p. 400.

General Wilhelm Gröner succeeded to Ludendorff's post. Like his predecessor, Gröner was an officer of humble birth who had risen to prominence by virtue of his ability. After performing brilliantly as chief of military railroad transport during the first two years of the conflict, he achieved excellent results as head of the War Ministry section that coordinated Germany's economic mobilization program. The most clear-minded German military leader at this point, Gröner had the misfortune to preside over the army during the last act of his country's unfolding tragedy.

CHANGES INSIDE GERMANY

Germany replied to Wilson's third note on the day following Ludendorff's departure. It again insisted that the promised constitutional reform was well underway and that the military would indeed be subject to the people's representatives. In reality the government had completed remodeling of the constitution on October 26, and the Reichstag approved the amending law two days later. The new system made the chancellor responsible to the Reichstag and, henceforth, all treaties as well as the declaration of war and conclusion of peace required Reichstag approval. These changes transformed Germany's government into a constitutional monarchy similar to that of Britain. In addition, the Prussian state government had initiated the process of placing its electorate on a democratic basis at long last.

Had Germany and Prussia adopted such far-reaching reforms earlier, the constitutional monarchy might have survived. Unfortunately for William II and his supporters, the transformation came much too late. The emperor also did not help his position when he suddenly departed for military headquarters in Belgium. William detested his new role as constitutional monarch and felt more secure in the company of his generals, but his action confirmed suspicions that he could not be trusted. It certainly did nothing to arrest Germany's rapid slide into revolution.

After more than four years of sacrifice and repeated assurances of victory, it was clear to the German people that the war was lost. Their desire for peace soared as a fifth wartime winter approached. Hunger to the point of starvation was rampant and the influenza pandemic had returned in its most virulent form. Morale was cracking, both at the front and at home. In this atmosphere of growing despair, much of the population shared Wilson's skepticism of the constitutional reforms and the role of the army. Opposition to the continuation of the monarchy grew by leaps and bounds.

Symbolically, the German navy, toward which the emperor had always lavished his greatest interest, mutinied on October 29. The morale of the High Seas Fleet had deteriorated steadily since 1916. At the same time, discipline had remained severe, and the sailors had grown resentful of the privileges enjoyed by officers, while they subsisted on meager rations. In July 1917, the crews of a few battleships had demonstrated against their treatment. Naval authorities sentenced 12 mutineers to death and actually executed two of them. In the following months, sullen resentment continued to fester. Interestingly, the battleship crews, who suffered from boredom, and not the U-boat crews who were fighting and dying, were those who resorted to mutiny.

When it became apparent late in October 1918 that the naval leaders were planning a sortie into the North Sea for a last battle to salvage the navy's honor, a number of crews mutinied. By November 4, the fleet was in the throes of a general uprising. Workers in the shipyards and on the docks at the naval base of Kiel supported the mutineers by going on strike. Both sailors and workers soon formed revolutionary councils similar to the soviets during the early stage of the Russian Revolution. The revolt quickly spread to other ports as well as inland cities where soldiers rebelled. It even reached Cologne, the vital rail center supplying the Western Front. An uprising of workers, led by the Independent Socialist Kurt Eisner, erupted in Munich on November 7, leading swiftly to the fall of the Bavarian monarchy. Two days later, workers also took to the streets in Berlin itself.

ALLIES PRESENT TERMS

Meanwhile, Allied leaders, showing no proclivity for indecent haste, conferred on November 4 and agreed on the final armistice terms. They included Allied occupation of the Rhineland and bridgeheads on the east bank of the Rhine as well as evacuation of German troops from all Allied territory. The Allies also required custody of much of the German fleet, including all its submarines, and Germany's renunciation of the Treaty of Brest-Litovsk. Finally, they stated that Germany must provide compensation for all damage sustained by Allied civilians and their property due to German aggression. On November 5, President Wilson informed Berlin that Marshal Foch had the authority to receive representatives of the German government to inform them of armistice terms.

Three days later, a German delegation, headed by Matthias Erzberger, reached Allied supreme headquarters at Compiègne, where Marshal Foch brusquely presented the terms. Although dismayed by their severity, Erzberger referred them to Berlin for consideration by Prince Max's government.

But Prince Max was to be spared the unhappy task of accepting the armistice. Events in Germany were moving too fast for that. The spread of revolution, the increasing un-

reliability of the army, and the growth of antimonarchical feeling placed both the government and the emperor in an untenable position. After conferring with other military leaders on November 9, Gröner and Hindenburg came to what they considered an inescapable conclusion. The emperor must abdicate. Later that day, Gröner impressed upon William that he no longer possessed the confidence of the army, and Hindenburg reluctantly agreed. Prince Max also pleaded with William to give up the throne. William refused to comply, but later in the day, it became clear to him that the revolt in Berlin was getting out of hand.

Vast numbers of workers converged on the imperial palace and Reichstag, demanding the downfall of the monarchy and the creation of a republic. Prince Max, acting on his own authority, now announced falsely that the emperor had abdicated. Next, he asked Friedrich Ebert, the head of the Social Democratic party, to succeed him as chancellor, and Ebert agreed. Early in the afternoon, Philipp Scheidemann, leader of the Social Democratic parliamentary delegation, proclaimed the establishment of a republic on the steps of the Reichstag building. He took this action to forestall a takeover by the Communist Spartacus League, which was raising the red flag of revolution. Confronted by the growing chaos in Berlin and the rest of the country as well as the desertion of both his generals and the government, William finally abdicated later on November 9. He went into exile in the Netherlands early the following morning, signalling the fall of the Hohenzollerns, the last of the three great Eastern European dynasties.

NOVEMBER 11: WAR ENDS IN EUROPE

Both Gröner and Hindenburg pledged their loyalty to the new provisional republican government in Germany and agreed that the armistice must be accepted. At 5 A.M. on November 11, the German and Allied delegations signed the armistice in the office car of Foch's train at Compiègne. The cease-fire went into effect at the eleventh hour of the eleventh day of the eleventh month of 1918. The most terrible war in history had finally ended. Huge crowds gathered in all the capitals of the belligerent countries and greeted the news with transports of joy. In some respects the celebrations resembled the great outpouring of naive enthusiasm that had greeted the outbreak of the conflict in 1914. However, this time bitter memories of over four years of death and suffering as well as fear of an uncertain future served to restrain the jubilation at least to some extent. Meanwhile, at long last, all was indeed quiet on the Western Front.

THE POSTWAR SETTLEMENT

When the cheering stopped, Europe began to take stock of what the war had cost—not merely for the Central Powers, but for the victorious Allies as well. The numbers were grimly impressive. At least 8 million men had lost their lives. Another 20 million had been wounded, perhaps as many as 7 million of them with permanent disabilities. These figures, ghastly though they are, may err on the side of understatement. Some estimates run considerably higher. The death toll for individual countries is also a matter of dispute and confusion, but it appears that Germany suffered approximately 1,800,000 dead and Russia an equal number. France sustained 1.4 million killed, Austria-Hungary 1.2 million, Britain 750,000, and Italy close to half a million. American losses numbered 115,000 dead, but most of these casualties occurred in a period of only a few weeks. In addition to the British losses, another 200,000 men from various parts of the British Empire died. Europe had been bled white and had slipped from its preeminent position in the world.

WOUNDS: PSYCHOLOGICAL AND MATERIAL

Few of the brave lads of 1914 who had greeted the war as a great adventure were still alive when it ended or were still physically able, if they had survived. The recruits who followed between 1915 and 1918 also had vast holes torn in their ranks. Many of those who eluded death or serious injury had suffered deep psychic wounds. As a British war correspondent observed in 1920:

Something was wrong. They put on civilian clothes again and looked to their mothers and wives very much like the young men who had gone to business in the peaceful days before August 1914. But they had not come back the same men. Something had altered in them. They were subject to queer moods and queer tempers, fits of profound depression alternating with a restless desire for pleasure. Many were easily moved to passion where they lost control of themselves, many were bitter in their speech, violent in opinion, frightening.[1]

But it was not only the returning soldiers who suffered from the lingering psychological impact of the conflict. There were few families that did not mourn the loss of loved ones and worry about the physical or mental condition of those who had come back. An atmosphere of gloom and uncertainty persisted long after the fighting stopped.

The material cost of the war had also been staggering. A painstaking report released in 1920 estimated the direct expense of the conflict at $186 billion and added another $151 billion under the heading of indirect costs. The latter category included such things as depreciation of capital, loss of peacetime profits, disruption of international trade, and the estimated value of the lives lost, obviously a difficult thing upon which to place a price tag. If these figures are correct, the total bill for both direct and indirect costs reached $337 billion, a stupendous amount for that time when prices were much lower compared to what they are today. One observer has deduced that the cost of the war "represented about six and a half times the sum of all the national debt accumulated in the world from the end of the eighteenth century up to the eve of the First World War."[2]

Europe had also suffered other economic wounds. Over four years of concentration on the production of war material had meant the almost total neglect of normal peacetime manufacturing and had disrupted the European economies. Imports surpassed exports by wide margins in Germany, Britain, France, and Italy. Russia's economy was a shambles, not only because of the war but also as a result of its revolution and ongoing civil war. Although Europe had paid a fearful price for the conflict, neutral powers had gained economically from their misfortune, most notably the United States during its long period of nonbelligerency. These countries, and especially America, had taken over market shares formerly belonging to European powers. The Allies were also deeply in debt to the United States, which had risen from the role of a debtor nation when the war began to a creditor nation on a massive scale well before 1918. Even Britain, which had attempted to fulfill its traditional role as banker to its allies, had been forced in the end to turn to America for financial aid.

The inflationary spiral that began early during the conflict continued into the postwar era. It became especially critical in Germany, which had financed much of its war effort through internal borrowing and by printing paper money, rather than by taxation. Large areas of Europe, such as northern France, Belgium, Poland, Serbia, and Russia, bore the scars of widespread and in some areas almost total devastation. Hunger bordering on starvation still remained a major problem for the former Central Powers, due in part to the refusal of the Allies to lift the blockade in the immediate aftermath of the war, a tragic and unnecessary vengeance. In Russia, the chaotic conditions created by the civil war and peasant resistance to the Communist government's agricultural policy led to a disastrous famine in 1921.

World War I had also unhinged the balance of power in Europe and left it strangely altered. The Hapsburg Empire had vanished completely, destroying the relative unity and stability that it had provided in Central Europe for centuries. In its place, a confusing

---

[1] Eric J. Leed, *No Man's Land: Combat and Identity in World War I* (Cambridge: Cambridge University Press, 1979), p. 187.
[2] D.H. Aldcroft, *The European Economy, 1914-1980* (Berkeley: University of California Press, 1977), p. 19.

array of small, weak countries had come into existence. The entire area had become a power vacuum. Although it had not suffered the terrible fate of Austria-Hungary, Russia had been seriously weakened by the war, revolution, and civil war. The Bolshevik government was fighting for its life against the White armies. In an atmosphere of growing chaos, it had been unable to reassert control over the territories lost as a result of the Treaty of Brest-Litovsk, despite the withdrawal of German forces. Instead, most of Eastern Europe had become another power vacuum as various nationalities scrambled to create a second jumble of small, weak states.

THE PARIS PEACE CONFERENCE

It was against this background that the victorious Allies met in Paris during January 1919 to draft the peace settlement. Hatred of the Germans ran high in both France and Britain after years of total war, dreadful casualties, and the cumulative impact of propaganda that portrayed the enemy as bloodthirsty Huns. The Western Allies, therefore, refused to invite any representatives from Germany or the other Central Powers to participate in the peace conference. As a result, the ensuing settlement inevitably took the form of a dictated peace. The Allies also barred Russia from participation. Resentment still lingered over the Bolshevik decision to quit the war, which had freed Ludendorff to undertake his 1918 offensives on the Western Front. None of the Allies had recognized the Bolshevik regime, and they all hoped that the Whites would win the civil war. Western forces, which had intervened in Russia in 1918, clearly confirmed where Allied sympathies lay by cooperating with the Whites and even providing them with equipment and supplies.

Despite the fact that 27 nations sent delegations to Paris, Wilson, Clemenceau, and Lloyd George made most of the major decisions

regarding the provisions of the settlement. At first, Italy's Prime Minister Vittorio Orlando shared in this task, but he left the conference in protest when the United States, Britain, and France refused to grant the extensive compensation promised to the Italians in the 1915 Treaty of London. Lloyd George and Clemenceau did not consider Italy's contribution to victory sufficient to warrant such a generous reward, especially as it conflicted with promises made to the South Slavs. Wilson objected to Italian acquisition of a large portion of the Adriatic coast because of its essentially South Slav population. The Western Allies also rejected Italy's claim to Albania and even denied Rome a share of the proceeds from the division of either Germany's colonies or the Ottoman Empire, except for recognition of Italy's conquest of Libya and the Dodecanese Islands in the Tripolitanian War. Otherwise, the Italians had to settle for the Trentino, Trieste, and Istria. Although Orlando did return later, the Big Three—Wilson, Clemenceau, and Lloyd George—acted as the real architects of the peace.

The overall settlement—the Peace of Paris—consisted of five separate treaties, one with each of the defeated Central Powers. By far the most important of these was the Treaty of Versailles, providing the settlement for Germany. It represented a compromise, essentially between the rival aims of Wilson and Clemenceau.

Wilson desired a peace of reconciliation based on his Fourteen Points as well as subsequent statements made by the president during the course of 1918. He hoped that a lenient peace would make the Germans grateful and, as a result, they would accept it as final. Wilson's experience as a war leader had strengthened his already firm conviction that he and the United States had a special calling to lead the world into a new age of peace and democracy. He saw himself as an alternative to the traditionally cynical approach of European power politics on the one hand and Lenin, the prophet of a new Marxist world order, on the other. The president hoped to build an international system based on democracy, liberal capitalism, and free trade with a League of Nations (of which more will be said in a later section) as its cornerstone. When he arrived in Europe before the conference convened, Wilson found himself greeted as a virtual messiah by huge crowds in London, Rome, and Paris.

THE TREATY OF VERSAILLES

Although Clemenceau had originally voiced support for Wilson's response to Germany's request for an armistice based on the Fourteen Points, he had grown increasingly critical of the president's approach. The premier desired a harsh peace that would cripple Germany permanently or at least greatly weaken its ability to make war. He had personally experienced two German invasions of his own country and was determined to prevent a third. To accomplish this goal, he hoped to reduce Germany's armed forces drastically, impose heavy reparations, and take away some German territory. Finally, he placed his faith not in a League of Nations but in a defensive military alliance that would bind both Britain and the United States to come to France's assistance if Germany did become aggressive again. Clemenceau looked upon Wilson as unrealistic, sanctimonious, and hypocritical. He graphically revealed his skepticism about the Fourteen Points when he remarked, "God gave us Ten Commandments, and we broke them. Wilson gave us his Fourteen Points—we shall see." Allegedly, he accused the president of talking "like Jesus Christ" but acting "like Lloyd George."

If indeed, Clemenceau made such a reference to Lloyd George, it was meant as a sarcastic comment on the prime minister's reputation for lack of principle. To be sure, Lloyd George had conducted himself in a most opportunistic manner in the immediate aftermath of the war. Soon after the armistice, with almost indecent haste, he called for the first British parliamentary election since 1910 to be held on November 21, 1918. In the ensuing campaign, he worked vigorously to gain the continuation of his wartime coalition in office as well as a mandate to preside over the nation's transition to peace. Taking advantage of a rabidly anti-German attitude among the electorate in this "Khaki election," he rivaled Clemenceau in his strident advocacy of a harsh peace. He urged the trial of William II for war crimes and insisted on severe reparations, going so far as to demand that Germany be squeezed "until the pips squeak."

By the time that the Paris Peace Conference convened, however, the popular British hostility toward Germany had cooled considerably, and Lloyd George's ferocity slackened accordingly. He now became a mediator between the more extreme positions of the French premier and the American president. In this role, Lloyd George left his mark as indelibly on the final settlement as did either of his more militant colleagues. Looking back on his labors later, he took pride in what he considered as good a performance "as might be expected, seated as I was between Jesus Christ and Napoleon Bonaparte."

Since it was a compromise, the Treaty of Versailles was neither as lenient as Wilson had desired nor as harsh as Clemenceau had intended. Both men yielded on many points to gain what they considered essential or at least what they could salvage from their original goals. Wilson won approval of his League of Nations, while Clemenceau gained restrictions on Germany, which he hoped would safeguard France's security. To the Germans, however, the treaty was terribly harsh. Appalled by its terms, they even briefly considered resistance. Perhaps naively, they had expected a much more lenient settlement, especially since they had met all the Allied conditions and had created a truly democratic republic based on a constitution drafted in the German town of Weimar. Chancellor Philipp Scheidemann resigned in protest, but the fledgling Weimar Republic could not avoid the responsibility of accepting the treaty. This grim necessity earned it the undying hatred of German nationalists.

CHANGES IN THE MAP OF EUROPE

Certainly the territorial provisions were not nearly as extensive as those of the Treaty of Brest-Litovsk, which Germany had dictated to Russia in March 1918. The French, of course, had made the reacquisition of Alsace-Lorraine one of their chief war aims, and Wilson had agreed to this in his Fourteen Points. As everyone, including the Germans, expected, the treaty returned the two provinces to France, and no plebiscite was held to determine the wishes of the population. Belgium also received minor border changes in its favor, and the Big Three provided for a plebiscite to determine possession of Germany's northern province of Schleswig, which bordered Denmark on the south. As a result of the voting, the predominantly Danish northern two-thirds of the province merged with Denmark, while the heavily German southern third remained in Germany.

The peacemakers also made two temporary changes in western Germany. Both involved compromises. Clemenceau asked for French annexation of the coal-rich Saar as compensation for the destruction of French coal mines during the war. Unfortunately, the Saar's population was solidly German, and both Wilson and Lloyd George refused on the basis of national self-determination. Instead, the Allied leaders placed administration of the area under League of Nations supervision

for 15 years. France received the right to operate the coal mines during this period. At the end of the 15 years, the people of the Saar would determine their permanent fate. When the plebiscite was held in 1935, they voted overwhelmingly to return to Germany, and the French sold the mines to German interests.

Far more important than the Saar was the question of the Rhineland. French war aims had focused on the need to establish an "independent" Rhenish state to the west of the Rhine River. This would create a buffer area to protect France and Belgium from a German attack utilizing the invasion route of 1914. However, when Clemenceau proposed this action, Wilson and Lloyd George declined to deal so drastically with a completely German-populated area. Eventually the three leaders agreed that the Rhineland would remain a part of Germany, but Allied troops would occupy the region as well as bridgeheads on the Rhine's opposite bank for 15 years. At the end of this period, they would withdraw, and the Rhineland, along with a 50-kilometer-wide strip of territory east of the river, would become a permanently demilitarized zone. To soften Clemenceau's disappointment, Wilson and Lloyd George agreed to a defensive military alliance with France. This "guarantee treaty" bound them to support the French militarily in case of a German attack. It represented a remarkable departure from the traditional peacetime policies of both powers.

By all odds, the most significant territorial changes took shape in the east. They were in keeping with Wilson's provision in the Fourteen Points for the creation of "an independent Poland, to include territories indisputably Polish, with free and secure access to the sea." Unfortunately, it proved impossible to determine whether certain areas were indisputably Polish. The ethnic pattern was so mixed that, unless the peacemakers insisted on wholesale population transfers, the Polish

**Territorial Settlements
in Europe, 1919-1926**

Areas lost:
- by Germany
- by Austria-Hungary
- by Russia
- by Bulgaria

·········· Boundaries of 1914 ——— Boundaries of 1926

Demilitarized areas (Rhineland, the Straits)

Allied Occupation Zone (Rhineland)

state would of necessity include a large German minority within its western areas.

The Big Three required Germany to cede the province and city of Posen (Poznan in Polish) and, most importantly, a strip of territory that provided Poland with an outlet to the Baltic Sea. Without this "Polish Corridor," the new state would be landlocked and dependent upon a hostile Germany for access to the sea. The Allied leaders made their decision to transfer these territories because they

had belonged to Poland before the partition of the country by its neighbors during the eighteenth century and because overall they contained a Polish majority. Unfortunately, the corridor had the effect of dividing the major part of Germany from East Prussia, a development that was bound to anger the Germans. One other area provided an especially difficult problem. This was the industrial region of Upper Silesia, which formed the southeastern extension of

Germany. It, too, contained a mixed German-Polish population. In this case, the peacemakers prescribed another plebiscite, which resulted in less than half the disputed territory going to Poland, although it contained a substantial German minority.

Even more troublesome was the question of the major port city of Danzig, which lay between the Polish Corridor and East Prussia. A solidly German city, Danzig was the only port of any size in the vicinity of the corridor, and the Poles hoped to bring it under their control. This would clearly violate the principle of self-determination. The result proved to be another compromise. Danzig and a small surrounding area became a free state with its own government but under League of Nations supervision. Poland, however, received the right to use the port facilities without any restrictions.

A final problem in the east concerned the smaller port of Memel at the extreme northeastern point of East Prussia. Although Memel was an overwhelmingly German city, a strip of territory extending southward contained a predominantly Lithuanian population. Again, the peacemakers placed the entire area under the overall authority of the League of Nations. However, in this case the new state of Lithuania seized the territory in 1921. The ability of such a small country to carry out this action demonstrated the weakness of Germany at the time.

GERMANY LOSES ITS COLONIES

While most of Germany's territorial losses in Europe could be justified, this was not true of the settlement for the German colonial empire. The Allies took away all of Germany's overseas possessions and divided them among themselves on the basis of greed. Britain, France, and the Union of South Africa became the chief beneficiaries in Africa. The British received German East Africa, which they renamed Tanganyika (today Tanzania), while South

Africa gained German South-West Africa (later Namibia). France obtained four-fifths of the Cameroons and Britain the remainder. The two powers also divided Togoland.

In the Far East, Japan gained German former rights in China's Shantung Peninsula as well as the Marshall, Caroline, and Mariana island chains in the Pacific. These islands became important Japanese bases, and during World War II some of them were to be the scenes of major battles with the United States. Australia was granted German New Guinea and the islands of the Bismarck Archipelago as well as the German Solomons. New Zealand acquired German Samoa.

According to the treaty, all of these areas were to be administered as "mandated territories" under League of Nations supervision. In theory, the occupying powers were to prepare the peoples who populated them for eventual self-government. In reality, they governed most of the territories as though they were colonies.

GERMAN MILITARY DISMANTLED

In keeping with Clemenceau's desire to weaken Germany's ability to make war, the Allies agreed to impose a number of disarmament provisions. They limited the German army to a volunteer force of 100,000 men and prohibited the use of conscription or any kind of reserve. The Big Three also insisted on the dissolution of the General Staff, War Academy, and cadet schools, which they considered breeding grounds for Prussian militarism. In addition, they barred Germany from maintaining a military air force or "offensive weapons," including tanks and heavy artillery. Finally, the treaty drastically reduced the size of the German navy. It was to possess only six warships, of not more than 10,000 tons displacement, as well as a few smaller supporting craft, and no submarines were allowed. The British, with memories of the prewar naval race and their disastrous losses to the U-boat offensive still fresh, were especially insistent on the latter provision.

THE QUESTION OF REPARATIONS

As everyone expected, the peace treaty decreed that Germany must pay reparations. The Germans had forced stringent repara-

tions upon Russia in the Treaty of Brest-Litovsk and, almost half a century earlier, had imposed a heavy war indemnity on France following the Franco-Prussian War. They had accepted the principle of paying reparations when they agreed to the armistice but were destined to be shocked by the size of the final bill. Actually, it could have been much higher. Clemenceau and Lloyd George had asked that reparations cover not only civilian dam-

FIGURE 20–1 Premier Clemenceau signs the Treaty of Versailles in the Hall of Mirrors. Photo courtesy of Roger Sherman

ages but all Allied costs incurred in waging the war. Wilson balked at such an extreme proposal, but he did finally agree that the reparations would include the expense of pensions for Allied soldiers. The United States did not ask compensation for itself. Because of the complexities of this problem, the Big Three delegated the power to set the final amount to a special commission. During the interim, Germany would pay $5 billion in cash and commodities as a first installment on its obligation.

The Reparations Commission studied the related problems of Allied costs and Germany's ability to pay and did not announce its decision until May 1921 when it set the final figure at $33 billion, an amount calculated to seriously weaken Germany economically. It provided for annual payments of $500 million for 66 years. American experts as well as the renowned British economist John Maynard Keynes attacked the reparations burden as beyond German ability to pay. Keynes warned that it would unhinge the postwar economy, not merely of Germany but of the world. The Germans denounced the decision as grossly unfair.

In an effort to justify the imposition of reparations, the Big Three inserted a clause in the treaty, Article 231, which charged "Germany and her allies" with responsibility for the "loss and damage" inflicted on the Allies because of their aggression. This "war guilt" clause deeply offended the Germans, who believed that it was much too simplistic an interpretation of the events and actions leading to the outbreak of war.

LEAGUE OF NATIONS ESTABLISHED

In addition to the settlement for Germany, the treaty contained the agreement, or covenant, that established the League of Nations. Wilson, of course, had enthusiastically championed the creation of a peacekeeping organization that would deter aggression and mediate disputes peacefully. As stipulated in the covenant, the League of Nations would include both an assembly and a council. All member nations would belong to the assembly, which would have the right to consider every issue that came before the League. The council was to consist of only nine members. Five of them—the United States, Britain, France, Italy, and Japan—were to be permanent, while the other four would be elected to limited terms on a rotating basis. The real power to make decisions in most cases lay with the council rather than the assembly.

According to the covenant, any quarrel between member nations should be submitted to the League for arbitration and settlement. If a member ignored this requirement, the League would be justified in taking action to force compliance. Unfortunately, a difference of opinion arose as to how to accomplish this objective. Clemenceau urged the creation of an international army that could be used to safeguard the security of all member nations and prevent or punish aggression. But, as with so many of Clemenceau's proposals, Wilson and Lloyd George refused to accept such a far-reaching commitment. Although Article X of the covenant did suggest that the League of Nations could use military force as the last resort, nothing came of this provision. Instead, Clemenceau and the League had to be content with economic sanctions as the organization's only real weapon in enforcing its decisions. Such sanctions would involve cutting off trade between member nations and an aggressor. The Big Three also weakened the moral authority of the League as an international body by refusing membership in the organization to either Germany or Russia.

WILSON AND REPUBLICANS CLASH

Ironically, despite Wilson's role as architect of the League of Nations, the United States never became a member. American membership was contingent on Senate confirmation of the treaty by a two-thirds majority. Unfortunately, the president's great dream collapsed when he became embroiled in a heated quarrel with the Republican party leadership in the Senate. Wilson, who was extremely partisan, had angered Republican leaders by refusing to include any of them in the U.S. delegation to the Paris Peace conference. To increase Wilson's dilemma, the Republicans had won control of the Senate in the November 1918 congressional election.

When he returned home after completion of the peace settlement, Wilson encountered varying degrees of opposition from senators who insisted on amendments that would protect American freedom of action from too close a dependence on League decisions. They particularly opposed Article X, which implied the use of force, if necessary, to preserve the territorial integrity and independence of all League members from aggression. Another unpopular provision granted votes in the assembly not only to Britain but also its four dominions and India, while the United States would only have one vote. The president stubbornly refused to compromise, demanding that the Senate ratify the League of Nations as established by the covenant. Had Wilson been willing to bargain with the more moderate of those who had reservations, he could have salvaged victory. Opponents of the League succeeded in attaching 14 reservations to the treaty, including one that would have virtually nullified Article X. When confronted by these changes, Wilson urged Democratic senators to vote against this version of the treaty, and 42 of them followed his advice. Thirteen irreconcilable Republican

opponents also cast no votes. Shortly afterward, when a vote was taken on ratification without reservations, only 38 senators, all but one of them Democratic, voted in favor, while 55 voted against. The peace treaty, and with it the League of Nations, had failed to gain ratification in either form. In 1921, the Senate finally passed a resolution approving the Paris peace settlement except for the covenant.

The guarantee treaty, designed to safeguard France's security, became another casualty of the dispute over the League of Nations and never made it to the floor of the Senate. Even without the turmoil over the League, it is highly unlikely that the Senate would have accepted such a far-reaching commitment. Britain subsequently used America's failure to honor Wilson's pledge to France as an excuse for reneging on its own responsibility as well. Not without reason, the French experienced a deep feeling of betrayal.

NEW COUNTRIES CREATED IN EUROPE

Since the Dual Monarchy had ceased to exist, two separate treaties provided the peace settlement for the new states of Austria and Hungary—the Treaty of St. Germain and the Treaty of Trianon, respectively. Essentially these treaties merely recognized the fact that Austria-Hungary had disintegrated and that a number of new states had come into being in Central Europe. Two of them had never existed before: Czechoslovakia and the Kingdom of Serbs, Croats, and Slovenes, later to become Yugoslavia.

Czechoslovakia was largely the creation of one man, Dr. Thomas Masaryk, a Slovak who was a native of the Czech province of Moravia. A university professor, a liberal, and a strong believer in democracy, Masaryk had been one of the leading advocates of federalism as the solution to the Dual Monarchy's nationalities problem prior to the war. Soon after the outbreak of hostilities, however, he switched to advocacy of outright independence for the Czechs. But he also believed that to create a viable state, the Czechs must unite with the kindred Slovaks. Thus, Masaryk became the father of "the Czechoslovak idea." He escaped from Austria-Hungary soon after the war began and made his headquarters in London where he worked to transform the idea into reality. Masaryk also visited the United States and won strong backing from Czechs and Slovaks, who had migrated to America. When Czechoslovakia was born during the last days of the Dual Monarchy, it represented a union of the Czech-inhabited provinces of Bohemia and Moravia with Slovakia. The country also included substantial German, Hungarian, Polish and Ukranian minorities as well.

The Kingdom of Serbs, Croats, and Slovenes united the three South Slav peoples of Austria-Hungary with Serbia. Inspiration for the new state had originated with the Croatian bishop Josef Strosmajer, who formulated the "Yugoslav idea" as far back as the 1860s. This concept took root among the Croats who lived along the Adriatic coast and feared Italian domination if the Dual Monarchy collapsed. The Croats of the interior never were enthusiastic about such a union, considering themselves culturally superior to the Serbs. The chief support for the Yugoslav idea among the Serbs came from those who resided within the Dual Monarchy. The Serbs of independent Serbia traditionally had thought primarily of taking over the Serbian-inhabited areas of Austria-Hungary, rather than of union with the Croats and Slovenes. Major differences persisted in religion, economic and cultural development, language, and, in the case of the Serbs and Croats who shared the same language, alphabet. Most of the Slovenes and Croats remained less than enchanted at the prospect of merger with the Serbs but feared that they would be too weak

to survive in separate states. Concern that the dissolution of Austria-Hungary would lead to an attempt by Italy to extend its influence into their areas contributed significantly to the decision to unite in the interest of greater security. The new state also contained other ethnic groups, including Hungarians, Bulgars, and Albanians.

Another Slavic group, the Poles of Galicia, united with their kinsmen in those territories formerly under German and Russian rule and proclaimed the independence of a reborn state of Poland. Unfortunately, they also forced the Ruthenes of eastern Galicia into their new "Polish" nation-state as well as substantial numbers of Belorussians and Lithuanians in the areas gained from Russia. There were also the German minorities in the western portions of the new country, granted by the Treaty of Versailles.

To the southeast, the Rumanians in the provinces of Transylvania and the Banat broke away from Magyar domination to join with Rumania. However, these areas also contained large concentrations of Magyars. Finally, the Italians in the Trentino, Trieste, and Istria merged with Italy. And, once again, other ethnic groups were present—Germans in the Trentino, and Croats and Slovenes in both Trieste and Istria.

The European states that came into existence or increased in size as a result of the demise of Austria-Hungary supposedly represented the triumph of the principle of self-determination of peoples. In reality, however, almost all of them inherited the fatal weakness of the Dual Monarchy. They were multi-national states in microcosm. While Austria-Hungary, for all its shortcomings, had been a significant power and provided Central Europe with a considerable degree of stability, none of the successor states, as they were called, came even remotely close to being a great power. They also did not prove to be good neighbors and soon fell to quarreling over border areas, which contained mixed populations or were important economically or strategically. The peacemakers established special commissions to help adjust borders as much as possible in keeping with self-determination. This proved a daunting task. Even when the ethnic character of an area was clear, economic and strategic considerations might prove more critical.

The Sudetenland, a narrow arc of territory comprising the frontier region of Bohemia-Moravia, represented the most significant example of such overriding factors taking precedence over self-determination. Although its population was overwhelmingly German, the Sudetenland was absolutely vital to Czechoslovakia. Heavily industrialized and blessed with important natural resources, it also consisted of hilly, heavily wooded terrain that was ideally suited for defense. Without the Sudetenland, the new Czechoslovak state would not be viable economically and would be left wide open to a possible German attack in the future. When confronted by these facts, even President Wilson agreed that the Sudetenland must become a part of Czechoslovakia rather than be divided between Germany and Austria.

The Big Three also violated the principle of self-determination in regard to Austria itself. When the empire disintegrated, many Austrians preferred the prospect of union with Germany rather than an uncertain future in a small, landlocked state. Accordingly, the government in Vienna asked that Austria be allowed to merge with Germany. However, the Allied leaders were in no mood to see their recent enemy increased in size, and they turned down the request.

In Eastern Europe, the areas that Russia had lost at Brest-Litovsk lay outside the scope of the Paris peace settlement. Nevertheless, they were of concern to the victorious Allies. Although Germany, in compliance with the armistice agreement, was withdrawing its forces from all these territories, the fate of this vast region was far from certain. Russian and local Bolshevik forces were still fighting nationalists as well as German troops in all of these areas as late as 1919.

In the far north, the Finns had created an independent Finland, with German assistance, as early as December 1917, while farther south along the Baltic coast three small countries had also declared their independence—Estonia, Latvia, and Lithuania—collectively referred to as the Baltic States. To the south and west of these new states, the Poles of Russian Poland joined with their kinsmen, who had lived under German and Austrian rule. On Poland's southeastern flank lay the sprawling area of the Ukraine, which also proclaimed its independence. Finally, Rumania seized Bessarabia, an area of mixed Rumanian and Ukranian population on its northeastern frontier. In all of these new "nations" no real consensus existed and chaos reigned for some time. Rival ethnic groups quarreled, and disputes flared over the type of political system that should be established. In the Baltic States, ethnic Germans were far from pleased when German forces departed.

In most cases, the Big Three took no action regarding Eastern Europe, other than to recognize the independence of the new nations. In the case of Poland, however, Lord Curzon, who succeeded Arthur Balfour as British foreign secretary in 1919, suggested that the eastern border of the new state follow roughly the linguistic division between the Poles to the west and the Belorussians and Ukrainians to the east. This was not to the liking of the Poles, who insisted on nothing less than the boundary that had existed before the eighteenth-century partitions of Poland. This would incorporate much of Belorussia and the Ukraine within the Polish state. In 1920, the Poles went to war with Russia to achieve this ambition but eventually had to settle for a frontier about 150 miles east of the "Curzon line."

TURKEY LOSES MUCH TERRITORY

The final treaties of the Peace of Paris provided the settlements for the minor Central Powers—Bulgaria and Turkey. Under the terms of the Treaty of Neuilly, Bulgaria lost its outlet on the Aegean Sea to Greece and ceded three small border areas to the new Yugoslav state. Turkey was the biggest loser of any of the defeated powers. The Treaty of Sèvres rewarded Greece with a generous slice of territory that pushed back the Turkish border to within 40 miles of Constantinople. It also gave the Greeks a number of Aegean islands as well as the right to administer the port city of Smyrna and its hinterland on the Aegean coast of Asia Minor for five years. When the time period expired, a plebiscite would determine the fate of this area, which contained a Turkish majority but a large Greek minority. Still another provision recognized the independence of Armenia and the autonomy of Kurdistan, two provinces in the extreme eastern portion of Turkey.

Finally, the treaty deprived the Turks of their Arab-inhabited territory. However, the Sykes-Picot Agreement took precedence over both the British promise of Arab independence and the Balfour Declaration pledging support for the creation of a homeland for the Jews in Palestine. France received a mandate over Syria and Lebanon, while Britain acquired mandates in Palestine, Transjordan, and Mesopotamia. King Hussein, who had hoped to unite all the Arab lands under his leadership, was not even to remain ruler of the Hejaz for long. In 1919, he became embroiled in a bloody struggle with Abdul-Aziz Ibn-Saud, emir of the neighboring territory of the Nejd. By 1924, Saud had forced Hussein into exile and brought the Hejaz completely under his rule during 1927. Five years later, he united his territories in the Kingdom of Saudi Arabia. The Treaty of

Sèvres was so draconian that outraged Turkish nationalists soon resorted to military action to reverse many of its terms.

GERMANS FEEL BETRAYED BY WEST

When Wilson, Clemenceau, and Lloyd George completed their labors, they all seemed reasonably satisfied with the peace settlement. Such was not the attitude of the former Central Powers. Most notably, the Germans attacked the Treaty of Versailles as a dictated peace. Both the republican government and the German people considered the territorial, disarmament, and reparations provisions quite unacceptable and viewed the "war guilt" clause as a distortion of reality. They still believed that they had entered the conflict to defend the Fatherland against Russian aggression. Since the treaty used the "war guilt" clause to justify payment of reparations, the Germans, feeling betrayed and employing reverse logic, saw it as an excuse for resisting reparations altogether. Opposition to such payments was already widespread well before Germany received the final accounting in 1921. Germans also considered the disarmament provisions unfair and degrading to a great power, especially since they made their country inferior militarily to their new upstart neighbors, Poland and Czechoslovakia. Accusing the peacemakers of hypocrisy, they charged that such reductions could only be justified if the Allies also agreed to undertake disarmament.

To the Germans, however, the most detestable of all the treaty's provisions were those separating Danzig and ceding Germany's eastern territories to Poland. Many of them could live with the loss of Alsace-Lorraine and the small parcels of land to Belgium and Denmark, but they had little sympathy for Polish claims based on self-determination and historic rights. The division of Germany by the Polish Corridor proved an especially hateful aspect of the settlement. Most Germans, regardless of political orientation, looked forward to a day in the indeterminate future when Germany might be strong enough to alter these provisions. They also criticized the refusal of the Big Three to allow union of Germany, not only with Austria but also with the Sudetenland. To them, this glaringly confirmed that the Allies employed the principle of self-determination only if it weakened Germany.

Unfortunately, German resentment over the peace settlement often took the form of anger toward the republican government in Germany, a government that had accepted the armistice and now the unpopular treaty. Despite the rising tide of war-weariness, demands for peace, and revolutionary outbreaks during the last days of the conflict, many Germans could not accept the fact that their country had actually suffered defeat. Allied troops did not reach German soil until after the armistice, and the only signs of destruction were those caused by a few bombing raids. German nationalists charged that the new Weimar Republic had betrayed the army by making a hasty armistice and accepting an unjust peace. In the forefront of those who spread this "stab in the back" legend was General Ludendorff, the man who had persisted in his offensives until the German army had been fatally weakened. It was also Ludendorff, of course, who in a near panic had urged the emperor to seek an armistice as early as August 1918. Now he proclaimed that the army could have fought on, had it not been for the treachery of the republican government. It is true that during 1918, despite their victories, Allied commanders were planning campaigns into 1919 and 1920, while Allied soldiers complained that German machine gunners were as deadly as ever. To be sure, the home front in Germany collapsed first, along with discipline in some units of the navy, but the republic was the product of that collapse, not its cause. Ironically, Friedrich Ebert, the Weimar Republic's first chancellor and soon afterward its first president, unwittingly helped perpetuate the "stab in the back" legend. When German troops arrived in Berlin from the front, he welcomed them home with the words, "As you return unconquered from the field of battle, I salute you." In the eyes of many Germans, the republic was never able to free itself from the stigma of accepting the peace settlement. In reality, it had no choice. Germany clearly could not resume hostilities. It was the republic's fate to accept the consequences of a war unleashed by the imperial government and lost by the imperial army.

OTHER CRITICS OF THE PEACE SETTLEMENT

The Germans were not the only critics of the Peace of Paris. The rump state of Austria decried the double standard employed by the Allies in rejecting its request for union with Germany. Hungary, Bulgaria, and Turkey all seethed over their territorial losses and looked forward to reversing them in the future.

The peace settlement even met with severe criticism among the Allies. Disillusionment grew rapidly in Britain where many came to the conclusion that the Treaty of Versailles was much too harsh. Agreeing with John Maynard Keynes that payment of the reparations bill was beyond Germany's capabilities, British opinion also turned against the prewar alliance with France and blamed the French for dragging Britain into war. Determination grew among both government leaders and the people that they must avoid such commitments in the future. To the British, it also seemed that the French were much too vindictive toward Germany and that it would be far wiser to pursue a conciliatory approach toward the recent enemy.

Disillusionment also blossomed in the United States, especially when the terms of the settlement seemed to contradict Wilson's idealistic wartime rhetoric. Despite the president's advocacy of a peace of reconciliation, it appeared to many that he had been a party to another cynical division of the spoils of war. Almost overnight, the superheated anti-German atmosphere of the war years dissipated, and numerous Americans concluded that Britain and France had lured them into a typical European power struggle. When the Senate refused to accept American membership in the League of Nations, the country returned to its traditional policy of isolation from European power politics. It did maintain its extensive economic relationship with Europe, however, insisting that war debts be paid, while trying to help solve the related problems of reparations and currency stabilization that persisted during the postwar years.

France, too, found little solace in the peace settlement. Although the French soon became the target of friend and foe alike because of their hostile attitude toward Germany, they were not at all certain that peace had brought them the security they so desperately desired. The war had left deep scars on France, both physically and psychologically. The deaths of almost 1.4 million French soldiers represented the heaviest loss suffered by any of the Great Powers in proportion to population. And, despite the reacquisition of Alsace-Lorraine and Germany's loss of territory to other countries, France's population still lagged behind that of its recent opponent by a margin of more than 20 million people. Four years of massive artillery bombardments, trench warfare, and deliberate German devastation had turned vast expanses of France's northern provinces into a wasteland. Even after major efforts to rehabilitate the land, large areas remained unfit for culti-

vation because of the danger from unexploded land mines and shells. To increase France's dissatisfaction still more, its former allies had reneged on their agreement to join in the guarantee treaty. In view of all these factors, it appeared to the French that the peace, far from being too harsh, was much too lenient.

Italy also felt a keen sense of betrayal because of the failure of its allies to honor their wartime promises of extensive compensation in the Adriatic, Middle East, and Africa. Orlando's government felt the lash of nationalistic outrage and soon felt obliged to resign. The desire to revise the settlement, if the opportunity should arise, remained strong among the more chauvinistic elements of the Italian population.

In Russia, the Bolshevik government harbored resentment over its exclusion from the peace conference as well as for the loss of Russia's western territories. Even though the peacemakers in Paris had not been responsible for these losses, they had endorsed them. Indeed, the changes in Eastern Europe pleased the Allied leaders because all the new states were anti-Russian and anti-Communist. Western powers soon referred to this entire tier of countries as the *cordon sanitaire*, a barrier that helped sanitize them against the spread of communism. Despite the civil war, however, by 1920 Communist Russia managed to regain control over the Ukraine. The Ukranians had never been able to consolidate their independence because of conflict between rival political factions and growing chaos. However, for the time being, Russia was not strong enough to do anything more to revise the map of Eastern Europe.

The well-nigh universal dissatisfaction with the peace settlement on the part of vanquished and victor alike underscored a tragic fact. Although the Allies had defeated the Central Powers, in a larger sense none of the belligerent powers of Europe had really

FIGURE 20–2   Victorious American troops receive a warm welcome from New York City following the war. National Archives

won the war. The fearful price of the conflict had left all of them in a seriously weakened condition and had dramatically changed the dominant position that Europe had so long enjoyed in the world. Leadership had passed to the United States even though the giant of the New World was not yet ready to fully accept this role. The war truly marked the great turning point of the twentieth century. Now that the war was over and the ink had dried on the peace treaties, Europe and the world looked to the future with hope, uncertainty, and not a little foreboding.

THE TROUBLED AFTERMATH

It was only natural that, during the seemingly endless years of the war, the peoples of the belligerent powers should look forward to a peace that would bring them a better life and help justify all the slaughter and suffering. Wartime propaganda and slogans, such as "a war to end war" and a war "to make the world safe for democracy," helped create this vision of the future. However, once the conflict finally ended, it did not take long for disillusionment to shatter the dream. Wartime disruption and the enormous problems of transition to a peacetime economy alone assured that the immediate postwar period would not create "a world fit for heroes to live in," as Lloyd George had promised. General dissatisfaction with the peace settlement confirmed this grim truth as did numerous other disturbing factors.

UNREST AT HOME

Many veterans of the various armed forces found that the reward for their sacrifice was unemployment or at best low-paying jobs. Not a few found the return to civilian life strange and full of bewildering adjustments. Some had become so accustomed to the brutal existence of the front that they found it difficult to abandon their old ways. They also could not shake off their long-standing contempt for civilians. In their frustration, they became part of an ongoing cult of violence. In Italy, such rootless men formed fighting bands, which soon became the basis for the Fascist movement led by Benito Mussolini. In Germany, they formed *Freikorps* (free corps), which sometimes cooperated with the new Weimar Republic in putting down Communist uprisings. In other cases they participated in right-wing revolts against the government. Many of these men eventually found a home in Adolf Hitler's National Socialist (Nazi) party. In Russia, violence continued to hold center stage as the civil war raged into the early 1920s. To the Bolsheviks, who had formerly denounced war as a tool of the capitalist exploiters, armed conflict now took the guise of a noble crusade to make Russia safe for communism. To the Whites, it was the mechanism through which they hoped to destroy communism. Violence also teamed with political instability in the form of revolution and even war in various parts of Central and Eastern Europe as well as the Middle East in the aftermath of the conflict.

In some of the new states of Central and Eastern Europe as well as Germany and Italy, fear of bolshevism reached near panic proportions. The prevailing economic and political turmoil in these countries led the property-owning classes to exaggerate the appeal of communism to the lower classes as well as the strength of the Communists within their own borders. Even the politically stable and relatively prosperous United States experienced a "Red Scare" during 1919–20. In large part this was the result of a fuzzy conception of what was actually involved in Marxist ideology. There was a tendency to equate communism with anarchism, which had inspired fear during the last few decades before the war and had been responsible for the assassination of President William McKinley in 1901. Along with this confusion, Americans tended to regard socialists in general with suspicion because of their opposition to the war. A number of violent labor strikes in the immediate postwar period also prompted concern that they were due to Communist inspiration, which in some cases was actually true.

INSTABILITY IN GERMANY

Germany found it especially difficult to adjust to the realities of the strange new world. Almost everything conspired against the youthful Weimar Republic, including political instability and severe economic problems. Political instability took the form of efforts by extremist groups on both the Left and Right to overthrow the new system. The first attempt came from the Left. It was the work of the Spartacus League, an extreme left-wing faction within the Independent Socialist party, that had split off from the majority Social Democrats because of its opposition to the war.

When the provisional German republic came into existence in November 1918, the Independent Socialists cooperated with the majority Socialists in establishing a Council of People's Commissars. This council was to rule until a constituent assembly could meet to draft a constitution for the permanent government. However, the Spartacists refused to participate, demanding instead a system modelled on that of the Soviet regime in Russia. Disagreements over policy also led to the resignation of the Independent Socialist members of the council on December 29. The following day, the Spartacus League broke away from the Independent Socialists altogether and formed the Communist party of Germany under the leadership of Karl Liebknecht and "Red" Rosa Luxemburg.

Meanwhile, General Wilhelm Gröner had recognized that the republican government was Germany's best hope for stability at this time. Fearing the danger of a left-wing seizure of power, he had pledged the army's support to Chancellor Freidrich Ebert as early as November 10. In return, Ebert agreed that the government would uphold the officer corps' authority over the army and would combat bolshevism.

The growing rift between the extreme Left and the provisional government erupted into an actual uprising on January 5, 1919, following the dismissal of the Independent Socialist Emil Eichhorn as chief of police in Berlin. The Communists along with the Independent Socialists and the Revolutionary Shop Stewards, another of the militant left-wing groups, demonstrated in protest. Both Liebknecht and Luxemburg realized that these dissident forces were not strong enough to seize power and proposed that they merely work to prepare the way for eventual revolution. But other members of the Spartacus League as well as the Shop Stewards insisted that the time was ripe for an uprising in Berlin, believing that soldiers and sailors in the capital would quickly join in such an action. Rather than splitting the newly established Communist party, Liebknecht and Luxemburg agreed to go along with this rash plan.

The ensuing "second revolution" soon became known as the Spartacist Uprising. It failed to gain the support of the soldiers and sailors, however, while *Freikorps* and units recruited from workers and other supporters of the republic easily crushed the revolt. Passions ran high on this occasion, and the *Freikorps* resorted to numerous atrocities, including the brutal murder of both Liebknecht and Luxemburg. The main effect of the abortive uprising was to instill a deep fear of Marxism among the German middle class. The fledgling republic became even more dependent on the *Freikorps* in March 1919 when it utilized the troops to crush another Communist revolt in Berlin. *Freikorps* also put down uprisings in a number of other cities, again to the accompaniment of bloody atrocities. But Bavaria had become the most chaotic region in all of Germany following the November revolution. Kurt Eisner, the Independent Socialist who had led the uprising that toppled the Bavarian monarchy, managed to stay in power until February 1919 with the support of the majority Socialists and a federation of peasants. However, when an assassin gunned down Eisner on February 19, the majority Socialists joined with the peasants to form a new government led by the Social Democrat Johannes Hoffmann. It was to have a stormy existence as left-wing elements became increasingly volatile. In April, a bizarre coalition of anarchists and radical Independent Socialists forced the government to flee Munich, the Bavarian capital, and established a soviet republic. It too, proved short-lived as Hoffmann recruited a volunteer force that overthrew it in less than a week. In the ensuing chaos, the Communists, who had remained aloof from the earlier revolt, formed a second soviet government. However, it soon fell victim to *Freikorps* and regular army forces. After heavy fighting, during which both sides resorted to atrocities, the Hoffmann government returned to power on May 3.

While turmoil gripped much of Germany, the provisional government held the elections for the constituent assembly on January 19. The voting resulted in a majority of 76 percent for three political parties that strongly supported the republic—the majority Social Democrats, the Center, and the Democrats, as the former Progressive party now called itself. These were the same parties that had favored democratic reforms before the war and had so worried the conservative supporters of the old monarchical system. The constituent assembly met in the city of Weimar in central Germany and completed its work on July 31, 1919. The new system featured a democratically elected president as head of state along with a chancellor and cabinet responsible to a Reichstag elected by all adult males and females. Although the Social Democrats had emerged from the elections as the largest single party with 37.9 percent of the vote, the constitution was the work of a coalition of all the republican parties and reflected the influence of the middle class.

The possibility for a socialist Germany had passed. Moreover, even before this, Ebert and the Social Democrats had made compromises that maintained strong links to the old regime. Not only did the army officer corps retain its former independence, but the Social Democrats maintained the old civil service intact, and most of its leading officials remained strongly devoted to the monarchy and contemptuous of the upstart republic. The judicial system also continued to be dominated by similarly inclined judges. While roughly, three-fourths of the electorate had endorsed the republic, the remaining fourth opposed the new regime and retained powerful positions in the army, civil service, and judiciary as well as the ownership and management of large industry.

THE WEIMAR REPUBLIC

The Weimar Republic also faced economic dislocation during its early years, which increased political instability. Germany's index of industrial production graphically reflected the economic dilemma as it plummeted from 98 points in 1913 to only 37 points in 1919. Unemployment also remained a serious problem. To stimulate the economy, the Reichsbank, which controlled both the flow of currency and the regulation of interest rates, authorized the printing of large amounts of paper money and kept interest rates low to provide much needed investment capital. Bank officials realized that these expedients would accelerate the inflationary trend that had begun during the war, but they hoped that the policy would lead to economic recovery, which would keep the rise in prices within reasonable limits. Unfortunately, the recovery did not materialize, and the inflation worsened dramatically. The German mark had already declined from its prewar value of 4.2 to the dollar to 8.9 in January 1919. By January 1921, it had skidded to 191.8 to the dollar, but this was only the

beginning of what was to become a remarkable and demoralizing slide. The government's refusal to raise taxes to reduce the enormous national debt contributed to this alarming trend, as did the need to pay reparations.

The French hoped to obtain early and regular payment of reparations to enable them to rebuild their devastated areas, but they gained relatively little. At first, they received payment in commodities such as timber and coal but, when Germany failed to deliver all of its quota in late 1922, Raymond Poincaré, now France's premier, reacted hostilely. He persuaded the Reparations Commission to proclaim Germany in default and, despite British opposition, his government ordered troops into the Ruhr, the most important German industrial area, in early 1923. Poincaré hoped to force Berlin's compliance on reparations payments and, in the meantime, planned to place the mines and railroads of the Ruhr under French operation. But German workers resorted to passive resistance, including strikes and delaying actions, and the government of the Weimar Republic subsidized the workers. France had accomplished nothing. This Ruhr crisis lasted for almost a year, while Germany's inflation soared out of control. By November 1923, the mark's value had fallen to the staggering figure of 4.2 trillion to the dollar. Salaries, savings, pensions, and insurance became worthless.

Germany now had no choice but to abandon its policy of passive resistance. France also realized that its occupation of the Ruhr was a failure and agreed to submit the entire question to an international commission chaired by the American banker Charles Dawes. In April 1924, this commission declared that reparations should be based on Germany's "index of prosperity." This resulted in the reduction of payments by half with the prospect for gradual increases later. The Dawes Commission also urged an international loan to Germany to help stabilize the currency and promote prosperity. American financial institutions provided more than half of the subsequent loan, which launched a program of U.S. financial assistance to Germany for the next five years. The influx of foreign capital contributed to a remarkable German economic recovery during this period. German leaders also introduced a new currency based officially on gold, which halted the inflation.

THREATS FROM THE RIGHT

After the failure of the various left-wing uprisings in 1919, the extreme Right posed the chief danger to the Weimar Republic. The first manifestation of this came in 1920 with the uprising known as the Kapp Putsch. This ill-conceived coup owed its inspiration to the right-wing politician Wolfgang Kapp and General Walther von Lüttwitz, commander of the army's Berlin division. On May 13, Kapp and Lüttwitz employed an anti-republican *Freikorps*, and some regular army units to seize Berlin. The republican government had no choice but to flee the capital. This episode clearly revealed the questionable loyalty of the army to the republic as its leadership refused to take action against the conspirators. It fell to the Social Democrats and the trade unions to foil the putsch by calling a general strike, which paralyzed Berlin, while the civil service refused to follow orders from the usurpers. The revolt collapsed within five days.

The last right-wing coup came in November 1923. It was triggered by the French occupation of the Ruhr and became known as the Beer Hall Putsch because its preliminaries took place in a Munich beer hall. This time, Adolf Hitler's Nazi party attempted to overthrow the state government of Bavaria, preliminary to a projected march on Berlin. Although General Ludendorff lent his still considerable prestige to the enterprise, it failed completely. However, it did bring Hitler to the attention of the German people. Convicted of

treason for his involvement in the putsch, Hitler benefitted from a sympathetic court, which sentenced him to only five years in prison. He actually served just nine months and used the time to dictate the first volume of *Mein Kampf* ("My Struggle") in which he revealed his plans if he ever came to power.

Hitler's goals included the establishment of a totalitarian regime designed to secure German domination of Europe as well as the systematic persecution of the Jews and Slavs. Hitler's unpleasant experience with the Beer Hall Putsch also prompted him to employ a change in strategy. Henceforth, he would seek to achieve power legally through the republic's own electoral system. Ultimately, this approach would serve him well and, with the renewed economic distress of the Great Depression in 1929, would lead to the undermining of the Weimar Republic and the establishment of a Nazi dictatorship in 1933.

FASCISTS TAKE CONTROL IN ITALY

Dictatorship came far more swiftly to Italy. Even though the Italians had emerged from the conflict on the winning side, they also entered the post-war era confronted by a multitude of problems. Italy's meager share of the spoils from the peace settlement outraged nationalists, who had clamored for war in 1915 as a prelude to a rich harvest of territorial gains. Those who had opposed the war were just as much at a loss to explain what the conflict had accomplished at such a dreadful price. To add to the malaise gripping Italian society, the democratic government, back in place after the wartime cabinet dictatorship, suffered from an unstable multiparty system, and it proved no more successful than Germany's Weimar Republic in solving the persistent postwar economic problems, including a huge debt, lagging industrial production, unemployment, a severe trade deficit, and inflation. To make matters still worse, it failed to fulfill the wartime government's promises of benefits to workers and a land reform program for the peasantry.

This lackluster performance led to growing unrest in Italy's cities, where strikes became increasingly frequent, as well as in the countryside, where peasants sometimes resorted to seizing land from wealthy landlords. In 1920, industrial workers, inspired by the Socialist party, briefly took control of many factories in northern Italy by means of sitdown strikes. Coming so soon after the Bolshevik Revolution in Russia, this action convinced many members of the property-owning classes that Italy faced a real danger of "Red Revolution." Despite these fears, the socialists made no attempt to seize power and, in fact, fell victim to a fatal three-way split soon after the end of the takeover of the factories.

It was against this background of chaos and growing disillusionment that fascism came into being. Composed originally of bands of former soldiers and disgruntled nationalists, the Fascists at first were united by little except their superheated nationalism and hostility toward the structure of Italian society and the ineptitude of the government. They soon came under the leadership of Benito Mussolini, a former socialist who had served in the Italian army, and who rose to the rank of corporal before being wounded. Gradually, a desire to gain power brought the Fascists together, although they did not coalesce into an actual political party until 1921. Mussolini and other Fascist leaders organized the fighting bands into an efficient paramilitary force known as the *squadristi*, or Black Shirts, and set out to broaden their support among the population.

Although Mussolini had initially favored cooperation with the moderate Socialists, other Fascist leaders opposed this orientation. Instead, the Fascist party assumed an anti-Socialist guise as the defender of law and order against the forces of "Red Revolution." The badly divided Italian government, distressed by the perceived danger from the Left, failed to see the growing threat from the Fascists on the Right. It tended to look on the movement as a bulwark against socialism and took no action when the Fascists forced many Socialists out of local governmental bodies and even seized a number of railroad stations and telegraph offices. The Fascists also gained considerable support in the officer corps of the army as well as the court of King Victor Emmanuel III.

It was not until Mussolini and the Fascists attempted to seize power by sending Black Shirt units on a march to Rome in October 1922 that the government awoke to the source of the real danger to the democratic system. At the eleventh hour, the Italian cabinet asked the king to declare martial law, but he refused, fearing possible civil war and the loss of his throne if he resisted and the Fascists won the struggle. It seemed safer to him to invite Mussolini to become premier, an offer that Mussolini could not refuse.

Once in office, Mussolini and the Fascists gradually consolidated their power, although it took them four years to complete the transition to dictatorship. In the process, the Fascists outlawed all other political parties, abolished labor unions, secured total control over local government and curtailed civil liberties. Fascism's triumph represented the first major defeat for democracy in Europe during the postwar period. It would not be the last.

DISCONTENT IN AUSTRIA

The fledgling democracies arising from the wreckage of the Dual Monarchy and the chaos of Russia's civil war also experienced turbulent times. The people of Austria, unlike those of other young countries of Central and Eastern Europe, lacked a well-developed sense of national consciousness. They considered themselves Germans rather than Austrians and believed that their national destiny lay in union with Germany, a goal denied them by the peacemakers. Some elements of the population even favored separation of their provinces from Austria altogether. This attitude was in part the legacy of long-standing provincialism, but it also reflected antagonism toward the centralized rule exercised by Vienna during the war years. The continuing food shortage and meager economic prospects added to the depressing atmosphere.

Like Germany, Austria lacked a democratic tradition, and the provisional republic, which came into being in late October 1918, soon found itself assailed by hostile groups similar to those that plagued the Weimar Republic—Communists on the Left as well as reactionary elements on the Right. Early in 1919, the Communists made two attempts to overthrow the government, but neither came remotely close to success. They failed because the rebels were far too few in number, while the Social Democrats, the dominant party in the Austrian government, made effective use of the *Volkswehr*, a new people's republican army recruited from unemployed workers. The *Volkswehr* crushed the revolts, enabling the republic to avoid the same sort of dependence on the old army leaders that afflicted the Weimar Republic.

By 1920, when the new democratic constitution went into effect, the Austrian republic was secure from any immediate threat of revolution. However, continued economic problems, coupled with growing hostility between the Social Democrats concentrated in Vienna and the conservative elements in the provinces, did not bode well for the future. Austria's democratic system had survived its first crisis, but it would face a much more severe test with the coming of the Great Depression in the early 1930s. By 1934, it would succumb to the forces of conservatism and dictatorship.

HUNGARY ABANDONS DEMOCRACY

Hungary did not have to wait that long. It made the transition to dictatorship in record time after a brief flirtation with democracy. Count Mihály Károlyi, who had led the republican uprising against King Charles, formed a provisional government as the Dual Monarchy split apart in the final days of the war. Károlyi and his ministers took steps to establish a democratic system and proposed a land reform program to benefit the traditionally exploited peasantry, but it had inherited a hopeless situation. Although the government proclaimed a policy of equal rights for all nationalities in the old Hungarian state, it was much too late. The other ethnic groups had declared their independence, and the Allied armistice terms granted occupation of southern Hungary to the Serbs and Transylvania to the Rumanians.

All of this led to a marked growth of radicalism, a trend exacerbated by a food shortage in the cities and a depressing economic picture. In early January 1919, the Károlyi government resigned, and a new regime, dominated by the Social Democrats, took power. However, when the Allies demanded that Hungary evacuate territory in Slovakia that was earmarked for occupation by the new Czechoslovak state, a growing chorus of protests led to the downfall of this government too. A coalition of Social Democrats and the new Communist party now formed a soviet republic within Hungary. The Communists, led by Béla Kun, a former prisoner of war who had joined the Bolshevik cause during the Russian Revolution, rapidly came to dominate the new regime. It began to nationalize industry and confiscate church property as well as that of the large landowners.

Kun soon emerged as the most important leader in the Hungarian soviet republic. However, the Communists had fallen heir to the same old problems, while quickly acquiring new ones. Kun attempted to foment revolts in the countries bordering Hungary, which earned his government the animosity of all of these neighboring states. Worse yet, he unwisely rejected an Allied offer to negotiate a new demarcation line with Rumania. The Rumanians responded by sending an army into Hungary in an effort to crush the Communist regime, and their forces drove to within 60 miles of Budapest. Meanwhile, a counterrevolutionary movement developed among former Hapsburg army officers, the landowners, and the wealthy middle class. The trade unions and peasantry also turned against the beleaguered and increasingly oppressive government. Confronted by this multitude of enemies as well as accelerating chaos, Kun and his fellow ministers resigned and fled to neighboring Austria.

After several more months of confusion, a counterrevolutionary regime took power in November 1919. Reactionary and ultra-nationalistic in character, it restored Hungary to the status of a kingdom but could not agree on who should be king. Although Charles returned to try to regain his throne, he was far too unpopular. In the fall of 1921, he went back into exile, this time on the island of Madeira, off the coast of Morocco, where he died the following year. In the absence of a monarch, Admiral Nicholas Horthy, former commander of the Austro-Hungarian navy, became regent. The new government introduced a bloody "White Terror," rounding up Communists as well as those suspected of being sympathizers and resorting to an orgy of torture and murder. By 1920, Hungary had already achieved the dubious distinction of becoming the first conservative and nationalist dictatorship in postwar Europe. It also remained totally unreconciled to any of the country's losses under the Treaty of Trianon. The intensity of its hostility created a major destabilizing influence in

Central Europe throughout the period between the two world wars.

CONFLICT IN YUGOSLAVIA

The new Yugoslav state also made the transition to dictatorship before the end of the 1920s. In this case, bitter hostility between the kindred Serbs and Croats provided the catalyst. Although the Serbs were more numerous, the Croats considered themselves culturally superior. Indeed, they had developed economically and culturally to a far greater degree than had the Serbs, most of whom had languished for centuries under the stultifying domination of the Turks. While the two peoples spoke the same Serbo-Croatian language, they were divided by both dialect and alphabet, the Croats using the Latin alphabet and the Serbs the Cyrillic. Religion provided still another source of cleavage. The Croats were devoutly Catholic, but the majority of the Serbs belonged to the Orthodox Church.

Serbian leaders had only agreed to union with the Croats, and Slovenes on condition that the new South Slav state would be a monarchy with the Serbian Karageorgevich dynasty as the ruling family. The Croats and Slovenes had accepted this proviso, and Serbia's King Alexander became the monarch of the Kingdom of the Serbs, Croats and Slovenes when the constitution for the new state took effect in 1921. The constitution also provided for a democratic electoral system, although King Alexander wielded extensive control over the army.

Another problem proved less amenable to solution. This concerned a dispute over whether the country should have a federal or unitary system of administration. The Croats insisted on a federal system that would enable them to govern Croatia itself, while being tied to a federal government in Belgrade in regard to foreign policy, military and naval affairs, and other matters concerning the entire kingdom. The Serbs were just as insistent on a unitary system in which the entire country would be administered from Belgrade, the capital.

Generally speaking, the Serbs looked upon the new state as, in effect, Greater Serbia. They intended to be the dominant ethnic group in the government. Since they outnumbered the Croats and gained the support of the Moslems in Bosnia, the constitution reflected their desires. But the Croats never ceased to agitate for autonomy. This division proved the fatal flaw in the new state. Hostility grew steadily more intense on this issue. An extremist Croat group even demanded outright independence for Croatia. When the Croatian leader Stephen Radich was assassinated in 1928, the two peoples teetered on the brink of civil war. The Croatian delegation withdrew in protest from the Yugoslav parliament, and the Croats established their own legislature in Zagreb. Croatia also demanded adoption of a federal system in which each state would have its own army. These demands were totally unacceptable to the Serbs, and in 1929, King Alexander used the army, dominated by Serbian officers, to impose a royal dictatorship. The king also officially changed the country's name to Yugoslavia.

Although King Alexander was dedicated to the Yugoslav idea and hoped to create a Yugoslav national consciousness among Serbs and Croats alike, his action merely made the Croats more sullen and resentful. In the years to come, the Serbs treated Croatia almost as though it were an occupied enemy province. The dictatorial regime also exploited the Serbian peasantry and enriched the corrupt politicians and army officers who dominated the country, while much of the population lived in poverty. The promise of the Yugoslav idea had degenerated into mutual hatred between the kindred Serbs and Croats, while the democracy proclaimed so hopefully

in 1921 had died before reaching adolescence. This tragedy created a legacy that was to haunt Yugoslavia for many decades to come.

ETHNIC DIVISIONS IN CZECHOSLOVAKIA

Ethnic divisions also bedeviled the new state of Czechoslovakia. In one respect, its problems resembled those of Yugoslavia. This took the form of quarreling between the kindred Czechs and Slovaks, although the degree of hostility never approached the intense hatred between Serbs and Croats. In another way, Czechoslovakia's dilemma was quite different and far more sinister from that confronting Yugoslavia. This focused on the presence in the Sudetenland of a large German population that harbored contempt for the predominant Slavic peoples of the country.

As in the case of Yugoslavia, the partners in the original decision to unite soon fell to squabbling. The Czechs outnumbered the Slovaks by a considerable margin, but unlike the dominant Serbs in Yugoslavia, they were more advanced culturally, economically, and in national consciousness than were the Slovaks. The Slovaks shared the Croat preference for a federal system and, indeed, Thomas Masaryk had promised to fulfill their desire as the price of union. But, as the new state took form, it became apparent that the Slovaks lacked a large enough pool of educated individuals to adequately administer Slovakia. By default, Czechoslovakia adopted a unitary system supervised from Prague, the capital. It was democratic and provided fair representation for all ethnic groups, but the task of administering Slovakia fell primarily to Czech officials. Although they handled matters in a generally enlightened manner, friction inevitably developed between the two factions.

In particular, the devoutly Catholic Slovaks found the religious attitudes of Czech administrators a source of irritation. Drawn primarily from the Czech middle class, these officials tended to be free thinkers and often anti-clerical. At the same time, the Czech provinces of Bohemia and Moravia, with well-developed industries and an efficient agricultural sector, enjoyed much greater prosperity than did Slovakia, with its mountainous, largely unproductive terrain and backward economy. Most Slovaks, nevertheless, favored continuation of the Czechoslovak state but pushed for a more decentralized system. Resentment was most intense among the Catholic clergy and the more reactionary Slovak conservatives.

Slovakia possessed a strip of rich agricultural territory along its southern border with Hungary. This area contained a predominantly Magyar population of almost a million people. However, the principle of self-determination proved less important to the disposition of this territory than did economic considerations. In this case, the argument that it was vital to Slovakia's economy carried the day. Unfortunately, the Magyar minority remained unreconciled to this decision.

On Slovakia's right flank lay Ruthenia, the narrow tail-like eastern extremity of Czechoslovakia. One of the most backward areas of Europe, it too had belonged to Hungary, but Ruthenes comprised the bulk of its population. Had self-determination prevailed here, the Ruthenes undoubtedly would have voted for union with their kinsmen in the Ukraine. Instead, Ruthenia became part of Czechoslovakia, largely because of the chaos in Hungary at the time of the Kun regime and the presence of Czech troops. As in the case of Slovakia, the Czechs promised autonomy for Ruthenia, but the Ruthenes, considerably more backward than the Slovaks, were even less able to provide the necessary competent officials. Hungary, under its ultra-nationalist and highly revisionist dictatorial regime, never reconciled itself to the loss of either Slovakia or Ruthenia.

By far the most serious aspect of Czechoslovakia's national divisions was the hostility harbored toward the Czechs by the German population of the Sudetenland. The Sudeten Germans held the distinction of being perhaps the most chauvinistic of all Germans. Convinced of their cultural superiority, they found it extremely difficult to accept the reality of Czech predominance. But eventually, necessity convinced them that for the foreseeable future no alternative existed to their inclusion in Czechoslovakia. By 1925, they had made their peace with the Czechs, at least outwardly, and two Sudeten German parties entered a coalition government. But the Sudeten Germans remained a potential Trojan horse within the Czechoslovak state. After Adolf Hitler came to power in Germany, the presence of three million Germans in the Sudetenland posed a latent threat to the continued existence of Czechoslovakia. In 1938, that threat became real and, under Hitler's skillful orchestration, led to the disintegration of the country.

Despite its nationalities problem, Czechoslovakia, alone of all the successor states, maintained its democratic government until it was completely undermined by Hitler's machinations. This achievement represented a tribute to Czech devotion to democracy as well as their generally fair treatment of minorities and the strength of the Czech economy. Their success posed a dramatic contrast to the utter failure of Yugoslavia to provide either ethnic peace or a stable democratic system. It also contrasted sharply with the failure of Poland, Czechoslovakia's neighbor to the northeast, to follow an enlightened policy toward its minorities or to prevent its democratic system from degenerating into chaos. Poland, like Yugoslavia, fell victim to a dictatorship in less than a decade.

DICTATORSHIP IN POLAND

Poland encountered difficulties that in certain respects were greater than those of the other successor states. Its creation necessitated the bringing together of three distinct areas, each of which had been ruled by a different Great Power since the partitions of the late eighteenth century. The question of Poland's eastern borders also did not become clear for over two years after the end of the war. Much of its territory had experienced widespread devastation during the fighting on the Eastern Front. From the start, the resurrected Polish state also became embroiled in border disputes with all of its neighbors except Rumania. These led to brief clashes with Germany, Czechoslovakia, and Lithuania as well as a more prolonged and full-scale conflict with Russia.

The Russo-Polish War of 1920–1921 resulted from Poland's insistence on its pre-1772 borders in the east, which would lead to the inclusion of millions of Ukrainians, Belorussians, and Lithuanians within the Polish state. Poland dispatched a note to Moscow in March 1920, asking restoration of these frontiers. The Communist government refused, and on April 25, Poland declared war. With French aid, the Poles invaded the Ukraine, which the Red Army had restored more or less to Russian control. Under the command of Marshal Józef Pilsudski, the Poles captured Kiev, the Ukrainian capital, and for a time drove well beyond the pre-1772 border. In fact, they advanced so far that their left flank proved vulnerable to a Russian counterattack. The Poles had to retreat with the Red Army in hot pursuit. For a time, it appeared that Warsaw itself would fall, but Pilsudski delivered a daring thrust into a gap between two enemy armies and forced them to flee in disorder.

The war ended in March 1921 with the signing of the Treaty of Riga, which estab-lished Poland's eastern frontier along the cease-fire line between the rival armies. While the war was still in progress, the Poles also seized the disputed but predominantly-Polish city of Vilna from Lithuania. Although it had not achieved its ambitious goal, Poland had acquired sizable territories. Unfortunately, they contained predominantly non-Polish populations. For the most part, the new additions were also wretchedly poor and did little to enhance Poland's economy. In the future, the Poles dominated the Ukrainians, Belorussians, and Lithuanians within their borders with little concern for their welfare, while trying to assimilate them into the Polish state.

Whatever the value of the spoils of war, they were welcome to the Polish people. An intense nationalism was one of the few things that tended to unite the Poles. Almost everything else divided them. Especially important were cultural differences in the three areas formerly under German, Russian and Austrian rule. There also were serious social divisions, most notably between the powerful landowning aristocracy, which controlled roughly half the country's agricultural land, and the hard-pressed peasants, who favored a redistribution of the land. A wide gap existed as well between conservatives, strongly influenced by the Catholic church, and the Socialists. To complicate matters still more, one-third of the population consisted of minorities with little or no loyalty to the Polish state. Most of these ethnic groups were also badly divided socially and politically.

The Polish constitution of 1921 provided for a democratic republic based on universal suffrage, which extended to all nationalities. It also created a weak president and a powerful parliament. The latter reflected the divided character of society in a multiparty system on a grand scale. Between 1921 and 1926, no fewer than 80 political parties existed, according to the best estimate, and 14 different cabinets rose and fell in the forlorn pursuit of a stable coalition. Finally, in 1926, Marshal Pilsudski, who enjoyed massive prestige by virtue of his role as one of the architects of Polish independence and his wartime exploits, used the army to carry out a coup. Motivated by great patriotism, Pilsudski had long believed that the parliamentary system was leading Poland to ruin. The marshal strengthened the power of the executive and curtailed that of the legislative.

In the process, he turned Poland into a dictatorship, which grew more thoroughgoing with the passage of time. Real power in this regime rested with a clique of army officers who often used it to enrich themselves rather than to benefit Poland. This became increasingly the case after Pilsudski's death in 1935. In addition to these unedifying internal developments, Poland looked to the future surrounded by enemies, most notably Germany and the Soviet Union, both of whom were to regain their power while Poland stagnated.

COMMUNISTS EXTEND THEIR GRIP IN RUSSIA

Indeed, by the time that the Russo-Polish War ended, the Communist regime in Russia had won the civil war and was at last able to take the first tentative steps toward what Lenin referred to as the "transition to socialism." Despite their early success in the civil war, the Whites never represented a united counter-revolutionary movement. The only thing that tended to bind them together was the mutual desire to destroy the Bolshevik regime. Politically, they ranged from conservative to moderate socialist, and the White military forces never effectively coordinated their efforts. In fact, White generals often viewed each other as rivals. While the counterrevolutionaries dissipated their initial advantage, Trotsky's remarkable organizational ability led to the rapid expansion of the Red Army. During the course of 1919, it grew to over three million men. It also improved in quality and ultimately turned out to be more than a match for the

FIGURE 21–1   Colonel George Stewart leads American forces in northern Russia during the Allied intervention in the Russian Civil War. National Archives

Whites. Utilizing interior lines of communication, Trotsky shifted his forces efficiently to combat each enemy threat as it arose.

The Allies had sent forces to intervene in Russia because they firmly believed that the Bolshevik regime had little support among the Russian people and was certain to collapse in the face of White pressure. Initially, the Allies were especially concerned that war material, which they had sent to Russia, would fall into the hands of the Germans. This fear took on greater urgency because of their mistaken conviction that the Bolsheviks had entered into a conspiracy with Germany as part of the Brest-Litovsk settlement.

The British intervened first, sending troops to the Arctic port of Murmansk as early as April 1918. French, American, and even Serbian reinforcements soon joined them, and in August, Allied units also occupied Archangel on the White Sea to the southeast. In July, Japanese and American forces landed at the Pacific port of Vladivostok. They, too, came ostensibly to safeguard war material as well as to cooperate with the Czechoslovak Legion, a force of 40,000 former prisoners of war who were making their way across Siberia, hoping to escape by way of Vladivostok. The Japanese also hoped to help themselves to some of Russia's Far Eastern territory, while the United States was determined to prevent this, a combination that did little to further harmony between the two powers. These Allied forces cooperated with Admiral Alexander Kolchak, who had established a counterrevolutionary government in Siberia and for a time seemed to represent the chief threat to the Bolsheviks.

In the south of European Russia, French forces intervened in the Ukraine, while Britain sent troops to the area southeast of the Don River as well as the Caucasus. The two powers even concluded an agreement in December 1917, authorizing the creation of economic spheres of influence in their respective areas.

Their troops soon cooperated with the White forces of General Anton Denikin.

The defeat of Germany removed the original stated purpose for the Allied intervention, but their troops lingered for some time. The forces at Murmansk and Archangel were the first to leave in October 1919, but those in Siberia continued to support Kolchak's armies, which for a time made progress against the Bolsheviks. Unfortunately, the admiral proved a poor military leader and also quarreled with his allies. When the Bolsheviks took the offensive against him in the summer of 1919, they scored an impressive victory. Before the end of the year, they had not only defeated his forces but had captured and executed Kolchak himself. In the aftermath of this collapse, Allied forces in Siberia began to evacuate during the course of 1920, although the Japanese remained until October 1922.

Meanwhile, the French troops found themselves caught up in the utter confusion that prevailed in the Ukraine during 1918–1919. Rival Ukrainian political groups fought among themselves as well as against Denikin's White army. By the spring of 1919, it became clear to the French that their intervention had failed, and they withdrew their troops. The British encountered similar problems in their sphere and evacuated during the summer, leaving Denikin's forces to fend for themselves. For a while, they did quite well, driving to within 200 miles of Moscow before suffering a major defeat in the spring of 1920. The White forces in the south were not yet finished, however, and under the command of General Peter Wrangel, they took the offensive one last time in the summer. However, after the Bolsheviks signed an armistice with the Poles in October 1920, they were able to shift strong forces to the southern front. Confronted by this influx of new strength, Wrangel had to accept defeat, and in November his men withdrew from ports on the Black Sea. The Bolsheviks had won.

It was not surprising that Lenin emerged from the civil war with an even more negative view of those Western powers who had indicated their hostility toward his government. The Allies had accomplished nothing through their intervention and now had to accept the hard fact that communism had triumphed in Russia. The Spartacist rebellion in Germany and Béla Kun's soviet republic in Hungary, short-lived though they were, also helped kindle Western fears of the continuing threat of "Red Revolution."

Even more ominously, in March 1919, Lenin established a new international organization, this time linking all the Communist parties outside Russia with the new Soviet regime. The Communist International, or Comintern, as it was called, maintained headquarters in Moscow and promoted the cause of world revolution. Even after it became clear that, for the foreseeable future, revolution was not likely to succeed outside Russia, the Comintern coordinated the actions of the worldwide Communist movement. During the 1920s and 1930s all Communist parties slavishly followed the party line laid down in Moscow.

Although Western relations with the Soviet government did improve to some extent after this turbulent beginning, mutual fear and suspicion lingered long afterward. When Hitler emerged as a menace to the peace of Europe in the 1930s, this unfortunate legacy prevented any meaningful cooperation between the Soviet Communists and the West toward a united effort to halt Hitler's aggressive actions.

As the Communists consolidated their control over other parts of the Russian Empire during the civil war, they created socialist republics, modeled on the Russian Republic, in Belorussia, the Ukraine, and Transcaucasia. In January 1924, a new constitution linked all four republics in the Union of Soviet Socialist Republics (USSR, or Soviet Union). This action reflected the fact that the country contained various nationalities, although the Great Russians were the most numerous. Their republic, by far the largest, included not only European Russia but also most of Siberia; it dominated the USSR. The Soviet leaders established additional republics in the following years in Central Asia and the Caucasus.

STALIN BECOMES SOVIET DICTATOR

In the same month that the Soviet Union came into existence, Lenin, who had suffered a series of strokes during the previous two years, died. Well before his death, a power struggle had developed among Communist leaders for the right to succeed the architect of the Soviet dictatorship. The two principal rivals were Leon Trotsky and the general secretary of the Communist party, Josif Dzhugashvili, who had taken the name Stalin, derived from the Russian word for steel. By 1928, Stalin had skillfully outmaneuvered Trotsky and several other leaders and had consolidated himself as dictator. He quickly embarked on an ambitious program to completely nationalize the economy and transform the Soviet Union into a major industrial power. Utilizing a series of Five-Year Plans and extremely ruthless tactics, Stalin succeeded to a large extent in modernizing the Soviet economy during the next 12 years. This achievement, gained at tremendous human suffering, would provide the basis for the country's survival in World War II.

UPHEAVAL IN TURKEY

Tumultuous events also took place in Turkey in the aftermath of the Treaty of Sèvres. The harshness of the peace settlement angered Turkish nationalists, who refused to accept the treaty as final. Mustapha Kemal, the hero of the defense of the Gallipoli Peninsula in 1915, now emerged as a leader of great inspirational qualities as well as organizational ability. He unified the various resistance groups that opposed the treaty and became a symbol of their cause. While willing to part with Turkey's Arab provinces, Kemal would not acquiesce in the partition of Anatolia, the core area of his country's Asian territory, or the loss of its European foothold to the west of Constantinople.

Nationalist anger increased sharply when Greek troops occupied Smyrna on the Aegean coast of Anatolia in May 1919. Kemal immediately capitalized on anger over the Greek invasion to create a mass nationalist political movement that won a majority in the parliamentary elections during the fall of 1919. When the Turkish parliament met in January 1920, it adopted a National Pact, proclaiming "the independence of Turkey within its national frontiers." The Allies reacted to this by sending more troops to Constantinople, and soon afterward, the Turkish sultan bowed to their pressure by dissolving parliament.

Kemal in turn responded by convening his own national parliament at Ankara in central Anatolia during April. When the sultan accepted the Treaty of Sèvres in August 1920, Kemal's rebel government denounced this action and vowed to resist. Having thrown down the gauntlet to both the sultan and the Allies, Kemal now reorganized the army and negotiated an agreement with Soviet Russia, which provided his forces with war material. By October, the Turkish army was ready to take the offensive. It struck first against the Armenians in the northeastern portion of the country. The Treaty of Sèvres had granted independence to Armenia, but the Armenians were in no condition to resist Kemal's army, which quickly crushed the Armenian forces.

Having established control in the east, Kemal turned westward to deal with the much more difficult task of defeating the Greeks. Starting in June 1920, Greek armies had penetrated from Smyrna into the interior of Anatolia. Although the Allies had originally sanctioned this action, they had expected the Greeks to exercise some restraint and had provided no military support. Once engaged in this operation, however, Greece became carried away with grandiose plans of conquest. Its forces advanced far beyond the limits of the territory granted to them by the Treaty of Sèvres. During 1921, they reached a point 400 miles beyond Smyrna and threatened Ankara. But, in a crucial battle along the Sakarya River, the Turks defeated the Greeks and gradually pushed them back. In August 1922, they unleashed a major offensive and swiftly smashed the enemy in a series of battles. The badly beaten Greeks retreated in disorder to Smyrna, and by September 18 they had evacuated all their troops from Anatolia. On November 1, the National Assembly in Ankara abolished the Ottoman sultanate, and Turkey became a republic.

The overwhelming Turkish success convinced the Allies that the Treaty of Sèvres was a dead letter. They convened a new peace conference at Lausanne, Switzerland, in November with Turkey represented as a full participant. The resulting Treaty of Lausanne, signed in July 1923, restored to Turkey all the territory it had lost to Greece in both Europe and Anatolia. Turkey also regained sovereignty over both Armenia and Kurdistan. Finally, the treaty abolished the legal privileges that foreign governments and individuals had enjoyed in Turkey before the war, thus removing this long-standing Turkish grievance.

Turkey's victory in the war with Greece, coming so soon after its defeat in World War I, and its ability to gain such a sweeping revision of the peace settlement represented a notable achievement for Kemal as well as his chief field commander, General Ismet Inönü, who also headed the Turkish delegation at Lausanne. Ismet proved a highly

FIGURE 21–2 General Mustapha Kemal, hero of Gallipoli and leader of the Turkish Nationalist Revolt. National Archives

skillful negotiator, more than able to hold his own against the imperious Lord Curzon, the British foreign secretary. Turkey's triumph also served as an inspiration to colonial and semicolonial peoples everywhere. It clearly demonstrated that it was possible to challenge the imperialist powers successfully, at least in certain cases.

BRITAIN AND THE IRISH QUESTION

This realization also was not lost on the two most important imperialist powers, Britain and France, although they would not experience a full-fledged colonial revolt until after World War II. Britain became especially aware of the need to make adjustments in its relationship with at least some members of its empire. The most pressing immediate problem, however, was posed by Ireland, a part of the United Kingdom itself. The issue of Irish Home Rule had created an exceptionally serious crisis shortly before the outbreak of World War I. The bitter opposition of the Protestants of Ulster (Northern Ireland) to the application of Home Rule there and the equally insistent demands of Irish nationalists for its extension to the entire island had threatened an armed clash in 1914. Only the coming of the European conflict had averted civil war. In the face of this greater challenge, the British postponed implementation of Home Rule until the return of peace.

However, this decision had not produced a solution to the problem, and during the war Irish nationalism took a more militant turn, especially in the "Easter Rebellion" of 1916. The Irish political party Sinn Fein, which means "We Ourselves" in Ireland's old Gaelic language, demanded outright independence. In the parliamentary election of November 1918, Sinn Fein won a resounding victory in Ireland. But its successful candidates refused to take their seats in the British Parliament. Instead, they attempted to establish an Irish parliament and claimed sovereignty over the entire island. Britain refused to accept this revolutionary act and took measures to crush Sinn Fein.

The rebels now resorted to a guerrilla war, which tormented Ireland for the next two years. It featured the Irish Republican Army, Sinn Fein's paramilitary force, against the Royal Irish Constabulary, augmented by units of British army veterans, referred to as "Black and Tans" because of the colors of their caps and uniforms. This nasty conflict took the form of hit-and-run attacks, ambushes, murders, arson, and the taking of hostages. It finally ended in 1921 when, in desperation, Lloyd George reached an agreement with representatives of Sinn Fein. Under its terms, the bulk of Ireland received dominion status as the Irish Free State, while six counties of Ulster obtained Home Rule and remained within the United Kingdom.

GREATER INDEPENDENCE GIVEN THE DOMINIONS

World War I also resulted in greater independence for Britain's older self-governing dominions—Canada, Australia, New Zealand, and the Union of South Africa. When the war began, they were technically still dependent on Britain in foreign affairs, but all of them had voluntarily joined the Mother Country in the conflict. They had fought well and suffered heavy casualties on many fronts. As a reward for their services, each nation had gained the right to send its own delegation to the Paris Peace Conference, and in 1926, Britain recognized the dominions as being, for all practical purposes, independent in foreign affairs. The sole remaining links to Britain were allegiance to the British monarch as head of state and membership in the Commonwealth of Nations, as the former British Empire was now called. All of this meant that in the future, London would have to pay close attention to the desires of the dominions, all of whom were determined to avoid stumbling into another war. British sensitivity to their wishes furthered the pursuit of a conciliatory policy toward Germany during the 1920s and 1930s.

UNREST IN BRITISH COLONIES

The debilitating effects of the war also made Britain less certain of its hold over other parts of the empire that had never received the right of self-government. India posed the most serious problem of this type. Although its soldiers had also fought valiantly and had sustained many casualties, India did not gain compensation even remotely close to that of the dominions. A nationalist movement had developed before the war but became much more militant afterward and demanded dominion status. But the British granted only a limited measure of self-government. As a result, dissatisfied Indian nationalists grew increasingly restless as the years passed.

A nationalist revolt in Egypt led to Britain's decision to grant independence to its former protectorate in 1922. The British also encountered resistance among the Arabs of Iraq, as Mesopotamia was now called. They responded by creating a kingdom under Prince Faisel in 1921, but they did not terminate their mandate until ten years later when Iraq became officially independent. In regard to both Egypt and Iraq, however, independence remained more apparent than real owing to the continued presence of British military, air and naval bases as well as strong political and economic influence. As a result, anti-British sentiment steadily increased. In Palestine, the British disappointed the national aspirations of Arabs and Jews alike when they established their rule over this area. The League of Nations mandate, which provided for Britain's authority in the region, called on the British to facilitate Jewish immigration and settlement in Palestine, but the ensuing influx of Jews led to opposition from Palestinian Arabs. In the following years, tension increased between the two groups, much to Britain's displeasure.

FRANCE SEEKS ALLIES

For the most part, France had fewer immediate worries over its empire, although from the start it had to contend with a hostile nationalist movement in newly acquired Syria. This hostility flared into rebellion in 1920 and again in a more intense form in 1925–1927. The French, also had to deal with a revolt by Riff tribesmen in Morocco during 1925–1926. While Nationalist movements in Tunisia and Indochina did not become large enough to create much concern until the 1930s. Resentment existed as well among the black populations of Senegal and Dahomey in Africa because of heavy losses among men recruited into the French army during the war.

France found much more to concern it on the European continent. With the refusal of the United States and Britain to enter into a collective security agreement or to insist on strict German compliance with the Treaty of Versailles, France took on the burden of enforcing the peace settlement almost single-handedly. This task soon proved beyond its capabilities.

The failure to achieve an alliance with Britain and the United States led the French to turn to lesser countries for help. In 1920, they made defensive military alliances with both Belgium and Poland and added another with Czechoslovakia the following year. All three of these countries shared France's fear of a revived Germany. Later in the decade, Paris also negotiated less binding agreements with Yugoslavia and Rumania. These merely required the partners to consult with each other in case of a threat to their independence. This system of collective security was a poor substitute for the wartime relationship among France, Britain, and the United States. France's dilemma took on an even more ominous aspect in view of the desire of not only Germany but also Italy and Russia to revise the 1919 peace settlement. Despite the mutual hostility of the Germans and Italians toward communism, it was possible that, in certain circumstances, their antagonism toward the settlement might bring the three powers together in at least limited cooperation, perhaps more.

The destruction of Austria-Hungary and the development of a power vacuum in Central Europe also created the potential for extension of German economic and political influence into this area in the future, despite Germany's postwar weakness. This situation reflected the economic realities of the region. Most of the successor states depended on exporting agricultural products but, while France was agriculturally self-sufficient, Germany needed to import large quantities of food. In the uncertain economic conditions of the postwar period, this combination of factors could bring Germany and the successor states closer together and undermine France's collective security system. It was clear to the French, if to no one else, that the key to their security was German weakness. It was by no means certain that France would be able to keep Germany in this condition permanently.

JAPAN WIDENS INFLUENCE IN EAST ASIA

In East Asia, Japan emerged from the war in a much stronger position. Japanese economic gains as a result of the conflict were second only to those of the United States. The country's steel production had doubled, and its exports had tripled. Like America, Japan suddenly had changed from a debtor to a creditor nation but on a lesser scale. Tokyo had also made the most of the opportunity to improve its position in China, while Russia, Britain, and France were preoccupied with the struggle in Europe. In 1915, Japan had confronted China with "twenty-one demands," which would have transformed China into a virtual protectorate. Although the Japanese subsequently bowed to pressure from President Wilson and relaxed their grip to some extent, they still emerged from the war as the strongest of the imperialist powers in East Asia. Their potential to dominate

China economically and politically was much like that of Germany in Central Europe. The war had eliminated German power in the Far East, and Japan had fallen heir to their interests in the Shantung Peninsula. Russia's massive internal problems also prevented it from interfering with Japanese efforts to encroach on China.

SOME BRIGHT SPOTS APPEAR

Despite the many ominous aftereffects of the war, all was not shrouded in gloom. Indeed, by the mid-1920s, the situation in much of the world looked far brighter. Germany began to emerge from its role as an outcast nation and even entered into better relations with the Soviet Union and France. In 1922, it negotiated the Treaty of Rapallo with the Soviets. This agreement provided for mutual diplomatic recognition and renunciation of war claims. However, on a more somber note, the German army entered into secret cooperation with the Red Army, enabling it to train tank and artillery units and test prototypes of weapons on Soviet soil in violation of the Treaty of Versailles.

Nevertheless, in 1925, Germany, France, and Belgium signed the Treaty of Locarno, in which the Germans reaffirmed their western borders as established at Versailles as well as the demilitarization of the Rhineland. This pact did not extend to Germany's eastern frontiers, however, and German leaders cherished hopes of someday gaining a revision of this portion of the peace settlement. In 1926, Germany entered the League of Nations. The end of the ruinous inflation and the availability of American loans also enabled the Weimar Republic to refurbish its economy and embark upon a period of prosperity. It was also able to make regular reparations payments. With the return of better economic conditions, the appeal of extremist political parties weakened and the Weimar Republic

gained greater acceptance. Field Marshal von Hindenburg even became its president in 1925, giving the republic a link with Germany's glorious past. Adolf Hitler seemed destined to remain the leader of a minor right-wing fringe party.

The former Allied powers joined Germany in what appeared to be a general economic recovery and made payments on their war debts to the United States. America, too, appeared prosperous, and its financial assistance had clearly underwritten the return to better days in Europe. During the same decade, Japan prospered and moved in the direction of democratic government, while following a more enlightened policy toward China. In 1922, Tokyo gave up its rights in the Shantung Peninsula to the Chinese. Military leaders also seemed to be losing their former dominant role in Japanese politics. Still another promising sign appeared in 1922 when Japan joined with the United States, Britain, France, and Italy in limiting the size of the fleets of the world's major naval powers. There was even talk about the possibility of general disarmament in the near future.

THE WAR'S GRIM LEGACY

The legacy of World War I proved too great to overcome. It had changed the world to an extent never imagined by the statesmen and generals who had plunged the Continent into the conflict in 1914. Europe's old predominance had vanished, and the balance of power lay shattered. Austria-Hungary had ceased to exist, and Central Europe had become a jigsaw puzzle of small, weak, multinational states. Despite improvement in the German economy during the second half of the 1920s, the war had gravely weakened Germany, while the new Soviet Union grappled with the lingering effects of the war, revolution, and civil war as well as its internal power struggle.

In view of German and Soviet weakness and Italy's continuing inferiority relative to other major countries, Britain and France loomed as the two most important European powers in the aftermath of the conflict. However, the war had diminished their strength as well. Britain's economic position had declined disastrously. France bore the psychological impact of hideous battles such as Verdun to perhaps a greater degree than any other power, especially in view of its numerical inferiority to Germany. The French believed that the Western powers must maintain the peace settlement and police the Continent but, of course, neither Britain nor the United States had been willing to undertake such an ambitious role. By default, France attempted to fulfill this formidable task alone, but after the failure of the ill-conceived Ruhr occupation, it realized that it could not succeed. As the years passed, France followed an increasingly passive role and tended to look to a reluctant Britain to provide leadership. As for the United States, it loomed as a potential superpower but refused to accept the responsibility and turned instead to its traditional policy of relative isolation from European political affairs while maintaining its close economic relationship to the European continent.

Although Germany and the Soviet Union languished for some time in their weakened condition, both had the potential for renewed greatness and would eventually recover their strength. Moreover, the disintegration of the Dual Monarchy and the emergence of the small multinational states in territories lost by Russia at Brest-Litovsk had created a huge power vacuum in much of Central and Eastern Europe. Eventually, both Germany and the Soviet Union would seek to fill this vacuum. Indeed, for a time, they shared a basis for cooperation in their mutual desire to revise the postwar settlement. In East Asia, the weakening of the European powers and their preoccupation with internal problems left Japan as the potential dominant power. But pursuit of a policy designed to achieve this goal might eventually bring it into a collision course with the United States, which retained a keen interest in that part of the world.

THE PSYCHOLOGICAL TOLL OF THE WAR

The war also had a profound impact on the philosophical, literary, and artistic outlook of Europe and the world. Philosophers, writers and artists reflected the prevailing gloom, dissatisfaction, and anxiety in their work. Many of them focused with extreme distaste on a society whose leadership could plunge their countries into the horror and carnage of the trenches and persist in their bloody quest for victory no matter what the cost. The creative work of the period cast doubt on the future of Western civilization and humanity in general, magnifying intellectual tendencies that were already present in prewar Europe.

Not surprisingly, the war discredited and undermined the position of the ruling classes in much of the Continent, while instilling great expectations among the middle and lower classes that its aftermath would produce a better world. At first, democracy seemed to hold the key to this dream. However, in the reality of the postwar era, these hopes turned to despair in the prevailing economic and political chaos. Democracy found it difficult to take root in the barren ground of nations with no previous experience with this difficult and often exasperating form of government. Since democracy did not seem to work, many people turned to more extreme remedies—communism, fascism, and nazism. Instead of entering an age of democracy, much of Europe would soon sink into totalitarianism.

ECONOMIC DESPAIR
AND POLITICAL INSTABILITY

Closely linked to all of these disturbing portents was the fact that, despite the hopes kindled by the improved economic conditions of the late 1920s, this recovery was deceptive and rested on flimsy foundations. In truth, the worldwide economy had not recovered from the dislocations created by the war. Before the decade closed, the greatest economic disaster in modern history had dispelled the renewed hopes for a better world. The Great Depression of the 1930s struck the United States with special intensity, putting an end to its crucial role in propping up the economic health of Europe. Indeed, America turned inward and followed a policy of protecting its domestic market from foreign competition, an action that helped unhinge the world economy still more.

The strength of democracy in Germany and Japan also proved more apparent than real. The Great Depression soon plunged Germany into both economic despair and deep political instability, providing the opportunity for Adolf Hitler and the Nazis to come to power in 1933. The impact of the Great Depression also discredited Japan's youthful democracy and heralded renewed meddling by the army in the country's politics as well as a return to an imperialist policy in China far more intense than anything that had preceded it. Finally, the economic disaster dealt harshly with Britain and France as well and left them in a demoralized and defeatist frame of mind just as Japan and Nazi Germany began to threaten the postwar status quo. Within another decade, both East Asia and Europe would be at war once again.

ADDITIONAL READING

Although its literature is not as immense as that of World War II, the First World War has inspired a vast number of works, both general and specialized. The following essay is not even remotely exhaustive. It merely attempts to cite some of the most notable works available in English.

GENERAL

Two of the oldest but still standard general histories that focus on the military aspects of the conflict are C.R.M.F. Cruttwell's *A History of the Great War* (Oxford: Clarendon Press, 1934); and B. H. Liddell Hart's *The Real War, 1914–1918* (London: Faber & Faber, 1930). Winston Churchill also published a five-volume history of the war, *The World Crisis* (New York: Scribner's, 1923–1931), but it deals primarily with Britain's role and especially Churchill's part in the war. Of more

recent vintage are Cyril Falls's *The Great War, 1914–1918* (New York: Capricorn Books, 1959), which also emphasizes Britain's contribution and is exceedingly favorable to Field Marshal Haig; and Vincent J. Esposito, ed., *A Concise History of World War I* (New York: Praeger, 1964). Other relatively brief surveys are James L. Stokesbury, *A Short History of World War I* (New York: William Morrow, 1981); Sir James E. Edmonds, *A Short History of World War I* (New York: Oxford University Press, 1951); and Marc Ferro, *The Great War, 1914–1918* (London: Routledge & Kegan Paul, 1973). The latter work is by far the briefest and stresses the social, economic, and human aspects of the conflict. The most thorough and balanced one-volume account is Bernadotte Schmitt and Harold Vedeler, *The World in the Crucible, 1914–1919* (New York: Harper & Row, 1984). Like Ferro, it deals with social, economic, and cultural aspects of the war but in more detail. Two brief works, René Albrecht-Carrié, *The Meaning of the First World War* (Englewood Cliffs, N.J.: Prentice-Hall, 1965); and Jack J. Roth, ed., *World War I: A Turning Point in Modern History* (New York: Knopf, 1967), succeed in placing the war's impact in the broader perspective of the twentieth century.

THE BACKGROUND FOR THE WAR

Gordon A. Craig's *Europe Since 1815* (New York: Holt, Rinehart & Winston, 1972) presents an excellent general account of the period 1815–1914. Among the best general texts on individual countries are R.C.K. Ensor, *England, 1870–1914* (Oxford: Clarendon Press, 1936); R.D. Anderson, *France, 1870–1914* (London: Edward Arnold, 1977); Gordon A. Craig, *Germany, 1866–1945* (Oxford: Oxford University Press, 1978); Arthur J. May, *The Hapsburg Monarchy, 1867–1914* (New York: W.W. Norton & Co., Inc., 1968); Marc Raeff, *Understanding Imperial Russia* (New York: Columbia University Press, 1984); and John A. Thayer, *Italy and the Great War: Politics and Culture, 1870–1915* (Madison: University of Wisconsin Press, 1964). An excellent recent diplomatic history of Europe during the nineteenth century is Norman Rich, *Great Power Diplomacy, 1814–1914* (New York: McGraw-Hill, 1992).

The origins of World War I constitute perhaps the most controversial issue in all of modern European history. Soon after the outbreak of war in 1914, the various belligerent powers hastened to publish a number of their diplomatic documents pertaining to the crisis of 1914. They selected those which portrayed their governments as blameless and cast their enemies in the role of aggressors. After the conflict, multivolume collections of documents, extending as far back as 1870, appeared in each country. Although they

were far more useful than the wartime propaganda efforts, they also were selective and tended to conceal material reflecting negatively on the individual country in question. During the 1920s and 1930s, historians of considerable renown published works dealing with the diplomatic background for the war during the period 1870–1914. Some of these attempted to present a balanced account that distributed blame for the war on virtually all the major powers as well as Serbia. Among the most notable of these early works are Sidney B. Fay, *The Origins of the World War*, 2 vols. (New York: Macmillan, 1928–1930); Bernadotte Schmitt, *The Coming of the War, 1914* (New York: Scribner's, 1930); and William L. Langer, *European Alliances and Alignments, 1871–1890* (New York: Knopf, 1950) and *The Diplomacy of Imperialism, 1890–1902* (New York: Knopf, 1935).

During the 1940s, Luigi Albertini's monumental three-volume *The Origins of the War of 1914* (Oxford: Oxford University Press, 1952–1957) presented an incredibly detailed study of the policies of the various powers, including special attention to Italy's role in the crisis of 1914 as well as the importance of the Balkans in creating European instability. Albertini was critical of the actions of all the powers but saw Germany as the chief culprit.

After World War II, a new wave of books on the origins of the Great War began to appear, making use of a vast amount of archival material uncovered by Allied forces when they overran Nazi Germany. The most influential and controversial of these is Fritz Fischer's *Germany's Aims in the First World War* (New York: W.W. Norton & Co., Inc., 1967). Fischer, a noted German historian, charges Germany with primary responsibility for the outbreak of the war and traces the development of extensive German aims during the conflict. He followed with *War of Illusions: German Policies from 1911 to 1914* (New York: W.W. Norton & Co., Inc., 1975), which focuses in highly critical fashion on Germany's prewar policies. In this work, Fischer contends that from as early as 1912 German leaders saw war as the means of deflecting internal forces seeking change in the country's social, political, and constitutional makeup. He also insists that Germany sought domination of Europe and the establishment of its position as a world power. Fischer saw civilian leaders, most notably Chancellor Bethmann-Hollweg, as instrumental in this approach along with the military. Other historians soon followed Fischer's lead and published works criticizing German foreign policy. Among them were Immanuel Geiss, *German Foreign Policy, 1871–1914* (London: Routledge & Kegan Paul, 1976); and Volker R. Berghahn, *Germany and the Approach of War in 1914* (New York: St. Martin's Press, 1973).

The contentions of the Fischer school did not go unchallenged. Another eminent German historian, Gerhard Ritter, in *The Sword and the Scepter*, 4 vols. (Princeton Junction, N.J.: Scholars Bookshelf, 1970–1988), denounced Fischer for distorting the record by quoting statements out of context and sometimes out of sequence. He especially disagreed with Fischer's interpretation of Chancellor Bethmann-Hollweg. While conceding the warlike teden-cies of the German General Staff, Ritter defended Bethmann-Hollweg and insisted that he did not seek war and even tried to moderate the military's desire for extensive war aims.

More recently, some historians have emphasized Austria-Hungary's role in provoking the war. These include Samuel R. Williamson, Jr., *Austria-Hungary and the Origins of the First World War* (New York: St. Martin's Press, 1991). Williamson points out that, despite Germany's "blank check," it was Austria-Hungary that made the initial decision for war, at the same time seeking German assurances and exploiting them once they were forthcoming. He also states that the leaders in Vienna pursued war against Serbia without giving sufficient consideration to the danger of Russian intervention. Joachim Remak in *The Origins of World War I, 1871–1914* (New York: Holt, Rinehart & Winston, 1967) singles out Austria-Hungary as the country most to blame for the outbreak of war, followed closely by Serbia. While not specifically distributing blame to individual nations, Laurence Lafore in *The Long Fuse: An Interpretation of the Origins of World War I* (Philadelphia: Lippincott, 1965) does see the Dual Monarchy's nationalities problem as well as Vienna's rivalries with Serbia and Russia as the most important factors in the coming of the war.

Russia also has had its share of detractors and defenders. Sidney Fay in his work cited above (*The Origins of the World War*) and L.C.F. Turner in *The Origins of the First World War* (New York: W.W. Norton & Co., Inc., 1970) are critical of the actions of not only Russia but also Serbia and France, both in the years prior to 1914 and during the July crisis. D.C.B. Lieven in *Russia and the Origins of the First World War* (New York: St. Martin's Press, 1983), while not uncritical of Russian policy, contends that "the major immediate responsibility for the outbreak of the war rested unequivocally on the German government."

Traditionally, historians have judged harshly the actions of President Poincaré of France and the French ambassador to St. Petersburg, Maurice Paleologue. They have accused Poincaré of extending what amounted to a "blank check" to Russia during his visit in July 1914. More recently, however, John F.V. Keiger's *France and the Origins of the First World War* (New York: St. Martin's Press, 1983) has attempted to revise this interpretation, while remaining critical of the behavior of Paleologue. Keiger contends that Poincaré was not as obsessed with the recovery of Alsace-Lorraine as is usually believed and, although Poincaré was a staunch proponent of the Triple Entente, he was primarily concerned with preserving the peace and desired better relations with Germany. Keiger's revisionist view has by no means convinced all historians. For example, Norman Rich states in his *Great Power Diplomacy*, cited above, that "It strains credulity to believe that Poincaré, native of Lorraine, passionate patriot, and fierce foe of Germany, was not tempted to take advantage" of the crisis of 1914, "if only to the extent of offering unconditional support to Russia and allowing the bungling Teutons to stumble to their doom." Conversely, not all historians would accept the extent of Rich's characterization of Poincaré's motives.

Zara S. Steiner in *Britain and the Origins of the First World War* (New York: St. Martin's Press, 1977) relates the growth of anti-German sentiment in Britain and the movement of British policy in the direction of closer cooperation with France and Russia. In *The Politics of Grand Strategy: Britain and France Prepare for War, 1904–1914* (Cambridge, Mass.: Harvard University Press, 1969), Samuel R. Williamson, Jr., also examines the tightening of Anglo-French relations and the creation of the Triple Entente. Both Steiner and Williamson reveal the confusion that prevailed among leaders in London regarding the extent of their commitment to the French as a result of the various agreements with Paris. The role of Italy receives consideration from both Albertini and Richard Bosworth in *Italy and the Approach of the First World War* (New York: St. Martin's Press, 1983).

The deterioration of relations between Britain and Germany is well documented in Paul Kennedy, *The Rise of Anglo-German Antagonism, 1860–1914* (London: Allen & Unwin, 1980); and R.J.S. Hoffman, *Great Britain and the German Trade Rivalry* (Philadelphia: University of Pennsylvania Press, 1933). E.L. Woodward's *Great Britain and the German Navy* (Oxford: Clarendon Press, 1935) is the classic study of the growth of the Anglo-German naval rivalry. Peter Padfield, *The Great Naval Race: The Anglo-German Naval Rivalry, 1900–1914* (New York: D. McKay, 1974) presents a more recent treatment of the same subject. Jonathan Steinberg deals with the background for the expansion of the German navy in *Yesterday's Deterrent: Tirpitz and the Birth of the German Battle Fleet* (New York: Macmillan, 1965) as does Ivo N. Lambi, *The Navy in German Power Politics, 1862–1914* (Boston: Allen & Unwin, 1984).

Other general studies of the period prior to the war include Dwight Lee, *Europe's Crucial Years: The Diplomatic Background for World War I, 1902–1914* (Hanover, N.H.: The University of New England Press, 1974); Oron J. Hale, *The Great Illusion, 1900–1914* (New York: Harper & Row, 1971); and James Joll, *The Origins of the First World War* (London: Longman, 1984). While Lee's work concentrates on diplomacy, Hale and Joll deal with other aspects of the period as well, Hale in considerably more detail. In *The Proud Tower* (New York: Macmillan, 1972), Barbara Tuchman turns her back on the diplomatic maneuvering that led to the war and attempts to explain "the underlying causes and deeper forces" that triggered the conflict. She fails in this endeavor but does provide some interesting, if not always accurate, vignettes of a number of prominent figures in European society during the prewar era.

Boyd C. Shafer's *Nationalism: Myth and Reality* (New York: Harvest Books, 1955) is a good study of the development of nationalism and its negative effects on Europe during the nineteenth century. For economic aspects of the prewar period, see Alan S. Milward and S.B. Saul, *The Development of Continental Europe, 1850–1914* (Cambridge, Mass.: Harvard University Press, 1977). Among the most useful works on imperialism are Wolfgang J. Mommsen, *Theories of Imperialism* (New York: Random House, 1980); Winfried Baumgart, *Imperialism: The Idea and Reality of British and*

French Colonial Expansion, 1880–1914 (Oxford: Oxford University Press, 1982); W.D. Smith, *The German Colonial Empire* (Chapel Hill: University of North Carolina Press, 1978); and Lewis H. Gann and Peter Duignan, eds., *Colonialism in Africa, 1870–1960*, 5 vols. (Cambridge: Cambridge University Press, 1969–1975).

Works on the Moroccan crises include E.N. Anderson, *The First Moroccan Crisis, 1904–1906* (Chicago: University of Chicago Press, 1930); and Geoffrey Barraclough, *From Agadir to Armageddon: Anatomy of a Crisis* (New York: Holmes & Meier, 1982). The tangled web of the Balkans and its crises have attracted much attention from historians. For an excellent general introduction, see Leften S. Stavrianos, *The Balkans Since 1453* (New York: Holt, Rinehart & Winston, 1958). Barbara Jelevich focuses on one of the region's most troubled periods in *The Great Powers and the Balkans, 1870–1887* (Bloomington: Indiana University Press, 1973). David MacKenzie deals with an issue of great importance in *The Serbs and Russian Pan-Slavism* (Ithaca, N.Y.: Cornell University Press, 1967). Andrew Rossos provides a broader perspective in *Russia and the Balkans: Inter-Balkan Rivalries and Russian Foreign Policy, 1908–1914* (Toronto: University of Toronto Press, 1981). Bernadotte Schmitt has written the classic account of the Bosnian crisis in *The Annexation of Bosnia* (Cambridge: Cambridge University Press, 1937), while Ernst C. Helmreich has done the same in *The Diplomacy of the Balkan Wars* (Cambridge, Mass.: Harvard University Press, 1938). Joachim Remak, *Sarajevo: The Story of a Political Murder* (New York: Criterion Books, 1959); and Vladimir Dedijer, *The Road to Sarajevo* (New York: Simon & Schuster, 1966) both relate the assassination of the Archduke Francis Ferdinand but take dramatically different positions on the role played by Colonel Dimitrijevich in the conspiracy. Remak sees him as the mastermind behind the crime, while Dedijer contends that he was only marginally involved.

WAR PLANS

Germany's Schlieffen Plan has attracted by far the most interest of any of the war plans prepared by the Great Powers before the conflict, primarily because it seemed to come so close to success, only to fail when General von Kluck's army was almost at the gates of Paris. In *The Schlieffen Plan: Critique of a Myth* (New York: Praeger, 1958), Gerhard Ritter effectively demolishes the legend that only blunders in executing the plan robbed Germany of victory. He clearly demonstrates that the plan itself was badly flawed. Martin van Creveld in *Supplying War* (Cambridge: Cambridge University Press, 1977) details the logistic weaknesses of the plan. Paul Kennedy, ed., *The War Plans of the Great Powers, 1880–1914* (London: Allen & Unwin, 1979) presents a number of essays on various plans for hostilities, including the Schlieffen Plan, the peculiarities of Austro-German cooperation, and the Russian mobilization plan. L.L. Farrar, Jr., in *The Short-War Illusion: German Policy, Strategy & Domestic Affairs* (Santa Barbara, Calif.: ABC-Clio, 1973), studies the plans of both Germany and the other belligerent powers and their failure in operation during 1914. Martin Kitchen has provided an excellent analysis of *The German Officer Corps, 1890–1914* (Oxford: Clarendon Press, 1968).

Samuel Williamson traces the change in Britain's military thinking regarding a continental commitment in *The Politics of Grand Strategy*, cited earlier as does John Gooch, *The Plans for War: The General Staff and British Military Strategy, 1900–1916* (London: John Wiley, 1974). Barbara Tuchman's engrossing *The Guns of August* (New York: Macmillan, 1962) deals with the planning of Germany, France, Britain, and Russia, while Douglas Porch analyzes the role of the French army in prewar decades in *The March to the Marne: The French Army, 1871–1914* (Cambridge: Cambridge University Press, 1981). Gunther Erich Rothenberg's *The Army of Francis Joseph* (West Lafayette, Ind.: Purdue University Press, 1976) surveys Austro-Hungarian planning and the shortcomings of the Hapsburg army in the context of the entire reign of Francis Joseph.

THE WESTERN FRONT

Corelli Barnett presents essays on top military commanders, including Moltke the Younger, Haig, Pétain, and Ludendorff in *The Swordbearers: Supreme Command in the First World War* (New York: William Morrow, 1964). Other biographies of British military leaders are Philip Magnus's critical *Kitchener: Portrait of an Imperialist* (London: Dutton, 1959); and Violet Bonham-Carter's, *Soldier True: The Life of Field Marshal Robertson* (London: Frederick Muller, 1964), which is excessively favorable to the British commander-in-chief. John Terraine's *Douglas Haig: The Educated Soldier* (London: Hutchinson, 1963), is in many respects an outstanding work but is overly sympathetic to the man who was responsible for the Somme and Third Ypres before hitting his stride in 1918. Biographies of French generals include Richard Griffiths, *Pétain* (London: Constable, 1970); Cyril Falls, *Marshal Foch* (London: Blackie, 1939); and Sir James Handyside Marshall-Cornwall, *Foch as Military Commander* (New York: Crane, Russak, 1972), while D.J. Goodspeed pays tribute to *Ludendorff: Genius of World War I* (London: Hart-Davis, 1966). More recently, Robert B. Asprey has written a highly critical work on *The German High Command at War: Hindenburg and Ludendorff Conduct World War I* (New York: William Morrow, 1991).

Among the military figures on the Allied side who have left memoirs are Field Marshal Sir William Robertson, *Soldiers and Statesmen,* 1914–1918, 2 vols. (New York: Scribner's, 1926); Marshal Joseph Joffre, *Personal Memoirs of Joffre*, 2 vols. (London: Geoffrey Bles, 1932); and Marshal Ferdinand Foch, *The Memoirs of Marshal Foch* (Garden City, N.Y.: Doubleday, Doran, 1931). General Erich von Falkenhayn, *The German General Staff, 1914–1916* (London: Hutchinson, 1920), recounts Falkenhayn's turbulent period as chief of staff. The two most powerful German military leaders published their memoirs soon after the war. These include Paul von Hindenburg, *Out of My Life* (New York: Cassel, 1920), and Erich Ludendorff, *Ludendorff's Own Story*, 2 vols. (New York: Harper, 1919). Robert Blake has edited *The Private Papers of Douglas Haig, 1914–1919* (London: Eyre & Spottiswoode, 1952).

In addition to Churchill's *The World Crisis*, cited earlier, autobiographical works by civilian leaders include Herbert Henry Asquith, *Memoirs and Reflections, 1852–1927*, 2 vols. (Boston: Little, Brown, 1928); David Lloyd George, *War Memoirs*, 6 vols. (Boston: Little, Brown, 1933–1937); Georges Clemenceau, *The Grandeur and Misery of Victory* (New York: Harcourt, 1930); and Theobold von Bethmann-Hollweg, *Reflections on the World War* (London: Thornton Butterworth, 1921).

Among the biographies of wartime political leaders are Roy Jenkins, *Asquith* (London: Collins, 1964); Thomas Jones, *Lloyd George* (Cambridge, Mass.: Harvard University Press, 1951); David Robin Watson, *Georges Clemenceau* (London: Eyre Methuen, 1974); Michael Balfour, *The Kaiser and His Times* (New York: W.W. Norton & Co., Inc., 1972); and Konrad Jarausch, *Bethmann-Hollweg and the Hubris of Imperial Germany* (New Haven, Conn.: Yale University Press, 1973). The first four volumes of Randolph S. Churchill and Martin Gilbert, *The Life of Winston Churchill*, 8 vols. (Boston: Little, Brown, 1966–1986), carry the future prime minister's story through 1922.

John Terraine has published a number of interesting essays on various aspects of *The*

Western Front, 1914–1918 (London: Hutchinson, 1973). Numerous studies are available on campaigns and battles, including Lyn MacDonald, 1914 (New York: Atheneum, 1988); Barbara Tuchman's The Guns of August, cited earlier, which covers both France's Plan 17 operations and the German offensive up to the start of the Battle of the Marne. Michael Keegan has provided a much briefer account of the 1914 campaign, including the Battle of the Marne, in The Opening Moves: August 1914 (New York: Ballantine, 1971). John Terraine focuses on Mons: Retreat to Victory (London: Batsford, 1960). Two works on the decisive battle that condemned Europe to four years of deadlock and slaughter are Georges Blond, The Marne (London: MacDonald, 1965); and Robert B. Asprey, The First Battle of the Marne (Philadelphia: Lippincott, 1962). General von Kluck provides his own personal account of The March on Paris and the Battle of the Marne, 1914 (London: Edward Arnold, 1920). The First Battle of Ypres is the subject of A.H. Farrar-Hockley's Death of an Army (New York: William Morrow, 1968).

Alan Clark offers an extremely critical account of British military leadership during the 1915 campaign in The Donkeys (London: Hutchinson, 1961). Alistair Horne has written a dramatic and highly readable account of the ghastly Battle of Verdun in The Price of Glory: Verdun 1916 (New York: Penguin, 1981), while A.H. Farrar-Hockley has related the equally grim carnage of The Somme (London: Batsford, 1964). Martin Middlebrook relies on a huge number of interviews with soldiers to capture the unbelievable horror of The First Day of the Somme (London: Allen Lane, 1971). The tragically misconceived Nivelle offensive of 1917 and the resulting mutinies provide the subject matter of Richard M. Watt's Dare Call It Treason (New York: Simon & Schuster, 1963), and Leon Wolff's In Flanders Fields (New York: Ballantine, 1960) presents a vivid depiction of the appalling Third Battle of Ypres and its preliminaries. The Battle of Arras receives attention in Edward L. Spears, Prelude to Victory (London: Jonathan Cape, 1939), while Alexander McKee tells the story of the great Canadian effort in The Battle of Vimy Ridge (New York: Stein & Day, 1967).

The final year of the war has attracted particular interest in such works as Bruce I. Gudmundson, Stormtroop Tactics: Innovation in the German Army (New York: Praeger, 1989); and Martin Middlebrook, The Kaiser's Battle, 21 March 1918: The First Day of the German Spring Offensive (London: Allen Lane, 1978), which again weaves an absorbing re-creation based on countless interviews. Other sources are Hubert Essame, The Battle for Europe, 1918 (New York: Batsford, 1972); Barrie Pitt, 1918: The Last Act (New York: W.W. Norton & Co., Inc., 1962); and John Terraine, To Win a War, 1918: The Year of Victory (New York: Doubleday, 1981). Gregory Blaxland, Amiens, 1918 (London: Frederick Muller, 1968); and Douglas Orgill, Armored Onslaught: 8th August 1918 (New York: Ballantine, 1972) both focus on the start of the final great British offensive.

E.M. Coffman details America's role on the Western Front in The War to End All Wars: The American Military Experience in World War I (New York: Oxford University Press, 1969). General John J. Pershing, the commander of the A.E.F., contributed a two-volume work titled My Experiences in the World War (New York: Stokes, 1931). General James G. Harbord, Pershing's first chief of staff who later took over the administration of supply for U.S. forces in Europe, wrote The American Army in France, 1917–1919 (Boston: Little, Brown, 1936). Laurence Stallings has provided a highly readable popular account in The Doughboys: The Story of the AEF in World War I (New York: Harper & Row, 1963). For a good biography of the American commander, see Frank E. Vandiver, Black Jack: The Life and Times of John J. Pershing, 2 vols. (College Station: Texas

A & M Press, 1977). General Hunter Liggett, who succeeded Pershing as commander of the First Army, wrote *A.E.F.: Ten Years Ago in France* (New York: Dodd, Mead, 1928). Russell F. Weigley makes some astute observations on the American role in the war in his *The American Way of War: A History of United States Military Strategy and Policy* (New York: Macmillan, 1973). Robert B. Asprey has described the nature of the battle in *At Belleau Wood* (New York: G.P. Putnam's, 1965).

In recent years, many writers have focused on life in the trenches during the long deadlock on the Western Front. Among the best of these is Eric J. Leed, *No-Man's Land: Combat & Identity in World War I* (Cambridge: Cambridge University Press, 1979), which concentrates on how the experience of war changed the soldiers who suffered in "utter defenselessness before authority and technology." Other excellent works include Tony Ashworth, *Trench Warfare, 1914–1918: The Live and Let Live System* (New York: Holmes & Meier, 1980); Denis Winter, *Death's Men: Soldiers of the Great War* (London: Allen Lane, 1978); and John Ellis, *Eye-Deep in Hell: Trench Warfare in World War I* (London: Croom Helm, 1976).

For the impact of technology on the war, see L.F. Haber, *The Poisonous Cloud: Chemical Warfare in the First World War* (Oxford: Clarendon Press, 1986); G.S. Hutchinson, *Machine Guns: Their History and Tactical Employment* (London: Macmillan, 1938); Aubrey Wade, *The War of the Guns: Western Front, 1917–1918* (London: Batsford, 1936); J.F.C. Fuller, *Tanks in the Great War* (London: J. Murray, 1920); and H.C.B. Rogers, *Tanks in Battle* (London: Seeley Service, 1965).

THE EASTERN FRONT

Far fewer works are available for the Eastern Front. Winston Churchill acknowledged this when he wrote *The Unknown War: The Eastern Front* (New York: Scribner's, 1931). More re-cently, Norman Stone has provided an excellent analysis and changed some traditional views in *The Eastern Front, 1914–1918* (New York: Scribner's, 1975). To some extent, Stone's book supersedes General Nicholas N. Golovine's *The Russian Army in the World War* (New Haven, Conn.: Yale University Press, 1932); and *The Russian Campaign of 1914* (Leavenworth, Kans.: The Command and Staff School Press, 1933). Stone especially challenges Golovine's positive appraisal of the Grand Duke Nicholas and negative depiction of General Sukhomlinov. Another good recent work is W. Bruce Lincoln, *Passage Through Armageddon: The Russians in War and Revolution, 1914–1918* (New York: Simon & Schuster, 1986). Alan Clark provides a brief account of the war in this theater of operations in *Suicide of the Empires: The Battles of the Eastern Front, 1914–1918* (New York: American Heritage Press, 1971).

General Aleksei Brusilov's memoirs appeared in *A Soldier's Notebook, 1914–1918* (New York: Macmillan, 1930), and General Basil Gourko has written his personal account of *Russia, 1914–1917: Memories and Impressions of War and Revolution* (New York: Macmillan, 1919). British general Sir Alfred Knox related his observations in *With the Russian Army, 1914–1917* (New York: Dutton, 1921). From the German side, the memoirs of Hindenburg and Ludendorff, cited earlier, detail their experiences on the Eastern Front from 1914 to 1916. General Max Hoffmann offers accounts that are both informative and sometimes misleading in *The War of Lost Opportunities* (New York: International Publishers, 1925) and *War Diaries and Other Papers*, 2 vols. (London: Eric Sutton, 1929).

The Battle of Tannenberg has attracted great interest and has inspired works such as Sir Edmund Ironside, *Tannenberg: The First Thirty Days in East Prussia* (Edinburgh: William Blackwood & Sons, 1925); Geoffrey Evans, *Tannenberg 1410, 1914* (London: Hamish

Hamilton, 1970); and more recently, Dennis Schowalter, *Tannenberg: Clash of Empires* (Hamden, Conn.: Archon Books, 1991). Gunther Rothenberg's *The Army of Francis Joseph*, cited earlier, pursues Austria-Hungary's military misfortunes as well as successes throughout the conflict. Gary W. Shanafelt's *The Secret Enemy: Austria-Hungary and the German Alliance, 1914–1918* (New York: Columbia University Press, 1985) examines Germany's growing ascendancy over the Dual Monarchy as the war continued. Gordon Brook-Shepherd relates the short, unhappy reign of the Emperor Charles in *The Last Hapsburg* (New York: Weybright & Talley, 1968). Allen Wildman's *The End of the Russian Army*, 2 vols. (Princeton, N.J.: Princeton University Press, 1979) traces the disintegration of the czarist forces under the stress of the long conflict.

THE ITALIAN FRONT AND GALLIPOLI

Accounts in English of Italy's contribution to the war are even more scarce than those for the Eastern Front. General histories include Luigi Villari, *The War on the Italian Front* (London: Cobden-Sanderson, 1932); Girard L. McEntee, *Italy's Part in Winning the World War* (Princeton, N.J.: Princeton University Press, 1937), and Sir James Edmonds and H. R. Davies, *Military Operations, Italy, 1915–1919* (London: H. M. Stationery Office, 1949). Antonio Salandra, Italy's premier during the first months of the war, has set forth his personal account of *Italy and the Great War* (London: Edward Arnold, 1932). Cyril Falls recounts the Italian disaster at *Caporetto* (Philadelphia: Lippincott, 1970). The Italian Supreme Command issued a published report on *The Battle of the Piave* (London: Hodder and Stoughton, 1921).

In contrast, British observers never seem to tire of writing about the forlorn Dardanelles campaign and speculating on whether, with different execution, the British could have succeeded and perhaps shortened the war. Winston Churchill certainly thought so as he explains in Volume II of his *World Crisis*, cited earlier. Trumbull Higgins is highly critical of Churchill's scheme as well as its execution in *Winston Churchill and the Dardanelles* (New York: Macmillan, 1963). Among the best of the many general accounts are Robert Rhodes James, *Gallipoli* (London: Batsford, 1965) and Alan Morehead, *Gallipoli* (New York: Harper, 1956). C.F. Aspinall-Oglander's *Military Operations, Gallipoli*, 2 vols. (London: Heinemann, 1929–1932) is the standard work on the land campaign. John Hargrave offers an eyewitness account of the *Sulva Bay Landing* (London: MacDonald, 1964). General Ian Hamilton, the commander of the invading Allied forces, provided an informative *Gallipoli Diary*, 2 vols. (New York: George H. Doran, 1920).

Ulrich Trumpener analyzes the background for Turkey's entry into the war as well as German-Turkish relations during the conflict in *Germany and the Ottoman Empire, 1914–1918* (Princeton, N.J.: Princeton University Press, 1968). Frank G. Weber, *Eagles on the Crescent* (Ithaca, N.Y.: Cornell University Press, 1970), also focuses on the relationship between Turkey and the Central Powers. General Otto Liman von Sanders relates his experiences as chief of Germany's military mission in *Five Years in Turkey* (Annapolis, Md.: United States Naval Institute, 1927). For the Allied forces tied down in northern Greece during 1915–1918, see A.W. Palmer, *The Gardeners of Salonika* (London: Andre Deutsch, 1965).

THE WAR OUTSIDE EUROPE

The literature on most of the colonial campaigns is small. Charles Burdick recounts Japan's major action in *The Japanese Siege of Tsingtau: World War I in Asia* (Hamden, Conn.: Archon Books, 1976). For Africa, see Charles

Miller, *Battle for the Bundu: The World War in East Africa* (New York: Macmillan, 1974); and Edmund H. Gorges, *The Great War in German West-Africa* (London: Hutchinson, 1930). General Paul von Lettow-Vorbeck recounts his brilliant *East African Campaigns* (New York: R. Speller, 1957). A.J. Barker's *The Bastard War: The Mesopotamian Campaign of 1914–1918* (New York: Dial Press, 1967) provides an informative account of the difficult nature of war in the Mesopotamian desert. Two accounts of the ordeal of the garrison trapped at Kut are Ronald Millar, *Kut: The Death of an Army* (London: Secker & Warburg, 1969); and Russell Braddon, *The Siege* (London: Jonathan Cape, 1969). An older general history of operations in Mesopotamia is Frederick J. Moberly, *The Campaign in Mesopotamia*, 4 vols. (London: H. M. Stationery Office, 1923–1927).

The campaigns in Arabia and Palestine have inspired much greater interest, largely due to the dramatic personality of T.E. Lawrence, who remains perhaps the most controversial figure of the war. He helped create his own legend with two finely crafted works: *The Revolt in the Desert* (New York: George H. Doran, 1927) and *The Seven Pillars of Wisdom* (New York: Doubleday, Moran, 1935). Actually, the American journalist Lowell Thomas had already started the legend in *With Lawrence of Arabia* (New York: Hutchinson, 1924) before Lawrence's works appeared. Thomas received help from the British writer Robert Graves in *Lawrence and the Arabs* (London: Jonathan Cape, 1928). Later, critical interpretations emerged in the works of Richard Aldington, *Lawrence of Arabia* (London: Collins, 1955); and Suleiman Mousa, *T.E. Lawrence: An Arab View* (Oxford: Oxford University Press, 1966). Mousa charges that Lawrence took credit for achievements that were actually those of the Arabs. A more balanced account is that of Philip Knightley and Colin Simson, *The Secret Lives of Lawrence of Arabia* (London: Nelson, 1969). The other

great British hero of the Palestine campaigns found an admiring biographer in General Sir Archibald Wavell, who wrote *Allenby: A Study in Greatness* (London: Harrap, 1940). Cyril Falls, *Armageddon* (Philadelphia: Lippincott, 1964), analyzes Allenby's last campaign, again with great admiration.

For the rise of Turkish nationalism during and immediately following the war, there is Bernard Lewis, *The Emergence of Modern Turkey* (London: Oxford University Press, 1961). For Arab nationalism, see Howard M. Sachar, *The Emergence of the Middle East, 1914–1924* (New York: Knopf, 1969).

THE WAR ON THE SEA AND IN THE AIR

Britain's official history of the war at sea, Sir Julian S. Corbett and Sir Henry Newbolt, *Naval Operations*, 5 vols. (London: Longmans, Green, 1920–1931), remains one of the standard works. Arthur J. Marder has provided the other in his outstanding *Dreadnought to Scapa Flow: The Royal Navy in the Fisher Era* (London: Oxford University Press, 1952–1959). Memoirs of naval leaders include Admiral John Jellicoe, *The Grand Fleet, 1914–1916* (New York: George H. Doran, 1919); Admiral Reinhard Scheer, *Germany's High Seas Fleet in the World War* (New York: Peter Smith, 1934); and Admiral Alfred von Tirpitz, *My Memoirs*, 2 vols. (New York: Dodd, Mead, 1919). Stephen Roskill has provided a good biography of *Admiral of the Fleet Earl Beatty* (New York: Atheneum, 1980), and John Winton has done the same for *Jellicoe* (London: Michael Joseph, 1981).

Richard Hough has written an excellent one-volume account of the naval war with emphasis on surface action and Britain's role in *The Great War at Sea, 1914–1918* (Oxford: Oxford University Press, 1983). Another fine general work is Geoffrey Bennett, *Naval Battles of the First World War* (London:

Batsford, 1968). Bennett has also written one of the best books on *Cornonel and the Falklands* (London: Pan, 1962) as well as an excellent recounting of *The Battle of Jutland* (London: David & Charles, 1972). Among the best books on the German submarine offensive and Allied countermeasures are R.H. Gibson and Maurice Prendergast, *The German Submarine War, 1914–18* (New York: R.R. Smith, 1931) and Sir William Jameson, *The Most Formidable Thing* (London: Hart-Davis, 1965). Colin Simpson relates the story of the sinking of *The Lusitania* (Boston: Little, Brown, 1972), and Daniel Horn analyzes *The German Naval Mutinies of World War I* (New Brunswick, N.J.: Rutgers University Press, 1969).

Walter Raleigh and H.A. Jones collaborated on the standard work on *The War in the Air*, 6 vols. (Oxford: Oxford University Press, 1922–1937). Robin Higham details the evolution of World War I aircraft in *Air Power: A Concise History* (New York: St. Martin's Press, 1972). Aaron Norman's *The Great Air War* (New York: Macmillan, 1968) provides a good general account. An excellent work on zeppelins is Douglas H. Robinson, *The Zeppelins in Combat* (London: Foulis, 1962). John H. Morrow, Jr., provides an analysis of *German Air Power in World War I* (Lincoln: University of Nebraska Press, 1982), which includes a chapter on Austro-Hungarian military aviation. For the British, see Raymond H. Fredette, *The Birth of the Royal Air Force* (London: Cassell, 1966) and for France, Herbert Molloy Mason, *High Flew the Falcons: The French Aces of World War I* (Philadelphia: Lippincott, 1965). Mason has also written *The Lafayette Escadrille* (New York: Random House, 1964). Neville Jones explores *The Origins of Strategic Bombing: A Study in the Development of British Strategic Thought Up to 1918* (London: Kimber, 1973). Raymond H. Fredette's *The Sky on Fire: The First Battle of Britain, 1917–1918* (New York: Harcourt Brace Jovanovich, 1973) focuses on the German bombing offensive.

WAR AIMS AND TOTAL WAR

Z.A.B. Zeman analyzes *The Diplomatic History of the First World War* (London: Weidenfeld & Nicholson, 1971). The essays contained in B. Hunt and A. Preston, eds., *War Aims and Strategic Policy in the Great War* (London: Croom Helm, 1977), constitute a good overview of the question of war aims. Fritz Fischer's *Germany's Aims in the First World War*, cited earlier, is the most influential and controversial work on the ambitions of the belligerent powers. Fischer sees Germany as desirous of dominating Europe as well as Africa politically and economically. Hans Gatzke in *Germany's Drive to the West: A Study of Germany's War Aims* (Baltimore: Johns Hopkins University Press, 1950) focuses on German aims in Western Europe. Gerhard Ritter in *The Sword and the Scepter*, cited earlier, attempts to refute Fischer's insistence that Chancellor Bethmann-Hollweg essentially shared the extreme aims of the German military but does not deny that the latter were excessive. For France, D. Stevenson provides the best source for *French War Aims Against Germany, 1914–1919* (Oxford: Clarendon Press, 1982). He points out that French political and social groups were divided on the extent of war aims, while France's allies exercised a restraining influence. Victor H. Rothwell analyzes Britain's ambitions in *British War Aims and Peace Diplomacy, 1914–1918* (Oxford: Clarendon Press, 1971); and C.J. Smith focuses on Russia's aims in *The Russian Struggle for Power, 1914–1917: A Study of Russian Foreign Policy During the First World War* (New York: Philosophical Library, 1956). Gary Shanafelt discusses the confusion over Austro-Hungarian war aims and disagreement between Vienna and Berlin on the future of Eastern Europe in *The Secret Enemy*, cited earlier. Gerald E. Silberson, *The Troubled Alliance: German-Austrian Relations, 1914–1917* (Lexington: University of Kentucky Press,

1970), deals with many of the same problems. K.L. Nelson examines the differences between the United States and its Allies regarding war aims in *Victors Divided: America and the Allies in Germany, 1918–1923* (Berkeley: University of California Press, 1975).

For the impact of total war on the home fronts, Jack J. Roth, ed., *World War I: A Turning Point in Modern History,* and René Albrecht-Carrié, *The Meaning of the First World War,* both cited earlier, focus on the changes that the conflict imposed on society and political institutions. Raymond Aaron's *The Century of Total War* (Boston: Beacon Press, 1954) places the war and its effects in the broader context of the historical development of the twentieth century. John Williams, *The Home Fronts: Britain, France and Germany, 1914–1918* (London: Constable, 1972), devotes more attention to the Western Allies, especially Britain, than to Germany. Alan Marwick has produced two excellent works on Britain during the conflict: *The Deluge: British Society and the First World War* (Boston: Little, Brown, 1965), and *Women in War, 1914–1918* (London: Croom Helm, 1977). More recently, J.M. Winter contributed *The Great War and the British People* (Cambridge, Mass.: Harvard University Press, 1986) in which he contends that, while soldiers suffered at the front and died in large numbers, the civilian population improved its life expectancy, apparently because of better nutrition. For Germany, see Jürgen Kocka, *Facing Total War: German Society, 1914–1918* (New York: Berg, 1984), and Albrecht Mendelssohn Bartholdy, *The War and German Society* (New Haven, Conn.: Yale University Press, 1939). Martin Kitchen traces the rise of Hindenburg and Ludendorff to prominence in the German government in *The Silent Dictatorship: Politics in the German High Command, 1916–1918* (New York: Holmes & Meier, 1976). Gerald D. Feldmann explores the impact of the war on industrial organization and labor relations in *Army Industry and Labor in Germany, 1914–*

1918 (Princeton, N.J.: Princeton University Press, 1966). In *The Great War and the French People* (New York: St. Martin's Press 1986), Jean Jacques Becker focuses on French public opinion and concludes that there was less enthusiasm among the French over the outbreak of the war than what is usually believed. He demonstrates, nevertheless, that confidence in victory remained firm among the majority of the French people throughout the conflict.

Richard Wall and Jay Winter, eds., *The Upheaval of War: Family, Work and Welfare in Europe* (Cambridge: Cambridge University Press, 1988) contains a series of revealing essays on the people of the warring countries and their living standards as well as the roles of women, social policy, and family ideologies. Avner Offer's *World War I: An Agrarian Interpretation* (Oxford: Oxford University Press, 1991) argues that Allied access to the major food supplies of the world and their ability to cut off the Central Powers from these resources were the crucial factors in winning the war. Archibald C. Bell also focuses on *The Blockade of Germany, Austria-Hungary, Bulgaria and Turkey* (London: H. M. Stationery Office, 1961) and its results. L. Margaret Barnett examines *British Food Policy During the First World War* (London: Allen & Unwin, 1985). For the organization and effect of British propaganda, see James M. Read, *Atrocity Propaganda, 1914–1919* (New Haven, Conn.: Yale University Press, 1941) and Cate Haste, *Keep the Home Fires Burning* (London: Allen Lane, 1977). In *The Great War and Modern Memory* (London: Oxford University Press, 1975), Paul Fussell has contributed a widely hailed work on the literary aspects of the conflict and its lasting impact on the consciousness of Western civilization.

THE RUSSIAN REVOLUTIONS

Hans Rogger provides the deep background for the coming of the Bolshevik Revolution in *Russia in the Age of Modernization and Revolution, 1881–1917* (London: Longman, 1983). Philip Pomper studies *The Russian Revolutionary Intelligentsia* (Arlington Heights, Ill.: Harlan Davidson, 1970). The standard account of the entire period of revolution is William H. Chamberlain, *The Russian Revolution: 1917–1921*, 2 vols. (New York: Grosset & Dunlap, 1935). More recent versions include Sheila Fitzpatrick, *The Russian Revolution* (Oxford: Oxford University Press, 1984) and Leonard Shapiro, *The Russian Revolution of 1917: The Origins of Modern Communism* (New York: Basic Books, 1984). George Katkov presents a critical account of *Russia, 1917: The February Revolution* (New York: Harper & Row, 1967). Richard Abraham has written a recent biography of *Alexander Kerensky* (London: Sidgwick & Jackson, 1987). John L.H. Keep, *The Russian Revolution: A Study in Mass Mobilization* (New York: W.W. Norton & Co., Inc., 1977), focuses on the growing power of the Soviets during the period of the Provisional Government.

For the Bolshevik Revolution, see Alexander Rabinowitch, *The Bolsheviks Come to Power: The Revolution of 1917 in Petrograd* (W.W. Norton & Co., Inc., 1976); Edward H. Carr, *The October Revolution, Before and After* (New York: Macmillan, 1969); and Adam Ulam, *The Bolsheviks* (New York: Collier Books, 1965). In addition to Ulam's work, which focuses on Lenin's career, biographies of the Bolshevik leader include Robert Service, *Lenin: A Political Life* (New York: Macmillan, 1985); David Shub, *Lenin*, rev. ed. (Harmondsworth: Penguin, 1966); and Louis Fischer, *The Life of Lenin* (New York: Harper & Row, 1964). Trotsky, *The Prophet Armed, 1879–1921* (New York: Oxford University Press, 1959), Vol. I of Isaac Deutscher's three-volume work on Lenin's second-in-command, covers the period of the Russian Revolution. For a thorough and critical account of the treaty forced on Russia by Germany, see John Wheeler-Bennett, *Brest-Litovsk: The Forgotten Peace, March 1918* (London: St. Martin's Press, 1938).

THE UNITED STATES AND THE WAR

For the period of the war prior to America's intervention, Ernest R. May's, *The World War and American Isolation, 1914–1917* (Chicago: Quadrangle, 1966), and Arthur S. Link's, *Woodrow Wilson and the Progressive Era, 1910–1917* (New York: Harper & Row, 1954), are the standard works. Both are generally sympathetic to Wilson's policies. For a brief but cogent interpretation, see Ross Gregory's *The Origins of American Intervention in the First World War* (New York: W.W. Norton & Co., Inc., 1971). Gregory contends that America hoped to reconcile its desire to remain neutral with its need for economic relations with Europe. In the end, this proved an impossible task. Still other important works on this subject are Patrick Devlin, *Too Proud to Fight: Woodrow Wilson's Neutrality* (New York: Oxford University Press, 1974); Jeffrey J. Safford, *Wilsonian Maritime Diplomacy* (New Brunswick, N.J.: Rutgers University Press, 1978); and Frederick S. Calhoun, *Power and Principle: Armed Intervention in Wilsonian Foreign Policy* (Kent, Ohio: Kent State University Press, 1986). Works on Wilson himself include Arthur Link's multivolume but unfinished *Wilson* (Princeton, N.J.: Princeton University Press, 1947–); and John Milton Cooper, *The Warrior and the Priest: Woodrow Wilson and Theodore Roosevelt* (Cambridge, Mass.: Harvard University Press, 1983).

The best book on American social history during the war is David M. Kennedy's well-researched, thoughtful, and brilliantly written *Over Here: The First World War and American Society* (New York: Oxford University Press, 1980). Other useful works are Robert H. Farrell, *Woodrow Wilson and World War I, 1917–1921* (New York: Harper & Row, 1985);

and Ronald Schaffer, *America in the Great War: The Rise of the War Welfare State* (New York: Oxford University Press, 1991). For the war economy and the close relations between government and industrial management, see Robert D. Cuff, *The War Industries Board: Business–Government Relations During World War I* (Baltimore: Johns Hopkins University Press, 1973); and Melvin C. Urofsky, *Big Steel and the Wilson Administration: A Study in Business–Government Relations* (Columbus: Ohio State University Press, 1969). The role of the Committee of Public Information is the subject of Stephen Vaughn's *Holding Fast the Inner Lines: Democracy, Nationalism, and the Committee of Public Information* (Chapel Hill: University of North Carolina Press, 1980). Among the works dealing with wartime dissent and both official and unofficial suppression are Paul L. Murphy, *World War I and the Origins of Civil Liberties in the United States* (New York: W.W. Norton & Co., Inc., 1979); Harry N. Schreiber, *The Wilson Administration and Civil Liberties, 1917–1921* (Ithaca, N.Y.: Cornell University Press, 1960); and William J. Breen, *Uncle Sam at Home: Civilian Mobilization, Wartime Federalism and the Council of National Defense, 1917–1919* (Westport, Conn.: Greenwood Press, 1984).

For the effect of the conflict on American women, see Maurine Weiner Greenwald, *Women, War, and Work: The Impact of World War I on Women Workers in the United States* (Westport, Conn.: Greenwood Press, 1980). Arthur E. Barbeau and Florette Henri focus on *The Unknown Soldiers: Black American Troops in World War I* (Philadelphia: Temple University Press, 1974). David Danbom treats the impact of the war on American agriculture and farmers in the context of what he refers to as *The Resisted Revolution: Urban America and the Industrialization of Agriculture, 1900–1930* (Ames: Iowa State University Press, 1979). Kathleen Burk's *Britain, America and the Sinews of War, 1914–1918* (Boston:

George Allen & Unwin, 1985) studies Anglo-American commercial and financial relations during the war and the loss of British financial leadership to the United States.

THE END OF THE WAR AND ITS AFTERMATH

Three excellent works on the collapse of Austria-Hungary are Arthur J. May, *The Passing of the Hapsburg Monarchy, 1914–1918*, 2 vols. (Philadelphia: University of Pennsylvania Press, 1968); Robert A. Kann, *The Hapsburg Empire: A Study in Integration and Disintegration* (New York: Praeger, 1957); and Z.A.B. Zeman, *The Break-Up of the Hapsburg Empire, 1914–1919* (New York: Oxford University Press, 1961). Karl R. Stadler traces *The Birth of the Austrian Republic, 1918–1921* (Leyden: A. W. Sitjhoff, 1966), while Ivan Völgyes, ed., *Hungary in Revolution, 1918–1919* (Lincoln: University of Nebraska Press, 1971), examines the chaos that tormented Hungary in the immediate postwar period. Arthur Rosenberg's *The Birth of the German Republic* (Oxford: Oxford University Press, 1931) is still useful for political developments in Germany during the war as well as the German revolution. Of more recent vintage is A.J. Ryder, *The German Revolution of 1918* (Cambridge: Cambridge University Press, 1967). C. Paul Vincent relates the postwar continuation of *The Politics of Hunger: The Allied Blockade of Germany, 1915–1919* (Athens: Ohio State University Press, 1985).

Many works that deal with the peace settlement also cover the entire period 1919–1939. Among the best of these are Raymond J. Sontag, *A Broken World, 1919–1939* (New York: Harper & Row, 1971) and Laurence Lafore, *The End of Glory* (Philadelphia: Lippincott, 1970). Sally Marks's *The Illusion of Peace: International Relations in Europe, 1918–1933* (London: St. Martin's Press, 1976) is excellent and covers a shorter period. John

Wheeler-Bennett, *Brest-Litovsk: The Forgotten Peace*, cited earlier, remains the standard work on the treaty that led ultimately to the creation of several of the small states of Eastern Europe. For the Paris Peace Conference and its treaties, Paul Birdsall's *Versailles Twenty Years After* (New York: Reynal & Hitchcock, 1941), although dated in some respects, is still important. Harold Nicolson, a British participant in the conference, presents his personal and highly critical appraisal in *Peacemaking, 1919* (Boston: Houghton Mifflin, 1933). More recent accounts include Charles L. Mee, *The End of Order: Versailles 1919* (New York: Dutton, 1980); and J.H. Elcock, *Portrait of a Decision: The Council of Four and the Treaty of Versailles* (London: Eyre Methuen, 1972). For the treaty dealing with Hungary, see Bela E. Kiraly, Peter Pastor, and Ivan Sander, eds., *Total War and Peacemaking: A Case Study of Trianon* (New York: Columbia University Press, 1982). Turkey receives attention in Paul C. Helmreich, *From Paris to Sèvres: The Partition of the Ottoman Empire at the Peace Conference of 1919–1920* (Columbus: Ohio State University Press, 1974). Arno Mayer's massive *Politics of Diplomacy and Peacemaking: Containment and Counterrevolution at Versailles, 1918–1919* (New York: Knopf, 1967) focuses critically on Allied attitudes toward Soviet Russia.

The famous economist John Maynard Keynes wrote a scathing analysis of the Treaty of Versailles in *The Economic Consequences of the Peace* (New York: Harcourt, Brace, 1920). Keynes was particularly critical of the reparations settlement, which he considered beyond Germany's capability to pay. Étienne Mantoux, in *The Carthaginian Peace, or the Economic Consequences of Mr. Keynes* (New York: Scribner's, 1952), challenged Keynes's thesis and launched a reevaluation of the reparations issue, which is still in progress. Among the more recent books on the subject is Marc Trachtenberg, *Reparations and World Politics* (New York: Columbia University Press, 1980). Trachtenberg argues that Germany did not suffer unduly from the reparations burden.

On the Russian civil war, see John F. N. Bradley's *Civil War in Russia, 1917–1920* (London: Batsford, 1975) and *Allied Intervention in Russia, 1917–1920* (New York: Basic Books, 1968). Titus Komarnichi covers *The Rebirth of the Polish Republic* (London: Heinemann, 1957), while Norman Davies presents a vivid picture of the Polish–Soviet War of 1919–1920 in *White Eagle, Red Star* (New York: St. Martin's Press, 1972). Thomas Masaryk, the founder of Czechoslovakia, wrote *The Making of a State* (London: Allen & Unwin, 1927), which is still valuable even though it reflects the author's obvious patriotism. For the creation of Yugoslavia, see Ivo J. Lederer, *Yugoslavia at the Paris Peace Conference* (New Haven, Conn.: Yale University Press, 1963). Stanley W. Page focuses on *The Formation of the Baltic States* (Cambridge: Mass.: Harvard University Press, 1959), while C. Jay Smith deals with *Finland and the Russian Revolution, 1917–1922* (Athens: University of Georgia Press, 1958), and John S. Reshetar treats the ill-fated *Ukranian Revolution, 1917–1920* (Princeton, N.J.: Princeton University Press, 1952).

Finally, Stephen J. Lee discusses the failure of democracy and the ascendancy of authoritarian government during the interwar years in *European Dictatorships, 1918–1945* (London: Methuen, 1987). A good introduction to the general topic of fascism is Alan Cassell's *Fascism* (Arlington Heights, Ill.: AHM Publishing Co., 1975), which analyzes Italian fascism as well as nazism and other versions of fascism. On Italy specifically, Adrian Lyttleton recounts *The Seizure of Power: Fascism in Italy, 1919–1929* (New York: Scribner's, 1973). For Germany, A.J. Nicholls focuses on *Weimar and the Rise of Hitler* (London: Macmillan, 1979).

INDEX